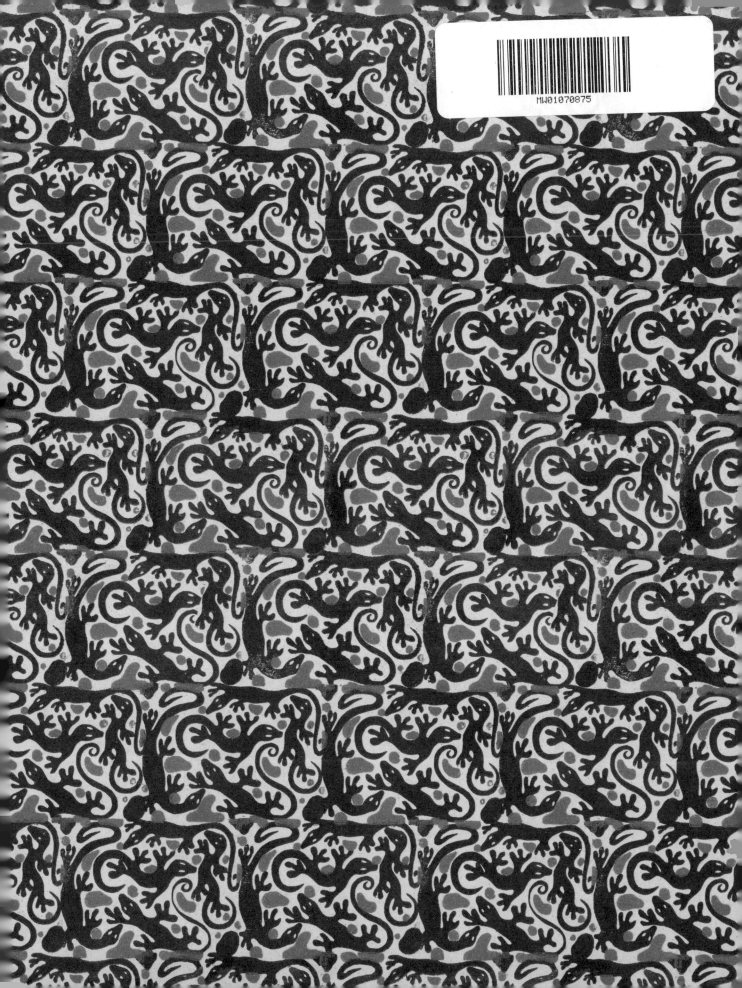

EPHEMERA

DIE GEBRAUCHSGRAFIK DER MAK-BIBLIOTHEK UND KUNSTBLÄTTERSAMMLUNG
THE GRAPHIC DESIGN OF THE MAK LIBRARY AND WORKS ON PAPER COLLECTION

EPHEMERA

DIE GEBRAUCHSGRAFIK DER MAK-BIBLIOTHEK UND KUNSTBLÄTTERSAMMLUNG
THE GRAPHIC DESIGN OF THE MAK LIBRARY AND WORKS ON PAPER COLLECTION

Herausgegeben von Edited by

CHRISTOPH THUN-HOHENSTEIN, KATHRIN POKORNY-NAGEL

Beiträge von Contributions by

THORSTEN BAENSCH, HEINZ DECKER, BERNHARD DENSCHER,
YASMIN DOOSRY, BRIGITTE FELDERER, INGRID HASLINGER, CLAUDIA KAROLYI,
ANNETTE KÖGER, ANITA KÜHNEL, KATHRIN POKORNY-NAGEL, TERESA PRÄAUER,
RAPHAEL ROSENBERG, ANNE-KATRIN ROSSBERG, STEFAN SAGMEISTER,
THOMAS SCHÄFER-ELMAYER, FRIEDER SCHMIDT, RAJA SCHWAHN-REICHMANN,
ELFIE SEMOTAN, DIETER STREHL, CHRISTOPH THUN-HOHENSTEIN

VERLAG FÜR MODERNE KUNST

Sämtliche Beiträge AUS DER SAMMLUNG von **Anne-Katrin Rossberg**, mit Ausnahme des Beitrags VI/A „Zur Entstehung der Sammlung" von **Kathrin Pokorny-Nagel**

All articles FROM THE COLLECTION are by Anne-Katrin Rossberg, with the exception of the article VI/A "On the Creation of the Collection" by Kathrin Pokorny-Nagel

VON DER BEDEUTUNG DES EPHEMEREN

Eine Publikation über Ephemeres lässt aufhorchen, denn der Begriff des Ephemeren versucht ja, das Kurzlebige und damit rasch Vergängliche zu beschreiben. Aus dem Altgriechischen ἐφήμερος (einen Tag dauernd) abgeleitet, findet er vor allem in der Biologie zur Bezeichnung besonders „kurzlebiger" Lebewesen oder Pflanzen eine dem unmittelbaren Wortsinn entsprechende Verwendung. Bildungssprachlich steht das Wort für „nur kurze Zeit bestehend" oder „vorübergehend". In diesem Sinne hat der Begriff auch Eingang in die bildende Kunst gefunden, von der Konzeptkunst über die Aktionskunst bis hin zu Formen der digitalen Kunst wie Internetkunst und „cyberpoetry". Auch für die Gebrauchsgrafik ist das „Ephemere" – verstanden als die auf kurze Zeit gerichtete Verwendung eines Gegenstandes – ein spannendes Feld.

Warum aber sammelt ein Museum für angewandte Kunst wie das MAK Gebrauchsgrafik, der eine vorübergehende, teilweise sogar nur einmalige Verwendung zugedacht ist? Was wird dabei nach welchen Kriterien gesammelt? Es ist der Zweck des Gegenstandes, der nicht nur bestimmt, ob wir von einem „ephemeren" Objekt reden können, sondern überhaupt zum Leitgedanken des Sammelns von Ephemerem wird. Das MAK hat im Lauf seiner Geschichte ein reichhaltiges Spektrum von Ephemera zusammengetragen: etwa Eintrittskarten, deren Gültigkeit bereits vor 100 Jahren obsolet geworden ist; Visitenkarten, deren Besitzer schon Jahrzehnte verstorben sind; Glückwunschkarten, deren Anlässe längst vergangen sind; Exlibris, Besitzervermerke in Büchern, die in alle Welt verstreut sind; Geschenkpapier, dessen Inhalt bereits seinen Adressaten gefunden hat; Spielkarten, deren Partien verloren wurden; Menüabfolgen zu längst Gegessenem oder Orangeneinwickelpapier von seit Langem Verdorbenem.

Doch was ist die Bedeutung dieser Dinge für das Heute? Welche Erinnerung gäbe es an Makarts Festzug der Stadt Wien 1879 ohne die chromolithografischen Wiedergaben durch Eduard Stadlin oder an den Wiener Spaziergang von Günter Brus 1965 ohne die Fotodokumentation von Ludwig Hoffenreich? Woher hätte Franz West seine Inspiration für den Teppich der Jubiläumsausstellung *Mozart. Experiment Aufklärung* genommen, wenn nicht aus dem reichen Fundus an Brokatmusterpapieren des 18. Jahrhunderts der MAK-Bibliothek und Kunstblättersammlung?

Das eigentliche ephemere Medium unserer Zeit, der sogenannten Digitalen Moderne, sind digitale Daten. Wie Vinton G. Cerf, einer der Väter des Internet, mahnt, sind unsere jetzigen Dateien künftig nur mehr digitaler Müll. Unzählige heute nicht mehr lesbare interaktive CD-ROMs sind traurige Zeitzeugen dieser Entwicklung. Im Gegensatz zu den papierenen Ephemera der MAK-Sammlung ist die Lesbarkeit der „Bits and Bytes" nicht einmal mehr als „Matrix" interpretierbar. Dieses Bewusstsein um die digitale Verflüchtigung und Vergänglichkeit bestätigt jedenfalls, wie wichtig es ist, dass Museen (auch) „analoge" Ephemera sammeln, bewahren, dokumentieren, erforschen und im (kunst)historischen Kontext präsentieren und vermitteln.

Die vorliegende Publikation beleuchtet somit nicht nur ephemere angewandte Kunst, sondern ist auch eine kulturgeschichtliche Schatztruhe. Wir erfahren Erstaunliches und können es mit den Gepflogenheiten unserer Gegenwart vergleichen. Über vieles mögen wir schmunzeln, manches wird uns zum Nachdenken anregen, und vielleicht können wir sogar das eine oder andere lernen. Auch in diesem Sinne bedanke ich mich bei allen, die zu diesem Projekt beigetragen haben.

Christoph Thun-Hohenstein, Generaldirektor, MAK

ON THE SIGNIFICANCE OF THE EPHEMERAL

A publication on the ephemeral is bound to attract attention; after all, the term "ephemeral" attempts to describe the short-lived and hence extremely temporary. Derived from the Ancient Greek ἐφήμερος (lasting one day), the word in its original meaning is mostly used in biological contexts to identify particularly "short-lived" creatures or plants. In more erudite texts, the word is synonymous with "existing for only a short time" or "transient." It is in this sense that the term has also entered the world of fine art, from concept and action art to forms of digital art such as internet art and cyber poetry. In the field of graphic design, "ephemera"—understood as objects intended to be used for just a short period—constitute an enthralling genre.

Why, though, would a museum of applied arts such as the MAK collect ephemera when it is destined for temporary —at times even single—use? What is collected—and according to which criteria?
It is the object's purpose, which not only defines whether we can call it "ephemeral," but which itself becomes the principle by which we collect ephemera. The MAK has compiled a rich spectrum of ephemera over the course of its history: such as admission tickets, whose validity became obsolete over a century ago; business cards whose owners passed away decades ago; greeting cards whose occasions long since became history; exlibris, ownership labels from books, which are scattered around the globe; wrapping paper whose contents have already found their recipient; playing cards from a game later lost; menu cards for meals eaten long ago; and orange wrappers for now rotten fruit.

Yet what is the significance of these things today? What reminder would there be of Makart's parade through the city of Vienna in 1879 without the chromolithograph renditions by Eduard Stadlin? Or of Günter Brus's Vienna Walk in 1965 without the photographic documentation by Ludwig Hoffenreich? How would Franz West have found inspiration for his carpet for the anniversary exhibition *Mozart. The Enlightenment: An Experiment in Vienna*, if not for the rich stock of 18th-century brocade paper samples in the MAK Library and Works on Paper Collection?

The truly ephemeral medium of our age, this so-called Digital Modernity, is digital data. As Vinton G. Cerf, one of the fathers of the internet, has criticized, our current documents will be nothing but digital trash in the future. Even now, countless interactive CD ROMS are no longer readable; they have become sorry contemporary witnesses to this development. In contrast to the paper ephemera of the MAK Collection, it is no longer even possible to interpret their bits and bytes as a matrix. This awareness of digital volatility and transience certainly confirms how important it is that museums (also) collect, preserve, document, research, exhibit, and educate visitors about "analog" ephemera in an (art) historical context.

Consequently, the publication in your hands not only shines a light on ephemeral applied art, but is also a treasure trove of cultural history. In it, you will discover astonishing things and can compare them with the conventions of our present age. Much may make you chuckle, some might provide you food for thought, and perhaps you will even learn a thing or two. For this reason as well, I would like to thank everyone who has contributed to this project.

Christoph Thun-Hohenstein, General Director, MAK

ZUR PUBLIKATION

Das 1863 gegründete k. k. Österreichische Museum für Kunst und Industrie (das heutige MAK) verstand sich als Vorbildersammlung für Künstler, Industrielle und KonsumentInnen sowie als Aus- und Weiterbildungsstätte für Entwerfer und Handwerker. Gleichsam als „Museum für alle" startet die Erfolgsgeschichte des ersten staatlichen Museums in der damaligen Habsburgermonarchie.

Im Sinne der Gründungsidee hatte die Bibliothek und Kunstblättersammlung den Auftrag, nicht nur Fachliteratur zu Kunst und Gewerbe, sondern ebenso grafische Entwürfe, Musterblätter und künstlerisch gestaltete Gebrauchsgrafik in den Bestand aufzunehmen. So entwickelte sie sich nach und nach zur größten Kunstbibliothek Österreichs. Bereits der erste Direktor Rudolf von Eitelberger interessierte sich für die Gebrauchsgrafik und trieb etwa den Aufbau einer Spielkarten-Sammlung voran. Den eigentlichen Grundstock des heute so umfassenden Bestandes verdanken wir jedoch Hans Ankwicz-Kleehoven, Leiter der Bibliothek und Kunstblättersammlung von 1925 bis 1939. Unter seiner Leitung wurden dem Museum zahlreiche Schenkungen zuteil, die er um gezielte Ankäufe ergänzte.

Auf dem Gebiet der Ephemera – grafische Arbeiten mit vorübergehendem Gebrauchswert – sammelt das MAK Brief- und Buntpapier, Buchumschläge, Einladungen, Eintrittskarten und Etiketten, Exlibris, Glückwunschkarten, Lesezeichen und Menükarten, Reklamemarken, Spielkarten, Tanzordnungen, Tischkarten, Visitenkarten und Werbematerial vom 18. Jahrhundert bis in die Gegenwart. Trotz ihrer Kurzlebigkeit zeichnen sich diese Drucksorten regelmäßig durch hohe gestalterische und technische Qualität aus und stellen damit zu jeder Zeit ein begehrtes Sammlungsgut dar. In ihnen spiegeln sich künstlerische Entwicklungen ebenso wider wie gesellschaftliche Riten, persönliche und kommerzielle Repräsentationsformen oder Werbestrategien. Wenngleich durch das Sammeln und Bewahren die „Gelegenheitsgrafik" ihres flüchtigen Charakters beraubt wird, ist darin ein nicht unwesentlicher Beitrag zum Erhalt des kulturellen Erbes zu sehen. Es verwundert daher nicht, dass gerade diese Objekte, angesiedelt im „Vorhof" der „hohen Künste", heute mehr und mehr Beachtung finden.

Die vorliegende Publikation repräsentiert die Stärken und die Ausgewogenheit der MAK-Bibliothek und Kunstblättersammlung auf dem Gebiet der Ephemera. Sie ist die Essenz eines langjährigen Forschungsprojektes, in dessen Verlauf die umfangreiche Gebrauchsgrafiksammlung des MAK systematisiert und digitalisiert wurde. Die Fakten zu den gescannten Objekten sind inzwischen online abrufbar – die Bestandsaufnahme allein, befinden wir, kann jedoch der außerordentlichen Qualität der Sammlung nicht gerecht werden. So soll dieser Band die flüchtigen Druckerzeugnisse festhalten und würdigen. In acht Kapiteln setzen sich ExpertInnen mit der Sammlung wissenschaftlich auseinander und werfen dabei ihren ganz persönlichen Blick auf das jeweilige Thema. Den Analysen des historischen Materials sind Kommentare von namhaften Persönlichkeiten aus der Praxis vorangestellt, die sich mit dem Entwurf, der Produktion oder dem Sammeln von Ephemera befassen. Beiträge zur Sammlungsgeschichte ergänzen schließlich die einzelnen Kapitel und gewähren weitere Einblicke in das überreiche Material.

Unser besonderer Dank gilt allen Mitarbeiterinnen und Mitarbeitern der MAK-Bibliothek und Kunstblättersammlung für ihr Engagement bei der Vorbereitung und Umsetzung dieser Publikation.

Kathrin Pokorny-Nagel, Anne-Katrin Rossberg

ON THE PUBLICATION

Founded in 1863, the Imperial Royal Austrian Museum of Art and Industry (the modern-day MAK) was conceived as an exemplary collection for artists, industrialists, and consumers, as well as a training and further education institution for designers and craftspeople. Hence it was as a "museum for everyone" that the success story of the first state museum in the then Habsburg monarchy began.

According to the founding principle of the museum, the task of the Library and Works on Paper Collection was to enrich the museum's holdings—not just with specialist literature on art and industry, but also with graphic designs, sample sheets, and artistic graphic design. This is how it gradually evolved into the largest art library in Austria. Even the museum's first director, Rudolf von Eitelberger, was interested in graphic design, among other things encouraging the expansion of the playing card collection. The solid foundation of today's so comprehensive holdings is, however, thanks to Hans Ankwicz-Kleehoven, head of the Library and Works on Paper Collection from 1925 to 1939. Under his management, numerous donations were bestowed on the museum, which he then supplemented with targeted purchases.

In the field of ephemera—works of graphic design with only temporary practical value—the MAK collects letter paper and decorated paper, dust jackets, invitations, admission tickets and labels, ex libris, greeting cards, bookmarks and menu cards, poster stamps, playing cards, dance cards, place cards, visiting cards, and promotional materials from the 18th century to the present day. Despite its ephemerality, this printed matter regularly exhibits exquisite designs and high technical quality, and hence constitutes a sought-after collector's item in every age. It reflects artistic developments as well as social rites, personal and commercial forms of representation, and advertising strategies. Even though collecting and preserving these "occasion graphics" robs them of their fleeting nature, the practice can be considered a significant contribution to the maintenance of our cultural heritage. It is therefore hardly surprising that precisely these objects—assigned to the "antechamber" of "high culture"—are attracting more and more attention today.

This publication represents the strengths and the balance of the MAK Library and Works on Paper Collection in the field of ephemera. It is the essence of a longstanding research project, during the course of which the MAK's comprehensive graphic design collection was systematized and digitized. The facts pertaining to the scanned objects are now accessible online; we feel, however, that this inventory alone cannot do justice to the exceptional quality of the collection. For this reason, this volume aims to record and pay tribute to these fleeting printed products. In eight chapters, experts explore the collection on an academic level while also taking a personal look at the respective topic. These analyses of the historical material are prefaced with comments by notable practitioners who concern themselves with the design, production, or collection of ephemera. Finally, articles on the collection's history supplement the individual chapters and afford further insights into the abundant material.

We would like to express special thanks to all our colleagues at the MAK Library and Works on Paper Collection for their involvement in the preparation and realization of this publication.

Kathrin Pokorny-Nagel, Anne-Katrin Rossberg

EPHEMERA

DIE EWIGE LIEBE ZUM VERGÄNGLICHEN

Teresa Präauer

Dem Papier hat meine erste Liebe gegolten, und sie wird meine letzte sein. Paper „was my first love, and it will be my last". Also habe ich mir aus dem ephemeren Material des Papiers einen Beruf fürs Leben gebaut – denn das Schreiben und das Zeichnen, beides findet, auch heute noch, auf dem Papier statt: Die Bücher in meinen Regalen sind auf Papier gedruckt, Plakate, die an der Wand hängen, daneben Bilder, Zeichnungen, Postkarten, die Einladungen und Tickets, die sich auf Tischen und Sesseln stapeln, die Rechnungen und Quittungen, die auf dem Boden liegen, um irgendwann einmal, unwillig, in eine Schachtel aus Karton einsortiert zu werden. Und so ist unser digitales Zeitalter wohl eines, in dem wir mehr Papier herstellen und verbrauchen als jemals zuvor in der statistisch auswertbaren Geschichte der Menschheit.

Dem Papier hat meine erste Liebe gegolten. Ich erinnere mich an den Moment, als mein erster Freund, vielleicht sind wir gerade 16 Jahre alt gewesen, etwas rasch ausgepackt und das Geschenkpapier sogleich zusammengeknüllt und weggeworfen hat. Dabei wäre das Eigentliche doch im Papier geschrieben gestanden! Würde ich mich je neu verlieben, dann aber in einen Buchdrucker und in einen Schriftsetzer, in einen Prägemeister und in einen Oberstanzer, in einen Verleimer und in einen Marmorierer, in einen Origamisten und in einen Reklamemarkenrückseiten-Abschlecker. Wir würden von Munken schwärmen und einander Wörter wie „chamoisfarben" zuflüstern. Wir würden über schwere, gestrichene Blätter mit wenig Körnung munkeln, wir würden über voluminierte, weiche Bögen mit viel Struktur tuscheln. All die Wörter, die ich gelernt habe: Vorsatz! Prägedruck! Kunstbillet! Netzkappenkarte! Mit Atlasseide! Mit Perlmutt! Hebelzugkarte! Blumenoblate! Brokatpapier! Immer würden wir mit unseren Fingern, wie über die Haut des anderen, über Papier gleiten. Und würde er mir Valentinsgrüße schicken: „Glück, Amor, Treue, handkoloriert" stände dort geschrieben. Und die Liebe zu Papier wird meine letzte sein. Ich kenne eine Zeichnerin, die recycelt, aus Trotz, aus Nostalgie, aus Faszination am Material, alte Karteikarten für ihre neuen Zeichnungen. Ja, ich glaube, es gibt kaum bildende Künstlerinnen und Künstler, die nicht einen starken emotionalen Bezug, nennen wir es Liebe, zum Medium Papier haben, und daher auch kaum welche, die am Papiermüll, der auf der Straße liegt, so einfach vorbeigehen. An Orangenpapier zum Beispiel: diesem halb durchscheinenden Seidenpapier, königsblau bedruckt, blutrot, dreckig-golden. Mit den altmodisch gewordenen Logos von Firmen aus Übersee, kolonialistischem Kitsch. Ich falte das Papier auf und streiche es glatt, lege es dann zwischen die Seiten eines Buches.

Es gibt auch diese Kinder, später werden daraus Liebhaber, die wissen, dass das Süßeste an den Bonbons manchmal eben ihre Verpackung ist. Die glänzende Alufolie des Eiskonfekts, gelb, blau, grün oder magentafarben, mit Sammelbildern darauf. Das weiße, an den Rändern in Fransen geschnittene Seidenpapier der Weihnachtsnaschereien auf dem Christbaum. Die Schokoladenverpackung aus Karton, mit Bildern bedruckt, die sich bewegen, wenn man die Schokolade aus der Verpackung schiebt. Immer hat es etwas an Papier gegeben, das nicht weggeworfen werden durfte, da doch noch eine Collage daraus gefertigt werden konnte. Eine alte Schuhschachtel mit Geschenkpapier neu überzogen. Ein Briefkuvert aus Zeitungspapier gefaltet, ein anderes mit bunten

EPHEMERA
OUR UNDYING LOVE OF THE SHORT-LIVED
Teresa Präauer

Paper "was my first love, and it will be my last." And so I made myself a job for life out of paper, that ephemeral material—after all, both writing and drawing are, even now, done on paper: the books on my shelves are printed on paper, the posters hanging on the wall, alongside pictures, drawings, postcards, the invitations and tickets piled on tables and chairs, the bills and receipts lying on the floor, waiting for the day when I reluctantly tidy them away into a cardboard box. Our digital age is arguably one in which we produce and use more paper than ever before in the annals of human history.

Paper was my first love. I remember the moment when my first boyfriend—we were probably only 16 years old—hastily unwrapped his present and promptly screwed up then threw away the wrapping paper. When in fact the most important part of the gift was written on that paper! If I ever fell in love again, then it would be with a printer or a typesetter, with a master embosser or a head pressman, with a bookbinder or a marbler, with an origamist or someone who licks the back of poster stamps. We would rhapsodize about Munken papers and whisper words like "chamois-colored" into each other's ears. We would purr about heavy, fine-grain, painted pages; we would speak in hushed tones about high-density, soft sheets with lots of texture. All the words I have learned: Endpaper! Embossing! *Kunstbillet*![1] *Netzkappenkarte*![2] With Atlas silk! With mother-of-pearl! Interactive cards! *Blumenoblate*![3] Brocade paper! We would run our fingers over paper as over each other's skin. And if he sent me valentines, they would bear the words "Happiness, Amor, Fidelity; hand-colored."

And my love of paper will also be my last. I know a draftswoman who recycles—out of spite, out of nostalgia, out of her fascination with the material—old index cards for her new drawings. Indeed, I believe there are hardly any fine artists who do not have a strong emotional attachment to—let's call it a love of—paper as a medium, and hence hardly any who would simply walk past waste paper lying on the street. Past orange wrappers, for example: that semi-translucent tissue paper, with royal blue print, blood red, dirty golden. With the now old-fashioned logos of companies from overseas, colonialist kitsch. I unfold the paper and smooth it out, then lay it between the pages of a book.

There are also those children—one day they will become fellow lovers—who know that sometimes the sweetest thing about candies is their packaging. The shiny aluminum foil of icy cups: yellow, blue, green, or magenta, with collectible pictures on them. The white tissue paper, cut into fringes at the ends, from Christmas treats on the tree. The chocolate wrapper made of cardboard and printed with pictures that move when you slide the chocolate out of the packaging. There has always been something about paper that has made people reluctant to throw it away. It could be used to make another collage. Or to cover an old shoe box in new wrapping paper. Or to fold an envelope out of newspaper, or to decorate another with colorful magazine illustrations. Oh, those ephemeral early loves! Paper was my first love, because my mother stirred cellulose into my baby food. As an apprentice, my father drew patterns; as a young man, he designed wallpaper and curtain fabrics,

[1] Card with artistic collage, popular in the early 19th century.

[2] Card with intricate paper cutting, which can be raised—often to reveal another motif below.

[3] Floral decoupage, often with lacelike edging.

Abbildungen aus Magazinen verziert. Ach, ihr ephemeren Jugendlieben! Dem Papier hat meine erste Liebe gegolten, denn meine Mutter hat mir Zellulose in den Babybrei gerührt. Mein Vater ist Musterzeichner im Lehrberuf gewesen, Tapeten und Vorhangstoffe hat er als Jugendlicher entworfen, und um ein Ornament nicht zu einem „Verbrechen" zu machen, hat er eben auch mathematisch-geometrisch denken müssen: Wie und wo überlappen zwei Schablonen, um etwas Drittes zu erzeugen? Später hat mein Vater Industrial Design studiert, in Linz und in London. Als Freiberufler in den 1980er Jahren hat er dann unter anderem die Geschäftspapiere von Firmen gestaltet. Diese Gebrauchspapiere habe ich mir als Kind unter den Nagel gerissen, um darauf unter Zuhilfenahme seiner elektrischen Schreibmaschine seriös-fantastische Briefe an eine Freundin zu verfassen – deren leichtgläubige Eltern den Inhalt eines dieser Briefe tatsächlich ernst genommen haben und daraufhin recht aufgebracht in der Bank nachgefragt haben, wie denn ihre Tochter einen Kredit zurückzahlen solle. „Tausendschillingblau", hätten die Bankbeamten darauf antworten können, „blutrot", „dreckig-golden".

Und noch eine Erinnerung an Gebrauchspapier und den bei dessen Herstellung entstehenden Abfall, der eben nicht gebraucht wird: Wir hatten immer einen endlosen Stapel an Notizkärtchen daheim, und noch immer, im verlassenen Zimmer meines Vaters, finde ich Stöße davon. Heute fällt mir auf, dass es sich dabei um die Überbleibsel von ausgestanzten Adressfeldern von Briefkuverts handelt, den Stanzabfall. Ist das nicht eigentlich poetisch: all unsere Notizen auf dem Abfall ausgestanzter Adressfelder? Mein Vater muss sie einmal nach der Erledigung eines Auftrags von der Druckerei mit nach Hause genommen haben. „Les petits papiers", hat Serge Gainsbourg einmal die kleinen Papiere in einem Chanson besungen, denn auch er hat etwas über die Liebe zu sagen gewusst: „Laissez glisser, papier glacé / Les sentiments, papier collant."

Und ja, aus dem Stanzabfall vom Lochen von Endlospapier werden ja auch manche Konfetti fürs Feiern von Fasching und Festen produziert. Aus dem alten Müll, scheint es, basteln wir uns den neuen Festtagsschmuck. „Die Geburt der Kunst aus der Tragödie des Bastelns", kalauere ich laut vor mich hin. Weil ich wirklich denke, dass sich so der Weg bei vielen Kindern darstellt, die später zu Liebhabern werden. Dass sie sich die Welt neu zusammenbauen aus dem, was andere nicht mehr benutzen. Dass man diese Erfahrung überhaupt je gemacht hat, und später wieder und wieder: dass man Dinge zerschneiden und mit Schere, Papier und Klebstoff neu zusammensetzen kann. Ha! Das nämlich ist sie, die umstürzlerische Kraft, die dem Basteln innewohnt. „Schere, Stein, Papier", so spielen wir.

Und schneiden Figuren aus dem Papier, Kleider, Hüte, zweidimensionale Ankleidepuppen. Die besten Kleider trug bei uns nicht der Kaiser, sondern: Prinz und Prinzessin. Und meine jüngere Schwester, noch ungelenk den Stift in der linken und die Schere in der rechten Hand, tat es mir nach: entstellter Prinz, verschnittene Prinzessin. „Verhoadagelt" heißt das treffende Dialektwort aus Kindheitstagen, wie verdreht, verhöhnt, verunstaltet. Und wie schön und lustig und liebevoll sind diese Figuren jetzt, in meiner Erinnerung. „Messer, Gabel, Schere, Licht", so spielen wir und spielen mit der Gefahr. Irgendjemand in der Nachbarschaft hat eine Zackenschere besessen, einen großen Schatz. Irgendjemand ein Falzbein, irgendjemand einen Brieföffner.

Die kleinen Schätze haben wir uns aus Papier selbst gebaut: Zündholzschachteln, die beim Aufziehen etwas Gefaltetes ausspucken, Eselsohren, die beim Auffalten die „Neugierdsnase" beschimpfen,

and to avoid a decoration becoming a "crime" he also had to think mathematically, geometrically: how and where do two stencils overlap to create something new? Later my father studied industrial design, in Linz and in London. As a freelancer in the 1980s, he designed companies' business documents, among other things. I pilfered that commercial paper as a child to write serious yet fantastical letters to a friend with the assistance of his electric typewriter—and her gullible parents actually took the content of those letters seriously. So much so that they went to the bank and anxiously asked how on earth their daughter should repay a loan. "One thousand schillings bluely," the bank clerks could have answered, "blood redly," "dirty goldenly."

And just one more memory of commercial paper and the leftover waste its production creates. We always had endless piles of notecards at home, and I still find stacks of them now in my father's abandoned room. Today I realized that they are the paper that is punched out of envelopes' address fields, the chad. Isn't that poetic: all of our notes are written on the waste paper punched from windowed envelopes. My father must have brought them home with him from the printing office after finishing an assignment. "Les petits papiers," Serge Gainsbourg once sung about such small pieces of paper in a chanson—as he, too, knew how to talk about love: "Laissez glisser, papier glacé / Les sentiments, papier collant."

And yes, some of the confetti we use to celebrate carnival and parties is actually the chad produced when punching holes in fanfolded paper. It seems that we craft our new festive decorations from old trash. "The Birth of Art: Out of the Spirit of Crafting," I joke to myself aloud. Because I genuinely believe that it paves the way for many children to become fellow lovers one day. That they put the world back together again with what others no longer use. That they have even had that experience, and later again and again: that they can cut things up and put them back together again with scissors, paper, and glue. Ha! You see, that is it, that is the subversive power that is inherent in crafting. "Rock, paper, scissors," that is how we play.

And cutting figures out of paper: clothes, hats, two-dimensional paper dolls. In our house, it was not the emperor who wore the best clothes, but the prince and the princess. And my younger sister, still ungainly with a pen in her left hand and scissors in her right, copied me: contorted prince, chopped princess. "Verhoadagelt" is the apt dialect word from our childhood, meaning distorted, ridiculed, deformed. And how beautiful and funny and lovely those figures are now, in my memory. "Messer, Gabel, Schere, Licht"[4]: that is how we play and how we dally with danger. One of our neighbors owned pinking shears, a great treasure. Another a bone folder, someone else a letter opener. We made our small treasures ourselves, out of paper: matchboxes that spit out a folded something when you open them, dog-ears that scold the "busybody" who unfolds them, flip-books that make your fingers sore. Paper can be delicate, yes, but it can also slice so sharply that it inflicts on you the occasional blood-red cut. It is pliable, yes, but when folded it becomes resilient and robust. What fascinates me about paper, pasteboard, and cardboard is the variability of the material. Like graphic design itself, which can be found in the many, many portfolios in the collection at the MAK, and which is subject to changes in trends and technology. We see the countless greeting cards and labels, printed using the relief printing technique with metal sorts and stereotypes; we see the late 18th-century decorated papers printed by hand with stamps; the Biedermeier visiting cards, made to shine with a layer of glue or gelatin; the offset printing of 20th-century posters and

4 "Knife, fork, scissors, fire," a nursery rhyme warning small children to keep away from dangerous objects.

Daumenkinos, die die Finger wund machen. Papier kann zart sein, ja, aber es kann auch so scharf schneiden, dass man davon manch blutroten Schnitt zugefügt bekommt. Es ist biegsam, ja, aber durch Falten wird es belastbar und stabil gemacht. Was mich an Papier, Pappe und Karton also auch fasziniert, ist die Wandelbarkeit des Materials.

So wie die Gebrauchsgrafik selbst, die sich in den vielen, vielen Mappen der Sammlung des MAK finden lässt, dem Wandel von Modegeschmack und Technik unterliegt. Wir sehen die zahllosen Grußkarten und Etiketten, bedruckt mittels Metalllettern und Klischees im Hochdruckverfahren, wir sehen die händisch mittels Stempel bedruckten Buntpapiere des späten 18. Jahrhunderts, die Biedermeier-Visitenkarten, zum Glänzen gebracht durch eine Schicht Leim oder Gelatine, den Offsetdruck der Plakate und Reiseprospekte des 20. Jahrhunderts bis hin zum gegenwärtig praktizierten Digitaldruck, geschnitten mit „Lasercut", hochglänzend durch Lack und Zellophanierung. Dem Papier hat unsere erste Liebe gegolten, und sie wird unsre letzte sein. Immer werden wir mit unseren Fingern, so wie über die matte Haut des Geliebten, über glänzendes Papier gleiten. Wir Kinder, die in ihren Alben Pickerl, Aufkleber, Sticker gesammelt haben, quietschbunt, glitzernd, beflockt, die Einträge in Poesiealben und Stammbücher geschrieben haben. Wir Kinder, die ihre Zeichnungen gefaltet haben, damit das nächste Kind einen Rumpf an einen verdeckten Kopf zeichnen kann, wieder gefaltet, weitergereicht, sodass das dritte Kind Beine und Schuhe an einen versteckten Rumpf zeichnen kann. Und wie wir dann, nach dem dritten oder vierten Kind, die gesamte Zeichnung aufgefaltet haben: welch Mensch-Tier-Mischwesen haben wir da auf dem Blatt Papier vorgefunden! Wir Kinder, denen die Mutter Zellulose in den Brei gerührt hat und der Vater Muster auf die Tapeten gezeichnet hat. Wir Liebhaber, wir „Ephemeristen".

Der Sammelwert, im Vergleich zu Möbeln und Immobilien: nicht allzu hoch. Jedoch einfacher zu erwerben und leichter aufzubewahren. Und wie sind sie eigentlich erhalten geblieben, diese filigranen Eintagsfliegen aus Papier: die Eintrittskarten, die Postkarten, Exlibris, Andachtsbilder? Nämlich über die Jahrhunderte, über die Umzüge, die Wasserschäden, die Brände und Kriege hinweg? Die Lesezeichen, die Spielkarten, die Kalender, die Briefe? Die Entwürfe der Schülerinnen und Schüler der Kunstgewerbeschule, die Musterproben von Dagobert Peche, Koloman Moser, Josef Hoffmann, Hilda Jesser, Wally Wieselthier, die Kunstbillets von Johann Joseph Endletzberger, die Plakate von Julius Klinger, Joseph Binder und Ernst Ludwig Franke, die Marmorpapiere aus der Sammlung Clerget, dies und das und außerdem zwischen alledem die Zeitschriften-Annonce für *Lutschi HUSTEN-PASTILLEN*. All dies hat jemand gesammelt und aufbewahrt, und das ist das eigentliche Wunder: die ewige Liebe zum Vergänglichen.

Die Autorin dankt dem MAK und seiner Mitarbeiterin Anne-Katrin Rossberg für viele Stunden vor aufgeschlagenen Mappen voll mit Papier.

travel brochures; everything, including the contemporary practice of digital printing, laser-cut and high-gloss thanks to dye ink and a cellophane coating.

Paper was our first love, and it will be our last. We will always run our fingers over glossy paper as over our lover's mat skin. We children whose albums contained collections of stickers—gaudy, glittery, flocked—who wrote inscriptions in autograph books. We children who folded our drawings so that the next child could draw a body onto a hidden head, then folded it again and passed it on so that the third child could draw legs and shoes onto a hidden body. And then, when we unfolded the entire drawing after the third or fourth child, what human-animal hybrids we discovered on those pieces of paper! We children whose mothers stirred cellulose into our baby food and whose fathers drew patterns on wallpaper. We fellow lovers, we ephemerists.

Compared to furniture and real estate, the collector's value is not very high. But they are easier to acquire and simpler to store. How have they survived, in fact, these delicate one-hit wonders made of paper: the admission tickets, the postcards, ex libris, devotional images? Over the centuries, despite moving house, water damage, fires, and wars? The bookmarks, the playing cards, the diaries, the letters? The designs by students at the School of Arts and Crafts; the pattern samples by Dagobert Peche, Koloman Moser, Josef Hoffmann, Hilda Jesser, Wally Wieselthier; the *Kunstbillets* by Johann Joseph Endletzberger; the posters by Julius Klinger, Joseph Binder, and Ernst Ludwig Franke; the marbled papers from the Clerget Collection; this and that and also, between all of the above, the magazine advertisement for *Lutschi HUSTEN-PASTILLEN*[5]. All of this someone collected and kept, and that is the real miracle: our undying love of the short-lived.

[5] Lutschi cough lozenges.

The author would like to thank the MAK and Anne-Katrin Rossberg for many happy hours spent in front of portfolios filled with paper.

Ernst Ludwig Franke
Etikett für *Lutschi HUSTEN-PASTILLEN*
um 1925
Klischee
Label for [Lutschi cough lozenges]
ca. 1925
Cliché
KI 13369-20-3, Ankauf purchased from
Ilka Franke 1959

BUNTPAPIER

KOMMENTAR von **Frieder Schmidt**

Raphael Rosenberg *Ornamentale Buntpapiere und die Bildexperimente der Wiener Secessionisten*

AUS DER SAMMLUNG
A   Brokatpapier aus dem 18. Jahrhundert
B   Marmorpapier aus der Sammlung Clerget
C   Buntpapier aus drei Jahrhunderten
D   Geschenk- und Packpapier
E   Orangenpapier aus den 1950er Jahren

DECORATED PAPERS

COMMENT by **Frieder Schmidt**

Raphael Rosenberg *Ornamental Decorated Papers and the Vienna Secessionists' Picture Experiments*

FROM THE COLLECTION
A   18th-Century Brocade Paper
B   Marbled Paper from the Clerget Collection
C   Three Centuries of Decorated Paper
D   Wrapping and Packing Paper
E   Orange Wrappers from the 1950s

FÜR DEN AUGENBLICK UND MANCHMAL, ABER NICHT IMMER, DARÜBER HINAUS FÜR EINE
HALBE EWIGKEIT GESCHAFFEN – das sind die Zeitgefüge, in denen sich jene Welt der Buntpapiere
bewegt, die aus dem Orient nach Europa kam und dort neuartige Ausprägungen fand. Was kann es
Flüchtigeres geben als Tinte, die auf Wasser schwimmt? Wird das entstandene Muster auf einen
Papierbogen übertragen, ist es gleichsam eingefangen und dauerhaft fixiert. In Japan sind älteste
Zeugnisse dieser Suminagashi-Technik aus dem 12. Jahrhundert überliefert. In Persien und in der
Türkei entwickelte sich die Marmoriertechnik, um 1600 gelangten solche Buntpapiere als „Türkisch
Marmor" nach Europa. Heutzutage verbindet man diese Erzeugnisse hauptsächlich mit Bucheinbän-
den, weil sie in den Beständen altehrwürdiger Bibliotheken anzutreffen sind. Dort finden sich auch
Belege für andere Techniken, die BuchbinderInnen in ihren Werkstätten ohne großen Aufwand
fabrizieren konnten, zum Beispiel Kleisterpapiere oder Spritzpapiere.

Wer sich auf die Welt des Buntpapiers einlässt, wird rasch feststellen, dass die Verwendung
desselben sich keineswegs nur auf das Reich der Bücher beschränkt. Eine wunderbare Welt der
handgedruckten Modelpapiere, die in ihrem Design dem Textildruck der Zeit glichen und daher
auch als Zitzpapiere bezeichnet wurden, findet sich in manchen Archiven in den langen Reihen der
Ratsprotokolle und Rechnungsbände. Wer sich für Antiquitäten interessiert, findet die Buntpapiere
als Innenverkleidung von Schränken und Schubladen. Fernrohre sind damit bezogen und die unbe-
druckten Seiten von Spielkarten damit beklebt worden. Brokatpapiere gleichen den Bilderbogen,
sie beeindrucken mit Prägungen und Metallglanz und sind die Zierde von Huldigungsschriften oder
Musikalien. Es kann nicht wundern, dass sich im 19. Jahrhundert eine ganze Buntpapierindustrie
entwickelte und den Weltmarkt bis nach Lateinamerika belieferte.

Heute sind es KünstlerInnen und RestauratorInnen, SammlerInnen und AntiquarInnen, die das Wissen um diese Welt und die praktischen Kenntnisse und Fertigkeiten hüten. Private und eine Reihe
wichtiger öffentlicher Sammlungen, unter anderem in London und Den Haag, in Berlin und München,
bewahren dieses ästhetische Vermächtnis. Regelmäßige Treffen und Workshops dienen ebenso
dazu. Nicht zuletzt das Vermächtnis des Wiener Papiersammlers und Hofrats Franz Bartsch in den
Sammlungen des Deutschen Buch- und Schriftmuseums der Deutschen Nationalbibliothek in Leipzig
trägt dazu bei, dass dieses seit dem Jahr 2004 als Treffpunkt für jährliche Buntpapier-Workshops
auserkoren ist. Dort finden Menschen zusammen, die sich für die Details alter Fertigungstechniken
interessieren und um eine exakte Terminologie zu deren Benennung ringen. Ein mehrsprachiges
Bestimmungsbuch ist dank der Energie von Susanne Krause aus diesen Aktivitäten entstanden,
das im Frühjahr 2016 in zweiter Auflage bei Hauswedell veröffentlicht wurde. Aufgrund der Initiative
der Kunsthistorikerin Julia Rinck ist unter www.buntpapier.org eine deutschsprachige Plattform
verfügbar, die in mustergültiger Weise die Welt der alten Papiere, aber auch gegenwärtiger künstlerischer Aktivitäten mit modernen Dokumentations- und Kommunikationsformen zusammenbringt.
Scheinbar obsolet Gewordenes erweist sich als sehr lebendig.

Frieder Schmidt, Leiter der Kultur- und Papierhistorischen Sammlungen des Deutschen Buch- und
Schriftmuseums, Deutsche Nationalbibliothek Leipzig

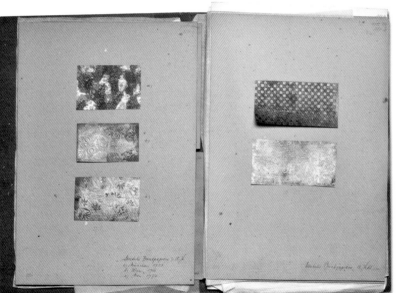

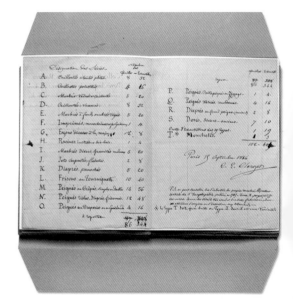

MADE FOR A SHORT MOMENT AND SOMETIMES, BUT NOT ALWAYS, FOR WHAT SEEMS TO BE AN ETERNITY: such is the range of life spans found within the world of decorated papers, which came to Europe from the East and evolved in their new home. What could be more fleeting than ink swimming on water? Yet when the resulting pattern is transferred to a sheet of paper, it is captured and recorded for posterity. In Japan the oldest evidence of this suminagashi technique dates from the 12th century. The marbling technique was developed in Persia and Turkey; this kind of decorated paper arrived in Europe around 1600, where it was known as "Turkish marbling." Nowadays, we mainly associate such items with book covers because they can be found in the collections of time-honored libraries. Those bibliophiles' paradises also house examples of other techniques, such as paste paper or sprinkled paper, which bookbinders could manufacture in their workshops without great difficulty.

Whoever becomes involved in the world of decorated paper will soon discover that its use is by no means restricted to the realm of books. A whole world of handmade block-printed papers—whose design resembled the textile printing of the time and hence led to them also being called chintz papers—can be found among the long rows of council minutes and account books in some archives. Those who are interested in antiques will find decorated papers used as linings for cabinets and drawers. They were used to cover telescopes and decorate the unprinted sides of playing cards. Brocade papers resemble Épinal prints, impressing their beholders with their embossing and metallic shine; they provide the adornment on written tributes or sheet music. It is hardly surprising that an entire industry dedicated to decorated paper developed in the 19th century, supplying a global market reaching as far as Latin America.

Now it is artists and restorers, collectors and antiquarians who safeguard our knowledge of this world, its practical skills and expertise. Both private as well as a number of important public collections—including those in London and The Hague, in Berlin and Munich—preserve this aesthetic legacy. Regular meetings and workshops serve the same purpose. The German Museum of Books and Writing at the German National Library in Leipzig has been selected as the venue for annual decorated paper workshops since 2004—in no small part due to the collections housing the bequest of the Viennese paper collector and privy councilor Franz Bartsch. It is a "place of pilgrimage" for people who are interested in the details of old production techniques and strive to know their precise terminology. Thanks to the efforts of Susanne Krause, a multilingual reference book has arisen from these activities, and Hauswedell published a revised edition in Spring 2016. By virtue of the initiative of art historian Julia Rinck, an exemplary German-language platform is available at www.buntpapier.org, which unites the world of these old papers with contemporary artistic activities while also making use of modern forms of documentation and communication. What had seemed obsolete has proven to be very much alive.

Frieder Schmidt, Head of the Cultural and Paper History Collections at the German Museum of Books and Writing, German National Library in Leipzig

ORNAMENTALE BUNTPAPIERE UND DIE BILDEXPERIMENTE DER WIENER SECESSIONISTEN
RAPHAEL ROSENBERG

Das MAK besitzt eine erlesene Sammlung von Buntpapieren aus vier Jahrhunderten. Sie geben Einblick in eine Gattung, mit der sich die Kunstgeschichte selten befasst. Einzigartig in der Sammlung ist der Bestand von Wiener Papieren des frühen 20. Jahrhunderts. Die zwei ersten Abschnitte des vorliegenden Aufsatzes skizzieren die Geschichte und beschreiben die Ästhetik des Buntpapiers. Der dritte stellt Blätter von drei Künstlern der Wiener Secession vor. Es gilt zu zeigen, dass Josef Hoffmann (1870–1956), Koloman Moser (1868–1918) und Leopold Stolba (1863–1929) mit Techniken des Buntpapiers regelrechte Bilder gestaltet haben und damit von der traditionellen ornamentalen Ästhetik und Funktion des Buntpapiers deutlich abgewichen sind. Stolba, der bei diesen Experimenten eine führende Rolle einnimmt, hat sie ab 1903 in der Secession mehrfach gezeigt. Jahre vor Wassily Kandinsky hat er damit in Kunstausstellungen abstrakte Bilder präsentiert. Im vierten und abschließenden Abschnitt wird die unterschiedliche Bedeutung, die Abstraktion für beide Künstler darstellte, diskutiert.

1. ZUR GATTUNG DES BUNTPAPIERS
Buntpapier ist ein Sammelbegriff: Er fasst Papiere zusammen, die mit verschiedenen Techniken hergestellt wurden. Das Gemeinsame liegt in der Funktion: Papierbögen werden ästhetisch veredelt, um andere Objekte zu verschönern. So definiert Wilhelm Exner Buntpapier 1869 als „Papier, dessen Oberfläche auf einer Seite desselben durch Auftragen von Farben (weiß und schwarz nicht ausgeschlossen), Firnissen, Metallen und verschiedenen anderen Stoffen ein von dem Habitus des gewöhnlichen Papiers wesentlich verändertes Aussehen erhalten hat und in Bogenformat in Handel gesetzt wird. Das Buntpapier wird auf die verschiedenartigste Weise, jedoch immer zum Überziehen von Gegenständen oder zum Anfertigen von solchen verwendet."[1]
Buntpapier sieht kostbar aus, ist raffiniert und dennoch in Herstellung und Material nicht zu kostspielig, sodass es für breite Schichten erschwinglich bleibt. In weiten Teilen Europas ist es seit dem 17. Jahrhundert sehr populär. Es kommt beim Binden von Büchern (Vorsatzpapiere, teils auch Buchdeckel), beim Auskleiden von Kästchen, Koffern, Schränken und bis heute als Geschenkpapier zum Einsatz. Hergestellt wurde es bis zum 19. Jahrhundert überwiegend von LohnarbeiterInnen, die in Buchbindereien und Papierhandlungen angestellt waren. Einzelne Buntpapiermacher sind seit 1700 als Verleger organisiert, damit wirtschaftlich selbstständig und namentlich fassbar. Die Darstellung einer *Gold u. allerley gefärbtes u. geprägtes Papiermacherin* (Abb. 001) zeigt, dass in Deutschland das Herstellen von Buntpapier um 1730 den Status eines eigenen Berufs hatte, für den es einen französischen Begriff gab (männlich „dominotier", weiblich „dominotière"), aber noch keinen zusammenfassenden deutschen.[2] Seit dem späten 18. Jahrhundert verlagert sich ein Großteil der Produktion in Verbund mit Papiertapeten in größere Manufakturen.[3]

2. DIE ÄSTHETIK DES BUNTPAPIERS: DAS PRINZIP DER WIEDERHOLUNG
Beeindruckend ist die Vielfalt der Formen: Buntpapiere kommen mit mimetischen Motiven, wie Blüten, Ranken, Tieren und Menschen, genauso wie amimetischen (d. h. ungegenständlichen) Kompositionen, geometrischen Strukturen, wilden Tupfen und fließenden Marmorierungen vor. Dessen ungeachtet lässt sich ein allen Blättern gemeinsames Gestaltungsprinzip ausmachen: das Prinzip der Wiederholung.

[1] Exner, Wilhelm Franz, *Die Tapeten- und Buntpapier-Industrie für Fabrikanten und Gewerbetreibende, sowie für technische Institute*, Weimar 1869, 1.

[2] Aus: Engelbrecht, Martin, *Neu-eröffnete Sammlung der mit ihren eigenen Arbeiten und Werkzeugen eingekleideten Künstlern, Handwerkern und Professionen*, Augsburg 1730, mit 170 Darstellungen von 85 Berufen, jeweils in männlicher und weiblicher Form. Das Vorkommen einer weiblichen „dominotière" ist deswegen kein Beleg für die Ausführung des Berufs durch Frauen. Dass dies der Fall war, schreibt Albert Haemmerle (*Buntpapier. Herkommen, Geschichte, Techniken, Beziehungen zur Kunst*, München 1961, 16) leider ohne systematische Nachweise. Die Begriffe „domino" und „dominotier" sind im französischen bereits 1514 und 1540 belegt (Rey, Alain, *Dictionnaire historique de la langue française*, 2 Bde., Paris 1993, Bd. I, 623). Der älteste mir bekannte Beleg für den zusammenfassenden deutschen Begriff „Buntpapier" stammt aus dem Jahr 1804 („Die Gräflische Bunt-Papier-Fabrik in Leipzig", in: *Journal für Fabrik, Manufactur, Handlung und Mode* (1) 26 1804, 45–48). Die englische Bezeichnung „decorated paper" ist offensichtlich noch jünger. Zur Terminologie der Buntpapiersorten siehe: Krause, Susanne/Rinck, Julia, *Buntpapier – Ein Bestimmungsbuch. Decorated Paper – A Guide Book*, Stuttgart 2016.

[3] Haemmerle 1961 (s. Anm. 2), 16–26.

ORNAMENTAL DECORATED PAPERS AND THE VIENNA SECESSIONISTS' PICTURE EXPERIMENTS
RAPHAEL ROSENBERG

The MAK owns an exquisite collection of decorated papers, which span four centuries. They provide an insight into a genre with which the history of art rarely concerns itself. Unique to the collection are holdings of papers by early 20th-century Viennese artists. The two initial sections of this essay outline the history and describe the aesthetics of decorated paper. The third section introduces papers by three artists from the Vienna Secession. It argues that Josef Hoffmann (1870–1956), Koloman Moser (1868–1918), and Leopold Stolba (1863–1929) designed veritable pictures using decorated paper techniques and hence departed appreciably from the traditional ornamental aesthetics and function of decorated paper. Stolba, who assumed a leading role in these experiments, showed his resulting work at the Secession on several occasions beginning in 1903. He therefore displayed abstract images in art exhibitions many years before Wassily Kandinsky. The fourth and final section discusses the different way in which both artists perceived abstraction.

1. DECORATED PAPER

Decorated paper is an umbrella term: it encompasses papers produced using a range of different techniques. What they all have in common is their function: sheets of paper are aesthetically enhanced to embellish the appearance of other objects. Wilhelm Exner described decorated paper in 1869 as "Paper whose surface has achieved a considerably altered appearance compared to that which is customary for ordinary paper due to the application of paint (white and black not precluded), varnishes, metals, and various other substances to one side of the same, and which is sold in the format of sheets. Decorated paper is used in a wide variety of different ways, however always to cover or to create objects."[1]

Decorated paper looks valuable, is elaborate and yet not particularly costly in terms of its production or materials, and is hence normally affordable for broad swathes of the population. In large parts of Europe, it has enjoyed great popularity since the 17th century. It is used when binding books (endpapers, sometimes also book covers), when lining boxes, suitcases, and cabinets, and to this day when wrapping presents. Until the 19th century it was mostly produced by laborers who were employed by bookbinders and paper merchants. Some decorated paper makers have been organized as publishers since 1700, thus making them economically independent and identifiable by name. The depiction of a "Female maker of gold and variously dyed and embossed paper" (*Gold u. allerley gefärbtes u. geprägtes Papiermacherin*) (ill. 001) shows that in Germany the production of decorated paper had the status of a separate profession around 1730, for which there was a French term (male "dominotier," female "dominotière"), though at that time neither an English nor an overarching German term.[2] Since the late 18th century the majority of its production has taken place in larger factories alongside wallpaper.[3]

2. THE AESTHETICS OF DECORATED PAPER: THE PRINCIPLE OF REPETITION

The variety of forms is impressive: decorated papers exist with mimetic motifs such as flowers, tendrils, animals, and people, as well as amimetic (i.e. non-representational) compositions, geometric structures, sprinkled blots, and flowing marbling. Nevertheless, it is possible to distinguish a design principle common to all decorated papers: the principle of repetition. There are precise repetitions with measurable

[1] Exner, Wilhelm Franz, *Die Tapeten- und Buntpapier-Industrie fur Fabrikanten und Gewerbetreibende, sowie fur technische Institute*, Weimar 1869, 1. Translated by Maria Slater.

[2] From: Engelbrecht, Martin, *Neu-eröffnete Sammlung der mit ihren eigenen Arbeiten und Werkzeugen eingekleideten Künstlern, Handwerkern und Professionen*, Augsburg 1730 with 170 illustrations of 85 professions, each with male and female variants. The incidence of a female "dominotière" is therefore not to be understood as evidence of women having carried out the profession. Albert Haemmerle (*Buntpapier. Herkommen, Geschichte, Techniken, Beziehungen zur Kunst*, Munich 1961, 16) argues that this was indeed the case, though sadly without giving systematic evidence. The terms "domino" and "dominotier" are recorded in French as early as 1514 and 1540 (Rey, Alain, *Dictionnaire historique de la langue française*, 2 vols., Paris 1993, vol. I, 623). The oldest supporting document of which I am aware for the synoptic German term "Buntpapier" comes from 1804 ("Die Gräffische Bunt-Papier-Fabrik in Leipzig," in: *Journal für Fabrik, Manufactur, Handlung und Mode* (1) 26 1804, 45–48).

The English designation "decorated paper" is evidently even younger. On the terminology of types of decorated paper, see: Krause, Susanne/Rinck, Julia, *Buntpapier – Ein Bestimmungsbuch. Decorated Paper – A Guide Book*, Stuttgart 2016.

[3] Haemmerle 1961 *(see note 2)*, 16–26.

Es gibt präzise Wiederholungen mit messbarem „Rapport", besonders bei Drucktechniken (s. S. 057 f., 060 f., 070–087), wie auch ungefähre Wiederholungen, bei denen nicht dieselben, sondern lediglich ähnliche Formen und Farben in nicht ganz regelmäßigen Abständen nebeneinander wiederholt werden – etwa bei Tunkpapieren (d. h. marmorierte Papiere), bei denen beispielsweise die Wiederholung analoger Flecken (sog. Steinmarmor, s. S. 064 f.), die Perpetuierung gleicher Strukturen oder die kunstvolle Aneinanderreihung ähnlicher Formen (sog. Kammmarmor oder Schnecken, s. S. 067 und 066) vorkommen. Die Grenze zwischen präzisen und unpräzisen Wiederholungen ist fließend, und es gibt zahlreiche Buntpapiere, die beide Formen spielerisch verknüpfen.

Nehmen wir dafür drei Beispiele, an denen auch das technische Spektrum der Herstellung solcher Papierbögen aufgezeigt werden kann. Das erste Beispiel entstand um die Mitte des 18. Jahrhunderts (Abb. 002). Es handelt sich um ein Brokatpapier, in Augsburg von Johann Michael Munck (gest. vor 1762) verlegt. Zwei Schichten liegen hier in gezielter Dissoziierung übereinander: ein in Reliefdruck hergestelltes Blumenmuster mit golden glänzendem Metall in den Vertiefungen und ein Teppich farbiger Flecken in Orange, Purpur, Violett, Türkis und Grün. Die Flecken scheinen wie wild auf das Blatt hingeworfen. Tatsächlich sind sie aber durch vorgeschnittene Schablonen aufgetragen. Diese farbige „Patronierung" erfolgte vor dem reliefierten Druck mit Metallblatt.[4] Das zweite Beispiel (Abb. 003) ist ein Kleisterpapier, das in drei Schritten hergestellt wurde – vermutlich in Herrnhut (Sachsen) in den Jahrzehnten um 1800.[5] Der Bogen wurde zuerst mit eingefärbtem Kleister gestrichen, um schachbrettartig purpurne und violette Quadrate mit abwechselnd gelben und grünen Tupfen in den Ecken zu erzeugen. Danach wurde das Blatt auf ein zweites gepresst und, solange der Kleister noch feucht war, wieder auseinandergezogen. Damit entstehen die für Kleisterpapiere charakteristischen Schlieren. Im dritten Schritt wurden die wellenförmigen Linien und Wirbel aus der noch feuchten Kleisterfarbe herausgeschabt, sodass sie ein Rautenmuster ergeben. Das Schachbrett der Farbverteilung und die Rauten der Wellenlinien folgen zwar dem Prinzip eines regelmäßigen Musters, sie sind aber händisch ausgeführt und damit voller Abweichungen. Bemerkenswert ist zudem, dass Rauten und Schachbrett sich nicht decken. Einschließlich der Schlieren gibt es also drei Ordnungen von Mustern. Alle drei haben Unregelmäßigkeiten und einen je eigenen Rapport. Das dritte Beispiel ist in nur einem Druckvorgang mit einem Holzmodel hergestellt (Abb. 004). Eine durchgehende Linie schlängelt sich mit zahlreichen Windungen durch das Blatt, Punkte füllen die Leerräume aus. Windungen und Punkte wiederholen sich zwar, aber nicht genau – sie scheinen zufällig gestreut, der Verlauf der Linie ist unberechenbar.

Man kann Ornament sowohl funktional (Ornament als bereichernde Hinzufügung) als auch formal (Ornament als Wiederholung von Mustern) definieren.[6] Buntpapier ist in beiderlei Hinsicht ornamental: funktional, weil es dazu dient, etwas anderes (Buch, Kästchen, Geschenk etc.) zu schmücken, und formal, weil die Gestaltung dem Prinzip der Wiederholung folgt.

3. BUNTPAPIERBILDER DER WIENER SECESSIONISTEN

Buntpapiere sind zunächst dem Geschick und der Fantasie von FacharbeiterInnen, die keine Akademie besucht haben und überwiegend anonym geblieben sind, zu verdanken. Das änderte sich in den letzten Jahren des 19. Jahrhunderts, als das Kunsthandwerk eine signifikante Aufwertung erfuhr. Namentlich bekannte und teils akademisch ausgebildete KünstlerInnen schufen damals Muster für Vorsatzpapiere und stellten Einzelblätter eigenhändig her. Ihre Werke wurden in Kunstzeitschriften abgebildet, diskutiert und in Ausstellungen gezeigt.[7] Von 1901 an entwarfen auch Künstler der Wiener Secession Vorsatzpapiere, ebenso wie die SchülerInnen der Kunstgewebeschule (s. S. 068).

[4] Für eine detaillierte Analyse der Technik und Geschichte des Brokatpapiers sowie ein Verzeichnis bekannter Blätter siehe Haemmerle 1961 (s. Anm. 2), 77–130, 197–245. Die deutliche Verschiebung zwischen Reliefdruck und schabloniertem Farbauftrag ist häufig und nicht nur bei diesem Beispiel beabsichtigt. Haemmerle

konnte dafür wenig Verständnis aufbringen (ebd., 90).

[5] Vgl. ebd., 139–144.

[6] Zur Definition von Ornament/ornamental siehe: Kroll, Frank-Lothar/Raulet, Gérard, „Ornament", in: Barck, Karlheinz et al. (Hg.), Ästhetische

Grundbegriffe. Historisches Wörterbuch in sieben Bänden, Bd. IV, Stuttgart 2002, 656–683.

[7] Wolfe, Richard J., Marbled Paper. Its History, Techniques, and Patterns, Philadelphia 1990, 124–136. Im deutschsprachigen Raum drucken von 1897 an zwei führende „Jugendstil"-

Zeitschriften regelmäßig Künstlerbuntpapiere ab: die Münchner Dekorative Kunst und die Darmstädter Deutsche Kunst und Dekoration. Letztere schließt in ihren Wettbewerbsausschreibungen von Anfang an auch Vorsatzpapiere ein (erste Ausschreibung zum 5. Juni 1898 in: Deutsche Kunst und Dekoration (1) I 1897/98, o. S.).

001
Martin Engelbrecht
**Une Dominotiere. Gold u. allerley
gefärbtes u. geprägtes Papiermacherin**
Augsburg, 1730
Aus: *Neu-eröffnete Sammlung der mit
ihren eigenen Arbeiten und Werkzeugen
eingekleideten Künstlern, Handwerkern
und Professionen*, Tafel 172
Kupferstich, koloriert
**[Female maker of gold and variously
dyed and embossed paper]**
Augsburg, 1730
From: *Neu-eröffnete Sammlung der mit
ihren eigenen Arbeiten und Werkzeugen
eingekleideten Künstlern, Handwerkern
und Professionen*, plate 172
Colored copperplate engraving
Germanisches Nationalmuseum Nürnberg
Nuremberg, Inv. Nr. Inv. No. 4° Vh 173, 1 [4]
© GNM

002
Johann Michael Munck
Brokatpapier
Augsburg, Mitte 18. Jh.
Prägedruck, Pochoirkolorierung
Brocade Paper
Augsburg, mid-18th c.
Embossing, pochoir coloring
147 x 193 mm
KI 3026-134, Ankauf purchased from
Antiquariat Mössel 1877

003
Anonym Anonymous
Kleisterpapier
Vermutl. Herrnhut, um 1800
Paste Paper
Prob. Herrnhut, ca. 1800
158 x 198 mm
KI 3026-142, Ankauf
purchased from Antiquariat
Mössel 1877

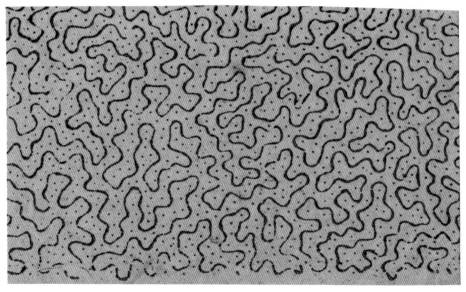

004
Anonym Anonymous
Modeldruckpapier
Österreich, um 1800
Block Printed Paper
Austria, ca. 1800
103 x 173 mm
KI 9080-30, Schenkung
donation from Karl Kock 1932

repeated patterns—especially common in printing techniques (see p. 057 f., 060 f., 070–087)—as well as irregular repeats, in which not the same but rather merely similar forms and colors are repeated next to one another in not entirely regular intervals: for example, in marbled papers, which feature a repetition of homogenous blots (so-called spot patterns; see p. 064 f.), and so-called Italian patterns with fine structures, or the artful concatenation of similar forms (so-called nonpareil or French curl; see p. 067 f.). The dividing line between precise and imprecise repetitions is fluid, and many decorated papers playfully combine the two forms. Let's consider three examples, which also demonstrate the technical spectrum associated with producing such sheets of paper.

The first example was created around the middle of the 18th century (ill. 002). It is a sheet of brocade paper, printed in Augsburg by Johann Michael Munck (d. pre-1762). Two layers lie on top of one another and are deliberately dissociated: a floral pattern produced by textured printing with shining golden metal in the recesses, and a carpet of colorful spots in orange, purple, violet, turquoise, and green. The spots look as though they have been thrown onto the sheet at random. In fact, however, they were applied using pre-cut stencils. This colorful stenciling was achieved prior to the textured print with metal leaf.[4] The second example (ill. 003) is a piece of paste paper that was produced in three steps, presumably in Herrnhut (Saxony) in the decades around 1800.[5] The sheet was first painted with a dyed paste to create a chessboard effect of purple and violet squares with alternating yellow and green dashes in the corners. Thereafter, it was pressed onto a second sheet and pulled apart again before the paste dried. This is how paste paper's characteristic streaks are created. In a third step, the wavelike lines and whirls were scraped out of the wet colored paste resulting in a diamond pattern. The chessboard color distribution and the diamond wavy lines may follow the principle of a regular pattern, but they are made by hand and as such replete with irregularities. It is also worth noting that the diamonds and chessboard are not congruent. Consequently, there are three arrangements of pattern including the streaks. All of them have irregularities and each has its own repeating pattern. The third example was produced in just one printing process with a wooden mold (ill. 004). A continuous line winds its way with numerous meanders through the sheet; dots fill the empty spaces. The twists and dots are admittedly repeated, but not precisely: they look as though they have been scattered at random, and the course of the line is erratic.

Ornament can be defined both functionally (ornament as an enriching addition) as well as formally (ornament as a repetition of patterns).[6] Decorated paper is ornamental in both respects: functionally because it serves to decorate something else (a book, cabinet, present, etc.), and formally because the design follows the principle of repetition.

3. DECORATED PAPER PICTURES BY THE VIENNA SECESSIONISTS

Decorated papers used to be made by skilled and imaginative workers who had not attended an academy and largely remained anonymous. That changed in the last years of the 19th century when the prestige of handicraft significantly increased. At the time, artists who were known by name—some of whom had been educated in academies—created patterns for endpapers and produced individual sheets themselves by hand. Their works were depicted and discussed in art periodicals, and even shown in exhibitions.[7] From 1901 onwards, artists of the Vienna Secession also designed endpapers, as did the students of the School of Arts and Crafts (see p. 069).

[4] For a detailed analysis of the technique and history of brocade paper, as well as a catalog of known sheets, see Haemmerle 1961 (see note 2), 77–130, 197–245. The explicit shift between textured printing and stenciled paint application is frequent and intentional—not only in this example. Haemmerle had little understanding for it (ibid., 90).

[5] Cf. ibid., 139–144.

[6] On the definition of ornament/ornamental, see: Kroll, Frank-Lothar/Raulet, Gérard, "Ornament," in: Barck, Karlheinz et al. (eds.), *Ästhetische Grundbegriffe. Historisches Wörterbuch in sieben Bänden*, vol. IV, Stuttgart 2002, 656–683.

[7] Wolfe, Richard J., *Marbled Paper. Its History, Techniques, and Patterns*, Philadelphia 1990, 124–136. In the German-speaking world, two leading Jugendstil periodicals regularly published artists' decorated papers from 1897 onwards: the Munich-based *Dekorative Kunst* and Darmstadt's *Deutsche Kunst und Dekoration*. From the outset, the latter also included endpapers in its competitions (first invitation for submission by 5 June 1898 in: *Deutsche Kunst und Dekoration* (1) I 1897/98, n. p.).

Das damalige k. k. Österreichische Museum für Kunst und Industrie hat diese Entwicklung aktiv gefördert und bereits 1903 eine *Ausstellung von Bucheinbänden und Vorsatzpapieren* präsentiert.[8]

Neben den gedruckten Vorsatzpapieren sticht aus der MAK-Sammlung eine wenig bekannte Gruppe von Blättern in Marmorier- und Kleistertechnik heraus. Gefertigt wurden sie von drei frühen Mitgliedern der Secession – Josef Hoffmann, Koloman Moser und Leopold Stolba –, teils im Gebäude der Secession am Karlsplatz,[9] wo man, vermutlich in Sommer 1901 in Vorbereitung der XIV. Ausstellung mit ihren neuartigen Materialien (so Klimts *Beethovenfries*), Ateliers eingerichtet hatte, in denen mit verschiedenen Stoffen gearbeitet und experimentiert wurde. Künstler des In- und Auslands scheinen hier einen geselligen Austausch gepflegt zu haben. Stolba wird von Zeitgenossen als „Hausherr" dieser „Versuchsstation" bezeichnet, die bis mindestens 1908 Bestand hatte.[10] In der Ausbildung als Bildhauer an der Wiener Akademie dürfte er ein breites Materialwissen gesammelt haben. Überliefert ist eine manische Leidenschaft für Papiere aller Art.[11] Wahrscheinlich haben Hoffmann und Moser die Papiermarmorierung bei dem älteren Kollegen gelernt bzw. mit ihm verfeinert. Die Tunkpapiere der drei Künstler sind so ähnlich, dass es „Marmorierungssitzungen" gegeben haben dürfte, bei denen sie gemeinsam Farben auf die Wasseroberfläche einer Wanne getropft und bewegt haben. Demgegenüber sind die Kleisterpapiere allem Anschein nach das alleinige Werk von Stolba, der diese Technik auf bemerkenswerte Weise entwickelte.[12] Der Bestand des MAK fasst insgesamt etwa 60 Blätter von Stolba, weniger als 40 von Moser und ein signiertes von Hoffmann, wobei die Zuschreibung der marmorierten Papiere angesichts der anzunehmenden gemeinsamen Autorschaft mancher Blätter nicht immer sinnvoll ist.

Diese Blätter sind mithilfe von Techniken hergestellt, die in Buchbindereien, nicht aber in Künstlerateliers gepflegt wurden. Sie unterscheiden sich dennoch in mehrfacher Weise von früheren Buntpapieren. Erstens, weil es den Künstlern nicht um die Produktion vieler ähnlicher Papierbögen ging – kaum ein Blatt gleicht dem anderen, jedes ist ein originelles Werk. Das ist typisch für Buntpapiere von KünstlerInnen, die sich damit von handwerklichen BuntpapiermacherInnen absetzen. Zweitens, weil viele Papiere der Wiener Secession nicht als *Ornament*, sondern als *Bild* konzipiert sind. Ich bezeichne sie deswegen als *Buntpapierbilder*. „Bild" meint hier nicht, dass sie etwas abbilden (obgleich das manchmal der Fall ist), sondern dass im Gegensatz zu den ornamentalen Buntpapieren Buntpapier*bilder* eine geschlossene Komposition formieren:[13] Im Gegensatz zu ornamentalen Buntpapieren haben bildhafte Buntpapiere der Wiener Secession ein bestimmtes Format und eine abgegrenzte Bildfläche, innerhalb derer Farben und Formen komponiert sind, wobei es verschiedene Gewichtungen zwischen Bildzentrum und Bildrändern gibt. Ornamentale Buntpapiere sind so konzipiert, dass man, je nach Bedarf, aus größeren Bögen Teile zuschneidet. Das geht bei Buntpapierbildern nicht: Würde man sie zuschneiden, so wäre die vom Künstler festgelegte Komposition zerstört. Auch die

[8] *Ausstellung von Bucheinbänden und Vorsatzpapieren, Ausstellungskatalog, k. k. Österreichisches Museum für Kunst und Industrie*, Wien 1903. Zur internationalen Wahrnehmung Wiener Vorsatzpapiere siehe auch: Jessen, Peter, „Einleitung", in: *Führer durch die Sonderausstellung Buntpapiere*, Ausst.kat. Königliche Museen Kunstgewerbe-Museum, Berlin 1907, bes. 10.

[9] Die Sekundärliteratur zu den Buntpapieren der Wiener Secessionisten ist heterogen. Einen ersten, wenn auch kurzen Überblick verdanken wir Pabst, Michael, *Wiener Grafik um 1900*, München 1984, 173–190. Die Buntpapiere Hoffmanns und Mosers sind mehrfach in einschlägigen Monografien abgebildet und kurz besprochen,

systematische Untersuchungen stehen aber aus. Zu Stolba siehe Zaunschirm, Thomas, „Wien und die Anfänge der Abstraktion", in: *Orient und Okzident im Spiegel der Kunst*, Graz 1986, 465–475, und Krist, Gabriela, *Leopold Stolba (1863–1929) und seine Tunk- und Kleisterpapiere*, phil. Diss., Salzburg 1989.

[10] Bisanz-Prakken, Marian, *Heiliger Frühling. Gustav Klimt und die Anfänge der Wiener Secession 1895–1905*, Wien 1999, 137–139. Weitere Quellen: Anonym, *Dekorative Kunst* (VII) 2 1903, 77; M. Z., „Der Riese und die Schmetterlinge. Erinnerung an den Maler Stolba", in: *Neues Wiener Journal*, 28.11.1930.

[11] Anonym, „Der Tod eines Sonderlings. Maler-Bildhauer Stolba gestorben", in: *Neues Wiener Tagblatt*, 20.11.1929. Vgl. Krist 1989 (s. Anm. 9), 64.

[12] Zwölf Kleisterpapiere, die vermutlich durch August Schestag (Direktor des Museums von 1927 bis 1931) in die Sammlung gelangten, sind rückseitig mit der Stampiglie „LS" versehen und unter Verwendung von Seiten des Versteigerungskatalogs *Theodor von Hörmann-Nachlass* entstanden. Sie wurden 1933 inventarisiert (KI 9074-1 bis 12). Weitere 41 unsignierte Kleisterpapiere auf solchen Katalogseiten wurden mit dem Hinweis „Alter Bestand" in den 1980er Jahren inventarisiert (KI 14292-1 bis 5, KI 14431-1 bis 29 und KI 14433) bzw. kamen 1929 über Koloman

Mosers Schwester Leopoldine Steindl in die Sammlung (KI 8678-1 bis 5 und KI 8678-7-1).

[13] Meyer Schapiro ("On some problems in the semiotics of visual art: field and vehicle in image-signs", in: *Semiotica* I 1969, 223–242) hat eine Geschichte des Bildes als begrenzte Planfläche skizziert. Nico Brömßer („Rahmung – Bildkonstitution – Ikonische Differenz", in: Günzel, Stephan/ Mersch, Dieter (Hg.), *Bild. Ein interdisziplinäres Handbuch*, Stuttgart 2014, 279–285) verweist in diesem Sinne auf Spencer-Browns Prinzip der Grenzziehung („draw a distinction") zwischen einer im Bild eingeschlossenen Einheit und der Welt außerhalb (Spencer-Brown, George, *Laws of form*, London 1969).

The then Imperial Royal Austrian Museum of Art and Industry actively supported this development and presented an exhibition of book covers and endpapers as early as 1903.[8]

Alongside the printed endpapers, a little-known group of sheets featuring marbling and paste techniques stands out in the MAK Collection. They were crafted by three early members of the Secession—Josef Hoffmann, Koloman Moser, and Leopold Stolba—partly in the Secession building on Vienna's Karlsplatz,[9] where studios were set up in which the artists worked and experimented with various media—presumably in the summer of 1901 in preparation for the 14th exhibition with its novel materials (as seen in Klimt's Beethoven Frieze). Artists from within and beyond Austria's borders appear to have nurtured a sociable rapport here. Contemporaries refer to Stolba as the "landlord" of this "experimental station," which endured until at least 1908.[10] We can assume that he would have accumulated a broad knowledge of materials during his training as a sculptor at the Viennese academy; what remained after those years was a manic passion for all kinds of paper.[11] Hoffmann and Moser probably learned paper marbling from their older colleague Stolba or refined their skills with him. The three artists' marbled papers are so similar that there must have been "marbling classes," during which they jointly dripped and manipulated colors on the surface of the water. In contrast, the paste papers are to all appearances the work of Stolba alone, who developed this technique in a remarkable manner.[12] The MAK's holdings contain a total of 60 sheets by Stolba, fewer than 40 by Moser, and just one signed by Hoffmann. Admittedly, in light of the assumable joint authorship of some sheets, ascribing the marbled papers to a single artist is not always judicious.

These sheets were produced with the aid of techniques, which had been cultivated by bookbinders, not in artists' studios. Nevertheless, they differ from earlier decorated papers in a number of ways. Firstly, because the artists were not interested in producing several similar sheets: hardly a single sheet resembles another, every one of them is an original work. That is typical for decorated papers by artists, which hence sets them apart from decorated papers by craftspeople. Secondly, because many papers by the Vienna Secession are not conceived as ornament, but as pictures. I therefore refer to them as decorated paper pictures. "Picture" in this context does not mean that they depict anything (although that is indeed sometimes the case), but that—in contrast to ornamental decorated papers—decorated paper pictures form a coherent composition:[13] Unlike ornamental decorated papers, pictorial decorated papers by the Vienna Secession have a specific format and a delimited image area within which colors and forms are composed, hence emphasis varies between the center and the edges of the picture. Ornamental decorated papers are designed such that it is possible to cut out parts from larger sheets as needed. That is not possible with decorated paper pictures: if they were cut, the composition defined by the artist would be destroyed. Nor is it possible

[8] *Ausstellung von Bucheinbänden und Vorsatzpapieren*, exhibition catalog, Imperial Royal Austrian Museum of Art and Industry, Vienna 1903. On the international perception of Viennese endpapers, see also: Jessen, Peter, "Einleitung," in: *Führer durch die Sonderausstellung Buntpapiere*, exh.cat. Königliche Museen Berlin, Kunstgewerbe-Museum, Berlin 1907, esp. 10.

[9] Secondary literature on decorated papers by the Vienna Secessionists is heterogeneous. Pabst, Michael, *Wiener Grafik um 1900*, Munich 1984, 173–190 gives an initial, though short, overview. The decorated papers by Hoffmann and Moser have been depicted and briefly discussed in multiple pertinent monographs; however,

systematic analyses are as yet lacking. On Stolba, see Zaunschirm, Thomas, "Wien und die Anfänge der Abstraktion," in: *Orient und Okzident im Spiegel der Kunst*, Graz 1986, 465–475, and Krist, Gabriela, *Leopold Stolba (1863–1929) und seine Tunk- und Kleisterpapiere*, doctoral thesis, Salzburg 1989.

[10] Bisanz-Prakken, Marian, *Heiliger Frühling. Gustav Klimt und die Anfänge der Wiener Secession 1895–1905*, Vienna 1999, 137–139. Further sources: Anonymous, *Dekorative Kunst* (VI)I 2 1903, 77; M. Z., "Der Riese und die Schmetterlinge. Erinnerung an den Maler Stolba," in: *Neues Wiener Journal*, 28 Nov 1930. Translated by Maria Slater.

[11] Anonymous, "Der Tod eines Sonderlings. Maler-Bildhauer Stolba gestorben," in: *Neues Wiener Tagblatt*, 20 Nov 1929. Cf. Krist 1989 (see note 9), 64.

[12] Twelve paste papers, which presumably entered the collection via August Schestag (director of the museum from 1927 to 1931), bear the stamp "LS" on their reverse and were created using pages from the auction catalog *Theodor von Hörmann-Nachlass* (see note 24). They were inventoried in 1933 (KI 9074-1 to 12). 41 additional unsigned paste papers on similar catalog pages were inventoried with the reference "Alter Bestand" (old holdings) in the 1980s (KI 14292-1 to 5, KI 14431-1 to 29, and KI 14433) or entered the collection in 1929 via Koloman Moser's

sister Leopoldine Steindl (KI 8678-1 to 5 and KI 8678-7-1).

[13] Meyer Schapiro ("On some problems in the semiotics of visual art: field and vehicle in image-signs," in: *Semiotica* I 1969, 223–242) sketched out a history of the picture as a limited plane surface. Nico Brömßer ("Rahmung – Bildkonstitution – Ikonische Differenz," in: Günzel, Stephan/Mersch, Dieter (eds.), *Bild. Ein interdisziplinäres Handbuch*, Stuttgart 2014, 279–285) refers in this sense to Spencer-Brown's principle of drawing a distinction between a unit embedded within a picture and the outside world (Spencer-Brown, George, *Laws of form*, London 1969).

Vergrößerung durch Wiederholung von Mustern ist hier kaum denkbar. Diese Bilder sind nicht zum Bekleiden von Büchern und Schachteln geeignet und waren bestimmt nicht dafür vorgesehen. Hoffmann, Moser und Stolba haben sowohl Blätter hergestellt, die sich formal und funktional in die Tradition des ornamentalen Buntpapiers einreihen, als auch Buntpapierbilder gestaltet, mit denen sie ein neuartiges Kapitel in der Geschichte des Buntpapiers aufschlagen. Soweit ich das beurteilen kann, wurde diese Innovation weder in zeitgenössischen Quellen noch von der späteren Kunstgeschichte erkannt. Eine systematische Einordnung der Buntpapierbilder im Rahmen der wenig erforschten Künstlerbuntpapiere des frühen 20. Jahrhunderts steht noch aus. Ich vermute allerdings, dass es sich um ein Charakteristikum der Wiener Secession handelt.[14] Die Buntpapierbilder der drei Secessionisten lassen sich in drei Gruppen einteilen: 1. Mimetische Tunkpapiere, 2. Bildgeschichten aus Buntpapiercollagen und 3. amimetische Buntpapierbilder.

3.1 DIE MIMETISCHEN TUNKPAPIERE

Zum typischen Formenspektrum von marmoriertem Papier zählen Flecken, Adern, Wellen, Hahnenkamm und Schnecken. Diese Benennungen rufen Naturassoziationen wach, die Muster sind dennoch amimetisch.[15] Die seltenen figürlichen Marmorierungen aus islamischen Ländern[16] dürften in Europa kaum bekannt gewesen sein, als Künstler wie Otto Eckmann (1865–1902) und Anker Kyster (1864–1939) beginnen, mimetische Tunkpapiere herzustellen (Abb. 005).[17] Hoffmann, Moser und Stolba schließen sich diesem Trend an. Sie lassen Vögel, Lurche und besonders häufig Fische in der Marmorierwanne entstehen. Groß ist der Bestand des MAK in diesem Bereich vor allem an Tunkpapieren Koloman Mosers. Er experimentiert mit verschiedenen Tierformen, die aus dem Fluss der Farbe entstehen, und bringt beispielsweise ein rotes, vogelartiges Wesen durch die Dynamik des umgebenden Blau zum Fliegen (Abb. 006). Vergleichbar sind Marmorierungen von Josef Hoffmann, der eine Ente in das aufgewühlte Wasser setzt (Abb. 007).[18] Stolba hat vor allem Fische marmoriert und diese Technik so perfektioniert, dass er 1904 auch Holztafeln ins Marmorbad tunkte und damit die grafische Technik auf das Niveau eines Gemäldes hob (Abb. 008).[19] Der Vergleich mit figürlichen Tunkpapieren anderer europäischer Künstler – neben Eckmann und Kyster etwa auch Johannes Rudel (1868–1955)[20] – macht die Besonderheit der Wiener Tierbilder deutlich: Jene Künstler haben mit hoher technischer Fertigkeit Blumen- und Tiermuster geschaffen, die ornamental nebeneinander – so regelmäßig es das Marmorbad erlaubt – wiederholt werden. Die Blätter der Wiener Secessionisten, besonders jene von Moser, sind im Vergleich dazu handwerklich weniger perfekt, dafür aber freier und fantasievoller. Sie spielen mit der zufälligen Bewegung der Farbe und schaffen immer neue, unvorhersehbare Bilder anstelle von sich wiederholenden Ornamenten.

---

[14] Julia Rinck (Leipzig) bereitet eine Dissertation vor, die einen ersten Überblick über Künstlerbuntpapiere um 1900 ermöglichen wird. Die weltweit wohl größte Sammlung in diesem Bereich ist jene, die der österreichische Finanzbeamte Franz Bartsch (1836–1910) der Deutschen Nationalbibliothek Leipzig gestiftet hat (siehe Schmidt, Frieder/Feiler, Sigrid, *Franz Bartsch: Papiersammler aus Wien. Rekonstruktion seiner Ausstellung Stuttgart 1909*, Deutsches Buch- und Schriftmuseum, Begleitmaterialien zur gleichnamigen Ausstellung, Leipzig 1998). Allein die Kästen mit Tunk- und Marmorpapieren beinhalten weit über 1 000 Buntpapiere, die Bartsch im ersten Jahrzehnt des 20. Jahrhunderts bei mehr als 50 europäischen KünstlerInnen und BuchbinderInnen eingekauft hat;

darunter 33 Papiere von Leopold Stolba (s. Anm. 34), neun von Koloman Moser (teils als Geschenke von Hoffmann) und vier von Josef Hoffmann. Viele von ihnen und nahezu sämtliche Blätter aller anderen Hersteller sind durchweg ornamental. Eine mit den Wiener Secessionisten vergleichbare Bildhaftigkeit ist nur bei einzelnen Papieren von Helene Dolmetsch aus Stuttgart (Inv. Nr. 12/2250, 12/2259) und der Firma Jacobi & Spilling aus Berlin (Inv. Nr. 12/2551, 12/2557) auszumachen.

[15] Weder die Sammlung Clerget noch Wolfe (s. Anm. 7) kennen Beispiele für mimetische Motive in der älteren europäischen Geschichte des Marmorpapiers.

[16] Die kunstvollsten Beispiele entstanden in Indien im 17. Jahrhundert. Siehe zuletzt Benson, Jake, „The Art of Abri: Marbled Album Leaves, Drawings, and Paintings of the Deccan", in: Haidar, Navina Najat/Sardar, Marika (Hg.), *Sultans of Deccan India 1500–1700*, New York 2015, 157–159.

[17] Bierbaum, Otto Julius, „Künstlerische Vorsatzpapiere", in: *Dekorative Kunst* (I) 3 1898, 127 u. 129.

[18] Siehe auch *Der Liebe Augustin* (I) 1904. Die kurzlebige literarische Zeitschrift druckte sieben farbige Abbildungen marmorierter Tierchen: zwei von Josef Hoffmann (123, 144), vier von Koloman Moser (o. S., Heft 9, 160, 207, 267) und eines ohne Angabe des Entwerfers (341).

[19] Krist 1989 (s. Anm. 9), 55, zählt insgesamt vier Beispiele, die allesamt auf 1904 datiert sind. Eine der Holztafeln (Pabst 1984, s. Anm. 9, 181, Abb. 185) ist allerdings offenbar mit Kleisterfarben gefertigt. Krists Annahme, wonach die Marmorierung der Tafel im MUMOK – Museum moderner Kunst Stiftung Ludwig Wien gemalt sei, dürfte irrig sein (so auch die vorläufige Beobachtung von Kathrine Ruppen und Susanne Neuburger, die das Werk demnächst einer eingehenderen Analyse unterziehen wollen). Zwei Tunkarbeiten auf Holz in Privatbesitz, ebenfalls auf 1904 datiert, in: Bisanz-Prakken 1999 (s. Anm. 10), 160, 204, Abb. 261, 262.

[20] Siehe *Deutsche Kunst und Dekoration* (4) XIV 1904, 577, 581, und Wolfe 1990 (s. Anm. 7), Pl. XXII.

005
Anker Kyster
Tunkpapier mit floralen Mustern
Marbled Paper with Floral Patterns
Aus From: *Dekorative Kunst* (I) 3 1898, 129

006
Koloman Moser
Tunkpapier
Wien, um 1904
Marbled Paper
Vienna, ca. 1904
260 x 380 mm
KI 8678-6, Ankauf purchased from Leopoldine Steindl 1929

007
Josef Hoffmann
Tunkpapier
Wien, 1904
Sign. Stampiglie JH
Marbled Paper
Vienna, 1904
Signed with JH stamping
286 x 223 mm
KI 8830, Ankauf purchased from
Josef Hoffmann 1930

008
Leopold Stolba
Fische
Wien, 1904
Beize auf Holz
Fishes
Vienna, 1904
Pickling liquor on wood
302 x 302 mm
mumok, museum moderner kunst
stiftung ludwig wien, Inv. Nr. Inv. No. B 206
© mumok

to enlarge them by repeating the pattern. Those pictures are not suitable for covering books and boxes and were certainly not intended for that purpose.

Hoffmann, Moser, and Stolba produced sheets, which are formally and functionally part of the tradition of ornamental decorated paper, as well as decorated paper pictures—with which they turned over a new leaf in the history of decorated paper. As far as I am able to judge, this innovation was recognized neither in contemporary sources nor by subsequent art historians. A systematic classification of decorated paper pictures in the context of the under-researched decorated papers by early 20th-century artists is still wanting. However, I conjecture that they are specific to the Vienna Secession.[14] The decorated paper pictures by the three Secessionists can be divided into three groups: 1) mimetic marbled papers, 2) stories from decorated paper collages, and 3) amimetic decorated paper pictures.

3.1 MIMETIC MARBLED PAPERS

Forms of marbled paper typically include spots, veins, waves, cockscombs, and curls. These names evoke associations with nature, but the patterns are nevertheless amimetic.[15] The rare specimen of figurative marbled papers from Islamic countries[16] appears to have been little known in Europe at the time when artists like Otto Eckmann (1865–1902) and Anker Kyster (1864–1939) started producing mimetic marbled papers (ill. 005).[17] Hoffmann, Moser, and Stolba joined this trend. They conjured birds, amphibians, and—especially common— fish in the marbling tank. The MAK has particularly large holdings of marbled papers in this vein by Koloman Moser. He experimented with various animal shapes created out of color flows, for example making a red, bird-like creature fly as a result of the dynamics of the surrounding blue (ill. 006). Some marbled sheets by Josef Hoffmann are comparable; i.e. a duck that appears in the turbulent water (ill. 007).[18] Stolba primarily marbled fish and perfected this technique to such a degree that he even dipped a wooden panel in the marbling tank in 1904, thereby raising the graphic technique to the status of painting (ill. 008).[19] The comparison with figurative marbled papers by other European artists—Johannes Rudel (1868–1955),[20] for instance, in addition to Eckmann and Kyster—reveals the noteworthiness of the Viennese animal images: with great technical skill the latter three artists created floral and animal patterns, which were repeated ornamentally alongside one another in as regular intervals as the marbling tank would allow. The sheets by the Vienna Secessionists—particularly those by Moser—are in comparison less perfect from a technical perspective, yet freer and more imaginative. They play with the serendipitous movement of the colors and create ever new, unpredictable images rather than repeating ornaments.

[14] Julia Rinck (Leipzig) is preparing a doctoral thesis, which will facilitate an initial overview of decorated papers by artists around 1900. Probably the world's largest collection in this area is that endowed by the Austrian Treasury official Franz Bartsch (1836–1910) to the German National Library in Leipzig (see Schmidt, Frieder/Feiler, Sigrid, *Franz Bartsch: Papiersammler aus Wien. Rekonstruktion seiner Ausstellung Stuttgart 1909*, Leipzig 1998). The marbled paper collection alone contains well above a thousand sheets, which Bartsch purchased in the first decade of the 20th century from over 50 European artists and bookbinders; they include 33 sheets by Leopold Stolba (see note 34), nine by Koloman Moser (partly as gifts from Hoffmann), and

four by Josef Hoffmann. Many of them and almost every single sheet by all other producers are ornamental. . I could only figure out a pictorial quality comparable to the work of the Vienna Secessionists in some papers by Helene Dolmetsch from Stuttgart (inv. no. 12/2250, 12/2259) and by the company Jacobi & Spilling from Berlin (inv. no. 12/2551, 12/2557).

[15] Neither the Clerget Collection nor Wolfe (see note 7) report examples of mimetic motifs in the older European history of marbled paper.

[16] The most elaborate examples were created in India in the 17th century. See most recently Benson, Jake, "The Art of Abri: Marbled Album Leaves,

Drawings, and Paintings of the Deccan," in: Haidar, Navina Najat/Sardar, Marika (eds.), *Sultans of Deccan India 1500–1700*, New York 2015, 157–159.

[17] Bierbaum, Otto Julius, "Künstlerische Vorsatzpapiere," in: *Dekorative Kunst* (I) 3 1898, 127, 129.

[18] See also *Der Liebe Augustin* (I) 1904. This short-lived literary periodical printed seven color illustrations of small marbled animals: two by Josef Hoffmann (123, 144), four by Koloman Moser (n. p., edition 9, 160, 207, 267), and one without a designer's name (341).

[19] Krist 1989 (see note 9), 55, counts four examples in total, all of which

are dated 1904. One of the wooden panels (Pabst 1984, see note 9, 181, ill. 185) was, however, obviously produced with colored pastes. Contrary to Krist's assumption the marbling on the panel in the mumok – Museum moderner Kunst Stiftung Ludwig Wien is not painted (this is confirmed by preliminary observations by Kathrine Ruppen and Susanne Neuburger, who want to subject the work to a more thorough analysis in the near future). Two privately owned marbled pictures on wood, also dated 1904, are published in: Bisanz-Prakken 1999 (see note 10), 160, 204, ill. 261, 262.

[20] See *Deutsche Kunst und Dekoration* (8) XIV 1904, 577, 581 and Wolfe 1990 (see note 7), Pl. XXII.

3.2 BILDGESCHICHTEN AUS BUNTPAPIERCOLLAGEN

Die Zeitschrift *Kind und Kunst* veröffentlichte 1906 ein von Koloman Moser signiertes „Bilderbuch". Abgebildet sind neun Seiten mit „ausgeschnittene[n] Papierfiguren auf Buntpapier geklebt" (Abb. 009). Am Ende der Bilderstrecke erläutert ein kurzer anonymer Text die Bilder. Fantasievoll wird das Dargestellte mit wenigen Zeilen einzeln kommentiert, ohne zusammenhängende Geschichte. Darauf folgen Beschreibungen der Buntpapiere und ihrer Farben. So heißt es über dem unteren Bild der hier wiedergegebenen Seite: „Adelaide und Violetta, die Sängerinnen. Ihr Gesang ist wie das Läuten feiner Glöckchen, wie das Zirpen der Grillen im Sommer. Und sie lächeln immer. Damit ihre Taille schmal bleibe, dürfen sie nur einmal in der Woche sich satt essen. Auch trinken sie die farbigen Wasser des Regenbogens; das erhält die Schönheit. – Hintergrund blau, mit Schwamm gemalt. Kleider grün, blau gemustert. Kragen, Manschetten Goldpapier. Perücken weiss mit schwarzen Scheibchen. Augen tiefschwarz. Mund grellrot."[21]

Es ist nicht bekannt, ob sich Mosers Kinderbuch erhalten hat. Bekannt sind aber fotografische Aufnahmen davon im Archiv der Wiener Werkstätte des MAK.[22] Darüber hinaus gibt es im MAK zwei Blätter im selben quadratischen Format und in derselben Technik: Collage auf Kleisterpapier (Abb. 010, 011). Die Figuren sind aus ähnlichen, teils japanischen, Buntpapieren ausgeschnitten wie jene, die in der Zeitschrift abgebildet sind.[23] Die Zuschreibung an Moser ist naheliegend und es ist anzunehmen, dass beide Collagen um 1905/1906 für das in *Kind und Kunst* abgedruckte Buch entstanden, aber unvollendet geblieben sind. Die Hintergründe mit Kleisterfarbe dürften allerdings Werke von Stolba sein. Erstens war diese Technik seine Spezialität, während nicht bekannt ist, dass Moser sie jemals verwendet hätte. Zweitens gibt es zwei Kleisterpapiere Stolbas im MAK, die den Hintergründen dieser Collagen in Muster und Farbe ähneln (man vergleiche die Abbildungen 010 und 012 sowie 011 und 013). Drittens ist der Karton der Collagen der gleiche, den Stolba für die allermeisten Kleisterpapiere verwendet hat. Es sind Rückseiten der Bildtafeln eines Versteigerungskataloges von 1899.[24]

3.3 AMIMETISCHE BUNTPAPIERBILDER

Leopold Stolba hat sowohl ornamentale als auch bildhafte amimetische Buntpapiere hergestellt. Ein Vergleich zweier Blätter soll den Unterschied deutlich machen (Abb. 014, 015). Beide sind mit Kleisterfarben, teils im selben Farbton, im selben Format, auf dem gleichen Karton hergestellt. Beide haben dieselbe Provenienz und sind um 1903 entstanden. Bei dem ornamentalen Papier (Abb. 014) hat Stolba mit drei verschiedenen Blautönen ein unregelmäßiges, senkrechtes Streifenmuster gebildet. In einem zweiten Arbeitsdurchgang kratzte er mit impulsiven waagerechten Strichen die noch feuchte Kleisterfarbe heraus und schuf damit ein zweites Muster. Man könnte beide Muster zu den Seiten, nach oben und nach unten fortsetzen und das Blatt als Vorsatzpapier auch für größere Formate verwenden. Tatsächlich wurde ein sehr ähnliches Papier von Stolba neuerdings als Buchdeckel eines Bandes der Insel-Bücherei verwendet.[25] Ganz anders verhält es sich

[21] *Kind und Kunst* (II) 1905/06, 154.

[22] Insgesamt zwölf Fotos (neun Blätter wie in der Zeitschrift und drei weitere): WWF 99-24-1 bis 4, WWF 99-25-1 bis 4, WWF 99-26-1 bis 4. Zu Mosers Kinderbüchern siehe Pichler, Gerd, „Kinderspielzeug von Kolo Moser", in: Leopold, Rudolf/Pichler, Gerd (Hg.), *Koloman Moser*, München 2007, 232–245.

[23] Die Figuren des Blattes KI 14292 sind aus einem japanischen Papier gemacht, von dem sich ein Muster in der MAK-Sammlung findet (KI 9388-88), vgl. Krist 1999 (s. Anm. 9), 63 f. Die Figuren von KI 14431-28 sind aus einem Papier ausgeschnitten, das 1897

veröffentlicht wurde und anscheinend mit alten venezianischen Druckstöcken hergestellt wurde, siehe Bierbaum, Otto J., „Venezianische Druckstöcke", in: *Dekorative Kunst* (I) 1 1897/1898, 21–24, hier 22.

[24] *Öffentliche Versteigerung des künstlerischen Nachlasses von Theodor von Hörmann im Ausstellungsgebäude der Vereinigung bildender Künstler Österreichs*, Wien I., Wienzeile 2, Ausstellung vom 22. bis 26. Februar, Wien 1899. Der Versteigerungskatalog hat zwölf Tafeln, die auf einem glatten Karton einseitig gedruckt wurden. Die Rückseiten blieben frei und eigneten sich offensichtlich gut für Stolbas Kleisterpapiere. Es ist anzunehmen,

dass mehrere Exemplare im Gebäude der Secession übrig geblieben waren. Die Fachbereichsbibliothek des Wiener Instituts für Kunstgeschichte besitzt ein Exemplar dieses Kataloges (aus dem Nachlass Ankwicz-Kleehoven, gebunden mit einem Kleisterpapier, das jenem von Stolba ähnelt). Die anlässlich einer Neubindung beschnittenen Seiten sind 230 x 265 mm groß. Das Originalmaß vor dem Beschnitt dürfte ca. 240 x 275 mm betragen haben.

[25] Kraus, Karl, *Die chinesische Mauer*, Frankfurt/Main 1999 (Insel-Bücherei Nr. 1199). Verwendet wurde ein Blatt, das Franz Bartsch 1903 bei Stolba erworben hat (vgl. Anm. 14, Inv. Nr.

12/06158a; über Buntpapiere in der Insel-Bücherei siehe Frieder Schmidt, „Buntpapier in den Sammlungen des Deutschen Buch- und Schriftmuseums", in: *Dialog mit Bibliotheken* 2012/1, 50–55). Farben und Muster gleichen jenen des Blattes im MAK (Abb. 014). Stolba hat dort aber keine zweite waagerechte Schicht hineingekratzt. Aufgrund der formalen und technischen Ähnlichkeiten dürften beide Blätter im MAK (Abb. 014, 015) zeitgleich wie jenes in der Sammlung Bartsch, also um 1903, entstanden sein. Stolba gestaltete mit nahezu gleichen Mustern auch die ebenfalls 1903 von Bartsch angekauften Blätter Inv. Nr. 12/06147, 12/06153a und 12/06156a.

3.2 STORIES FROM DECORATED PAPER COLLAGES

In 1906 the magazine *Kind und Kunst* published a picture book signed by Koloman Moser. It reproduced nine pages with cut-out paper figures stuck on decorated paper (ill. 009). At the end of the series of pictures a short, anonymous text explains the images. The depictions are imaginatively annotated with a few lines, without a coherent story. They are followed by descriptions of the decorated papers and their colors. Hence the text about the lower image on the page reproduced here reads: "Adelaide and Violetta, the singers. Their singing is like the chiming of small, fine bells, like the chirring of crickets in summertime. And they always smile. So that their waists remain slender, they are only allowed to eat their fill once a week. They also drink the colorful water of the rainbow; it contains beauty. – Background blue, sponge painted. Dresses green with blue pattern. Collar, cuffs gold foil. Wigs white with small black discs. Eyes jet black. Mouth bright red."[21]

It is unknown whether or not Moser's picture book has survived. However, photographs of it are known to be in the MAK's Wiener Werkstätte archive.[22] Furthermore, there are two sheets at the MAK with the same square format and which use the same technique: collage on paste paper (ill. 010, 011). The figures are cut from similar—in part Japanese—decorated paper as those reproduced in the magazine.[23] Their ascription to Moser is obvious and it can be assumed that both collages, though unfinished, were created around 1905/1906 for the book published in *Kind und Kunst*. Despite that, the colored paste backdrops appear to have been works by Stolba: Firstly, the technique was his specialty, whereas it is not known whether it was ever used by Moser. Secondly, there are two paste papers by Stolba at the MAK, which resemble the backdrops to these collages in both pattern and color scheme (compare the illustrations 010 and 012, as well as 011 and 013). Thirdly, the cardboard used for the collages is the same as that which Stolba used for the majority of his paste papers. They are the reverse sides of plates from an auction catalog from 1899.[24]

3.3 AMIMETIC DECORATED PAPER PICTURES

Leopold Stolba produced both ornamental and pictorial amimetic decorated papers. A comparison of two of his sheets (ill. 014 and 015) makes the difference clear: Both are made with colored pastes, partly of the same shade, in the same format, on the same cardboard. Both have the same provenance and were created around 1903. For the ornamental paper (ill. 014) Stolba composed an irregular, vertical striped pattern with three different shades of blue. In a second step he scratched the wet colored paste with impulsive, horizontal strokes, thereby creating a second pattern. One could extend the two patterns to the sides, above, and below and use the sheet as an endpaper for larger formats, too. Indeed, a very similar piece of paper by Stolba was recently used as the book cover for a volume of the Insel-Bücherei series.[25] The method is very different in illustration 015. The sheet is painted with just one turquoise-blue colored paste. A cloudy texture

[21] *Kind und Kunst* (II) 1905/06, 154. Translated by Maria Slater.

[22] A total of 12 photos (9 sheets as in the magazine and three others): WWF 99-24-1 to 4, WWF 99-25-1 to 4, WWF 99-26-1 to 4. On Moser's children's books, see Pichler, Gerd, "Kinderspielzeug von Kolo Moser," in: Leopold, Rudolf/Pichler, Gerd (eds.), *Koloman Moser*, Munich 2007, 232–245.

[23] The figures on the sheet KI 14292 are made from a piece of Japanese paper of which a sample can be found in the MAK Collection (KI 9388-88), cf. Krist 1999 (see note 9), 63 f. The figures from KI 14431-28 were cut from a sheet of paper published in 1897 and

apparently produced with old Venetian printing blocks, see Bierbaum, Otto J., "Venezianische Druckstöcke," in: *Dekorative Kunst* (I) 1 1897/98, 21–24, here 22.

[24] *Öffentliche Versteigerung des künstlerischen Nachlasses von Theodor von Hörmann im Ausstellungsgebäude der Vereinigung bildender Künstler Österreichs*, 1010 Vienna, Wienzeile 2, exhibition from 22 to 26 February, Vienna 1899. The auction catalog has 12 plates, which were printed single-sided on smooth cardboard. The reverse sides were left blank and were obviously well suited to Stolba's paste papers. It can be assumed that several copies were left over in the Secession

building. The library of the Department of Art History at the University of Vienna owns a copy of this catalog (from the Ankwicz-Kleehoven bequest, bound with paste paper, which resembles Stolba's). Cut for the purposes of rebinding, the pages are 230 x 265 mm. The original measurements prior to being trimmed must have been approx. 240 x 275 mm.

[25] Kraus, Karl, *Die chinesische Mauer*, Frankfurt/Main 1999 (Insel-Bücherei no. 1199). It uses a sheet purchased by Franz Bartsch from Stolba in 1903 (cf. note 14, inv. no. 12/06158a; on decorated papers in the Insel-Bücherei, see Frieder Schmidt, "Buntpapier in den Sammlungen des Deut-

schen Buch- und Schriftmuseums," in: *Dialog mit Bibliotheken* 2012/1, 50–55). Colors and patterns correspond to those of the sheet at the MAK (ill. 014). However, Stolba did not scratch a second horizontal layer into the latter. Due to the formal and technical similarities, both sheets at the MAK (ill. 014, 015) must have been produced at the same time as that in the Bartsch Collection, i.e. around 1903. In 1903 Bartsch bought further papers by Stolba with almost identical patterns (inv. no. 12/06147, 12/06153a, and 12/06156a).

bei Abb. 015. Das Blatt ist mit nur einer türkisblauen Kleisterfarbe gestrichen. Durch Auftrag mit breitem Pinsel und anschließendes Abziehen entstand eine wolkige Struktur. In einem zweiten Arbeitsgang hat Stolba auch hier mit schwungvollen Zügen die Farbe verdrängt. Die mit parallelen Gesten ausgeführten Striche ähneln denen des anderen Blattes. Ein für die Wirkung entscheidender Unterschied liegt aber darin, dass die Strichreihen nicht über das gesamte Blatt hinweg durchlaufen. Die dicksten Linien drängen sich energisch von links in die Mitte vor. Damit entsteht ein Bild interagierender dynamischer Kräfte. Es kann mimetische Assoziationen wecken – etwa Vögel, die an einem windigen Tag über ein Getreidefeld flattern – und bleibt dennoch zweifelsfrei ein amimetisches Bild. Es gibt im MAK rund 15 vergleichbare amimetische Bilder von Stolba, überwiegend in Kleisterfarbe. Sie zeugen von seiner Lust am Experimentieren. Gemalte Striche kombiniert er mit Abzugstechnik (Abb. 012), verwendet Textilabdrucke (Abb. 016) und schafft Monotypien, die an Dendriten erinnern (Abb. 013).

4. STOLBA VERSUS KANDINSKY

Wozu und wann hat Leopold Stolba amimetische Buntpapierbilder gemacht? Den Katalogen der Wiener Secession ist zu entnehmen, dass er von 1900 an regelmäßig an den Gruppenausstellungen teilnimmt, diese auch mehrfach mitorganisiert. Auffällig ist, dass Buntpapiere mehr als die Hälfte dessen ausmachen, was er über die Jahre ausstellt – erstmals im März 1903, damals mit der Bezeichnung „Vorsatzpapiere".[26] Der Kunstkritiker und Secessionsfreund Ludwig Hevesi erwähnt sie damals kurz und wohlwollend: „Die getunkten Buntpapiere von Stolba sind sehr amüsant zu sehen; manche könnten nicht effektvoller komponiert sein."[27] Höhepunkt von Stolbas Ausstellungstätigkeit in diesem Bereich ist die XXIII. Ausstellung im März 1905 mit mindestens acht „Monotypien"[28] und neun „Zeichnungen in Marmoriertechnik".[29] Ein Jahr danach befinden sich laut Katalog im Saal VII der XXVI. Ausstellung vier „Monotypien" nebst sechs Holzschnitten und zwei Temperas von Wassily Kandinsky (1866–1944).[30] Weitere „Monotypien" und „Vorsatzpapiere" stellte Stolba im November 1906 aus (u.a. vermutlich Abb. 017).[31] Danach zeigt er nur noch zweimal Buntpapiere in der Secession: „Acht Monotypien" 1910 und eine nicht genauer definierte Anzahl „Getunkter Papiere" 1912.[32] Die Titelgebung in den Ausstellungskatalogen macht deutlich, dass es für Stolba drei verschiedene Arten von Buntpapier-Blättern gibt: 1. „Vorsatzpapiere": Damit sind vermutlich ornamentale Blätter gemeint, die sich durch Wiederholung von Mustern für Bucheinbände eignen (Abb. 014). 2. „Zeichnungen in Marmoriertechnik" bzw. „getunkte Papiere": Im Gegensatz zu den vorherigen ornamentalen Blättern sind das *Bilder* aus der Marmorierwanne – vermutlich sowohl die mimetischen (Fische) als auch die amimetischen (Abb. 017). 3. Als „Monotypien" bezeichnet Stolba zweifellos Blätter in Kleistertechnik (Abb. 012, 013, 015, 016). Vermutlich unterscheidet er dabei nicht zwischen figürlichen und nicht figürlichen Motiven, wobei erstere offensichtlich um 1903/04, nicht aber später entstanden.[33] Mangels Quellen ist eine präzise Zuordnung der erhaltenen Blätter zu den einzelnen Ausstellungen nicht möglich. Bemerkenswert ist aber, dass Stolba seine Buntpapierbilder montiert hat, die Blätter rückseitig und/oder auf den Passepartouts signiert und teilweise

26 XVII. Ausstellung, Nr. 253. Siehe auch Nr. 283 „Muster und Holzschnitt". Eine Liste aller Ausstellungsbeteiligungen in: Krist 1999 (s. Anm. 9), 165 f. Betitelungen der Ausstellungskataloge sind nur teilweise wiedergegeben.

27 Hevesi, Ludwig, *Acht Jahre Sezession (März 1897 – Juni 1905). Kritik – Polemik – Chronik*, Klagenfurt 1984, 134, erstmalig am 2.4.1903 veröffentlicht.

28 Nr. 156, 158, 165, 169, 172, 174, 175. Nr. 156 als „Monotypien" im Plural, also mindestens zwei, alle weiteren im Singular.

29 Nr. 164, 168, 170, 171, 173, 176, 177, 179, 180. Franz Bartsch (vgl. Anm. 14) vermerkt in seinen Notizen zu Stolba: „Bei der 23 Austellg der Secession 3-5/905 unter den # 164.8.170.1.3.176. 7.179.180 als Zeichnungen in Marmoriertechnik auf ein farbigem Marmorgrunde fische [sic]." [Randanmerkung:] „9/v.[?] [1]903" (Deutsches Buch- und Schriftmuseum der Deutschen Nationalbibliothek Leipzig, Franz Bartsch, Wien, Notizen zum Buntpapier, 1004).

30 Stolba: Nr. 223–226, Kandinsky: 249–252, 268–271.

31 XXVII. Ausstellung, Nr. 285, 289, 306–308. Hierzu vermerkt Bartsch: „Bei der November 1906 eröffneten Ausstellung der Secession waren ausser den Tunkp. von Stolba älterer Art auch andere in entschiedenen farben [sic] (Orange u Schwarz) die an feine Maserung erinnert" (s. Anm. 29, 1004 verso).

32 XXXVI. Ausstellung, Nr. 168; XLI. Ausstellung, Nr. 164, 167.

33 Zwei figürliche Kleisterpapiere sind abgebildet in: *Dekorative Kunst* XII, 1904, 72. Alle sieben Abbildungen der Werke Stolbas in diesem Aufsatz sind zwar in den Bildlegenden pauschal als Vorsatzpapiere bezeichnet. Der anonyme Text (77) erwähnt jedoch Stolbas „grafische Versuche", die sich u. a. aus „auf Glasplatten flüchtig hingeworfenen Skizzen durch den Abdruck auf Papier ergeben – wir bringen einige Abbildungen solcher Monotypes auf Seite 72". Pabst 1984 (s. Anm. 9, Abb. 110, 112) bildet zwei figürliche Monotypien aus Privatbesitz ab. Die Sammlung Bartsch (vgl. Anm. 14) beinhaltet eine rückseitig signierte und 1903 datierte figürliche Monotypie (Apfelbaum, Inv. 12/06150). Dass Stolba später weniger oder gar keine figürlichen Kleisterpapiere gemacht hat, leite ich aus der Tatsache ab, dass weder im MAK noch in der Wiener Akademie solche figürlichen Blätter vorkommen. Die Bestände dieser Häuser haben das Atelier des Künstlers erst zu einem späteren Zeitpunkt verlassen.

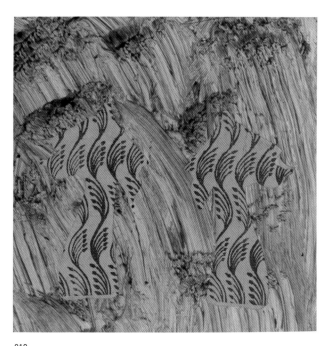

009
Koloman Moser
„**Bilderbuch**" [Picture book]
Aus From: *Kind und Kunst* (II) 1905/06, 151

010
Koloman Moser, Leopold Stolba
Collage auf Kleisterpapier
Wien, um 1905
Collage on Paste Paper
Vienna, ca. 1905
205 x 205 mm
KI 14431-28, alter Bestand , inv. old holdings, inventoried in 1986

011
Koloman Moser, Leopold Stolba
Collage auf Kleisterpapier
Wien, um 1905
Collage on Paste Paper
Vienna, ca. 1905
205 x 205 mm
KI 14292-1, alter Bestand, inv.
old holdings, inventoried in 1983

012
Leopold Stolba
Kleisterpapier
Wien, um 1905
Paste Paper
Vienna, ca. 1905
273 x 234 mm
KI 14431-10, alter Bestand, inv. old holdings,
inventoried in 1986

013
Leopold Stolba
Kleisterpapier
Wien, um 1905
Paste Paper
Vienna, ca. 1905
210 x 210 mm
KI 14292-4, alter Bestand, inv. old holdings,
inventoried in 1983

was created by briefly applying an object to and then removing it from the drying paste. In a second step Stolba once again scratched the color with sweeping strokes. Achieved with parallel movements, the strokes resemble those on the other sheet. However, a key difference to the effect lies in the fact that the rows of lines do not continue across the entire sheet. The thickest lines energetically sweep from the left to the center. The result is an image of interacting, dynamic forces. It can prompt mimetic associations—such as birds flapping their wings above a grain field on a windy day—yet it nevertheless remains an amimetic picture. There are some 15 comparable amimetic pictures by Stolba at the MAK, predominantly in colored paste. They testify to his love of experimentation. He juxtaposes painted strokes and pulled textures (ill. 012), uses textile imprint (ill. 016), and creates monotype reminiscent of dendrites (ill. 013).

4. STOLBA VERSUS KANDINSKY

Why and when did Leopold Stolba make amimetic decorated paper pictures? It can be gathered from the catalogs of the Vienna Secession that he regularly participated in group exhibitions from 1900 onwards, and indeed helped to organize them on a number of occasions. It is striking that decorated papers constitute more than half of the works, which he exhibited over the years—for the first time in March 1903, at which point they were referred to as endpapers.[26] The art critic and acquaintance of the Secession Ludwig Hevesi mentions these sheets then briefly and favorably: "The marbled decorated papers by Stolba are very enjoyable to see; some could not have been more effectively composed."[27] The highlight of Stolba's exhibition activity in this field is the 23rd exhibition in March 1905, which included at least eight "monotypes"[28] and nine "drawings using the marbling technique."[29] One year later four "monotypes" were exhibited in the 7th room of the 26th exhibition alongside six woodcuts and two temperas by Wassily Kandinsky (1866–1944).[30] Stolba exhibited other "monotypes" and "endpapers" in November 1906 (presumably including ill. 017).[31] Thereafter he only showed decorated papers at the Secession on two more occasions: "Eight monotypes" in 1910 and an indefinite number of "marbled papers" in 1912.[32] The titles assigned in the exhibition catalogs reveal that Stolba differentiated between three kinds of decorated paper sheets:

1. "Endpapers": which presumably means ornamental sheets whose repetition of patterns makes them suitable for the covers or endpapers of books (ill. 014).

2. "Drawings using the marbling technique" or "marbled papers": in contrast to the previous ornamental sheets, these are pictures from the marbling tank—presumably both mimetic (fish) and amimetic (ill. 017).

3. With "monotype" Stolba is undoubtedly referring to sheets using the paste technique (ill. 012, 013, 015, 016). He probably did not differentiate between figurative and non-figurative motifs, though the former were obviously only created around 1903/04 and no later.[33]

Due to a lack of sources, a precise attribution of the surviving sheets to the individual exhibitions is not possible. Nevertheless, it is

[26] 17th exhibition, no. 253. See also no. 283 "Muster und Holzschnitt." There is a list of all participations in exhibitions in: Krist 1999 (see note 9), 165 f. However, the titles of Stolba's pictures from the exhibition catalogs are incomplete.

[27] Hevesi, Ludwig, *Acht Jahre Sezession (März 1897 – Juni 1905). Kritik – Polemik – Chronik*, Klagenfurt 1984, 134, first published on 2 Apr 1903. Translated by Maria Slater.

[28] No. 156, 158, 165, 169, 172, 174, 175. No.156 as "monotypes" in the plural, so at least two; all others are in the singular.

[29] No. 164, 168, 170, 171, 173, 176, 177, 179, 180. Franz Bartsch (cf. note 14) mentions in his notes on Stolba: "At the 23rd exhibition of the Secession 3-5/905 among the # 164.8.170.1.3. 176.7.179.180 as drawings using the marbling technique on a colored marble ground fish." [Marginal note:] "9/v.[?] [1]903" (German Museum of Books and Writing at the German National Library in Leipzig, Franz Bartsch, Vienna, Notes on decorated paper, 1004).

[30] Stolba: no. 223–226, Kandinsky: 249–252, 268–271.

[31] 27th exhibition, no. 285, 289, 306–308. In this regard Bartsch notes: "At the Secession exhibition which opened in November 1906, works other than the older marbled papers by Stolba were in key colors (orange & black), which are reminiscent of fine grain" (see note 29, 1004 verso).

[32] 36th exhibition, no. 168; 41st exhibition, no. 164, 167.

[33] Two figurative paste papers are reproduced in: *Dekorative Kunst* XII, 1904, 72. All seven reproductions of Stolba's works in this article are admittedly given the blanket term of endpapers in the captions. The anonymous text (77), however, mentions Stolba's "graphic attempts," which are among other things "the result of sketches fleetingly thrown onto glass plates and applied to paper—we have reproduced some such monotypes on page 72." Pabst 1984 (see note 9, ill. 110, 112) reproduces two privately owned figurative monotypes. The Bartsch Collection (cf. note 14) contains a monotype representing an apple tree signed on the reverse and dated 1903 (nv. 12/06150). That Stolba later made fewer or no figurative paste papers is something I deduce from the fact that neither at the MAK nor at the Vienna Academy are there any such figurative sheets. The holdings of these institutions only left the artist's studio at a later date.

auch datiert hat (Abb. 017).[34] Buntpapiere anderer Künstler sind öfters signiert. Signierte Montierungen, wie sie Stolba öfters machte, sind mir von keinem anderen Buntpapiermacher dieser Zeit bekannt. Sie dürften bei ihm im Hinblick auf Ausstellungen entstanden sein. Leopold Stolba stellt also von 1903 an dutzende ungegenständliche Blätter in der Secession aus, rechteckig bis nahezu quadratisch, von ähnlichem Format (die längste Seite bleibt meistens unter 270 mm). Einige Blätter sind ornamentale „Vorsatzpapiere", viele jedoch komponierte Bilder, auf vielfältige Weise gestaltet. Abhängig von der Technik bezeichnet er sie als „Monotypien" oder „Zeichnungen in Marmoriertechnik". Diese Blätter sind teilweise signiert und mehrfach datiert. Stolba ist damit einer der weltweit allerersten Künstler, die abstrakte Bilder als Kunst ausstellen.[35] Allemal früher als Kandinsky: Als beide im März 1906 im selben Raum der Secession nebeneinander präsentiert wurden, waren neben Stolbas abstrakten Blättern gegenständliche Temperas und Holzschnitte von Kandinsky zu sehen.[36]

Man kann die Tatsache, dass Stolba abstrakte Bilder mehrere Jahre vor Kandinsky ausstellte, aus heutiger Sicht als ein epochales Ereignis beschreiben. Stolba dürfte seine Tätigkeit aber weniger pathetisch begriffen haben. Darin liegt ein fundamentaler Unterschied zu Kandinsky. Letzterer verstand die Absage an die Mimesis als Revolution der Kunst. Diese Revolution hat er systematisch mit einer doppelgleisigen Strategie verfolgt – Ausstellungspraxis und schriftlicher, propagandistischer Diskurs. Von 1910 an stellt Kandinsky in avantgardistischen Ausstellungen Bilder aus, die zunehmend weniger gegenständlich erkennbar sind.[37] Mit der Veröffentlichung von *Über das Geistige in der*

[34] Stolbas Blätter im MAK befinden sich nicht (mehr?) auf originalen Montierungen. Bekannt sind allerdings vier Konvolute von Buntpapieren mit originalen Montierungen, Signaturen und Datierungen (von 1903, 1904, 1905 und, weit überwiegend, 1906):

1) 33 Buntpapiere im Deutschen Buch- und Schriftmuseum der Deutschen Nationalbibliothek Leipzig (vgl. Anm. 14): fünf marmorierte Fischbilder (allesamt in Passepartouts, zwei davon rechts unten auf dem Passepartout signiert und 1903 datiert: Inv. Nr. 12/4133 und 12/4135), eine Monotypie (s. Anm. 33) und 27 weitere Kleisterpapiere. Die Monotypie und der Großteil der Kleisterpapiere sind auf den Rückseiten des Hörmann Versteigerungskatalogs (s. Anm. 24) angefertigt (außer 12/06144-06147 und 12/06161). Die Monotypie und sämtliche Kleisterpapiere sind auf Trägerkartons montiert, teils zwei Blätter auf einem Karton, durchwegs ohne Passepartouts. Montierungen kommen in der Sammlung Bartsch sonst kaum vor (eine Ausnahme: Inv. 12/06165, Karton mit vier marmorierten Papieren von Koloman Moser). Sie könnten von Stolba selbst stammen, zeugen jedenfalls von der besonderen Wertschätzung der Blätter Stolbas innerhalb der Sammlung. Dafür spricht auch die Tatsache, dass 1909 ein Großteil seiner Werke in der von Bartsch organisierten

Ausstellung in Stuttgart zu sehen war (Schmidt/Feiler 1998, s. Anm. 14, 38). Die Umstände der Ankäufe lassen sich aus den von Bartsch angebrachten Stempeln auf den Rückseiten der Blätter sowie aus schriftlichen Aufzeichnungen des Sammlers entnehmen. Demnach hat er „20 Blatt Kleisterpapiere à 3 K[ronen] durch die Secession Juni 1903" erworben und im November desselben Jahres „3 Bl[ätter] à 6 K[ronen] [und] 15 B[lätter] à 3 Kr[onen]" (vgl. Anm. 29). Diese Preise übersteigen, soweit ich es nach einer ersten Übersicht beurteilen kann, sehr deutlich den Durchschnitt der Ankäufe: Die allermeisten der überwiegend größeren Blätter hat Bartsch für 25 Pfennig bis maximal 2 Mark pro Stück erworben. Teurer war der damals bereits sehr angesehene, verstorbene Ernst Leistikow. Bartsch zahlte 1899 für Blätter aus dessen Nachlass 5 Mark (Mark und Krone wiegen in dieser Zeit jeweils 5 Gramm Silber, mit geringen Unterschieden im Feingehalt).

2) 105 Buntpapiere im Kupferstichkabinett der Akademie der bildenden Künste Wien. Viele davon vom Künstler auf Kartons montiert. Zwei Drittel der Blätter tragen auf der Montierung und/oder Rückseite eine Signatur in Bleistift und/oder ein mit violetter Tinte gestempeltes Monogramm „LS" (Stempel in der Regel auf Rückseite der Blätter, bei Inv. HZ 27355-35 auf

Rückseite der Montierung, der gleiche Stempel findet sich auch auf der Rückseite vieler Kleisterpapiere im MAK). 30 Blätter sind neben der Signatur auch eigenhändig datiert – je einmal 1904 und 1905, 28-mal 1906.

3) Signiert und datiert (1902–1906) sind nach Aussage des Versteigerungskataloges auch zehn marmorierte Blätter, die bei Bonhams, New York, am 4.12.2006 (Los 6182) mit Provenienz Hilde Wittgenstein unter den Hammer kamen.

4) Die Galerie Walfischgasse verzeichnet in einem Katalog (*Wiener Grafik des Jugendstils*, Wien 2012, https://www.yumpu.com/de/document/view/5871757/wiener-grafik-des-jugendstils-galerie-walfischgasse/33, 27.7.2016) drei marmorierte Fische aus der Hand Stolbas, alle drei auf Passepartout signiert, zwei davon 1903 datiert. Zwei davon sind mit den Ziffern 11 und 13 nummeriert.

[35] Wie andernorts dargestellt (Rosenberg, Raphael, *Turner – Hugo – Moreau: Entdeckung der Abstraktion*, Ausst.kat. Schirn Kunsthalle Frankfurt, München 2007), hat es lange vor 1900 viele ungegenständliche Bilder, die von KünstlerInnen gemacht, jedoch nicht als Kunstwerke deklariert und also nicht in Kunstausstellungen gezeigt worden sind, gegeben. Eine scheinbare Ausnahme ist die Ausstellung von

Georgiana Houghton (1814–1884) 1871 in der New British Gallery in London. Auf eigene Kosten zeigte sie damals amimetische Zeichnungen, jedoch nicht als Kunstwerke, sondern als „spirit drawings" (Grant, Simon et al., *Georgiana Houghton – Spirit drawings*, London 2016).

[36] Bei den Temperas handelte es sich um die Werke *In den sechziger Jahren* (Ausst. Kat. Nr. 250; Endicott Barnett, Vivian, *Kandinsky. Werkverzeichnis der Aquarelle*, 2 Bde., München 1992 und 1994, Bd. I, 182, Nr. 200), *Italienischer Hafen* (Ausst. Kat. Nr. 269; Barnett, 182, Nr. 199), zusätzlich vielleicht außer Katalog auch *Waschtag* (Barnett, 183, Nr. 201). Die Identifikation der Holzschnitte ist mangels Betitelung im Secessionskatalog weniger eindeutig. Kandinsky machte 1906 keine Holzschnitte. Keines der Blätter bis 1904/1905 ist auch nur annähernd ungegenständlich, siehe Röthel, Hans Konrad, *Kandinsky. Das graphische Werk*, Köln 1970.

[37] Rosenberg, Raphael, „Was There a First Abstract Painter? Af Klint's Amimetic Images and Kandinsky's Abstract Art", in: Almquist, Kurt/Belfrage, Louise (Hg.), *Hilma af Klint – The art of seeing the invisible*, Stockholm 2015, 87–100, 322–323, hier 99.

remarkable that Stolba mounted his decorated paper pictures, signed the sheets on the reverse and/or on their passe-partouts, and partly also dated them (ill. 017).[34] Though decorated papers by artists were often signed. I know of no comparable artist using signed passe-partouts for decorated papers at that time. Stolba's signed mounts were probably made in view of exhibitions.

Leopold Stolba exhibited dozens of non-representational sheets at the Secession from 1903 onwards; they were rectangular to almost square and in a similar format (the longest side mostly remains under 270 mm). Some sheets are ornamental "endpapers," though many are composed pictures, created in diverse ways. Depending on the technique, he refers to them as "monotypes" or "drawings using the marbling technique." These sheets are partly signed and, on a number of occasions, dated. Stolba is hence one of the very first artists to exhibit abstract pictures as art.[35] Certainly earlier than Kandinsky: when the two were displayed alongside one another in the same room at the Secession in March 1906, Stolba's abstract sheets were facing representational temperas and woodcuts by Kandinsky.[36]

From today's perspective, the fact that Stolba exhibited abstract images several years before Kandinsky can be described as an epochal sensation. Stolba himself, however, must have comprehended his actions in less lofty terms. Therein lies a fundamental difference compared to Kandinsky. The latter interpreted his rejection of mimesis as an artistic revolution. He pursued this revolution systematically with a twofold strategy: exhibition practice and written, propagandistic discourse. From 1910 onwards, the pictures shown by Kandinsky in avant-garde exhibitions were less and less representational.[37] Furthermore, the publication of *Concerning the Spiritual in Art* in December

[34] Stolba's sheets at the MAK are not (or no longer?) on their original mounts. However, four bundles of decorated paper with original mounts, signatures, and dates are known (from 1903, 1904, 1905, and, far outweighing the other years, 1906):

1) 33 decorated papers at the German Museum of Books and Writing at the German National Library in Leipzig (cf. note 14): five marbled fish pictures (all in passe-partouts, two of them signed on the bottom-right of the passe-partout and dated 1903: inv. no. 12/4133 and 12/4135), a monotype (see note 33), and 27 other paste papers. The monotype and the majority of the paste papers were produced on the reverse of the Hörmann auction catalog plates (see note 24, except 12/06144-06147 & 12/06161). The monographs and the paste papers are mounted on cardboard, sometimes with two sheets on one board, without passe-partouts. Otherwise, mounts are hardly found in the Bartsch Collection (an exception: inv. 12/06165, board with four marbled papers by Koloman Moser). I suppose that they were done by Stolba himself; in any event, they testify to the high appreciation of Stolba's sheets in the collection. As does the fact that in 1909 a large proportion of his works was on display in the exhibition organized by Bartsch in Stuttgart

(Schmidt/Feiler 1998, see notes 14, 38). The circumstances of their purchase can be gathered from Bartsch's stamps on the reverse of the sheets as well as the collector's written records. According to these sources, he purchased "20 sheets of paste paper for 3 K[ronen] by the Secession, June 1903" and in November of the same year "3 sheets for 6 K[ronen] [and] 15 sheets for 3 Kr[onen]" (cf. note 29). As far as I can judge after an initial review, these prices significantly exceed the average for all purchases: Bartsch bought the vast majority of the predominantly larger sheets for between 25 pfennigs and a maximum of 2 marks per piece. Only in the case of the deceased Ernst Leistikow, who was already well-respected at that time, did Bartsch pay 5 marks for sheets from his estate in 1899 (Marks and Kronen weighed 5 grams of silver each at this time, with minimal differences in assay).

2) 105 decorated papers in the Graphic Collection of the Academy of Fine Arts Vienna. Many of them were mounted on board by the artist. Two thirds of the sheets bear a signature in pencil and/or the monogram "LS" stamped in violet ink on the mount and/or the reverse side (the stamp is generally on the reverse of the sheets, but for inv. HZ 27355-35 on the reverse of the mount; the same stamp can be found on the

reverse of many paste papers at the MAK). 30 sheets are also dated next to the signature in the same handwriting—once each for 1904 and 1905, and 28 are dated 1906.

3) 10 marbled sheets signed and dated (1902–1906, according to the auction catalog), were sold at Bonhams, New York, on 4 Dec 2006 (lot 6182), previously owned by Hilde Wittgenstein.

4) Galerie Walfischgasse records three marbled fish by Stolba's hand in a catalog (*Wiener Grafik des Jugendstils*, Vienna 2012, https://www.yumpu.com /de/document/view/5871757/wiener-grafik-des-jugendstils-galerie-walfisch-gasse/33, 27 Jul 2016). All three are signed on the passe-partout, two of them are dated 1903. Two of them are numbered, one 11 and one 13.

[35] As illustrated elsewhere (Rosenberg, Raphael, *Turner – Hugo – Moreau: Entdeckung der Abstraktion*, exh.cat. Schirn Kunsthalle Frankfurt, Munich 2007), there were many amimetic pictures made by artists, though not declared as artworks, long before 1900. However, they were not displayed in art exhibitions. An apparent exception is the 1871 exhibition by Georgiana Houghton (1814–1884) at the New British Gallery in London. In it, she displayed amimetic drawings at

her own expense, though as "spirit drawings" not as art works (Grant, Simon et al., *Georgiana Houghton – Spirit drawings*, London 2016).

[36] The temperas were *In den sechziger Jahren* (exhib. cat. no. 250; Endicott Barnett, Vivian, *Kandinsky. Werkverzeichnis der Aquarelle*, 2 vols., Munich 1992 and 1994, vol. I, 182, no. 200), *Italienischer Hafen* (exhib. cat. no. 269; Barnett, 182, no. 199), additionally perhaps, though not in the catalog: *Waschtag* (Barnett, 183, no. 201). The identification of the woodcuts is less straightforward due to a lack of titles in the Secession catalog. Kandinsky did not do any woodcuts in 1906. None of the sheets is even slightly non-representational until 1904/1905, see Röthel, Hans Konrad, *Kandinsky. Das graphische Werk*, Cologne 1970.

[37] Rosenberg, Raphael, "Was There a First Abstract Painter? Af Klint's Amimetic Images and Kandinsky's Abstract Art," in: Almquist, Kurt/Belfrage, Louise (ed.), *Hilma af Klint – The art of seeing the invisible*, Stockholm 2015, 87–100, 322–323, here 99.

014
Leopold Stolba
Kleisterpapier
Wien, um 1903
Sign. Stampiglie LS (rückseitig)
Paste Paper
Vienna, ca. 1903
Signed with LS stamping (on the back)
269 x 233 mm
KI 9074-9, Geschenk donation from
August Schestag 1932

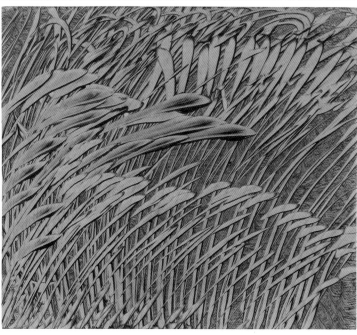

015
Leopold Stolba
Kleisterpapier
Wien, um 1903
Sign. Stampiglie LS (rückseitig)
Paste Paper
Vienna, ca. 1903
Signed with LS stamping (on the back)
233 x 269 mm
KI 9074-4, Geschenk donation from
August Schestag 1932

016
Leopold Stolba
Kleisterpapier
Wien, um 1903–1906
Paste Paper
Vienna, ca. 1903–1906
208 x 272 mm
KI 14432-6, alter Bestand, inv.
old holdings, inventoried in 1986

017
Leopold Stolba
Tunkpapier
Wien, 1906
Sign. Leop. Stolba 1906
Marbled Paper
Vienna, 1906
Signed Leop. Stolba 1906
268 x 201 mm
Kupferstichkabinett der Akademie
der bildenden Künste Wien Academy
of Fine Arts, Graphic Collection,
Inv. Nr. Inv. No. HZ 27355-12
© Kupferstichkabinett

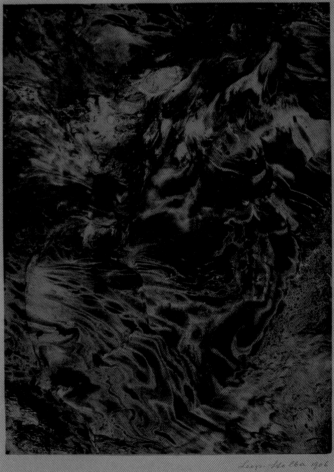

Kunst im Dezember 1911 beginnt außerdem eine Reihe von Publikationen, in denen er Abstraktion als *die* Zukunft der Kunst propagiert.[38] Für Stolba war dagegen Abstraktion kein Bekenntnis, sondern eine von vielen Möglichkeiten künstlerischer Gestaltung. Neben den amimetischen Buntpapieren stellte er immer auch mimetische Werke aus. Von 1913 bis zu seinem Tod 1929 sind seine Ausstellungsbeiträge nur noch figürlicher Art.[39]

Kunsttheoretische Äußerungen von Stolba sind nicht überliefert. Da er seit 1900 ordentliches Mitglied der Secession (Vereinigung bildender Künstler Österreichs) war und 1902/1903 zum Mitglied des Redaktionskomitees des *Ver Sacrum*, der Zeitschrift dieser Vereinigung, ernannt wurde, kann man davon ausgehen, dass er die zentralen Ansichten der Secessionisten teilte. Dazu gehörte die Ablehnung des Kultes des Kunstwerks als Meisterwerk, wie er sich im 19. Jahrhundert etabliert hatte. So heißt es in der programmatischen Einleitung des ersten Heftes des *Ver Sacrum* (Januar 1898): „Wir kennen keine Unterscheidung zwischen ‚hoher Kunst' und ‚Kleinkunst'."[40] Zudem wird seit der XIV. Ausstellung (eröffnet im April 1902) das Einzelwerk dem Gesamtraum untergeordnet. So wird das Ziel der XVII. Ausstellung (März 1903), jene in der Stolba erstmals Buntpapiere zur Schau stellte, folgendermaßen erklärt: „Unsere XVII. Ausstellung will zeigen, unter welchen Bedingungen sich auch mit dem mobilen, nicht für den betreffenden Platz eigens hergestellten Kunstwerke dekorative Innenraumwirkungen erzielen lassen."[41] Das einzelne Bild zählt nicht an sich, sondern als Teil einer Gesamtraumwirkung.[42] Unter diesem Vorzeichen wird aber der Unterschied von ornamental und bildhaft, wie auch von figürlich und nicht figürlich, nachrangig. Stolba ist unter den Wiener Secessionisten nicht der erste und einzige, der mit bildhafter Abstraktion experimentierte.[43] Kein anderer aber hat sich in Wien in den ersten Jahren des 20. Jahrhunderts so intensiv in diese Experimente vertieft.

Mein Dank geht an Tanja Jenni, Julia Rinck, Heidrun Rosenberg und Anne-Katrin Rossberg, die zu den Recherchen für diesen Aufsatz beigetragen und das Manuskript kritisch gelesen haben. Wichtige Hinweise verdanke ich ferner Nourane Ben Azzouna, Thomas Kaminsky, Eva Knels, Martina Manecke-Frey, Susanne Neuburger, Markus Ritter, Kathrine Ruppert, Frieder Schmidt, Klaus Speidel, Ilse Sturkenboom und Johannes Wieninger.

[38] Rosenberg 2007 (s. Anm. 35), 312–317.

[39] Krist 1999 (s. Anm. 9), 167.

[40] „Weshalb wir eine Zeitschrift herausgeben?", in: *Ver Sacrum* (I) 1 1898, 6.

[41] „Vorwort", in: *XVII. Ausstellung der Vereinigung Bildender Künstler Österreichs Secession Wien*, Ausstellungskatalog, 1903, 13.

[42] Zum Meisterwerkbegriff und seiner Kritik siehe Belting, Hans, *Das unsichtbare Meisterwerk. Die modernen Mythen der Kunst*, München 1998. Zum Wiener Konzept von Raumkunst siehe Forsthuber, Sabine, *Moderne Raumkunst. Wiener Ausstellungsbauten von 1898 bis 1914*, Wien 1991.

[43] Die in diesem Zusammenhang am häufigsten diskutierten Werke sind die zwei „Schmucktafeln" (so die Bezeichnung im Ausstellungskatalog) von Josef Hoffmann über den Türen der Seitensäle der XIV. Ausstellung der Secession (April 1902). Siehe dazu die differenzierte Analyse von Bogner, Dieter, „Die geometrischen Reliefs von Josef Hoffmann", in: *Alte und moderne Kunst* XXVII 184/185 1982, 24–32. In der XV. Ausstellung (November 1902) stellt Else Unger „Stoffmuster und Vorsatzpapiere" aus (Nr. 203); in der XXIII. Ausstellung (März 1905) Josef Engelhart „Monotypien. Einzige Exemplare" (Nr. 11); in der XXVII. Ausstellung des Hagenbundes war ein „Vorsatzpapier" von Heinrich Lefler zu sehen.

1911 launches a series of publications in which he propagates abstraction as the future of art.[38] For Stolba, in contrast, abstraction was no creed, but rather one of several possibilities of artistic work. Alongside his amimetic decorated papers, he consistently exhibited mimetic pictures, too. From 1913 to his death in 1929 his contributions to exhibitions were exclusively figurative.[39]

There are no records of any art theoretical statements by Stolba. However, as he was a full member of the Secession from 1900 and was appointed a member of the editorial board of *Ver Sacrum*, the union's magazine, in 1902/1903, we can assume that he shared the core sentiments of the Secessionists. They included the rejection of the cult of an artwork as a masterpiece, as it had become established in the 19th century. Hence, the programmatic introduction to the first edition of *Ver Sacrum* (January 1898) states: "We acknowledge no difference between 'high art' and 'minor arts.'"[40] Additionally, since the 14th exhibition (opened in April 1902) individual works were subordinate to the space as a whole. Thus the aim of the 17th exhibition (March 1903), in which Stolba exhibited decorated papers for the first time, was declared as follows: "Our 17th exhibition aims to show under which conditions decorative interior design effects can be achieved even with a mobile artwork, which has not been produced specifically for the place in question."[41] The individual picture does not matter in itself, but only as part of the effect created by an entire space.[42] Under this banner, however, a differentiation between ornamental and pictorial, as well as figurative and non-figurative, is of secondary importance. Among the Vienna Secessionists, Stolba was not the first and not the only artist to experiment with pictorial abstraction.[43] Yet there was no other artist in early 20th-century Vienna who immersed themselves in these experiments with such intensity.

I would like to thank Tanja Jenni, Julia Rinck, Heidrun Rosenberg, and Anne-Katrin Rossberg, who contributed to the research for this article and read the manuscript with a critical eye. For their pertinent advice I would also like to thank Nourane Ben Azzouna, Thomas Kaminsky, Eva Knels, Martina Manecke-Frey, Susanne Neuburger, Markus Ritter, Kathrine Ruppert, Frieder Schmidt, Klaus Speidel, Ilse Sturkenboom, and Johannes Wieninger.

[38] Rosenberg 2007 (see note 35), 312–317.

[39] Krist 1999 (see note 9), 167.

[40] "Weshalb wir eine Zeitschrift herausgeben?," in: Ver Sacrum (I) 1 1898, 6. Translated by Maria Slater.

[41] "Vorwort," in: *XVII. Ausstellung der Vereinigung Bildender Künstler Österreichs Secession Wien*, exhibition catalog, 1903, 13. Translated by Maria Slater.

[42] On the term "masterpiece" and its criticism, see Belting, Hans, *Das unsichtbare Meisterwerk. Die modernen Mythen der Kunst*, Munich 1998. On the Viennese concept of "Raumkunst" (spatial art), see Forsthuber, Sabine, *Moderne Raumkunst. Wiener Ausstellungsbauten von 1898 bis 1914*, Vienna 1991.

[43] The works discussed most frequently in this context are the two "decorative panels" (as described in the exhibition catalog) by Josef Hoffmann over the doors of the side rooms of the 14th exhibition of the Secession (April 1902). On this, see the nuanced analysis by Bogner, Dieter, "Die geometrischen Reliefs von Josef Hoffmann," in: *Alte und moderne Kunst* XXVII 184/185 1982, 24–32. In the 15th exhibition (November 1902) Else Unger exhibited "fabric patterns and endpapers" (no. 203); in the 23rd exhibition (March 1905) Josef Engelhart showed "Monotypes. Sole copies" (no. 11); in the 27th exhibition of the Hagenbund there was an "endpaper" by Heinrich Lefler.

BROKATPAPIER AUS DEM 18. JAHRHUNDERT

Die ersten mit Blattmetall geprägten Papiere – sogenannte Brokatpapiere – gelangten 1877 in die Sammlung der Bibliothek. Georg Mössel, Antiquar aus Nürnberg, bot Direktor Rudolf von Eitelberger ein Konvolut von Buntpapieren „für 35 Mark" an, das vom Kustos und Bibliothekar Eduard Chmelarz unter der Nummer 3026 inventarisiert wurde. Darunter befanden sich Augsburger Brokatpapiere der bedeutenden Verleger Georg Christoph Stoy (1670–1750), Johann Michael Munck (gest.1762) und Josef Friedrich Leopold (1669–1727), deren Signaturen auf den Fragmenten teilweise erhalten sind (Abb. 002, 018). Weitere 16 Muster aus Augsburg wurden 1886 inventarisiert, ohne Angabe der Provenienz (Abb. 020, 026, 027).

Augsburg war seit ca. 1700 das Zentrum der Brokatpapiererzeugung, ab 1720 nahm auch Fürth eine führende Rolle ein. Vom dortigen Verleger Johann Lechner (1766–1839) haben sich 24 vollständige Bogen erhalten, die 1985 von der Textilsammlung in die Bibliothek wechselten, ursprünglich aber bereits 1917 von der Wiener Antiquitätenhändlerin Rosa Wandner erworben worden waren (Abb. 021–025). Auf deren Informationen beruht wohl die Bemerkung im Inventarbuch: „Stammt aus einem Wiener Kloster". Die Verwendung von Brokatpapieren in Klosterbibliotheken ist vor allem aus Göttweig bekannt, wo 1984 die Ausstellung *Europäische Buntpapiere* stattfand. Gregor M. Lechner und Hanna Egger (von 1982 bis 2000 Leiterin der MAK-Bibliothek und Kunstblättersammlung) arbeiteten hierfür die Bestände des Stifts und des Museums erstmals systematisch auf.[1] Dabei zeigten sich auch die unterschiedlichen Sammlungsgeschichten. Während das Museum seine Objekte bewusst als Vorbilder für EntwerferInnen, ErzeugerInnen und KonsumentInnen erworben hatte, entstand die Göttweiger Sammlung durch den direkten Gebrauch der Papiere, mit denen seit der Barockzeit Kleinschriften und Mappen eingebunden worden waren. Umschlag und Inhalt sind jeweils gemeinsam erhalten. Im Museum hingegen, wo man den Ordnungsprinzipien des 19. Jahrhunderts folgte, interessierte das Papier und nicht seine Funktion, was – aus heutiger Sicht – zu gewaltsamen Maßnahmen führte: des Inhalts beraubt und auseinandergeklappt, erinnert allenfalls ein Etikett an die ursprüngliche Broschüre (Abb. 019).

Die Augsburger Brokatpapiere der MAK-Kunstblättersammlung zeigen vorwiegend Rankenornamente aus Blüten, Blättern und Früchten, teils verbunden mit Figuren und Tieren (Abb. 020). Granatäpfel, Tulpen, Nelken, Schachbrettblumen und Trauben zeugen vom Ursprung der Ornamentik im Orient, die durch Musterbücher in Europa verbreitet worden war. Auch die Berufsbezeichnung „Türkisch Papiermacher" für den Verleger erinnert an die Herkunft dieser Art Papier. In der zweiten Hälfte des 18. Jahrhunderts kommen bilderbogenartige Dekore dazu, die Alphabete, Handwerkerszenen oder Tiermotive aneinanderreihen (Abb. 021, 023, 024). Auch finden sich vermehrt geometrische Muster oder Rankendekore geometrisch patroniert (Abb. 022, 025). Die Blütezeit der Brokatpapiere ist jedoch bereits vorbei – orientalische Üppigkeit und technische Präzision sind einer gewissen Beliebigkeit in der Motivwahl und einer vergröberten Ausführung gewichen. Die Gegenüberstellung zweier Tafeln aus der Sammlung Clerget (s. folgendes Kapitel) mag diese Entwicklung noch einmal veranschaulichen (Abb. 028, 029).

[1] Egger, Hanna/Lechner, Gregor M., *Europäische Buntpapiere. Barock bis Jugendstil*, Schriften des Museums für angewandte Kunst 26, Wien 1984.

18TH-CENTURY BROCADE PAPER

The first papers embossed with metal leaf—so-called brocade papers—to enter the collection of the library did so in 1877. Georg Mössel, a bibliopole from Nuremburg, had offered the director Rudolf von Eitelberger a bundle of decorated papers "for 35 marks," which was later inventoried under the number 3026 by the conservator and librarian Eduard Chmelarz. The bundle included brocade papers from Augsburg, Germany, by the eminent publisher Georg Christoph Stoy (1670–1750), Johann Michael Munck (d. 1762), and Josef Friedrich Leopold (1669–1727), whose signatures have been partly preserved on the fragments (ill. 002, 018). A further 16 patterns from Augsburg were inventoried in 1886, though their provenance was not recorded (ill. 020, 026, 027).

Augsburg had been the center of brocade paper production since ca. 1700; from 1720 Fürth, Germany, also played a leading role. 24 complete sheets by the Fürth-based publisher Johann Lechner (1766–1839) have survived, which were moved from the textile collection to the library in 1985, but which had originally been acquired by the Viennese antiques dealer Rosa Wandner as early as 1917 (ill. 021–025). It is probably information from her on which the comment in the inventory is based: "Comes from a Viennese cloister." The use of brocade papers in cloistral libraries is best known from Göttweig, Austria, where an exhibition on European decorated paper was held in 1984. For the purpose of the show, Gregor M. Lechner and Hanna Egger (head of the MAK Library and Works on Paper Collection from 1982 to 2000) systematically reviewed the holdings of both the abbey and the museum for the first time.[1] This process also revealed the differences in the histories of the two collections. While the museum had intentionally acquired its objects as exemplars for designers, producers, and consumers, the Göttweig Collection had arisen as a result of the straightforward use of the papers, with which files and short documents had been bound since the baroque period. In every case, the cover and content had been preserved together. In the museum, in contrast, which had obeyed 19th-century classification principles, the paper and not its function had been of interest, which led to—from today's perspective—violent measures: bereft of their content and unfolded, a label at most serves as a reminder of the original brochure (ill. 019).

The brocade papers of Augsburg origin in the MAK Works on Paper Collection predominantly bear tendril-based ornamentation comprising flowers, leaves, and fruit, partly accompanied by figures and animals (ill. 020). Pomegranates, tulips, carnations, *fritillaria meleagris*, and grapes bear witness to the origins of this kind of ornamentation in the East, which was disseminated in Europe by means of pattern books. Even the publisher's job description—"Turkish papermaker"— is a reminder of the provenance of this kind of paper. In the second half of the 18th century, Épinal-like decorations emerge, which concatenate alphabets, scenes of craftspeople, and animal motifs (ill. 021, 023, 024). There is also an increasing number of geometric patterns or geometrically stenciled tendril decorations (ill. 022, 025). The heyday of brocade paper has, however, already passed: Eastern opulence and technical precision have given way to a certain arbitrary choice of motifs and more imprecise workmanship. A comparison of two boards from the Clerget Collection (see next section) illustrates this development quite clearly (ill. 028, 029).

[1] Egger, Hanna/Lechner, Gregor M., *Europäische Buntpapiere. Barock bis Jugendstil*, Schriften des Museums für angewandte Kunst 26, Vienna 1984.

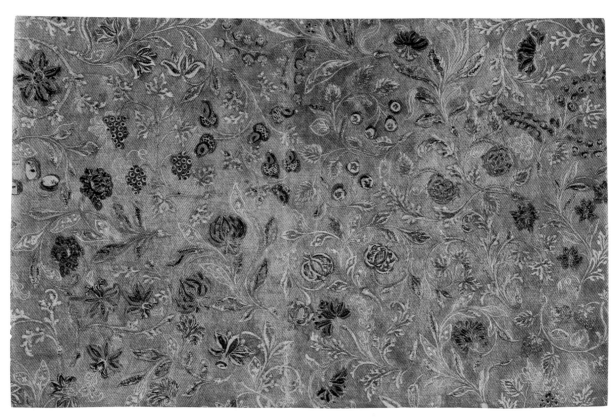

018
Georg Christoph Stoy
Brokatpapier
Augsburg, 1. Hälfte 18. Jh.
Prägedruck, handkoloriert
Brocade Paper
Augsburg, 1st half 18th c.
Embossing, hand colored
217 x 341 mm
KI 3026-124, Ankauf purchased from
Antiquariat Mössel 1877

019
Anonym Anonymous
Bucheinband mit Brokatpapier
Augsburg, 2. Hälfte 18. Jh.
Prägedruck, Pochoirkolorierung
Book Cover with Brocade Paper
Augsburg, 2nd half 18th c.
Embossing, pochoir coloring
176 x 208 mm
KI 3026-17, Ankauf purchased from
Antiquariat Mössel 1877

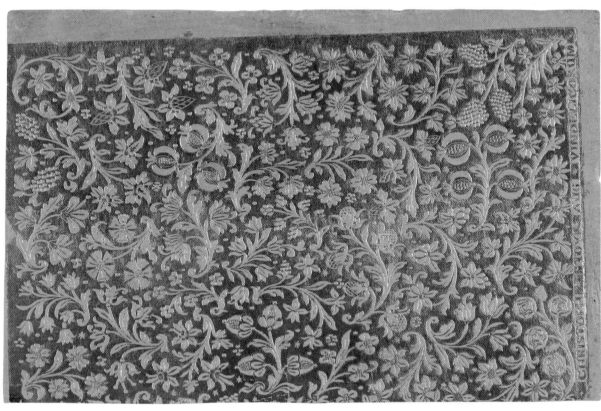

020
Georg Christoph Stoy
Brokatpapier
Augsburg, 1. Hälfte 18. Jh.
Prägedruck auf Grundierung
Brocade Paper
Augsburg, 1st half 18th c.
Embossing on primer
212 x 333 mm
KI 5259-4, inv. inventoried in 1886

021
Johann Lechner
Brokatpapier
Fürth, letztes Viertel 18. Jh.
Prägedruck auf Grundierung
Brocade Paper
Fürth, last quarter 18th c.
Embossing on primer
358 x 422 mm
KI 14436-1, Ankauf purchased from
Rosa Wandner 1917

022
Johann Lechner
Brokatpapier
Fürth, letztes Viertel 18. Jh.
Prägedruck auf Grundierung
Brocade Paper
Fürth, last quarter 18th c.
Embossing on primer
358 x 435 mm
KI 14435-1, Ankauf purchased
from Rosa Wandner 1917

023
Johann Lechner
Brokatpapier
Fürth, letztes Viertel 18. Jh.
Prägedruck auf Grundierung
Brocade Paper
Fürth, last quarter 18th c.
Embossing on primer
360 x 422 mm
KI 14435-10, Ankauf purchased
from Rosa Wandner 1917

024
Johann Lechner
Brokatpapier
(Kopie nach Johann Carl Munck)
Fürth, letztes Viertel 18. Jh.
Prägedruck
Brocade Paper
(Copy of Johann Carl Munck)
Fürth, last quarter 18th c.
Embossing
356 x 420 mm
KI 14436-2, Ankauf purchased
from Rosa Wandner 1917

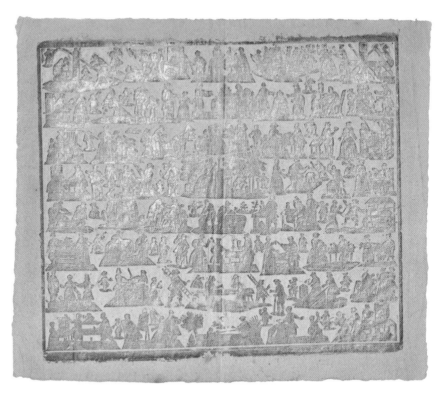

025
Johann Lechner
Brokatpapier
Fürth, letztes Viertel 18. Jh.
Prägedruck, Pochoirkolorierung
Brocade Paper
Fürth, last quarter 18th c.
Embossing, pochoir coloring
374 x 428 mm
KI 14435-8, Ankauf purchased
from Rosa Wandner 1917

026
Josef Friedrich Leopold
Brokatpapier
Augsburg, 1. Hälfte 18. Jh.
Prägedruck auf Grundierung
Brocade Paper
Augsburg, 1st half 18th c.
Embossing on primer
187 x 337 mm
KI 5259-2, inv. inventoried in 1886

027
Vermutl. Prob.
Johann Michael Schwibecher
Brokatpapier
Augsburg, 1. Hälfte 18. Jh.
Prägedruck auf Grundierung
Brocade Paper
Augsburg, 1st half 18th c.
Embossing on primer
165 x 204 mm
KI 5259-6, inv. inventoried in 1886

028
Anonym Anonymous
Zwei Brokatpapiere auf Karton
1720 und 1704
Modeldruck
Two Brocade Papers on cardboard
1720 and 1704
Block printing
221 x 295 mm
KI 16711-101, Sammlung
Charles Ernest Clerget Collection

029
Anonym Anonymous
Zwei Brokatpapiere auf Karton
1764 und 1766
Prägedruck
Two Brocade Papers on cardboard
1764 and 1766
Embossing
221 x 295 mm
KI 16711-97, Sammlung
Charles Ernest Clerget Collection

MARMORPAPIER AUS DER SAMMLUNG CLERGET

Wann und durch wen die Buntpapiersammlung von Charles Ernest Clerget (1812–ca. 1870) an
das Museum geriet, ist nicht überliefert: Weder die Inventare noch das Aktenarchiv geben darüber
Auskunft. Erstmals genauer beschrieben wurde sie im Katalog zur Ausstellung *Europäische Bunt-*
papiere. Barock bis Jugendstil, die 1984/85 im Stift Göttweig und anschließend im Österreichischen
Museum für angewandte Kunst stattgefunden hatte.[1] Clara Radunsky unternahm 2011 im Zuge
ihrer Diplomarbeit die genaue Inventarisierung der zuvor als Konvolut aufgenommenen Blätter.[2]
Die Sammlung beeindruckt nicht nur aufgrund des Materials, sondern erhält einen zusätzlichen
Reiz durch dessen besondere Aufbereitung. 404 ca. 80 x 120 mm große Muster von hauptsächlich
Marmor-, aber auch Kleister-, Modeldruck- und Brokatpapieren wurden jeweils in Vierergruppen
auf graublaue Kartons kaschiert und dabei sorgfältig mit Blei- und Buntstiftstrichen umrahmt.
Alle Beispiele sind mit einer Datierung versehen und umfassen damit einen Zeitraum von 1644
bis 1866. Anhaltspunkt für die Datierungen war das jeweilige Erscheinungsjahr der Bücher, aus
denen Clerget die Beispiele (Vorsatzpapiere) herausgelöst hatte. So ergaben sich konkrete Jahres-
zahlen, die aber letztlich nur Annäherungswerte darstellen, wie Clerget in seiner Einleitung betont.
Das betrifft auch die sporadischen Angaben zur Herkunft der Muster: „allemand" (Abb. 032),
„Londres" oder „Espagne".

Aus dem handgeschriebenen Verzeichnis (Abb. S. 028), datiert mit 19. September 1866, ist die
Ordnung der Sammlung ersichtlich: Die Buchstaben A bis T (auf den Kartons jeweils oben links)
bezeichnen die unterschiedlichen Kategorien, etwa „Punktierter Steinmarmor" (Abb. 031), „Granit-
artig in moderner Technik" (Abb. 033) oder „Löckchenmarmor" (Abb. 034). Diese Systematik ist
sicher der Funktion Clergets als Bibliothekar der Union Centrale des Beaux Arts appliqués à
l'industrie in Paris zu verdanken. Die bildhafte Inszenierung jedoch verweist auf den Künstler und
Ornamentstecher Clerget, der an verschiedenen kunstgewerblichen Vorlagewerken beteiligt war.
1837 etwa erschien das großformatige Opus *Mélanges d'ornements de tous les styles*, das 1875
vom Museum angekauft wurde.[3]

Auch als Theoretiker trat er in Erscheinung. In seiner Abhandlung *Von der typographischen Ver-*
zierung beklagt Clerget den Qualitätsverlust innerhalb der Buchgestaltung durch die industrielle
Herstellung. Das Buch wurde 1859 von der k. k. Hof- und Staatsdruckerei verlegt und erschien in
deutscher und französischer Sprache.[4] Demnach unterhielt Clerget Beziehungen zu Wien und
kannte – als Mitbegründer der Union Centrale 1864 – mit Sicherheit das k. k. Österreichische
Museum für Kunst und Industrie, weil beide Institutionen dieselben Ideen verfolgten. Womöglich
überließ er noch zu Lebzeiten seine Sammlung der Bibliothek.

[1] Egger, Hanna/Lechner, Gregor M.,
Europäische Buntpapiere. Barock bis Jugend-
stil, Schriften des Museums für angewandte
Kunst 26, Wien 1984.

[2] Radunsky, Clara, *Marmorpapier. Vom*
Gebrauchsgegenstand zum Kunstobjekt,
am Beispiel der Sammlung Charles Ernest
Clerget im Museum für angewandte Kunst
in Wien, Diplom-Arbeit, Wien 2012.

[3] Clerget, Charles Ernest, *Mélanges*
d'ornements de tous les styles – persan,
mauresque, arabe, grec, gothique, renais-
sance, principalement XVIe et XVIIe siècles.
Composés, dessinés et gravés par Clerget,
Paris 1837.

[4] Clerget, Charles Ernest, *Von der*
typographischen Verzierung. Ein Versuch über
Ornamentik in ihrer Anwendung auf die Ver-
zierung der Bücher, Wien 1859.

MARBLED PAPER FROM THE CLERGET COLLECTION

When and via whom the decorated paper collection of Charles Ernest Clerget (1812–ca. 1870) arrived at the museum is not recorded: neither the inventories nor the archive of files provide any information in this regard. The collection was first described in more detail in the catalog for the exhibition on European decorated paper from baroque to art nouveau, which took place in Göttweig Abbey and subsequently the Austrian Museum of Applied Arts in 1984/1985.[1] As part of her thesis, Clara Radunsky created a precise inventory of these sheets in 2011, which had previously only been recorded as a bundle.[2]

The collection is impressive: not merely due to the material, but it gains additional appeal due to its unusual preparation. 404 ca. 80 x 120 mm exemplars of predominantly marbled, but also paste, block printed, and brocade papers were each attached in groups of four to gray-blue boards and carefully framed with lines in lead and colored pencil. All of the examples are dated and cover a period from 1644 to 1866. A reference point for these dates was supplied by the publication date of the books from which Clerget had taken the examples (endpapers). This provided him with specific years, though they were ultimately mere approximations, as Clerget emphasizes in his introduction. That description also applies to the sporadic information relating to the origins of the patterns: "allemand" (ill. 032), "Londres," or "Espagne."

The handwritten register (ill. p. 028), dated 19 September 1866, makes the organization of the collection evident: the letters A to T (always top left on the boards) designate the different categories, such as "dotted Gloster" (ill. 031), "granite-like using modern technique" (ill. 033), and "French curl marbling" (ill. 034). This classification can undoubtedly be explained by Clerget's function as the librarian of the Union Centrale des Beaux Arts appliqués à l'industrie in Paris. The embellished presentation, however, points to the artist and ornamental engraver Clerget, who was involved in various publications of arts-and-crafts exemplars. In 1837, for example, he completed his large-format opus *Mélanges d'ornements de tous les styles*, which was acquired by the museum in 1875.[3] He also worked as a theorist. In his essay *Von der typographischen Verzierung* [On typographic ornament], Clerget laments the loss of quality in book design as a result of industrial production. The book was published in 1859 by the Imperial Royal Court and State Printers; it was released in both French and German.[4] Thereafter, Clerget maintained connections with Vienna and—as the co-founder of the Union Centrale in 1864—most certainly knew the Imperial Royal Austrian Museum of Art and Industry, as both institutions pursued the same ideas. Indeed, it is possible that he donated his collection to the library during his lifetime.

[1] Egger, Hanna/Lechner, Gregor M., *Europäische Buntpapiere. Barock bis Jugendstil*, Schriften des Museums für angewandte Kunst 26, Vienna 1984.

[2] Radunsky, Clara, *Marmorpapier. Vom Gebrauchsgegenstand zum Kunstobjekt, am Beispiel der Sammlung Charles Ernest Clerget im Museum für angewandte Kunst in Wien*, degree thesis, Vienna 2012.

[3] Clerget, Charles Ernest, *Mélanges d'ornements de tous les styles – persan, mauresque, arabe, grec, gothique, renaissance, principalement XVIe et XVIIe siècles. Composés, dessinés et gravés par Clerget*, Paris 1837.

[4] Clerget, Charles Ernest, *Von der typographischen Verzierung. Ein Versuch über Ornamentik in ihrer Anwendung auf die Verzierung der Bücher*, Vienna 1859.

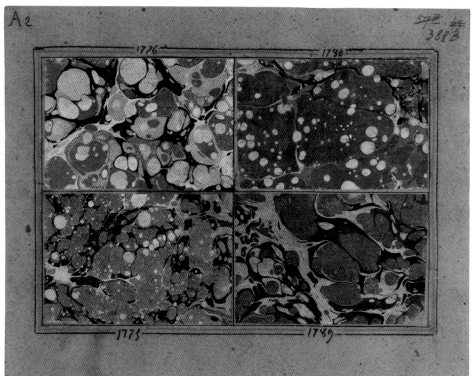

030
Anonym Anonymous
Vier Marmorpapiere auf Karton
(A: Cailloutés a Peintes plates)
1775–1789
Four Sheets of Marbled Paper
on cardboard (A: Cailloutés
a Peintes plates)
1775–1789
225 x 291 mm
KI 16711-3, Sammlung
Charles Ernest Clerget Collection

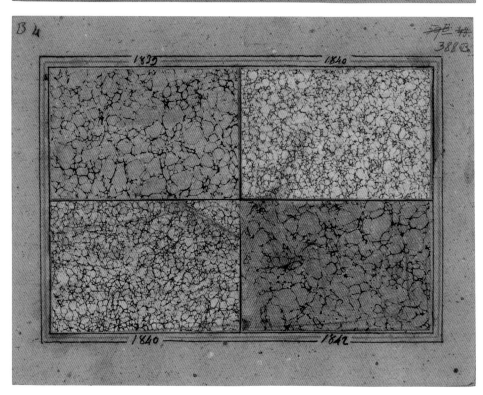

031
Anonym Anonymous
Vier Marmorpapiere auf Karton
(B: Cailloutés pointillés)
1839–1842
Four Sheets of Marbled Paper
on cardboard (B: Cailloutés
pointillés)
1839–1842
225 x 291 mm
KI 16711-13, Sammlung
Charles Ernest Clerget Collection

032
Anonym Anonymous
Vier Marmorpapiere auf Karton
(E: Marbrés à fonds ombrés rayés)
1849–1852
Four Sheets of Marbled Paper
on cardboard (E: Marbrés à fonds
ombrés rayés)
1849–1852
225 x 291 mm
KI 16711-30, Sammlung
Charles Ernest Clerget Collection

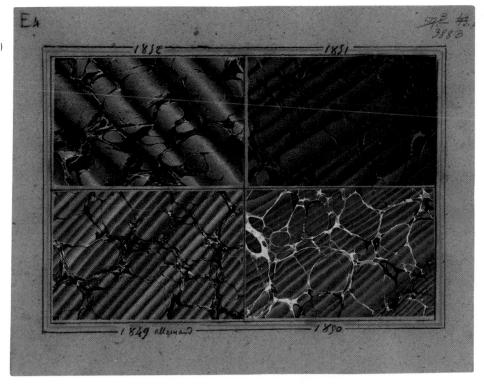

033
Anonym Anonymous
Vier Marmorpapiere auf Karton
(I: Marbrés Divers,
Granités modernes)
1860 und 1859
Four Sheets of Marbled Paper
on cardboard (I: Marbrés Divers,
Granités modernes)
1860 and 1859
225 x 291 mm
KI 16711-36, Sammlung
Charles Ernest Clerget Collection

034
Anonym Anonymous
Vier Marmorpapiere auf Karton
(L: Frisons ou Tourniquets)
1741–1768
Four Sheets of Marbled Paper on cardboard
(L: Frisons ou Tourniquets)
1741–1768
221 x 295 mm
KI 16711-49, Sammlung Charles Ernest Clerget Collection

035
Anonym Anonymous
Vier Marmorpapiere auf Karton
(M: Peignés ou Crêpés, simples ou doubles)
1644–1690
Four Sheets of Marbled Paper on cardboard
(M: Peignés ou Crêpés, simples ou doubles)
1644–1690
221 x 295 mm
KI 16711-58, Sammlung Charles Ernest Clerget Collection

BUNTPAPIER AUS DREI JAHRHUNDERTEN

„11 Bogen mit je 10 Mustern von einer alten Buntpapiermusterkarte" offerierte Georg Mössel, Antiquar aus Nürnberg, der Bibliothek des k. k. Österreichischen Museums für Kunst und Industrie (ÖMKI) am 29. März 1877. Sie stammen aus der zweiten Hälfte des 18. Jahrhunderts und zeigen ca. 75 x 50 mm große Beispiele von Modeldruckpapieren (Abb. 040–042). Zur Zeit ihrer Entstehung waren sie als Kattunpapiere bekannt, weil Technik und Motive auf dem Textildruck basierten. Raffinierte Kombinationen aus floralem und linearem Dekor wechseln sich mit teilweise skurrilen figuralen und streng geometrischen Motiven ab.

Ein Konvolut von Buntpapieren aus dem späten 18. und frühen 19. Jahrhundert kam laut Inventarbuch als „Geschenk des Provisors Karl Kock, Hausleiten b. Stockerau" 1932 in die Sammlung des Museums. Darin finden sich verschiedene Versionen des ausgefallenen, im Walzendruck erzeugten Wolkenbandmusters (Abb. 043). Rechnungsbücher aus der Gemeinde Reuenthal (1820er bis 1850er Jahre) zeigen die Verwendung der Papiere als Umschläge, deren wappenähnliche Etiketten die Bedeutung des Inhalts unterstreichen (Abb. 044, 045).

Im Frühjahr 1903 richtete das ÖMKI eine *Ausstellung von Bucheinbänden und Vorsatzpapieren* aus, um sowohl vorbildliche Beispiele der Vergangenheit als auch die Entwicklungen der Gegenwart vorzustellen. In der Hauspublikation *Kunst und Kunsthandwerk* findet sich eine Ausstellungskritik von Ludwig Hevesi, worin der Autor die Vielfältigkeit der modernen Entwürfe hervorhebt: „Ein Saal voll Vorsatzpapiere ist heutzutage ungemein amüsant, ein Stelldichein der verschiedensten Geister."[1] Neben den japanischen Blättern, die er ausführlich beschreibt (Abb. 046), beeindrucken ihn die Leistungen der KunstgewerbeschülerInnen: „Auch das Vorsatzpapier unserer Monatsschrift stammt aus diesem Kreise, es ist von Else Unger."[2] (Abb. 053) Ein schönes Beispiel für die Verschränkung der beiden gemeinsam gegründeten Institutionen: Eine (womöglich durch Vorbilder aus der Museumssammlung angeregte) Arbeit aus der Schule wird im Museum präsentiert und zugleich für dessen Hauszeitschrift verwendet.

Buntpapiere von Josef Hoffmann, Koloman Moser und seinen SchülerInnen sowie Maria von Uchatius, einer Schülerin Carl Otto Czeschkas, gelangten 1936 als Geschenk von Hans Ankwicz-Kleehoven in das ÖMKI. Als Leiter der Bibliothek von 1925 bis 1939 hatte Ankwicz-Kleehoven einen enormen Anteil am Ausbau der Gebrauchsgrafiksammlung, die durch Legate und Ankäufe aus seinem Nachlass 1963/1964 noch einmal erweitert wurde. Maria von Uchatius war mit ihren Holzstöckeldrucken auf der Buntpapier-Ausstellung 1907 im Berliner Kunstgewerbemuseum vertreten und wurde im Katalog ausdrücklich erwähnt.[3]

Drei Jahre später erhielten die SchülerInnen der Wiener Kunstgewerbeschule die Gelegenheit, ihre Arbeiten in einer eigenen umfangreichen Buntpapier-Ausstellung zu präsentieren. Erzherzog Rainer, Protektor des ÖMKI, besuchte sie am 25. April 1910, „interessierte sich lebhaft für die Herstellungsarten der verschiedenen Entwürfe" und äußerte sich am Ende „wiederholt sehr befriedigt über das Gesehene".[4] Dieser Notiz in *Kunst und Kunsthandwerk* geht eine kurze Rezension mit Abbildungen voran, die einen Teil der vom Museum erworbenen Buntpapiere zeigen.[5] Insgesamt wurden 28 Arbeiten um 980 Kronen direkt aus der Ausstellung angekauft, darunter Linolschnitte und Modeldrucke ebenso wie Originalentwürfe; auf der Rückseite der Blätter sind jeweils die EntwerferInnen und die Einzelpreise angegeben.

[1] Hevesi, Ludwig „Die Ausstellung von Bucheinbänden und Vorsatzpapieren im Österr. Museum", in: *Kunst und Kunsthandwerk* (V)I 4 1903, 146.

[2] Ebd., 148.

[3] Jessen, Peter, „Einleitung", in: *Führer durch die Sonderausstellung Buntpapiere*, Ausstellungskatalog, Königliche Museen Berlin, Kunstgewerbemuseum, Berlin 1907, 18.

[4] „Kunstgewerbeschule", in: *Kunst und Kunsthandwerk* (XIII) 5 1910, 337.

[5] „Ausstellung von Buntpapieren in der Kunstgewerbeschule des Österreichischen Museums", in: *Kunst und Kunsthandwerk* (XIII) 5 1910, 319.

THREE CENTURIES OF DECORATED PAPER

"11 sheets with 10 patterns on each, from an old decorated paper sample card" were offered by Georg Mössel, a bibliopole from Nuremburg, to the library of the Imperial Royal Austrian Museum of Art and Industry (ÖMKI) on 29 March 1877. They dated back to the second half of the 18th century and show ca. 75 x 50 mm examples of block printed papers (ill. 040–042). At the time they were produced, they were known as "Kattunpapiere" (from English *cotton*), as the technique and motifs were based on textile printing. Elaborate combinations of floral and linear decorations alternate with—at times bizarre—figurative and strictly geometric motifs.

A bundle of decorated papers from the late 18th and early 19th centuries entered the museum's collection in 1932, according to the inventory as a "gift from the administrator Karl Kock, Hausleiten b. Stockerau [Austria]." His donation includes several versions of an unusual band of cloud pattern, produced using rotary printing (ill. 043). Accounts books from the municipality of Reuenthal (1820s to 1850s) reveal that the papers were used as covers; their heraldic labels emphasize the significance of their contents (ill. 044, 045).

In spring 1903 the ÖMKI organized an exhibition on book covers and endpapers for the purpose of displaying both exemplary styles from the past and present developments. In the in-house publication *Kunst und Kunsthandwerk* there is a review of the exhibition by Ludwig Hevesi, in which the author underscores the diversity in the modern designs: "Nowadays, a room filled with endpapers is profoundly enjoyable, a rendezvous for an array of spirits."[1] In addition to the Japanese sheets, which he describes in detail (ill. 046), he is impressed by the achievements of the students from the School of Arts and Crafts: "Even the endpaper in our monthly journal comes from this group; it is by Else Unger."[2] (ill. 053) This is a wonderful example of the close connection between the two jointly founded institutions: a work from the school (possibly inspired by exemplars in the museum's collection) is displayed in the museum and simultaneously used for the in-house magazine.

Decorated papers by Josef Hoffmann, Koloman Moser, and his students, as well as Maria von Uchatius, a student of Carl Otto Czeschka, arrived at the ÖMKI in 1936 in the form of a donation by Hans Ankwicz-Kleehoven. As the head of the library from 1925 to 1939, Ankwicz-Kleehoven made a major contribution to the expansion of the ephemera collection, which was expanded once again in 1963/1964 with bequests and acquisitions from his estate. Maria von Uchatius's woodblock prints were displayed in the decorated paper exhibition in Berlin's Museum of Decorative Arts in 1907; she was also explicitly mentioned in the catalog.[3]

Three years later, the students of Vienna's School of Arts and Crafts were given the opportunity to present their works in a large-scale dedicated exhibition on decorated paper. Archduke Rainer, protector of the ÖMKI, who attended the show on 25 April 1910, "was exceedingly interested in the methods of production behind the various designs" and at the end "repeatedly" voiced his "great satisfaction with what he had seen."[4] This note in *Kunst und Kunsthandwerk* precedes a short review with illustrations depicting some of the decorated papers acquired by the museum.[5] In total, 28 works were purchased straight from the exhibition for 980 Kronen, including linocuts and block prints as well as original designs; the reverse of each sheet shows the designer and unit price.

The way in which the attention paid to the topic of decorated paper intensified during the first decade of the 20th century is striking. What had previously only been collected by public bodies

1 Hevesi, Ludwig, "Die Ausstellung von Bucheinbänden und Vorsatzpapieren im Österr. Museum," in: *Kunst und Kunsthandwerk*, (VI) 4 1903, 146. Translated by Maria Slater.

2 Ibid., 148. Translated by Maria Slater.

3 Jessen, Peter, "Einleitung," in: *Führer durch die Sonderausstellung Buntpapiere*, exhibition catalog, Königliche Museen Berlin, Museum of Decorative Arts, Berlin 1907, 18.

4 "Kunstgewerbeschule," in: *Kunst und Kunsthandwerk* (XIII) 5 1910, 337. Translated by Maria Slater.

5 "Ausstellung von Buntpapieren in der Kunstgewerbeschule des Österreichischen Museums," in: *Kunst und Kunsthandwerk* (XIII) 5 1910, 319.

Es ist auffallend, wie sich die Beschäftigung mit dem Thema Buntpapier in der ersten Dekade des 20. Jahrhunderts intensivierte. Was zuvor von öffentlicher oder privater Hand gesammelt worden war, wurde nun ausgestellt und publiziert, in den Schulen gehörten neue Dessins zu den Aufgabenstellungen und in den Museen zum Sammlungsgut. Der Forderung Wilhelm Exners 1869, bei der Buntpapierfabrikation mehr Schönheitssinn walten zu lassen, wurde im Zuge verschiedenster Reformbewegungen entsprochen.[6] Institutionen wie die 1903 gegründete Wiener Werkstätte trieben die Entwicklungen voran und verhalfen dem Ephemeren zu einem starken Auftritt. So zeigte die Hoffmann-Schule in der Ausstellung 1910 auch – anhand von Briefpapierkassetten oder Menükartenumschlägen –, wie vielfältig Buntpapiere einsetzbar waren. Zugleich nutzte man die Gelegenheit zur Präsentation weiterer Gebrauchsgrafiken wie Prospekte, Geschäftsformulare oder Visitenkarten.

[6] Exner, Wilhelm F., *Die Tapeten- und Buntpapier-Industrie*, Weimar 1869, 2. Der Gründer des Technologischen Gewerbemuseums in Wien war dem ÖMKI als sogenannter Korrespondent verbunden. Das Museum ernannte Korrespondenten in ganz Europa und erstellte damit ein Netzwerk, das dem Austausch von Informationen, der Vermittlung von Ausstellungen und dem Aufbau der Sammlung dienen sollte.

036
Anonym Anonymous
Modeldruckpapier
um 1800
Block Printed Paper
ca. 1800
77 x 77 mm
KI 9080-10, Schenkung
donation from Karl Kock 1932

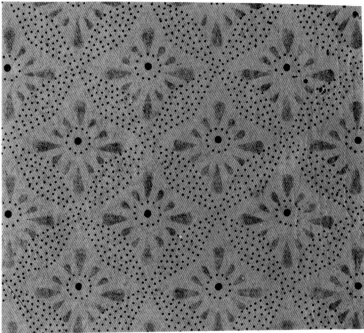

037
Anonym Anonymous
Modeldruckpapier
um 1800
Block Printed Paper
ca. 1800
82 x 95 mm
KI 9080-3, Schenkung
donation from Karl Kock 1932

[6] Exner, Wilhelm F., *Die Tapeten- und Buntpapier-Industrie*, Weimar 1869, 2. The founder of the Technologisches Gewerbemuseum in Vienna was connected to the ÖMKI as a so-called correspondent. The museum appointed correspondents across Europe and thereby created a network that was intended to guarantee an exchange of information, notification about exhibitions, and the growth of the collection.

or private individuals was now exhibited and published; new designs were now part of the assignments in schools and of the collections in museums. Wilhelm Exner's insistence from 1869 that there should be a sense of beauty to the production of decorated paper was finally heeded in the course of diverse reform movements.[6] Institutions such as the Wiener Werkstätte, founded in 1903, furthered these developments and helped the ephemeral to come into the limelight. This led to the Hoffmann school showing in the 1910 exhibition the wide range of ways in which decorated papers could be used by reference to boxes of letter paper and menu covers. At the same time, this opportunity was taken to display other ephemera such as flyers, business forms, and visiting cards.

038
Anonym Anonymous
Modeldruckpapier
um 1800
Block Printed Paper
ca. 1800
91 x 105 mm
KI 9080-13, Schenkung
donation from Karl Kock 1932

039
Anonym Anonymous
Modeldruckpapier
um 1800
Block Printed Paper
ca. 1800
95 x 108 mm
KI 9080-16, Schenkung
donation from Karl Kock 1932

040
Anonym Anonymous
Zwei Bögen mit Modeldruckpapieren
2. Hälfte 18. Jh.
Two Sheets with Block Printed Papers
2nd half 18th c.
360 x 190 mm
KI 3026-18 bis -27, -38 bis -47, Ankauf
purchased from Antiquariat Mössel 1877

041
Anonym Anonymous
Modeldruckpapier
2. Hälfte 18. Jh.
Block Printed Paper
2nd half 18th c.
50 x 76 mm
KI 3026-33, Ankauf purchased
from Antiquariat Mössel 1877

042
Anonym Anonymous
Modeldruckpapier
2. Hälfte 18. Jh.
Block Printed Paper
2nd half 18th c.
49 x 76 mm
KI 3026-64, Ankauf purchased
from Antiquariat Mössel 1877

043
Anonym Anonymous
Modeldruckpapier
um 1800
Block Printed Paper
ca. 1800
160 x 86 mm
KI 9080-19, Schenkung
donation from Karl Kock 1932

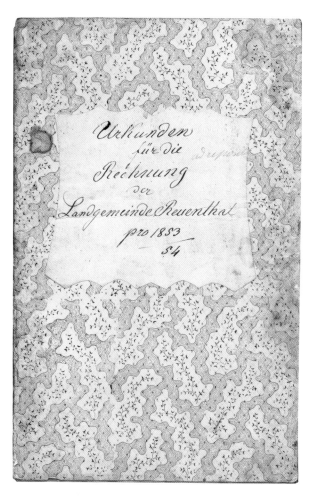

044
Rechnungsbuch der Gemeinde Reuenthal
Reuenthal (Dinkelsbühl), 1845–1846
Modeldruck
Account Book of the Municipality Reuenthal
Reuenthal (Dinkelsbühl), 1845–1846
Block printing
340 x 212 mm
KI 14714-6, Ankauf purchased from Dietrich Hecht 1990

045
Rechnungsbuch der Gemeinde Reuenthal
Reuenthal (Dinkelsbühl), 1853–1854
Modeldruck
Account Book of the Municipality Reuenthal
Reuenthal (Dinkelsbühl), 1853–1854
Block printing
344 x 218 mm
KI 14391-4, Ankauf purchased from Dietrich Hecht 1985

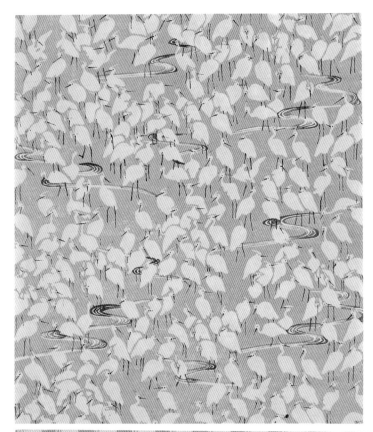

046
Anonym Anonymous
**Japanisches Modeldruckpapier
mit Wasservögeln**
Japan, vor 1897
Ausführung: R. Wagner, Berlin, 1897
**Japanese Block Printed Paper
with Water Birds**
Japan, before 1897
Execution: R. Wagner, Berlin, 1897
206 x 234 mm
KI 9388-84, Schenkung donation from
Hans Ankwicz-Kleehoven 1936

047
Josef Hoffmann
Vorsatzpapier
Wien, 1902
Lithografie
Endpaper
Vienna, 1902
Lithograph
262 x 360 mm
KI 9388-25, Schenkung donation from
Hans Ankwicz-Kleehoven 1936

048
Josef Hoffmann
Vorsatzpapier
Wien, 1902
Lithografie
Endpaper
Vienna, 1902
Lithograph
233 x 276 mm
KI 9388-27, Schenkung donation from
Hans Ankwicz-Kleehoven 1936

049
Koloman Moser
Vorsatzpapier
Wien, 1902
Lithografie
Endpaper
Vienna, 1902
Lithograph
229 x 255 mm
KI 9388-32, Schenkung donation from
Hans Ankwicz-Kleehoven 1936

050
Josef Manfreda/Fachklasse
specialized class Franz Čižek
**Entwurf für die Ausstellung von
Buntpapieren in der Kunstgewerbe-
schule 1910**
Wien, 1910
Deckfarben
**Design for the Exhibition of Decorated
Paper at the School of Arts and
Crafts 1910**
Vienna, 1910
Coating paint
250 x 393 mm
KI 7756-4, Ankauf purchased 1910

051
Maria von Uchatius/Fachklasse
specialized class C. O. Czeschka
Vorsatzpapier in Holzstöckeldruck
Wien, 1906–1907
Endpaper in Woodblock Print
Vienna, 1906–1907
390 x 268 mm
KI 9388-8, Schenkung donation from
Hans Ankwicz-Kleehoven 1936

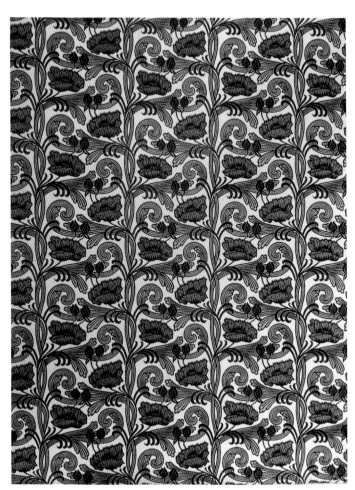

052
Maria von Uchatius/Fachklasse
specialized class C. O. Czeschka
Vorsatzpapier in Holzstöckeldruck
Wien, 1906–1907
Endpaper in Woodblock Print
Vienna, 1906–1907
177 x 91 mm
KI 9388-10, Schenkung donation from
Hans Ankwicz-Kleehoven 1936

053
Else Unger
Vorsatzpapier der Zeitschrift
Kunst und Kunsthandwerk
Jahrgang V, Wien 1902
Klischee
Endpaper of the magazine
[Art and Applied Art]
Year V, Vienna 1902
Cliché
BI 2148, 1902

054
Anton Hofer/Fachklasse
specialized class Franz Čižek
**Entwurf für die Ausstellung von
Buntpapieren in der Kunstgewerbe-
schule 1910**
Wien, 1910
Deckfarben
**Design for the Exhibition of
Decorated Paper at the School
of Arts and Crafts 1910**
Vienna, 1910
Coating paint
300 x 205 mm
KI 7756-3, Ankauf purchased 1910

055
Anonym Anonymous
Fachklasse specialized class Koloman Moser
Modeldruckpapier
Wien, um 1905
Block Printed Paper
Vienna, ca. 1905
188 x 214 mm
KI 9388-47, Schenkung donation from
Hans Ankwicz-Kleehoven 1936

056
Anonym Anonymous
Fachklasse specialized class Koloman Moser
Modeldruckpapier
Wien, um 1905
Block Printed Paper
Vienna, ca. 1905
191 x 217 mm
KI 9388-54, Schenkung donation from
Hans Ankwicz-Kleehoven 1936

057
Walter Weber/Fachklasse
specialized class Franz Čižek
**Entwurf für die Ausstellung
von Buntpapieren in der
Kunstgewerbeschule 1910**
Wien, 1910
Modeldruck
**Design for the Exhibition of
Decorated Paper at the School
of Arts and Crafts 1910**
Vienna, 1910
Block printing
250 x 180 mm
KI 7756-6, Ankauf purchased 1910

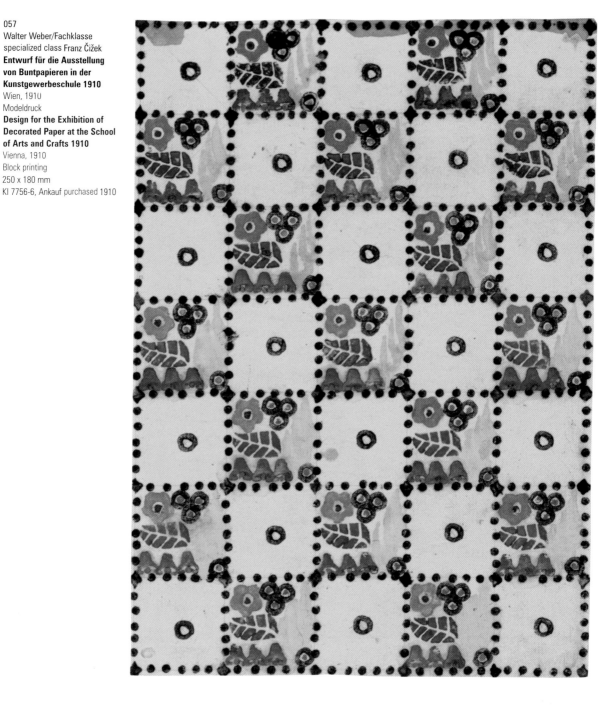

058
Ludmilla Pietsch/Fachklasse specialized class
Franz Čižek
**Entwurf für die Ausstellung von Buntpapieren
in der Kunstgewerbeschule 1910**
Wien, 1910
Deckfarben
**Design for the Exhibition of Decorated Paper
at the School of Arts and Crafts 1910**
Vienna, 1910
Coating paint
245 x 183 mm
KI 7756-7, Ankauf purchased 1910

059
Friedrich Wüttrich
**Entwurf für die Ausstellung von Buntpapieren
in der Kunstgewerbeschule 1910**
Wien, 1910
Deckfarben
**Design for the Exhibition of Decorated Paper
at the School of Arts and Crafts 1910**
Vienna, 1910
Coating paint
272 x 220 mm
KI 7756-10, Ankauf purchased 1910

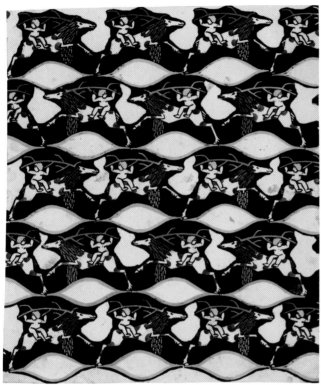

060
Karl Schwetz/Fachklasse specialized class
Bertold Löffler
**Entwurf für die Ausstellung von Buntpapieren
in der Kunstgewerbeschule 1910**
Wien, 1910
Linolschnitt
**Design for the Exhibition of Decorated Paper
at the School of Arts and Crafts 1910**
Vienna, 1910
Linocut
393 x 250 mm
KI 7756-5, Ankauf purchased 1910

061
Anonym Anonymous/Fachklasse specialized class
Koloman Moser
Modeldruckpapier
Wien, um 1905
Block Printed Paper
Vienna, ca. 1905
157 x 116 mm
KI 9388-20, Schenkung donation from
Hans Ankwicz-Kleehoven 1936

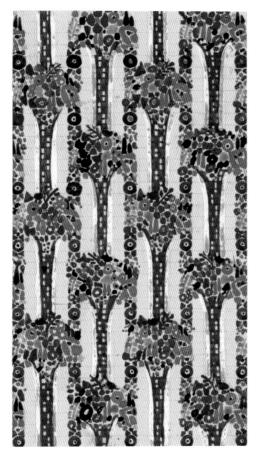

062
Franz Fochler/Fachklasse specialized class
Josef Hoffmann
**Entwurf für die Ausstellung von Buntpapieren
in der Kunstgewerbeschule 1910**
Wien, 1910
Deckfarben
**Design for the Exhibition of Decorated Paper
at the School of Arts and Crafts 1910**
Vienna, 1910
Coating paint
245 x 183 mm
KI 7756-8, Ankauf purchased 1910

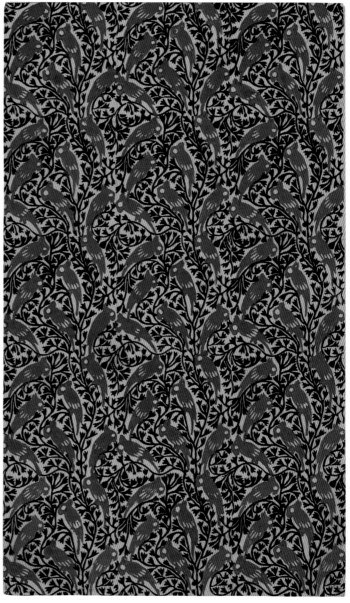

063
Karl Massanetz
**Entwurf für die Ausstellung von Buntpapieren
in der Kunstgewerbeschule 1910**
Wien, 1910
Modeldruck
**Design for the Exhibition of Decorated Paper
at the School of Arts and Crafts 1910**
Vienna, 1910
Block printing
564 x 340 mm
KI 7756-20, Ankauf purchased 1910

064
Maria von Uchatius/Fachklasse
specialized class C. O. Czeschka
Vorsatzpapier in Holzstöckeldruck
Wien, 1906–1907
Endpaper in Woodblock Print
Vienna, 1906–1907
432 x 298 mm
KI 9388-2, Schenkung donation from
Hans Ankwicz-Kleehoven 1936

GESCHENK- UND PACKPAPIER

Neben den Buntpapieren kamen auch etliche Geschenk- und Einwickelpapiere durch Hans Ankwicz-Kleehoven in die Museumssammlung. Aus seinen eigenen Beständen steuerte er Verpackungs-materialien der Wiener Werkstätte, des Österreichischen Werkbunds, der Wiener Glühlampen-Firma FerroWatt und des New Yorker Warenhauses Macy's sowie des Kaufhauses Gerngross bei. Originalentwürfe von Maria Strauss-Likarz gelangten durch die Übernahme des Wiener Werkstätte-Archivs 1955 an das Museum (Abb. 069). Das Archiv aus dem Besitz von Alfred Hofmann, dem letzten Geschäftsführer und schließlich Liquidator der Wiener Werkstätte, umfasst Tausende Entwurfszeichnungen, diverse Modellbücher, Fotobände und Korrespondenzakten; mit ihm verfügt das MAK über eine einzigartige Quelle zur Geschichte dieser weltberühmten Institution. Von Anbeginn entwickelte die Wiener Werkstätte eine eigene Corporate Identity, die sich mit den Firmenzeichen – WW-Logo, Wort- und Rosenmarke – auch auf den Packpapieren niederschlug (Abb. 065–067). Später reichte die Anbringung des Namenszuges innerhalb der Gestaltungen der jeweiligen EntwerferInnen.

Unter ihnen befand sich auch die ungarische Grafikerin Kató Lukáts (Abb. 070), ausgebildet an der Wiener Kunstgewerbeschule und vor allem bekannt durch ihre Einwickelpapiere und Pralinen-schachteln für Altmann & Kühne, die bis heute erzeugt werden. Eine der wenigen Quellen zu Leben und Werk der Künstlerin ist ein Artikel in *Alte und Moderne Kunst*, der Zeitschrift des Österreichischen Museums für angewandte Kunst von 1956 bis 1985, worin sie als „Meisterin des Packaging-Designs" bezeichnet wird.[1]

Mit Verpackungsmaterial für Süßwaren beschäftigte sich auch Joseph Binder, dessen gesamter Nachlass 1978 bzw. 1995/96 in die Sammlung des Museums gelangte. Sowohl für den jüdischen Schokoladehersteller Barricini als auch für dessen Konkurrenten Barton's entwarf der seit 1936 in New York ansässige Grafikdesigner Einwickelpapiere für Schokoladentafeln und Bonbonnieren (Abb. 075, 077, 078). Ihre geometrischen Dekore aus den späten 1950er Jahren entsprechen Binders Hinwendung zur abstrakten Malerei, der er sich in seinem letzten Lebensjahrzehnt gänzlich widmen sollte. Auch die amerikanische Niederlassung des *Wiener Zuckerl*-Erzeugers Heller zählte zu Binders Kunden: In einem Verpackungsdesign legte er die Farben und Sterne der US-Flagge über eine abstrahierte New Yorker Skyline gleichsam als Bekenntnis der Firma zu ihrem Standort in der Neuen Welt (Abb. 076). Ein trauriges Schicksal ist mit dem Auftraggeber Richard Wieselthier ver-bunden, Betreiber einer Kragen- und Manschettenfabrik in Wien, der sich 1940 in der holländischen Emigration mit seiner Frau das Leben nahm.[2] Joseph Binder entwarf für ihn Pack- und Briefpapier mit dem sprechenden Dekor eines Wiesels über dem Namenszug (Abb. 073).

Zeitgenössische Beispiele bereichern die MAK-Sammlung durch Schenkungen von Ingeborg Strobl und Bernhard Cella, deren Geschenkpapiere als Editionen in Bregenz und Wien erschienen. Strobls *Bestiarium* (Abb. 079), das aus zehn Motiven besteht, erinnert an die Arbeiten von Maria von Uchatius, die ähnlich ironisch das Tier in Ornamente einspannte (vgl. Abb. 051). Bernhard Cella, der den Salon für Kunstbuch im 21er Haus führt, entwickelte die Geschenkpapier-Edition gemeinsam mit Gilbert Bretterbauer, Siggi Hofer, Sabina Hörtner, Tillman Kaiser und Leo Schatzl (Abb. 080). Sie entstand aus der Absicht, Museumsshop und Kunstproduktion stärker zu verbinden.

[1] Bánszky-Kiss, Eva, „Die Konfiserie Altmann & Kühne, 1935", in: *Alte und moderne Kunst* (XXX) 198/199 1985, 30–33 (mit falschen Bildunterschriften); siehe auch: „Decoration – with reference to Hungarian Confectionery Wrappers", in: *Commercial Art and Industry* 10 (XIX) 1935, 106–111.

[2] www.joodsmonument.nl/nl/page/232150/richard-wieselthier (29.4.2016).

WRAPPING AND PACKING PAPER

In addition to the decorated papers, a number of wrapping and packing papers entered the museum collection via Hans Ankwicz-Kleehoven. From his own holdings, he contributed packing materials by the Wiener Werkstätte, the Austrian Werkbund, the Viennese lightbulb company FerroWatt, Macy's department store in New York, as well as the Gerngross mall in Vienna.

Original designs by Maria Strauss-Likarz came to the museum in 1955 when it acquired the Wiener Werkstätte Archive (ill. 069). From the estate of Alfred Hofmann, the last manager and ultimately the liquidator of the Wiener Werkstätte, the archive consists of thousands of design drawings, diverse catalogs of work, volumes of photographs, and correspondence files; the MAK thus has in its possession a unique fountain of knowledge about the history of this world-famous institution. From the outset, the Wiener Werkstätte developed its own corporate identity, the logo of which—WW monogram, word and rose trademarks—also appeared on the packing papers (ill. 065–067). Later, it was sufficient to integrate the company name into the works of the respective designers. Among them was the Hungarian graphic designer Kató Lukáts (ill. 070), educated at Vienna's School of Arts and Crafts and best known for her wrappers and chocolate boxes for Altmann & Kühne, which are still produced today. One of the few sources on the life and work of the artist is an article in *Alte und Moderne Kunst*, the magazine of the Austrian Museum of Applied Arts from 1956 to 1985, in which she is identified as a "master of packaging design."[1]

Packaging material for confectionery was also a focus of Joseph Binder, whose entire estate would enter the museum collection in 1978 and 1995/1996. Both for the Jewish chocolate manufacturer Barricini and the company's competitor Barton's, the graphic designer—who was based in New York from 1936—designed wrappers for bars and boxes of chocolate (ill. 075, 077, 078). Their geometric decorations from the late 1950s bear witness to Binder turning his attention to abstract painting, to which he would dedicate all of his creative endeavors in the last decade of his life. Binder also counted the American branch of the *Wiener Zuckerl* manufacturer Heller among his clients: in one packaging design he laid the colors and stars of the U.S. flag over an abstract New York skyline as if to proclaim that the company had a base in the New World (ill. 076). One man who commissioned work from Binder ultimately met a tragic fate: Richard Wieselthier, who ran a cuff and collar factory in Vienna, and his wife took their lives in 1940 after emigrating to the Netherlands.[2] Joseph Binder had designed packaging and letter paper for him with the expressive embellishment of a weasel (*Wiesel* in German: the name Wieselthier literally means "weasel animal") above the signature (ill. 073).

The MAK Collection has been enhanced by contemporary examples thanks to donations by Ingeborg Strobl and Bernhard Cella, whose wrapping papers were published as editions in Bregenz and Vienna. Strobl's *Bestiarium* [Bestiary] (ill. 079), which is composed of ten motifs, is reminiscent of the works by Maria von Uchatius, whose ornamentations harnessed animals with similar irony (cf. ill. 051). Bernhard Cella, who runs the Salon für Kunstbuch at Vienna's 21er Haus, jointly developed the wrapping paper edition with Gilbert Bretterbauer, Siggi Hofer, Sabina Hörtner, Tillman Kaiser, and Leo Schatzl (ill. 080); it was the result of their aim to establish a closer connection between the museum shop and the production of art.

[1] Bánszky-Kiss, Eva, "Die Konfiserie Altmann & Kühne, 1935," in: *Alte und moderne Kunst* (XXX) 198/199 1985, 30–33 (with incorrect picture credits); see also: "Decoration – with reference to Hungarian Confectionery Wrappers," in: *Commercial Art and Industry* 10 (XIX) 1935, 106–111. Translated by Maria Slater.

[2] www.joodsmonument.nl/nl/page/232150/richard-wieselthier (29 Apr 2016).

065
Anonym Anonymous
Papier der Wiener Werkstätte
Wien, 1917
Klischee
Paper of the Wiener Werkstätte
Vienna, 1917
Cliché
353 x 220 mm
KI 10177-7, aus dem Archiv der WW, inv.
from the archives of the WW, inventoried in 1940

066
Anonym Anonymous
Papier der Wiener Werkstätte
Wien, ab 1903
Klischee
Paper of the Wiener Werkstätte
Vienna, from 1903
Cliché
315 x 243 mm
KI 9050-5, Schenkung donation from
Hans Ankwicz-Kleehoven 1935

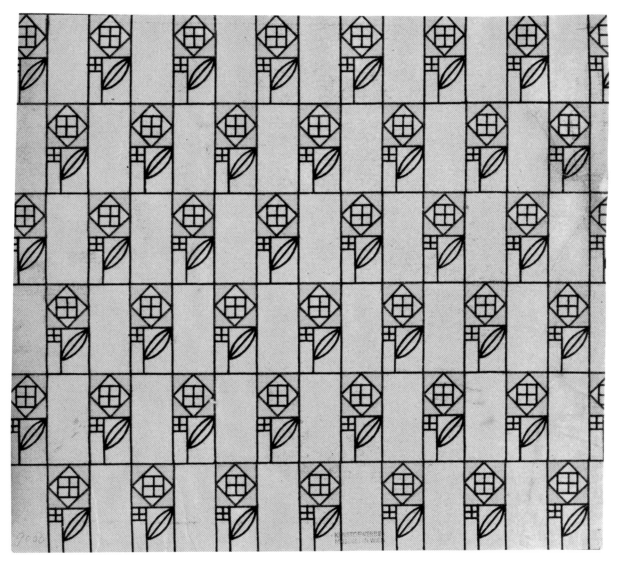

067
Koloman Moser
Papier der Wiener Werkstätte
Wien, ab 1903
Klischee
Paper of the Wiener Werkstätte
Vienna, from 1903
Cliché
630 x 272 mm
KI 9050-9, Schenkung donation from
Hans Ankwicz-Kleehoven 1935

068
Anonym Anonymous
Papier des Österreichischen Werkbundes
Wien, um 1928
Klischee
Paper of the Austrian Werkbund
Vienna, ca. 1928
Cliché
332 x 204 mm
KI 9096, Schenkung donation from
Hans Ankwicz-Kleehoven 1933

069
Maria Likarz
Entwurf für ein Papier der Wiener Werkstätte
Wien, um 1928
Bleistift, Deckfarben
Design for a Paper of the Wiener Werkstätte
Vienna, ca. 1928
Pencil, coating paint
587 x 460 mm
KI 12295-6, Schenkung donation from
Alfred Hofmann 1955

070
Kató Lukáts
Papier der Wiener Werkstätte
Wien, um 1930
Klischee
Paper of the Wiener Werkstätte
Vienna, ca. 1930
Cliché
310 x 239 mm
KI 9050-6, Schenkung donation from
Hans Ankwicz-Kleehoven 1935

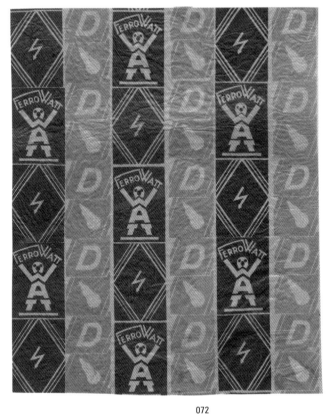

071
Anonym Anonymous
Papier der Firma Macy's
New York, um 1930
Modeldruck
Paper of the Company Macy's
New York, ca. 1930
Block printing
370 x 243 mm
KI 9389-3, Schenkung donation from
Hans Ankwicz-Kleehoven 1936

072
Bernd Steiner
Papier der Firma FerroWatt
Wien, um 1928
Modeldruck
Paper of the Company FerroWatt
Vienna, ca. 1928
Block printing
230 x 187 mm
KI 9389-1, Schenkung donation from
Hans Ankwicz-Kleehoven 1936

073
Joseph Binder
Entwurf für ein Papier der Firma
Richard Wieselthier
Wien, vor 1936
Bleistift, Deckfarben
Design for a Paper of the Company
Richard Wieselthier
Vienna, before 1936
Pencil, coating paint
134 x 252 mm
KI 14145-69, Legat bequest from
Carla und and Joseph Binder 1978

074
Anonym Anonymous
Papier der Firma Gerngross
Wien, um 1930
Klischee
Paper of the Company Gerngross
Vienna, ca. 1930
Cliché
370 x 243 mm
KI 9389-4, Schenkung donation from
Hans Ankwicz-Kleehoven 1936

075
Joseph Binder
Papier der Firma Barricini
USA, um 1960
Offsetdruck
Paper of the Company Barricini
USA, ca. 1960
Offset printing
281 x 219 mm
KI 14145-213, Legat bequest from
Carla und and Joseph Binder 1978

076
Joseph Binder
Papier der Firma Heller für die
Bonbonniere *Manhattan*
USA, 1950
Offsetdruck
Paper of the Company Heller
for the Bonbonniere *Manhattan*
USA, 1950
Offset printing
120 x 197 mm
KI 14145-944-3, Legat bequest from
Carla und and Joseph Binder 1995/96

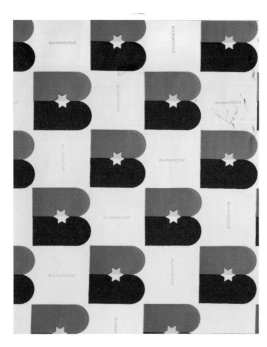

077
Joseph Binder
Papier der Firma Barricini
USA, um 1950
Siebdruck
Paper of the Company Barricini
USA, ca. 1950
Screen printing
367 x 334 mm
KI 14145-946-11, Legat bequest from
Carla und and Joseph Binder 1995/96

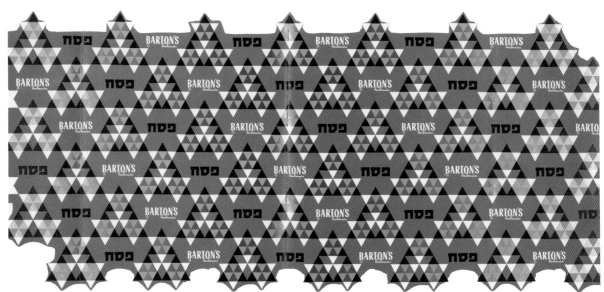

078
Joseph Binder
Papier der Firma Barton's
USA, um 1957
Offsetdruck
Paper of the Company Barton's
USA, ca. 1957
Offset printing
292 x 788 mm
KI 14145-946-8, Legat bequest from
Carla und and Joseph Binder 1995/96

079
Ingeborg Strobl
Geschenkpapier *Bestiarium*
Edition, Kunsthaus Bregenz, 1994
Offsetdruck
Wrapping Paper [Bestiary]
Edition, Kunsthaus Bregenz, 1994
Offset printing
590 x 840 mm
KI 15721-3, Ankauf purchased
from Ingeborg Strobl 2003

080
Bernhard Cella
Packpapier
Edition Salon für Kunstbuch
Wien, 2013
Offsetdruck
Wrapping Paper
Edition Salon für Kunstbuch
Vienna, 2013
Offset printing
650 x 948 mm
KI 20866-2, Schenkung
donation from Bernhard Cella 2013

ORANGENPAPIER AUS DEN 1950ER JAHREN

2008 schenkte Paul Kurt Schwarz der MAK-Bibliothek und Kunstblättersammlung ein Konvolut von 43 Orangenpapieren, die er selbst in den 1950er Jahren gesammelt hatte. Der 1916 in St. Pölten geborene Grafiker studierte von 1932 bis 1938 an der Wiener Kunstgewerbeschule u. a. bei Franz Čižek (Ornamentale Formenlehre), Rudolf von Larisch (Schrift und Heraldik) und Paul Kirnig (Malerei und Druckgrafik), dessen Lehrstuhl Schwarz 1954 übernahm. Schenkungen aus seiner Sammlung (neben den Orangen- auch Geschenkpapiere, Werbebroschüren, Post- und Einladungskarten) und eigener Arbeiten (Plakate, Buchumschläge, Briefpapier, Kataloge und Signets) erfolgten von 1999 bis zu seinem Tod 2010.

Sammlungen von Orangenpapieren sind nicht so ungewöhnlich, wie es scheint. Es gibt sie in Frankreich, den USA, den Niederlanden und in Deutschland, wo etwa der Autor und Kunstsammler Lothar-Günther Buchheim Hunderte Beispiele zusammengetragen hat; eine Auswahl davon wurde 2012 in dem nach ihm benannten Museum gezeigt.[1] Eine weitere private Initiative ist das virtuelle OPIUM – Orangenpapiermuseum, das Dirik von Oettingen, Besitzer von über 40 000 Blättern, seit 1999 betreibt.[2] Bereits um 1900 interessierte sich der österreichische Buntpapier-Sammler Franz Bartsch für Orangenpapier, das 1878 zum Patent angemeldet worden war.[3]

Auch öffentliche Sammlungen schenken dem Thema Beachtung. Das Mudac – Musée de design et d'arts appliqués contemporains in Lausanne widmete ihm 2008 eine eigene Ausstellung. 2015 zeigte das Historische Museum Regensburg die Ephemera-Sammlung Färber, deren Bestandskatalog knapp 800 Einwickelpapiere für Zitrusfrüchte verzeichnet.[4] Bereits 1985 erkannte das Victoria and Albert Museum den speziellen Reiz der dünnen Schutzhüllen und publizierte 21 Faksimiles spanischer und italienischer „fruit wrappers".[5]

Derselben Herkunft entstammen auch die Orangenpapiere der Sammlung Schwarz; ihre Aufdrucke verweisen auf Betriebe in Sizilien, Kalabrien und der Provinz Valencia. Die viereckigen Blätter zeigen ein meist kreisförmiges Motiv mit dem Logo des Herstellers oder der Bezeichnung der Marke im Zentrum; weitere Illustrationen und Aufschriften erschließen sich erst nach dem Auseinanderfalten. Die Gestaltungen reichen von zurückhaltend über mit Goldauflagen nobilitiert bis hin zu bild- und wortreich erzählend. Dabei werden entweder die Herkunftsländer vermarktet und damit verbundene Sehnsüchte bedient (Sonne, sizilianische Sehenswürdigkeiten) oder Identifikationsmomente mit dem Importland hergestellt (*Struwwelpeter* oder *Vater und Sohn* für den deutschsprachigen Raum). Die Marke *Liebe Wien* versammelt selbstredend die berühmtesten Baudenkmäler der Stadt um einen rot-weiß-rot gerahmten Stephansdom.

[1] Segieth, Clelia, *Pop Art mit Orangenduft. Orangenpapiere aus der Sammlung Buchheim*, Feldafing 2008.

[2] Oettingen, Dirik von, *Verhüllt um zu verführen. Die Welt der Orange*, Potsdam 2007; www.opiummuseum.de (3.10.2016).

[3] Schmidt, Frieder/Feiler, Sigrid (Red.), *Franz Bartsch: Papiersammler aus Wien. Rekonstruktion seiner Ausstellung Stuttgart 1909*, Deutsches Buch- und Schriftmuseum, Begleitmaterialien zur gleichnamigen Ausstellung, Frankfurt/Main 1998.

[4] Neiser, Wolfgang, *Luxuspapier, Buntpapier und Ephemera. Die Sammlung Helmut und Dr. Juliane Färber im Historischen Museum der Stadt Regensburg*, Regensburg 2015.

[5] *Oranges & Lemons. Fruit Wrappers from the Victoria & Albert Museum. A selection of twenty one original designs faithfully reproduced in full colour*, London 1985.

ORANGE WRAPPERS FROM THE 1950S

In 2008 Paul Kurt Schwarz donated a bundle of 43 orange wrappers to the MAK Library and Works on Paper Collection, which he had collected himself in the 1950s. Born in St. Pölten, Austria, in 1916, the graphic designer studied at Vienna's School of Arts and Crafts from 1932 to 1938 among others under Franz Čižek (theory of ornamental form), Rudolf von Larisch (lettering and heraldry), and Paul Kirnig (painting and printed graphics), whose professorship Schwarz took over in 1954. He donated parts of his collection (in addition to the orange wrappers, this also includes wrapping papers, advertising brochures, postcards, and invitation cards) and his own works (posters, book jackets, letter paper, catalogs, and publisher's marks) to the MAK from 1999 to his death in 2010. Collections of orange wrappers are not as uncommon as one might assume. They can be found in France, the U.S.A., the Netherlands, and in Germany, where for example the author and art collector Lothar-Günther Buchheim has compiled hundreds of examples; a selection was shown in the museum named after him in 2012.[1] Another private initiative is the virtual OPIUM – Orangenpapier-museum, which Dirik von Oettingen, owner of over 40 000 wrappers, has run since 1999.[2] As early as 1900 the Austrian decorated paper collector Franz Bartsch became interested in orange wrappers, a patent for which was registered in 1878.[3]

Public collections, too, attach value to the topic. The Mudac – Musée de design et d'arts appliqués contemporains in Lausanne, Switzerland, dedicated an entire collection to it in 2008. In 2015 the Historisches Museum Regensburg presented the Färber ephemera collection, whose inventory catalog lists almost 800 wrappers for citrus fruit.[4] As early as 1985 the Victoria and Albert Museum recognized the special appeal of these thin protective covers and duly published 21 facsimiles of Spanish and Italian fruit wrappers.[5]

The orange wrappers in the Schwarz Collection share the same origin; their printed matter points to companies in Sicily, Calabria, and the province of Valencia. The square sheets bear a mostly circular motif with the producer's logo or brand name in the center; other illustrations and wording are only revealed when the fruit is unwrapped. The designs range from modest to luxury—complete with gilding—and narratively rich with words and pictures. They either promote their countries of origin and hence revolve around associated desires (sun, Sicilian tourist attractions) or create a sense of identification with the importing country (*Struwwelpeter* or E. O. Plauen's *Vater und Sohn* for the German-speaking world). The brand *Liebe Wien* (literally "love Vienna") naturally opted to gather the city's most famous historic buildings around a St. Stephen's Cathedral framed in the Austrian flag.

[1] Segieth, Clelia, *Pop Art mit Orangenduft. Orangenpapiere aus der Sammlung Buchheim*, Feldafing 2008.

[2] Oettingen, Dirik von, *Verhüllt um zu verführen. Die Welt der Orange*, Potsdam 2007; www.opiummuseum.de (3 Oct 2016).

[3] Schmidt, Frieder/Feiler, Sigrid (eds.), *Franz Bartsch: Papiersammler aus Wien. Rekonstruktion seiner Ausstellung Stuttgart 1909*, German Museum of Books and Writing, materials accompanying the exhibition of the same name, Frankfurt/Main 1998.

[4] Neiser, Wolfgang, *Luxuspapier, Buntpapier und Ephemera. Die Sammlung Helmut und Dr. Juliane Färber im Historischen Museum der Stadt Regensburg*, Regensburg 2015.

[5] *Oranges & Lemons. Fruit Wrappers from the Victoria & Albert Museum. A selection of twenty one original designs faithfully reproduced in full colour*, London 1985.

081
Orangenpapier der Firma Aldo Becca, Imola
Italien, 1950–1960
Ausführung: Giovanni Foschini, Massa Lombarda
Klischee
Orange Wrapper of the Company Aldo Becca, Imola
Italy, 1950–1960
Execution: Giovanni Foschini, Massa Lombarda
Cliché
197 x 193 mm
KI 15826-38, Schenkung donation from Paul Kurt Schwarz 2008

082
Orangenpapier der Marke *Liebe Wien*
Spanien, 1950–1960
Ausführung: Fabbri, Valencia
Klischee
Orange Wrapper of the Brand [Love Vienna]
Spain, 1950–1960
Execution: Fabbri, Valencia
Cliché
244 x 247 mm
KI 15826-13, Schenkung donation from Paul Kurt Schwarz 2008

083
Maria Likarz
Orangenpapier der Firma Angelo Tringale & Figli, Catania
Italien, 1950–1960
Klischee
Orange Wrapper of the Company
Angelo Tringale & Figli, Catania
Italy, 1950–1960
Cliché
395 x 395 mm
KI 15826-10, Schenkung donation from Paul Kurt Schwarz 2008

084
Orangenpapier der Marke *Bagu 3*
Italien, 1950–1960
Entwurf: Anonym, Spanien, vermutl. 1950–1960
Klischee
Orange Wrapper of the Brand *Bagu 3*
Italy, 1950–1960
Design: Anonymous, Spain, prob. 1950–1960
Cliché
250 x 185 mm
KI 15826-2, Schenkung donation from Paul Kurt Schwarz 2008

085
**Zitrusfruchtpapier der Firma F. A. O. Vagelli,
Verona**
Italien, 1950–1960
Ausführung: Giovanni Foschini, Massa Lombarda
Klischee
**Citrus Fruit Wrapper of the Company
F. A. O. Vagelli, Verona**
Italy, 1950–1960
Execution: Giovanni Foschini, Massa Lombarda
Cliché
94 x 94 mm
KI 15826-1, Schenkung donation from Paul Kurt Schwarz 2008

086
Orangenpapier der Marke *Principessina dei Mori – Sanguinello*
Italien, 1950–1960
Ausführung: Fabbri, Vignola
Klischee
Orange Wrapper of the Brand *Principessina dei Mori – Sanguinello*
Italy, 1950–1960
Execution: Fabbri, Vignola
Cliché
205 x 190 mm
KI 15826-23, Schenkung donation from Paul Kurt Schwarz 2008

087
Orangenpapier der Marke *Oscar*, Cooperativa Agricola de Gandia
Spanien, 1950–1960
Ausführung: Fabbri, Valencia
Klischee
Orange Wrapper of the Brand *Oscar*, Cooperativa Agricola de Gandia
Spain, 1950–1960
Execution: Fabbri, Valencia
Cliché
240 x 190 mm
KI 15826-29, Schenkung donation from Paul Kurt Schwarz 2008

088
Orangenpapier der Firma Tarfi Export, Valencia
Spanien, 1950–1960
Klischee
Orange Wrapper of the Company Tarfi Export, Valencia
Spain, 1950–1960
Cliché
180 x 235 mm
KI 15826-22, Schenkung donation from Paul Kurt Schwarz 2008

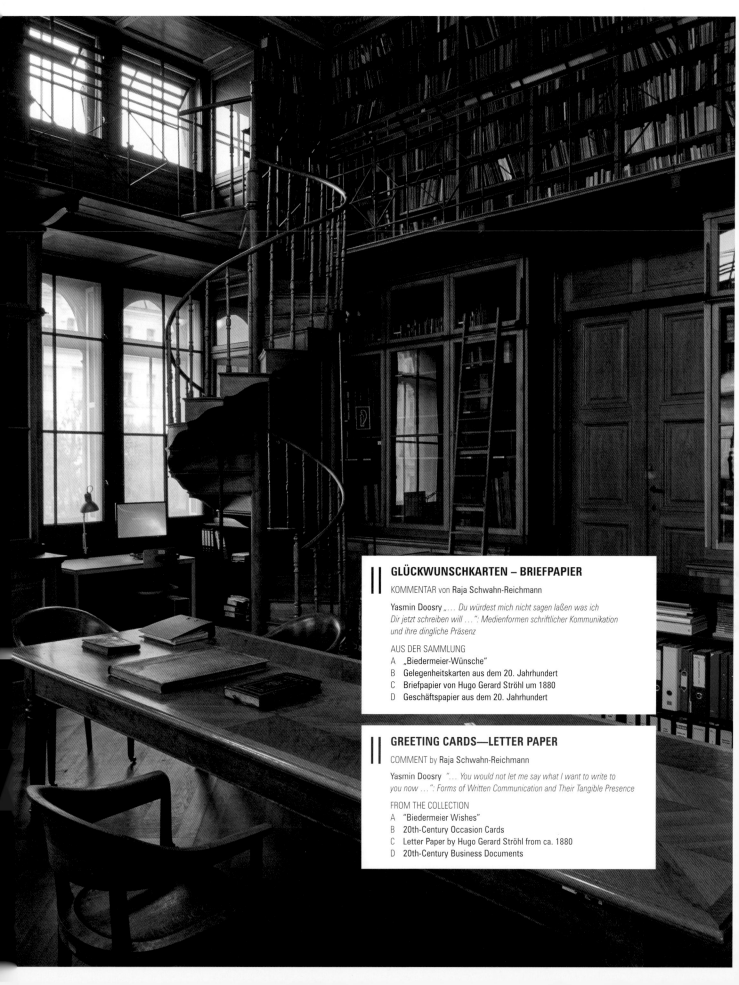

GLÜCKWUNSCHKARTEN – BRIEFPAPIER

KOMMENTAR von Raja Schwahn-Reichmann

Yasmin Doosry „… *Du würdest mich nicht sagen laßen was ich Dir jetzt schreiben will …"*: *Medienformen schriftlicher Kommunikation und ihre dingliche Präsenz*

AUS DER SAMMLUNG

A   „Biedermeier-Wünsche"
B   Gelegenheitskarten aus dem 20. Jahrhundert
C   Briefpapier von Hugo Gerard Ströhl um 1880
D   Geschäftspapier aus dem 20. Jahrhundert

GREETING CARDS—LETTER PAPER

COMMENT by Raja Schwahn-Reichmann

Yasmin Doosry *"… You would not let me say what I want to write to you now …"*: *Forms of Written Communication and Their Tangible Presence*

FROM THE COLLECTION

A   "Biedermeier Wishes"
B   20th-Century Occasion Cards
C   Letter Paper by Hugo Gerard Ströhl from ca. 1880
D   20th-Century Business Documents

THE NOT-ENTIRELY-THOUGHT-THROUGH, THE SYMPATHETICALLY VULNERABLE NATURE OF EACH NEW BEGINNING
IS INHERENT TO PAPER. By definition it is usually within reach—so that we can grab it, turn it over, fold it, unfold it,
unwrap it, write on it, etc.—yet it is also defenselessly sensitive, pure and appetizing.

That presents a challenge to the creative predator. The lascivious innocence of the fresh sheet sparks lust and a thrill.
Hungry for an idea, we yearn for it—as for a sandwich in the late afternoon! What would remain of that idea—now
finally found—without that greedily grabbed, hopefully handy, fresh sheet of paper? And what is a snack without that
crinkling, crunching foreplay with its appetizing paper wrapping?

Paper bears everything that must not or cannot grow old—such as food and greetings. Destined—both in terms of
content and form—not for a long life but for the right moment, the right occasion. Wonderfully enough, these one-hit
wonders made of paper sometimes survive. Once scented greetings, lace-framed paper portraits, and paper surprises
unfolded for just a moment endure in a nook of time. They then find themselves, astonished and astonishing, bundled
together as collector's items, as a fragile symbol of our imperative need for beauty, made from the most precious
materials of the age.

After all, think how precious a simple piece of paper used to be: until the end of the 18th century, it could only be
produced by hand from equally hand-produced material! And then there is the lovingly, lavishly resplendent paper
of the lace-framed portraits of that time, like Brussels lace. Or the Biedermeier greeting cards, boisterously parading
the young, luminous achievements of half-industrial possibilities: embossing, prints, folds, material additions with
gauze, silk, one outdoing the other in its delicacy. Decorated paper and endpapers from the 19th century: The worse
the industrial paper, the more it is dressed up with a precious surface, with moiré, velour, gold print, or a chromolithograph. But this sickliness, this birth defect makes the rare surviving papers all the more lovable.

Then a paper shop, closed decades before, opens its storeroom like a floodgate: defenseless, the unsuccessful
non-collector—i.e. me—is overwhelmed by so much defenselessness, moved by the vulnerable permanence of the
ultimately impermanent. Even in the shadows of the storeroom, bright crepe paper from the early 20th century has
lost some of its colorfulness and, as pristine as it was 80 years ago, it waits, rustling, to be used. Factory-fresh letter
paper with the suburban elegance of the 1930s. Between helplessly badly printed greeting cards, the poverty of
the post-war era has been preserved in this storeroom in the form of soon unsaleable cardboard Christmas tree
decorations, once again proving the immortality of wallflowers and bad sellers.

And all of this we must love, have. Why does the defenseless make us so defenseless, why is a paper forget-me-not
so dangerous? Perhaps it is a case of momentary mischief triumphing over time. Because if it determines history,
it is a precious contradiction, a rare, absolute miracle. To loosely quote Elfriede Gerstl:

Some never stop marveling,
Some never start.
So off to the paper garden!
I want to be tirelessly lazy there.

Raja Schwahn-Reichmann, artist and restorer, Vienna

DEM PAPIER WOHNT DAS NICHT-ZU-ENDE-GEDACHTE, DAS SYMPATHISCH VERLETZLICHE JEDEN BEGINNES INNE. Von seiner Bestimmung her meistens zum Greifen nahe, zum Angreifen, Umblättern, Entfalten, Auswickeln, Falten, Beschreiben usw. – aber doch wehrlos empfindlich, rein und appetitlich. Das fordert das schöpferische Raubtier heraus. Die laszive Unschuld des frischen Blattes ist Lust und Nervenkitzel. Hungrig nach einer Idee verzehrt man sich nach ihr – wie nach einer Wurstsemmel am späten Vormittag! Was bliebe dann von dieser endlich gepackten Idee, ohne das gierig hergenommene, hoffentlich griffbereite frische Blatt Papier. Und was ist eine Jause ohne dieses knitternde, knusprige Vorspiel des appetitlichen Papierdrumherums.

Papier ist Träger für alles, was eigentlich nicht alt werden darf oder kann – wie Lebensmittel oder Glückwünsche –, dem inhaltlich und formal kein langes Leben, aber der richtige Moment, der Anlass zugedacht ist. Auf wundersame Weise überleben diese papierenen Eintagsfliegen manchmal. Ehemals duftende Glückwünsche, Papierspitzenbilder, sich für einen Augenblick entfaltet habende Papierüberraschungen überdauern in einem Winkel der Zeit, finden sich dann wieder, erstaunt und erstaunlich, als Sammelgut versammelt, als zerbrechliches Zeichen eines unbedingten Schönheitswollens mit kostbarsten Mitteln zur jeweiligen Zeit.

Denn wie kostbar war ein Stück Papier, das bis Ende des 18. Jahrhunderts nur händisch aus ebenso händisch hergestelltem Stoff erzeugt werden konnte! Und dann noch in den Spitzenbildern dieser Zeit liebevoll aufwendig prangend, wie eine Brüsseler Spitze daherkommend. Oder die biedermeierlichen Glückwunschbillets, übermütig die jungen, leuchtenden Errungenschaften halbindustrieller Möglichkeiten zur Schau tragend: Prägungen, Drucke, Faltungen, stoffliche Ergänzungen mit Gaze, Seide, das alles sich an Zartheit überbietend. Schmuck- und Vorsatzpapiere des 19. Jahrhunderts: Je schlechter das industrielle Papier, umso mehr wird mit kostbarer Oberfläche geprunkt, mit Moiré, Velours, Golddruck und Chromolithografie. Aber diese Kränklichkeit, diese Geburtsfehler machen die raren überlebenden Papiere so liebenswert.

Dann öffnet eine vor Jahrzehnten geschlossene Papierhandlung ihr Lager wie eine Schleuse: Wehrlos wird die erfolglose Nichtsammlerin, also ich, von so viel Wehrlosem überwältigt, gerührt von der verletzlichen Beständigkeit des doch so Unbeständigen. Buntes Krepppapier des frühen 20. Jahrhunderts hat sogar in der Dunkelheit des Lagers etwas von seiner Farbigkeit eingebüßt und harrt doch frisch wie vor 80 Jahren knisternd der Verwendung. Fabrikneues Briefpapier mit der Vorstadteleganz der 1930er Jahre. Die Nachkriegsärmlichkeit hat sich in diesem Lager in bald unverkäuflich gewordenem Karton-Christbaumschmuck zwischen hilflos schlecht gedruckten Glückwunschkarten erhalten, was wieder die Unsterblichkeit von Mauerblümchen und Ladenhütern beweist.

Und all das muss man lieben, haben. Warum macht Wehrloses so wehrlos, wird einem ein Papiervergissmeinnicht so gefährlich? Es ist vielleicht der Triumph des flüchtigen Unfugs über die Zeit. Denn setzt er Geschichte an, ist das ein kostbarer Widerspruch, ein Orares wahres Wunder. Mit Elfriede Gerstl (frei zitiert):

Manche kommen aus dem Staunen nicht heraus,
Manche nie hinein.
Darum auf in den papierenen Garten!
Unermüdlich faul will ich da sein.

Raja Schwahn-Reichmann, Künstlerin und Restauratorin, Wien

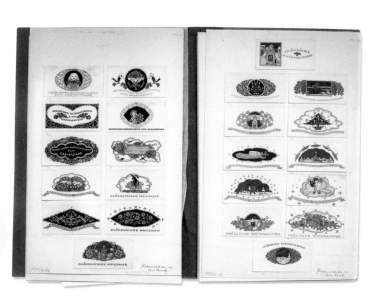

„… DU WÜRDEST MICH NICHT SAGEN LASSEN
WAS ICH DIR JETZT SCHREIBEN WILL …"[1]
MEDIENFORMEN SCHRIFTLICHER KOMMUNIKATION UND IHRE DINGLICHE PRÄSENZ
YASMIN DOOSRY

Zu den populären deutschsprachigen Ratgebern des 19. Jahrhunderts gehörte Amalia Schoppes *Briefsteller für Damen*. Er erschien 1834 in erster Auflage in Berlin mit einem beschaulichen Titelkupfer und Titelblatt von Peter Carl Geissler (Abb. 089).[2] Der Nürnberger Illustrator zeichnete ein Medaillon mit allegorischen Randverzierungen und einer für den spezifischen Ton und Inhalt des Regelwerks programmatischen häuslichen Szene: In einem biedermeierlich-bürgerlichen Interieur sitzt an der geöffneten Klappe eines Schreibsekretärs, auf dem Schreibfedern, Tinte und Streusandgefäß stehen, eine schlicht gekleidete Frau. Die übrigen Schreibutensilien wie Postpapier und Kuverts sind, wie wohl auch die private Korrespondenz, in den zahlreichen Schubladen und Fächern des Möbels einsortiert. Die junge Frau hält im Schreiben inne und nimmt von einem Postillon d'amour einen gesiegelten Umschlag entgegen. Die gesellschaftliche Bedeutung der hier im Bild eingefangenen privaten Briefkultur als Ausweis konventioneller Bildung einerseits und als Träger freundschaftlicher Gefühle und Gedanken andererseits deutet das Rahmenwerk des Titelkupfers mit einer Symbolwelt aus überbordenden Blumengirlanden, Liebespfeilen und antikisierenden Versatzstücken an. Der Briefverkehr war, als Amalia Schoppe ihr Kompendium veröffentliche, ein herausragendes Kommunikationsmittel der Zeit. Davon zeugen nicht zuletzt die Brieftaube und die Schreibutensilien auf dem Titelkupfer sowie die von Post überquellenden Füllhörner auf dem Titelblatt.

Brieflehrbücher, die die Regularien der Privatkorrespondenz praktisch erläuterten, waren keine Erfindung des 19. Jahrhunderts. Mit dem wachsenden Bedürfnis nach einem persönlichen schriftlichen Austausch im 18. Jahrhundert erfuhr der zweckmäßige und unpersönliche Duktus dieser Ratgeberliteratur jedoch einen Wandel. Im „Zeitalter des Briefes", in dem eine leidenschaftlich betriebene Korrespondenz eine Modeerscheinung war, hatten zunächst 1742 und 1751 Christian Fürchtegott Gellert und 1783 Karl Philipp Moritz eine radikale Briefreform gefordert: Der Schreibstil sollte gleich einem lebhaften Gespräch von Leichtigkeit, Zufälligkeiten sowie von persönlichen Eigenheiten und Gedanken bestimmt sein.[3] Geleitet von diesen Prämissen entwickelte sich die private Korrespondenz zu einem bedeutsamen Bestandteil der bürgerlichen Geselligkeit und zu einem Mittel der Selbstdarstellung. Persönliche Briefe zirkulierten nicht mehr allein zwischen zwei Menschen, vielmehr las man sie in kleinen und großen Runden Familienmitgliedern oder FreundInnen vor und erörterte sie anschließend eingehend: Eine per se intime Kommunikationsform wandelte sich zu einem Gegenstand öffentlichen Interesses.[4]

Gellerts und Moritz' Ausführungen führten keineswegs zu einem Popularitätsverlust der traditionellen Briefsteller, sie hinterließen aber deutliche Spuren in den Kompendien. So forderte Schoppe, bei „Beachtung aller üblichen Formen" eine klare, wohlklingende und abwechslungsreich-lebhafte und von eigenen Gedanken geleitete Sprache.[5] Ansonsten hielt sie am kanonischen Schema der Handbücher fest, die auch bürgerliches Wohlverhalten einüben sollten.[6] Ihr Ratgeber beschreibt die äußere Form eines Briefes, stellt die korrekte Anwendung von Titulaturen, Anreden und Grußformen vor, erklärt die Schreib- und Sprachlehre und liefert 320 fingierte Briefe und einen Anhang mit

1 Brief von Sophie Leisewitz an ihren Mann Johann zum 19. Hochzeitstag im Jahr 1800, abgedruckt in: Dülmen, Andrea von (Hg.), *Frauenleben im 18. Jahrhundert*, München/Leipzig/Weimar 1992, 84.

2 Schoppe, Amalie, *Briefsteller für Damen. Ein Fest- und Toilettengeschenk für Deutsche Frauen*, 2. Auflage, Berlin 1837.

3 Anderegg, Johannes, *Schreibe mir oft! Das Medium Brief von 1750 bis 1830*, Göttingen 2001, 13–19; Kording, Inka K., „Wovon wir reden können, davon können wir schreiben. Briefsteller und Briefknigge", in: Beyer, Klaus/Täubrich, Hans-Christian, *Der Brief. Eine Kulturgeschichte der schriftlichen Kommunikation*, Heidelberg 1997, 27–33, hier 33; Schlaffer, Hannelore, „Glück und Ende des privaten Briefs", in: Beyer/Täubrich 1997, 34–45; Furger, Carmen, *Briefsteller. Das Medium Brief im 17. und frühen 18. Jahrhundert*, Weimar/Wien 2010, 42, 45, 171 f.

4 Vgl. Schlaffer 1997 (s. Anm. 3), 36, 40.

5 Schoppe 1837 (s. Anm. 2), IV, V, 107–109.

6 Vgl. Ertel, Susanne, *Anleitung zur schriftlichen Kommunikation. Briefsteller von 1880 bis 1980*, Tübingen 1984, 241; Furger 2010 (s. Anm. 3), 67–69.

1 Letter from Sophie Leisewitz to her husband Johann on their 19th wedding anniversary in 1800, printed in: Dülmen, Andrea von (ed.), *Frauenleben im 18. Jahrhundert*, Munich/Leipzig/Weimar 1992, 84. Translated by Maria Slater.

2 Schoppe, Amalie, *Briefsteller für Damen. Ein Fest- und Toilettengeschenk für Deutsche Frauen*, 2nd edition, Berlin 1837.

3 Anderegg, Johannes, *Schreibe mir oft! Das Medium Brief von 1750 bis 1830*, Göttingen 2001, 13–19; Kording, Inka K., "Wovon wir reden können, davon können wir schreiben. Briefsteller und Briefknigge," in: Beyer, Klaus/Täubrich, Hans-Christian, *Der Brief. Eine Kulturgeschichte der schriftlichen Kommunikation*, Heidelberg 1997, 27–33, here 33; Schlaffer, Hannelore, "Glück und Ende des privaten Briefs," in: Beyer/ Täubrich 1997, 34–45; Furger, Carmen, *Briefsteller. Das Medium Brief im 17. und frühen 18. Jahrhundert*, Weimar/Vienna 2010, 42, 45, 171 f.

4 Cf. Schlaffer 1997 (see note 3), 36, 40.

5 Schoppe 1837 (see note 2), IV, V, 107–109. Translated by Maria Slater.

6 Cf. Ertel, Susanne, *Anleitung zur schriftlichen Kommunikation. Briefsteller von 1880 bis 1980*, Tübingen 1984, 241; Furger 2010 (see note 3), 67–69.

"… YOU WOULD NOT LET ME SAY WHAT I WANT TO WRITE TO YOU NOW …"[1]
FORMS OF WRITTEN COMMUNICATION AND THEIR TANGIBLE PRESENCE
YASMIN DOOSRY

One of the popular German-language guides to letter writing in the 19th century was Amalia Schoppe's *Briefsteller für Damen*. The first edition was published in Berlin in 1834 with a serene copperplate frontispiece and title page by Peter Carl Geissler (ill. 089).[2] This illustrator from Nuremberg had drawn a medallion with allegorical border decorations and a domestic scene, which sets the specific tone and content of these guidelines: In a bourgeois Biedermeier interior, a modestly dressed woman sits at the dropped lid of a secretary, on which quills, ink, and a pounce pot stand. The remaining writing utensils such as letter paper and envelopes are doubtless tidied away in the secretary's numerous drawers and pigeonholes, probably along with her private correspondence. The young woman has paused from her writing to take delivery of a sealed envelope from love's messenger. That this picture captures the social significance of private correspondence culture as proof of conventional education on the one hand and as a bearer of amicable feelings and thoughts on the other is suggested by the vignette around the copperplate frontispiece, which features a world of symbols including exuberant garlands of flowers, Cupid's arrows, and antique-like clichés. At the time when Amalia Schoppe published her compendium, correspondence was a prominent means of communication. This is shown not least by the messenger pigeon and the writing implements on the copperplate frontispiece, as well as the cornucopias overflowing with post on the title page. Letter-writing handbooks, which practically explained the rules of private correspondence, were no 19th-century invention. Nevertheless, with the growing need for personal written communication in the 18th century, the functional and impersonal style of this advisory literature did indeed undergo a change. In the "age of letter writing," when a passionate engagement in correspondence was extremely fashionable, a radical reform of letter writing had first been called for by Christian Fürchtegott Gellert in 1742 and 1751 and by Karl Philipp Moritz in 1783: the writing style should resemble a lively conversation and be dominated by ease, haphazardness, as well as by personal idiosyncrasies and thoughts.[3] Led by these premises, private correspondence developed into a significant aspect of bourgeois social life and into a means of self-representation. Personal letters now no longer circulated merely between two people, but rather they were read aloud in smaller and larger circles of family members or friends, and were subsequently discussed at length: what was per se an intimate form of communication had become an object of public interest.[4] Gellert's and Moritz's remarks by no means led to a decline in the popularity of the traditional guides to letter writing, though they certainly left their mark in the compendia. Thus Schoppe urged a clear, melodious, varied, and lively language drawn from the writer's own thoughts, while also "heeding all the usual forms."[5] In other respects, she adhered to the canonical formula of handbooks, which were also supposed to teach good bourgeois conduct.[6] Her guide describes the outward appearance of a letter, introduces the reader to the correct use of titles, forms of address, and salutations, explains spelling and grammar, and provides 320 fictitious letters as well as an appendix with maxims and aphorisms for every possible occasion for writing letters, every life situation, and every

Sentenzen und Denksprüchen für alle erdenklichen Schreibanlässe, Lebenssituationen und möglichen Kombinationen von KorrespondenzpartnerInnen. Der Erfolg von Schoppes Briefsteller, der in mehreren Auflagen erschien, offenbart das Bedürfnis einer breiten Öffentlichkeit nach einer gründlichen Einweisung in die formalen und sozialen Regeln der Briefetikette. Nicht einmal in weiten Kreisen des Bürgertums gehörte die Beherrschung der Orthografie, geschweige denn die Fähigkeit zum schriftlichen Ausdruck oder der Einblick in gesellschaftliche Konventionen zu den selbstverständlichen Fähigkeiten und Kenntnissen.

Einen Weg aus diesem Dilemma wiesen Glückwunschbillets, die sich Ende des 18. Jahrhunderts als neues Kommunikationsmedium etablierten. Unabhängig von Bildung und sozialem Status waren sie weiten Bevölkerungskreisen zugänglich. Ihre Wurzeln hatten sie in der französischen Erfindung der Besuchskarte, die man nicht nur als „billet de visite" an Freunde und Bekannte verteilte, sondern auch mit kurzen Mitteilungen beschrieb. Die Gepflogenheit, sie ebenfalls als Neujahrsgruß zu verschenken, verbreitete sich bald über Frankreichs Grenzen hinaus und generierte innerhalb des populären Grafikmarkts den neuen Geschäftszweig der Gratulationskarten. Bereits 1771 kündigte eine Anzeige „Neujahrswünsche in Octav, teils in roter, teils in schwarzer Einfassung, mit einem sauberen Kupferstich in Farbe en médaillon" an.[7] Zum Zentrum ihrer Produktion entwickelte sich Wien mit etwa 40 von 80 europäischen Verlagen, die neuartige Artikel unverzüglich auf den Markt brachten und in wortreichen Annoncen bewarben.[8] Glückwunschbillets kursierten nicht nur innerhalb einer Familie und eines Freundes- und Bekanntenkreises, Dienstleistende wie Theaterdiener, Zeitungsträger, Kellner, Barbiere oder Schornsteinfeger überreichten sie ihren KundInnen in Erwartung eines Trinkgeldes. Postboten, Lakaien oder die GratulantInnen selbst verteilten, wie ein Zeitgenosse bereits 1796 anschaulich berichtete, zum Jahreswechsel Tausende von Neujahrszetteln in der ganzen Stadt.[9] Der allmählich überbordenden Sitte begegnete man 1830 schließlich mit der Einführung kostenpflichtiger amtlicher Enthebungs- oder Entschuldigungskarten, deren Erlös wohltätigen Zwecken zufloss: An Haustüren geheftet, sollten sie unerwünschte GratulantInnen fernhalten (s. Abb. 126).[10] Fand der Austausch von Glückwunschbillets ursprünglich ausschließlich zum Jahreswechsel und an Namenstagen statt, dehnte man diese Sitte rasch auf weitere familiäre und öffentliche Feste aus und entdeckte sie auch als Freundschafts- und Liebesbeweis. Die Gratulationskarte erweiterte sich zum Gelegenheitsbillet, das man zu jedem erdenklichen Anlass oder Ereignis verschenkte. Diesen Funktionswandel förderten die Kartenmacher mit einem bunten Sortiment, das für jede Person und jede Okkasion die passenden Stücke in großer Anzahl und Vielfalt bereithielt. Dabei handelte es sich zunächst meist um kleinformatige, kolorierte Radierungen, die im ganzen Bogen oder zerschnitten in Päckchen angeboten wurden. Zu den Exemplaren der ersten Stunde gehörten Artikel mit ornamentalem Rahmenwerk oder Kartuschen in der Tradition der Visitenkarte. Ferner setzten sich geschwind Bildbillets auf dem Markt durch, die Einzelmotive oder szenische Darstellungen mit einem Begleitvers verbanden:[11] Auf einem Beispiel von etwa 1810 steuert ein junger Mann mit dem Kommentar „Ihnen meine Achtung zu beweisen scheue ich keine Gefahr" ein Boot durch die mächtigen Eisschollen eines Flusses (Abb. 090). Ebenso eindeutig ist die Botschaft einer zwischen 1810 und 1820 entstandenen Bildkarte mit dem überkommenen Motiv der ineinandergelegten Hände als Zeichen eines ewigen Bündnisses. Ein Seidenband, das eine Taube als Liebessymbol im Schnabel hält, umschlingt die Hände eines Paares. Ihre Liebe und Freundschaft wird, so der Kartenspruch, unsterblich sein (Abb. 091).

[7] Zit. nach Zur Westen, Walter von, *Vom Kunstgewand der Höflichkeit. Glückwünsche, Besuchskarten und Familienanzeigen aus sechs Jahrhunderten*, Berlin 1921, 51. Zur Entwicklung der Glückwunschbillets vgl. ebd., 36 f.; Pazaurek, Gustav E. „Künstlerische Besuchskarten", in: *Mitteilungen des Württembergischen Kunstgewerbevereins* (6) 2 1907/1908, 53–74, hier 55–58, 63, 69; Zur Westen, Walter von, „Zur Kunstgeschichte der Besuchs- und Glückwunschkarte", in: *Exlibris, Buchkunst und angewandte Graphik* (18) 3/4 1908, 90–126, hier 93, 106 f.; Gugitz, Gustav, „Alt-Wiener Neujahrswunschkarten", in: *Jahrbuch für Exlibris und Gebrauchsgraphik* (34) 1939, 10–20, hier 12; Egger, Hanna, *Herrn Biedermeiers Wunschbillet*, Ausst.kat. ÖMKI, Wien 1978, 7, 9 f.; Egger, Hanna, *Glückwunschkarten im Biedermeier. Höflichkeit und gesellschaftlicher Zwang*, München 1980, 17; Ehret, *Gloria, Freundschafts- und Glückwunschkarten im Biedermeier*, München 1982, 26.

[8] Zu Wien als Zentrum der Glückwunschkartenproduktion im Biedermeier vgl. Pazaurek 1907/1908, 70 f.; Pazaurek, Gustav E., *Biedermeier-Wünsche*, Stuttgart 1908, 7, 15; Zur Westen 1921, 31, 59, 99; Gugitz 1939,17; Böhmer, Günter, *Sei glücklich und vergiß mein nicht. Stammbuchblätter und Glückwunschkarten*, München 1973, 78, 96; Egger 1978, 13; Witzmann, Reingard, *Freundschafts- und Glückwunschkarten aus dem Wiener Biedermeier*, hg. vom Historischen Museum der Stadt Wien, Dortmund 1979, 167 f.; Egger 1980, 18. Zur extensiven Bewerbung der Biedermeier-Glückwunschkarten in Zeitungsannoncen vgl. Pazaurek 1908, 15; Gugitz 1939, 12, 14 f.; Egger 1978, 9; Egger 1980, 17 f. (alle s. Anm. 7).

[9] Gugitz 1939 (s. Anm. 7), 10–12.

[10] Pazaurek 1908 (s. Anm. 8), 1, 24; Gugitz 1939, 19; Egger 1978, 14; Egger 1980, 63 (s. Anm. 7).

[11] Zu den Motiv- und Bildbillets vgl. Pazaurek 1907/1908 (s. Anm. 7), 3; Pazaurek 1908 (s. Anm. 8), 58, 63; Zur Westen 1921 (s. Anm. 7), 57; Doosry, Yasmin, *Käufliche Gefühle. Freundschafts- und Glückwunschbillets des Biedermeier. Mit einem Beitrag von Jutta Zander-Seidel: Freundschafts- und Erinnerungsschmuck*, Ausst.kat. Germanisches Nationalmuseum, Nürnberg 2004, 26–28.

089
Peter Carl Geissler
Titelkupfer und Titelblatt zu
Amalia Schoppes *Briefsteller*
für Damen
2. Auflage, Berlin 1837
Copperplate Title Page
and Title Page for Amalia
Schoppe's [Guide to letter
writing for ladies]
2nd edition, Berlin 1837
Germanisches Nationalmuseum
Nürnberg Nuremberg, Inv. Nr.
Inv. No. 8° Gs 2084 h
© GNM

090
Anonym Anonymous
Bildbillet
Pest, um 1810
Ausführung: J. Müller
Radierung, koloriert
Illustrated Card
Pest, ca. 1810
Execution: J. Müller
Etching, colored
85 x 110 mm
KI 8774-1, Ankauf purchased from
Josef Kuderna 1930

091
Anonym Anonymous
Bildbillet
Wien, 1810–1820
Ausführung: Anton Tessaro
Punktiermanier, koloriert
Illustrated Card
Vienna, 1810–1820
Execution: Anton Tessaro
Stipple engraving, colored
92 x 71 mm
KI 8759-1, Ankauf purchased from
Josef Kuderna 1930

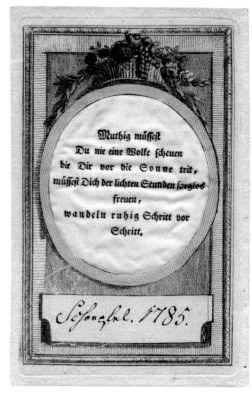

092
Anonym Anonymous
Medaillonbillet
Gewidmet von „Schoepfl 1785"
Seide, Radierung, koloriert
Medallion Card
Dedicated by "Schoepfl 1785"
Silk, etching, colored
135 x 87 mm
KI 8763-3, Ankauf purchased from
Josef Kuderna 1930

093
Jeremias Paul Schweyer
Klappkarte
Frankfurt/Main, 1801–1810
Radierung, Aquatinta
Lift-the-Flap Card
Frankfurt/Main, 1801–1810
Etching, aquatint
136 x 80 mm
KI 8760-2, Ankauf purchased from
Josef Kuderna 1930

[7] Quoted in Zur Westen, Walter von, *Vom Kunstgewand der Höflichkeit. Glückwünsche, Besuchskarten und Familienanzeigen aus sechs Jahrhunderten*, Berlin 1921, 51. Translated by Maria Slater. On the development of greeting cards cf. ibid., 36 f.; Pazaurek, Gustav E. "Künstlerische Besuchskarten," in: *Mitteilungen des Württembergischen Kunstgewerbevereins* (6) 2 1907/1908, 53–74, here 55–58, 63, 69; Zur Westen, Walter von, "Zur Kunstgeschichte der Besuchs- und Glückwunschkarte," in: *Exlibris, Buchkunst und angewandte Graphik* (18) 3/4 1908, 90–126, here 93, 106 f.; Gugitz, Gustav, "Alt-Wiener Neujahrskarten," in: *Jahrbuch für Exlibris und Gebrauchsgraphik*, Vienna 1939, 10–20, here 12; Egger, Hanna, *Herrn Biedermeiers Wunschbillet*, exh.cat. ÖMKI, Vienna 1978, 7, 9 f.; Egger, Hanna, *Glückwunschkarten im Biedermeier. Höflichkeit und gesellschaftlicher Zwang*, Munich 1980, 17; Ehret, Gloria, *Freundschafts- und Glückwunschkarten im Biedermeier*, Munich 1982, 26.

[8] On Vienna as the center of greeting card production in the Biedermeier period cf. Pazaurek 1907/1908, 70 f.; Pazaurek, Gustav E., *Biedermeier-Wünsche*, Stuttgart 1908, 7, 15; Zur Westen 1921, 31, 59, 99; Gugitz 1939,17; Böhmer, Günter, *Sei glücklich und vergiß mein nicht. Stammbuchblätter und Glückwunschkarten*, Munich 1973, 78, 96; Egger 1978, 13; Witzmann, Reingard, *Freundschafts- und Glückwunschkarten aus dem Wiener Biedermeier*, pub. by the Historisches Museum der Stadt Wien, Dortmund 1979, 167 f.; Egger 1980, 18. On the extensive advertisement of Biedermeier greeting cards in newspapers cf. Pazaurek 1908, 15; Gugitz 1939, 12, 14 f.; Egger 1978, 9; Egger 1980, 17 f. (for all see note 7).

[9] Gugitz 1939 (see note 7), 10–12.

[10] Pazaurek 1908 (see note 8), 1, 24; Gugitz 1939, 19; Egger 1978, 14; Egger 1980, 63 (see note 7).

[11] On motif and illustrated cards cf. Pazaurek 1907/1908 (see note 7), 3; Pazaurek 1908 (see note 8), 58, 63; Zur Westen 1921 (see note 7), 57; Doosry, Yasmin, *Käufliche Gefühle. Freundschafts- und Glückwunschbillets des Biedermeier. Mit einem Beitrag von Jutta Zander-Seidel: Freundschafts- und Erinnerungsschmuck*, exh.cat. Germanisches Nationalmuseum, Nuremberg 2004, 26–28.

possible combination of correspondence partners. The success of Schoppe's guide to letter writing, which appeared in several editions, lays bare the need of a wider public for exhaustive instruction in the formal and social rules of letter-writing etiquette. Not even in wide sections of the bourgeoisie was a command of orthography—much less the ability to express themselves in writing or have an insight into social conventions—a skill, which could be taken for granted.

A way out of this dilemma was provided by greeting cards, which became established as a new medium of communication at the end of the 18th century. They were accessible to broad sections of the population, irrespective of education and social status. Their roots lie in the French invention of the visiting card, which was not just handed out to friends and acquaintances as a "billet de visite," but also bore short hand-written messages. The practice of also giving them away as a New Year's greeting soon spread beyond the French borders and led to the creation of congratulations cards as a new line of business within the popular graphic design market. As early as 1771 an advertisement announced "New Year's greetings in octavo, partly with red, partly with black edging, with a clean copperplate print in color en médallion."[7] With approximately 40 of 80 European publishers, Vienna evolved into the center of their production. Novel articles were introduced onto the market without delay and advertised in verbose announcements.[8] Greeting cards not only circulated within a family or a circle of friends and acquaintances, but service providers such as theater employees, newspaper deliverers, waiters, barbers, and chimney sweeps presented them to their customers in anticipation of a tip. At the turn of the year mailmen, footmen, and well-wishers themselves distributed thousands of New Year's cards across the entire city, as a contemporary vividly described as early as 1796.[9] The increasingly excessive custom was eventually met with the introduction in 1830 of official relief or apology cards, the proceeds from the sale of which were donated to charities: fastened to front doors, their purpose was to keep unwelcome well-wishers at bay (see ill. 126).[10]

Although greeting cards were originally only exchanged at the turn of the year and on name days, the custom quickly expanded to include other familial and public celebrations, and they soon also served as tokens of love and friendship. The congratulations card evolved into an occasion card, which was presented on every conceivable occasion or occurrence. The card makers encouraged this extended use with a colorful assortment, offering a large number and variety of appropriate items for every person and every event. Initially, this assortment mainly comprised small-format, colorized etchings, which were sold by the sheet or cut to size in packets. Among the earliest examples were articles with ornamental borders or cartouches in the same tradition as visiting cards. Furthermore, illustrated cards soon gained acceptance on the market; they combined individual motifs or scenic depictions with an accompanying verse.[11] On one example from ca. 1810 a young man steers a boat between the massive ice floes on a river, with the comment: "To prove my high esteem for you, I balk at no danger" (ill. 090). Equally unambiguous is the message of an illustrated card from 1810/1820 with the traditional motif of holding hands as a symbol of an eternal alliance. Held in a dove's beak as a symbol of love, a silk ribbon is wound around the couple's hands. The line on the card assures us that their love and friendship is undying (ill. 091).

The Viennese manufacturers did not leave it at simple illustrated cards, although these did comprise the bulk of their product range. Homeworkers would cut rectangles or medallions from the etchings and fill these windows with maxims printed on paper or Atlas silk (ill. 092). They soon used the

Die Wiener Produzenten beließen es nicht bei den einfachen Bildkarten, obwohl sie die Masse ihrer Kollektionen bildeten. HeimarbeiterInnen trennten aus den Radierungen Rechtecke oder Medaillons heraus und hinterlegten die Fenster mit auf Papier oder Atlasseide gedruckten Sentenzen (Abb. 092). Alsbald nutzten sie die ausgeschnittenen Bildteile als bewegliche Klappen:[12] Auf einem um 1800 angebotenen Stück erscheint auf einer mandelförmigen Abdeckung ein Mann, der im Wald sitzt und in ein Buch vertieft ist. Seine Hoffnung auf die Erwiderung seiner Liebe offenbart sich, sobald man die Klappe lüftet, in den Worten „[…] Sey glücklich! / liebe mich dabei, / damit auch ich / ganz glücklich / sey." (Abb. 093). Als Träger versteckter Mitteilungen boten sich desgleichen zweilagige Netzkappenkarten an. Die Radierung ihres Deckblattes weist ein fein geschnittenes Gitterwerk auf. Hebt man das Gespinst mit einem Faden empor, enthüllt es den Vers oder das Bild der Unterlage.[13] Zu den Klapp- und Netzkappenkarten gesellten sich Faltbillets, die ihre Botschaft ebenfalls erst auf den zweiten Blick preisgeben. In der schlichtesten Variante stellen sie sich in der Art von Patenbriefen als Papierbogen mit bedruckten oder aufgeklebten Bildern dar, die zu Umschlägen zusammengefaltet werden (Abb. 094). Darin konnten Freunde und Liebende einen anspielungsreichen Spruch oder eine mit einer vertraulichen Nachricht beschriebene Karte, aber ebenso ein Liebespfand in Form einer Haarlocke verschenken.[14]

Mit den beweglichen Billets kam eine zweite Gruppe von Gelegenheitskarten auf, die zwischen 1810 und 1830 ihre Blüte erlebte. Die ersten mechanischen Stücke waren in Wien bereits zwischen 1796 und 1797 in den Werkstätten von Joseph Frister und Hieronymus Löschenkohl entstanden, deren Beispiel Heinrich Friedrich Müller und Jeremias Bermann folgten. Diese zweischichtigen Billets mit geschlitzten Oberflächen verhüllen in ihrem Futter ein weiteres Bildmotiv oder gar mehrere Bildteile. Je nach Kartenart besitzen sie eine mehr oder weniger knifflige Technik, die aus papiernen Zugstreifen, Hebeln, Gelenken und geknoteten Drehpunkten besteht. Zieht man an einer Zunge oder Drehscheibe, setzt sich die Maschinerie in Bewegung: Sie lässt über die Schlitze Bildelemente im Inneren eines Billets verschwinden oder befördert sie an ihre Oberfläche und erzeugt so einen fortwährenden Szenenwechsel. Eine schier unübersehbare Vielfalt von Zug-, Dreh-, Hebelzug-, Teilungs-, Vorhangzug-, Schwebezug-, Türflügel- oder Etagenkulissenkarten sorgte in ganz Europa für Entzücken. Auf geheimnisvolle Weise entfaltete sich vor einem staunenden Publikum eine fantastische Welt mit sprießender Natur, bewegten Figuren, wechselnden Interieurs und Bildern voller Wunder, Abenteuer, dramatischer Aktion, rührseliger Schwärmerei oder drastischer Komik:[15] Heinrich Friedrich Müller stellte zwischen 1810 und 1820 eine Hebelzugkonstruktion her, die einen Astrologen mit Himmelsglobus und Fernrohr zeigt. Zieht man an einer Lasche, versinkt der Sternendeuter samt Sternenhimmel im Billetfutter. Er macht einem jungen Mann Platz, der mit einer Hand auf seinem Herzen den Sinn des Kartenspruchs erschließt, indem er ihn vollendet: „Die Zukunft giebt Dir tausend Glück, / Es ist gar nicht zu nennen – / Mich wirst Du jeden Augenblick / Als treuen Freund erkennen." (Abb. 095). Begeisterung lösten mit ihren überraschenden optischen Gaukeleien auch Transparentkarten aus, die aus zwei Papierlagen mit je einer Darstellung oder einer Bild-Text-Kombination zusammengesetzt sind.[16] Bogenförmig überspannen auf der durchsichtigen Oberseite eines Exemplars die Worte „Wie die Liebe zart und rein" eine Lilie, das Symbol der Reinheit. Gegenlicht entschleiert die auf der Unterlage versteckte Versicherung „Muß die wahre Liebe sein" (Abb. 096). Die Glanzstücke der biedermeierlichen Wunschkartenproduktion bilden überaus artifizielle Ausfertigungen aus kostbar scheinenden Materialien. Neben Präge- und Stanzspitzenkarten zählen vor allem

[12] Zum Typus der Klappkarte vgl. Pazaurek 1908 (s. Anm. 8), 3 f.; Zur Westen 1908 (s. Anm. 7), 107; Zur Westen 1921 (s. Anm. 7), 38 f.; Egger 1978 (s. Anm. 7), 12; Egger 1980 (s. Anm. 7), 19; Doosry 2004 (s. Anm. 11), 29 f.

[13] Zum Typus des Netzkappenbillets vgl. Pazaurek 1908 (s. Anm. 8), 4; Zur Westen 1921 (s. Anm. 7), 39; Doosry 2004 (s. Anm. 11), 33–35.

[14] Zum Typus der Faltkarte vgl. Pazaurek 1908 (s. Anm. 8), 4 f.; Zur Westen 1908 (s. Anm. 7), 109; Zur Westen 1921 (s. Anm. 7), 39 f.; Böhmer 1973 (s. Anm. 8), 75; Doosry 2004 (s. Anm. 11), 31 f.

[15] Zur besonders großen Gruppe der mechanischen Billets mit ihren vielen Spielarten vgl. Pazaurek 1908 (s. Anm. 8), 5–9; Zur Westen 1908, 108, 110 f.; Zur Westen 1921 (s. Anm. 7), 40–45; Gugitz 1939 (s. Anm. 7), 14 f.; Böhmer 1973 (s. Anm. 8), 78 f., 81–91; Egger 1978, 13; Egger 1980, 21 f.; Egger 1980 (s. Anm. 7), 21 f.; Ehret 1982, 50, 62 f. (s. Anm. 7); Doosry 2004 (s. Anm. 11), 35–47.

[16] Zum Typus der Transparentkarte vgl. Pazaurek 1908 (s. Anm. 8), 5; Zur Westen 1921 (s. Anm. 7), 42; Gugitz 1939 (s. Anm. 7), 15 f.; Böhmer 1973 (s. Anm. 8), 75; Doosry 2004 (s. Anm. 11), 48–51. Im Zusammenhang mit dem Typus der Transparentkarte stellte Zur Westen fest: „[…] eigentlich Unanständiges findet man fast niemals", s. Zur Westen 1908 (s. Anm. 7), 107. Sämtliche Publikationen zu Biedermeierbillets betonen ihre harmlos-idyllischen Motive und Themen. Dazu sei angemerkt, dass die umfangreiche Sammlung Anton Maximilian Pachinger an Gelegenheitskarten auch pornografische Hebelzugkarten enthält (heute in der Graphischen Sammlung des Germanischen Nationalmuseums, Nürnberg).

[12] On the genre of interactive cards cf. Pazaurek 1908 (see note 8), 3 f.; Zur Westen 1908, 107; Zur Westen 1921, 38 f.; Egger 1978, 12; Egger 1980 (see note 7), 19; Doosry 2004 (see note 11), 29 f.

[13] Cards with intricate paper cutting, which can be raised—often to reveal another motif below.

[14] On the genre of *Netzkappenkarten* cf. Pazaurek 1908 (see note 8), 4; Zur Westen 1921 (see note 7), 39; Doosry 2004 (see note 11), 33–35.

[15] On the genre of folded cards cf. Pazaurek 1908 (see note 8), 4 f.; Zur Westen 1908 , 109; Zur Westen 1921 (see note 7), 39 f.; Böhmer 1973 (see note 8), 75; Doosry 2004 (see note 11), 31 f.

[16] On the particularly large array of mechanical cards in their various forms cf. Pazaurek 1908 (see note 8), 5–9; Zur Westen 1908, 108, 110 f.; Zur Westen 1921, 40–45; Gugitz 1939 (see note 7), 14 f.; Böhmer 1973 (see note 8), 78 f., 81–91; Egger 1978, 13; Egger 1980, 21 f.; Egger 1980, 21 f.; Ehret 1982, 50, 62 f. (see note 7); Doosry 2004 (see note 11), 35–47.

[17] On the genre of transparent cards cf. Pazaurek 1908 (see note 8), 5; Zur Westen 1921, 42; Gugitz 1939 (see note 7), 15 f.; Böhmer 1973 (see note 8), 75; Doosry 2004 (see note 11), 48–51. Regarding the genre of transparent cards, Zur Westen stated: "[…] actually indecent motifs are almost never found," see Zur Westen 1908 (see note 7), 107. Translated by Maria Slater. All publications on Biedermeier cards emphasize their harmless and idyllic motifs and themes. To this one might add that Anton Maximilian Pachinger's comprehensive collection of occasion cards also includes pornographic interactive cards with levers (now in the Department of Prints and Drawings at the Germanisches Nationalmuseum, Nuremberg).

[18] Card with artistic collage, popular in the early 19th century.

[19] Zur Westen 1921 (see note 7), 58.

cut-out image components as movable flaps:[12] On a piece sold around 1800, an almond-shaped covering shows a man sitting in the forest and engrossed in a book. His hope that his love will be requited is divulged once the flap is lifted in the words" […] Be happy! Love me so that I, too, can be happy." (ill. 093). Likewise bearers of hidden messages were dual-layered *Netzkappenkarten*[13]. The etching of their cover sheet features finely cut latticework. When the gossamer is raised with a thread, it reveals the verse or the picture on the layer below.[14] Similar to interactive cards and *Netzkappenkarten* are folded cards, which similarly only disclose their message at second glance. The simplest variety were—in the fashion of godparent request letters—a sheet of paper featuring printed or attached pictures, which were folded together to create envelopes (ill. 094). In them, friends and lovers could send each other an allusive line or a card bearing a confidential message, or equally a love token in the form of a lock of hair.[15]

In interactive cards, a second group of occasion cards emerged, which enjoyed their heyday between 1810 and 1830. The first mechanical pieces had already been made in Vienna between 1796 and 1797 in the workshops of Joseph Frister and Hieronymus Löschenkohl, and Heinrich Friedrich Müller and Jeremias Bermann followed their lead. These dual-layered cards with slit surfaces disguise another image motif or even several image components in their lining. Depending on the type of card, they feature one more or less fiddly mechanism, which consists of pullable paper tabs, levers, joints, and knotted pivots. Pulling a tab or dial sets the machinery in motion: via the slits it causes the elements of the image inside the card to vanish or rise to the surface, thereby creating a continual change of scene. A thoroughly immense variety of interactive cards—featuring elements, which could be pulled, rotated, levered, divided, pulled apart like curtains, hung, opened like doors, or which had layers of scenery—enchanted people throughout Europe. By means of these mysterious mechanisms, a wide-eyed audience watched a fantastical world unfold with flourishing nature, moving figures, changing interiors, and images filled with marvels, adventure, dramatic action, sentimental rhapsody, or crude humor.[16] For example, Heinrich Friedrich Müller produced a lever construction in 1810/1820 showing an astrologer with a celestial globe and tele-scope. When a tab is pulled, the astrologer sinks into the card's lining along with the starry sky. He makes space for a young man, who with his hand on his heart completes the card's verse and thus reveals its meaning: "The future will give you a thousand pleasures, / So many they cannot be named— / You will instantly recognize— / A loyal friend in me" (ill. 095). With their surprising optical illusions, transparent cards also caused excitement; they were composed of two layers of paper with an illustration or combination of image and text on each.[17] In an arc spanning the transparent upper side of one example are the words "As tender and pure as love" and a lily, the symbol of purity. Only when held against the light is the hidden assertion on the bottom layer unveiled: "True love must be" (ill. 096).

The pièce de résistance of Biedermeier greeting card production is a range of overtly artificial items made of seemingly precious materials. In addition to embossed and punched lace cards, it is mostly the Viennese *Kunstbillets*[18], which belong to this type. The use of relief on the surface of embossed cards—first advertised in 1787 and 1790[19]—was created by squeezing the material between two rollers, one a raised and one a recessed die. Though initially paper—which may also have been coated with colored Atlas silk—was the sole raw material, going forward even straw, birch bark, and tin were worked in this way. As cards in the style of bisque or Wedgwood, embossed cards

die Wiener Kunstbillets zu diesem Typus. Die reliefplastische Oberfläche von Prägekarten – sie wurden erstmals 1787 und 1790 annonciert[17] – entstand durch Pressung des Materials zwischen zwei Walzen mit einer Positiv- und einer Negativdruckform. Diente anfangs nur Papier als Rohstoff, das obendrein mit farbiger Atlasseide kaschiert sein konnte, sollten künftig selbst Stroh, Birkenrinde und Zinn als Material verarbeitet werden. Als Billets in Biskuit- oder Wedgwoodmanier fanden Prägekarten zahlreiche AbnehmerInnen:[18] Der cremefarbene Ton des reinen Papiers erinnerte sie an Biskuitporzellan, das ohne Glasur die samtgleiche Oberfläche hellen Marmors besitzt. Prägekarten imitieren jedoch nicht nur das seit Ende des 18. Jahrhunderts für die Herstellung von Ziergegenständen und Kleinplastiken außerordentlich geschätzte Hartporzellan. Sie ahmen ebenso die seit 1775 von Josiah Wedgwood angebotenen keramischen Gefäße und Plaketten nach, bei denen plastische Dekorelemente aus weißem Ton auf einem pastellfarbenen Fond aufliegen. Diese Jasperware lieferte die Vorlage für eine Prägekarte in dem von Wedgwood favorisierten klassizistischen Stil (Abb. 097). Ihr weißes, nur teilweise gefasstes Relief hebt sich von einem rosafarbenen Hintergrund ab. Zwei Genien bekränzen einen Freundschaftsaltar. Gehalten von geflügelten Gestalten schweben über ihm tiefrote, von einem Band umschlungene und einer Blumengirlande gerahmte Herzen. Damit vereint das Billet eine von der Antike inspirierte Symbolwelt mit populären Sinnbildern des 19. Jahrhunderts: Herzen und Blumen, die durch ihre leuchtende Farbigkeit besonders hervorgehoben sind. Dies trifft auch auf eine Klappkarte mit einem Rahmen aus Stanzspitzenpapier zu, die eine antikisierende Urne mit üppigen Blumenverzierungen paart (Abb. 098).[19] Der eigentliche Reiz des Stücks liegt jedoch in seiner Materialvielfalt, die ihm eine erlesene Anmutung verleiht: Atlasseide, geprägtes Silberpapier und geprägte Goldfolie sowie Stanzspitzenpapier.

Als Meister der Kombination unterschiedlichster Stoffe im Wien der Biedermeierzeit etablierte sich Johann Joseph Endletsberger, der zwischen1820 und 1830 mit Unterstützung der Künstler Franz Steinfeld, Ferdinand Georg Waldmüller und Josef Danhauser neuartige Glückwunsch- und Freundschaftskarten schuf.[20] Der Münzgraveur fertigte aus Gaze und Krepp, geprägtem und ausgeschlagenem Papier, Elfenbein, Perlmutt und Schildpatt, winzigen Spiegeln und Messing, ferner Stroh und Moos, Federn und Haaren, außerdem Gold- und Silberfäden, Glassteinen, Glasstaub und Glimmerstreusand dreidimensionale, tiefgestaffelte Collagen. Die mit geprägtem Messingblech oder kunstvoll applizierten Papierstreifen gerahmten Miniaturwerke erzielten mit 2 bis 5 Gulden die höchsten Preise im Kartenhandel – üblich waren 3 Kreuzer für einfache, 20 für mechanische, 40 für geprägte und ein Gulden für besonders feine Billets.[21] Als begehrte Sammlerstücke wurden sie prompt unter anderem von Joseph Riedl erfolgreich kopiert. Endletsberger versuchte seine handgefertigten Einzelstücke von den Nachschöpfungen durch sein Monogramm abzusetzen: Signierte Karten waren damals ein Novum, gaben doch Verleger mit Blick auf zahlreiche Konkurrenten ihr Sortiment allein unter ihrem Namen heraus. Sie unterschlugen die kleinen entwerfenden Künstler und GelegenheitsdichterInnen, die wesentlich zum Erfolg ihrer Artikel beitrugen. Erzeugnisse aus Endletsbergers Werkstatt zeichnen sich nicht allein durch ungewöhnliche Materialkombinationen aus. Sie decken darüber hinaus ein breites Motiv- und Themenspektrum ab, was übrigens auch für die Artikel der restlichen Kartenhersteller gilt. Meisterhaft arrangierte Symbole – Uhren als Vanitasmetaphern, Fortunas Füllhorn als Gleichnis für Reichtum und Glück, Amors Pfeile, schnäbelnde Täubchen, Veilchen und Rosen als Liebeszeichen oder Händepaare und Hunde als Treueembleme – gehören ebenso dazu wie erzählerisch bunte Szenen voller sinnbildhafter Anspielungen.[22] So feiert ein Kunst-

[17] Zur Westen 1921 (s. Anm. 7), 58.

[18] Zum Typus der Prägekarte mit ihren Varianten vgl. Pazaurek 1908 (s. Anm. 8), 3 f.; Zur Westen 1921 (s. Anm. 7), 39, 58; Böhmer 1973 (s. Anm. 8), 74 f.; Egger 1978, 12 f.; Egger 1980 (s. Anm. 7), 19 f.; Doosry 2004 (s. Anm. 11), 52–55.

[19] Zum Typus des Spitzenbillets vgl. Zur Westen 1908, 111; Zur Westen 1921, 39; Egger 1978, 13; Egger 1980, 20 (s. Anm. 7).

[20] Zur Gruppe der Wiener Kunstbillets aus der Endletsberger-Werkstatt vgl. Pazaurek 1908 (s. Anm. 8), 13 f.; Zur Westen 1908, 111; Zur Westen 1921, 60 f.; Gugitz 1939, 18 (s. Anm. 7); Böhmer 1973 (s. Anm. 8), 91–96; Egger 1978 (s. Anm. 7), 13 f.; Egger 1980 (s. Anm. 7), 27 f., 31; Doosry 2004 (s. Anm. 11), 56–66.

[21] Pazaurek 1908 (s. Anm. 8), 15; Zur Westen 1908,111; Zur Westen 1921, 60; Egger 1980, 18 (s. Anm. 7).

[22] Zu den Symbolen, Motiven und Themen der Biedermeierbillets vgl. u. a. Pazaurek 1908, 12, 17–23; Zur Westen 1921, 52–55 (s. Anm. 8); Egger 1978 (s. Anm. 7), 7 f.; Witzmann 1979 (s. Anm. 8), 171–173, 178 f., 181–183; Egger 1980 (s. Anm. 7), 24; Doosry 2004 (s. Anm. 11), 67–76.

094
Anonym Anonymous
Faltbillet in Form eines Umschlags
Entwurf: Anonym, um 1830
Geprägte Goldborten, Radierung, koloriert
Folded Card in the shape of an envelope
Design: Anonymous, ca. 1830
Embossed gold borders, etching, colored
185 x 135 mm
KI 8764-4, Ankauf purchased from Josef Kuderna 1930

095
Anonym Anonymous
Hebelzugkarte
Wien, 1810–1820
Ausführung: Heinrich Friedrich Müller
Kupferstich, koloriert
Pull-Tab Card
Vienna, 1810–1820
Execution: Heinrich Friedrich Müller
Copper engraving, colored
92 x 71 mm
KI 14137-1, Ankauf purchased from
Antiquariat Heck 1980

096
Anonym Anonymous
Transparentkarte
Gewidmet von J. Prokupek, 1808
Punktiermanier, koloriert
See-Through Card
Dedicated by J. Prokupek, 1808
Stipple engraving, colored
103 x 75 mm
KI 8765-3, Ankauf purchased from
Josef Kuderna 1930

097
Anonym Anonymous
Prägekarte in Wedgwoodmanier
Wien, 1800–1820
Tusche; Prägedruck, koloriert
**Embossed Card in Wedgwood
Style**
Vienna, 1800–1820
Ink; embossing, colored
128 x 93 mm
KI 8773-9, Ankauf purchased from
Josef Kuderna 1930

098
Anonym Anonymous
Stanzspitzenbillet
Wien, um 1810
Atlasseide, Silberpapier u. Goldfolie,
geprägt; Stanzspitze, koloriert
Punched Lace Card
Vienna, ca. 1810
Atlas silk, silver paper and gold leaf,
embossed; punched lace, colored
100 x 75 mm
KI 8773-5, Ankauf purchased from
Josef Kuderna 1930

20 On the genre of embossed cards and their variants cf. Pazaurek 1908 (see note 8), 3 f.; Zur Westen 1921 (see note 7), 39, 58; Böhmer 1973 (see note 8), 74 f.; Egger 1978, 12 f.; Egger 1980 (see note 7), 19 f.; Doosry 2004 (see note 11), 52–55.

21 On the genre of lace cards cf. Zur Westen 1908, 111; Zur Westen 1921, 39; Egger 1978, 13; Egger 1980, 20 (see note 7).

22 On Viennese *Kunstbillets* from the Endletsberger workshop cf. Pazaurek 1908 (see note 8), 13 f.; Zur Westen 1908, 111; Zur Westen 1921, 60 f.; Gugitz 1939, 18 (see note 7); Böhmer 1973 (see note 8), 91–96; Egger 1978, 13 f.; Egger 1980 (see note 7), 27 f., 31; Doosry 2004 (see note 11), 56–66.

23 Pazaurek 1908 (see note 8), 15; Zur Westen 1908, 111; Zur Westen 1921, 60; Egger 1980, 18 (see note 7).

24 On the symbols, motifs, and themes of Biedermeier cards cf. among others Pazaurek 1908, 12, 17–23; Zur Westen 1921, 52–55 (see note 8); Egger 1978 (see note 7), 7 f.; Witzmann 1979 (see note 8), 171–173, 178 f., 181–183; Egger 1980 (see note 7), 24; Doosry 2004 (see note 11), 67–76.

25 Pieske, Christa, with the cooperation of Vanja, Konrad, and others, *Das ABC des Luxuspapiers. Herstellung, Verarbeitung und Gebrauch 1860 bis 1930*, Berlin 1983, 87, 269–275; Rickards, Maurice, compl. by Michael Twyman, *The Encyclopedia of Ephemera: A guide to the fragmentary documents of everyday life for the collector, curator, and historian*, London 2000, 165–167.

found numerous buyers:[20] the cream shade of immaculate paper reminded them of bisque porcelain, which being unglazed has the velveteen surface of light marble. However, embossed cards not only imitate this hard porcelain, which had been highly valued for the production of ornamental objects and small sculptures since the end of the 18th century. They also emulate the ceramic receptacles and plaquettes supplied by Josiah Wedgwood since 1775, on which sculptural decorative elements in white clay rest on a pastel-colored ground. This jasperware provided the template for an embossed card in Wedgwood's preferred classical style (ill. 097). Its white, only partly set relief sets itself apart from a pale pink background. Two genii are laying a garland on an altar of friendship. Held by winged figures, deep red hearts framed in a floral wreath and wound in a ribbon hover over it. The card thus combines a world of symbols inspired by antiquity with popular 19th-century allegories: hearts and flowers, which are particularly prominent due to their bright colors. This is applied to an interactive card with a border made of punched lace paper, which couples an antique-like urn with lavish floral embellishments (ill. 098).[21] The actual charm of the piece, however, lies in its diverse materials, which give it an exquisite appearance: Atlas silk, embossed silver paper, and embossed gold foil as well as punched lace paper.

During the Biedermeier period in Vienna, Johann Joseph Endletsberger established himself as a master of combining different fabrics. He created novel kinds of greeting and friendship cards between 1820 and 1830 with the support of the artists Franz Steinfeld, Ferdinand Georg Waldmüller, and Josef Danhauser.[22] The coin engraver produced three-dimensional, deeply staggered collages from gauze and crepe, embossed and rejected paper, ivory, mother-of-pearl, and tortoiseshell, minute mirrors and brass, in addition to straw and moss, feathers and hair, as well as gold and silver threads, rhinestones, ground glass, and powdered mica glitter. Sold for between two and five gulden, these miniature works framed with embossed sheet brass or artistically applied strips of paper were the most expensive items in the card trade: common prices include 3 kreuzers for simple cards, 20 for mechanic, 40 for embossed, and one gulden for especially fine cards.[23]

As sought-after collector's items they were promptly copied—successfully by Joseph Riedl among others. Endletsberger tried to set his unique handmade specimens apart from their imitations by using his monogram: signed cards were a novelty at that time, seeing as publishers issued their assortment only under their own name in view of their numerous competitors. They thereby defrauded the small designing artists and occasional poets who had made considerable contributions to the success of their articles. Products from Endletsberger's workshop stood out not just as a result of their unusual combinations of materials. Additionally, they covered a broad spectrum of themes and motifs—which is incidentally also true of the articles by the other card producers. Masterfully arranged symbols—clocks as vanitas metaphors, Fortuna's cornucopia as an allegory of wealth and fortune, Amor's arrow, billing little doves, violets, and roses as tokens of love, or pairs of hands and dogs as emblems of fidelity—are as much a part of this tradition as narratively colorful scenes alive with symbolic allusions.[24] For example, one *Kunstbillet* from Endletsberger's workshop from ca. 1826 depicts a happy and pleasant life and eternal friendship in equal measure (ill. 099). With the introduction of the apology card for New Year's Day in 1830, the exchange of occasion cards temporarily experienced a sharp decline. From ca. 1845 an emergent luxury paper industry once again produced cards after the exemplars of the Biedermeier period, featuring illustrations, flaps, pull tabs, rotating elements, scenery, and display cards (ill. 100)[25]—the only cards to find no

099
Johann Joseph Endletsberger
Kunstbillet
Wien, 1820–1830
Geprägtes Messingblech, Krepp- u.
Glanzpapier, koloriert
Card with Artistic Collage
Vienna, 1820–1830
Embossed brass sheet, crepe paper
and gilt paper, colored
80 x 95 mm
KI 7946-12, Schenkung donation from
Technologisches Gewerbemuseum 1914

100
Anonym Anonymous
Aufstellkarte
Österreich, um 1900
Klischee, Prägedruck
Display Card
Austria, ca. 1900
Cliché, embossing
115 x 70 mm
KI 13452-1, Schenkung
donation from
Lorenz Fettinger 1959

101
Anonym Anonymous
**Glückwunschbrief eines
Enkels an seinen Großvater**
Wien, 1818
Radierung, koloriert
**Greeting Letter from a
Grandson to His Grandfather**
Vienna, 1818
Etching, colored
265 x 215 mm
KI 8791-41, Ankauf purchased from
Josef Kuderna 1930

[26] Zur Westen 1908 (see note 7), 99–102; Pieske 1983 (see note 25), 128 f., 130–132, 135–137; Stiftung Nordfriesland, Schloss vor Husum (ed.), *Papier im Reiche des Luxus und der Phantasie*, with contributions by Christa Pieske/Rolf Kuschert, Husum 1987, 16 f.; Rickards, Maurice, Collecting Ephemera, Oxford 1988, 154–157; Rickards (see note 25), 91 f., 348 f.

[27] On the definition of *"Umschlagkarte (envelope card)"* see Pieske 1983 (see note 25), 270.

[28] Detailed explanations of the diverse materials used in envelope cards in the 2nd half of the 19th century in: Pieske 1983 (see note 25), 294–297, 298 f., 302 f., 306; cf. also Rickards 1988 (see note 26), 94–97, 98–100; Rickards 2000 (see note 25), 132–134.

[29] Rammler, Otto Friedrich/Traut, Heinrich Theodor (rev.), Otto Friedrich Rammlers *Universal-Briefsteller oder Musterbuch zur Abfassung aller in den allgemeinen und freundschaftlichen Lebensverhältnissen sowie im Geschäftsleben Briefe, Documente und Aufsätze*, 46th edition, Leipzig 1876, 55.

[30] Quoted in Giuriato, Davide, "Briefpapier," in: Bohnkamp, Anne/Wiethölter, Waltraud (eds.), *Der Brief – Ereignis & Objekt*, exh.cat. Freies Deutsches Hochstift Frankfurt – Frankfurter Goethe-Museum, Frankfurt am Main/Basel 2008, 1–18, here 3, see note 10. Translated by Maria Slater.

successor were the exclusively handmade Viennese *Kunstbillets*. Furthermore, the increasing complexity of social life and an interest beyond one's own country's borders yielded occasion cards for particular junctures, which had previously not been marked with written greetings. This led to people giving congratulations cards for confirmations from the 1890s as well as Valentine's and Christmas cards, which had been commonplace in the United Kingdom and the U.S.A. since the 1840s and 1860s. In contrast, Easter cards only became customary after the turn of the century.[26] Elaborate products from the second half of the 19th century—to differentiate them from the new invention of picture postcards, they were also called envelope cards as they were sent in envelopes because they were so fragile[27]—are usually characterized by one more or less conspicuous feature. Particularly delicate pieces could be made of leaf gelatin, embossed and punched glazed, shiny, metallic, pearlescent, and alabaster paper, partly with silver and gold edging and with silver and gold-colored coatings, in addition to being embellished with ornately cut-out and shaped paper decorations, applications of detailed chromo-relief scraps or embossed textiles like silk and gauze, as well as bearing ornamentations made of mica and so-called Venetian dew in the form of minute glass beads, and imitation snow made of ground glass, and finally featuring the scintillating colorfulness of chromolithographs.[28] Even though such exclusive creations managed to survive into the 20th century, they were increasingly superseded by examples made of unrefined paper at the end of the 19th century; as mass-produced goods, the latter had always been part of the range of cards on offer. Among the well-made examples of this kind are illustrated cards, whose designers turned away from the rampant pictorial decorations and ornamental adornments of historicism and art nouveau and, influenced by the Werkkunst movement, favored a reduced language of pictures and forms along with clear typography. Exemplary works along these lines are the art cards by the Wiener Werkstätte, which became popular from the beginning of the 20th century.

As already mentioned, occasion cards provided members of all classes with a means of communication, which conformed with society's rules. Nevertheless, the bourgeoisie enthusiastically continued to write private letters. In terms of style, content, and choice of letter paper, they predominantly aligned themselves with the traditional advisory literature. Thus it was Otto Friedrich Rammler who decisively explained the criteria for the correct use of different types of paper. According to him, the simple letter sheet in a square format was reserved for correspondence with relations, friends, acquaintances, and business partners. Sheets with gold borders qualified for love letters, and those with black borders were appropriate for death announcement letters. Decorated papers were saved for family members and close friends.[29] Even Karl Philipp Moritz emphasized the importance of the paper for a letter's message and intention. He warned against sparing the expense of a good letter sheet or vellum paper, since "even in a letter, clothes make the man, and some letters are cast aside and disregarded as a result of their clothes …"[30]

Decorated writing paper had been established since the end of the 18th century and enjoyed great demand in the 19th century. Consumers had the choice between simple and reasonably priced or exclusive and expensive single and double sheets. They could buy simple paper and affix pre-produced borders to them. Furthermore, they had the choice of examples with colorized, embossed, or lacy and openwork-like edges, or with ornamental decorated borders printed in one or multiple colors. In addition, they could turn to designs with a rich pictorial decoration comprising scattered flower motifs, romantic vignettes, or scenic narrations on the upper edge or in the middle of the

billet aus Endletsbergers Werkstatt von etwa 1826 gleichermaßen ein glückliches und frohes Leben und ewige Freundschaft (Abb. 099).

Mit der Einführung der Enthebungskarte zum Neujahrstag 1830 erfuhr der Austausch von Gelegenheitskarten einen vorübergehenden Einbruch. Seit etwa 1845 produzierte eine aufstrebende Luxuspapierindustrie nach dem Vorbild der Biedermeierzeit erneut Bild-, Klapp-, Zug-, Dreh-, Kulissen- und Aufstellkarten (Abb. 100)[23] – allein die ausschließlich in Handarbeit gefertigten Wiener Kunstbillets fanden keine Nachfolger. Die zunehmende Differenzierung des Gesellschaftslebens und der Blick über die eigenen Landesgrenzen hinaus brachten außerdem Gelegenheitskarten für bestimmte Anlässe hervor, die man bisher nicht mit schriftlichen Wünschen bedacht hatte. So verschenkte man ab den 1890er Jahren zur Konfirmation eine Gratulationskarte und die seit den 1840er und 1860er Jahren in England und den USA üblichen Valentins- und Weihnachtskarten, während der Ostergruß erst ab der Jahrhundertwende üblich war.[24]

Elaborierte Erzeugnisse der zweiten Hälfte des 19. Jahrhunderts – im Unterschied zur neuen Erfindung der Bildpostkarten bezeichnet man sie, weil sie wegen ihrer Empfindlichkeit in Kuverts versandt wurden, auch als Umschlagkarten[25] – sind gewöhnlich durch eine mehr oder weniger auffällige Ausstattung charakterisiert. Besonders delikate Stücke können aus Gelatinefolie, aus geprägtem und gestanztem Glacé-, Glanz-, Metall-, Perlmutt-, und Eispapier bestehen, teilweise mit Silber- und Goldschnitt und mit silber- und goldfarbenen Auflagen, außerdem mit kunstvoll ausgeschnittenen und geformten Papierverzierungen, Applikationen aus kleinteiligen Glanzbildchen oder geprägten Textilien wie Seide und Gaze dekoriert sein, ferner Verzierungen aus Glimmer und dem sogenannten Venezianischen Tau in Form winziger Glasperlen und Schneeimitationen aus gemahlenem Glas besitzen und schließlich die brillante Farbigkeit von Chromolithografien aufweisen.[26] Auch wenn sich derartig exklusive Schöpfungen bis ins 20. Jahrhundert hinein behaupteten, wurden sie Ende des 19. Jahrhunderts zunehmend von Exemplaren aus nicht veredelten Papieren verdrängt, die von jeher als Massenware zum üblichen Kartensortiment gehört hatten. Zu den gelungenen Beispielen dieser Art zählen Bildkarten, deren Entwerfer sich vom wuchernden Bild- und Ornamentschmuck des Historismus und Jugendstils abwandten und unter dem Einfluss der Werkkunstbewegung eine reduzierte Bild- und Formensprache und eine klare Typografie favorisierten. Vorbildlich sind dafür die Künstlerkarten der Wiener Werkstätte, die seit Anfang des 20. Jahrhunderts ihre LiebhaberInnen fanden.

Die Gelegenheitskarten erlaubten, wie bereits erwähnt, eine schichtenübergreifende gesellschaftskonforme Kommunikation. Gleichwohl pflegte das Bürgertum weiterhin den privaten Briefverkehr nachdrücklich. Dabei orientierte es sich in Stil, Inhalt und in der Wahl des Schreibpapiers überwiegend an der traditionellen Ratgeberliteratur. So erklärte Otto Friedrich Rammler dezidiert die Kriterien für die korrekte Verwendung unterschiedlicher Sorten. Demnach war der schlichte Bogen im Quartformat der Korrespondenz mit Verwandten, FreundInnen, Bekannten und GeschäftspartnerInnen vorbehalten. Blätter mit Goldschnitt kamen für Liebes- und mit schwarzem Rand für Trauerbriefe infrage. Verzierte Papiere waren für Familienmitglieder und nahe FreundInnen reserviert.[27] Sogar Karl Philipp Moritz hob die Bedeutung des Schreibträgers für die Aussage und Intention eines Briefes hervor. Er warnte davor, die Kosten für ein gutes Post- oder Velinpapier zu scheuen. Denn „selbst bei Briefen machen Kleider Leute, und mancher Brief wird des Kleides wegen unbeachtet zur Seite gelegt …".[28]

[23] Pieske, Christa, unter Mitarbeit von Vanja, Konrad, u. a., *Das ABC des Luxuspapiers. Herstellung, Verarbeitung und Gebrauch 1860 bis 1930*, Berlin 1983, 87, 269–275; Rickards, Maurice, ferstiggestellt von Michael Twyman, *The Encyclopedia of Ephemera: A guide to the fragmentary documents of everyday life for the collector, curator, and historian*, London 2000, 165–167.

[24] Zur Westen 1908 (s. Anm. 7), 99–102; Pieske 1983 (s. Anm. 23), 128 f., 130–132, 135–137; Stiftung Nordfriesland, Schloss vor Husum (Hg.), *Papier im Reiche des Luxus und der Phantasie*, mit Beiträgen von Christa Pieske/Rolf Kuschert, Husum 1987, 16 f.; Rickards, Maurice, *Collecting Printed Ephemera*, Oxford 1988, 154–157; Rickards (s. Anm. 23), 91 f., 348 f.

[25] Zur Definition „Umschlagkarte" s. Pieske 1983 (s. Anm. 23), 270.

[26] Ausführliche Erläuterungen der Materialvielfalt der Umschlagkarten der 2. Hälfte des 19. Jahrhunderts bei: Pieske 1983 (s. Anm. 23), 294–297, 298 f., 302 f., 306; vgl. auch Rickards 1988 (s. Anm. 24), 94–97, 98–100; Rickards 2000 (s. Anm. 23), 132–134.

[27] Rammler, Otto Friedrich/Traut, Heinrich Theodor (Bearb.), *Otto Friedrich Rammlers Universal-Briefsteller oder Musterbuch zur Abfassung aller in den allgemeinen und freundschaftlichen Lebensverhältnissen sowie im Geschäftsleben Briefe, Documente und Aufsätze*, 46. Auflage, Leipzig 1876, 55.

[28] Zitiert nach Giuriato, Davide, „Briefpapier", in: Bohnkamp, Anne/Wiethölter, Waltraud (Hg.), *Der Brief – Ereignis & Objekt*, Ausst.kat. Freies Deutsches Hochstift Frankfurt – Frankfurter Goethe-Museum, Frankfurt am Main/Basel 2008, 1–18, hier 3, Anm. 10.

[31] Pieske 1983, 99; Rickards 2000, 360 f. (see note 25).

[32] Pieske 1983 (see note 25), 267 f.; Pieske/Kuschert 1987 (see note 26), 16.

[33] Rickards 2000 (see note 25), 193, 135–137, 311.

[34] Pieske 1983 (see note 23), 195 f.

[35] Detailed explanation of the development of business documents in: Apel, Claus, "Gestalt- und Aussagewandlungen des illustrierten Firmenbriefkopfes im 19. Jahrhundert," in: Korzus, Bernard (ed.), *Fabrik im Ornament. Ansichten auf Firmenbriefköpfen des 19. Jahrhunderts*, exh.cat. Westfälisches Landesmuseum and Stiftung Westfälisches Wirtschaftsarchiv Dortmund, Münster 1980, 84–98. Cf. also Lewis, John, *Printed Ephemera: The changing uses of type and letterforms in English and American Printing*, Ipswich 1962, 194–216; Pieske 1983 (see note 25), 100; Rickards 1988 (see note 26), 20–23, 113–117; Rickards 2000 (see note 24), 49–52, 193 f.

[36] Behal, Vera J., *Möbel des Jugendstils. Sammlung des Österreichischen Museums für angewandte Kunst in Wien*, Munich 1988, 59.

sheet, the exemplars for which were often provided by occasion cards.[31] For example, a depiction known from Biedermeier cards with the line "Out of childlike affection" adorns an anonymous congratulatory letter sent from a grandson to his grandfather in 1818: two children are crowning garden urns with floral wreaths in a park with a temple and an altar to friendship (ill. 101). Even more obviously than in that case, the close relationship between occasion cards and letter paper is illustrated in an English product from the mid 19th century: The front of a double sheet with punched lace edging is printed with a colorful bouquet of flowers cut in the same way as on a *Netzkappenkarte* (ill. 102). That the secret message under the bouquet was a Valentine's surprise is revealed by a poem.

The majority of letter paper destined for private correspondence in the 19th century was furnished with motifs and decorations, which had to satisfy different addressees and tasks: their actual purpose was only defined once they had been given a printed verse or a handwritten text. Among the letter paper whose embellishments were intended to convey a specific application from the outset was principally paper with black borders for announcements of death, condolences, and thank-you letters for expressions of sympathy. Their traditional black borders gradually gave way to more elaborate solutions (ill. 103).[32] Together with this kind of paper, the industry also offered envelopes in matching formats and designs—as it did for the rest of its assortment (ill. 104). Until the advent of ready-made envelopes in the United Kingdom in 1820 as well as small round or angular paper seals, letters had been protected from unauthorized eyes by artfully folding their paper and sealing them with wax and a signet.[33] Whereas previously sheets and envelopes had been sold loose, for the sale of particularly exquisite versions the Berlin-based manufacturer Max Krause produced imposing boxed letter-writing sets from the 1870s. The resounding success of this packaging idea—around 1900 German luxury paper manufacturers generated a turnover of ca. 50 million marks by exporting these boxes—was not least thanks to their extravagant designs. They ranged from magnificently adorned examples to whimsical pieces in the shape of a dovecote (see ill. 148) or furniture, such as a closet in the grandiose neo-Renaissance style (ill. 105).[34]

Decorated letter paper likewise influenced the business correspondence of tradesmen and manufacturers throughout the entire 19th century; they used delivery notes, invoice forms, and letter paper for information and advertising purposes in equal measure. From 1820 they had their company letters printed with small-format vignettes and dingbats, which they replaced around 1845 with impressive illustrations as an expression of their trustworthiness, capability, and economic power. Views of retail businesses and factory complexes developed into the leading design feature of letterheads until the 1920s. They depict business premises featuring main and adjacent buildings with smoking chimneys, modern transportation, industrious workers, and curious passers-by, often supplemented by allegories, artisanal and industrial products, medals, and garlands of flowers.[35] As early as 1903 the furniture factory of Julius & Josef Hermann, which had been founded in Vienna in 1878, used this type of image in its advertising; the company produced every style of simple and high-quality furniture and exhibited entire room arrangements in a dedicated department store[36] (ill. 106). In contrast, Thonet-Mundus AG presented itself entirely differently; established in 1922, the company's correspondence paper bears an unusual connection between the writing and the image: the letterhead is dominated by a modern sans serif combined font similar to Paul Renner's Futura black; the tubular steel furniture—produced by Thonet after designs by Marcel Breuer—sold

Ausgeschmücktes Schreibpapier war seit Ende des 18. Jahrhunderts bekannt und erfreute
sich im 19. Jahrhundert großer Nachfrage. Die KonsumentInnen hatten die Wahl zwischen
einfach-preiswerten und exklusiv-teuren Einzel- und Doppelbogen. Sie konnten schlichte Papiere
kaufen und sie mit vorfabrizierten Bordüren bekleben. Außerdem standen ihnen Exemplare mit
kolorierten, geprägten, spitzenartig durchbrochenen Rändern oder mit ein- oder mehrfarbig bedruck-
tem ornamentalen Rahmenwerk zur Verfügung. Ferner konnten sie auf Ausführungen mit einem
reichen Bildschmuck aus vereinzelten Blumenmotiven, romantischen Vignetten, szenischen Erzählungen am oberen Rand oder in der Mitte eines Blattes zurückgreifen, für den oft Gelegenheitskarten
das Vorbild lieferten.[29]

[29] Pieske 1983, 99; Rickards 2000, 360 f.
(s. Anm. 23).

So ziert eine von Biedermeierbillets her bekannte Darstellung mit dem Zusatz „Aus kindlicher Liebe"
einen anonymen Glückwunschbrief, den ein Enkel 1818 artig seinem Großvater widmete: ein
Kinderpaar, das in einem Park mit Freundschaftstempel und Freundschaftsaltar Gartenurnen mit
Blumengirlanden bekränzt (Abb. 101). Noch offensichtlicher als in diesem Fall stellt sich die enge
Verwandtschaft zwischen Gelegenheitskarten und Briefpapier bei einem englischen Erzeugnis aus
der Mitte des 19. Jahrhunderts dar: Die Vorderseite eines Doppelbogens mit gestanztem Spitzen-
rand ist mit einem bunten, zu einer Netzkappe aufgeschnittenen Blumenbukett bedruckt (Abb. 102).
Dass die geheime Botschaft des Gebindes eine Valentinsüberraschung war, verrät ein Gedicht.
Das Gros der für die private Korrespondenz bestimmten Briefpapiere war im 19. Jahrhundert mit
Motiven und Dekoren versehen, die unterschiedlichen AdressatInnen und Aufgaben gerecht werden
mussten: Ihre eigentliche Zweckbestimmung erhielten sie erst durch einen gedruckten Vers oder
einen handschriftlichen Text. Zu den Beispielen, deren Verzierungen hingegen von vornherein auf
bestimmte Anlässe hinweisen sollten, gehörten vornehmlich Trauerpapiere für Todesanzeigen,
Kondolenzen und Danksagungen für die Beileidsbezeugungen. Ihr traditioneller schwarzer Rand wich
schrittweise elaborierten Lösungen (Abb. 103).[30] Zusammen mit den Trauerbogen bot der Handel –

[30] Pieske 1983 (s. Anm. 23), 267 f.;
Pieske/Kuschert 1987 (s. Anm. 24), 16.

wie bei seinem übrigen Sortiment auch – in Format und Gestaltung passende Kuverts an (Abb.104).
Bis zum Aufkommen konfektionierter Umschläge 1820 in England sowie kleiner Papiersiegel in
runder und eckiger Form hatte man Briefe durch kunstvolles Falten ihres Papiers und Plombieren mit
Siegellack und Petschaft vor unberechtigtem Zugriff geschützt.[31] Für den Verkauf von besonders ex-
quisiten Garnituren stellte der Berliner Fabrikant Max Krause seit den 1870er Jahren repräsentative
Papierkassetten her: Bis dahin waren Bogen und Kuverts lose angeboten worden. Der durchschla-
gende Erfolg dieser Verpackungsidee – um 1900 erzielten deutsche Luxuspapierfabrikanten mit dem
Export der Schachteln einen Umsatz von ca. 50 Millionen Mark – verdankte sich nicht zuletzt den
extravaganten Entwürfen. Sie reichten von prächtig verzierten Exemplaren bis zu skurrilen Stücken
in Form eines Taubenschlags (s. Abb. 148) oder Möbels wie das eines Kastenschranks im pracht-
vollen Neorenaissancestil (Abb. 105).[32]

[31] Rickards 2000 (s. Anm. 23), 193, 135–137,
311.

[32] Pieske 1983 (s. Anm. 23), 195 f.

Ausgeschmückte Briefpapiere bestimmten das gesamte 19. Jahrhundert hindurch ebenfalls die Ge-
schäftskorrespondenz Gewerbetreibender und Fabrikanten, die Lieferscheine, Rechnungsformulare
und Briefbogen gleichermaßen als Informations- und Reklameträger einsetzten. Seit 1820 ließen sie
ihr Firmenpapier mit kleinformatigen Vignetten und Schmuckzeichen bedrucken, die sie um 1845
durch eindrucksvolle Illustrationen als Ausdruck von Vertrauenswürdigkeit, Leistungsfähigkeit und
wirtschaftlicher Potenz ersetzten. Zum leitenden, noch bis in die 1920er Jahre gültigen Gestaltungs-
merkmal der Briefköpfe entwickelten sich Ansichten von Ladengeschäften und Fabrikanlagen. Sie

102
Anonym Anonymous
Netzkappenbriefpapier
Großbritannien, 1840–1850
Stanzspitze, Seidenpapier, Seidenfaden, Lithografie, koloriert
Letter Paper with Raisable Paper Cutting
Great Britain, 1840–1850
Punched lace, silk paper, silk thread, lithograph, colored
238 x 196 mm
KI 8791-36, Ankauf purchased from Josef Kuderna 1930

103
Hugo Gerard Ströhl
Trauerbogen
Wien, 1880–1885
Ausführung: Röder, Baus & Comp.
Lithografie
Mourning paper
Vienna, 1880–1885
Execution: Röder, Baus & Comp.
Lithograph
291 x 232 mm
KI 7752-131, Schenkung donation from Hugo Gerard Ströhl 1910

104
Hugo Gerard Ströhl
Trauerbriefpapier mit Kuverts und Bordüren
Berlin, um 1880
Ausführung: Max Krause
Klischee
Mourning Letter Paper with Envelopes and Bordures
Berlin, ca. 1880
Execution: Max Krause
Cliché
177 x 112 mm; 96 x 119 mm
KI 7752-135, Schenkung donation from Hugo Gerard Ströhl 1910

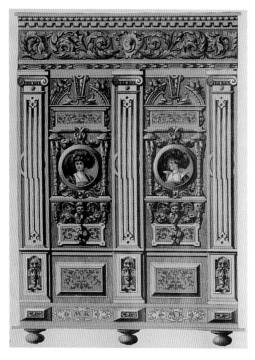

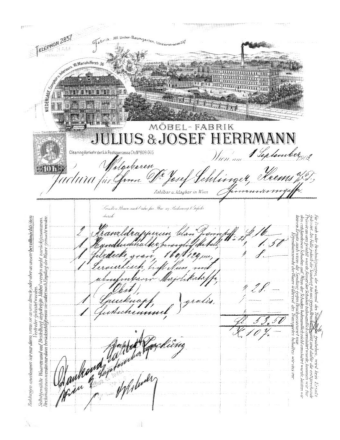

105
Hugo Gerard Ströhl
Etikett für eine Briefpapierkassette in Form eines Kastenschranks
Berlin, um 1880
Ausführung: Max Krause
Chromolithografie
Label for a Letter Paper Box in the Shape of a Wardrobe
Berlin, ca. 1880
Execution: Max Krause
Chromolithograph
216 x 149 mm
KI 7752-195-1, Schenkung donation from Hugo Gerard Ströhl 1910

106
Anonym Anonymous
Rechnungsbogen der Möbelfabrik Julius & Josef Herrmann, ausgestellt 1903
Wien, 1903
Klischee
Invoice Paper of the Furniture Company Julius & Josef Herrmann, issued 1903
Vienna, 1903
Cliché
271 x 209 mm
KI 15760-8, Schenkung donation from Waltraud Neuwirth 2005

107
Robert Haas
Briefpapier des Hotel Wandl
Wien, nach 1925
Ausführung: Officina Vindobonensis
Buchdruck
Letter Paper of the Hotel Wandl
Vienna, after 1925
Execution: Officina Vindobonensis
Letterpress print
124 x 227 mm
KI 8882-5, Schenkung donation from
Officina Vindobonensis 1930

by the company was depicted in a rectangle in the lower left corner of the sheet. Here, it is no longer ostentatious representation, which is revered, but rather modern design, linked to an advertisement, which has been reduced to the bare essentials (see ill. 159).

Two exemplary business documents from the late 1920s dispensed with illustrations entirely: Robert Haas designed a letterhead for the Viennese Hotel Wandl, which was equipped with all modern comforts. In doing so, he followed a Bauhaus principle according to which typography requires an emphatic form in order to convey a clear message (ill. 107). The name, address, and telephone number of this long-standing hotel on the Petersplatz appeared in uppercase Futura on white paper. The main and ancillary information is differentiated by use of different colors, sizes, and font weight for the letters as well as by their arrangement as a portrait or landscape rectangle. The business documents of the Atelier Hans Neumann srepresent his modern design and advertising principles even more clearly. When he reopened his advertising studio at Vienna's Stock-im-Eisen-Platz after the turmoil of the First World War, the busy graphic designer introduced a studio stamp in 1920 with which he signed his designs, including his numerous posters:[37] a circular signet with changing colors and the name of the agency in Futura, which could also contain his address details (ill. 108). As a distinctive trademark on the company correspondence paper and as the identifying feature of the company, it met all of the requirements for a logo—as stipulated by modern advertising: concision and recognizability (see ill. 168).

In its rich diversity, the material record of written communication documents multifarious manifestations of cultural history from the end of the 18th to the beginning of the 20th century. Congratulations cards and congratulatory letters, which accompanied people on their journeys through life, powerfully reflect the emotional culture, desires, and standards of conduct of the middle and upper classes. However, this betrays neither the social and political conflicts of the wars of liberation from 1813 to 1815, the Restoration period from 1815 to 1848, the Revolutions of 1848/1849, nor the radical changes to working and living conditions as a result of intensifying industrialization in the second half of the 19th century. At best, these themes are briefly reflected in illustrated cards via a caricature of Napoleon or a depiction of a hot-air balloon;[38] most of all, however, they find expression in a delight in playfulness, with hidden notes and messages doubling as an astonishing means of internalizing political restrictions.

Congratulations cards and congratulatory letters demonstrate a withdrawal into the private sphere and the nurturing of relationships with family and friends. They manifest the significance of the culture of friendship and memory, and are moreover part of a social culture, which transported the 19th-century delight in media spectacles—with their optical phenomena and moving pictures—into the domestic sphere. Furthermore, they bear witness to a new kind of consumer behavior in the second half of the 19th century, in which ostentatious self-representation superseded the genteel modesty of the Biedermeier period. In this context, elaborate occasion cards and letter paper with their luxury features and imitation of expensive materials such as gold and silver, porcelain and lace are testament to a profound change in taste, which would once again be called into question at the end of the 19th century. Additionally, they make plain the need of broader sections of the population to define their social situation through their consumption of goods. In their battle for these customers and new sales markets, tradespeople, manufacturers, and service companies discovered correspondence sheets as effective advertising media whose appearance they continually adapted

[37] On Hans Neumann cf. Doosry, Yasmin (rev.), *Plakativ! Produktwerbung im Plakat*, exh.cat. Germanisches Nationalmuseum, Nuremberg, Ostfildern 2009, 548 (in which further literature is listed).

[38] Cf. Zur Westen 1921 (see note 7), 52 f. In 1813/1814 a satirical portrait of Napoleon was sold as a New Year's greeting, several versions of which had been published after the Battle of Leipzig in October 1813, cf. Langemeyer, Gerhard (ed.), *Bild als Waffe. Mittel und Motive der Karikatur in fünf Jahrhunderten*, exh.cat. Wilhelm Busch-Museum Hannover, Munich 1984, No. 126.

geben Betriebsstätten mit Haupt- und Nebengebäuden mit rauchenden Schornsteinen, modernen Transportmitteln, fleißigen ArbeiterInnen und neugierigen PassantInnen wieder, oft ergänzt durch Allegorien, Handwerks- und Industrieprodukte, Preismedaillen und Blumengirlanden.[33] Noch 1903 warb die 1878 in Wien gegründete Möbelfabrik Julius & Josef Herrmann, die einfache und hochwertige Möbel aller Stilarten herstellte und ganze Zimmereinrichtungen in einem eigenen Warenhaus ausstellte,[34] mit diesem Bildtypus (Abb. 106). Vollkommen anders präsentierte sich hingegen die 1922 gegründete Thonet-Mundus AG, deren Korrespondenzpapier eine ungewöhnliche Schrift-Bild-Verknüpfung zeigt: Den Briefkopf beherrscht eine moderne serifenlose Kombinationsschrift, ähnlich der Renner'schen Futura black; in einem Rechteck in der unteren linken Blattecke sind die vom Unternehmen vertriebenen Stahlrohrmöbel aus der Produktion von Thonet nach Entwürfen von Marcel Breuer abgebildet. Hier wird nicht mehr einer pompösen Repräsentation gehuldigt, sondern modernes Design mit einer auf das Wesentliche reduzierten Werbung verknüpft (s. Abb. 159). Einen vollständigen Verzicht auf Illustrationen weisen beispielhaft zwei Geschäftspapiere aus den späten 1920er Jahren auf: Robert Haas entwarf einen Briefkopf für das komfortable Wiener Hotel Wandl. Dabei folgte er einem Grundsatz des Bauhauses, wonach die Typografie als Instrument einer klaren Mitteilung einer eindringliche Form bedarf (Abb. 107). Name, Anschrift und Telefonnummer des Traditionshauses am Petersplatz erscheinen in Futura-Versalien auf weißem Papier. Dabei sind Haupt- und Nebeninformationen durch Farbe, Größe und Schriftstärke der Buchstaben sowie durch ihre Anordnung zum Hoch- und Querrechteck unterschieden. Noch greifbarer vertritt das Atelier Hans Neumann moderne Gestaltungs- und Reklamegrundsätze. Nach der Wiedereröffnung seines Werbestudios am Stock-im-Eisen-Platz in Wien nach den Wirren des Ersten Weltkriegs führte der vielbeschäftigte Grafiker 1920 einen Atelier-Stempel ein, mit dem er seine Entwürfe kennzeichnete, darunter seine zahlreichen Plakate:[35] Ein kreisrundes Signet mit wechselnden Farben und dem Namen der Agentur in Futura, das auch eine Adressenangabe enthalten kann (Abb. 108). Als markante Schriftmarke erfüllt es auf dem Firmenkorrespondenzbogen alle Anforderungen, die die moderne Werbung an ein Logo als Identifikationsmerkmal eines Unternehmens stellt: Prägnanz und Wiedererkennbarkeit (s. Abb. 168).

Mit ihrem Facettenreichtum dokumentiert die dingliche Überlieferung der schriftlichen Kommunikation vielfältige Erscheinungsformen der Kulturgeschichte vom ausgehenden 18. bis zum beginnenden 20. Jahrhundert. Gratulationskarten und Glückwunschbriefe, die die Menschen in ihrem Lebenslauf begleiteten, spiegeln eindringlich die Gefühlskultur der Mittel- und Oberschichten mit ihren Wunschvorstellungen und Verhaltensnormen. Darin scheinen jedoch weder die politischen und gesellschaftlichen Konflikte der Befreiungskriege von 1813 bis 1815, der Restaurationszeit von 1815 bis 1848 sowie der bürgerlichen Revolution von 1848/1849 noch die tief greifende Umgestaltung der Arbeits- und Lebensumstände durch die sich verstärkende Industrialisierung in der zweiten Hälfte des 19. Jahrhunderts auf. Bestenfalls finden sie einen flüchtigen Reflex in Bildkarten mit einer Napoleon-Karikatur oder der Darstellung eines Heißluftballons,[36] vor allem aber in der Lust am Spiel mit versteckten Botschaften und Mitteilungen als einer erstaunlichen Form der Verinnerlichung politischer Restriktionen.

Gratulationskarten und Glückwunschbriefe veranschaulichen den Rückzug ins Private und die Pflege familiärer und freundschaftlicher Beziehungen. Sie manifestieren die Bedeutung der Freundschafts- und Erinnerungskultur und sind obendrein Teil einer Geselligkeitskultur, die die Freude des

[33] Ausführliche Erläuterung zur Entwicklung des Geschäftspapiers bei: Apel, Claus, „Gestalt- und Aussagewandlungen des illustrierten Firmenbriefkopfes im 19. Jahrhundert", in: Korzus, Bernard (Hg.), *Fabrik im Ornament. Ansichten auf Firmenbriefköpfen des 19. Jahrhunderts*, Ausst.kat., Westfälisches Landesmuseum und Stiftung Westfälisches Wirtschaftsarchiv Dortmund, Münster 1980, 84–98. Vgl. auch Lewis, John, *Printed Ephemera: The changing uses of type and letterforms in English and American Printing*, Ipswich 1962, 194–216; Pieske 1983 (s. Anm. 23), 100; Rickards 1988 (s. Anm. 24), 20–23, 113–117; Rickards 2000 (s. Anm. 23), 49–52, 193 f.

[34] Behal, Vera J., *Möbel des Jugendstils. Sammlung des Österreichischen Museums für angewandte Kunst in Wien*, München 1988, 59.

[35] Zu Hans Neumann vgl. Doosry, Yasmin (Bearb.), *Plakativ! Produktwerbung im Plakat*, Ausst.kat. Germanisches Nationalmuseum Nürnberg, Ostfildern 2009, 548 (mit weiteren Literaturangaben).

[36] Vgl. Zur Westen 1921 (s. Anm. 7), S. 52 f. 1813/1814 wurde ein satirisches Napoleon-Porträt als Neujahrsgruß vertrieben, das in mehreren Varianten nach der Völkerschlacht bei Leipzig im Oktober 1813 erschienen war, vgl. Langemeyer, Gerhard (Hg.), *Bild als Waffe. Mittel und Motive der Karikatur in fünf Jahrhunderten*, Ausst.kat. Wilhelm Busch-Museum Hannover, München 1984, Nr. 126.

[39] On the production of (luxury) paper as well as on the new printing techniques in the 19th century cf. Böhmer 1978 (see note 8), 99 f.; Pieske 1983 (see note 25), 35—41, 250–253; Pieske/Kuschert 1987 (see note 26), 4–6; Giuriato 2008 (see note 30), 2.

to the latest principles of advertising art. Innovative printing techniques such as lithography, chromolithography, collotype, and halftone printing as well as the development of groundbreaking machines for the economical manufacture and refinement of paper facilitated the production of a wider range of occasion cards and letter paper as reasonably priced, mass-produced goods. Moreover, these technical innovations superseded the manual labor of the printing shop and home-worker's quarters.[39]

108
Atelier Hans Neumann
Plakat für Briefpapier und Kuverts der Marke Ibus
Wien, 1924
Auftraggeber: Julius Baumgarten & Söhne
Lithografie
Poster for Letter Paper and Envelopes by the Brand Ibus
Vienna, 1924
Client: Julius Baumgarten & Söhne
Lithograph
1 260 x 950 mm
Pl 121, Schenkung donation 1929

19. Jahrhunderts am Medienspektakel mit optischen Phänomenen und bewegten Bildern ins häusliche Umfeld transportiert. Sie sind außerdem Zeugnisse eines neuen Konsumverhaltens in der zweiten Hälfte des 19. Jahrhunderts, in der die repräsentative Selbstdarstellung die vornehme Bescheidenheit der Biedermeierzeit ablöst. In diesem Kontext belegen luxuriöse Gelegenheitskarten und Briefpapiere mit ihrer reichen Ausstattung und der Imitation teurer Materialien wie Gold und Silber, Porzellan und Spitze einen tief greifenden Geschmackswandel, den man Ende des 19. Jahrhunderts wieder infrage stellte. Darüber hinaus verdeutlichen sie das Bedürfnis weiter Bevölkerungskreise, ihre soziale Stellung über den Warenkonsum zu definieren. Im Kampf um diese KundInnen und um neue Absatzmärkte entdeckten Gewerbetreibende, Fabrikanten und Dienstleister Korrespondenzbogen als wirksame Werbeträger, deren Erscheinungsbild sie fortlaufend den jeweils aktuellen Grundsätzen der Reklamekunst anpassten. Innovative Druckverfahren wie die Lithografie, Chromolithografie, der Licht- und Rasterdruck sowie die Entwicklung wegweisender Maschinen für die wirtschaftliche Herstellung und Veredelung von Papier förderten die Produktion einer breiten Palette von Gelegenheitskarten und Briefpapieren als preiswerte Massenware. Die technischen Neuerungen lösten überdies die Handarbeit in den Offizinen und den Unterkünften der HeimarbeiterInnen ab.[37]

37 Zur Herstellung von (Luxus-)Papier sowie zu neuen Druckverfahren im 19. Jahrhundert vgl. Böhmer 1978 (s. Anm. 8), 99 f.; Pieske 1983 (s. Anm. 23), 35–41, 250–253; Pieske/Kuschert 1987 (s. Anm. 24), 4–6; Giuriato 2008 (s. Anm. 28), 2.

"BIEDERMEIER WISHES"

In 1896 the *Wiener-Congress* exhibition took place at the Imperial Royal Austrian Museum of Art and Industry (ÖMKI); it triggered in the contemporary generation a longstanding, profound interest in their grandparents' furnishing style and arts and crafts. It led to the language of form of the Wiener Werkstätte, which was established in 1903 and found therein its very own, future-oriented answer to French art nouveau. Even Gustav E. Pazaurek's publication *Biedermeier-Wünsche*, released in 1908 and purchased by the museum's library in the same year[1], resulted from this interest. This art historian who was skilled at identifying lapses of taste in arts and crafts[2] testified to the utmost quality of the greeting cards, particularly the Viennese examples: "Surely no one would deny that they should be considered superior to similar kinds of graphic products—such as visiting cards, invitations, ex libris, menus, etc."[3]

The first examples and indeed the best of their kind entered the collection of the ÖMKI in 1914, having been acquired from the Technologisches Gewerbemuseum: twelve *Kunstbillets*[4] by Johann Joseph Endletsberger (1779–1856). His colorized collages—elaborately produced using mother-of-pearl, enamel, mirrors, and embossed gilt paper—are signed and set in a frame of thin sheet brass (ill. 111, 112, 114). As such, they are not just greeting cards, but also artistic wall decorations. These *Kunstbillets* were distributed to broader sections of society via imitations of varying quality—Endletsberger's only competitor worth naming was Joseph Riedl (d. 1830) (ill. 109, 110, 113). Another bundle arrived at the MAK Library and Works on Paper Collectionin 1994 via a bequest and is stored en bloc in a frame for safekeeping.

In 1930 over 270 greeting cards were purchased from Josef Kuderna, a collector from Langenzersdorf, Austria. They show the entire spectrum of design styles used for these cards, which were predominantly exchanged on name days and at the turn of the year: interactive (with pulls and flaps) and folded cards; *Netzkappenkarten*[5]; embossed and stitched cards; tin foil, gelatin, silk, and Atlas silk cards; *Augenkarten*[6] and rebus cards; as well as collages. They were the starting material for Hanna Egger's study *Herrn Biedermeiers Wunschbillet* from 1978, which the then employee and later head of the MAK Library developed into an extensive source book published two years later.[7] In the course of this pursuit, acquisitions from the Viennese antiquarian bookshops Heck and Gilhofer as well as from the Wölfle antiquarian bookshop in Munich were added to the museum's collection. It is from the latter that an example of the truly enchanting *Netzkappenkarten* comes (ill. 121), while from Gilhofer there is one of the so-called apology cards, which came into circulation from 1830 (ill. 126). Bestowing New Year's greetings—coupled with a small donation to the deliverer (ill. 124)—had grown so out of hand that it became possible to make a donation to a charity in order to eschew this custom. However, this solution "halted the thriving development of the greeting card."[8]

[1] Inventoried under BI 14672.

[2] Pazaurek, Gustav E., *Geschmacksverirrungen im Kunstgewerbe. Führer für die neue Abteilung im königl. Landes-Gewerbe-Museum Stuttgart*, Stuttgart 1909.

[3] Pazaurek, Gustav, E., *Biedermeier-Wünsche*, Stuttgart 1908, 11. Translated by Maria Slater.

[4] Card with artistic collage, popular in the early 19th century.

[5] Cards with intricate paper cutting, which can be raised—often to reveal another motif below.

[6] "Eye card," type of transparent card.

[7] Egger, Hanna, *Glückwunschkarten im Biedermeier. Höflichkeit und gesellschaftlicher Zwang*, Munich 1980.

[8] Pazaurek 1908 (see note 3), 24. Translated by Maria Slater.

„BIEDERMEIER-WÜNSCHE"

1896 fand im k. k. Österreichischen Museum für Kunst und Industrie (ÖMKI) die *Wiener-Congress-Ausstellung* statt und löste eine jahrelange, intensive Beschäftigung mit dem Einrichtungsstil und Kunsthandwerk der Großväter-Generation aus. Sie führte zur Formensprache der 1903 gegründeten Wiener Werkstätte, die damit eine ureigene und zukunftsweisende Antwort auf den französischen Jugendstil fand. Auch Gustav E. Pazaureks Publikation *Biedermeier-Wünsche*, erschienen 1908 und im selben Jahr von der Bibliothek des Museums erworben[1], resultiert aus dieser Beschäftigung. Der Kunsthistoriker, der sich auf *Geschmacksverirrungen im Kunstgewerbe*[2] verstand, bescheinigte den Wunschkarten, namentlich den Wiener Exemplaren, höchste Qualität: „Daß sie unter den graphischen Erzeugnissen ähnlicher Art – wie Besuchskarten, Einladungen, Ex-libris, Menükarten usw. – an die Spitze zu stellen sind, wird wohl niemand leugnen."[3]

Die ersten Exemplare und gleich die besten ihrer Art kamen 1914 durch Übernahme aus dem Technologischen Gewerbemuseum in die Sammlung des ÖMKI: zwölf Kunstbillets von Johann Joseph Endletsberger (1779–1856). Seine kolorierten, unter Verwendung von Perlmutt, Email, Spiegeln und geprägtem Goldpapier aufwendig hergestellten Collagen sind signiert und mit Rahmen aus dünnem Messingblech eingefasst (Abb. 111, 112, 114). Damit waren sie nicht nur Grußkarten, sondern auch künstlerischer Wandschmuck. Durch Nachahmungen unterschiedlichster Qualität – einzig nennenswerter Konkurrent Endletsbergers war Joseph Riedl (gest. 1830) – fanden die Kunstbillets ihre Verbreitung (Abb. 109, 110, 113). Ein weiteres Konvolut gelangte 1994 durch eine Verlassenschaft in die MAK-Bibliothek und Kunstblättersammlung und wird als Ganzes in einem Rahmen verwahrt. 1930 wurden über 270 Glückwunschkarten von Josef Kuderna, einem Sammler aus Langenzersdorf, angekauft. Sie zeigen die ganze Bandbreite an Gestaltungsweisen dieser vor allem zum Namenstag und Jahreswechsel überbrachten Billets: Zug-, Klapp- und Faltkarten, Netzkappenkarten, Präge- und Nadelstichkarten, Stanniol-, Gelatine-, Seiden- und Atlaskarten, Augen- und Rebuskarten sowie Collagen. Sie waren Ausgangsmaterial für Hanna Eggers Studie *Herrn Biedermeiers Wunschbillet* von 1978, die die damalige Mitarbeiterin und spätere Leiterin der MAK-Bibliothek zu einem umfangreichen, zwei Jahre später publizierten Quellenwerk ausbaute.[4] Im Zuge dieser Beschäftigung wurde die Sammlung des Museums um Ankäufe aus den Wiener Antiquariaten Heck und Gilhofer sowie dem Münchner Antiquariat Wölfle erweitert. Von letzterem stammt ein Exemplar der im wahrsten Sinn zauberhaften Netzkappenkarten (Abb. 121), von Gilhofer eine der sogenannten Enthebungskarten, die ab 1830 in Umlauf kamen (Abb. 126). Das Verschenken von Neujahrswünschen, verbunden mit einem Obolus an den Überbringer (Abb. 124), hatte derart überhandgenommen, dass man sich mit einer Spende an eine wohltätige Organisation freikaufen konnte. Damit aber war „die gedeihliche Weiterentwicklung der Wunschkarten unterbunden".[5]

[1] Inventarisiert unter BI 14672.

[2] Pazaurek, Gustav E., *Geschmacksverirrungen im Kunstgewerbe. Führer für die neue Abteilung im königl. Landes-Gewerbe-Museum Stuttgart*, Stuttgart 1909.

[3] Pazaurek, Gustav, E., *Biedermeier-Wünsche*, Stuttgart 1908, 11.

[4] Egger, Hanna, *Glückwunschkarten im Biedermeier. Höflichkeit und gesellschaftlicher Zwang*, München 1980.

[5] Pazaurek 1908 (s. Anm. 3), 24.

109
Joseph Riedl
Kunstbillet
Wien, vor 1830
Geprägtes Goldpapier, Krepp- und
Glanzpapier, Gouache
Card with Artistic Collage
Vienna, before 1830
Embossed gilt paper, crepe paper and
shiny paper, gouache
67 x 82 mm
KI 7946-1-3, Schenkung donation from
Technologisches Gewerbemuseum 1914

110
Anonym Anonymous
Kunstbillet
Wien, 1820–1830
Geprägtes Gold- und Glanzpapier, koloriert;
Gaze; Messingblech
Card with Artistic Collage
Vienna, 1820–1830
Embossed gilt paper and shiny paper,
colored; gauze; brass sheet
70 x 90 mm
KI 14135-2, Ankauf purchased from
Antiquariat Wölfle 1980

111
Johann Joseph Endletsberger
Kunstbillet
Wien, 1820–1830
Geprägtes Messingblech; Glanz- u. Goldpapier,
koloriert; Perlmutt, Spiegelglas
Card with Artistic Collage
Vienna, 1820–1830
Embossed brass sheet; shiny paper and gilt paper, colored;
mother-of-pearl, mirror glass
95 x 80 mm
KI 7946-7, Schenkung donation from
Technologisches Gewerbemuseum 1914

112
Johann Joseph Endletsberger
Kunstbillet
Wien, 1820–1830
Geprägtes Messingblech; Krepp- u. Goldpapier, koloriert;
Email, Perlmutt, Deckfarbe
Card with Artistic Collage
Vienna, 1820–1830
Embossed brass sheet; crepe paper and gilt paper, colored;
enamel, mother-of-pearl, coating paint
95 x 80 mm
KI 7946-8, Schenkung donation from
Technologisches Gewerbemuseum 1914

113
J. S.
Kunstbillet
Wien, 1830
Geprägtes Messingblech;
Krepp- u. Goldpapier, koloriert
Card with Artistic Collage
Vienna, 1830
Embossed brass sheet;
crepe paper and gilt paper, colored
82 x 65 mm
KI 7946-1-1, Schenkung donation from
Technologisches Gewerbemuseum 1914

114
Johann Joseph Endletsberger
Kunstbillet
Wien, 1820–1830
Geprägtes Messingblech; Krepp- u.
Goldpapier, koloriert; Perlmutt, Deckfarbe
Card with Artistic Collage
Vienna, 1820–1830
Embossed brass sheet; crepe paper and
gilt paper, colored; mother-of-pearl, coating paint
85 x 95 mm
KI 7946-5, Schenkung donation from
Technologisches Gewerbemuseum 1914

115
Anonym Anonymous
Hebelzugkarte
Wien, um 1811
Ausführung: Johann Adamek
Radierung, koloriert
Pull-Tab Card
Vienna, ca. 1811
Execution: Johann Adamek
Etching, colored
100 x 80 mm
KI 14137-4, Ankauf purchased from
Antiquariat Heck 1980

116
Anonym Anonymous
Prägekarte in Bisquitmanier
Prag, 1805–1810
Ausführung: Johann Seidan
Tüll, Seide, Prägedruck
Embossed Card in Bisque Style
Prague, 1805–1810
Execution: Johann Seidan
Tulle, silk, embossing
79 x 90 mm
KI 8760-6, Ankauf purchased from
Josef Kuderna 1930

117
Anonym Anonymous
Transparentkarte (sog. Augenkarte)
Wien, 1805–1820
Radierung, koloriert
See-Through Card (so-called Eye Card)
Vienna, 1805–1820
Etching, colored
60 x 98 mm
KI 8765-8, Ankauf purchased from
Josef Kuderna 1930

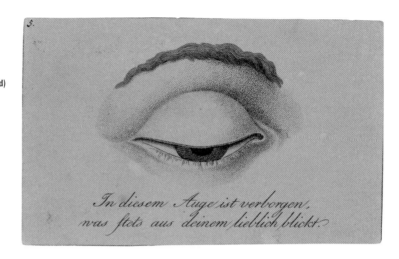

118
Anonym Anonymous
Hebelzugkarte
Wien, um 1815
Ausführung: Anton Leitner
Kupferstich, koloriert
Pull-Tab Card
Vienna, ca. 1815
Execution: Anton Leitner
Copperplate engraving, colored
99 x 64 mm
KI 8765-12, Ankauf purchased from Josef Kuderna 1930

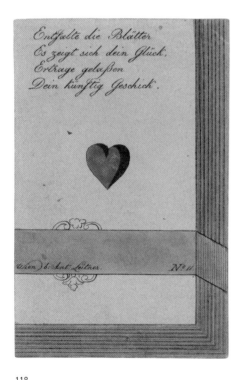

119
Anonym Anonymous
Durchsteckkarte
Wien, 1810–1815
Ausführung: Heinrich Friedrich Müller
Radierung, koloriert
Tuck-In Card
Vienna, 1810–1815
Execution: Heinrich Friedrich Müller
Etching, colored
95 x 74 mm
KI 8765-10, Ankauf purchased from Josef Kuderna 1930

120
Anonym Anonymous
Teilungsbillet
Berlin, 1810–1815
Ausführung: J. G. Hasselberg
Lithografie
Pull-Apart Card
Berlin, 1810–1815
Execution: J. G. Hasselberg
Lithograph
125 x 197 mm
KI 8776-8, Ankauf purchased
from Josef Kuderna 1930

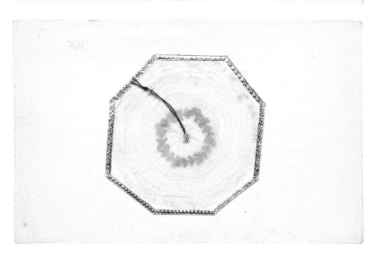

121
Anonym Anonymous
Netzkappenbillet
Wien, gewidmet am 25.12.1841
Geprägte Goldborte, Seidenpapier, Seidenfaden,
Deckfarben
Card with Raisable Paper Cutting
Vienna, dedicated on 25 Dec 1841
Embossed gold border, silk paper, silk thread,
coating paint
100 x 165 mm
KI 14134-1, Ankauf purchased
from Antiquariat Wölfle 1980

122
Anonym Anonymous
Prägekarte
Prag, um 1815
Ausführung: Johann Seidan
Satin, Tüll, Silberpapier u. Goldfolie, geprägt
Embossed Card
Prague, ca. 1815
Execution: Johann Seidan
Satin, tulle, silver paper and gold leaf, embossed
115 x 80 mm
KI 8779-5, Ankauf purchased from
Josef Kuderna 1930

123
Anonym Anonymous
Collagebillet
Österreich, 1790–1810
Eichenblatt, Federn, Papier, koloriert
Collage Card
Austria, 1790–1810
Oak leaf, feathers, paper, colored
135 x 75 mm
KI 8761-8, Ankauf purchased from
Josef Kuderna 1930

Mein Wunsch ist zwar einfach, doch hat er Gehirn,
Er lautet: nie fehle es Ihnen an Zwirn.

124
Anonym Anonymous
Bildbillet
Österreich, 1810–1820
Radierung, koloriert
Illustrated Card
Austria, 1810–1820
Etching, colored
82 x 66 mm
KI 8778-7, Ankauf purchased from
Josef Kuderna 1930

125
Anonym Anonymous
Rebuskarte
Österreich, um 1805
Radierung, koloriert
Rebus Card
Austria, ca. 1805
Etching, colored
46 x 60 mm
KI 8764-1, Ankauf purchased from
Josef Kuderna 1930

126
Franz Kollarz
Glückwunsch-Enthebungskarte für das Jahr 1849
Wien, 1848
Prägedruck, Lithografie
New Year's Apology Card 1849
Vienna, 1848
Embossing, lithograph
128 x 178 mm
KI 14141-2, Ankauf purchased from
Antiquariat Gilhofer 1980

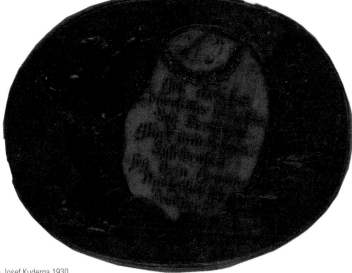

127
Anonym Anonymous
Gelatinebillet
Österreich, um 1820
Gelatinefolie, geprägt
Gelatine Card
Austria, ca. 1820
Gelatine foil, embossed
75 x 95 mm
KI 8761-1-1, Ankauf purchased from Josef Kuderna 1930

GELEGENHEITSKARTEN AUS DEM 20. JAHRHUNDERT

Während die Biedermeier-Wünsche wort- und bildreich Freundschaft und Glück für die Beschenkten beschworen, wurden in der Folgezeit die Anlässe, zu denen man Grüße versandte, immer bestimmender. Die Karten wünschten nun „Fröhliche Ostern" bzw. Weihnachten oder ein „Glückliches Neujahr", zeigten eine Verlobung oder Heirat an, äußerten Dank oder „Herzliches Beileid". Die knappen Botschaften und einschlägigen Motive reizten dabei viele KünstlerInnen, dem Sujet ihren eigenen Ausdruck zu verleihen. In Wien etablierte sich die „Künstler-Postkarte" seit 1895 und fand mit über 1 000 Motiven der Wiener Werkstätte (WW) zwischen 1907 und 1920 ihren Höhepunkt.[1] Zu deren wichtigsten EntwerferInnen zählte Mela Koehler, die auch für den Postkartenverlag Brüder Kohn arbeitete (Abb. 135). Im Ersten Weltkrieg erschien hier eine Serie Propagandakarten, in der Koehler politische Botschaften mit der WW-Ästhetik verband und in anrührende Kinderszenen einbettete (Abb. 134).

Sie kam 1930 durch Schenkung in die Sammlung des Österreichischen Museums für Kunst und Industrie (ÖMKI), zu einer Zeit, als Hans Ankwicz-Kleehoven die Bibliothek leitete und sich der Gebrauchsgrafik besonders annahm. Er ließ für sich selbst etliche Visitenkarten, Exlibris, Einladungen sowie Gelegenheitskarten (Abb. 139) anfertigen und stiftete sie dem Museum. Zugleich erwirkte er Schenkungen diverser Kunstschaffender, denen er als Sammler sowie durch seine Arbeit für das Künstlerlexikon Thieme-Becker verbunden war, etwa Hubert Woyty-Wimmer (Abb. 138), Maria Likarz (Abb. 141) oder Carl Krenek (Abb. S. 109). In diese Zeit fällt auch das Legat des Verlegers Artur Wolf (1887–1932), der dem ÖMKI seine umfangreiche Exlibris-Sammlung hinterließ. Darunter befindet sich eine Kassette mit Gelegenheitsgrafiken, die die technisch aufwendigsten Beispiele dieses Kapitels darstellen: Es sind vorwiegend von deutschen KünstlerInnen geschaffene Radierungen aus der ersten Hälfte des 20. Jahrhunderts, die sich weniger als Gebrauchs- denn als Sammlungsgut verstanden. Der Österreicher Kurt Libesny ist mit einem Glückwunsch-Billet Rudolf von Höfkens vertreten (Abb. 132), dessen Visitenkarten-Sammlung 1930 an das Museum gelangte (s. S. 218).

Die als Holzschnitt gefertigte Vermählungsanzeige des WW-Künstlers Dagobert Peche (Abb. 133) entstammt einem Konvolut, das 1925 aus den Mitteln der sogenannten „Tauschaktion" der Witwe Nelly Peche abgekauft wurde. Diese Art der Objekt- bzw. Geldmittelbeschaffung – Doubletten oder Objekte aus dem Depot wurden verkauft oder getauscht – war bis in die frühen 1960er Jahre üblich und wurde mit dem methodischen Ausbau der Sammlungen begründet.[2]

Im Nachlass Joseph Binders hat sich eine Reihe von Weihnachtsgrüßen erhalten, die der Grafiker vor allem für private Zwecke, aber auch als Art Director der US Navy Recruiting Stations entwarf, eine Funktion, die er von 1948 bis 1963 innehatte. Sterne und Strahlen sind dabei die bevorzugten Motive (Abb. 144). Sie erfahren über die Jahre eine beständige Reduktion und sind zuletzt nur mehr Andeutungen aus geometrischen Formen (Abb. 145) – eine subtile Anknüpfung an Binders Wiener Wurzeln (vgl. Abb. 137).

1 Schmuttermeier, Elisabeth/Witt-Dörring, Christian, *Postcards of the Wiener Werkstätte. A Catalogue Raisonné*, Neue Galerie, New York 2010.

2 Judtmann, Fritz, „Der ‚Hoftiteltaxfond' und das Kunstgewerbemuseum", in: *Alte und moderne Kunst* (X) 78 1965, 23.

20TH-CENTURY OCCASION CARDS

While Biedermeier wishes prayed for the friendship and happiness of their recipients in a wealth of words and images, in the following period the occasions when greetings were sent became increasingly specific. The cards now wished "Happy Easter," "Merry Christmas," or "Happy New Year," announced an engagement or marriage, expressed thanks or "Heartfelt Sympathy." The short messages and pertinent motifs inspired many artists to develop their own approaches to those themes. In Vienna the art postcard became established from 1895 and enjoyed its heyday between 1907 and 1920 when the Wiener Werkstätte produced over 1 000 motifs.[1] Among their most important designers was Mela Koehler, who also worked for the postcard publisher Brüder Kohn (ill. 135). During the First World War, a series of propaganda cards was printed in which Koehler combined political messages with WW aesthetics and embedded them in touching scenes of children (ill. 134). This series entered the collection of the Austrian Museum of Art and Industry (ÖMKI) via a donation in 1930, at a time when Hans Ankwicz-Kleehoven ran the library and paid particular attention to ephemera. He had quite a number of visiting cards, ex libris, invitations, as well as occasion cards (ill. 139) made and endowed them to the museum. At the same time, he effected donations from diverse artists with whom he was associated as a collector as well as through his work for the Thieme-Becker dictionary of artists, such as Hubert Woyty-Wimmer (ill. 138), Maria Likarz (ill. 141), and Carl Krenek (ill. p. 109). It was also during this period that the bequest of publisher Artur Wolf (1887–1932) entered the museum's collection: he had left the ÖMKI his extensive ex libris collection. This included a box with occasion graphics, which comprise the most technically elaborate examples of this chapter: they are predominantly etchings created by German artists in the first half of the 20th century, which were understood less as commodities than as collector's items. The Austrian Kurt Libesny is represented with a greeting card from Rudolf von Höfken (ill. 132), whose visiting card collection arrived at the museum in 1930 (see p. 219).

The marriage announcement produced as a woodcut by WW artist Dagobert Peche (ill. 133) comes from a bundle purchased in 1925 with the funds of his widow Nelly Peche's so-called "exchange event." This kind of object or fund exchange—whereby duplicates or objects from a portfolio were sold or exchanged—was common until the early 1960s and was justified as the systematic expansion of collections.[2]

A series of Christmas greetings was preserved in Joseph Binder's estate, which the graphic designer had created mostly for private purposes, but also in his role as the art director of the US Navy Recruiting Stations, an office he held from 1948 to 1963. Stars and rays are his preferred motifs in these works (ill. 144). They consistently reduced over the years, in the last pieces becoming mere suggestions comprised of geometric shapes (ill. 145)—a subtle connection to Binder's Viennese roots (cf. ill. 137).

[1] Schmuttermeier, Elisabeth/Witt-Dörring, Christian, *Postcards of the Wiener Werkstätte. A Catalogue Raisonné*, Neue Galerie, New York 2010.

[2] Judtmann, Fritz, "Der 'Hoftiteltaxfond' und das Kunstgewerbemuseum," in: *Alte und moderne Kunst* (X) 78 1965, 23.

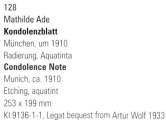

128
Mathilde Ade
Kondolenzblatt
München, um 1910
Radierung, Aquatinta
Condolence Note
Munich, ca. 1910
Etching, aquatint
253 x 199 mm
KI 9136-1-1, Legat bequest from Artur Wolf 1933

129
Walter Helfenbein
Dankesblatt Dr. Walter und Margarete Vogel
Dresden, 1924
Radierung, Aquatinta
Thank-You Note Dr. Walter and Margarete Vogel
Dresden, 1924
Etching, aquatint
219 x 155 mm
KI 9136-13, Legat bequest from Artur Wolf 1933

130
Adolf Kunst
Neujahrskarte Hanns Heeren
München, 1924
Radierung
New Year's Card Hanns Heeren
Munich, 1924
Etching
150 x 118 mm
KI 9136-286, Legat bequest from Artur Wolf 1933

131
Karl Michel
Neujahrskarte Karl Michel
Berlin, 1922
Radierung
New Year's Card Karl Michel
Berlin, 1922
Etching
155 x 119 mm
KI 9136-293, Legat bequest from Artur Wolf 1933

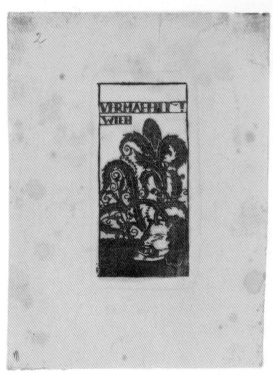

132
Kurt Libesny
Glückwunschkarte Rudolf von Höfken
Wien, um 1910
Radierung, Aquatinta
Greeting Card Rudolf von Höfken
Vienna, ca. 1910
Etching, aquatint
135 x 99 mm
KI 9136-3581, Legat bequest from Artur Wolf 1933

133
Dagobert Peche
Vermählungsanzeige Nelly und Dagobert Peche
Wien, 1911
Holzschnitt
Wedding Announcement Nelly and Dagobert Peche
Vienna, 1911
Woodcut
247 x 185 mm
KI 8402, Ankauf purchased from Nelly Peche 1925

134
Mela Koehler
Propagandapostkarte
Wien, 1914–1915
Ausführung: Postkartenverlag Brüder Kohn
Klischee, Farblithografie
Propaganda Postcard
Vienna, 1914–1915
Execution: Postkartenverlag Brüder Kohn
Cliché, color lithograph
141 x 90 mm
KI 8876-79, Schenkung donation 1930

135
Mela Koehler
Weihnachtspostkarte
Wien, um 1915
Ausführung: Postkartenverlag Brüder Kohn
Klischee
Christmas Postcard
Vienna, ca. 1915
Execution: Postkartenverlag Brüder Kohn
Cliché
138 x 90 mm
KI 8876-106, Schenkung donation 1930

136
Richard Paulus
Neujahrskarte
Prag, 1921
Radierung
New Year's Card
Prague, 1921
Etching
172 x 156 mm
KI 9136-294, Legat bequest from Artur Wolf 1933

137
Rudolf Hancke
Neujahrskarte Chwala's Druck
Wien, 1911
Ausführung: Chwala's Druck
Klischee
New Year's Card Chwala's Druck
Vienna, 1911
Execution: Chwala's Druck
Cliché
159 x 159 mm
KI 8783-4, Ankauf purchased from
Josef Kuderna 1930

138
Hubert Woyty-Wimmer
Osterkarte Hubert Woyty-Wimmer
Wien, 1932
Holzstich
Easter Card Hubert Woyty-Wimmer
Vienna, 1932
Wood engraving
79 x 110 mm
KI 8996-2, Schenkung donation from
Hubert Woyty-Wimmer 1932

9203/3

139
Otto Feil
Neujahrskarte Hans Ankwicz-Kleehoven
Wien, 1926
Linolschnitt
New Year's Card Hans Ankwicz-Kleehoven
Vienna, 1926
Linocut
155 x 104 mm
KI 9203-3, Schenkung donation from Hans Ankwicz-Kleehoven 1937

9061/10

140
Rose Reinhold
Dankeskarte Hans Ankwicz-Kleehoven
Wien, 1933
Holzschnitt, koloriert
Thank-You Card Hans Ankwicz-Kleehoven
Vienna, 1933
Woodcut, colored
104 x 150 mm
KI 9061-10, Schenkung donation from
Rose Reinhold 1933

141
Maria Likarz
**Entwurf für eine Weihnachtskarte
der Wiener Werkstätte**
Wien, um 1928
Bleistift, Deckfarben
**Design for a Christmas Card from
the Wiener Werkstätte**
Vienna, ca. 1928
Pencil, coating paint
230 x 147 mm
KI 12281-4, Schenkung donation from
Alfred Hofmann 1955

142
Lois Gaigg
Neujahrskarte Lois Gaigg
Wien, 1936
Klischee
New Year's Card Lois Gaigg
Vienna, 1936
Cliché
96 x 119 mm
KI 13441, Schenkung donation from
Ilka Franke 1959

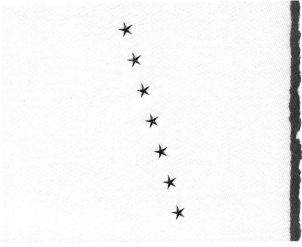

143
Joseph Binder
Weihnachtskarte mit Kuvert
Mr. & Mrs. Joseph Binder
New York, um 1960
Siebdruck
Christmas Card with Envelope
Mr. & Mrs. Joseph Binder
New York, ca. 1960
Screen printing
121 x 164 mm
KI 14145-917-10, Legat bequest from
Carla und and Joseph Binder 1995/96

144
Joseph Binder
Weihnachtskarte der US Navy
New York, um 1950
Offsetdruck
Christmas Card from the US Navy
New York, ca. 1950
Offset printing
159 x 115 mm
KI 14145-917-7-1, Legat bequest from
Carla und and Joseph Binder 1995/96

145
Joseph Binder
Probedruck für eine Weihnachtskarte
New York, um 1960
Siebdruck
Test Print for a Christmas Card
New York, ca. 1960
Screen printing
170 x 369 mm
KI 14145-919-31-2, Legat bequest from
Carla und and Joseph Binder 1995/96

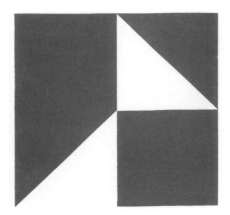

BRIEFPAPIER VON HUGO GERARD STRÖHL UM 1880

Der Jahresbericht des k. k. Österreichischen Museums für Kunst und Industrie vermerkt für das Jahr 1910: „Als Geschenke erhielt die Bibliothek im verflossenen Jahre unter anderen […] von Herrn Hugo Gerard Ströhl in Mödling einen Sammelband mit 953 Blättern, Abdrücke der graphischen Arbeiten Ströhls aus den Jahren 1876 bis 1885."[1] Der 1851 in Wels geborene Zeichner, Illustrator und Heraldiker (gest. 1919) war dem Museum in mehrfacher Hinsicht verbunden. Er studierte ab 1873 an der sich damals noch im Haus befindenden Kunstgewerbeschule bei Ferdinand Laufberger (der seinerseits an der künstlerischen Ausstattung des Gebäudes am Stubenring umfassend beteiligt war) und legte dort 1877 die Lehramtsprüfung ab. Zwischen 1899 und 1913 verfasste Ströhl zahlreiche Artikel für die museumseigene Zeitschrift *Kunst und Kunsthandwerk* zu seinem Spezialgebiet Heraldik.

Das Musterbuch dokumentiert seine Arbeit als selbstständiger Entwerfer und ist eine reiche Quelle an Beispielen historistischer Gebrauchsgrafik. Es enthält diverse Drucksorten, sorgfältig aufkaschiert und mit Angaben zu Techniken und Herstellern versehen. Einen großen Teil nehmen Briefpapiere, Karten und Umschläge ein, entworfen für Max Krause in Berlin, Röder, Baus & Comp. in Wien und M. Mayer in Koblenz. Krause war der große Innovator auf dem Gebiet der Papierausstattung (ein Begriff, der auf ihn zurückgeht). Er erfand die Briefpapier-Kassette, worin die zuvor einzeln verkauften Bögen und Kuverts in gleicher Anzahl (z. B. 25:25) sicher und edel verpackt wurden. Die Kassetten erfreuten sich großer Beliebtheit, wurden aufbewahrt und weiterverwendet, und Krause etablierte damit eine Marke, die in einem späteren Slogan – „Schreibste mir, schreibste ihr, schreibste auf M.-K.-Papier!" – werbewirksam Ausdruck fand.[2]

Ströhl gestaltete die Pappkassetten als Miniaturmöbel im Stil der Neorenaissance und stellte mit Kommode, Kasten und Buffet, Tisch und Stuhl, Ofen, Spiegel und Uhr gleich ein ganzes Interieur bereit, ergänzt um ein Taubenhaus, das den Bezug zum Inhalt wieder sinnfällig macht (Abb. 146–148).

Die Etiketten für die einfache Schachtelform fallen oft noch repräsentativer aus. Ihre Ornamentik orientiert sich an der Buchgestaltung, wobei Medaillons mit Schriftlogo, Markenzeichen oder dem Signet der Wiener Weltausstellung 1873 das Produkt zusätzlich nobilieren (Abb. 151). Von besonderer Feinheit und technischer Qualität sind die Drucksorten für die Trauerkorrespondenz. Ströhl entwarf Briefpapier und Kassetten für Max Krause sowie Trauerbogen für die 1880 gegründete Firma Röder, Baus & Comp. (Abb. 149). Schließlich enthält das Musterbuch diverse Motiv-Briefpapiere, deren Schachtel- oder Hüllendekore die Gestaltung des Inhalts ankündigen (Abb.150, 152). Wie Ströhl in seiner Einleitung bemerkt, illustrieren auch sie den damals „herrschenden Geschmack im Kreise der Besteller und Abnehmer" (Abb. S. 109).

[1] *Jahresbericht des k. k. Österr. Museums für Kunst und Industrie für das Jahr 1910*, Wien 1911, 8.

[2] Schmidt-Bachem, Heinz, *Aus Papier. Eine Kultur- und Wirtschaftsgeschichte der Papier verarbeitenden Industrie in Deutschland*, Berlin/Boston 2011, 377 f.

LETTER PAPER BY HUGO GERARD STRÖHL FROM CA. 1880

The annual report of the Imperial Royal Austrian Museum of Art and Industry for the year 1910
notes: "As gifts, the Library received over the past year among other things [...] from Mr. Hugo
Gerard Ströhl in Mödling, Austria, an omnibus volume with 953 sheets, copies of Ströhl's graphic
works from the years 1876 to 1885."[1] Born in Wels, Austria, in 1851, the draftsman, illustrator, and
heraldist (d. 1919) was connected to the museum in a number of ways. From 1873 he had studied
under Ferdinand Laufberger (who for his part was deeply involved in the artistic decor of the building
on Stubenring) at the School of Arts and Crafts, which at that time was still housed in the museum,
and passed his teaching qualification there in 1877. Between 1899 and 1913 Ströhl wrote numerous
articles on his specialty—heraldry—for the museum's own magazine *Kunst und Kunsthandwerk*.
The catalog of work documents his profession as a self-employed designer and is a rich source
of examples of historical ephemera. It contains diverse printed matter, carefully mounted and
annotated with information about techniques and producers. A large proportion comprises letter
paper, cards, and envelopes designed for Max Krause in Berlin; Röder, Baus & Comp. in Vienna;
and M. Mayer in Koblenz, Germany. Krause was a great innovator in the field of paper provisions
(indeed, the term in German, *Papierausstattung*, can be traced back to him). He invented the boxed
letter-writing set, in which the sheets and envelopes—previously sold loose—were packaged
safely and stylishly in equal number (e.g. 25:25). These boxes gained huge popularity, were kept
and reused, and Krause even established a brand dedicated to them, which found expression and
advertising appeal in a later slogan: "Write to me, write to her, write on MK paper!"[2]
Ströhl designed these cardboard boxes as miniature pieces of furniture in the neo-Renaissance style
and supplied almost an entire interior with a chest of drawers, wardrobe, and buffet, table and chair,
oven, mirror, and clock, in addition to a dovecote, with which the reference to its contents once
again became evident (ill. 146–148). The labels for the simpler box shape are often even more
ostentatious. Their ornamentation is aligned with book design, with medallions—featuring a written
logo, trademark, or the signet of the 1873 Vienna world's fair—additionally ennobling the product
(ill. 151). The print materials for correspondence related to a death are of particularly fine
technical quality. Ströhl designed letter paper and boxes for Max Krause as well as paper with
black borders for the company Röder, Baus & Comp., which had been founded in 1880 (ill. 149).
Finally, the catalog of work contains diverse kinds of letter paper with motifs, whose box or wrapper
decorations declare the design of their contents (ill. 150, 152). As Ströhl notes in his introduction,
these items also illustrate the then "prevailing taste within the circle of purchasers and customers"
(ill. p. 109).

[1] *Jahresbericht des k. k. Österr. Museums für Kunst und Industrie für das Jahr 1910*, Vienna 1911, 8. Translated by Maria Slater.

[2] Schmidt-Bachem, Heinz, *Aus Papier. Eine Kultur- und Wirtschaftsgeschichte der Papier verarbeitenden Industrie in Deutschland*, Berlin/Boston 2011, 377f.

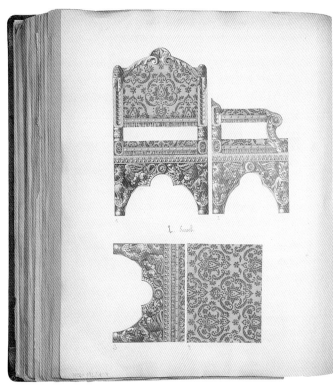

146
Hugo Gerard Ströhl
Etiketten für eine Briefpapierkassette
in Form eines Sessels
Berlin, um 1880
Ausführung: Max Krause
Chromolithografie
Labels for a Letter Paper Box
in the shape of an armchair
Berlin, ca. 1880
Execution: Max Krause
Chromolithograph
340 x 285 mm
KI 7752-192-1, Schenkung donation from
Hugo Gerard Ströhl 1910

147
Hugo Gerard Ströhl
Etiketten für eine Briefpapierkassette
in Form einer Kommode
Berlin, um 1880
Ausführung: Max Krause
Chromolithografie
Labels for a Letter Paper Box
in the shape of a chest of drawers
Berlin, ca.1880
Execution: Max Krause
Chromolithograph
340 x 285 mm
KI 7752-191, Schenkung donation from
Hugo Gerard Ströhl 1910

148
Hugo Gerard Ströhl
Etikett für eine Briefpapierkassette
in Form eines Taubenhauses
Berlin, um 1880
Ausführung: Max Krause
Lithografie
Labels for a Letter Paper Box
in the shape of a dovecote
Berlin, ca. 1880
Execution: Max Krause
Lithograph
215 x 142 mm
KI 7752-212-2, Schenkung donation from
Hugo Gerard Ströhl 1910

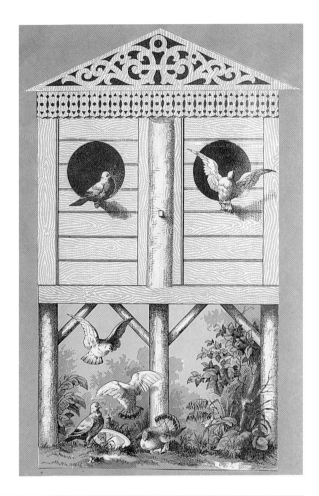

149
Hugo Gerard Ströhl
Trauerbogen
Wien, 1880–1885
Ausführung: Röder, Baus & Comp.
Lithografie
Mourning Paper
Vienna, 1880–1885
Execution: Röder, Baus & Comp.
Lithograph
232 x 291 mm
KI 7752-132, Schenkung donation from
Hugo Gerard Ströhl 1910

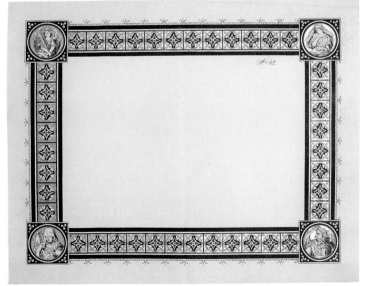

150
Hugo Gerard Ströhl
Etikett für eine Briefpapierkassette
Wien, 1880–1885
Ausführung: Röder, Baus & Comp.
Lithografie
Labels for a Letter Paper Box
Vienna, 1880–1885
Execution: Röder, Baus & Comp.
Lithograph
158 x 215 mm
KI 7752-243, Schenkung donation from
Hugo Gerard Ströhl 1910

151
Hugo Gerard Ströhl
Etikett für eine Briefpapierkassette
Berlin, 1876–1877
Ausführung: Max Krause
Klischee
Labels for a Letter Paper Box
Berlin, 1876–1877
Execution: Max Krause
Cliché
146 x 162 mm
KI 7752-160, Schenkung donation from
Hugo Gerard Ströhl 1910

152
Hugo Gerard Ströhl
Acht Briefbögen mit figurativen Vignetten
Wien, 1880–1885
Ausführung: Röder, Baus & Comp.
Strichätzung
Eight Sheets of Writing Paper with Figurative Vignettes
Vienna, 1880–1885
Execution: Röder, Baus & Comp.
Line etching
Je 149 x 97 mm each
KI 7752-245, Schenkung donation from Hugo Gerard Ströhl 1910

GESCHÄFTSPAPIER AUS DEM 20. JAHRHUNDERT

Im Jahr 2008 erwarb die MAK-Bibliothek und Kunstblättersammlung Teile des Archivs der 1898 gegründeten Buch- und Steindruckerei August Chwala. Über 1.400 Druckerzeugnisse geben einen Überblick über die Produktpalette aus acht Jahrzehnten – vom Aufkleber bis zum Plakat. Ihre moderne Ausrichtung und der hohe Qualitätsanspruch machten die Firma zur Anlaufstelle der Wiener Künstlerschaft und ließen sie schnell reüssieren. In einer Anzeige der Zeitschrift *Gebrauchsgraphik* wurde 1927 auf diese Entwicklung zurückgeblickt: Die ständige Erweiterung des Unternehmens, das 1911 ein eigenes Haus in der Zieglergasse 61 bezog, sowie internationale Preise (Pariser Weltausstellung 1900, Bugra – Internationale Ausstellung für Buchgewerbe und Graphik 1914) wiesen auf einen Erfolg, den man ausdrücklich Künstlern wie Koloman Moser, Josef Hoffmann und Otto Wagner zu verdanken wusste.[1] Deren Unterstützung setzte zugleich die Aufgeschlossenheit des Firmengründers voraus, der nach einer Setzerlehre in Prag seine Kenntnisse u.a. in Deutschland, der Schweiz und Italien erweitert hatte.[2] 1892 verfasste August Chwala (1857–1931) einen Artikel „Ueber die alte und neue Richtung im Accidenzsatze" und hob darin das moderne amerikanische Grafikdesign hervor, das den Fokus auf die Hauptsache lege und dennoch durch Effekte besteche.[3] Nicht nur stilistisch, sondern auch technisch blickte er „Vorwärts!" (so das Schlusswort seines Artikels) und arbeitete relativ früh mit dem Offset-Druckverfahren.

Das Firmen-Briefpapier aus der Mustersammlung von Chwala's Druck liefert einen Querschnitt seiner besten Gestaltungsformen. Es zeigt die klassische Repräsentation mit der Darstellung des Firmengebäudes im Kopf um 1900 genauso wie um 1912 und 1930, jeweils im Zeitstil interpretiert (Abb. 155, 156, 158). Alternativ werden bestimmte Produkte beworben (Auto, Film, Stahlrohrmöbel) oder es stehen ein Ornament, das Signet oder die Schrift im Vordergrund. Vor allem mit letzteren Mitteln gelangen klare Lösungen; sie stammen von Künstlern wie Ernst Lichtblau, Julius Klinger und Hans Neumann, der sein Markenzeichen gleichsam auf den Punkt brachte (Abb. 162, 164, 168). Chwalas Signet – eine aus dem Namen gebildete Rosenblüte – wird Koloman Moser zugeschrieben und entstand ca. 1909; es war bis Anfang der 1950er Jahre im Einsatz (Abb. 161).

In Zusammenarbeit mit Moser und Hoffmann fertigte Chwala's Druck das berühmte Arbeitsprogramm der Wiener Werkstätte sowie deren Papierausstattung zwischen 1905 und 1907 (Abb. 165). In den späten 1920er Jahren wurden die Drucksachen von Maria Likarz gestaltet und vermutlich von der WW selbst produziert (Abb. 166, 167). Sie zeigen die Verbindung von geometrischem Jugendstil und Art Déco und ergänzen den Schwarz-Weiß-Kontrast um die rote Farbe – ein (nicht nur) in der Wiener Grafikszene beliebter Dreiklang. Joseph Binder arbeitete vielfach und über Jahre mit dieser Farbstellung (Abb. 153, 154), ebenso Paul Kurt Schwarz, dessen Briefpapiere und -kuverts 2000 in die MAK-Sammlung gelangten (Abb. 169).

[1] *Chwala's Druck*, Anzeige unter Verwendung einer Originalzeichnung von Julius Klinger, in: *Gebrauchsgraphik* (IV) 11 1927, o. S.

[2] Durstmüller, Anton, *500 Jahre Druck in Österreich*, Bd. 2, Wien 1986, 270; siehe auch Bd. 3, Wien 1989, 222 f.

[3] Chwala, August, „Ueber die alte und neue Richtung im Accidenzsatze", in: Faber, Heinrich (Hg.), *Almanach für Buchdruckerei*, Wien 1892, 27–38.

20TH-CENTURY BUSINESS DOCUMENTS

In 2008 the MAK Library and Works on Paper Collection acquired parts of the archive of the August Chwala book and stone printing company, which was founded in 1898. Over 1 400 printed items provide an overview of a product range spanning eight decades—from stickers to posters. Its modern style and high standards of quality made the company the first port of call for Viennese artists and enabled it to quickly gain success. An advertisement in the magazine *Gebrauchsgraphik* looked back on this development in 1927: the constant expansion of the company, which moved into a dedicated building at Zieglergasse 61 in 1911, as well as international awards (Paris world's fair in 1900, the Bugra international book trade and graphic exhibition in 1914) point to a success, which it expressly knew it owed to artists such as Koloman Moser, Josef Hoffmann, and Otto Wagner.[1] Their support simultaneously relied on the open-mindedness of the company's founder, who after completing a typesetting apprenticeship in Prague had added to his skills in Germany, Switzerland, and Italy among other places.[2] In 1892 August Chwala (1857–1931) wrote an article „Ueber die alte und neue Richtung im Accidenzsatze" [On the old and new school of thought in commercial printing] and in it emphasized modern

American graphic design, which focused on the main issue and yet still stood out as a result of its effects.[3] Not just stylistically but also technically, he looked "Onward!" (according to the final word of the article) and worked with the offset printing technique at quite an early stage.

The company letter paper in the sample collection called Chwala's Druck provides a cross section of his best design styles. It shows a classic representation with a depiction of the company building in the letterhead around 1900 just as in 1912 and 1930, in each case reinterpreted in the style of the age (ill. 155, 156, 158). Alternatively, particular products are advertised (car, movie, tubular steel furniture), or an ornament, the signet, or the wording is foregrounded. It was above all with the latter means that the company achieved clear solutions; they come from artists such as Ernst Lichtblau, Julius Klinger, and Hans Neumann, who boiled his trademark down to an essence, as it were (ill. 162, 164, 168). Chwala's signet—a rose blossom formed out of the company name—is ascribed to Koloman Moser and was created in ca. 1909; it was used until the beginning of the 1950s (ill. 161).

In cooperation with Moser and Hoffmann, Chwala's Druck manufactured the famous work program of the Wiener Werkstätte as well as its paper provisions between 1905 and 1907 (ill. 165). In the late 1920s its printed materials were designed by Maria Likarz and presumably produced by the WW itself (ill. 166, 167). They show the connection between geometric Jugendstil and French art deco, and add the color red to the black-and-white contrast—a trio popular (not only) on the Viennese graphic scene. Joseph Binder frequently worked with this color combination over many years, as did Paul Kurt Schwarz, whose letter paper and envelopes entered the MAK Collection in 2000 (ill. 169).

[1] *Chwala's Druck*, Advertisement using an original drawing by Julius Klinger, in: *Gebrauchsgraphik* (IV) 11 1927, n.p.

[2] Durstmüller, Anton, *500 Jahre Druck in Österreich*, vol. 2, Vienna 1986, 270; see also vol. 3, Vienna 1989, 222 f.

[3] Chwala, August, "Ueber die alte und neue Richtung im Accidenzsatze," in: Faber, Heinrich (ed.), *Almanach für Buchdruckerei*, Vienna 1892, 27–38.

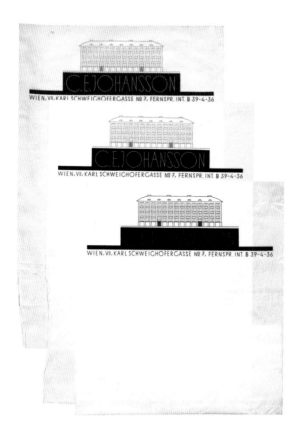

153
Joseph Binder
Briefpapier Joseph Binder
New York, nach 1936
Offsetdruck
Letter Paper Joseph Binder
New York, after 1936
Offset printing
279 x 216 mm
KI 14145-916-11, Legat
bequest from Carla und and
Joseph Binder 1995/96

154
Joseph Binder
Briefpapier der Importfirma Arabia
Wien, 1931–1935
Offsetdruck
**Letter Paper of the Import
Company Arabia**
Vienna, 1931–1935
Offset printing
281 x 221 mm
KI 14145-184, Legat bequest from
Carla und and Joseph Binder 1978

155
Anonym Anonymous
**Briefpapier des Warenhandels
C. E. Johansson**
Wien, 1930
Ausführung: Chwala's Druck
Klischee
**Letter Paper of the Trading Company
C. E. Johansson**
Vienna, 1930
Execution: Chwala's Druck
Cliché
302 x 200 mm
KI 20085-141, Ankauf Teilnachlass purchased from
part of the estate of Chwala's Druck 2008

156
Anonym Anonymous
Briefpapier des Verlags Friedrich Wolfrum & Co.
Wien, um 1912
Ausführung: Chwala's Druck
Klischee
**Letter Paper of the Publishing
House Friedrich Wolfrum & Co.**
Vienna, ca. 1912
Execution: Chwala's Druck
Cliché
283 x 218 mm
KI 20085-70, Ankauf Teilnachlass purchased from
part of the estate of Chwala's Druck 2008

157
Anonym Anonymous
Briefpapier des Autohauses Adolf Heilig
Wien, um 1920
Ausführung: Chwala's Druck
Klischee
Letter Paper of the Car Dealer Adolf Heilig
Vienna, ca. 1920
Execution: Chwala's Druck
Cliché
294 x 229 mm
KI 20085-74, Ankauf Teilnachlass Chwala's Druck
purchased from part of the estate of Chwala's Druck 2008

158
Anonym Anonymous
Briefkopf der Maschinenfabrik Josef Oser Krems
Wien, um 1900
Ausführung: Chwala's Druck
Klischee
Letterhead of the Engineering Works Josef Oser Krems
Vienna, ca. 1900
Execution: Chwala's Druck
Cliché
105 x 226 mm
KI 15848-1-1, Ankauf Teilnachlass purchased from
part of the estate of Chwala's Druck 2008

159
Anonym Anonymous
**Briefpapier der Thonet-Mundus
Ges.m.b.H.**
Wien, um 1930
Ausführung: Chwala's Druck
Klischee
**Letter Paper of the Thonet-Mundus
Ges.m.b.H.**
Vienna, ca. 1930
Execution: Chwala's Druck
Cliché
296 x 211 mm
KI 20085-176, Ankauf Teilnachlass purchased
from part of the estate of Chwala's Druck 2008

160
Anonym Anonymous
Briefpapier der Zenit-Film Gesellschaft
Wien, 1920–1929
Ausführung: Chwala's Druck
Klischee
Letter Paper of the Zenit-Film Company
Vienna, 1920–1929
Execution: Chwala's Druck
Cliché
277 x 216 mm
KI 20085-73, Ankauf Teilnachlass purchased
from part of the estate of Chwala's Druck 2008

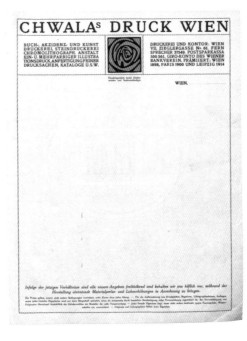

161
Anonym Anonymous
Briefpapier der Druckerei Chwala
Wien, nach 1914, Ausführung: Chwala's Druck
Klischee
Letter Paper of the Printing House Chwala
Vienna, after 1914, Execution: Chwala's Druck
Cliché
294 x 229 mm
KI 20085-1, Ankauf Teilnachlass purchased from
part of the estate of Chwala's Druck 2008

ARCHITEKT Ö·W·B·
K·K·
PROFESSOR
ERNST
LICHTBLAU
WIEN·XIII·
OBER·ST·VEIT
SCHWEIZERTAL-
STR.50·TEL·H512/II
POSTSP.-K. 146.955

162
Anonym Anonymous
Briefpapier des Architekten Ernst Lichtblau
Wien, um 1926
Ausführung: Chwala's Druck
Klischee
Letter Paper of the Architect Ernst Lichtblau
Vienna, ca. 1926
Execution: Chwala's Druck
Cliché
281 x 216 mm
KI 20085-23-2, Ankauf Teilnachlass purchased
from part of the estate of Chwala's Druck 2008

163
Vermutl. Prob. Urban Janke
Briefpapier des Malerateliers
Rudolf Jüttner & Bruder
Wien, 1911
Ausführung: Chwala's Druck
Klischee
Letter Paper of the Painting Studio
Rudolf Jüttner & Bruder
Vienna, 1911
Execution: Chwala's Druck
Cliché
296 x 230 mm
KI 20085-95, Ankauf Teilnachlass purchased from
part of the estate of Chwala's Druck 2008

164
Julius Klinger
Briefpapier des Werbeateliers
Klinger-Plakate
Wien, 1920–1925
Ausführung: Chwala's Druck
Klischee
Letter Paper of the Advertising
Studio Klinger-Plakate
Vienna, 1920–1925
Execution: Chwala's Druck
Cliché
293 x 228 mm
KI 20085-44, Ankauf Teilnachlass purchased from
part of the estate of Chwala's Druck 2008

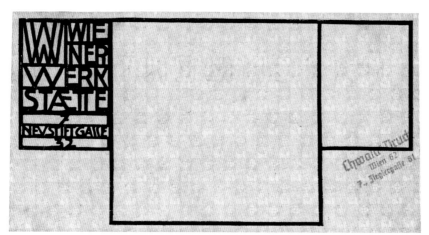

165
Koloman Moser
Kuvert der Wiener Werkstätte
Wien, 1905
Ausführung: Chwala's Druck
Klischee
Envelope of the Wiener Werkstätte
Vienna, 1905
Execution: Chwala's Druck
Cliché
94 x 182 mm
KI 15848-3-2-2, Ankauf Teilnachlass purchased
from part of the estate of Chwala's Druck 2008

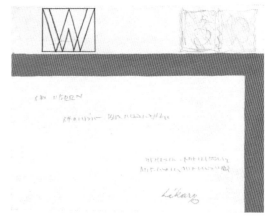

166
Maria Likarz
Entwurf für ein Kuvert der Wiener Werkstätte
Wien, 1927–1928
Bleistift, Deckfarbe
**Design for an Envelope of the
Wiener Werkstätte**
Vienna, 1927–1928
Pencil, coating paint
125 x 157 mm
KI 12281-13, Schenkung donation from
Alfred Hofmann 1955

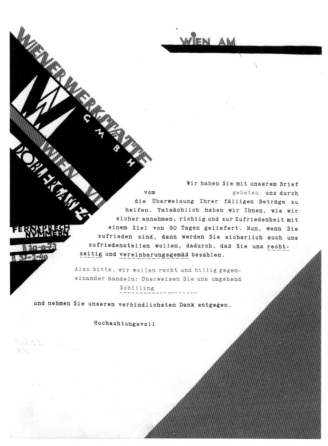

167
Maria Likarz
Briefpapier der Wiener Werkstätte, Zahlungserinnerung
Wien, 1927–1928
Klischee
Letter Paper of the Wiener Werkstätte, payment reminder
Vienna, 1927–1928
Cliché
283 x 218 mm
KI 12281-10, Schenkung donation from Alfred Hofmann 1955

168
Hans Neumann
Briefpapier des Ateliers Hans Neumann
Wien, um 1928
Ausführung: Chwala's Druck
Klischee
Letter Paper of Atelier Hans Neumann
Vienna, ca. 1928
Execution: Chwala's Druck
Cliché
284 x 220 mm
KI 20085-158, Ankauf Teilnachlass purchased from
part of the estate of Chwala's Druck 2008

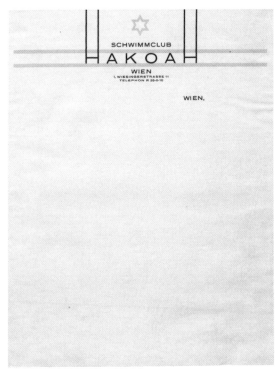

170
Anonym Anonymous
**Briefpapier des Schwimmclubs
Hakoah**
Wien, um 1930
Ausführung: Chwala's Druck
Klischee
**Letter Paper of the Swimming
Club Hakoah**
Vienna, ca. 1930
Execution: Chwala's Druck
Cliché
294 x 227 mm
KI 20085-180, Ankauf Teilnachlass
purchased from part of the estate of
Chwala's Druck 2008

169
Paul Kurt Schwarz
**Briefpapier der Möbelfabrik
Anton Herrgesell**
Wien, 1958
Klischee
**Letter Paper of the Furniture
Factory Anton Herrgesell**
Vienna, 1958
Chliché
210 x 148 mm
KI 15623-8, Schenkung donation from
Paul Kurt Schwarz 2000

III SPIELKARTEN – VISITENKARTEN

KOMMENTAR von Dieter Strehl

Annette Köger *Klein, aber fein: die MAK-Spielkartensammlung*

AUS DER SAMMLUNG

A   Spielkarten als Wissens- und Geschichtsquelle
B   Spielkarten aus Künstlerhand
C   Spielkarten als Makulatur
D   Spielkarten als Visitenkarten
E   „Künstlerische Besuchskarten"

III PLAYING CARDS—VISITING CARDS

COMMENT by Dieter Strehl

Annette Köger *Good Things Come in Small Packages:
The MAK's playing card collection*

FROM THE COLLECTION

A   Playing Cards as a Source of Knowledge and History
B   Playing Cards by Artists
C   Playing Cards as Spoilage
D   Playing Cards as Visiting Cards
E   "Artistic Visiting Cards"

VIELE KÜNSTLERINNEN HABEN SPIELKARTEN ENTWORFEN: Salvador Dalí, Arnold Schönberg, Sonia Delaunay, Christian Ludwig Attersee, Alfred Kubin, Karl Korab, Arik Brauer, Max Ernst, Anton Lehmden, Ditha Moser, Jean Dubuffet. Diese Auswahl ist ungeordnet und stellvertretend für eine große Anzahl weiterer KünstlerInnen. Möglicherweise hat sie die Aufgabe fasziniert, einen Artikel zu gestalten, bei dem man kreativ stark eingeschränkt ist: Sollen die Karten verwendet werden, muss schließlich der Herz-König als solcher erkennbar sein.

Allen diesen Entwürfen ist jedoch gemeinsam, dass ihnen kein kommerzieller Erfolg beschieden war. KartenspielerInnen wollen und wollten sie nicht verwenden. Diese Feststellung soll nicht als negative Kritik verstanden werden, stand doch die Massenverbreitung dieser Werke wahrscheinlich gar nicht im Fokus der künstlerischen Arbeit. Der Grund dafür lag vielmehr darin, dass auf wichtige Details für die Verwendung zu wenig geachtet wurde.

Schön sieht man das z.B. bei dem von Ditha Moser, der Gemahlin von Koloman Moser, entworfenen *Jugendstil-* oder *Sezessions-Tarock*. Es ist ein prachtvolles Spiel, das aber zum Gebrauch ungeeignet ist: Die Figuren sind einander so ähnlich, dass man in der Hitze des Spiels leicht Könige mit Buben verwechseln kann, auch die Damen sind nicht leicht zu erkennen. Schwerwiegender ist das Anbringen der römischen Zahlen der Tarocke in den falschen Ecken der Karten: der rechten oberen und linken unteren. Beim üblichen Auffächern in der Hand sind die Zeichen verdeckt, es ist nicht klar, welche Trümpfe man in der Hand hält.

Die Kritik an Künstlerkarten lenkt aber die Aufmerksamkeit auf die Gestaltung „normaler" Spielkarten und deren Qualität. In einem jahrhundertelangen Prozess haben sich in Europa spezifische Kartenbilder-Typen entwickelt. Wenn man sich Gedanken über die Ikonografie von Spielkarten macht, fällt auf: Die – in den meisten Fällen – anonymen Entwerfer, Stecher, Spielkartenmaler waren wirkliche Meister ihres Fachs. Fast alle Standardbilder sind ungemein prägnant, der kleine zur Verfügung stehende Raum wird perfekt genützt, die Kolorierung ist – trotz der Verwendung von nur drei oder vier Buntfarben – ausgewogen und gleichmäßig, die Übergänge der Figuren bei den gedrehten (nicht gespiegelten, wie manchmal fälschlich gemeint wird) doppelfigurigen Bildern sind perfekt gemacht, die Gesichter sympathisch, freundlich. Die Bilder sind so gelungen, dass sie den Spielenden gar nicht auffallen, obwohl sie sie stundenlang konzentriert betrachten.

Zahlreich sind die Versuche, diese Meisterwerke anonymer „Handwerker" zu „modernisieren". Obwohl im Offsetdruck hergestellt, ahmen die üblichen Bilder noch immer die alte, handkolorierte Stahlstichmanier nach und werden manchmal irrtümlich als veraltet angesehen. Das Resultat dieser Versuche ist regelmäßig ein Misserfolg: Die neuen Entwürfe werden von der Kartenspielgemeinde abgelehnt, man wünscht sich die „richtigen" Bilder zurück.

Bekanntlich ändert die Massenherstellung nichts am Kunstcharakter, auch nicht dem der Spielkarten. So empfinden viele die traditionellen Kartenbilder trotz Millionenauflagen als echte Kunstwerke. KartenspielerInnen sind den Bildern, die sie liebgewonnen haben, treu; sie verbinden sie mit triumphal gewonnenen Spielen, lustigen Kartenabenden im Freundeskreis und vielen Stunden, in denen der Alltag vergessen werden konnte.

Dieter Strehl, Geschäftsführer und Gesellschafter der Wiener Spielkartenfabrik Ferd. Piatnik & Söhne

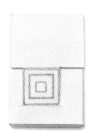

MANY ARTISTS HAVE DESIGNED PLAYING CARDS: Salvador Dalí, Arnold Schönberg, Sonia Delaunay, Christian Ludwig Attersee, Alfred Kubin, Karl Korab, Arik Brauer, Max Ernst, Anton Lehmden, Ditha Moser, Jean Dubuffet. This random selection of names represents a large number of other artists. It is conceivable that they were fascinated by the task of designing an article with such strict creative limitations: ultimately, if the cards are to be used, the king of hearts must be identifiable as such.

What all of these designs have in common, however, is that they were met with no commercial success. Card players do not and did not want to use them. This observation should not be understood as negative criticism; after all, the mass circulation of these works was quite probably not the artists' intention. Rather, the explanation is that too little attention had been paid to important details.

This fact can be seen clearly in the art nouveau or Secession-style tarot cards designed by Ditha Moser, wife of Koloman Moser, for instance. It is a magnificent—though utterly impractical—set: The figures resemble each other so closely that it would be easy to mistake kings for jacks in the heat of a game—indeed, even the queens are not easily recognizable. A more serious error is the placing of the Roman numerals in the wrong corners of the tarot cards: the top right and the bottom left. Fanning out the cards in one's hand in the usual way would leave these numbers hidden, meaning that the player would not know which trumps they were holding.

However, this criticism of artists' cards turns the spotlight on the design and quality of "normal" playing cards. Over the centuries, specific types of card designs developed in Europe. When considering the iconography of playing cards, one thing becomes clear: the—in most cases—anonymous designers, engravers, and playing card painters were true masters of their art. Almost all standard designs are exceptionally succinct, the small space made available to them being used perfectly; the coloration is balanced and uniform—despite the use of just three or four chromatic colors; the way the figures transition into their rotated (not mirrored, as is sometimes wrongly assumed) second torso is perfectly executed; the faces are kind, friendly. The pictures are so well made that the players do not even notice them, in spite of the fact that they often study them for hours.

The attempts to "modernize" these masterpieces by anonymous "craftspeople" are numerous. Although they are produced using offset printing, the conventional pictures still imitate the old, hand-colored steel engraving technique and as such are sometimes mistakenly believed to be old-fashioned. These attempts regularly result in failure: the new designs are rejected by the card-playing community, who want the "original" pictures back.

It is common knowledge that mass production does not affect the nature of art, and the same can be said of playing cards. Certainly, many people consider the traditional card designs to be genuine works of art—despite being manufactured by the million. Card players are faithful to the pictures of which they have grown fond; they associate them with triumphantly won games, fun evenings playing cards with friends, and many pleasant hours when they could forget about their everyday troubles.

Dieter Strehl, CEO and Partner of Wiener Spielkartenfabrik Ferd. Piatnik & Söhne

KLEIN, ABER FEIN: DIE MAK-SPIELKARTENSAMMLUNG
ANNETTE KÖGER

„An die Spiele überhaupts. Ode.

[…] Durch Euch erwirbt sich mit der Zeit / Dies Buch noch viele edle Kenner; / Mein Fleiß Gewinn,
Zufriedenheit, / Und meine Dienste manchen Gönner. / Wer seinen Witz im Spiel recht übt, /
Und in dem prächtigen Wien gewesen, / Wird, da er Welt und Wohlstand liebt, / Mein Buch,
zu eurer Ehre, lesen."[1]

Die Spielkartensammlung des MAK lässt sich wie fünf Finger einer Hand in fünf Bereiche unterteilen:
Tarocke, Standard-Spielkarten, Gesellschaftsspiele, Künstler-Entwürfe sowie Zweitverwendung als
Makulatur bzw. Visitenkarten. Nach einer kurzen Betrachtung zur Spielkartengeschichte werden
einzelne Kartenspiele aus den vier ersten Bereichen vorgestellt. Auf die Zweitverwendung wird im
Katalogteil näher eingegangen.

Die Spielkarten, vom Maß der Hand abgeleitet, waren ein steter Begleiter der Menschen. Seit ihrem
Auftauchen in Europa Ende des 14. Jahrhunderts haben sie sich rasant verbreitet. Sie waren sowohl
beim Adel als auch bei der Bevölkerung beliebt: leicht transportierbar, handlich und preiswert, über-
all verfügbar. Damit ähneln sie den gut in der Hand liegenden und sich heutzutage in aller Hände
befindlichen Mobiltelefonen.

Spielkarten werden der Grafik zugeordnet, weil es sich bei ihnen meist – zumindest im europäischen
Kontext – um Papier oder Karton als Bildträger handelt. Sie reagieren mit Farbverlust bei allzu
häufiger Ausstellungspräsenz, was dem Konservierungsauftrag entgegensteht. Als nebensächliche
Alltagsgegenstände im großen Sammelkomplex historischer Zeugnisse und Mustervorlagen führen
die Spielkarten im MAK verständlicherweise einen Dornröschenschlaf. Dies wiederum schützt die
Bestände vor lichtintensiver oder mechanischer Beanspruchung.

Trotz ihres vermuteten Ursprungs in Asien bewahren die Spielkarten bis heute das Geheimnis ihrer
Entstehung. Die ältesten Erwähnungen der Spielkarten weisen ins 7. und 8. Jahrhundert nach China,
wo seit dem 1. Jahrhundert n. Chr. die Papierherstellung bekannt war. Nach der am häufigsten
vertretenen Lehrmeinung wanderten Spielkarten wohl auf den alten Handelswegen vom Fernen
Osten mit den Kaufleuten und Händlern in Richtung Mittelmeer und landeten zunächst in Italien.
Die Alpen stellten im 14. Jahrhundert zwar ein Hindernis dar, doch gelangte die Kenntnis um die
Karten fast zeitgleich in Regionen auch nördlich der Gebirgskette. Die Verbreitung fand erstaunlich
rasch statt, was sich an den erhaltenen Verboten, mit Karten zu spielen, ablesen lässt. Die erteilten
Verbote lesen sich wie das Who's Who der wichtigen mittelalterlichen Handelszentren: Florenz
1376, Viterbo 1377, Basel 1377, Regensburg 1378, St. Gallen 1379, Brabant 1379, Nürnberg 1380,
Lille 1382, Konstanz 1388, Zürich 1389, Augsburg 1391, Frankfurt/Main 1392, Straßburg 1394 etc.
Nach Osten breitete sich das Kartenspiel langsamer aus, Mitte des 15. Jahrhunderts tauchte es im
heutigen Österreich und Polen auf.[2] Zunächst noch wie Buchmalerei ausgeführt, entwickelte sich die
Spielkartenproduktion anhand der jeweils neuesten Druckverfahren vom Holzschnitt und Kupferstich
über die Lithografie zum Offset- oder Laserdruck. Als Spielinstrumente für alle werden Karten seit
ungefähr 1500 in Europa von den Kartenmachern manufakturmäßig produziert.

[1] Philidor, François Danican, *Die Kunst die Welt mitzunehmen in den verschiedenen Arten der Spiele, so in Gesellschaften höhern Standes, besonders in der Kayserl. Königl. Residenz-Stadt Wien üblich sind. Nebst einem Anhang, von dem neuen Spiel Lotto di Genova*, Bd. 1, Wien-Nürnberg 1756, 3 v.

[2] Hoffmann, Detlef, *Die Welt der Spielkarte*, München 1972; Hargrave, Catherine Perry, *A History of Playing Cards*, unabridged republ. of the ed. 1930, New York 1966; Radau, Sigmar/Himmelheber, Georg, *Spielkarten*, Kataloge des Bayerischen Nationalmuseums, Bd. 21, München 1991; Köger, Annette, „Spielkarten", in: *Lexikon des gesamten Buchwesens*, Bd. 7, Stuttgart 2007, 170 f.; Ulm, Dagmar (Hg.), *Diese Karden seind zu finden bey – Spielkarten aus Oberösterreich*, Kataloge der Oberösterreichischen Landesmuseen, Linz 2010; Husband, Timothy B., *The World in Play. Luxury Cards 1430–1540*, The Metropolitan Museum of Art, New York 2015, dort Angaben zur einschlägigen Literatur.

GOOD THINGS COME IN SMALL PACKAGES: THE MAK'S PLAYING CARD COLLECTION
ANNETTE KÖGER

"To Games in General. An Ode.
[…] In time, this book—with your blessings— / Will earn many a noble admirer; / My efforts
satisfaction, earnings / And my labors a wealthy inquirer. / Those who practice their quips in games, /
And can testify to Vienna's claims, / Will—the world and wealth do not forsake!— / Read my book
for their reputation's sake."[1]

Like the five fingers of a hand, the MAK's collection of playing cards can be divided into five groups: tarot cards, standard playing cards, parlor games, artists' designs, and those with a dual purpose as spoilage or business cards. After an overview of the history of playing cards, a few card games from the first four groups will be described. Their dual purpose will be considered in more detail in the catalog section.

Playing cards, derived from the size of a hand, have been humanity's constant companion. After their emergence in Europe at the end of the 14th century, they spread rapidly. They were popular both among the aristocracy as well as among the general population: easy to transport, handy, and reasonably priced, they were available everywhere. In this regard, they resemble another hand-sized object, which can be found in everyone's hands today: cell phones.

Playing cards are associated with works on paper because they are mostly—at least in the European context—made of paper or cardboard. When displayed too frequently, their colors fade, which can be counteracted by conservation efforts. As incidental everyday objects in a large and complex collection of historical evidence and exemplars, the playing cards at the MAK understandably lay dormant. This in turn protects the holdings from bright lights or mechanical strain.

Despite their presumed origins in Asia, playing cards have managed to keep the secret of their evolution. The oldest mentions of playing cards point to 7th and 8th-century China, where paper-making had been established since the 1st century CE. According to the most common school of thought, playing cards probably migrated with the merchants and traders along the old trade routes from the Far East towards the Mediterranean Sea, landing first in Italy. Although the Alps admittedly presented an obstacle in the 14th century, knowledge of the cards arrived in regions to the north of the mountain range at almost the same time as the south. Their distribution was astoundingly swift, as can be deduced from the surviving prohibitions on playing with cards. The imposed bans read like a who's who of important medieval trade centers: Florence 1376, Viterbo 1377, Basel 1377, Regensburg 1378, St. Gallen 1379, Brabant 1379, Nuremberg 1380, Lille 1382, Konstanz 1388, Zurich 1389, Augsburg 1391, Frankfurt/Main 1392, Strasbourg 1394, etc.

Card games spread more slowly to the east; only in the mid-15th century did they arrive in modern-day Austria and Poland.[2] Initially created in a method resembling illumination, the production of playing cards evolved in line with the latest printing techniques—from woodblock and copperplate printing to lithography to offset or laser printing. As universal tools for play, these cards have been manufactured by card makers in Europe since ca. 1500.

[1] Philidor, François Danican, *Die Kunst die Welt mitzunehmen in den verschiedenen Arten der Spiele, so in Gesellschaften höhern Standes, besonders in der Kayserl. Königl. Residenz-Stadt Wien üblich sind. Nebst einem Anhang, von dem neuen Spiel Lotto di Genova*, vol. 1, Vienna/Nuremberg 1756, 3 v. Translated by Maria Slater.

[2] Hoffmann, Detlef, *Die Welt der Spielkarte*, Munich 1972; Hargrave, Catherine Perry, *A History of Playing Cards*, unabridged republ. of the ed. 1930, New York 1966; Radau, Sigmar/Himmelheber, Georg, *Spielkarten*, Kataloge des Bayerischen Nationalmuseums, vol. 21, Munich 1991; Köger, Annette, "Spielkarten," in: *Lexikon des gesamten Buchwesens*, vol. 7, Stuttgart 2007, 170 f.; Ulm, Dagmar (ed.), *Diese Karden seind zu finden bey – Spielkarten aus Oberösterreich*, Catalogs of the Oberösterreichische Landesmuseen, Linz 2010; Husband, Timothy B., *The World in Play. Luxury Cards 1430–1540*, The Metropolitan Museum of Art, New York 2015, in which relevant literature is listed.

Spielkarten und ihre Regeln für Kartenspiele geben Einsicht in alte Sitten und Gebräuche. An ihnen lässt sich die Kulturgeschichte der Welt im Kleinen ablesen. Die alltägliche Nebensache Spielkarten erlaubt einen streiflichtartigen Blick in die Geschichte, mit Annäherung an menschliche Triumphe, ja Glücksgefühle, aber auch unangenehme Debakel. So ist das gesamte Spektrum menschlicher Emotionen an sie geknüpft.

Bei einigen ausgewählten Stücken der MAK-Spielkartensammlung lohnt sich ein zweiter oder gar dritter Blick. So werden im Folgenden Tarocke, Standardspielkarten, Gesellschaftsspiele mit Lehrkarten sowie Künstlerkarten vorgestellt. Original-Entwürfe sind das besondere Schmuckstück jeder Sammlung. Auch in diesem Bereich kann die MAK-Sammlung glänzen. Einzigartig sind die Entwürfe des Whists sowie des *Jugendstil-Tarocks* von Ditha Moser.

TAROCKE

Ein Tarockspiel besteht aus 78 Blatt: 16 Figurenkarten (Hofkarten), 40 Zahlenkarten, 21 Tarocke plus 1 Narr (Skys, Le Fou). Mit französischen Farben sind sie als Tiertarock seit dem 2. Viertel des 18. Jahrhunderts entstanden. Dabei orientierten sich die Kartenmacher an den Vorbildern aus Lyon oder Paris. Seit ca. dem 3. Viertel des 18. Jahrhunderts wurden die Tiermotive durch andere Darstellungen ersetzt. Ein gelungenes Beispiel dafür stellt das *Hochzeitszug-Tarock* des Andreas Benedickt Göbl von ca.1765 dar (Abb. 171, 172). Es entstand anlässlich der Hochzeit von Maria Josepha, Prinzessin von Bayern und Böhmen, mit Joseph, der noch im selben Jahr als Joseph II. neuer Kaiser und Mitregent seiner Mutter Maria Theresia von Österreich wurde. Die Karten sind in Zeichnung und Kolorierung sorgfältig ausgeführt. Leuchtende Farben werden durch Gold- und Silberhöhungen noch betont.

Diese Hochzeit und die damals bevorstehende Fastnacht ließen letztmalig einen seit 1682 nachgewiesenen Usus aufleben: Mitglieder des kurfürstlichen Hofes zogen als Bauern verkleidet während eines Festumzugs durch München und beendeten das Spektakel mit einem großen Festessen, der sogenannten Wirtschaft. Auf den Tarocken ist der Festzug dargestellt, angeführt vom Hochzeitslader (I), gefolgt von Wirt und Wirtin (II), von Braut und Bräutigam (IV), von Pastor und Pastorin (VI), von Zigeuner (VIII), Jäger (X) und Bauern (XII, XIV), Musik (XVIII),[3] Jubelrufer (XIX), Prinzen und Prinzessinnen (XX) sowie von allgemeiner Freude mit dem „Bruder" (XXI).

Die Abbildungen der Tarocke wurden im Laufe des 19. Jahrhunderts abwechslungsreicher. Inspirationsquellen konnten sein: Fabeln nach La Fontaine, Meeresfabelwesen, historische Themen, Reisedarstellungen, literarische Vorlagen, Theateraufführungen, Genreszenen etc. Besonders auf 54 Blatt verkürzte Formen fanden bereits zu Beginn des 19. Jahrhunderts als *Industrie & Glück Tarock* (Abb. 173) in der österreichisch-ungarischen Monarchie weite Verbreitung.[4] Zur Kategorie der Tarocke nach literarischen Vorlagen und Reisedarstellungen zählen das Literatur-Tarock sowie die Souvenir-Tarocke von Wien und Paris.

Das Literatur-Tarock (Abb. 174, 175) zeigt Szenen z.B. aus dem Liederzyklus *Fräulein vom See* (1810), den Novellen *Waverley* (1814) und *Guy Mannering* (1815) sowie den historischen Romanen des schottischen Dichters und Schriftstellers Sir Walter Scott. Die literarische Wirkung seiner Werke war enorm und beeinflusste u.a. die Literatur der deutschen Romantik. Mit Übernahme des Uffenheimer Kartenmacher-Betriebs 1848 produzierte Josef Glanz bis ca. 1870 dieses beliebte Literatur-Tarock.[5] Das Veduten-Tarock von Carl Titze zeigt Wiener Sehenswürdigkeiten auf den

3 Köger, Annette, „Musikalische Spielkarten", in: Bauer, Günther G. (Hg.), *Musik und Spiel. Homo Ludens – Der spielende Mensch*, Internationale Beiträge des Institutes für Spielforschung und Spielpädagogik an der Hochschule Mozarteum Salzburg, 10, 2000, München/Salzburg, 288 f.

4 Reisinger, Klaus, „Die bedeutendsten Wiener Kartenmacher mit ihren Tarocken", in: Ders., *Tarocke. Kulturgeschichte auf Kartenbildern*, Bd. 1, Wien 1996, 49–61.

5 Reisinger, Klaus, *Tarocke. Kulturgeschichte auf Kartenbildern*, Bd. 2, Wien 1996, 283–304.

Playing cards and rules for card games give an insight into old customs and conventions. In them it is possible to trace the cultural history of the world in microcosm. The everyday ephemera of playing cards enable a fleeting glimpse of the past, with an intimation of human triumphs—indeed happiness—but also unpleasant debacles. As such, they are inextricably linked to the entire spectrum of human emotions.

With some select pieces in the MAK's playing card collection, it is worth taking a second or even third look. Consequently, tarot cards, standard playing cards, parlor games with didactic cards, as well as artists' cards are all described below. Original designs are the particularly rare jewels of any collection. In this regard, too, the MAK Collection excels: unique to the collection are the designs for *Whist* as well as the art nouveau tarot deck by Ditha Moser.

TAROT CARDS

A tarot deck consists of 78 cards: 16 face cards (court cards), 40 pip cards, 21 tarots, plus 1 fool (skys, excuse, le fou). With French suits they emerged as animal tarot from the 2nd quarter of the 18th century. The card makers of the time aligned their designs with exemplars from Lyon or Paris. From ca. the 3rd quarter of the 18th century, the animal motifs were replaced with other patterns. A successful example is the wedding procession tarot deck by Andreas Benedict Göbl from ca. 1765 (ill. 171, 172). It was created on the occasion of the marriage of Maria Josepha, Princess of Bavaria and Bohemia, to Joseph, who became Joseph II, the new emperor and co-regent of Austria with his mother Maria Theresa, in the same year. The drawing and coloring of the cards have been carefully executed. Luminous colors are further emphasized with gold and silver highlights.

This wedding and the then forthcoming Shrovetide revived for the last time a custom for which there is evidence dating back to 1682: dressed as peasants, members of the elector's court would make their way through Munich during a festival procession; the spectacle would end with a large banquet called a "Wirtschaft." This procession is depicted on the tarot cards, led by the wedding inviter (I), followed by host and hostess (II), bride and bridegroom (IV), pastor and pastor's wife (VI), gypsy (VIII), hunter (X), and farmers (XII, XIV), musicians (XVIII),[3] a cheering crowd (XIX), princes and princesses (XX), as well as by general happiness with the "fellow man" (XXI).

The illustrations on the tarot cards became more varied over the course of the 19th century. Sources of inspiration included: fables after La Fontaine, mythical sea creatures, historical themes, depictions of journeys, literary references, theater performances, genre scenes, etc. It was especially versions reduced to just 54 cards known as *Industrie & Glück Tarock*, which gained wide currency in the Austro-Hungarian Empire as early as the beginning of the 19th century (ill. 173).[4] Literature tarot decks as well as souvenir tarot decks from Vienna and Paris belong to the category of tarot cards with literary references and depictions of journeys.

The literature tarot deck (ill. 174, 175) shows scenes e.g. from the lieder cycle *Fräulein vom See* (1810), the novels *Waverley* (1814) and *Guy Mannering* (1815), as well as other historical novels by Scottish poet and author Sir Walter Scott. The literary impact of his works was enormous and influenced among others the literature of German romanticism. Having taken over the Uffenheimer Kartenmacher-Betrieb in 1848, Josef Glanz produced this popular literature tarot deck until ca. 1870.[5] The veduta tarot deck by Carl Titze shows Viennese tourist attractions on the tarots, with each bearing a view in landscape format (see ill. 205–207). In the Viennese directories from 1857

[3] Köger, Annette, "Musikalische Spielkarten," in: Bauer, Günther G. (ed.), *Musik und Spiel. Homo Ludens – Der spielende Mensch*, Internationale Beiträge des Institutes für Spielforschung und Spielpädagogik an der Hochschule Mozarteum Salzburg, 10, 2000, Munich/Salzburg, 288f.

[4] Reisinger, Klaus, "Die bedeutendsten Wiener Kartenmacher mit ihren Tarocken," in: id., *Tarocke. Kulturgeschichte auf Kartenbildern*, vol. 1, Vienna 1996, 49–61.

[5] Reisinger, Klaus, *Tarocke. Kulturgeschichte auf Kartenbildern*, vol. 2, Vienna 1996, 283–304.

171
Andreas Benedict Göbl
Tarock XVIII aus einem *Hochzeitszug-Tarock*
München, um 1765
Kupferstich, handkoloriert
Tarot 18 from a [Wedding procession tarot]
Munich, ca. 1765
Copperplate engraving, handcolored
109 x 57 mm
KI 13393, alter Bestand, inv. old holdings,
inventoried 1960

172
Andreas Benedict Göbl
Tarock X aus einem *Hochzeitszug-Tarock*
München, um 1765
Kupferstich, handkoloriert
Tarot 10 from a [Wedding procession tarot]
Munich, ca. 1765
Copperplate engraving, handcolored
109 x 57 mm
KI 13393, alter Bestand, inv. old holdings,
inventoried 1960

173
Anonym Anonymous
Tarock II aus *The Finest Ladies-Tarok*
(Industrie & Glück)
Budapest, nach 1896
Ausführung: Ferd. Piatnik & Söhne
Chromolithografie
Tarot 2 from *The Finest Ladies-Tarok*
(Industrie & Glück)
Budapest, after 1896
Execution: Ferd. Piatnik & Söhne
Chromolithograph
100 x 54 mm
KI 14068, Ankauf purchased from
Auktionshaus Wendt 1976

and 1858, Carl Titze is listed as the "Owner of an imperial royal privilege for so-called comfort cards, which afford players a considerable advantage when playing;" Michael Schinkay is named as his business partner from 1859. The landscape-format views became very fashionable from 1875. The playing card manufacturer C. Titze & Schinkay also modernized the original edition; over half of the views now showed buildings from the construction period of Vienna's Ringstrasse. In ca. 1850 Georg Mayer—who worked as a card maker in Pest, Hungary, from 1841 to 1856—copied the veduta tarot deck, which had first been published by Max Uffenheimer in Vienna, with views of Paris (see ill. 207–209). In contrast to the original, an accompanying sheet explaining the motifs would no longer be necessary because the names of the sights were printed on the cards themselves. Exclusively in vivid puce, the views are reminiscent of old photographs. It is possible that this was the intended effect: the description accompanying the earlier Uffenheimer edition names as a subtitle *PARIS (nach Daguerreotypen)* ("after daguerreotypes"). Mayer took the face cards including the pagat (1 of tarots or le petit) and skys (fool or excuse) from his *Chineser Tapp-Tarock* (ill. 176).

STANDARD PLAYING CARDS

The suits of the standard cards had become established by 1500. Depending on these suits, the playing cards were described as decks with e.g. Latin (Ital./Span.), German, or French suits: "In fact there are three main kinds of playing cards, [...] namely the Italian, (the so-called *Traplier-karten*) the German, and the French: the first appear to be the oldest and the last the newest. [...] Each of these playing cards has its own specific colors and suits: the first has many suits, namely Spadi (swords), Bastoni (clubs), Denari (coins), Coppe (cups): the face or court cards are king, queen, knight, and knave. The second has four different colors and suits, they are: red, representing hearts; green or leaves; bells, which are bright yellow; and acorns, which are green and yellow; the face cards are the king, the over (Ober) and under (Unter) knave or peasant. The last playing cards, however, have only two colors, but four suits: the reds have hearts (Coeur), and diamonds (Carreau); the blacks have spades or shovels (Pique), and clover or clubs (Trefle). The face or court cards are: the king, queen, and knave or knight."[6]

There is also evidence dating back to before 1500 for playing cards with German suits, which bear a remarkable diversity of pattern designs on the pip cards. The rich language of forms was passed on and, where necessary, adapted across regions and through the ages in the guilds of the card-making trade.[7] Consequently, the most descriptive scenes often differ geographically. Often town or country names are used to make this clear. The German card patterns were also widespread beyond the German-speaking world—in Eastern Europe, Bohemia, Hungary, Poland, and Russia.[8] In the meantime, the former wealth of diversity has been reduced to just a few two-headed standard patterns. While the basic structure of the court and pip cards has remained the same to the present day, originally the German deck comprised 52 cards. Over the course of time it has diminished e.g. for a game of skat to just 32 cards.[9]

An example of the design of German suits is provided by the 1843 Tyrolean pattern (ill. 177–179) by Franz Krapf from Bolzano (South Tyrol, today Italy) and working there between ca. 1835 and 1858, he is part of the Tyrolean card-making tradition, for which there is evidence dating back

[6] Philidor, François Danican, *Die Kunst die Welt mitzunehmen in den verschiedenen Arten der Spiele, so in Gesellschaften höhern Standes, besonders in der Kayserl. Königl. Residenz-Stadt Wien üblich sind. Mit einer Nachricht von andern mehrern, auch unter leuten niedern Standes gewöhnlichen Spielarten und einigen der neuesten Künste mit Karten*, vol. 2, Vienna/Nuremberg 1756, 96 f. Translated by Maria Slater.

[7] Radau/Himmelheber 1991 (see note 2), 69; Hoffmann, Detlef, *Altdeutsche Spiel-karten 1500–1600*, Nuremberg 1993, 25–30, 149–153; Hausler, Manfred, "Das schwäbische Bild. Ein Standardbild – drei Typen," in: *Das Blatt* 44, Berlin 2011, 89–95, Radau, Sigmar/Kranich, Jürgen F., *Das Schwäbische Bild*, Studien zur Spielkarte 37, Berlin 2016, 1. From ca. 1470 there is also evidence of the Ulm-Munich or Swabian card design. The German standard design, coming from Ulm, Augsburg, or Frankfurt via Munich, led in the 16th century to standard designs like the Stukeley cards (ca. mid-16th century).

[8] Radau/Himmelheber 1991 (ibd.), 68. The Old Bavarian pattern is considered the precursor of many card designs used in the Austro-Hungarian Empire or in southern Germany such as the Salzburg, Tyrolean, Prague, Bavarian, and Franconian standard designs. The Hungarian standard design, previously called *Neue Schweizer Deutsche* or *Tellkarte*, in Austria *Deutsche* or *Doppeldeutsche*, still exists today. By contrast, other patterns dating back to the former Austro-Hungarian Empire such as the Linz card, the Sopron, Lviv (also called Moor card or later *Polnische Nationalkarte*), and Tyrolean design are no longer produced.

[9] Radau/Himmelheber 1991 (see note 7), 67. The first reduction was from 52 cards to 48 cards (1 disappears). The 2 of the deuce took on the function of the ace from the French suit. In the 18th century the deck was reduced to 36 cards, with the pip cards 3 and 5 disappearing. At the beginning of the 19th century, the 6 was removed when playing and hence the deck was reduced to just 32 cards.

Tarocken mit je einer Ansicht im Querformat (s. Abb. 205–207). In den Wiener Adressbüchern von 1857 und 1858 ist Carl Titze als „Besitzer eines k. k. Privilegiums auf sog. Comfort-Karte, welche dem Spieler einen wesentlichen Vortheil beim Spielen gewähren", aufgelistet, ab 1859 mit dem Geschäftspartner Michael Schinkay. Ab 1875 kamen die querformatigen Ansichten sehr in Mode. Die Spielkartenfabrik C. Titze & Schinkay modernisierte die ursprüngliche Ausgabe. Mehr als die Hälfte der Ansichten zeigt nun Gebäude aus der Bauzeit der Wiener Ringstraße.

Georg Mayer – von 1841 bis 1856 in Pest als Kartenmacher tätig – kopierte um 1850 das von Max Uffenheimer in Wien erstmalig herausgebrachte Veduten-Tarock mit Pariser Ansichten (s. Abb. 208–210). Im Unterschied dazu war nun kein die Motive erklärendes Begleitblatt mehr nötig, weil die Bezeichnung der Sehenswürdigkeiten direkt auf die Karten gedruckt wurde. Die in Lebhaftbraunrot gehaltenen Ansichten erinnern an alte Fotografien. Möglicherweise war dieser Effekt gewollt: Die beigelegte Beschreibung der früheren Uffenheimer Ausgabe nennt im Untertitel *PARIS (nach Daguerreotypen)*. Die Figurenkarten samt Pagat und Skys entnahm Mayer seinem *Chineser Tapp-Tarock* (Abb. 176).

STANDARDSPIELKARTEN

Die Farbzeichen der Standardkarten sind bereits um das Jahr 1500 ausgeprägt. Die Spielkarten werden diesen Zeichen entsprechend als Spielkarten mit z.B. lateinischen (ital./span.), deutschen oder französischen Farben beschrieben: „Eigentlich sind dreyerley Haupt-Spielkarten, […] nemlich die Italiänischen, (die sogenannten Traplierkarten) die Deutschen, und die Französischen: Die erstern scheinen die ältesten und die leztern die neuesten zu seyn. […] Jede von diesen Spielkarten hat ihre besonderen Farben und Figuren: die erstere hat viererley Figuren, nemlich Spadi (Schwerter), Bastoni (Stäbe), Denari (Pfennige), Coppe (Becher): die Figuren oder Bilder sind König, Königin, Reuter und Bub. Die zweyte hat vier unterschiedliche Farben und Figuren, als: Roth, so Herzen vorstellet, Grün oder Laub, Schellen, welche hochgelb, und Eicheln, welche grün und gelb: Die Bilder sind der König, Ober- und Untermann oder Bauer. Die letzteren Spielkarten aber haben nur zweyerley Farbe, aber vier Figuren: die Rothe hat Herze (Coeur), und Rauten (Carreau); die schwarze Spaden oder Schüppen, (Pique), und Klee (Trefle). Die Figuren oder Bilder sind, der König, Dame und Bub oder Knecht."[6]

Ebenfalls bereits vor 1500 nachweisbar, zeichnen sich die Spielkarten mit deutschen Farben durch Vielfalt der Bildgestaltung auf den Zahlenkarten aus. Die reiche Formensprache wurde über Räume und Zeiten hinweg weitergegeben und, wenn nötig, angepasst.[7] Somit unterscheiden sich die meist sprechenden Szenen regional. Oft werden Städte- oder Ländernamen verwendet, um sie zu benennen. Die deutschen Kartenbilder waren auch außerhalb des deutschsprachigen Raums in Osteuropa, Böhmen, Ungarn, Polen und Russland verbreitet.[8] Inzwischen hat sich der ehemalige Variantenreichtum auf wenige doppelköpfige Standardbilder reduziert. Das Grundschema der Hof- und Zahlenkarten blieb zwar bis heute erhalten, doch ursprünglich umfasste die Anzahl der deutschen Karte 52 Blatt. Im Laufe der Zeit wurde sie z.B. für Skat bis auf 32 Blatt verringert.[9]

Ein Beispiel für die Gestaltung von deutschen Farben stellt das Tiroler Bild (Abb. 177–179) des Franz Krapf aus Bozen von 1843 dar. Dort zwischen ca. 1835 und 1858 tätig, gehört er zu der seit 1522 mit Hans Perkhamer in Innsbruck belegbaren, annähernd 400 Jahre währenden Tiroler

6 Philidor, François Danican, *Die Kunst die Welt mitzunehmen in den verschiedenen Arten der Spiele, so in Gesellschaften höhern Standes, besonders in der Kayserl. Königl. Residenz-Stadt Wien üblich sind. Mit einer Nachricht von andern mehrern, auch unter leuten niedern Standes gewöhnlichen Spielarten und einigen der neuesten Künste mit Karten*, Bd. 2, Wien/Nürnberg 1756, 96f.

7 Radau/Himmelheber 1991 (s. Anm. 2), 69; Hoffmann, Detlef, *Altdeutsche Spielkarten 1500–1600*, Nürnberg 1993, 25–30, 149–153; Hausler, Manfred, „Das schwäbische Bild. Ein Standardbild – drei Typen", in: *Das Blatt* 44, Berlin 2011, 89–95; Radau, Sigmar/Kranich, Jürgen F., *Das Schwäbische Bild*, Studien zur Spielkarte 37, Berlin 2016, 1. Ab ca. 1470 ist das Ulm-Münchner oder auch Schwäbische Kartenbild nachweisbar. Das Deutsche Standardbild, ausgehend von Ulm, Augsburg oder Frankfurt über München, führte im 16. Jahrhundert zu den Standardbildern wie den Stukeley Cards (ca. Mitte des 16. Jahrhunderts).

8 Radau/Himmelheber 1991 (ebd.), 68. Das altbayerische Bild gilt als Vorläufer vieler in der österreichisch-ungarischen Monarchie oder im süddeutschen Raum verwendeter Kartenbilder wie des Salzburger, des Tiroler, des Prager, des bayerischen oder des fränkischen Standardbildes. Das ungarische Standardbild, früher auch als *Neue Schweizer Deutsche* oder *Tellkarte*, in Österreich als *Deutsche* oder *Doppeldeutsche* bezeichnet, existiert noch heute. Hingegen werden weitere in die Epoche der ehemaligen Donaumonarchie zurückreichende Bilder wie die Linzer Karte, das Ödenburger Bild, das Lemberger (auch Mohrenkarte oder später *Polnische Nationalkarte*) und das Tiroler Bild nicht mehr hergestellt.

9 Radau/Himmelheber 1991 (s. Anm. 7), 67. Die erste Reduktion erfolgte von 52 Blatt auf 48 Blatt (1 verschwindet). Die 2 des Daus erhält die Funktion des As der französischen Karte. Im 18. Jahrhundert wird auf 36 Blatt reduziert, die Zahlenkarten 3 bis 5 verschwinden. Anfang des 19. Jahrhunderts wird zum Spielen die 6 entfernt und damit auf 32 Blatt gekürzt.

174
Anonym Anonymous
Das Fräulein vom See,
Tarock II aus einem Literaturtarock
Wien, 1845
Ausführung: Max Uffenheimer
Stahlstich, koloriert
[The Lady of the Lake],
Tarot 2 from a literature tarot
Vienna, 1845
Execution: Max Uffenheimer
Steel engraving, colored
102 x 54 mm
KI 14067-1, Ankauf purchased from
Auktionshaus Wendt 1976

175
Anonym Anonymous
Waverley,
Tarock XVI aus einem Literaturtarock
Wien, 1845
Ausführung: Max Uffenheimer
Stahlstich, koloriert
***Waverley*, Tarot 16 from a literature tarot**
Vienna, 1845
Execution: Max Uffenheimer
Steel engraving, colored
102 x 54 mm
KI 14067-15, Ankauf purchased from
Auktionshaus Wendt 1976

176
Georg Mayer
Kreuz-Bube aus einem Veduten-Tarock
(*Chineser Tapp-Tarock*)
Wien, um 1850
Ausführung: Georg Mayer
Kupferstich
Knave of Clubs from a veduta tarot
(*Chineser Tapp-Tarock*)
Vienna, ca. 1850
Execution: Georg Mayer
Copperplate engraving
104 x 55 mm
KI 14023-1, alter Bestand, inv. old holdings,
inventoried 1974

177
Johann Albrecht
Herz-7 aus einem Tiroler Bild
Bozen, 1843
Ausführung: Franz Krapf
Holzschnitt, schablonenkoloriert
Seven of Hearts from a Tyrolean pattern
Bolzano, 1843
Execution: Franz Krapf
Woodcut, stencil-colored
89 x 50 mm
KI 14031-1, Ankauf purchased from Anton Hofer 1974

178
Johann Albrecht
Eichel-Ober aus einem Tiroler Bild
Bozen, 1843
Ausführung: Franz Krapf
Holzschnitt, schablonenkoloriert
Over of Acorns from a Tyrolean pattern
Bolzano, 1843
Execution: Franz Krapf
Woodcut, stencil-colored
89 x 50 mm
KI 14031-3, Ankauf purchased from Anton Hofer 1974

179
Johann Albrecht
Laub-König aus einem Tiroler Bild
Bozen, 1843
Ausführung: Franz Krapf
Holzschnitt, schablonenkoloriert
King of Leaves from a Tyrolean pattern
Bolzano, 1843
Execution: Franz Krapf
Woodcut, stencil-colored
89 x 50 mm
KI 14031-10, Ankauf purchased from Anton Hofer 1974

to 1522 with Hans Perkhamer in Innsbruck, and which as such has lasted almost 400 years. The Tyrolean standard pattern was probably developed by Johann Albrecht in the 1790s on the basis of the Old Bavarian standard pattern. It has an acorn over with a tankard and sickle, for labor in a field or vineyard, as well as an acorn Unter with a flower and roses in the crook of his arm—peaceful accessories in the otherwise distinctly military card hierarchy of officers and soldiers. This deck of cards is complete and has been preserved in immaculate condition. The strong coloring is striking; the vibrant orange and dark carmine red shades in particular affect and emphasize the stout figures, which almost burst through the borders. Two kings (acorn and leaves) wear turbans instead of crowns as a result of Turkish influence. Their shields—in the tradition of card maker Andreas Benedict Göbl—bear heraldic animals: the Habsburg double-headed eagle, a unicorn, the sun in a corona, and a dog.

PARLOR GAMES—DIDACTIC CARDS

At quite an early stage, playing cards were also used for fortunetelling and teaching. The idea of exploiting people's inherent instinct and desire to play for educational purposes goes back to the age of the Renaissance and humanism. The emergence of didactic cards coincided with the European expeditions around 1500.[10] It is generally considered that the first didactic card game is the *Logica memorativa – Chartiludium logicae*, which was published as a book edition in 1507 by the Strasbourg-based Franciscan monk Thomas Murner (1475–1537). This popular preacher, humanist, and poet achieved great success with his invention to "learn through play."[11] As a bearer of information in its function as the page of a book, things worth knowing can also be found on a playing card, for example—depending on the date it was created—about mythology, astronomy, mathematics, music, religion, literature, history, art, geography, heraldry, technology, or languages, etc.

One notable example is the signed and dated mythological game (ill. 180) by Johann Georg Staindorffer from 1688. An unusual version, it combines Italian, German, and Swiss suits like "Trappola." It is unlikely that it was created for a mere simple game. The colorful depiction of the figures captured in energetic movement reveal Johann Staindorffer to have been a proficient baroque painter. The dictionary of artists confirms this impression: He is listed there as the painter of side altarpieces in the church in Biberbach, Lower Austria, in 1681.[12] "As a simple letter or card painter who was a member of a guild, Staindorffer should indisputably be ranked among the most proficient," finds Eduard Chmelarz; he even attests to "the repercussions of Rubens' influence in Germany" in Staindorffer's work with regard to his color scheme and drawing style.[13] The 28 surviving cards appear to have been created "as a commission for a distinguished gentleman."[14] As Staindorffer worked as an altar painter, it is conceivable that he was commissioned by a member of the clergy. The iconography shows figures from classical mythology whose names are recorded on the cards. The emblematic meaning was either known to the observer or could have been taught to them using the cards. The fine paintings and miscellaneous suits were probably not ideally suited to a trivial game of cards. The marbled reverse sides, too, are testament to their high-quality execution. Their good state of preservation indicates their careful and rare use.

In contrast to this presumably unique item, the three cards from a heraldic didactic deck from Lyon, designed in ca. 1660 by Claude Oronce Finé, known as de Brianville, with at least 15 other editions, are evidence of its substantial success; today we would call it a bestseller. This can be explained by

[10] Köger, Annette, *Spielend lernen – Lehrkarten aus vier Jahrhunderten*, exh.cat. Schlossmuseum Aulendorf 1998, Leinfelden-Echterdingen 1998, 1.

[11] Radau/Himmelheber 1991 (see note 2), 331–366.

[12] Thieme-Becker, *Allgemeines Lexikon der bildenden Künstler*, Munich 1992, unaltered reprint of the original edition, Leipzig 1937/1938, vol. 31/32, 449; Hoffmann, Detlef, *Gemalte Spielkarten*, Frankfurt/Main 1985, 64f.

[13] Chmelarz, Eduard, "Die Spielkarten in der Bibliothek des Oesterr. Museums," in: *Mittheilungen des k. k. Oesterr. Museums für Kunst und Industrie* (XVII) 207 1882, 268. Translated by Maria Slater.

[14] Ibid., 266. Translated by Maria Slater.

Kartenmachertradition. Das Tiroler Standardbild wurde wohl von Johann Albrecht in den 1790er
Jahren aus dem altbayerischen Standardbild entwickelt. Es hat einen Eichel-Ober mit Krug und
Sichel für die Arbeit im Feld oder im Weinberg sowie einen Eichel-Unter mit einer Blume und Rosen
in den Armbeugen – friedliches Zubehör in der ansonsten militärisch geprägten Kartenhierarchie
von Offizieren und Soldaten. Das vorliegende Kartenspiel ist vollständig und in makellosem Zustand
erhalten. Auffällig ist die kräftige Farbgebung, besonders die lebhaftorangen und dunkelkarminroten
Töne wirken und betonen die untersetzten, beinahe den Rahmen sprengenden Figuren. Zwei Könige
(Eichel und Laub) tragen infolge des türkischen Einflusses Turbane statt Kronen. Auf den Schilden
sind, in der Tradition des Kartenmachers Andreas Benedict Göbl stehend, Wappentiere zu sehen:
habsburgischer Doppeladler, Einhorn, Sonne in Strahlenkranz, Hund.

GESELLSCHAFTSSPIELE – LEHRKARTEN

Spielkarten dienten schon ziemlich früh außer zum Spielen auch zum Wahrsagen oder Lehren.
Die Idee, den im Menschen angelegten Spieltrieb und die Lust daran für pädagogische Zwecke
einzusetzen, reicht bis ins Zeitalter der Renaissance bzw. des Humanismus zurück. Das Aufkommen
der Lehrkarten fällt zusammen mit den europäischen Entdeckungsreisen um 1500.[10] Als erstes
Lehrkartenspiel gilt allgemein das als Buchausgabe 1507 erschienene *Logica memorativa – Chartilu-
dium logicae* des Straßburger Franziskanermönchs Thomas Murner (1475–1537). Der Volksprediger,
Humanist und Dichter hatte mit der Erfindung, „spielend zu lernen", großen Erfolg.[11] Als Inform-
ationsträger in Funktion einer Buchseite kann sich so Wissenswertes je nach Entstehungszeit zu
Mythologie, Astronomie, Mathematik, Musik, Religion, Literatur, Geschichte, Kunst, Geografie,
Heraldik, Technik oder Sprachen etc. auf einer Spielkarte finden.
Ein bemerkenswertes Spiel stellt das signierte und datierte mythologische Spiel (Abb. 180) des
Johann Georg Staindorffer von 1688 dar. Als Sonderform kombiniert es italienische, deutsche und
Schweizer Farbzeichen wie ein „Trappolierspiel". Für ein nur simples Spielchen war es wohl nicht
geschaffen. Die farbenprächtige Darstellung der in schwunghafter Bewegung erfassten Figuren
lassen in Johann Staindorffer einen geübten Barockmaler erkennen. Das Künstlerlexikon bestätigt
diese Vermutung: Er ist dort als Maler der Seitenaltarblätter von 1681 in der Kirche zu Biberbach
(NÖ) verzeichnet.[12] „Als einfacher zunftmäßiger Brief- oder Kartenmaler wäre Staindorffer unbe-
streitbar unter den tüchtigsten zu vermerken", befindet Eduard Chmelarz, sogar „die Nachwirkung
des Rubens'schen Einflusses in Deutschland" attestiert er ihm hinsichtlich Farbgebung und Zeichen-
stil.[13] Die noch erhaltenen 28 Karten scheinen „im besonderen Auftrage für einen hohen Herrn"
entstanden zu sein.[14] Da Staindorffer als Altarmaler tätig war, ist ein Auftrag auch aus geistlichen
Kreisen vorstellbar. Das Bildprogramm zeigt Figuren aus der antiken Mythologie, deren Namen
auf den jeweiligen Karten vermerkt sind. Der emblematische Sinngehalt war dem Betrachtenden
bekannt oder konnte ihm damit beigebracht werden. Die feinen Malereien und die vermischten
Farbzeichen eigneten sich wohl weniger zum trivialen Kartenspiel. Auch die marmorierten Rückseiten zeugen von der qualitätsvollen Ausführung. Der gute Erhaltungszustand verweist auf einen
pfleglichen und seltenen Gebrauch.
Im Unterschied zu diesem vermuteten Unikat sind die drei Blatt einer heraldischen Lehrkarte aus
Lyon, um 1660 entworfen von Claude Oronce Finé, gen. de Brianville, in mindestens 15 weiteren
Auflagen Teil eines beachtlichen Erfolgs, heute würde man Bestseller dazu sagen. Zur Grundlage

[10] Köger, Annette, *Spielend lernen –
Lehrkarten aus vier Jahrhunderten*,
Ausst.kat. Schlossmuseum Aulendorf 1998,
Leinfelden-Echterdingen 1998, 1.

[11] Radau/Himmelheber 1991 (s. Anm. 2),
331–366.

[12] Thieme-Becker, *Allgemeines Lexikon der
bildenden Künstler*, München 1992,
unveränderter Nachdruck der Original-
Ausgabe Leipzig 1937/1938, Bd. 31/32, 449;
Hoffmann, Detlef, *Gemalte Spielkarten*,
Frankfurt/Main 1985, 64f.

[13] Chmelarz, Eduard, „Die Spielkarten in der
Bibliothek des Oesterr. Museums", in:
*Mittheilungen des k. k. Oesterr. Museums
für Kunst und Industrie* (XVII) 207 1882, 268.

[14] Ebd., 266.

180
Johann Georg Staindorffer
Meleager/Atalanta, **Herz-Ober**
aus einem mythologischen Kartenspiel,
Vorder- und Rückansicht
Österreich, 1688
Tusche, Deckfarbe auf Karton, Marmorierung
Meleager/Atalanta, **Over of Hearts**
from a mythological deck of cards,
front and back
Austria, 1688
Ink, coating paint, marbling
93 x 55 mm
KI 13382-1, alter Bestand, inv.
old holdings, inventoried 1960

der Bildung junger Adliger gehörten nämlich Kenntnisse in Wappenkunde. Diese waren wichtig, um z. B. die in Umlauf befindlichen unterschiedlichen Zahlungsmittel auseinanderhalten und deren Wert richtig einschätzen zu können.

Die drei erhaltenen Karten der Farben Kreuz-9, -7 und -4 zeigen Wappen europäischer Adelshäuser, hier italienischer und französischer Städte, sowie ihrer Machthaber von Mailand, Modena, Mirande, Monaco und Massa (Abb. 181, 182). Das Farbzeichen mit dem Kartenwert darin ist in der linken Ecke platziert, rechts die Wappennennung, im unteren Kartenteil ein französischer Erläuterungstext. Die erste Auflage wurde 1658/1659 hergestellt, mindestens 15 weitere Auflagen folgten mit z. T. veränderten Wappen. In einer Neuauflage musste de Brianville nach Beschwerden einiger Prinzen die Buben in Chevaliers und die Asse in Princes umbenennen. Deshalb wurden die üblichen Buchstaben R, D, V, A (Roi, Dame, Valet, As) ersetzt durch R, D, C, P (Roi, Dame, Chevalier, Prince).[15]

Die Tradition, Wappenkunde, Geschichte oder Rechnen, Lesen und Schreiben samt Sprachen spielend mit Spielkarten zu erlernen, erreichte im Zeitalter der Aufklärung einen Höhepunkt. Es entstanden ABC-Spiele, mehrsprachige Spiele, die etwa einen französischen Satz in zwei weitere Sprachen wie Portugiesisch und Englisch oder Deutsch und Italienisch übersetzten. In zahlreichen europäischen Ländern verlangten die Napoleonischen Feldzüge mit ihren „multi-nationalen" Truppen vor allem von den Kommandeuren Mehrsprachigkeit. Bis zu jenen Tagen zeigten alle Lehrspiele noch Farbzeichen und ermöglichten somit ebenfalls „normales" Kartenspielen. Mit dem Verschwinden der Farbzeichen auf Lehrkarten Ende des 18. Jahrhunderts entstanden Vorläufer der heute bekannten Quartett-Spiele. Der Übergang von Spielkarten über Quartette zu Gesellschaftsspielen ist fließend.[16]

Karten ohne Farbzeichen sind etwa die Vogel- oder Hexenkarten (Abb. 183, 184), deren weitere Bezeichnungen Cucuspiel, Coucou, Cambio, Gnav, Kis Kis oder Kille lauten. Ihr Ursprung wird in Italien vermutet, von wo aus sie sich über Frankreich und Deutschland bis nach Dänemark, Norwegen und Schweden unter jeweils anderen Namen verbreitet haben. Heute sind sie nur noch in Italien, Dänemark und Schweden bekannt.

Die Karten zeigen Figuren und Nummern. Die höchste Karte (XV) ist der Cucu, der „Herr des Spiels" genannt. Es folgen die Figur des Bragone (XIV), ein Pferd (XIII), eine Katze (XII) und ein Wirtshaus (XI) bis zur Nummer (I) und schließlich die Nulla (0), ein Eimer und ein Larvengesicht, jeweils weniger als die vorherige Karte geltend. Vor Spielbeginn wird eine vereinbarte Menge an Geld in eine Tasse (Kassette) gelegt und „eine gewisse Zahl der Zeichen (Marquen)" von den Spielern genommen. Jeder erhält eine Karte und tauscht diese mit seinem Nachbarn, um eine höherwertige Karte zu erlangen. Sieben Karten von Cucu bis Wirtshaus sind privilegiert vom Tausch ausgenommen. „Wer aber nicht tauschen will mit seinem Gespan, wird eine Marque in die Taze sezzen, und das so lang, als er deren hat; der aber der lezte seyn wird von allen, und seine Marque nicht zugesezzet, hat gewonnen."[17]

Im zweiten Teil des 1756 in Nürnberg und Wien erschienenen Spielregelbuchs von François Danican Philidor wird „Das Cucuspiel" erstmals im deutschen Sprachraum erwähnt.[18] Einführend wird erläutert, dass es in Italien erfunden wurde, „um damit eine zahlreiche Gesellschaft vollkommen zu unterhalten, ohne daß sich die Spielere in eine Gefahr sezzen dörffen".[19] Die dafür benötigten 38 Blatt „besondere Karten" finde „man aber nicht so leicht in Deutschland".[20] Die in der MAK-Sammlung vorhandenen 18 Blatt zeigen bis auf eine fehlende Karte alle Motive eines Cucu-Spiels und können somit einen fast vollständigen Eindruck dieses Spiels geben.

[15] Radau/Himmelheber 1991 (s. Anm. 2), 337–339.

[16] Selbst die Religion fand z. B. mit Zitaten aus dem Alten und Neuen Testament Eingang in Spielkarten. In Graz wurden Ende des 18. Jahrhunderts *Biblische Lehrkarten für das Alphabet* entwickelt. Jeder Buchstabe war mit einer biblischen Figur verknüpft, sodass lesen lernen mit einer Bibeleinführung gekoppelt war. Damit sollte wohl ein religiöser Bezug hergestellt und die von der Kirche als „des Teufels Gebetsbuch" gebrandmarkten Spielkarten geläutert werden. Heutzutage sind technische Errungenschaften eindeutig in den Vordergrund der Motivauswahl gerückt.

[17] Philidor 1756, Bd. 2 (s. Anm. 6), 231.

[18] Ebd., 229–234.

[19] Ebd., 230.

[20] Ebd.

the fact that knowledge of heraldry was considered one of the foundations of education for young aristocrats. It was important e.g. to distinguish between the various currencies in circulation and to correctly assess their value.

The three surviving cards—the nine, seven, and four of clubs—bear the arms of noble European families, here Italian and French cities, as well as their rulers from Milan, Modena, Mirande, Monaco, and Massa (ill. 181, 182). The symbol of the suit containing the card's value is placed in the left corner, right the name of the coat of arms, and in the lower part of the card is an explanatory text in French. The first edition was produced in 1658/1659; at least 15 further editions followed with sometimes altered coats of arms. In a new edition, de Brianville had to rename the knaves chevaliers and the aces princes after complaints from a few real-life princes. For this reason, the customary letters R, D, V, A (roi, dame, valet, ace) were replaced with R, D, C, P (roi, dame, chevalier, prince).[15]

The tradition of playfully learning heraldry, history, or reading, writing, and arithmetic as well as languages reached its heyday in the age of Enlightenment. There arose ABC games, multilingual games, which for example translated a French sentence into two other languages such as Portuguese and English or German and Italian. In numerous European countries the Napoleonic campaigns with their "multinational" troops demanded multilingualism of their commanders above all. Until that time all didactic games still bore suits and hence still facilitated "normal" card games. The disappearance of the suits on the didactic cards at the end of the 18th century brought precursors of the now famous quartets. The transition from card games to quartets to parlor games is fluid.[16]

Cards without suits include, for example, Gnav cards (ill. 183, 184), used for a game which is also known as Vogelspiel or Hexenspiel, as well as Cuccù, Coucou, Cambio, Kis Kis, and Kille. It is presumed to have originated in Italy, from whence it spread via France and Germany to Denmark, Norway, and Sweden, gaining a different name in each place. Today the cards are only known in Italy, Denmark, and Sweden.

The cards bear figures and numbers. The highest card (XV) is the cuckoo, known as the "lord of the game." It is followed by the figure of the knight (XIV), a horse (XIII), a cat (XII), and an inn (XI), as well as the numbers (I), and finally a zero (0), a pot, and a scary face, with each being worth less than the previous card listed. Before the game begins, an agreed sum of money is placed in a cup (box) and the players take "a certain number of the tokens (chips)." Every player is given a card, which they then swap with their neighbor to gain a higher-value card. Known as matadors, the seven highest cards—from cuckoo to inn—cannot be swapped. "However, those who do not want to swap with their neighbors must put a chip in the cup. This continues as long as they still have chips; the player who is the last not to have added their chip to the others is the winner."[17]

"The cuckoo game" is mentioned for the first time in the German-speaking world in the second part of François Danican Philidor's game rulebook, which was published in Nuremberg and Vienna in 1756.[18] The introduction explains that it was invented in Italy, "to thoroughly entertain a large society, without the players having to face any danger."[19] The required deck of 38 "special cards" could "not however be found very easily in Germany."[20] The 18 cards in the MAK Collection show all but one of the motifs and hence give an almost complete impression of the game of Gnav.

[15] Radau/Himmelheber 1991 (see note 2), 337–339.

[16] Even religion found its way onto playing cards, e.g. with quotations from the Old and New Testament. In Graz, Austria, *Biblische Lehrkarten für das Alphabet* were developed at the end of the 18th century. Every letter was associated with a biblical character, meaning that learning to read was coupled with an introduction to the Bible. This was probably intended to establish a religious connection and hence purify playing cards, which had been denounced as "the devil's prayer book" by the Church. Nowadays, technical accomplishments have unambiguously been given priority in the choice of motifs.

[17] Philidor 1756, vol. 2 (see note 6), 231. Translated by Maria Slater.

[18] Ibid., 229–234.

[19] Ibid., 230. Translated by Maria Slater.

[20] Ibid. Translated by Maria Slater.

ENTWÜRFE VON KÜNSTLERINNEN

Die Sammlung weist einige Sonderformen an Kartenspielen auf, die als Künstler-Entwürfe Aufmerksamkeit verdienen. Dabei handelt es sich um die Cotta'schen Transformationskarten, das *Botanische Kartenspiel* von Johann Hieronymus Löschenkohl sowie Entwürfe von Fedor Alexis Flinzer und Ditha Moser. Als Zeitgenosse der politischen und gesellschaftlichen Umbrüche um 1800 gestaltete und verlegte Hieronymus Löschenkohl (1753–1807) um die 700 Kupferstiche, sogenannte *Bilder des Tages*, und schuf damit eine Art Vorgänger der illustrierten Zeitung. Er selbst bezeichnete sich als Graveur.[21] Ein von ihm 1781 in der Wiener Zeitung veröffentlichter Silhouetten-Kupferstich zum Todestag Kaiserin Maria Theresias brachte ihm zugleich Bekanntheit und wirtschaftlichen Erfolg.[22] Er war, wie man sagen könnte, ein „Tausendsassa", ein kreativer Kopf voller Ideen, mit Geschäftsräumen am Kohlmarkt, einem idealen Handelsstandort.[23]

Das *Botanische Kartenspiel* (Abb. 185–187) versammelt Blumen und Blüten auf den Zahlenkarten sowie Theaterfiguren auf den Hofkarten. Die darstellerische Erweiterung auf Spielkarten, die die Farbzeichen in die Illustration integriert, findet sich bereits in den Spielkarten-Almanachen des Verlegers Johann Friedrich Cotta, die in Tübingen zwischen 1805 und 1811 herausgegeben wurden.[24] Löschenkohl, allen Neuerungen gegenüber aufgeschlossen, nutzte geschickt Aktuelles und Beliebtes für seine Karten. Bei seinen Spielkarten mit Blumen zeigen die Hofkarten Figuren aus Theaterstücken diverser Autoren. Gekleidet nach der damaligen Mode und dem Zeitgeschmack geben sich dort z. B. Maria Stuart und Wilhelm Tell (Schiller), Iphigenie (Goethe), Rodogüne (Corneille) und Athalia (Racine) ein Stelldichein. Kenntnis von Literatur und Theaterleben konnte zu der Zeit vorausgesetzt werden, gehörte der Austausch darüber doch zu den Gepflogenheiten der Salons. Solche mit reichlich Inhalt versehene Karten konnten und wollten wohl auch zur Konversation anregen.[25]

Im Juni 1806 wirbt eine ganzseitige Annonce in der Wiener Zeitung für „Zeitvertreib bei schlechter Witterung" als „Winterunterhaltung" für vier von Löschenkohl hergestellte Spielkarten-Sets mit Musik, Karikaturen, SchauspielerInnen und Gedichten sowie Blumen.[26] Seine Spielkarten-Konkurrenz wusste deren Verbreitung mit einem Magistratsurteil vom 14. August 1806 zu verhindern. Dies mag der Grund für die geringe Zahl noch existierender Exemplare sein.[27]

Einen Höhepunkt der Spielkartensammlung des MAK stellen die Original-Entwürfe des *Sezessions-Tarocks* von Ditha Moser aus dem Jahr 1906 dar. Hersteller der gedruckten Fassung waren Albert Berger und Josef Glanz (Abb. 188, 189). Herz-As zeigt: „Druck Berger Wien VIII". Die moderne geometrische Formensprache verleiht den Karten eine besondere Note. Das quadratische Grundraster strukturiert alle Karten auf ihrer Vorder- und Rückseite (Abb. 190, 191). Die Quadrate in den Ecken sind entweder mit den Farbzeichen oder bei den Tarocken mit den römischen Zahlen I bis XXI gefüllt. Die Wiener Spielkartenfabrik Ferd. Piatnik & Söhne übernahm um 1910 die Firma Glanz und damit auch deren Archiv-Bestände, worunter sich Exemplare des Tarocks von Ditha Moser sowie eine von der Künstlerin mit verwandten Motiven handbemalte Spielkartenschatulle aus Holz befanden. Der Begeisterung für das farbenprächtige Spiel vom Beginn des 20. Jahrhunderts folgte ein Nachdruck durch die Firma Piatnik im Jahr 1972, der noch von Karl Moser, Sohn von Ditha und Koloman, begleitet wurde. Zehn Jahre später wurde das Spiel als *Jugendstil-Tarock* erneut in einer nummerierten Sonderedition aufgelegt und mit einem Textbändchen auf Deutsch und Englisch versehen. Bei der Beantwortung der Frage, weshalb sich die neue Gestaltungsform in einem Tarockspiel

[21] Egger, Hanna, *Botanisches Kartenspiel des Johann Hieronymus Löschenkohl*, Wien 1978, 17.

[22] Ebd., 10 f., Verkauf zu 2 Gulden von 7 000 Exemplaren innerhalb weniger Tage.

[23] Ebd., 22. Löschenkohls Angebotspalette war groß: Er druckte Fächer und Kalender mit Stichen aller Art. Mit Silhouetten auf Visitenkarten hatte er ebenso geschäftlichen Erfolg wie mit Dosen, Noten, Knöpfen, Scherzartikeln oder dem ersten Wiener Modejournal. 1786 führte er die Glückwunschkarte in Wien ein, ein sehr geschätzter Artikel zur Zeit des Biedermeiers.

[24] Radau/Himmelheber 1991 (s. Anm. 2), 228. Sogenannte Transformationskarten in Karten-Almanachen wurden in der Nachfolge von Kalendern und Taschenbüchern entwickelt. Das Taschenbuch für 1801 des Braunschweiger Vieweg Verlags zeigt Kupferstiche, die in die Darstellung erstmals Farbzeichen von Spielkarten integrieren.

[25] Auflistung der Figuren und Blumen in: Egger 1978 (s. Anm. 21), 49 f.

[26] Ebd. 24.

[27] Ebd. 25.

181
Claude Oronce Finé gen. de Brianville
Kreuz-4 aus dem heraldischen Kartenspiel
Jeu de Blason
Lyon, um 1660
Kupferstich, koloriert
**Four of Clubs from the Heraldic Deck of
Cards** *Jeu de Blason*
Lyon, ca. 1660
Copperplate engraving, colored
87 x 55 mm
KI 13396, alter Bestand, inv.
old holdings, inventoried 1960

182
Claude Oronce Finé gen. de Brianville
Kreuz-9 aus dem heraldischen Kartenspiel
Jeu de Blason
Lyon, um 1660
Kupferstich, koloriert
**Nine of Clubs from the Heraldic Deck of
Cards** *Jeu de Blason*
Lyon, ca. 1660
Copperplate engraving, colored
87 x 55 mm
KI 13396, alter Bestand, inv. old holdings,
inventoried 1960

183
Anonym Anonymous
**Secchia manco di nulla [Eimer zählt
weniger als Null] aus dem Spielkartenset**
Alla Colomba (sog. Hexenspiel)
Mailand oder Turin, 1. Hälfte 19. Jh.
Holzschnitt, schablonenkoloriert
**Secchia manco di nulla [Pot counts less
than zero] from the Deck of Cards** *Alla
Colomba* (so-called Gnav)
Milan or Turin, 1st half 19th c.
Woodcut, stencil-colored
97 x 53 mm
KI 14060-3-18, Ankauf purchased from
Anton Hofer 1974

184
Anonym Anonymous
Chu Chu XV aus dem Spielkartenset
Alla Colomba (sog. Hexenspiel)
Mailand oder Turin, 1. Hälfte 19. Jh.
Holzschnitt, schablonenkoloriert
Chu Chu XV from the Deck of Cards
Alla Colomba (so-called Gnav)
Milan or Turin, 1st half 19th c.
Woodcut, stencil-colored
97 x 53 mm
KI 14060-3-17, Ankauf purchased from
Anton Hofer 1974

185
Johann Hieronymus Löschenkohl
Rodogüne, Karo-Dame aus dem
Botanischen Kartenspiel
Wien, 1806
Stecher: Mayer
Kupferstich, handkoloriert
Rodogüne, Queen of Diamonds from the
[Botanical deck of cards]
Vienna, 1806
Engraver: Mayer
Copperplate engraving, handcolored
86 x 58 mm
KI 13391-1, alter Bestand, inv. old holdings, inventoried 1960

186
Johann Hieronymus Löschenkohl
Betonie, Kreuz-As aus dem
Botanischen Kartenspiel
Wien, 1806
Stecher: Mayer
Kupferstich, handkoloriert
Betony, Ace of Clubs from
the [Botanical deck of cards]
Vienna, 1806
Engraver: Mayer
Copperplate engraving, handcolored
86 x 58 mm
KI 13391-1, alter Bestand, inv.
old holdings, inventoried 1960

187
Johann Hieronymus Löschenkohl
Wilhelm Tell u. Walter dessen Sohn, Pik-König
aus dem Botanischen Kartenspiel
Wien, 1806
Stecher: Mayer
Kupferstich, handkoloriert
Wilhelm Tell and Walter His Son, King of Spades
from the [Botanical deck of cards]
Vienna, 1806
Engraver: Mayer
Copperplate engraving, handcolored
86 x 58 mm
KI 13391-1, alter Bestand, inv. old holdings, inventoried 1960

ARTISTS' DESIGNS

The collection features several unusual versions of card games; these are artists' designs and deserve closer attention. They include Cotta's transformation cards, the *Botanisches Kartenspiel* [Botanical deck of cards] by Johann Hieronymus Löschenkohl, as well as designs by Fedor Alexis Flinzer and Ditha Moser. A contemporary of the social and political turmoil around 1800, Hieronymus Löschenkohl (1753–1807) designed and published approximately 700 copperplate prints, so-called *Bilder des Tages* ("pictures of the day"), and thereby created a kind of precursor of the magazine. He himself described his profession as that of an engraver.[21] A silhouette copperplate print by him published in the Wiener Zeitung in 1781 upon the anniversary of Empress Maria Theresa's death brought him both fame and financial success.[22] One could say that he was a "jack-of-all-trades": He had a creative mind filled with ideas, and an office on Vienna's Kohlmarkt, an ideal commercial location.[23] The *Botanisches Kartenspiel* (ill. 185–187) assembles flowers and blossoms on the pip cards and theater characters on the court cards. This theatrical rendition on the playing cards, which integrates the suits into the illustration, can already be found in the playing card almanacs by publisher Johann Friedrich Cotta, which were released in Tübingen, Germany, between 1805 and 1811.[24] Löschenkohl, open to any innovation, skillfully used contemporary and popular themes for his cards. In his floral playing cards, the court cards bear figures from stage plays by various authors. Dressed according to the fashion and taste of the time, the figures who tryst on these cards include Mary Stuart and William Tell (Schiller), Iphigenia (Goethe), Rodogune (Corneille), and Athalie (Racine). Knowledge of literature and the theater could be taken for granted at that time, considering that discussing these topics was customary in the salons. Cards such as these featuring rich content could and were probably intended to stimulate conversation.[25]

In June 1806 a full-page advertisement in the Wiener Zeitung announced "Diversion in bad weather" and "winter entertainment" with four playing card sets produced by Löschenkohl bearing music, caricatures, actors, and poems as well as flowers.[26] His competitors in the playing card industry managed to prevent their distribution via a municipal decree dated 14 August 1806. This may be the reason for the small number of surviving copies.[27]

A highlight of the MAK's playing card collection is provided by the original designs for an *Sezessions-Tarock* [Secession tarot deck] by Ditha Moser from 1906. The producers of the printed version were Albert Berger and Josef Glanz (ill. 188, 189): the ace of hearts shows "Druck Berger Wien VIII" (printed by Berger in Vienna's 8th district). The modern, geometric language of forms lends the cards a special effect. The square underlying grid provides structure to all of the cards on their front and reverse sides (ill. 190, 191). The squares in the corners are either filled with the suits or, on the tarots, with the Roman numerals I to XXI.

The Wiener Spielkartenfabrik Ferd. Piatnik & Söhne took over the Glanz company around 1910—and hence also its archival holdings, which included copies of the tarot deck by Ditha Moser as well as a wooden playing card box hand-painted by the artist with related motifs. The enthusiasm for this colorful game from the beginning of the 20th century was followed by a reproduction by the company Piatnik in 1972, which was supervised by Karl Moser, son of Ditha and Koloman. Ten years later, the game was republished as *Jugendstil-Tarock* in a numbered limited edition and furnished with a short volume of text in German and English.

[21] Egger, Hanna, *Botanisches Kartenspiel des Johann Hieronymus Löschenkohl*, Vienna 1978, 17.

[22] Ibid., 10 f., sale at 2 gulden of 7 000 copies within just a few days.

[23] Ibid., 22. Löschenkohl had a large product range: He printed fans and calendars with all kinds of engravings. With silhouettes on visiting cards he had as much commercial success as with tins, musical scores, buttons, joke items, and the first Viennese fashion journal. In 1786 he introduced the greeting card to Vienna, a highly valued article into the Biedermeier period.

[24] Radau/Himmelheber 1991 (see note 2), 228. So-called transformation cards in card almanacs subsequently developed into calendars and diaries. The diary for 1801 by the Braunschweiger Vieweg publishers shows copperplate engravings, which integrate playing cards' suits in the illustrations for the first time.

[25] List of figures and flowers in: Egger 1978 (see note 21), 49f.

[26] Ibid. 24. Translated by Maria Slater.

[27] Ibid. 25.

188
Ditha Moser
Herz-As des *Sezessions-Tarock*
Wien, 1906
Ausführung: Josef Glanz
Druckerei: Albert Berger
Lithografie
Ace of Hearts of the [Secession tarot deck]
Vienna, 1906
Execution: Josef Glanz
Printing: Albert Berger
Lithograph
116 x 55 mm
KI 13965-3, Ankauf purchased from
Ernst Köhler 1968

189
Ditha Moser
Titelblatt des *Sezessions-Tarock*
Wien, 1906
Ausführung: Josef Glanz
Druckerei: Albert Berger
Lithografie
Front Page of the [Secession tarot deck]
Vienna, 1906
Execution: Josef Glanz
Printing: Albert Berger
Lithograph
116 x 55 mm
KI 13965-3, Ankauf purchased from
Ernst Köhler 1968

190
Ditha Moser
**Entwurf für die Spielkarte des Sküs
aus dem *Sezessions-Tarock***
Wien, 1906
Bleistift, Tusche, Deckfarbe auf Karton
**Design for the Excuse playing card
of the [Secession tarot deck]**
Vienna, 1906
Pencil, ink, coating paint on cardboard
154 x 141 mm
KI 8979-39, Schenkung donation 1932

191
Ditha Moser
**Entwürfe für die Zahlenkarten
des *Sezessions-Tarock***
Wien, 1906
Bleistift, Tusche, Deckfarbe
**Design for the pip cards
of the [Secession tarot deck]**
Vienna, 1906
Pencil, ink, coating paint
142 x 200 mm
KI 8979-38, Schenkung donation 1932

192
Ditha Moser
**Entwurf für Tarock I aus dem
*Sezessions-Tarock***
Wien, 1906
Bleistift, Tusche, Deckfarbe auf Karton
**Design for Tarot 1 from the
[Secession tarot deck]**
Vienna, 1906
Pencil, Ink, coating paint on cardboard
154 x 141 mm
KI 8979-23, Schenkung donation 1932

mit 78 Karten ausdrückte, stößt man auf ein wichtiges Familienfest. In der elterlichen Familie der Künstlerin, der Familie Mautner Markhof, wurde immer wieder vom großen Ereignis der goldenen Hochzeit von Adolf Ignaz und Marcelline Mautner Markhof erzählt, die am 27. Juni 1881 (zwei Jahre vor Dithas Geburt) stattgefunden hatte. Das Jubelpaar hatte zu der Zeit nicht weniger als 72 Enkel-kinder. Und bei diesem Fest wurde Tarock mit lebenden Figuren gespielt. Die Enkelkinder waren samt und sonders als Tarockspielkarten gekleidet. „Blattweise" gruppierten sie sich durch Aufruf der dirigierenden Tarockspieler in „Stichen" und wurden zusammengeführt.[28] Das Fest blieb zweifellos sowohl bei den „tarockierenden" Kindern als auch den anwesenden Gästen in lebhafter Erinnerung. Vielleicht waren die Erzählungen davon eine Inspirationsquelle für Ditha Mosers moderne Kreation zu Beginn des 20. Jahrhunderts.

SPIELKARTEN – EIN TRIUMPHZUG AN FARBEN UND IDEEN IM TASCHENFORMAT

Je nach Spielregel sind Kartenspiele für Jung und Alt leicht erlernbar und einfach spielbar. Die gesellige Runde kann sich in Wirtshäusern, auf Jahrmärkten, hinter Klostermauern oder an der Front im Kriegseinsatz zusammenfinden und versuchen, „das Glück" zu erspielen. Begabte Kartenkünstle-rInnen erfreuen die Runde mit Zauberkunststücken. Doch seit ihrem Erscheinen stehen Spielkarten auch in einem Spannungsfeld zwischen Amüsement und Verdammnis. Von ihrem negativen Image, ein Werk des Teufels zu sein (wie es der Franziskanermönch Bernhardin von Siena in einer berühmt gewordenen Predigt 1424 in Bologna formulierte) konnten sich die Spielkarten nie ganz befreien. Denn undurchschaubar bleiben die Wechselfälle von Glück, Zufall, Strategie und Geschick beim Umgang mit diesen kleinen beschrifteten, nummerierten und bemalten Kärtchen. So mahnte um das Jahr 1820 der Braunschweiger Kartenmacher Friedrich Vieweg auf einem Kartenspiel mit Sprüchen wie: „Spiele ja nicht in der Fremte, sonst verlirs tu Rock und Hempte, Leib und Ehre, Hab und Guth, mercke diß, du Junges Bluth."[29] Die Spielfreude der Menschen unabhängig von sozialem Stand oder Geschlecht konnte jedoch weder durch Verbote und Erlasse noch durch angedrohte Strafen wesentlich erschüttert werden.

Wer der geniale Erfinder der eingängigen Spielkartensymbole war, bleibt wohl ein Geheimnis. Trotz einiger Erwähnungen von Spielkarten in frühen Nachschlagewerken wie *Zedlers Grosses Universallexikon* oder Diderots und d'Alemberts *Encyclopédie* sowie Kruenitz' *Oeconomische Encyclopädie*[30] und zahllosen weiteren Untersuchungen und Veröffentlichungen bis in die jüngste Zeit ließ sich dieses Rätsel bisher nicht lüften. Werbefachleute verdienten hohes Lob, würden solche eingängigen, einfachen und formal starken Logos oder neudeutsch Corporate-Identity-Symbole von ihnen kreiert – und dies quasi ohne Verfallsdatum, denn die Kartensymbole sind bereits seit Jahrhunderten gültig. Spielkarten haben eine längere Haltbarkeit als die Papierscheine der Geld-währungen. Nach modernen Gesichtspunkten sind sie eine wirklich nachhaltige Erfindung. Sie sind über Generationen, Sprach- und Ländergrenzen hinweg wiedererkennbar und mit den französischen Farbzeichen sogar weltweit verbreitet. Und schließlich sind Spielkarten auch Projektionsträger, sie fungieren als Angelhaken, um die Imagination zu einzufangen. Mit jeder Karte kann eine Fantasie-reise beginnen. „Auch da, wo von dem Drang der Arbeit sich ein Geist / Um wieder neue Kraft zu sammeln, froh entreißt, / Muß eine Nahrung seyn, die Witz und Denken stärket, / Und wo Er bey der Lust die Absicht mit bemerket, / Die unsre kluge Welt beym Zeitvertreibe setzt, / Daß stets ein edler Geist nach Regeln sich ergötzt."[31]

[28] Ragg, Ernst Rudolf, *Jugendstil-Tarock Ditha Moser*, Begleitheft zum Kartenspiel, Piatnik Edition, Wien 1982, 15.

[29] Sammlung Deutsches Spielkartenmuseum Leinfelden-Echterdingen, (DSM Inv. Nr. B 13 a), Eichel-7.

[30] Zedler, Johann Heinrich (1706–1751), *Grosses vollständiges Universallexikon aller Wissenschaften und Künste*, 64 Bde., 1732–1754; Diderot, Denis/d'Alembert, Jean-Baptiste le Rond, *Encyclopédie ou Dictionnaire raisonné des sciences, des arts et des métiers*, 35 Bde., 1751–1780; Kruenitz, Johann Georg, *Oeconomische Encyclopädie oder allgemeines System der Staats-Stadt-Haus- u. Landwirthschaft, in alphabetischer Ordnung*, 242 Bde., 1773–1858.

[31] Philidor 1756, Bd. 1 (s. Anm. 1), Rückseite Titelkupfer, Gedicht von Christian Fürchtegott Gellert (1715–1769).

Why did the new design find its expression in a tarot deck with 78 cards? The answer can be found in an important family celebration. The artist's paternal family, named Mautner Markhof, frequently used to recount tales about the sensation that was the golden wedding anniversary of Adolf Ignaz and Marcelline Mautner Markhof, which had taken place on 27 June 1881 (two years before Ditha's birth). The couple had no fewer than 72 grandchildren at the time—and so the party's guests played tarot with living figures. The grandchildren were dressed one and all as tarot cards. "Card by card" they formed groups of "tricks" when called by the directing tarot players and were gathered together.[28] The party undoubtedly remained a vivid memory—both for the "tarot-playing" children as well as the guests present. Perhaps these reminiscences were a source of inspiration for Ditha Moser's modern creation at the beginning of the 20th century.

PLAYING CARDS: A POCKET-SIZED TRIUMPH OF COLORS AND IDEAS

Depending on the rules, card games are easy to learn and play for young and old alike. The social group can meet in pubs, at county fairs, behind abbey walls, or at the front during wartime, and see whether they have the luck of the draw. Talented card magicians can delight the group with conjuring tricks. Yet since their advent, playing cards have found themselves torn between amusement and damnation. Playing cards have never been able to rid themselves of their negative image of being the work of the devil (as the Franciscan monk Bernardino of Siena described them in a now famous sermon in Bologna in 1424). After all, the vicissitudes of luck, chance, strategy, and skill when dealing with these small, inscribed, numbered, and painted cards remain inscrutable. This led to the Braunschweig-based card maker Friedrich Vieweg warning players with adages on a pack of cards from 1820 such as: "Do not play with strangers, or you will lose the shirt off your back, your life and honor, and all your worldly belongings; remember this, young players."[29] Nevertheless, the joy people found when playing—regardless of social status or gender—could not be materially shaken either by prohibitions and decrees or by threats of punishment.

The identity of the ingenious inventor of playing cards' catchy symbols will probably never be known. Despite some mentions of playing cards in early reference works such as *Zedler's Grosses Universallexikon* or Diderots and d'Alembert's *Encyclopédie*, as well as Kruenitz's *Oeconomische Encyclopädie*,[30] and despite countless other investigations and publications up to the recent past, this mystery has not yet been solved. Advertising specialists would have earned high praise had they created such catchy, simple, and formally strong logos or corporate identity symbols—and that without an expiry date, as it were, because those card symbols have remained the same for centuries. Playing cards are more durable than the paper bills of the world's currencies. From a modern perspective they are a truly sustainable invention. They are recognizable across generations, across linguistic and political borders, and the French suits are even known the world over. And finally, we also project our thoughts onto playing cards; they are as fishhooks, which capture our imagination. A new imaginary journey can begin with every card.

"There, where a spirit from the stress of labor, / To rally his strength, wrests himself with savor; / He needs nourishment, which bolsters wit and cognition, / And where in his zeal he also notes the intention, / Which our clever world in its pastimes doth create: / Rules will a noble spirit always celebrate."[31]

28 Ragg, Ernst Rudolf, *Jugendstil-Tarock Ditha Moser*, booklet accompanying the deck of cards, Piatnik Edition, Vienna 1982, 15.

29 Collection of Deutsches Spielkartenmuseum Leinfelden-Echterdingen, (DSM Inv. No. B 13 a), 7 of acorns. Translated by Maria Slater.

30 Zedler, Johann Heinrich (1706–1751), *Grosses vollständiges Universallexikon aller Wissenschaften und Künste*, 64 vols., 1732–1754; Diderot, Denis/d'Alembert, Jean-Baptiste le Rond, *Encyclopédie ou Dictionnaire raisonné des sciences, des arts et des métiers*, 35 vols., 1751–1780; Kruenitz, Johann Georg, *Oeconomische Encyclopädie oder allgemeines System der Staats-Stadt-Haus- u. Landwirthschaft, in alphabetischer Ordnung*, 242 vols., 1773–1858.

31 Philidor 1756, vol. 1 (see note 1), reverse copperplate frontispiece, poem by Christian Fürchtegott Gellert (1715–1769). Translated by Maria Slater.

SPIELKARTEN ALS WISSENS- UND GESCHICHTSQUELLE

Bereits Rudolf von Eitelberger (1817–1885), erster Professor für Kunstgeschichte sowie Gründer und erster Direktor des k. k. Österreichischen Museums für Kunst und Industrie, beschäftigte sich mit dem Thema Spielkarten.[1] Es verwundert daher nicht, dass die frühesten Beispiele der Gebrauchsgrafiksammlung Einzelkarten bzw. Kartenspiele sind. Interessant ist, wie Eitelberger seine Beschäftigung begründet. An erster Stelle beschreibt er den Reiz der Kartenspiele für den Kulturwissenschaftler: „Denn die Völker, wie den einzelnen Menschen, lernt man am besten in ihren Leidenschaften und in ihren Spielen kennen, und es ist für sie gleich interessant, die Gattung des Spieles, wie die Art und Weise, wie sie sich beim Spielen benehmen." Aber auch für den Kunstforscher sei das Thema attraktiv – zum einen hinsichtlich der Gestaltung der Spiele, zum anderen aufgrund der verwendeten Technik. Diese stand im Vordergrund, als für das neue Haus am Stubenring eine „permanente Ausstellung der zeichnenden reproducirenden Künste" geplant wurde; darin sollten in der „I. Gruppe. Schnitt in Holz und Metall" auch die Spielkarten zur Ansicht kommen.[2] 1882 erschien in den *Mittheilungen des k. k. Oesterr. Museums* ein ausführlicher Artikel von Bibliothekar Eduard Chmelarz zu den bis dato erworbenen Karten.[3] Darunter befanden sich auch zwei Lehrspiele aus dem späten 17. Jahrhundert: ein Tarock-Kartenspiel mit mythologischen Figuren von Johann Georg Staindorffer (Abb. 193–195) und das Augsburger Kartenspiel *Fürtreffliche Welt-Berühmte Mænner* von Johann Stridbeck dem Jüngeren (1665–1714). Um Ersteres „lesen" zu können, wurden gewisse Kenntnisse bereits vorausgesetzt. Im anderen Fall boten Bild und Text reichlich Informationen, und das nicht nur über prominente Männer: Chmelarz nennt ausdrücklich alle Repräsentantinnen der Dame-Blätter und zitiert vollständig die Biografie der Dichterin Sappho, während das starke Geschlecht nur im Zusammenhang mit dem Ziertitel Erwähnung findet (Abb. 196–198). Eine ähnliche Aufteilung – Bildmedaillon und erklärende Zeilen – zeigt ein mythologisches Kartenspiel aus dem frühen 19. Jahrhundert, das in der originalen Hülle in Form eines kostbar scheinenden Büchleins erhalten ist (Abb. S. 172). Gänzlich auf Text konzentriert (selbst die Kartenfarben sind beschrieben) ist hingegen ein italienisches Frage-Antwort-Spiel, das Marianne von Kinsky, eine Nichte Marie von Ebner-Eschenbachs, 1895 dem Museum stiftete (Abb. 199). Neben der antiken Helden- und Götterwelt ist auch die unmittelbare Historie Gegenstand der Themen-Tarocke – so etwa in einem Spiel zum Gedenken an die Völkerschlacht bei Leipzig, die Heilige Allianz und den Wiener Kongress, das der Linzer Verleger Friedrich Emanuel Eurich 1817 herausbrachte (Abb. 200, 201). Vom Wiener Spielkartenerzeuger Josef Glanz stammt die spätere Version eines solchen Gedenkblattes, dessen Pathos der dokumentierenden Biedermeier-Serie gänzlich entgegensteht (Abb. 202, 203). Insofern bemerkte Ludwig Hevesi sehr treffend in *Kunst und Kunsthandwerk*, der Fortsetzung der *Mittheilungen*: „Die Spielkarten werden ja nachgerade tatsächlich Geschichtsquellen; kleine Handspiegel, in denen sich die ganze Zeitgeschichte Zug für Zug spiegelt. Die Phantasie-, Unterrichts-, Genre- und Karikaturenspiele des XVIII. und XIX. Jahrhunderts sind füglich schon als das anzusehen, was in unserer Zeit die allgegenwärtige und alles aufgreifende ‚Ansichtskarte' bedeutet."[4] Eine solche im klassischen Sinn spiegelt sich in den Veduten-Karten wider (Abb. 204–210). Drei Spiele mit Ansichten von Schweizer, Pariser und Wiener Sehenswürdigkeiten wurden zu einer Zeit erworben, als man sich dem Thema erneut widmete und 1973 eine Ausstellung ausrichtete. Der begleitende Katalog wurde 1974 durch einen Artikel in *Alte und moderne Kunst* noch einmal erweitert.[5]

1 Eitelberger, Rudolf von, *Über Spielkarten. Mit besonderer Rücksicht auf einige in Wien befindliche alte Kartenspiele*, Wien 1860.

2 „Programm für eine permanente Ausstellung der zeichnenden reproducirenden Künste alter und neuer Zeit im Oesterr. Museum", in: *Mittheilungen des k. k. Oesterr. Museums für Kunst und Industrie* (VII) 78 1872, 65.

3 Chmelarz, Eduard, „Die Spielkarten in der Bibliothek des Oesterr. Museums", in: *Mittheilungen des k. k. Oesterr. Museums für Kunst und Industrie* (XVII) 207 1882, 265–272.

4 Hevesi, Ludwig, „Das Spielkartenwerk von H.-R D'Allemagne", in *Kunst und Kunsthandwerk* (IX) 2 1906, 719.

5 Dornik-Eger [spätere Egger], Hanna, *Spielkarten und Kartenspiele*, Schriften der Bibliothek des Österreichischen Museums für angewandte Kunst 10, Wien 1973; Dies., „Spielkarten und Kartenspiele im Österreichischen Museum für angewandte Kunst", in: *Alte und moderne Kunst* (XIX) 135 1974, 15–21.

PLAYING CARDS AS A SOURCE OF KNOWLEDGE AND HISTORY

¹ Eitelberger, Rudolf von, *Über Spielkarten. Mit besonderer Rücksicht auf einige in Wien befindliche alte Kartenspiele*, Vienna 1860. Translated by Maria Slater.

Even Rudolf von Eitelberger (1817–1885), first professor of art history as well as founder and first director of the Imperial Royal Austrian Museum of Art and Industry, paid attention to the topic of playing cards.[1] It is therefore hardly surprising that the earliest items in the ephemera collection are individual playing cards or card games. What is interesting is how Eitelberger justifies the attention he pays to them. Firstly, he describes the attraction of card games to the cultural scientist: "Since one can best get to know peoples—as we can individuals—through their passions and their games, and the type of game is equally as interesting as the way in which they behave when playing." Secondly, the subject is also appealing to art researchers—on the one hand as a result of the design of the games, on the other due to the technique used. The latter was at the fore when a "permanent exhibition of the arts of reproducing drawings" was planned for the new museum on Vienna's Stubenring; the "1st group [in the show would be] engravings in wood and metal" and would also include playing cards.[2]

² "Programm für eine permanente Ausstellung der zeichnenden reproducirenden Künste alter und neuer Zeit im Oesterr. Museum," in: *Mittheilungen des k. k. Oesterr. Museums für Kunst und Industrie* (VII) 78 1872, 65. Translated by Maria Slater.

³ Chmelarz, Eduard, "Die Spielkarten in der Bibliothek des Oesterr. Museums," in: *Mittheilungen des k. k. Oesterr. Museums für Kunst und Industrie* (XVII) 207 1882, 265–272.

In 1882 a detailed article on the cards hitherto acquired was written by the librarian Eduard Chmelarz and published in the *Mittheilungen des k. k. Oesterr. Museums*.[3] Among them were two didactic card games from the late 17th century: a tarot deck with mythological figures by Johann Georg Staindorffer (ill. 193–195) and the Augsburg deck *Fürtreffliche Welt-Berühmte Mænner* [Virtuous world-famous men] by Johann Stridbeck the Younger (1665–1714). Specialized knowledge was essential in order to even "read" the former. In the latter case, the imagery and text provided ample information—and not only for the prominent men of the title: Chmelarz explicitly names all of the figures represented on the queen cards and quotes in full the biography of the poet Sappho, whereas the stronger sex is only mentioned in connection with the decorative title (ill. K196–198). A similar division—pictorial medallion and explanatory notes—occurs in a mythological card game from the early 19th century, which has survived in its original case in the form of a small and see-mingly valuable book (see ill. p. 172). In contrast, an Italian question-and-answer game is entirely focused on text (even the cards' suits are described); it was donated to the museum in 1895 by Marianne von Kinsky, a niece of Marie von Ebner-Eschenbach (ill. 199). In addition to the world of heroes and gods, recent history also features as the subject of themed tarot decks, as is the case in a deck to commemorate the Battle of Leipzig, the Holy Alliance, and the Congress of Vienna, which was released by the Linz-based publisher Friedrich Emanuel Eurich in 1817 (ill. 200, 201). The Viennese playing card manufacturer Josef Glanz produced a later version of such a commemorative deck, whose pathos is in sharp contrast to the documentary nature of the Biedermeier deck (ill. 202, 203). In this respect Ludwig Hevesi noted very aptly in *Kunst und Kunsthandwerk*, the continuation of the *Mittheilungen*: "Indeed, the playing cards are well-nigh historical sources; small handheld mirrors in which all contemporary history is reflected, step by step. The fantasy, didactic, genre, and carica-ture decks of the 18th and 19th centuries should be justifiably considered as comparable to that which is symbolized in our age by the ubiquitous and all-capturing 'postcard.'"[4] Just such a deck in the classical sense is reflected in the veduta cards (ill. 204–210). Three decks with views of Swiss, Parisian, and Viennese tourist attractions were acquired at a time when there was a renewed focus on the subject; indeed, an exhibition was dedicated to it in 1973. The accompanying catalog was expanded in 1974 with an article in *Alte und moderne Kunst*.[5]

⁴ Hevesi, Ludwig, "Das Spielkartenwerk von H.-R D'Allemagne," in *Kunst und Kunsthandwerk* (IX) 2 1906, 719. Translated by Maria Slater.

⁵ Dornik-Eger [later Egger], Hanna, *Spielkarten und Kartenspiele*, Schriften der Bibliothek des Österreichischen Museums für angewandte Kunst 10, Vienna 1973; id., "Spielkarten und Kartenspiele im Österreichischen Museum für angewandte Kunst," in: *Alte und moderne Kunst* (XIX) 135 1974, 15–21.

193
Johann Georg Staindorffer
Actaeon, **Herz-Unter**
aus einem mythologischen Kartenspiel
Österreich, 1688
Tusche, Deckfarbe auf Karton
Actaeon, **Under of Hearts**
from a mythological deck of cards
Austria, 1688
Ink, coating paint on cardboard
93 x 55 mm
KI 13382-1, alter Bestand, inv.
old holdings, inventoried 1960

194
Johann Georg Staindorffer
Schellen-9
aus einem mythologischen Kartenspiel
Österreich, 1688
Tusche, Deckfarbe auf Karton
Nine of Bells
from a mythological deck of cards
Austria, 1688
Ink, coating paint on cardboard
93 x 55 mm
KI 13382-1, alter Bestand, inv.
old holdings, inventoried 1960

195
Johann Georg Staindorffer
Bachus, **Schellen-Reiter aus**
einem mythologischen Kartenspiel
Österreich, 1688
Tusche, Deckfarbe auf Karton
Bachus, **Knight of Bells**
from a mythological deck of cards
Austria, 1688
Ink, coating paint on cardboard
93 x 55 mm
KI 13382-1, alter Bestand, inv.
old holdings, inventoried 1960

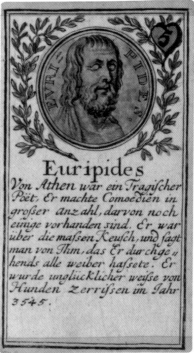

196
Johann Stridbeck d. J. the Younger
Ziertitel des Kartenspiels
Fürtreffliche Welt-Berühmte Maenner
Augsburg, 1685
Kupferstich, handkoloriert
**Decorative Front Page of the Deck
of Cards [Virtuous world-famous men]**
Augsburg, 1685
Copperplate engraving, hand colored
98 x 55 mm
KI 13395-1, alter Bestand, inv.
old holdings, inventoried 1960

197
Johann Stridbeck d. J. the Younger
Euripides, **Herz-5 aus dem Kartenspiel**
Fürtreffliche Welt-Berühmte Maenner
Augsburg, 1685
Kupferstich, handkoloriert
Euripides, **Five of Hearts from the Deck
of Cards [Virtuous world-famous men]**
Augsburg, 1685
Copperplate engraving, hand colored
98 x 55 mm
KI 13395-2, alter Bestand, inv.
old holdings, inventoried 1960

198
Johann Stridbeck d. J. the Younger
Sappho, **Herz-Dame aus dem Kartenspiel**
Fürtreffliche Welt-Berühmte Maenner
Augsburg, 1685
Kupferstich, handkoloriert
Sappho, **Queen of Hearts from the Deck
of Cards [Virtuous world-famous men]**
Augsburg, 1685
Copperplate engraving, hand colored
98 x 55 mm
KI 13395-1, alter Bestand, inv.
old holdings, inventoried 1960

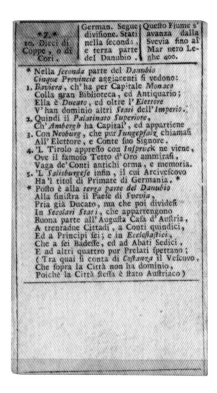

199
Anonym Anonymous
Kelch-10 bzw. Herz-10 aus einem
geografischen Lehrspiel
Italien, 18. Jh.
Buchdruck
Ten of Cups or Ten of Hearts from
a geographic didactic game
Italy, 18th c.
Letterpress print
95 x 54 mm
KI 7021-3, Schenkung donation from
Marianne von Kinsky 1895

200
Anonym Anonymous
Tarock II aus einem Kartenspiel zum
Gedenken an den Wiener Kongress,
die Heilige Allianz und die Völkerschlacht
bei Leipzig
Linz, 1817
Ausführung: Friedrich Emanuel Eurich
Kupferstich
Tarot 2 from a Deck of Cards
Commemorating the Congress of Vienna,
the Holy Alliance, and the Battle of Leipzig
Linz, 1817
Execution: Friedrich Emanuel Eurich
Copperplate engraving
100 x 50 mm
KI 4001-1, Ankauf purchased from
Friedrich Deckelmayer 1883

201
Anonym Anonymous
Tarock VII aus einem Kartenspiel zum
Gedenken an den Wiener Kongress,
die Heilige Allianz und die Völkerschlacht
bei Leipzig
Linz, 1817
Ausführung: Friedrich Emanuel Eurich
Kupferstich
Tarot 7 from a Deck of Cards
Commemorating the Congress of Vienna,
the Holy Alliance, and the Battle of Leipzig
Linz, 1817
Execution: Friedrich Emanuel Eurich
Copperplate engraving
100 x 50 mm
KI 4001-1, Ankauf purchased from
Friedrich Deckelmayer 1883

203
Anonym Anonymous
Heldentod, Tarock X
aus einem Kriegstarock
Wien, um 1850
Ausführung: Josef Glanz
Kupferstich, schablonenkoloriert
[Heroic death], Tarot 10
from a war tarot
Vienna, ca. 1850
Execution: Josef Glanz
Copperplate engraving, stencil-colored
103 x 55 mm
KI 14239, Ankauf purchased 1974

202
Anonym Anonymous
Graf Radetzky, Tarock XX
aus einem Kriegstarock
Wien, um 1850
Ausführung: Josef Glanz
Kupferstich, schablonenkoloriert
[Count Radetzky], Tarot 20
from a war tarot
Vienna, ca. 1850
Execution: Josef Glanz
Copperplate engraving, stencil-colored
103 x 55 mm
KI 14239, inv. inventoried 1983

204
Johannes Müller
Thonne/Vevey, Pik-Ass
aus einem Schweizer Veduten-Tarock
Schaffhausen, um 1880
Kupferstich, schablonenkoloriert
Thonne/Vevey, **Ace**
of Spades from a Swiss veduta tarot
Schaffhausen, ca. 1880
Copperplate engraving, stencil-colored
92 x 60 mm
KI 14012-1, Ankauf purchased 1973

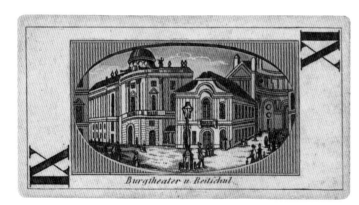

205
Anonym Anonymous
***Burgtheater und Reitschul*, Tarock IX**
aus einem Wiener Veduten-Tarock
Wien, 1859
Ausführung: C. Titze & Schinkay
Lithografie
[Burgtheater and riding school],
Tarot 9 from a Viennese veduta tarot
Vienna, 1859
Execution: C. Titze & Schinkay
Lithograph
53 x 101 mm
KI 14066-8, Ankauf purchased from
Auktionshaus Wendt 1976

206
Anonym Anonymous
***Weilburg bei Baden*, Tarock X**
aus einem Wiener Veduten-Tarock
Wien, 1859
Ausführung: C. Titze & Schinkay
Lithografie
[Weilburg near Baden], Tarot 10
from a Viennese veduta tarot
Vienna, 1859
Execution: C. Titze & Schinkay
Lithograph
53 x 101 mm
KI 14066-9, Ankauf purchased from
Auktionshaus Wendt 1976

207
Anonym Anonymous
***Kärntnerstraße*, Tarock XX**
aus einem Wiener Veduten-Tarock
Wien, 1859
Ausführung: C. Titze & Schinkay
Lithografie
***Kärntnerstraße*, Tarot 20**
from a Viennese veduta tarot
Vienna, 1859
Execution: C. Titze & Schinkay
Lithograph
53 x 101 mm
KI 14066-16, Ankauf purchased from
Auktionshaus Wendt 1976

208
Georg Mayer
Magdalenenkirche, Tarock 8 aus
einem Veduten-Tarock (*Chineser Tapp-Tarock*)
Wien, um 1850
Ausführung: Georg Mayer
Kupferstich
[La Madeleine], Tarot 8 from a
veduta tarot (*Chineser Tapp-Tarock*)
Vienna, ca. 1850
Execution: Georg Mayer
Copperplate engraving
55 x 104 mm
KI 14023-2, alter Bestand, inv.
old holdings, inventoried 1974

209
Georg Mayer
Ansicht von Paris, Tarock 21 aus
einem Veduten-Tarock (*Chineser Tapp-Tarock*)
Wien, um 1850
Ausführung: Georg Mayer
Kupferstich
[View of Paris], Tarot 21 from a
veduta tarot (*Chineser Tapp-Tarock*)
Vienna, ca. 1850
Execution: Georg Mayer
Copperplate engraving
55 x 104 mm
KI 14023-2, alter Bestand, inv.
old holdings, inventoried 1974

210
Georg Mayer
Juliussäule, Tarock 3 aus einem
Veduten-Tarock (*Chineser Tapp-Tarock*)
Wien, um 1850
Ausführung: Georg Mayer
Kupferstich
[July Column], Tarot 3 from a
veduta tarot (*Chineser Tapp-Tarock*)
Vienna, ca. 1850
Execution: Georg Mayer
Copperplate engraving
104 x 55 mm
KI 14023-2, alter Bestand, inv.
old holdings, inventoried 1974

SPIELKARTEN AUS KÜNSTLERHAND

Piatnik-Geschäftsführer Dieter Strehl wies einleitend darauf hin, viele KünstlerInnen hätten Spielkarten entworfen, und nannte beispielhaft solche des 20. Jahrhunderts. Der Kreis lässt sich schnell
erweitern, denn seit der Verbreitung des Kartenspiels um 1400 haben sich Künstler mit dessen
Gestaltung befasst. Dabei vereinten sie oft mehrere Funktionen, sollten doch die Karten auch bilden
und unterhaltsam sein (was teilweise auf Kosten der Spielbarkeit ging). Das Augenmerk auf fanta-
sievolle Motive weckte frühzeitig das Interesse von SammlerInnen, wovon die ersten und ältesten
in die Bibliothek gelangten Spielkarten zeugen. Es sind Kupferstiche des Nürnberger Künstlers Virgil
Solis (1514–1562), die entweder zu Sammelzwecken oder auch als Vorlagen erzeugt worden waren.
1868/1869 erfolgte der Ankauf eines ersten Blattes (Abb. 212) aus Solis' Tarockspiel, welches die
deutschen Farbzeichen Schelle, Eichel, Grün und Rot als Löwe, Affe, Pfau und Papagei zeigt;
weitere 21 Blätter wurden bis 1882 erworben (Abb. 213, 214). Rudolf von Eitelberger bescheinigt
diesen Arbeiten große Lebendigkeit sowie einen feinen Humor und betont des Künstlers Produktivi-
tät und „bürgerliche Tüchtigkeit".[1] Im Gedenkblatt zu Virgil Solis' Tod wurde daraus buchstäblich sein
Alleinstellungsmerkmal generiert: „ES THET MIRS KEINR GLEICH MIT ARB[EI]T VEIN / DRU[M] HIS
ICH BILLICH SOLIS ALLEI[N]" (Abb. 211).

Mit den Farbzeichen spielten auch die sogenannten Transformationskarten aus dem Tübinger Verlag
J. G. Cotta, die zwischen 1805 und 1811 als jährliche Almanache erschienen. Die Ausgabe des
Jahres 1807 wurde von Wilhelm Christian Faber du Faur (1780–1857) mit Figurinen-Karten zu
Schillers *Wallenstein* gestaltet, während die Zahlkarten mehr oder minder gelungene „Verwandlun-
gen" zeigen: Treff, Pik, Herz und Karo finden sich in teils karikierende, teils dokumentierende
Szenarien eingebaut. „Die schwarze Weste eines ehrsamen Bürgers umspannt mühsam dessen
stattlichen Schmerbauch", beschreibt Eduard Chmelarz etwa das Pik-As in seinem Artikel über die
Spielkarten der Bibliothek, und „die Durchkreuzungen und Bekrönungen eines eisernen Gitters
eignen sich unschwer zur Anbringung der Treff" (Abb. 215, 216).[2] Insgesamt kann der Autor
den Humor nicht nachvollziehen und hält die meisten Motive für geschmacklos und gezwungen
(Abb. 217, 218).

Während Chmelarz' Bibliotheksleitung wurde auch ein zeitgenössisches Kartenspiel erworben.
Es handelt sich um ein deutsches Blatt, gedruckt in Leipzig um 1880 nach Entwurf von Fedor
Alexis Flinzer (1832–1911), einem bedeutenden Illustrator des Historismus (Abb. 219, 220).
Die Bezeichnung „Ovale Salon-Spielkarten" sowie Rokoko-Motive in den Figurinen-Karten weisen
auf den intendierten Spielort und die Zielgruppe: aristokratische Damen, die im (oft im Stil des
18. Jahrhunderts dekorierten) Salon ihren Repräsentationspflichten nachkamen.

An die Transformationskarten schließt ein Spiel aus der Gegenwart an, das Julius Deutschbauer
und Gerhard Spring anlässlich ihrer 2008 im MAK gezeigten Ausstellung *Nur 100 Plakate*
produzierten (Abb. 221). Die Platzierung der Farbzeichen im Zentrum der Plakatmotive ergab
oft stimmige inhaltliche Bezüge. Ein 2012 entstandenes Wien-Spiel (Abb. 227) des niederländischen
Studio Formafantasma wiederum bezieht sich auf die Formensprache der Zeit um 1905, als Ditha
Moser ihre außergewöhnlichen Whist- und Tarockkarten erfand. Die Künstlerin, eine geborene
Mautner von Markhof, studierte ab 1902 bei Josef Hoffmann an der Wiener Kunstgewerbeschule,
wo sie Koloman Moser, ihren späteren Ehemann, kennenlernte.

[1] Eitelberger. Rudolf von, *Über Spielkarten.
Mit besonderer Rücksicht auf einige in
Wien befindliche alte Kartenspiele*,
Vienna 1860, 14.

[2] Chmelarz, Eduard, "Die Spielkarten in der
Bibliothek des Oesterr. Museums," in:
*Mittheilungen des k. k. Oesterr. Museums
für Kunst und Industrie* (XVII) 207 1882,
265–272, hier 271.

PLAYING CARDS BY ARTISTS

The CEO of Piatnik, Dieter Strehl mentioned in his introduction that many artists had designed play-ing cards, suggesting some 20th-century names by way of example. It is not difficult to add others to this category: since the initial spread of card games around 1400, many artists have turned their attention to their design. They have often combined several functions, considering that the cards should both educate and entertain (which at times came at the expense of their playability).

A focus on imaginative motifs soon gained the interest of collectors, to which the first and oldest playing cards to arrive in the MAK Library bear witness. They are copperplate prints by the Nurem-berg-based artist Virgil Solis (1514–1562), which were either produced as collector's items or as exemplars. The first card (ill. 212) from Solis's tarot deck was purchased in 1868/1869, which bears the German suits bell, acorn, green, and red as lion, monkey, peacock, and parrot; a further 21 cards were purchased in the period up to 1882 (ill. 213, 214). Rudolf von Eitelberger attests to these works' great vitality as well as their subtle humor, and emphasizes the artist's productivity and "bourgeois proficiency."[1] On the memorial sheet for Virgil Solis's death, this was quite literally mentioned as his unique selling point: "No one's work compares to mine / Which is why I, Solis, rightly stand alone" (ill. 211).

The suits were also played with in the so-called transformation cards by the Tübingen-based publisher J. G. Cotta, which were released as annual almanacs between 1805 and 1811. The 1807 edition was designed by Wilhelm Christian Faber du Faur (1780–1857) with face cards representing Schiller's *Wallenstein*, while the pip cards show more or less successful "transformations": club, spade, heart, and diamond are incorporated into partly caricatural, partly documentary scenarios. "The black vest of an honorable citizen girdles his considerable potbelly," is, for example, how Eduard Chmelarz describes the ace of spades in his article about the library's playing cards, and "the crisscrosses and finials of an iron grid are easily suited to bearing the club" (ill. 215, 216).[2] By and large the author cannot comprehend the humor and considers most motifs to be tasteless and forced (ill. 217, 218).

While Chmelarz was head of the library, a contemporary deck of cards was also acquired. It is a German deck, printed in Leipzig around 1880 after a design by Fedor Alexis Flinzer (1832–1911), an important historicist illustrator (ill. 219, 220). The description "Oval salon playing cards" and rococo motifs on the face cards point to the game's intended venue and target group: aristocratic ladies who performed their prestigious duties at a salon (which were often decorated in the 18th-century style).

Related to the transformation cards is a deck from the present day, which Julius Deutschbauer and Gerhard Spring produced on the occasion of their 2008 exhibition *Only 100 Posters* at the MAK (ill. 221). By placing the suits in the center of the posters' designs, they generated often harmonious content references. A Vienna deck (ill. 227) produced in 2012 by the Dutch Studio Formafantasma, on the other hand, makes reference to the language of forms of the era around 1905, when Ditha Moser invented her exceptional whist and tarot cards.

The artist, née Editha Mautner von Markhof, studied under Josef Hoffmann at the Vienna School of Arts and Crafts from 1902, where she met Koloman Moser, who would later become her husband. Under his influence she produced a straightforward yet highly remarkable work of ephemera, most

[1] Eitelberger, Rudolf von, *Über Spielkarten. Mit besonderer Rücksicht auf einige in Wien befindliche alte Kartenspiele*, Vienna 1860, 14. Translated by Maria Slater.

[2] Chmelarz, Eduard, "Die Spielkarten in der Bibliothek des Oesterr. Museums," in: *Mittheilungen des k. k. Oesterr. Museums für Kunst und Industrie* (XVII) 207 1882, 265–272, here 271. Translated by Maria Slater.

Unter seinem Einfluss entstand ein überschaubares, aber höchst bemerkenswertes gebrauchsgrafisches Werk, dessen Originalentwürfe sich großteils in der Kunstblättersammlung des MAK erhalten haben. Ein Exemplar des von Josef Glanz verlegten *Whist-S*piels gelangte 1927 durch Dithas ältesten Sohn Karl in die Bibliothek; es wurde 1985 von der Firma Piatnik reproduziert (Abb. 226). Die streng geometrische Gestaltung spannt Farbzeichen und Figuren in ein schwarzes bzw. rotes Raster ein und folgte damit der aktuellen Ästhetik – Hoffmanns „Quadratlstil" – weit mehr als dem Anspruch der Spielbarkeit.

Um ein (sehr persönliches) Kunstwerk handelt es sich auch bei Mosers Tarockspiel, das zu Weihnachten 1906 ebenfalls bei Glanz erschien. Die Entwürfe zu diesem Spiel kamen 1932 durch einen unbekannten Spender in die Sammlung. Ludwig Hevesi widmete Mosers *Sezessions-Tarock* einen ausführlichen Artikel im *Fremden-Blatt* und machte darin besonders auf die familiären Beziehungen hinter den Motiven aufmerksam.[4] Da ist die Mutter der Künstlerin „auf dem Neunzehner, die freundliche alte Dame mit den grauen Scheiteln, im schwarz-weiß gestreiften Kleide" und auf dem Zwanziger die Mautner'sche Brauerei auf der Landstraßer Hauptstraße (Abb. 223, 225). Die übrigen Tarocke zeigen vor allem Genreszenen. Ihre Inszenierung als Spielzeugwelt empfindet Hevesi als „einzigen, symbolisch richtigen [Stil], denn was ist der Mensch anders als eine Puppe?". Einmal mehr erweist sich hier der Kunstkritiker als Philosoph – dabei würdigt er eine Gestaltung, die einem Testspiel letztlich nicht standhalten sollte, denn die Trumpfkarten waren zu ähnlich geraten. „Man habe Treffkönig für Pikdame gehalten", so Hevesi, und „Kaval für Bub angesehen" (Abb. 222, 224).

4   Hevesi, Ludwig, „Sezessions-Tarock", in: *Fremden-Blatt*, 1. Jänner 1907, abgedruckt in: Ragg, Ernst Rudolf, *Jugendstil-Tarock Ditha Moser*, Begleitheft zum Kartenspiel, Piatnik Edition, Wien 1972 (1. Aufl.), 1982 (2. Aufl.), 22–31.

211
Balthasar Jenichen
Portrait von Virgil Solis d. Ä.
Nürnberg, nach 1562
Kupferstich, Radierung
Portrait of Virgil Solis Sen.
Nuremberg, after 1562
Copperplate engraving, etching
123 x 88 mm
KI 1777, Ankauf purchased from
Kunsthandlung Artaria & Co. 1868

of the original designs for which have been preserved in the MAK Works on Paper Collection. An example of her *Whist* deck—printed by Josef Glanz—arrived at the library in 1927 thanks to Ditha's oldest son Karl; it was reproduced by the Piatnik company in 1985 (ill. 226). The strict geometric design captures suits and figures in a black or red grid and hence complies with the contemporary aesthetic—Hoffmann's "square style"—far more than any aspirations to playability.

A (very personal) work of art can also be found in Moser's tarot deck, which was also printed by Glanz, this time for Christmas 1906. The designs for the deck entered the collection in 1932 via an unknown benefactor. Ludwig Hevesi dedicated an entire article to Moser's Secession-style tarot deck in *Fremden-Blatt*, in which he drew readers' particular attention to the familial relations underlying the motifs.[4] The artist's mother is depicted "on the nineteen, the friendly old lady with the gray parting, in a black-and-white striped dress" and the Mautner brewery on Vienna's Landstraßer Hauptstraße features on the twenty (ill. 223, 225). The other tarots predominantly bear genre scenes. Their depiction as a toy world is something Hevesi considers the "only symbolically correct [style], since what are people other than dolls?" Once again the art critic proves to be a philosopher—while appreciating a design, which ultimately could not even withstand a trial game, as the trump cards were too similar. "We mistook the king of clubs for the queen of spades," says Hevesi, and "thought the knight a knave" (ill. 222, 224).

[4]   Hevesi, Ludwig, "Sezessions-Tarock," in: *Fremden-Blatt*, 1 January 1907, reprinted in: Ragg, Ernst Rudolf, *Jugendstil-Tarock Ditha Moser*, booklet accompanying the deck of cards, Piatnik Edition, Vienna 1972[1], 1982[2], 22–31.

212
Virgil Solis
Rot-4 (Papagei) aus einem Tarockspiel
Nürnberg, um 1544
Kupferstich
Red 4 (Parrot) from a tarot deck
Nuremberg, ca. 1544
Copperplate engraving
101 x 69 mm
KI 1832, Ankauf purchased from
Kunsthandel Alexander Posonyi 1868/69

213
Virgil Solis
Rot-Ober (Papagei) aus einem Tarockspiel
Nürnberg, um 1544
Kupferstich
Red Over (Parrot) from a tarot deck
Nuremberg, ca. 1544
Copperplate engraving
101 x 69 mm
KI 2408-1, Ankauf purchased from
Galerie Miethke & Wawra 1873

214
Virgil Solis
Grün-5 (Pfau) aus einem Tarockspiel
Nürnberg, um 1544
Kupferstich
Green 5 (Peacock) from a tarot deck
Nuremberg, ca. 1544
Copperplate engraving
92 x 61 mm
KI 3942-8, Ankauf purchased from
Kunsthandlung J. C. Wawra 1882

215
Wilhelm Christian Faber du Faur
Pik-Ass aus einem Transformations-Kartenspiel
Tübingen, 1807
Ausführung: J. G. Cotta
Kupferstich
Ace of Spades from a transformation deck of cards
Tübingen, 1807
Execution: J. G. Cotta
Copperplate engraving
98 x 69 mm
KI 13390-3-2, alter Bestand, inv.
old holdings, inventoried 1960

216
Wilhelm Christian Faber du Faur
Kreuz-10 aus einem Transformations-Kartenspiel
Tübingen, 1807
Ausführung: J. G. Cotta
Kupferstich
Ten of Clubs from a transformation deck of cards
Tübingen, 1807
Execution: J. G. Cotta
Copperplate engraving
98 x 69 mm
KI 13390-3-16, alter Bestand, inv.
old holdings, inventoried 1960

217
Wilhelm Christian Faber du Faur
Kreuz-Ass aus einem Transformations-Kartenspiel
Tübingen, 1807
Ausführung: J. G. Cotta
Kupferstich
Ace of Clubs from a transformation deck of cards
Tübingen, 1807
Execution: J. G. Cotta
Copperplate engraving
98 x 69 mm
KI 13390-1-11, alter Bestand, inv.
old holdings, inventoried 1960

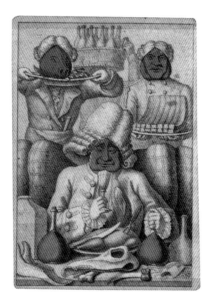

218
Wilhelm Christian Faber du Faur
Herz-5 aus einem Transformations-Kartenspiel
Tübingen, 1807
Ausführung: J. G. Cotta
Kupferstich
Five of Hearts from a transformation deck of cards
Tübingen, 1807
Execution: J. G. Cotta
Copperplate engraving
98 x 69 mm
KI 13390-1-13, alter Bestand, inv.
old holdings, inventoried 1960

219
Fedor Alexis Flinzer
Herz-Daus aus dem Set
Ovale Salon-Spielkarten
Leipzig, um 1880
Ausführung: A. Twietmeyer
Lithografie
Deuce of Hearts from the Set
[Oval parlor playing cards]
Leipzig, ca. 1880
Execution: A. Twietmeyer
Lithograph
103 x 67 mm
KI 4127-1, Ankauf purchased from
Buchhandlung Gerold & Co. 1884

220
Fedor Alexis Flinzer
Laub-König aus dem Set
Ovale Salon-Spielkarten
Leipzig, um 1880
Ausführung: A. Twietmeyer
Lithografie
King of Leaves from the Set
[Oval parlor playing cards]
Leipzig, ca. 1880
Execution: A. Twietmeyer
Lithograph
103 x 67 mm
KI 4127-1, Ankauf purchased from
Buchhandlung Gerold & Co. 1884

221
Julius Deutschbauer, Gerhard Spring
4 Karten aus dem Kartenspiel
Nur 100 Plakate
Wien, 2008
Herausgeber: MAK – Österreichisches Museum
für angewandte Kunst / Gegenwartskunst
Offsetdruck
4 Cards from the Deck of Cards
[Only 100 Posters]
Vienna, 2008
Publisher: MAK – Austrian Museum of Applied
Arts / Contemporary Art
Offset printing
Je 100 x 60 mm each
KI 22394, inventarisiert inventoried 2008

222
Ditha Moser
Entwurf für Kreuz-Reiter aus dem *Sezessions-Tarock*
Wien, 1906
Bleistift, Tusche, Deckfarbe auf Karton
Design for Knight of Clubs from the [Secession tarot deck]
Vienna, 1906
Pencil, ink, coating paint on cardboard
154 x 141 mm
KI 8979-27, Schenkung donation 1932

223
Ditha Moser
Entwurf für Tarock XIX aus dem *Sezessions-Tarock*
Wien, 1906
Bleistift, Tusche, Deckfarbe auf Karton
Design for Tarot 19 from the [Secession tarot deck]
Vienna, 1906
Pencil, ink, coating paint on cardboard
154 x 141 mm
KI 8979-23, Schenkung donation 1932

224
Ditha Moser
Entwurf für Kreuz-Bube aus dem *Sezessions-Tarock*
Wien, 1906
Bleistift, Tusche, Deckfarbe auf Karton
Design for Knave of Clubs from the [Secession tarot deck]
Vienna, 1906
Pencil, ink, coating paint on cardboard
154 x 141 mm
KI 8979-28, Schenkung donation 1932

225
Ditha Moser
Entwurf für Tarock XX aus dem *Sezessions-Tarock*
Wien, 1906
Bleistift, Tusche, Deckfarbe auf Karton
Design for Tarot 20 from the [Secession tarot deck]
Vienna, 1906
Pencil, ink, coating paint on cardboard
154 x 141 mm
KI 8979-24, Schenkung donation 1932

226
**Andruckbogen für das *Whist*-Spielkartenset
von Ditha Moser**
Wien, 1985
Ausführung: Ferd. Piatnik & Söhne
Offsetdruck
**Proof Sheet for the *Whist* Deck of Cards
by Ditha Moser**
Vienna, 1985
Execution: Ferd. Piatnik & Söhne
Offset printing
450 x 600 mm
KI 22934, Schenkung donation from
Ernst R. Ragg 1985, inv. inventoried 2015

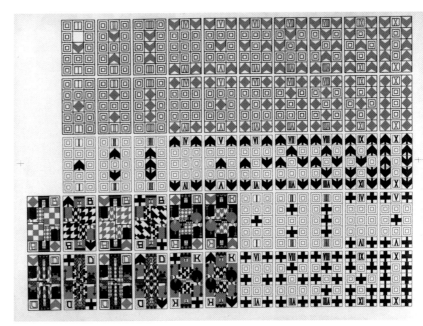

227
Studio Formafantasma
Vienna Now or Never
Amsterdam, 2012
Offsetdruck
Vienna Now or Never
Offset printing
Je 122 x 71 mm each
KI 22393 inventarisiert
inventoried 2012

SPIELKARTEN ALS MAKULATUR

Spielkarten sind auf Umwegen erhalten geblieben, wenn sie als Makulatur etwa zur Verstärkung von Buchdeckeln gedient haben. 28 solcher Karten eines deutschen Blattes wurden um 1880 angekauft und entstammten einem Bucheinband von 1569. Eduard Chmelarz hält in seinem Artikel 1882 nur 23 davon für nennenswert, u.a. Herz-Ober, -Unter, -3, -4 und Laub-Ober (Abb. 230), welche „recht gut gezeichnete Costümfiguren mit Federhut und Pelzwerk [bringen], deren Meister auf Herz-6 mit M.S.H. monogrammirt ist". Eichel-As zeigt die Datierung 1564 auf einer Banderole über einem Löwen mit Wappenschild (Abb. 231).[1] Die Karten sind als Holzschnitte ausgeführt und teilweise bemalt, waren aber offenbar so mangelhaft, dass sie einer anderen Verwendung zugeführt wurden. Häufiger findet man ganze Bögen mit unbearbeiteten Kartenandrucken als Einbandfutter – wie sie 1881 und 1886 in die Sammlung gelangten (Abb. 228, 229).[2]

Einen ungewöhnlichen Kartenfund – König, Bube und zwei Damen (Abb. 232) – machte man 1970 bei der Restaurierung eines spanischen Kabinettschränkchens, das 1940 aus dem Kunsthistorischen Museum übernommen worden war. „Der Möbeltischler hatte die Karten als Seitenwände von zwei kleinen Schubladen verwendet", hatte Vorder- und Rückseite der Laden damit verbunden (daher die Nagellöcher) und sie dann mit grüner Seide überzogen – so beschreibt Detlef Hoffmann in der Museumsschrift *Alte und moderne Kunst* die Konstruktion.[3] Dabei wurde ausgerechnet die Karte mit dem Namen des Produzenten verwertet: Auf dem Pik-Buben sind „andrien.perrozet" und seine Initialen zu lesen, ebenso wie das Monogramm „M" für den Holzschneider. Hoffmann ordnet Ersteren der bekannten Kartenmacher-Familie Perrocet in Lyon zu und datiert das Spiel um die Mitte des 16. Jahrhunderts. Ist Andrien Perrozet mit André Perrocet ident, der von 1491 bis 1524 in Lyon nachweisbar ist, kann das Blatt auch schon früher entstanden sein.

Im selben Jahrhundert jedenfalls dienten die Karten – durch Export nach Spanien gelangt – der Anfertigung des Kabinettschränkchens, das schließlich die Kunst- und Wunderkammer des Tiroler Erzherzogs Ferdinand II. (1529–1595) bereicherte. Unvollständige Spiele durch verloren gegangene Karten (die später unter Fußböden oder hinter Wandverkleidungen auftauchten und dadurch überdauerten) benutzte man oft als Schreibmaterial und notierte auf der blanken Rückseite der Karte Schulden oder Rechnungen. Hoffmann weist darauf hin, dass sich etwa in der Pariser Bibliothèque Nationale überwiegend solche Karten in Zweitverwendung erhalten haben, auch jene, die den später weit verbreiteten Brauch illustrieren, Spiel- als Visitenkarten einzusetzen.

[1] Chmelarz, Eduard, „Die Spielkarten in der Bibliothek des Oesterr. Museums", in: *Mittheilungen des k. k. Oesterr. Museums für Kunst und Industrie* (XVII) 207 1882, 265f. Datierung hier fälschlicherweise mit 1560 angegeben.

[2] Dornik-Eger [spätere Egger], Hanna, *Spielkarten und Kartenspiele*, Schriften der Bibliothek des Österreichischen Museums für angewandte Kunst 10, Wien 1973, 11. Die Autorin irrt bei der Angabe, die Bögen stammten ebenfalls aus dem Buchdeckel von 1569; sie sind anderer Provenienz.

[3] Hoffmann, Detlef, „Vier Spielkarten aus Lyon und ein Kabinettschränkchen aus Spanien", in: *Alte und moderne Kunst* (XVI) 116 1971, 18–21.

PLAYING CARDS AS SPOILAGE

Playing cards survive in a roundabout way when they have served as spoilage e.g. to reinforce book covers. 28 such cards from a German suit were purchased around 1880 and came from a book cover from 1569. Eduard Chmelarz only considers 23 of them noteworthy in his article from 1882, including the over, under, three, and four of hearts and the ober of leaves (ill. 230), which show "genuinely well-drawn costumed figures with plumed hats and furs, whose master's name is monogrammed as M. S. H. on the 6 of hearts." The ace of acorns bears the date 1564 on a banderole above a lion with a heraldic shield (ill. 231).[1] The cards were executed as woodcuts and partly painted, but were obviously so flawed that they were given a different purpose. More frequently, entire sheets of unfinished card proofs are found as the stuffing for book covers—as entered the collection in 1881 and 1886 (ill. 228, 229).[2]

An unusual card find—king, knave, and two queens (ill. 232)—occurred in 1970 when restoring a small Spanish cabinet, which had been acquired from the Kunsthistorisches Museum in 1940. "The cabinetmaker had used the cards as the side panels for two small drawers," had availed himself of them to connect the front to the back of the drawers (hence the nail holes) and then covered them in green silk—according to a description of the construction by Detlef Hoffmann in the museum's publication *Alte und moderne Kunst*.[3] Incredibly, the card chosen for this purpose by the cabinetmaker is that which bears the name of its producer: on the knave of spades "andrien.perrozet" and his initials are legible, as is the monogram "M" for the woodcutter. Hoffmann identifies the former as a member of the well-known card-making family Perrocet from Lyon and dates the deck to the mid-16th century. If Andrien Perrozet is in fact the same person as André Perrocet, who can be traced to Lyon from 1491 to 1524, the card may well have been made even earlier.

It was undoubtedly in the same century that the cards—having been exported to Spain—assisted in the production of this small cabinet, which would ultimately enrich the Chamber of Art and Curiosities of the Tyrolean Archduke Ferdinand II (1529–1595). Incomplete decks as a result of lost cards (which later reappeared under flooring or behind wall paneling and have hence survived) were often used as writing material, with debts or bills noted on their blank reverse. Hoffmann points to the fact that it is predominantly such cards with a dual purpose, which have been preserved in the Bibliothèque Nationale in Paris, for example, including those whose function was the later widespread custom of using illustrated playing cards as visiting cards.

[1] Chmelarz, Eduard, "Die Spielkarten in der Bibliothek des Oesterr. Museums," in: *Mittheilungen des k. k. Oesterr. Museums für Kunst und Industrie* (XVII) 207 1882, 265f. Translated by Maria Slater.—Date here erroneously stated as 1560.

[2] Dornik-Eger [later Egger], Hanna, *Spielkarten und Kartenspiele*, Schriften der Bibliothek des Österreichischen Museums für angewandte Kunst 10, Vienna 1973, 11. The author is mistaken when she states that the sheets also originated from the book cover from 1569; their provenance is another.

[3] Hoffmann, Detlef, "Vier Spielkarten aus Lyon und ein Kabinettschränkchen aus Spanien," in: *Alte und moderne Kunst* (XVI) 116 1971, 18–21. Translated by Maria Slater.

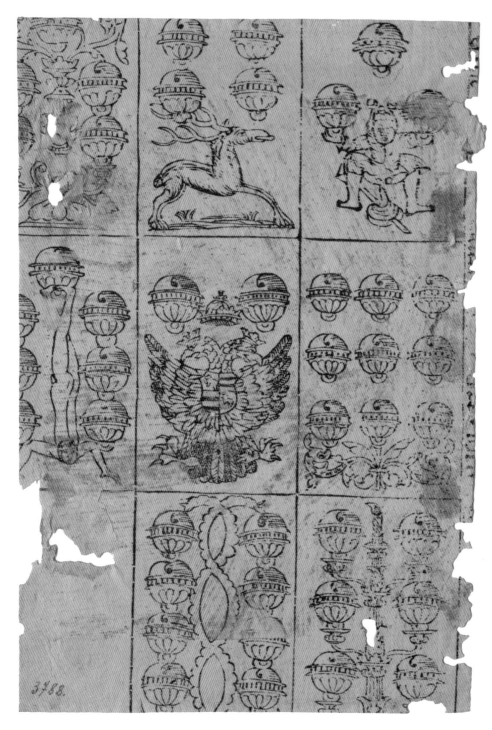

228
Anonym Anonymous
**Bogen eines ungeschnittenen
deutschen Blattes**
Deutschland, Mitte 16. Jh.
Holzschnitt
Sheet of Uncut German Cards
Germany, mid-16th c.
Woodcut
274 x 184 mm
KI 3788-1, Ankauf purchased from
Hr. Mr. Möringer 1881

229
Anonym Anonymous
**Bogen eines ungeschnittenen
deutschen Blattes**
Deutschland, Mitte 16. Jh.
Holzschnitt
Sheet of Uncut German Cards
Germany, mid-16th c.
Woodcut
304 x 197 mm
KI 4779-3, aus einem alten Einband gelöst
removed from an old book cover 1886

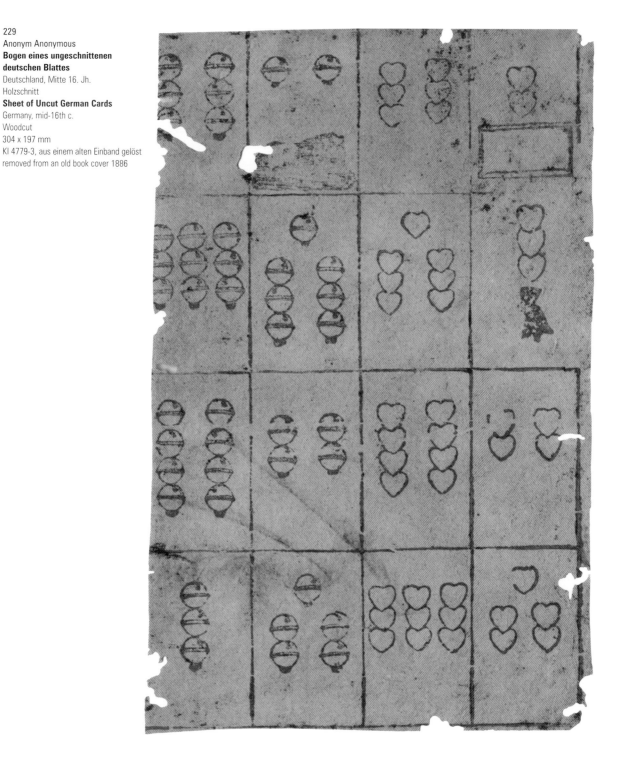

230
M. S. H.
**Laub-Ober, Spielkarte aus einem
Buchdeckel von 1569**
vermutl. Sachsen, 1564
Holzschnitt
**Over of Leaves, Playing Card from
a Book Cover from 1569**
prob. Saxony, 1564
Woodcut
75 x 60 mm
KI 3692-2-1, Ankauf purchased from
Wagner 1880

231
M. S. H.
**Eichel-Ass, Spielkarte aus einem
Buchdeckel von 1569**
vermutl. Sachsen, 1564
Holzschnitt
**Ace of Acorns, Playing Card from
a Book Cover from 1569**
prob. Saxony, 1564
Woodcut
75 x 60 mm
KI 3692-2-13, Ankauf purchased from
Wagner 1880

232
Andrien Perrozet
**4 Spielkarten aus einem
französischen Blatt**
Lyon, 1. Hälfte 16. Jh.
Holzschnitt
**4 Playing Cards from a
French Deck of Cards**
Lyon, 1st half 16th c.
Woodcut
Je 87 x 54 mm each
KI 14203, bei Restaurierung eines
Kabinettschränkchens aufgefunden
discoverd during restoration of a cabinet 1970

SPIELKARTEN ALS VISITENKARTEN

In seiner Abhandlung *Zur Geschichte der Besuchskarte* macht Walter von Zur Westen, Berliner
Jurist, Kunsthistoriker und Verfasser umfangreicher Werke über Gebrauchsgrafik, auf eine eigen-
tümliche Sitte aufmerksam: „Vielleicht hat man sich schon damals [um 1710] zu diesem Behufe
der Spielkarte bedient, auf deren Rückseite der Name geschrieben oder gedruckt wurde. […]
In Deutschland war diese seltsame und wenig geschmackvolle Benutzung der Spielkarte zu
Besuchszwecken sehr verbreitet und hielt sich merkwürdig lange. Sie ist noch gegen Ende des
18. Jahrhunderts nachweisbar. Man zerschnitt die Karten meist in vier oder sechs Streifen."[1]
Mag dieser Zweitverwendung tatsächlich etwas Grobes anhaften, so wurden doch unvollständig
gewordene Spiele einer neuen Funktion zugeführt; zudem konnten mit den entsprechenden Farben
und Figurenkarten auch bestimmte Botschaften (Identifikationen, Herzensangelegenheiten)
transportiert werden.

In der Bibliothek sind 19 solcher Besuchskarten aus der Sammlung des Numismatikers Rudolf von
Höfken (1861–1921) überliefert. Zusammen mit einem Konvolut weiterer Visiten- sowie Glück-
wunschkarten waren sie im November 1929 von Josef Kuderna um 1.200 Österreichische Schilling
offeriert und ein halbes Jahr später um etwa die Hälfte des Preises angekauft worden (Abb. S. 172).
Die Spielkarten sind hier oftmals ganz oder längs bzw. quer halbiert erhalten und tragen auf ihren
Rückseiten französisierte deutsche Namen und Titel, entweder handschriftlich notiert oder aufge-
druckt. Graf Maximilian von Königsegg-Rothenfels (1757–1831), Domkapitular von Straßburg und
Köln, empfahl sich unter Angabe seiner Adresse („logirt beÿ") mit einem Kreuz-Buben (Abb. 234),
Baronin Anna Clara Louise von Vrints geb. von Kielmansegg (1741–1813) wählte Herz-5, wobei
diese Farbe nicht den Damen vorbehalten war (Abb. 233, 235). Auf einer längs halbierten Karo-10
verewigte sich eine Baronin von Keller, Hofdame einer Prinzessin Reuß von Plauen, und nutzte dabei
fünf Karos offenbar für eine Sprachspielerei (Abb. 236).

Die aus dem späten 18. Jahrhundert stammenden Beispiele illustrieren einen Brauch, der sich
etwa ein Jahrhundert zuvor in Paris etabliert hatte. Im Laufe der Zeit wurden die behelfsmäßigen
Spielkarten durch eigens gestaltete Visitenkarten ersetzt und ein neues künstlerisches Genre
entstand. Anspielungen auf die Zweitverwendung finden sich bei der bereits zum Massenartikel
entwickelten Drucksorte noch im späten 19. Jahrhundert (Abb. 237). Rudolf Höfken Ritter von
Hattingsheim war als Gründer und Präsident der österreichischen Exlibris-Gesellschaft offenbar
daran interessiert, dem Thema Visitenkarte – als Bestandteil der sogenannten Kleinkunst – zu
erneuter Aufmerksamkeit zu verhelfen. So erschienen in den Jahrbüchern der ÖEG 1908 und 1909
zwei Artikel von Moritz von Weittenhiller, der hierfür aus Höfkens Sammlung schöpfen durfte.[2] Sie
fallen in die Zeit eines wahren Booms, angeregt 1907 durch die erste Besuchskarten-Ausstellung im
Königlichen Landesgewerbemuseum Stuttgart.

[1] Zur Westen, Walter von, „Zur Geschichte der
Besuchskarte", in: *Exlibris, Buchkunst und
angewandte Graphik* (29) 1919, 1–14.

[2] Weittenhiller, Moritz von, „Einiges über
illustrierte Besuchskarten" [I und II],
Sonderdrucke aus dem VI. und VII. Jahrbuch
der Österreichischen Exlibris-Gesellschaft,
Wien 1908 und 1909. Die Exemplare in der
MAK-Bibliothek und Kunstblättersammlung
tragen eine handschriftliche Widmung
Weittenhillers an Höfken.

PLAYING CARDS AS VISITING CARDS

In his treatise *Zur Geschichte der Besuchskarte*, Walter von Zur Westen, a Berlin-based lawyer, art historian, and writer of voluminous works on ephemera, drew his readers' attention to a curious practice: "Perhaps even then [ca. 1710] one resorted to this purpose for playing cards, writing or printing one's name on the reverse. […] In Germany this strange and rather tasteless use of playing cards for visiting purposes was very widespread and persisted for a remarkably long time. There is even evidence of it dating to the end of the 18th century. The cards would mostly be cut into four or six strips."[1] Despite the fact that this secondary purpose might indeed be considered rather crude, it nevertheless meant that now incomplete decks were given a new function; moreover, the respective suits and face cards could be used to convey specific messages (identifications, affairs of the heart).

In the library 19 such visiting cards survive from the collection of the numismatist Rudolf von Höfken (1861–1921). Together with a bundle of other visiting as well as greeting cards, they were offered by Josef Kuderna in November 1929 for 1 200 Austrian schilling and purchased half a year later for approximately half the price (ill. p. 172). These playing cards have often been preserved whole or halved lengthwise or crosswise and bear French names and titles on their reverse, either hand-written or printed. Count Maximilian von Königsegg-Rothenfels (1757–1831), canon of Strasbourg and Cologne, took his leave by stating his address ("lorgit beÿ" [lodging at]) on a knave of clubs (ill. 234), Baroness Anna Clara Louise von Vrints née von Kielmansegg (1741–1813) chose the five of hearts, though this suit was not exclusively reserved for ladies (ill. 233, 235). A Baroness von Keller, lady-in-waiting of a Princess Reuß von Plauen, immortalized herself on a ten of diamonds halved lengthwise, evidently using the five remaining diamonds for a pun (ill. 236).

The examples dating from the late 18th century illustrate a custom, which had become established in Paris roughly a century before. Over the course of time the improvised playing cards were replaced by specially designed visiting cards, thus heralding the advent of a new artistic genre. Allusions to the dual purpose can still be found on the printed matter—by that time a mass-produced item—in the late 19th century (ill. 237). As the founder and president of the Austrian Bookplate Society, Rudolf Höfken Ritter von Hattingsheim was clearly interested in helping the subject of visiting cards—as part of the so-called minor arts—gain renewed attention. As such, two articles were published in the 1908 and 1909 yearbooks of the Austrian Bookplate Society by Moritz von Weittenhiller, who was permitted access to Höfken's collection for this purpose.[2] They emerged at the time of a genuine boom, induced in 1907 by the first visiting card exhibition at the Königliches Landesgewerbemuseum in Stuttgart.

[1] Zur Westen, Walter von, "Zur Geschichte der Besuchskarte," in: *Exlibris, Buchkunst und angewandte Graphik* (29) 1919, 1–14. Translated by Maria Slater.

[2] Weittenhiller, Moritz von, "Einiges über illustrierte Besuchskarten" [I and II], offprints from the 6th and 7th yearbook of the Austrian Bookplate Society, Vienna 1908 and 1909. The examples in the MAK Library and Works on Paper Collection bear a hand-written dedication by Weittenhiller to Höfken.

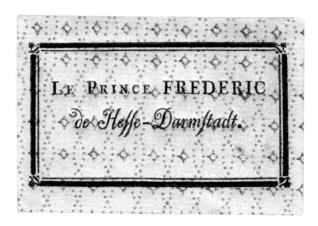 

233
Anonym Anonymous
Visitenkarte des Prinzen Friedrich von Hessen-Darmstadt auf Herz-6,
Vorder- und Rückansicht
Deutschland, um 1800
Kupferstich, Model- und Schablonendruck
Prince Friedrich von Hessen-Darmstadt's Visiting Card on a
Six of Hearts, front and back
Germany, ca. 1800
Copperplate engraving, block print and stencil print
55 x 80 mm
KI 8697-2, Ankauf purchased from Josef Kuderna 1930

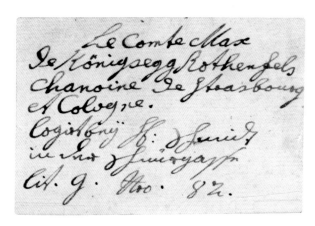 

234
Anonym Anonymous
Visitenkarte des Grafen Maximilian von Königsegg-Rothenfels auf
Kreuz-Bube, Vorder- und Rückansicht
Straßburg, um 1800
Ausführung der Spielkarte: Louis Carey
Holzschnitt, koloriert
Count Maximilian von Königsegg-Rothenfels' Visiting Card on
a Knave of Clubs, front and back
Strasbourg, ca. 1800
Execution of the playing card: Louis Carey
Woodcut, colored
55 x 90 mm
KI 8697-4, Ankauf purchased from Josef Kuderna 1930

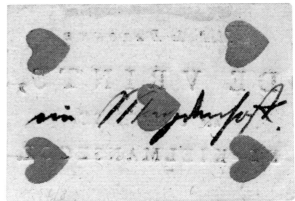

235
Anonym Anonymous
Visitenkarte der Baronin Anna Clara Louise von Vrints auf Herz-5,
Vorder- und Rückansicht
Deutschland, um 1780–1790
Kupferstich, Schablonendruck
Baronesse Anna Clara Louise von Vrints' Visiting Card on
a Five of Hearts, front and back
Germany, ca. 1780–1790
Copperplate engraving, stencil print
55 x 83 mm
KI 8697-8, Ankauf purchased from Josef Kuderna 1930

236
Anonym Anonymous
Visitenkarte der Baronin von Keller
auf einer beschnittenen Karo-10, Vorder- und Rückansicht
Deutschland, um 1780–1790
Schablonendruck
Baronesse von Keller's Visiting Card on a Cut
Ten of Diamonds, front and back
Germany, ca. 1780–1790
Stencil print
30 x 85 mm
KI 8697-16, Ankauf purchased from Josef Kuderna 1930

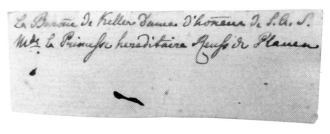

237
Anonym Anonymous
Visitenkarte des Cafetiers Johann Rauch
Wien, um 1880–1890
Lithografie
Cafetier Johann Rauch's Visiting Card
Vienna, ca. 1880–1890
Lithograph
58 x 100 mm
KI 8725-7, Ankauf purchased from Josef Kuderna 1930

„KÜNSTLERISCHE BESUCHSKARTEN"

Im Jahr 1907 beschäftigte sich erstmals eine eigene Ausstellung mit dem Thema Visitenkarten, ausgerichtet vom Königlichen Landesgewerbemuseum Stuttgart. Sie war Anregung für eine Studie von Gustav E. Pazaurek unter dem Titel *Künstlerische Besuchskarten*[1] und womöglich auch für ein Preisausschreiben, das am Ende des Jahres von der Königlichen Akademie der graphischen Künste Leipzig und dem Deutschen Buchgewerbeverein erlassen wurde. Die Ausstellung basierte hauptsächlich auf der Sammlung Albert Figdor, welche man einige Jahre später in den Schriften des Österreichischen Museums für Kunst und Industrie ausführlich beschrieben findet.[2] Zum Sammlungsgegenstand von Interesse wurde die Visitenkarte jedoch erst in der Ära Ankwicz-Kleehoven, der 1926 zu diesem Thema publizierte und 1930 über 700 Beispiele für die Bibliothek erwarb.[3] Sie stammen aus dem späten 18. bis frühen 20. Jahrhundert und illustrieren die Ausführungen Pazaureks auf sehr qualitätsvolle Weise. Dieser unterscheidet zwei Arten von „billets de visite": die personifizierte Karte mit eingedrucktem Namen und die Rahmenkarte, auf der man sein Autogramm und zunehmend auch kleine Mitteilungen hinterließ. Denn die bei der Dienerschaft hinterlassenen Karten zeigten nicht nur einen vergeblichen Besuch an, sondern überbrachten auch Dank, Glückwünsche oder die Nachricht über den bevorstehenden Abschied (wenn auch nur in „SMS-Form": p.p.c., „pour prendre congé", Abb. 239). Die Rahmenkarten gab es in jeglicher Ausführung; ab den 1780er Jahren wurden verschiedene Motive auf einen Bogen gedruckt, um nicht immer mit der gleichen Karte aufwarten zu müssen (Abb. 238). Den Randornamenten stehen die bildfüllenden Darstellungen gegenüber, die aus den Besuchs- imposante Ansichtskarten machen (Abb. 240) oder feine kleine Kunstwerke entstehen lassen (Abb. 241, 242). Eine eigene Gruppe bilden die geprägten Karten, die aufwendig gestaltet sein können (Abb. 244), sowie die mit Bleiweiß und Fischleim überglänzten Karten ab den 1820er Jahren, in denen Pazaurek aber schon die Bedeutungslosigkeit der Besuchskarte angekündigt findet (Abb. 243). Der Ankauf 1930 enthält auch Ergebnisse des erwähnten Preisausschreibens, das zur Wiederbelebung der illustrierten Visitenkarte animieren wollte und drei Entwürfe verlangte: Namenskarten für die deutsche Kronprinzessin Cecilie, die Prinzessin Johann Georg Herzogin zu Sachsen sowie für eine Privatperson.[4] Eine Auswahl der Arbeiten wurde 1908 in einer Wanderausstellung präsentiert und fand in der Fachpresse recht kritische Resonanz. So auch in Wien: Felix Poppenberg bemerkte in *Kunst und Kunsthandwerk*, es habe hier mehr Gegenbeispiele als Fruchtbares gegeben.[5] Nicht sehr glücklich ist er auch mit dem preisgekrönten Entwurf Heinrich Vogelers für Prinzessin Cecilie, dem er die flau nachempfundene Formensprache des 18. Jahrhunderts attestiert (Abb. 246). Vogelers Arbeiten, die zwei erste und einen vierten Preis erhielten, überzeugten auch Erich Willrich, den Direktor des Deutschen Buchgewerbemuseums, nicht gänzlich, denn, so befand er, was sei die Karte für Prinzessin Johann Georg anderes als eine Landschaft mit Figur und einem ausgesparten Teil für die Schrift (Abb. 245).[6]
Beide Autoren sehen in der Schrift die Hauptsache, die Gestaltung der Namenskarte sei typografischer Natur. Poppenberg hebt etwa einen Entwurf für Prinzessin Johann Georg von Rudolf Koch hervor, vergleichbar mit Abb. 247. Die weitere Entwicklung sollte ihnen recht geben. Exemplarisch hierfür stehen Visitenkarten aus den 1920er Jahren solchen von Stefan Sagmeister gegenüber (Abb. 250). In beiden Fällen offenbart sich die Schrift als großes Experimentierfeld, wo mit wenigen Mitteln Sinn, Humor und Individualität erzeugt werden können.

[1] Pazaurek, Gustav E., „Künstlerische Besuchskarten", in: *Archiv für Buchgewerbe* (44) 11/12 1907, 445–452.

[2] Guglia, Eugen, „Die Besuchs- und Gelegenheitskarten der Sammlung Figdor in Wien", in: *Kunst und Kunsthandwerk* XIV, 1911, 73–121.

[3] Ankwicz-Kleehoven, Hans, *Künstlerische Visitkarten*, Sonderdruck, Wien 1926.

[4] Weittenhiller, Moritz von, „Einiges über illustrierte Besuchskarten" [!], Sonderdrucke aus dem VI. und VII. Jahrbuch der Österreichischen Exlibris-Gesellschaft, Wien 1908, 3f. Die in der Ausschreibung als „Prinzessin Johann Georg" bezeichnete Gattin Johann Georgs von Sachsen ist ident mit Prinzessin Maria Immacolata Cristina Pia Isabella von Bourbon-Sizilien.

[5] Poppenberg, Felix, „Berlin. Chronik der angewandten Künste" [Kleine Nachrichten], in: *Kunst und Kunsthandwerk* (XI) 11 1908, 608f.

[6] Willrich, Erich, „Künstlerische Besuchskarten", in: *Die Woche* (10) 30 1908, 1317.

"ARTISTIC VISITING CARDS"

In 1907 the first exhibition dedicated to the topic of visiting cards was hosted by the Königliches Landesgewerbemuseum in Stuttgart. It provided the incentive for a study by Gustav E. Pazaurek entitled *Künstlerische Besuchskarten*[1] and possibly also for a competition, which was announced at the end of the year by the Königliche Akademie der graphischen Künste in Leipzig and the Deutscher Buchgewerbeverein. The exhibition was largely based on the collection of Albert Figdor, a detailed description of which could be found a few years later in the publication by the Austrian Museum of Art and Industry.[2] However, the visiting card only became interesting as a collector's item in the era of Ankwicz-Kleehoven, who published an article on this topic in 1926 and acquired over 700 examples for the library in 1930.[3]

These works date from the late 18th to early 20th century and excellently illustrate Pazaurek's observations. He differentiates between two kinds of "billets de visite": the personalized card with a printed name, and the bordered card on which one would leave one's signature and, increasingly, a short message. After all, the cards left with servants did not just represent an unsuccessful visit, but also conveyed thanks, good wishes, or notice of imminent parting (if only in "SMS style": p. p. c., "pour prendre congé," ill. 239). Bordered cards were available in all manner of styles; from the 1780s various motifs were printed on one sheet so that it was no longer necessary to wait on friends with the same card every time (ill. 238). These border decorations contrast with the space-consuming depictions, which transform visiting cards into imposing picture postcards (ill. 240) or result in small yet fine works of art (ill. 241, 242). A dedicated category is reserved for embossed cards, some of which had elaborate designs (ill. 244), as well as those cards glazed with white lead and isinglass from the 1820s, which Pazaurek believed already heralded the future irrelevance of the visiting card (ill. 243). The 1930 purchase also includes the results of the aforementioned competition, which hoped to revive the illustrated visiting card and required three designs: name cards for the German Crown Princess Cecilie; Princess Johann Georg, Duchess of Saxony; as well as for a private individual.[4] A selection of these works was presented in a traveling exhibition in 1908 and was met with a truly critical response in the specialized press. This was also the case in Vienna: Felix Poppenberg noted in *Kunst und Kunsthandwerk* that there were more counterexamples than fruitful works.[5] Nor was he content with the award-winning design by Heinrich Vogeler for Princess Cecilie, to which he attested a spiritless language of forms modeled on that of the 18th century (ill. 246). Vogeler's works, which won two first and one fourth prize, also failed to persuade the director of the Deutsches Buchgewerbemuseum, Erich Willrich, as he questioned whether the card for Princess Johann Georg was in fact anything more than a landscape with a figure and a part left blank for the text (ill. 245).[6]

Both authors see the text as essential; the nature of designing a name card was typographical. Poppenberg, for example, pointed out a design for Princess Johann Georg by Rudolf Koch, comparable to ill. 247. The subsequent development of the genre would prove them right. By way of example, contrast the visiting cards from the 1920s with the business cards by Stefan Sagmeister (ill. 250). In both cases the text manifests itself as a large space for experimentation on which with limited means sense, humor, and individuality can be created.

1 Pazaurek, Gustav E., "Künstlerische Besuchskarten," in: *Archiv für Buchgewerbe* (44) 11/12 1907, 445–452.

2 Guglia, Eugen, "Die Besuchs- und Gelegenheitskarten der Sammlung Figdor in Wien," in: *Kunst und Kunsthandwerk* (XIV) 2 1911, 73–121.

3 Ankwicz-Kleehoven, Hans, *Künstlerische Visitkarten*, offprint, Vienna 1926.

4 Weittenhiller, Moritz von, "Einiges über illustrierte Besuchskarten" [I], Vienna 1908, 3 f. The wife of Johann Georg of Saxony was described in the competition announcement as "Princess Johann Georg"; her name is in fact Princess Maria Immacolata Cristina Pia Isabella of Bourbon-Two Sicilies.

5 Poppenberg, Felix, "Berlin. Chronik der angewandten Künste" [short notices], in: *Kunst und Kunsthandwerk* (XI) 11 1908, 608 f.

6 Willrich, Erich, "Künstlerische Besuchskarten", in: *Die Woche* (10) 30 1908, 1317.

238
Karl Schneeweis
6 Blanko-Visitenkarten auf einem Bogen
Salzburg, 1780–1790
Radierung
6 Blank Visiting Cards on a sheet
Salzburg, 1780–1790
Etching
197 x 176 mm
KI 8698-1, Ankauf purchased from Josef Kuderna 1930

239
Anonym Anonymous
Visitenkarte Graf von Hoya
Deutschland, um 1780
Kupferstich
Count von Hoya's Visiting Card
Germany, ca. 1780
Copperplate engraving
62 x 87 mm
KI 8703-7, Ankauf purchased from Josef Kuderna 1930

240
Wenzel Engelmann
Visitenkarte Joachim Ballás
Österreich, um 1800
Kupferstich
Joachim Ballás's Visiting Card
Austria, ca. 1800
Copperplate engraving
96 x 125 mm
KI 8723-4, Ankauf purchased from Josef Kuderna 1930

241
Jacob Gauermann
Visitenkarte
Wien, um 1800
Radierung
Visiting Card
Vienna, ca. 1800
Etching
51 x 72 mm
KI 8704-8, Ankauf purchased from Josef Kuderna 1930

242
Karl Heinrich Rahl
Visitenkarte
Wien, 1800–1820
Kupferstich
Visiting Card
Vienna, 1800–1820
Copperplate engraving
74 x 106 mm
KI 8713-11, Ankauf purchased from Josef Kuderna 1930

243
Vermutl. prob. Jiří Döbler
Visitenkarte Hauptmann Brökl von Brokenstein
Prag, 1820–1830
Glanzpapier, Stahlstich
Captain Brökl von Brokenstein's Visiting Card
Prague, 1820–1830
Shiny paper, steel engraving
64 x 90 mm
KI 8721-8, Ankauf purchased from Josef Kuderna 1930

244
Anonym Anonymous
Visitenkarte Friedrich Wilhelm Gallas
Dresden, gewidmet am 23.8.1842
Prägedruck
Friedrich Wilhelm Gallas's Visiting Card
Dresden, dedicated 23 Aug 1842
Embossing
76 x 104 mm
KI 8720-18, Ankauf purchased from Josef Kuderna 1930

245
Heinrich Vogeler
Probedruck einer Visitenkarte für Prinzessin Johann
Georg Herzogin zu Sachsen (Erster Preis eines Wettbewerbs)
Worpswede, 1908
Radierung
Proof of a Visiting Card for Princess Johann
Georg Duchesse of Saxony (First prize in a competition)
Worpswede, 1908
Etching
90 x 115 mm
KI 8730-2, Ankauf purchased from Josef Kuderna 1930

246
Heinrich Vogeler
Probedruck einer Visitenkarte für die deutsche
Kronprinzessin Cecilie (Erster Preis eines Wettbewerbs)
Worpswede, 1908
Radierung
Proof of a Visiting Card for the German Crown
Princess Cecilie (First prize in a competition)
Worpswede, 1908
Etching
93 x 121 mm
KI 8730-7, Ankauf purchased from Josef Kuderna 1930

247
Rudolf Koch
Visitenkarte Walter von Zur Westen
Offenbach/Main, um 1908
Klischee
Visiting Card Walter von Zur Westen
Offenbach/Main, ca. 1908
Cliché
76 x 125 mm
KI 8743-1, Ankauf purchased from Josef Kuderna 1930

248
Rudolf Köhl
Visitenkarte Rudolf Köhl
Wien, um 1920
Holzschnitt
Visiting Card Rudolf Köhl
Vienna, ca. 1920
Woodcut
56 x 100 mm
KI 8745-5, Ankauf purchased from
Josef Kuderna 1930

249
Robert Haas
Visitenkarte Hansi Fritsche
Wien, um 1928
Klischee
Visiting Card Hansi Fritsche
Vienna, ca. 1925
Cliché
63 x 104 mm
KI 8894-7, Schenkung donation from
Hans Ankwicz-Kleehoven 1930

250
Stefan Sagmeister
Visitenkarte Stefan Sagmeister mit Plastikhülle
New York, 1988
Offsetdruck
Business Card Stefan Sagmeister with plastic cover
New York, 1988
Offset print
52 x 88 mm
KI 15735-31-1, Schenkung donation from
Stefan Sagmeister 2003

IV EINLADUNGEN – EINTRITTSKARTEN TANZORDNUNGEN – BALLSPENDEN TISCH- UND MENÜKARTEN – ETIKETTEN

Aus einem GESPRÄCH mit Thomas Schäfer-Elmayer

Ingrid Haslinger *Versprechen auf Papier*

AUS DER SAMMLUNG
A Gelegenheitsgrafik zu Fest- und Tischkultur
B Einladungen zu Ausstellungen und Besichtigungen

IV INVITATIONS—ADMISSION TICKETS DANCE CARDS—LADIES' GIFTS PLACE AND MENU CARDS—LABELS

From an INTERVIEW with Thomas Schäfer-Elmayer

Ingrid Haslinger *Paper Promises*

FROM THE COLLECTION
A Occasion Graphics for Social and Dining Culture
B Invitations to Exhibitions and Viewings

INVITATION

The program for the annual Elmayer-Kränzchen ball is now provided as a PDF. Does that replace the invitation?

Well, there are also proper invitations for the guests of honor—on deckle-edge paper with "Thomas Schäfer-Elmayer would be honored" printed on them, very classic. We mail approximately a thousand of those. Formerly the name used to be added by hand, but that task is now done by the computer—but in an attractive Allegro typeface! We give the ball program to all students and course participants; we don't mail it, but it can be downloaded. It has to be really well designed because it's truly essential to the ball's image. At my parents' house in Dornbirn, Austria, there's an archive of the dance school, which was founded back in 1919. All sorts of things are preserved there, such as admission tickets, invitations, thank-you cards, as well as dance cards. One day I'll probably bring it to Vienna.

DANCE CARD

The sequence of the dances used to be printed in small booklets in which the ladies made a note of which gentleman they had promised to spend each dance with. I imagine nothing along those lines exists now, does it?

People keep trying to revive it at various balls, but to only moderate success—because nowadays the ladies are much more enthusiastic dancers than the gentlemen. In fact, it would be better to reverse the tradition, so that the ladies could reserve dances with the gentlemen. As far as the dances themselves are concerned, much has changed. Those we have in our program now are almost all more or less African American/Caribbean. One really good idea was the world dance program at the beginning of the 1960s, which included set rules and steps for particular dances. Previously it was the case that a student from the Elmayer dance school had difficulties dancing a waltz with a student from the Fränzl dance school, because they'd been taught different versions. Now practically everyone around the world can dance with each other.

LADIES' GIFT

The dance card evolved into the ladies' gift, which was at times very elaborate. Today it's usually a promotional gift.

Very often, yes. I have an aversion to these ladies' gifts in principle, because it's usually some piece of junk and people are so crazy about them. If someone doesn't get a ladies' gift, then it's the end of the world! That happened to us once: We had ladies' gifts from a company whose employees thought they would be stuck with the goods because the ball was almost over and no one had come. So they simply gave them to the cloakroom women and other members of staff. Then, when the guests came just before the end of the ball, there wasn't much left and some people left empty-handed. You would not believe how badly I was told off. The entire ball was ruined just because some people hadn't gotten a little bottle of perfume.

PLACE CARDS

Place cards are used to establish a specific seating plan. Is it possible to ignore that plan?

I have known people to simply change it. Sadly, it happens. But even if you had been looking forward to spending the evening next to Ms. Smith and then find yourself sitting next to Ms. Jones, you should never swap cards. Incidentally, I think place cards should have writing on both sides so that people can find their seats more easily and also know who they are sitting opposite.

LABELS AND ETIQUETTE

The connection between the words label (in German: *Etikett*) and etiquette (German: *Etikette*; as a term for ways of behaving) is revealing. How did that happen?

The origin is said to be as follows. The gardener of Louis XIV used to get annoyed about the distinguished gentlemen walking or galloping over his beautiful floral borders in Versailles. So he put up signs, the *Etiketten*. And those gentlemen obviously couldn't care less about what the gardener had done. So he went to the king and declared: "The etiquette must be observed!" Which led to the creation of court etiquette.

Bottle labels are hugely important, especially in the context of a ball. I recently went to the presentation of the Life Ball wine for 2016. The labels had been designed by students from the New Design University in St. Pölten, Austria. The Life Ball wine will be served at lots of events, though the ball itself is not being held this year.

Thomas Schäfer-Elmayer, CEO, Willy Elmayer-Vestenbrugg Dance School, Vienna (Excerpt from a conversation with Anne-Katrin Rossberg in April 2016)

EINLADUNG

Zum jährlichen Elmayer-Kränzchen gibt es heutzutage das Ballprogramm als PDF. Ersetzt das die Einladung?

Na ja, es gibt auch noch richtige Einladungen an die Ehrengäste – auf Büttenpapier mit dem Aufdruck „Thomas Schäfer-Elmayer gibt sich die Ehre", ganz klassisch. Davon werden ungefähr tausend Stück versandt. Früher wurde der Name handschriftlich eingetragen, das übernimmt inzwischen der Computer – aber in einer schönen Allegro-Schrift! Das Ballprogramm geben wir allen Schülern und Kursteilnehmern mit, versenden tun wir's nicht, aber man kann es herunterladen. Das muss wirklich gut gestaltet werden, weil das ja ganz wesentlich für das Image des Balls ist. In meinem Elternhaus in Dornbirn gibt es ein Archiv der Tanzschule, die ja schon 1919 gegründet wurde. Darin ist alles Mögliche verwahrt, also Eintrittskarten, Einladungen, Dankeskarten und auch Tanzordnungen. Irgendwann werde ich's wohl nach Wien bringen.

TANZORDNUNG

Die Reihenfolge der Tänze war früher in kleinen Heften abgedruckt, worin die Damen vermerkten, welchem Herrn sie den jeweiligen Tanz versprochen hatten. So etwas gibt es heute sicher nicht mehr?

Man versucht es immer wieder auf verschiedenen Bällen, aber nur mit mäßigem Erfolg, weil ja die Damen heutzutage viel tanzbegeisterter sind als die Herren. An sich müsste man das umgekehrt machen, dass die Damen sich bei den Herren Tänze reservieren. Was die Tänze betrifft, hat sich vieles verändert. Die, die wir heute im Programm haben, sind ja fast alle mehr oder weniger afroamerikanisch-karibisch. Eine wirklich gute Idee war Anfang der 1960er Jahre das Welttanzprogramm, das fixe Regeln und Schritte für bestimmte Tänze enthielt. Davor war es so, dass ein Schüler aus der Tanzschule Elmayer Schwierigkeiten hatte, einen Walzer mit einer Schülerin aus der Tanzschule Fränzl zu tanzen, weil ihn beide verschieden gelernt hatten. Jetzt kann praktisch auf der ganzen Welt jede mit jedem tanzen.

BALLSPENDE

Aus der Tanzordnung hat sich die Ballspende entwickelt, die sehr aufwendig gestaltet sein konnte. Heute ist das meist ein Werbegeschenk.

Sehr oft, ja. An sich hab ich ja eine Aversion gegen diese Ballspenden, weil es meistens irgendein Glumpert ist und die Leute so verrückt danach sind. Wenn einer keine Ballspende kriegt, ist das der Weltuntergang! Das ist uns einmal passiert: Wir hatten Ballspenden von einer Firma, deren Mitarbeiter gedacht haben, sie bleiben auf den Sachen sitzen, weil der Ball schon fast zu Ende war und niemand kam. Also haben sie sie einfach an die Garderobe-Frauen und anderes Personal verteilt. Als dann die Gäste kurz vor Ballende gekommen sind, war ziemlich viel weg und einige Leute gingen leer aus. Was ich da zu hören bekommen hab, das kann man sich nicht vorstellen. Der ganze Ball war verdorben, weil mancher das Flascherl Parfum nicht gekriegt hat.

TISCHKARTEN

Durch die Tischkarten wird eine bestimmte Sitzordnung festgelegt. Darf man sich darüber hinwegsetzen?

Ich hab's schon erlebt, dass Leute das einfach ändern. Kommt leider vor. Aber auch wenn man sich gefreut hat, dass man heute Abend bestimmt neben dem Fräulein Müller sitzt und sitzt dann neben Frau Mayer, darf man die Karten nie austauschen. – Ich finde ja, man sollte die Tischkarte auf beiden Seiten beschriften, dann findet man seinen Platz leichter und weiß auch, wer einem gegenübersitzt.

ETIKETT UND ETIKETTE

Aufschlussreich ist die Verbindung der Wörter Etikett (für das Hinweisschild) und Etikette (als Bezeichnung für Umgangsformen). Wie ist es dazu gekommen?

Der Ursprung soll folgender sein: Der Gärtner von Ludwig XIV. hat sich immer so geärgert, dass die hohen Herrschaften über seine wunderschönen Blumenrabatten in Versailles spaziert oder galoppiert sind. Er hat deswegen Schilder aufgestellt, die Etiketten. Und diese Herrschaften haben sich natürlich überhaupt nicht drum geschert, was der Gärtner da aufstellt. Daraufhin ging er zum König und der hat deklariert: „Die Etikette ist zu beachten!" Daraus ist die Hofetikette entstanden. Flaschenetiketten sind ein Riesenthema, gerade im Zusammenhang mit Bällen. Zuletzt war ich bei der Vorstellung des Life-Ball-Weins 2016. Die Etiketten wurden von Studierenden der New Design University in St. Pölten entworfen. Der Life-Ball-Wein wird auf vielen Veranstaltungen serviert, nur der Ball selber findet heuer nicht statt.

Thomas Schäfer-Elmayer, CEO,
Tanzschule Willy Elmayer-Vestenbrugg, Wien (Auszug aus einem Gespräch mit Anne-Katrin Rossberg im April 2016)

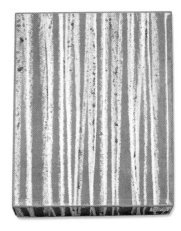

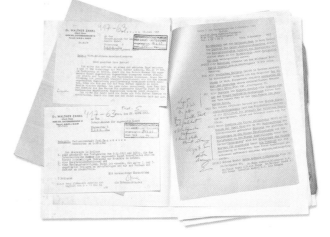

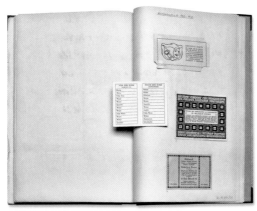

VERSPRECHEN AUF PAPIER
INGRID HASLINGER

„Nicht zufrieden mit der Rolle, die die nüchterne Geschäfts- und Utilitätsindustrie ihm angewiesen, überschreitet das Papier die Grenzen des Alltäglichen und betritt das Reich des Luxus und der Phantasie in Gestalt von Blumen und Blättern, von reich verzierten Liebesbriefen, Karten, Bonbonnièren und Cartons, präsentiert sich als glänzende Etikette, als Orden, als Lichtmanschette, als Fächer und Bouquethalter, als Tellerpapier und Serviette, und Tausende von Menschenhänden sind heute in allen civilisirten Ländern damit beschäftigt […]"[1]

In Anlehnung an Sinnsprüche und Dekorationen auf Porzellan findet man ab dem Ende des 18. Jahrhunderts Ähnliches auf Papier für verschiedene Anlässe – seien es Briefköpfe oder kleine Billets mit Wappen, floralen Verzierungen oder Monogrammen der Schreibenden. Im Lauf der Zeit entstand eine wahre Flut an gedruckten Helfern, mit denen man eine kurze, intime Nachricht durch die Dienerschaft besorgen lassen konnte, Einladungen und Glückwünsche aussprach oder sich mittels einer Notiz auf der Visitenkarte bei Verhinderung entschuldigen ließ. Denn erst die sich weiterentwickelnde Druckkunst machte diese kleinen, ephemeren Papierwerke möglich und zumindest den reichen Schichten zugänglich. Für Kinder adeliger oder herrschender Familien ließ man schon zur Biedermeierzeit spezielle Briefpapiere anfertigen, um die Freude am Schreiben zu fördern und die jungen Menschen auf die Führung umfangreicher Korrespondenz vorzubereiten – in einer Zeit, in der Korrespondenz ausschließlich auf Papier erfolgte.

Bis weit über die zweite Hälfte des 19. Jahrhunderts hinaus boten professionelle Schreiber ihre Dienste an, bei denen man Ansuchen, offizielle Schreiben oder seinen Lebenslauf verfassen lassen konnte. Aber nicht alle Inhalte waren für Fremde bestimmt, und oft war die Nachricht zu wenig bedeutend, um einen Schreiber zu bemühen. Überdies nahm das Druckgewerbe in Wien und im übrigen Europa einen gewaltigen Aufschwung: Aus England importierte Spezialmaschinen erleichterten den Druck und reduzierten die Kosten, allerdings wurden dadurch im Druckereiwesen viele arbeitslos – ein Umstand, der neben vielen anderen die Habsburgermonarchie in die Revolution 1848 schlittern ließ. Der Fortschritt der Technik ermöglichte die Herstellung einer immer größeren Zahl an Druckwerken, Pamphleten, Zeitungen (vor allem mit der Pressefreiheit ab 1848) und kleineren Schriften. Für alle möglichen Gelegenheiten und Anlässe gab es nun Drucksorten, zu deren Gestaltung häufig namhafte Maler, Grafiker und bildende Künstler herangezogen wurden. Zu den wenigen Beispielen aus der Biedermeierzeit gesellt sich eine Fülle künstlerischer Entwürfe aus verschiedenen Stilperioden: vom Historismus über den Jugendstil bis zum Art déco. In dieser Gebrauchsgrafik finden sich oft künstlerische Anspielungen auf die Profession der Auftraggeber und den Anlass für die Anfertigung, oder es wurden – wie bei Ballspenden und Faschingsgaben – Motive zur Erbauung der Gäste benutzt.

Auch wenn bei Papierwerken Ornamentik, Grafik und Bilder eine wichtige Rolle spielen, wurde das geschriebene Wort nicht obsolet. Denn alle Mitteilungen – seien sie grafisch noch so suggestiv – benötigen das Wort zur Übermittlung von Informationen bezüglich Veranstaltung, Termin, Ort, Produkt, Firmenanschrift etc. Der Text weist auf den eigentlichen Zweck der Karte hin, für den sie hergestellt wurde, während Ornamente auf den Geschmack der Auftraggeber schließen lassen.

[1] Beschreibung eines Berichterstatters von der Wiener Weltausstellung 1873, zitiert in: Pieske, Christa, *Das ABC des Luxuspapiers. Herstellung, Verarbeitung und Gebrauch 1860 bis 1930*, Ausst.kat. Museum für Deutsche Volkskunde, Staatliche Museen Preußischer Kulturbesitz, Berlin 1984, 10.

PAPER PROMISES
INGRID HASLINGER

"Not content with the role given it by the sober business and utilities industry, paper crosses the boundaries of the everyday and enters the realm of luxury and fantasy in the form of flowers and leaves, of richly embellished love letters, cards, boxes of candy, and cardboard boxes, presenting itself as shiny labels, as awards, as bobeches, as fans and bouquet holders, as paper doilies and napkins, and thousands of people in all civilized countries are now employed in paper [...]"[1]

From the end of the 18th century, designs in the style of epigrams and decorations on porcelain can be found on paper for various occasions—whether letterheads or small cards bearing coats of arms, floral decorations, or the writers' monograms. Over the course of time, a veritable flood of printed media arose, with which one could receive a short intimate message via one's servants, express invitations and congratulations, or send one's apologies in the form of a note on a visiting card when otherwise engaged. It was only the evolving art of printing, which made these small, ephemeral works of paper possible and available to at least the richest classes of society. As early as the Biedermeier period, special letter paper was produced for the children of aristocratic or ruling families in order to encourage the joy of writing and to prepare the younger generation for copious quantities of correspondence—at a time when written communication exclusively took place on paper. Professional writers offered their services until long after the second half of the 19th century: one could have them write requests, official letters, or one's résumé. However, not all content was intended for strangers, and often the message was of too little import to be worth employing the services of a professional. Moreover, the printing industry in Vienna and the rest of Europe underwent a tremendous boom: special machines imported from England made printing easier and reduced costs, although this admittedly resulted in many people in the world of printing being made redundant—one of the many circumstances, which led to the Habsburg realm sliding into revolution in 1848. The progress of technology facilitated the production of ever greater numbers of printed matter, polemical pamphlets, newspapers (especially after the freedom of the press from 1848), and shorter documents. For every possible opportunity and occasion there was now printed matter available, for the design of which the services of well-known painters, graphic designers, and fine artists were enlisted. Alongside the few examples from the Biedermeier era is a plethora of artistic designs from various other stylistic periods: from historicism to art nouveau and art deco. In this ephemera the artists often allude to their customer's profession and the occasion for which the work was commissioned, or—as is the case with ladies' gifts at balls and carnival presents—motifs intended to give pleasure to the guests.

Even though ornamentation, artwork, and images played an important role in ephemera, the written word did not become obsolete. After all, every message—as graphically suggestive as it may be—needs words to convey information regarding the event, date and time, venue, product, company address, etc. The text states the actual purpose for which the card was produced, whereas the decorations are simply indicative of the taste of the person who commissioned it.

[1] Reporter's description of the 1873 Vienna world's fair, quoted in: Pieske, Christa, *Das ABC des Luxuspapiers. Herstellung, Verarbeitung und Gebrauch 1860 bis 1930*, exh.cat., Museum of German Folklore, Staatliche Museen Preußischer Kulturbesitz, Berlin 1984, 10. Translated by Maria Slater.

GESCHÄFTSLEBEN

Zu den ältesten Drucksorten zählt wohl die Visitenkarte. Man kann sie ab Anfang des 17. Jahrhunderts immer wieder nachweisen – als Besuchskarte gehörte sie zum guten Ton des Adels in Frankreich, Österreich und England. Allerdings war sie eben nur ein Instrument der Visite: Wer jemanden aufsuchte oder zum Kaiser zur Audienz zugelassen war, gab beim Domestiken seine Karte ab, auf der in goldenen oder silbernen Lettern nur der Name und vielleicht der Titel standen. Gegen Ende des 19. Jahrhunderts waren nur mehr schwarze Lettern modern. In Visitenkartenschalen wurden die Karten dem Zeremonienmeister, dem Hausherrn oder der Hausfrau präsentiert, die dann entschieden, ob sie empfingen oder nicht. Bei höfischen Festen dienten die Visitenkarten dem Zeremonienmeister zur öffentlichen Ankündigung der Gäste.

Auch Geschäftsleute bedienten sich des Druckmediums für „Annonçirungs"-Zwecke. Dazu gehörten Gasthäuser, Restaurants, Modehäuser etc. (Abb. 251). Schon im *Wiener Diarium* (später: *Wiener Zeitung*) sind solche Anzeigen im 18. Jahrhundert zu finden; im letzten Drittel des 19. Jahrhunderts werden sie immer häufiger. Um dieselbe Zeit entdeckten Geschäftsleute die individuelle Visitenkarte als Geschäftskarte, die man unter Angabe von Namen, Adresse, Branche – später auch „Téléphon" und „Télégraph" – einer Person übergeben konnte, um Geschäftskontakte zu knüpfen. Denn die Kundenschar nahm stetig zu: Zum kleinen Kreis zahlungskräftiger Auftraggeber wie dem Kaiserhof, Adelshäusern, Industriellen und Angehörigen des Großbürgertums kamen nun kleinere Geschäftsleute und Haushalte, die ebenfalls immer wieder für Drucksorten Aufträge erteilten. Auch heute spielen Visitenkarten in dieser Hinsicht eine wichtige Rolle.

Die kleine, handliche Visitenkarte vergrößerte sich zwischen 1880 und 1920 gelegentlich bis zum A5-Format. Die Gestaltungen wurden aufwendig, mit Anspielungen auf den Beruf der Auftraggeber, Allegorien, das Angebot des jeweiligen Geschäfts. Firmen im Gastronomiebereich (Wein, Sekt, Liebig, Maggi) stellten oft Blanko-Menü- bzw. Speisekarten für Restaurants und Gasthäuser mit dem eigenen Logo zur Verfügung (Abb. 252). Zu den Bestellern dieser heute bibliophilen Kostbarkeiten in den Wiener Druckereien, deren Gestaltung namhafte Künstler besorgten, gehörten Emilie Flöge, die Wiener Werkstätte, die Bugholzfirma Kohn, die Hofphotographen Scolik und C. Angerer & Göschl, die Hoflieferanten[2] Johann Kattus, Johann Stifft, Johann Backhausen & Söhne, Julius Meinl – der erfolgreiche Selfmade-Geschäftsmann, dessen ursprünglicher Geschäftserfolg daher rührte, dass er seinen Kaffee frisch, d.h. vor dem Verkauf röstete, ein wichtiger Faktor in Zeiten vor den sogenannten Aromaverpackungen – und zahlreiche andere Firmen. Sie alle zählten zur Kundschaft der Wiener Druckereien, von denen v.a. Chwala's Druck und Johann Klein eng mit Künstlern zusammenarbeiteten. Von beiden Firmen haben sich Mustermappen im MAK erhalten, die beredtes Zeugnis von der Vielfalt der künstlerischen Produkte, ihrer hohen Qualität, aber auch vom Angebot an schlichten, eleganten Ausführungen ablegen. Die Wiener Druckereien nahmen sich auch der Gestaltung aufwendiger Briefköpfe und Rechnungsformulare an, beispielsweise für die Wiener Pflanzenfettfabrik Herrmann Finch, den Hofzuckerbäcker Christoph Demel oder die Weingroßhandlung A. Schwartzer's Nachfolge (Abb. 255). Die Briefköpfe und Rechnungsformulare zeigen meist die Produktions- oder Verkaufsstätten, den charakteristischen Namenszug des Inhabers, Hinweise auf sein Gewerbe, eventuelle Auszeichnungen bei Gewerbe-Ausstellungen oder Medaillen sowie Standort und Adresse.

[2] Zur Geschichte der k.u.k. Hoflieferanten vgl. Haslinger, Ingrid, *Kunde: Kaiser*, Wien 1996.

THE WORLD OF WORK

The visiting—later business—card probably ranks among the oldest printed matter. There is evidence of it dating from the beginning of the 17th century, when the visiting card came to be part of the bon ton of the French, Austrian, and English aristocracy. However, it served merely as a tool when visiting: Those who called on someone or were granted an audience with the emperor would hand their card to the domestics; it bore nothing but their name and perhaps their title in gold or silver letters. Towards the end of the 19th century only black letters were fashionable. The cards were presented to the master of ceremonies or the head of the household in visiting card trays; they would then decide whether or not they would receive their caller. At courtly festivities visiting cards enabled the master of ceremonies to publicly announce the arrival of each guest.

Businesses, too, availed themselves of this printed medium for the purposes of "Annonçirung" (announcement). They included inns, restaurants, couture houses, etc. (ill. 251). Such announcements can be found in the *Wiener Diarium* (later: *Wiener Zeitung*) as early as the 18th century; their frequency increases in the last third of the 19th century. Around the same time business people reinterpreted the individual visiting card as a business card featuring their name, address, branch—and later "Téléphon" and "Télégraph"—which could be handed over in the hope of making business contacts. With time, the customer base for these visiting or business cards grew steadily: in addition to the small circle of affluent customers such as the imperial court, the aristocracy, industrialists, and members of the upper classes, minor business people and households would now also commission printed matter. Even today, business cards play an important role in this regard.

The small, handy visiting card increased in size between 1880 and 1920—at times even to A5 format. The designs became elaborate, with allusions to the owner's profession, allegories, and the range offered by their respective business. Companies in the gastronomy sector (wine, sparkling wine, Liebig, Maggi) often provided restaurants and inns with blank menus and menu cards bearing their own logo (ill. 252). Among the bestsellers of what are now bibliophiles' treasures by Viennese printing houses, with designs by famous artists, are Emilie Flöge, the Wiener Werkstätte, the bentwood company Kohn, the court photographers Scolik and C. Angerer & Göschl, the purveyors to the court[2] Johann Kattus, Johann Stifft, Johann Backhausen & Söhne, Julius Meinl—the successful self-made businessman whose original business masterstroke was based on him roasting his coffee fresh, i.e. just before it was sold, an important factor at a time before modern aroma-preserving packaging—and countless other companies. All of them were customers of Viennese printing houses, among which Chwala's Druck and Johann Klein most notably worked closely with artists. Sample portfolios from both companies have been preserved at the MAK, which eloquently attest to the diversity of these artistic products, their high quality, but also their spectrum of simple yet elegant workmanship. The Viennese printing houses also supplied designs for elaborate letterheads and billing forms, for example for Herrmann Finch's Viennese vegetable fat factory, the imperial royal confectioner Christoph Demel, and the wine wholesaler A. Schwartzer's Nachfolge (ill. 255). The letterheads and billing forms mostly show the production or sales facilities, the owner's distinctive signature, references to his trade, any awards or medals bestowed at trade exhibitions, as well as the company's location and address.

[2] On the history of the purveyors to the imperial royal court cf. Haslinger, Ingrid, *Kunde: Kaiser*, Vienna 1996.

251
Anonym Anonymous
Geschäftskarte Hotel und Restaurant *Riedhof*
Wien, um 1912
Ausführung: Chwala's Druck
Buchdruck
Business Card Hotel and Restaurant *Riedhof*
Vienna, ca. 1912
Execution: Chwala's Druck
Letterpress print
100 x 149 mm
KI 15854-21-2, Ankauf Teilnachlass purchased
from part of the estate of Chwala's Druck 2008

252
Anonym Anonymous
Blanko-Menükarte Sekt-Kellereien
Johann Kattus
Wien, um 1900
Lithografie
Blank Menu Card Sparkling Wine
Producer Johann Kattus
Vienna, ca. 1900
Lithograph
173 x 116 mm
KI 21484-23-7, Ankauf purchased from
Kunstarchiv Werner J. Schweiger 2015

In the last third of the 19th century, companies started to replace their often small-format price lists or brochures with more comprehensive printed media. Here, artistic design was no longer merely relevant for the external appearance of the media; the interior presented the company's products and their prices in the format of engravings or the increasingly affordable medium of photography. Alongside these illustrations there were technical descriptions and dimensions to facilitate efficient ordering. These humble beginnings would eventually evolve into price and sample catalogs—such as those by the Arthur Krupp metal goods factory—comprising up to 400 pages from which retailers and customers could select their purchases. This development underwent a rapid downturn with the First World War and the collapse of the Habsburg monarchy, as long-established companies now either faced a reduction in their markets or had to cease operations entirely.

LABELS, PAPER SEALS

An early form of label had existed since the Middle Ages. Entirely unembellished pieces of paper were stuck to crates and barrels to declare their contents—an important approach considering the numerous customs and tollbooths. Later, labels were increasingly needed for wares sold in smaller containers. While for a long time wine and beer were exclusively traded in barrels and only poured into bottles and jugs for consumption purposes, in the second half of the 18th century—when the quality of these beverages took on greater significance—wine started to be bottled. Consequently, it became necessary to label the bottles to differentiate between the varieties. Indeed, the production of champagne only became possible with the advent of bottling.[3] This change took place much later for beer, which was only bottled after long-lasting lager was developed;[4] glass bottles were expensive and bore labels.

The results of research by Nicolas Apperts (1749–1841) and other chemists revealed that it was possible to preserve food in cans; later jars were also used, predominantly for fruit and vegetables. All of these containers were given labels to identify their contents. The Julius Meinl company, for example, had labels for jams, tea, mustard, coffee, chocolate, cocoa, etc.; lemonade bottles, too, were furnished with labels (ill. 253, 254).

From the Middle Ages important documents had been sealed—mostly with red wax. The monogram, coat of arms, or crown embossed on it confirmed to the commonalty, who could neither read nor write, that the content of the document was authorized by the emperor, feudal lord, or a lower-ranking authority and was hence legitimate. This custom spread to correspondence, which was also sealed with wax; the sender's coat of arms or initials was impressed on the documents with a signet. In the second half of the 19th century, businesspeople found a slightly easier way to seal a letter: small, stamp-shaped paper seals came into general use, which despite their small size were lovingly graphically designed—with symbols, coats of arms, crowns, signatures, addresses, etc. (ill. 256). These small paper seals were round, oval, or rectangular, gummed, and attached to the back of an envelope at the edge of the sealed overlap. These sealing stamps represented a transition to the gradually less expensive postal correspondence—even at that time, thrift was essential.

[3] For champagne, the first process involves fermenting the base wine in barrels. After being transferred to champagne bottles, cane or beet sugar and some yeast are added. This leads to a second fermentation and carbonation. For weeks, the bottles are moved from a horizontal to a vertical position (bottle neck facing down) on remuage racks. This leads to the lees—the yeast—collecting by the cork. The neck of the bottle is briefly deep-frozen before the bottle is opened and the excess pressure forces out the frozen lees. Before being sealed with a champagne cork, the bottle is filled up with the *dosage* (mostly sweet wine). Depending on the quantity and the composition of the *dosage*, one speaks of extra dry, sec, demi-sec, or doux champagnes.

[4] Anton Dreher sen. (1810–1863) developed this light, bottom-fermented lager in Schwechat, Austria, in 1840/1841.

Im letzten Drittel des 19. Jahrhunderts begannen Firmen ihre oft nur kleinformatigen „Preiscourants" oder Prospekte durch umfangreichere zu ersetzen. Hier ging es nur mehr bei der Außengestaltung um künstlerisches Design. Das Innenleben wartete mit Stichen bzw. den allmählich erschwinglicher werdenden Fotografien auf, die Produkte der Firmen zeigten und die Preise angaben. Daneben gab es noch technische Beschreibungen und Abmessungsangaben, die eine effiziente Bestellung möglich machten. Aus diesen Anfängen sollten sich – wie beispielsweise bei der Metallwarenfabrik Arthur Krupp – bis zu 400 Seiten starke Preis- und Musterkataloge entwickeln, aus denen Händler und Kunden auswählen konnten. Diese Entwicklung nahm mit dem Ersten Weltkrieg und mit dem Zusammenbruch der Habsburgermonarchie einen raschen Abschwung, denn die alteingesessenen Firmen waren nun mit einem beschränkten Absatzgebiet konfrontiert oder mussten ihren Betrieb schließen.

ETIKETTEN, PAPIERSIEGEL

Eine frühe Form der Etiketten gab es bereits ab dem Mittelalter. Kisten und Fässer wurden mit völlig schmucklosen Papieren beklebt, um den Inhalt zu deklarieren, was für die zahlreichen Zoll- und Mautstellen von Bedeutung war. Etiketten wurden später zunehmend für Waren benötigt, die in kleinen Gebinden verkauft wurden. Während Wein und Bier lange Zeit nur in Fässern gehandelt und für den Konsum in Flaschen und Krüge abgefüllt wurden, begann man in der zweiten Hälfte des 18. Jahrhunderts – als die Qualität der Getränke immer mehr an Bedeutung gewann – Weine in Flaschen abzufüllen. Somit wurde eine Beschriftung nötig, um die Sorten auseinanderzuhalten. Die Herstellung von Champagner wurde überhaupt erst durch Abfüllen in Flaschen möglich.[3] Bei Bier kam dies viel später: Bier wurde erst nach Entwicklung des haltbareren Lagerbiers[4] in Flaschen abgefüllt – Glasflaschen waren teuer – und mit Etiketten versehen.

Auf Basis der Ergebnisse von Forschungen Nicolas Apperts (1749–1841) und anderer Chemiker konnte man Lebensmittel in Konserven haltbar machen, später kamen Gläser v. a. für Obst und Gemüse hinzu. Alle diese Behälter bekamen Etiketten, um den Inhalt zu identifizieren. Die Firma Julius Meinl hatte Etiketten für Marmeladen, Tee, Senf, Kaffee, Schokolade, Kakao etc.; auch Limonadenflaschen wurden mit Etiketten versehen (Abb. 253, 254).

Wichtige Dokumente sicherte man seit dem Mittelalter mit einem – meist roten – Wachssiegel. Das darauf befindliche Monogramm oder Wappen bzw. die Krone bestätigte dem einfachen Volk, das weder schreiben noch lesen konnte, dass der Inhalt des Dokuments vom Kaiser, Landesherrn oder einer nachgeordneten Behörde autorisiert war und daher volle Geltung hatte. Dieser Gebrauch übertrug sich auch auf die Korrespondenz, die man mit Wachssiegel verschloss; den Dokumenten wurden mit einem Petschaft Wappen oder Initialen der Absender aufgedrückt. In der zweiten Hälfte des 19. Jahrhunderts fanden Geschäftsleute eine etwas leichtere Art, einen Brief zu siegeln: Kleine markenförmige Papiersiegel kamen in Gebrauch, die selbst in dieser Größe liebevoll grafisch gestaltet waren – mit Symbolen, Wappen, Kronen, Namenszügen, Adressen etc. (Abb. 256). Diese kleinen Papiersiegel waren rund, oval oder rechteckig, gummiert und wurden an der Hinterseite eines Briefkuverts am Rand der Klebestelle angebracht. Die Siegelmarken stellten einen Übergang zur allmählich weniger kostspielig werdenden postalischen Korrespondenz dar – auch damals war Sparen angesagt.

[3] Für Champagner wird in einem ersten Arbeitsgang der Grundwein in Fässern vergoren. Nach dem Abfüllen in die Champagnerflasche wird ihm Rohr- oder Rübenzucker und etwas Germ zugesetzt. Dies führt zu einer zweiten Gärung und der Entstehung der Kohlensäure. Die Flaschen werden auf Rüttelpulten über Wochen von der waagrechten Lage in die Senkrechte gedreht (Flaschenhals nach unten). Somit sammelt sich beim Stoppel das Depot bzw. die Germ. Der Flaschenhals wird kurz tiefgefroren, die Flasche geöffnet und durch den Überdruck schießt das gefrorene Depot heraus. Vor dem Verschließen mit dem Champagnerkorken wird die Flasche mit der Dosage (meist Süßwein) aufgefüllt. Je nach Menge und Zusammensetzung der Dosage spricht man von extra trockenen, trockenen, halbtrockenen oder süßen Getränken.

[4] Anton Dreher sen. (1810–1863) entwickelte 1840/1841 in Schwechat das helle, untergärige Lagerbier.

253
Rudolf Köhl
**Etikett für Ribisel-Marmelade
der Firma Heller**
Wien, um 1920
Farbdruck
**Label for Red Currant Jam
by the Company Heller**
Vienna, ca. 1920
Color print
90 x 45 mm
WWGG 771-5, Nachlass bequest from
Hans Ankwicz-Kleehoven 1963/64

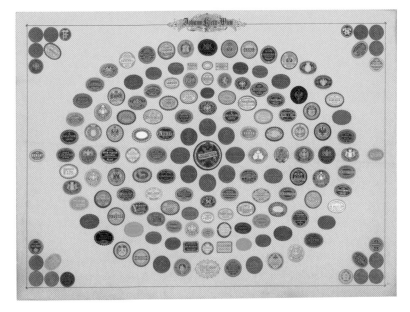

254
Ernst Ludwig Franke
**Etikett für Himbeer-Limonade
von Julius Meinl**
Wien, um 1925
Lithografie
Label for Raspberry Lemonade by Julius Meinl
Vienna, ca. 1925
Lithograph
81 x 102 mm
KI 13369-8-1, Ankauf purchased from Ilka Franke 1959

255
Anonym Anonymous
**Mustertafel mit Etiketten, Briefköpfen etc. der
Druckerei Johann Klein**
Wien, 1870–1887
**Sample Board with Labels, Letterheads, etc. by
the Printer Johann Klein**
Vienna, 1870–1887
467 x 633 mm
KI 22214-58, alter Bestand, inv.
old holdings, inventoried 2015

256
Anonym Anonymous
**Mustertafel mit Verschlussmarken
der Druckerei Johann Klein**
Wien, 1870–1887
**Sample Board with Seals
by the Printer Johann Klein**
Vienna, 1870–1887
467 x 633 mm
KI 22214-80, alter Bestand, inv.
old holdings, inventoried 2015

LIEBIG'S SAMMELBILDER

Nicht bei jedem Werbematerial einer Firma war sofort der kommerzielle Zweck zu erkennen. Zu dieser Kategorie gehörten Liebig's Sammelbilder.[5] Die ersten Liebig-Bilder erschienen um 1875 in Paris und wurden in Serien von drei, vier, fünf, sechs, acht, zehn und in einem Fall 24 Bildern gedruckt. „Sie dienten als Schulbuch-Ergänzung und -Ersatz und prägten das Weltbild junger Menschen vermutlich in ganz beträchtlichem Maße [...]."[6] Die kleinen bunten Bilder, die grafisch von keinem hohen künstlerischen Wert waren, hatten pädagogische Funktion: Auf ihnen waren Marktszenen in fremden Ländern abgebildet, bekannte Gebäude, Soldaten in Uniformen, Szenen aus Märchen, Urmenschen auf Büffeljagd; geografische, naturkundliche und geschichtliche Themen wurden angesprochen. Die Namen der Grafiker sind nicht überliefert. Da die Bilder in vielen Ländern erschienen, wiesen sie keinen nationalen Bezug auf und waren meist konfessionsfrei. In einem Zeitraum von 100 Jahren erschienen 1870 Serien mit rund 11 500 Bildern in zwölf Sprachen. Heute werden nur mehr kleine Auflagen in Italien gedruckt. Die alten Serien sind teure und begehrte Sammelobjekte, für die es schon zu ihrer Entstehungszeit Sammelalben gab. Sie waren nicht in den Liebig-Produkten mitverpackt. Die Kaufleute erhielten sie mit den Gebinden und verteilten sie nach Gutdünken an ihre Kundschaft, die Fleischextrakt bei ihnen besorgte (Abb. 257).

FESTE, BÄLLE, KONZERTE, OPERN, AUSSTELLUNGEN, BALLETTE

Vergnügungen dieser Art waren lange Zeit – bis zur Mitte des 19. Jahrhunderts – insbesondere dem Adel und dem Monarchen vorbehalten, die Besucheranzahl daher einigermaßen bekannt und beschränkt. Einladungen erfolgten zu jener Zeit mündlich durch oberste Ämterinhaber oder Kammerdiener oder schriftlich durch kleine persönliche Billetts. Doch als Kaiser Franz II. (I., 1768–1835) allen anständig gekleideten Wiener Bürgern und ausländischen Reisenden Zutritt zu seinen öffentlichen Tafeln gewährte, wurden Eintrittskarten notwendig. Denn auf andere Weise konnte man sich des Andrangs nicht erwehren bzw. die Besucherzahl nicht mehr überblicken. Beim Wiener Kongress (1814/1815) gab es Veranstaltungen mit bis zu 8 000 (!) Besuchern.[7]
Diese Eintrittskarten waren wohlgemerkt *nicht* mit einem Eintrittsgeld verbunden, sie dienten nur der Kontrolle. Ebenso verhielt es sich bei Eintrittskarten für die kaiserliche Fußwaschung am Gründonnerstag oder bei Eintrittskarten für Fensterplätze in der Hofburg, an denen Geladene bei Prozessionen, Fronleichnamsumzug, Denkmalenthüllungen oder Truppenparaden zusehen konnten. Genauso verhielt es sich mit Bällen, Redouten, Konzerten und Lesungen für karitative Zwecke: Dafür gab es ebenfalls Einladungen bzw. Eintrittskarten (Abb. 258). Eintrittsgeld war nicht zu bezahlen; die Veranstalter erwarteten sich jedoch von den Gästen entsprechend hohe Spenden. Auch künstlerische Ausstellungen jeder Art konnten von Mitgliedern der kaiserlichen Familie und des Adels jederzeit ohne Eintrittsgeld besucht werden, denn hier erwartete man sie als zahlungskräftige Kundschaft, die das eine oder andere Gemälde oder Kunstobjekt erwarb, um es in der Hofburg, in Schönbrunn, im Belvedere oder in ihren Palais aufzuhängen bzw. aufzustellen.
Bürgerliche Etablissements, in denen Bälle abgehalten wurden, Vorstadttheater, Zirkusse, die damals beliebten Vergnügungsetablissements (Apollosaal, Sofiensäle, Gschwandner etc.) sowie die im 19. Jahrhundert bekannte Feuerwerkerfamilie Stuwer verlangten für ihre Vorführungen sehr wohl Eintrittsgeld (Abb. 259, 260). Bei privaten Hausbällen gab es wohl Einladungen, aber keine Eintrittskarten. Auch Künstlerzirkel luden mit manchmal skurril-sinister gestalteten Karten zu Bällen,

5 Die Bilder wurden nach dem Chemiker Justus von Liebig (1803–1870) benannt, ebenso wie der von ihm entwickelte Fleischextrakt aus Rindfleisch.

6 Pieske 1984 (s. Anm. 1), 235.

7 Zum Wiener Kongress vgl. Haslinger, Ingrid, „Tafeln für Kaiser und Könige. Die Hofwirtschaft am Wiener Kongress", in: Just, Thomas/Maderthaner, Wolfgang/Maimann, Helene (Hg.), *Der Wiener Kongress. Die Erfindung Europas*, Wien 2014.

LIEBIG'S COLLECTIBLE CARDS

The commercial purpose of a company's promotional materials was not always immediately identifiable. Liebig's collectible cards belonged to this category.[5] The first Liebig cards emerged in Paris around 1875 and were printed in series of three, four, five, six, eight, ten, and in one case 24 pictures. "They served as a supplement to and replacement for school textbooks and presumably left quite a considerable impression on young people [...]"[6] The small, colorful pictures, which were not of high artistic value from a graphic perspective, had an educational function: they depicted market scenes in foreign lands, famous buildings, soldiers in uniform, scenes from fairy tales, prehistoric man hunting buffalo; topics from geography, natural history, and human history were addressed. There is no record of the graphic artists' names. As the pictures were published in several countries, they exhibit no national references and were mostly undenominational. Over a period of one hundred years, 1870 series were published with some 11500 pictures in twelve languages. Today only small editions are still published in Italy. The old series are expensive and sought-after collector's items for which collector's albums already existed at the time they were made. These were not packaged with the Liebig products, however; the traders received them with the food containers and distributed them at their own discretion to the customers who bought Liebig meat extract from them (ill. 257).

PARTIES, BALLS, CONCERTS, OPERAS, EXHIBITIONS, BALLETS

Amusements of this kind were reserved for the aristocracy, and monarchs in particular, for a long time—indeed until the mid-19th century—and as such the attendance was to some extent both foreseen and limited. At this time, invitations were extended verbally by the house steward or butler, or in writing on small, personalized cards. Yet when Emperor Francis II (& I, 1768–1835) granted admission to his public banquets to all properly dressed Viennese citizens and foreign travelers, admission tickets became necessary. Without them it would not have been possible to ward off the crowds nor maintain an overview of the number of visitors. At the Congress of Vienna (1814/1815) there were events with up to 8000 (!) attending.[7]

It should be noted that these admission tickets were *not* connected to an admission charge; they served exclusively supervisory purposes. There was a similar intention behind admission tickets for the imperial foot-washing on Maundy Thursday or admission tickets for window seats at the Hofburg Palace, where invited guests could watch religious processions, Corpus Christi processions, the revealing of memorials, or military parades. The same applied to ordinary and masked balls, concerts, and readings for charitable purposes: they, too, used invitations or admission tickets (ill. 258). There was no admission charge; the event organizers did, however, expect their guests to make donations of an appropriate sum. Even all manner of artistic exhibitions could be visited by the imperial family and the aristocracy at any time without an admission charge, as here they were expected as affluent customers who might purchase one or two paintings or art objects in order to hang or exhibit them at the Hofburg Palace, at Schönbrunn Palace, at the Belvedere, or in their own residences.

Bourgeois establishments where balls were held, suburban theaters, circuses, the then popular amusement sites (Vienna's Apollosaal, Sofiensäle, Gschwandner, etc.), as well as the pyrotechnician family Stuwer—who were famous in the 19th century—did indeed charge admission to their

[5] The pictures were named after the chemist Justus von Liebig (1803–1870), as was the meat extract made of beef, which he developed.

[6] Pieske 1984 (see note 1), 235. Translated by Maria Slater.

[7] On the Congress of Vienna cf. Haslinger, Ingrid, "Tafeln fur Kaiser und Könige. Die Hofwirtschaft am Wiener Kongress," in: Just, Thomas/Maderthaner, Wolfgang/Maimann, Helene (eds.), *Der Wiener Kongress. Die Erfindung Europas*, Vienna 2014.

258
Vermutl. Prob. Fanny Zakucka
**Einladungskarte zum
Hohewarte-Gartenfest**
Wien, 1906
Ausführung: Chwala's Druck
Klischee
**Invitation Card for the Hohewarte Garden
Party**
Vienna, 1906
Execution: Chwala's Druck
Cliché
166 x 86 mm
KI 15854-41-3, Ankauf Teilnachlass
purchased from part of the
estate of Chwala's Druck 2008

259
E. Bartl
Eintrittskarte zum 31. Krummholz-Kränzchen
Wien, 1910
Ausführung: Chwala's Druck
Autotypie
**Admission Ticket for the 31st Krummholz
Party**
Vienna, 1910
Execution: Chwala's Druck
Halftone
100 x 165 mm
KI 15854-37-2, Ankauf Teilnachlass
purchased from part of the
estate of Chwala's Druck 2008

260
Anonym Anonymous
**Eintrittskarte zum Kostüm-Kränzchen des
Tanz-Instituts Kadur**
Wien, 1908
Ausführung: Chwala's Druck
Klischee
**Admission Ticket for the Costume Party at
the Dance School Kadur**
Vienna, 1908
Execution: Chwala's Druck
Cliché
150 x 90 mm
KI 15854-39-2, Ankauf Teilnachlass
purchased from part of the
estate of Chwala's Druck 2008

257
Hugo Gerard Ströhl
**Druckbogen für drei Liebig-Sammelkarten
aus der Serie *Le Monde renversé* [Die verkehrte Welt]**
Paris, 1880–1885
Chromolithografie
**Print Sheet for three Liebig Trading Cards
from the Series [The reversed world]**
Paris, 1880–1885
Chromolithograph
211 x 108 mm
KI 7752-427-2, Schenkung donation from
Hugo Gerard Ströhl 1910

261
**Tanzordnung zum Kränzchen
der Kunstgewerbe-Schüler**
Wien, 1895
Illustratoren: Koloman Moser, Joseph Urban,
Alfred Cossmann u.a.
Samt, Leder, Seidenband, Prägedruck
**Dance Sequence for a Party of the Students
of the School of Arts and Crafts**
Vienna, 1895
Illustrators: Koloman Moser, Joseph Urban,
Alfred Cossmann, et al.
Velvet, leather, silk ribbon, embossing
210 x 110 mm
KI 8687-2, Ankauf purchased from
Leopoldine Steindl 1929

262
Otto Nowak
Ballspende zum Concordia-Ball
Wien, 1925
Ausführung: Druckerei Waldheim-Eberle
Lithografie
Ladies' Gift at the Concordia-Ball
Vienna, 1925
Execution: Printer Waldheim-Eberle
Lithograph
115 x 165 mm
BI 61412-3, Ankauf purchased from
Kunsthandlung Nebehay 1997

263
Koloman Moser
Ballspende zum Ball der Stadt Wien
Wien, 1901
Ausführung: Druckerei Martin Gerlach & Co.
Stoff, Messing, Email, Autotypie
Ladies' Gift at the Ball of the City of Vienna
Vienna, 1901
Execution: Printer Martin Gerlach & Co.
Cloth, brass, enamel, halftone
162 x 177 mm
KI 8687-1, Ankauf purchased from
Leopoldine Steindl 1929

Gschnasfesten oder Ausstellungen ihrer Mitglieder. Besonders das Wiener Künstlerhaus war in dieser Hinsicht sehr aktiv (s. Abb. 279–282). Die Erlöse aus solchen Veranstaltungen wurden häufig notleidenden oder kranken Kollegen zur Verfügung gestellt – eine besonders in den 1920er und 1930er Jahren wichtige Einrichtung.

Ballspenden für die Damen haben in Wien Tradition. Dieser Usus entwickelte sich aus den Tanzkarten, die sich Damen beim Ball ans Handgelenk, an den Fächer oder an den Gürtel ihrer Toilette hängen konnten. Meist waren es kleine, gebundene Hefte, mit einer Schlaufe versehen, in der ein Bleistift steckte (Abb. 261). Im Heft befanden sich Name und Datum des Balls sowie die Tanzordnung, denn ein Ball war bis zum Zusammenbruch der Monarchie – was die Tänze betraf – einem strengen Ablauf unterworfen. Als Beispiel möge die Tanzordnung für den Kammerball bei Hof vom 17. Februar 1863[8] dienen:

[8] HHStA, NZA K 89, r. VII, 1861–1864. Der Cotillon setzt sich aus verschiedenen Tänzen zusammen, dabei gibt es keinen Partnerwechsel; Polka tremblante: gemischte Polka; Française: französische Polka; Lançe: Galopp.

	Anfang		*Ende*
8.45	**1.**	1ter Walzer	8.51
8.56	**2.**	1te Française	9.11
9.16	**3.**	1te Polka tremblante	9.22
9.27	**4.**	2ter Walzer	9.33
9.38	**5.**	2te Française	9.53
10.00	**6.**	Cotillon	11.00
		Souper	
11.45	**7.**	3ter Walzer	11.50
11.54	**8.**	Lançe	12.14
12.18	**9.**	2te Polka tremblante	12.23
12.27	**10.**	3te Française	12.42
12.46	**11.**	4ter Walzer	12.51
12.55	**12.**	3te Polka tremblante	1.00

Neben den Tänzen konnten sich die Damen mit dem Bleistift die Namen der Tänzer eintragen (s. Abb. 284), wobei bei Hof und in Adelshäusern vorher bekannt gegeben werden musste, wer am Tanz teilnahm oder nicht. Eine spätere andere Entscheidung war nicht möglich, um zu großes Gedränge auf der Tanzfläche zu vermeiden. Die kleinen Hefte wurden mit der Zeit grafisch immer aufwendiger gestaltet, oft auch mit Fotos versehen, die auf die Ballveranstalter Bezug nahmen. Als im Laufe des 20. Jahrhunderts diese strengen Ballordnungen verschwanden, wurden auch die Tanzhefte obsolet. Man behielt aber die Tradition der Damenspende bei, die ein kleines praktisches Geschenk (Süßigkeiten, ein kleines Parfumfläschchen, kleine Taschen, eine themenbezogene Broschüre etc.) sein kann (Abb. 263). Weiterhin blieben jedoch die Einladungen und Eintrittskarten zu Tanzveranstaltungen ein Anliegen der (Wiener) Künstler und Druckanstalten. Eine Ballspende des Concordia-Balls im Jahr 1925 zeigt ein tanzendes Paar und ein Wienpanorama (Abb. 262). Das erweiterte Büchlein enthält Bilder, Noten, Lieder (mit Texten) und schließlich die Tänze: zwei Ländler, ein Menuett, zwei deutsche Tänze, einen Walzer, den *Dornbacher Ländler* von Josef Lanner (1801–1843), den *Täuberl-Walzer* von Johann Strauss Vater (1804–1849), den *D'Schwamma-Tanz* und den *Schellerl-Tanz* von Johann Schrammel (1850–1893).

performances, however (ill. 259, 260). At private balls there were probably invitations but no admission tickets. Even artists' circles extended invitations to balls, fancy-dress parties, or exhibitions by their members with at times bizarre or sinister card designs. Vienna's Künstlerhaus was particularly active in this regard (see ill. 279–282). The proceeds of such events were frequently offered to needy or sick colleagues—an important arrangement, especially in the 1920s and 1930s.

Ladies' gifts at balls are a tradition in Vienna. This custom developed from the dance cards, which ladies could hang on their wrists, fans, or the belts of their gowns. These were mostly small, bound notebooks with a loop for a pencil (ill. 261). In the notebook were the name and date of the ball as well as the dance sequence: until the collapse of the monarchy, balls were subject to a strict chronology—at least regarding the dances. By way of example, consider the dance sequence for the *Kammerball* at court from 17 February 1863[8]:

Start		End
8:45	**1.** 1st waltz	8:51
8:56	**2.** 1st *Française*	9:11
9:16	**3.** 1st *Polka tremblante*	9:22
9:27	**4.** 2nd waltz	9:33
9:38	**5.** 2nd *Française*	9:53
10:00	**6.** Cotillion	1:00
	Dinner	
11:45	**7.** 3rd waltz	11:50
11:54	**8.** *Lançe*	12:14
12:18	**9.** 2nd *Polka tremblante*	12:23
12:27	**10.** 3rd *Française*	12:42
12:46	**11.** 4th waltz	12:51
12:55	**12.** 3rd *Polka tremblante*	1:00

[8] HHStA, NZA K 89, r. VII, 1861–1864. The cotillion is comprised of various dances, without changing partners; *polka tremblante:* mixed polka; *Française:* French polka; *Lançe:* galop.

The ladies would write the names of their dancing partners alongside the dances in pencil (see ill. 284); at courtly and aristocratic balls it was necessary to give prior notice of who would participate in which dances. It was not possible to alter one's decision at a later point in order to avoid the dance floor becoming overcrowded. The small notebooks were designed ever more elaborately as time went by, often even bearing photographs, which made reference to the ball's organizer.

As these strict ball sequences disappeared over the course of the 20th century, the dance cards also became obsolete. However, the tradition of the ladies' gift has survived; it might be a small, practical present (candies, a little bottle of perfume, small bags, a booklet related to the topic, etc.; ill. 263). Despite this change, the invitations and admission tickets for dance events remained a matter for (Viennese) artists and printing houses. A ladies' gift at the Concordia Ball in 1925 shows a dancing couple and a panorama of Vienna (ill. 262). The remaining booklet contains pictures, notes, songs (with lyrics), and finally the dances: two *Ländler*, a minuet, two German dances, a waltz, the *Dornbacher Ländler* by Josef Lanner (1801–1843), the *Täuberl-Walzer* by Johann Strauss the Elder (1804–1849), the *D'Schwamma-Tanz* and the *Schellerl-Tanz* by Johann Schrammel (1850–1893).

SPEISEKARTEN, MENÜKARTEN, TISCHKARTEN, FÜHRKARTEN

Lange Zeit gab es keine schriftlichen Aufzeichnungen darüber, was in Gasthäusern angeboten, bzw. keine Menülisten, was bei vornehmen Tafeln serviert wurde. Doch bereits 1716 ermöglichten Wein- listen den Gästen in Wiener Adelskreisen, sich beim Personal das gewünschte Getränk zu bestellen. Lady Montagu berichtete von einer ersten Weinkarte im frühen 18. Jahrhundert: „Ich habe bereits die Ehre gehabt, von verschiedenen Personen vom ersten Range zur Mittagsmahlzeit geladen zu werden, und ich muß gerecht sein zu gestehen, daß der gute Geschmack und die Pracht ihrer Tafeln dem, der in ihren Möbeln herrscht, sehr wohl entspricht […]. Doch die Verschiedenheit und der Reichtum ihrer Weine scheint das meiste Erstaunen zu verdienen. Es ist gewöhnlich, eine Liste von denselben neben die Serviette auf die Teller zu legen, und ich habe zuweilen bis auf achtzehn ver- schiedene Gattungen, die in ihrer Art alle auserlesen waren, gezählet."[9]

Um die Mitte des 18. Jahrhunderts scheint ein Wandel eingetreten zu sein. In den *Oesterreichischen Bausteinen zur Kultur- und Sittengeschichte* (1745) erschien eine „Notification, kraft welcher hiemit jedermänniglich kund und zu wissen gemacht wird, daß in nachstehenden Wirths-Häusern allhier in der königl. Haupt- und Residentz Stadt Wien um verschiedenen geringen Preiss die Kost für die Dinstinctions-Personen sowol, als vor gemeine Leut zu bekommen seye, auch was und wie viel Gerichte man selben vor solchen Preis aufsetze". Damit konnte man erstmals ablesen, welche Speisen ein Wirtshaus bot und was sie kosteten. Allerdings gab es damals noch keinen Platten- oder Tellerservice. Alle Speisen wurden gleichzeitig auf die Tafel gestellt und man bediente sich von dem, was man gerne mochte. So verhielt es sich insbesondere in adeligen Kreisen und am Kaiserhof, wo nach dem „service à la française" serviert wurde: Die Speisen wurden zu Trachten zusammenge- fasst und gemeinsam auf die Tafel gestellt. Die Tafelgäste sahen also, was geboten wurde. Aber die Table d'Hôte – mehrere Leute speisen zugleich am selben Tisch und können daher sehen, was alles aufgetragen wird – gab es in Wien nur sehr selten. Die Wiener speisten lieber allein an indivi- duellen kleinen Tischen. Dabei mussten sie aber wissen, welches Angebot es im Gasthaus gab. Diese Art der Tafel in Wien wurde von ausländischen Gästen oft beklagt.

Dennoch hielt sich in Wien noch sehr lange der Brauch, dass der Kellner dem Gast die Speisekarte ansagte. Besondere Tagesspezialitäten wurden auf Schiefertafeln aufgeschrieben. Gedruckte Speisekarten von Gasthäusern bzw. Hotelrestaurants sind bereits aus der Biedermeierzeit bekannt. Sogenannte bessere Häuser konnten sich den Druck leisten. Tagesgerichte wurden nach wie vor auf Tafeln vermerkt. Dies ist im Großen und Ganzen bis heute so geblieben. Ein „Kuchl Zeddl" aus dem Jahr 1784 ist vom Wiener Wirtshaus Roter Apfel bekannt.

Der Wandel von „service à la française" zu „service à la russe" führte bei Hof, in Adels- und Groß- bürgerhäusern dazu, dass bei jedem Couvert eine Menükarte aufgelegt wurde, auf der von Austern über Vorspeise, Suppe, diverse Zwischenspeisen bis zu Braten, Gemüse und Mehlspeisen sowie Nachspeisen alles angeführt war (Abb. 264). Oft wurden noch die Getränke, die zu den einzelnen Gängen serviert wurden, vermerkt. Auch im bürgerlichen Bereich gab es zumindest bei besonderen Anlässen Menüs, die häufig grafisch besonders attraktiv gestaltet waren, bei jedem Couvert lagen und von den Tischgenossen als Andenken mitgenommen werden konnten. Diese Menükarten waren auch in Wien meist in Französisch – *der* Küchen- und Tafelsprache – abgefasst (Abb. 265). Bei Tafeln, die zeremoniellen Charakter hatten bzw. an denen viele Gäste teilnahmen, war es üblich,

9 Wortley Montagu, Mary, *Briefe, geschrieben während ihrer Reise nach Europa, Asien und Afrika*, Mannheim (deutsche Über- setzung) 1784. Lady Montagu (1689–1762) reiste 1716 mit ihrem Mann, der Botschafter im Osmanischen Reich wurde, nach Konstantinopel. Sie hielten sich einige Zeit auch in Wien auf.

264
Anonym Anonymous
**Handgeschriebene Menükarte
des Hotel Meissl & Schadn**
Wien, 1891
Klischee, Tusche
**Handwritten Menu Card from
the Hotel Meissl & Schadn**
Vienna, 1891
Cliché, ink
160 x 106 mm
KI 21484-23-5, Ankauf purchased from
Kunstarchiv Werner J. Schweiger 2015

265
Anonym Anonymous
**Menükarte zur Feier des
70. Geburtstags von Otto Wagner
Vorder- und Innenansicht**
Wien, 1911
Ausführung: Verlagsanstalt Brüder Rosenbaum
Radierung
**Menu Card for the Party for
Otto Wagner's 70th Birthday
front and interior**
Vienna, 1911
Execution: Publishing house Brüder Rosenbaum
Etching
215 x 158 mm
WWGG 760, Nachlass bequest from
Hans Ankwicz-Kleehoven 1963/64

266
Anonym Anonymous
Speisekarte des Restaurants in der Ausstellung der Künstlerkolonie in Darmstadt
Darmstadt, 1901
Buchdruck
Food Menu of the Restaurant at the Exhibition of the Artists' Colony in Darmstadt
Darmstadt, 1901
Letterpress print
275 x 415 mm
BI 12749, Ankauf vor Ort purchased on site 1901

267
Auguste Bénard
**Menükarte zum Bankett
des Cercle Athlétique Liégeois**
Lüttich, 1901
Lichtdruck, Buchdruck
**Menu Card for the Banquet
of the Cercle Athlétique Liégeois**
Lüttich, 1901
Collotype, letterpress print
245 x 155 mm
KI 9136-73, Legat bequest from Arthur Wolf 1933

268
Paul Bürck
**Getränkekarte des Restaurants in der
Ausstellung der Künstlerkolonie in
Darmstadt, Vorder- und Rückansicht**
Darmstadt, 1901
**Drinks Menu of the Restaurant at the
Exhibition of the Artists' Colony
in Darmstadt, front and back**
Darmstadt, 1901
490 x 250 mm
BI 12750, Ankauf vor Ort purchased on site 1901

MENUS, MENU CARDS, PLACE CARDS, ESCORTING CARDS

For a long time, there were no written records stating what was sold at inns nor menu lists explaining what was served at aristocratic banquets. Yet as early as 1716 wine lists enabled guests in the Viennese aristocracy to order their desired drink from the servants. Lady Montagu told of one of the first wine menus in the early 18th century: "I have already had the honour of being invited to dinner by several of the first people of quality; and I must do them the justice to say, the good taste and magnificence of their tables, very well answered to that of their furniture. […] But the variety and richness of their wines, is what appears the most surprising. The constant way is, to lay a list of their names upon the plates of the guests, along with the napkins; and I have counted several times to the number of eighteen different sorts, all exquisite in their kinds."[9]

A change appears to have occurred around the mid-18th century. In the *Oesterreichische Bausteine zur Kultur- und Sittengeschichte* (1745), a "notification [was published], on the strength of which everyone was informed and made known that in the subsequently named inns—all here in the royal seat and capital of Vienna—fare for persons of distinction as well as the commonalty could be received for various low prices, also what and how many dishes are served for such a price."[10]

This was the first time that one could read which dishes were served at an inn and how much they cost. Having said this, at that time meals were not served on an individual platter or plate. All dishes were put on the table at the same time and the diners helped themselves to what they wanted. This was particularly the case among the aristocracy and at the imperial court, where meals were served according to the "service à la française": all dishes eaten per course were brought to the table simultaneously. The guests at table could therefore see everything that was available. However, the table d'hôte—when several people eat together at the same table and can thus see all that is being served—was very rare in Vienna. The Viennese preferred to eat alone at small, individual tables, which meant that they had to know what food was cooked at that inn. This kind of dining in Vienna was much bemoaned by foreign guests.

Nevertheless, the convention whereby the waiter would announce the menu to the guest lasted a long time in Vienna. The specials of the day were written on slate boards. Despite this, there is evidence of printed menus by inns or hotel restaurants dating back to the Biedermeier period: higher-end establishments could afford to have theirs printed, though the specials of the day were still written on boards. This has largely remained the same up to the present day. Furthermore, a "Kuchl Zeddl" (kitchen sheet) dating from 1784 has survived from the Roter Apfel inn in Vienna. At the court, in aristocratic and upper-class homes, the transition from "service à la française" to "service à la russe" led to a menu card being placed on every couvert, on which all dishes were listed: from oysters to the starter, soup, diverse entremets, the roast meat, vegetables, and pastries as well as desserts (ill. 264). Often the drinks served with each course were also mentioned. There were even menus among the bourgeoisie—at least on special occasions—whose graphic designs were frequently very attractive, and which were placed on every couvert and could be taken as a keepsake by the diners. Even in Vienna, these menu cards were mostly written in French—*the* language of cuisine and dining (ill. 265). At meals with a ceremonial character or at which many guests took part, it was common for place cards bearing the people's names to be put alongside the place setting. Escorting cards or lists determined which gentleman would accompany which lady into the dining room (see ill. 293).

[9] Wortley Montagu, Mary, *Letters of the Right Honourable Lady Mary Wortley Montagu; Written during Her Travels in Europe, Asia, and Africa, to Persons of Distinction, Men of Letters, &c. in Different Parts of Europe*, London 1790. In 1716 Lady Montagu (1689–1762) traveled to Constantinople with her husband, who became ambassador in the Ottoman Empire. They also stayed a while in Vienna.

[10] Translated by Maria Slater.

Tischkarten mit den Namen der Personen zu den Gedecken zu stellen. Führkarten oder -listen bestimmten, welcher Herr welche Dame in den Speisesaal begleitete (s. Abb. 293).

Die Gestaltung der Menükarten unterlag prinzipiell keiner Konvention. In Adelshäusern und bei Hof waren sie meist recht schlicht, häufig mit dem entsprechenden Wappen bzw. der Krone versehen, manchmal auch mit den Initialen des Namens der Gastgeber. Die Prägung war weiß erhaben, konnte aber auch in Gold oder Silber gehalten sein. Menükarten waren mit Landschaften dekoriert oder mit einer Ansicht des herrschaftlichen Palais der Besitzer, Hinweisen auf den Anlass (Hochzeitssymbole, jagdliche Szenen, Champagnergläser und Flaschen für Silvester, Köche, Kochgeschirr, Kellner mit Schüsseln, vor denen sich Hunde begehrlich aufrichteten) – der Fantasie waren keine Grenzen gesetzt. Besonders humorvoll ist eine Menükarte in der Sammlung des MAK: Der Cercle Athlétique Liégois veranstaltete im Jahr 1901 ein Dîner. Auf der Menükarte ist eine Harlekindame abgebildet, die mit kleinen Beinchen versehene Schüsseln, auf denen bereits die Speisen angerichtet sind, durch einen Reifen springen lässt (Abb. 267).

Eine besondere Rarität besitzt das Museum in der Speise- und Weinkarte der Darmstädter Künstlerkolonie aus dem Jahr 1901. Die Künstlerkolonie wurde 1899 gegründet und konnte 1901 ihre erste Ausstellung veranstalten. Anlässlich dieses Ereignisses gab es ein Hauptrestaurant der Künstlerkolonie, das mit Speise- und Weinkarte bestückt war (Abb. 266, 268). Obwohl das Angebot – in drei Sprachen (Deutsch, Englisch, Französisch) – vor allem auf die damalige Speisenauswahl internationaler Speisekarten ausgerichtet war und mit Spezialitäten wie Hummer, Kaviar, Sardellen, Austern, Suppen (Kraftbrühen, Hummer, Schildkröten etc.), diversen englischen Rindfleischgerichten, Pasteten, Geflügel, Käse und Desserts aufwartete, ist erfreulich, dass auch Wiener Spezialitäten wie Wiener Backhendl, Wiener Schnitzel, Kaiserschnitzel, gebackener Kalbskopf und Gugelhupf angeboten wurden – schließlich gehörte mit Joseph Maria Olbrich (1867–1908) auch ein Wiener Künstler dieser eindrucksvollen Kolonie an. Von der ganz schlicht gehaltenen Speisekarte hebt sich die dazugehörige Weinkarte stark ab. Das deutsche und internationale Wein- und Getränkeangebot wird mit Abbildungen aus den jeweiligen Landschaften und mit Szenen aus der Mythologie illustriert, auch Anspielungen zur Sinneslust finden sich. Die Liste umfasst zahlreiche deutsche Weine, Bordeaux, Burgunder, Sekte, Champagner, Dessert- und Süßweine sowie Cognac und Liköre.

Am Ende dieser eindrucksvollen Broschüre zeigt die Grafik eine Frau mit Totenkopf in den Händen, worunter die folgenden Verse zu lesen sind:

„Der Sinne Taumel ist verflogen
Man hat sich schliesslich selbst betrogen
Ja soll der Nachgeschmack Dir fehlen
Musst Du nur Nektar Dir erwaehlen"

In principle, the design of the menu cards was not subject to any convention. Among the aristocracy and at court, they were usually very simple, often featuring the respective coat of arms or crown, sometimes also the host's initials. The embossing was raised and white, but could also be gold or silver. Menu cards were decorated with landscapes, with a view of the owner's grand residence, or with references to the occasion (wedding symbols, hunting scenes, champagne glasses and bottles for New Year's Eve, chefs, cookware, waiters bearing bowls and dogs raised towards them in covetous anticipation)—there were no limits to the designers' imagination. One particularly humorous menu card in the MAK Collection is that for the dinner organized by the Cercle Athlétique Liègois in 1901. The menu card shows an illustration of a female harlequin who makes dishes with little legs—on which meals have already been served—jump through a hoop (ill. 267).

The museum owns a particular rarity in the food and wine menu of the Darmstadt Artists' Colony from 1901. The Artists' Colony was founded in 1899 and was able to organize its first exhibition in 1901. To celebrate this occasion, one of the Artists' Colony's main restaurants was furnished with food and wine menus (ill. 266, 268). Although the meals and wines offered—in three languages (German, English, French)—were mostly aligned with the typical dishes on menus of the time and included specialties such as lobster, caviar, anchovies, oysters, soups (consommés, lobster, turtle, etc.), various English beef dishes, pâtés, poultry, cheese, and desserts, it is gratifying that Viennese specialties such as Viennese *Backhendl* (fried chicken), Wiener schnitzel, *Kaiserschnitzel* (veal schnitzel), baked calf's head, and *Gugelhupf* (Bundt cake) were also offered—after all, Joseph Maria Olbrich (1867–1908), a member of this formidable colony, was a Viennese artist. The wine menu certainly sets itself apart from the very simple food menu. The range of German and international wines and drinks is illustrated with depictions of the respective landscapes and with mythological scenes, including allusions to sensual pleasure. The list comprises numerous German wines, Bordeaux, burgundy, sparkling wine, champagne, dessert and sweet wines, as well as cognac and liqueurs. At the end of this impressive brochure, there is an image of a woman holding a skull in her hands, underneath which the following verse is printed:

"The frenzy of the senses has faded,
You have deceived no one but yourself;
Should you yet find your taste buds wanting,
It is up to you to find your nectar."[11]

[11] Translated by Maria Slater.

GELEGENHEITSGRAFIK ZU FEST- UND TISCHKULTUR

Ephemera gelangen oft eher zufällig in eine Museumssammlung, besonders solche, die einem einmaligen Anlass dienten und daher kaum aufbewahrt wurden, wie etwa Einladungen oder Eintritts-
karten. Im MAK haben sie sich als Künstler-Entwürfe erhalten – so in einer frühen Arbeit Koloman
Mosers (Abb. 271) – oder innerhalb von Musterbüchern (Abb. 269, 273), als Beigabe zur großen
Exlibris-Sammlung von Artur Wolf oder innerhalb der Schenkung einer Grafikerin (Abb. 270, 275).
Eine Besonderheit bildet die Eintrittskarte zu einem Gschnasfest, die sich bereits 1886 im Inventar-
buch findet und aufgrund des Entwerfers Ferdinand Laufberger sowie ihrer Plakat-Dimension für die
Museumssammlung interessant gewesen sein dürfte (Abb. 272).

Im Jahr 1985 wurden über 100 Einladungen zu Wiener Tanzveranstaltungen aus dem Besitz des
Kunsthistorikers Wolfgang Prohaska erworben, hauptsächlich zusammengetragen von dessen
Urgroßvater Julius Schmid (1854–1935), Maler und Professor an der Akademie der bildenden
Künste. Sie umfassen den Zeitraum von 1885 bis 1939 und bitten zu Bällen, Redouten, Schützen-
kränzchen und Faschingsfesten vor allem im Künstlerhaus (1907 ist Schmids Frau Leopoldine eine
der Ehrenpräsidentinnen, Abb. 279), aber auch in der Secession, den Sofiensälen oder im Musikverein. Die Gestaltungen namhafter Künstler liefern eine Stilgeschichte im Kleinen und sind dabei
von einer Qualität, die auch vor den zahlreichen Kinderfesten nicht Halt macht (Abb. 280, 282).

„Schön, aber fad", befand ein Besucher die Opernredoute 1928, deren Programmheft Joseph Binder
gestaltet hatte; sein Cover belebte die Modenschau *Wienerinnen von einst* mit einem eleganten
Beispiel aus der Gegenwart (Abb. 283). Die aufwendige Inszenierung eines Balles spiegelt sich in
solchen Einlagen wie auch in den Listen der Beteiligten wider, besonders aber in den Damenspenden, die sich aus den Tanzordnungen zu luxuriösen (Buch-)Geschenken entwickelten (Abb. 285).

Gustav E. Pazaurek wundert es nicht, dass das Wien der kunstvollen Biedermeierbillets „noch heutzutage liebenswürdige Galanterie-Pimpeleien mit ebenso unnachahmlicher Virtuosität und Vielseitig-
keit in den Tanzordnungen (‚Damenspenden') hervorzuzaubern versteht".[1] Ein meisterhaftes Beispiel
hierfür ist der kleine Ballführer zum Kränzchen der Kunstgewerbe-Schüler 1895 mit Illustrationen
u. a. von Koloman Moser (von dessen Schwester er angekauft wurde), Joseph Urban und Alfred
Cossmann, ausgestattet mit einem Einband aus Samt und Leder, Seidenschleife, einem Bleistift mit
Elfenbeindekor und einer Kordel zur Anbringung an die Abendrobe; die 5. Quadrille wurde übrigens
an Josef Hoffmann vergeben (Abb. 286, s. Abb. 261).

Zur Fest- gehört die Tischkultur, der man sich im Österreichischen Museum für Kunst und Industrie
(ÖMKI) gleichsam missionarisch widmete. Im Rahmen der einstigen Donnerstag-Vorlesungen hielt
der erste Kustos und Vizedirektor Jacob von Falke im Februar 1870 einen Vortrag über die Speiseta-
fel. Er hatte „den Zweck, den Hörern zum Bewusstsein zu bringen, dass dem ästhetisch Gebildeten
auch die gedeckte Tafel wie ein würdiges, wenn auch nur für den Augenblick entstandenes Kunstwerk erscheint", heißt es in den hauseigenen *Mittheilungen*.[2] Die Gelegenheitsgrafik für ein solch
ephemeres Ereignis besteht in den Tisch- und Menükarten. Ein größeres Konvolut letzterer kam
1901 als Geschenk des Handelsministeriums in die Sammlung des ÖMKI, vermittelt durch Wilhelm
Exner, den General-Commissär für die Pariser Weltausstellung 1900.[3] Die Karten stammen sämtlich
aus der Druckerei Nathan Weill und wurden direkt auf der Weltausstellung erworben. Den dekorati-
ven Motiven etwa eines Alfons Mucha steht vielfach die Karikatur gegenüber (Abb. 287–289).

[1] Pazaurek, Gustav E., *Biedermeier-Wünsche*,
Stuttgart 1908, 15.

[2] „Vorlesungen im Museum", in: *Mittheilungen
des k. k. Oesterr. Museums für Kunst und Industrie* (V) 55 1870, 134–135.

[3] Zu Wilhelm Exner s. S. 070, Anm. 6.

OCCASION GRAPHICS FOR SOCIAL AND DINING CULTURE

Ephemera often enter a museum's collection in a rather incidental manner; this is particularly true of ephemera, which were produced for a onetime occasion and were hence hardly kept, such as invitations or admission tickets. At the MAK they have been preserved as artists' designs—as in an early work by Koloman Moser (ill. 271)—or inside catalogs of work (ill. 269, 273), as an addition to the large ex libris collection of Artur Wolf, or as part of a donation by a graphic designer (ill. 270, 275). One exceptional piece is an admission ticket to a fancy-dress party, which found its way into the inventory as early as 1886 and may have been of interest to the collection of the museum due to its designer, Ferdinand Laufberger, as well as its poster dimensions (ill. 272).

In 1985 over 100 invitations to Viennese dance events from the estate of the art historian Wolfgang Prohaska were purchased, most of which had been collected by his great-grandfather, Julius Schmid (1854–1935), a painter and professor at the Academy of Fine Arts. They cover a period from 1885 to 1939 and invite the recipient to ordinary and masked balls, shooters' and carnival parties, mostly at Vienna's Künstlerhaus (Schmid's wife Leopoldine became one of its honorary presidents in 1907; ill. 279), but also at the Secession, the Sofiensälen, or the Musikverein. Designs by prestigious artists provide a miniature history of styles and are of such quality that it even extends to numerous children's parties (ill. 280, 282).

"Nice but boring" is the opinion of one visitor to the opera's masked ball in 1928, whose program had been designed by Joseph Binder; its cover revived the fashion show *Wienerinnen von einst* [Viennese women of old] with an elegant contemporary example (ill. 283). Although the elaborate staging of a ball is reflected in such inserts as well as in lists of attendees, it is especially clear in the ladies' gifts, which had evolved from dance cards into luxury presents (sometimes books, ill. 285). Gustav E. Pazaurek is not surprised that the Vienna of ornate Biedermeier cards "even nowadays knows how to conjure amiably gallant bad taste with equally inimitable virtuosity and versatility in dance cards ('ladies' gifts')."[1] A masterly example of this is the small ball guide for the dance of the students at the School of Arts and Crafts in 1895 with illustrations by Koloman Moser (from whose sister it was purchased), Joseph Urban, and Alfred Cossmann among others, and furnished with a cover made of velvet and leather, silk ribbon, a pencil with ivory decoration, and a cord to attach it to one's evening gown; incidentally, she danced the 5th quadrille with Josef Hoffmann (ill. 286, see ill. 261).

Social culture includes table culture, to which the Austrian Museum of Art and Industry (ÖMKI) dedicated itself in an almost missionary manner. In the context of the former Thursday lectures, the first custodian and deputy director Jacob von Falke held a lecture in February 1870 about the dining table. According to the in-house publication *Mittheilungen*, its "purpose [was] to make listeners aware that even the laid table appears to the aesthetically educated as a worthy, if only momentary, work of art."[2] The occasion graphics for such an ephemeral event are found in place and menu cards. Quite a large bundle of the latter entered the collection of the ÖMKI in 1901 as a gift from the trade ministry, negotiated by Wilhelm Exner, the general commissioner of the Paris world's fair in 1900.[3] All of the cards come from the Nathan Weill printing house and were purchased at the world's fair itself. The decorative motifs, such as one by Alfons Mucha, often contrast with caricatures (ill. 287–289). Both design styles can also be found in two gold-colored menu cards by the

[1] Pazaurek, Gustav E., *Biedermeier-Wünsche*, Stuttgart 1908, 15. Translated by Maria Slater.

[2] "Vorlesungen im Museum," in: *Mittheilungen des k. k. Oesterr. Museums für Kunst und Industrie* (V) 55 1870, 134–135. Translated by Maria Slater.

[3] On Wilhelm Exner see p. 071, note 6.

Beide Gestaltungsweisen finden sich auch in zwei goldfarbenen Menükarten der Wiener Werkstätte (WW), welche 1906 die Ausstellung *Der gedeckte Tisch* ausrichtete (Abb. 290, 291). Zu den hierfür angefertigten Drucksachen gehörte auch die bereits aus der Mode gekommene, von der WW wiederbelebte Tischführungskarte (Abb. 293).

Weinetiketten von Josef Divéky zeugen ebenfalls vom Interesse der WW an der künstlerischen Gestaltung von Gelegenheitsgrafik (Abb. 295). Die Epoche davor dokumentieren sorgfältig arrangierte Mustertafeln der Wiener Druckerei Johann Klein aus der Zeit zwischen 1870 und 1887, als sich der Firmenstandort im 3. Bezirk, Ungargasse 11, befand. Sie bilden vor allem Etiketten ab, u. a. für Bonbonnieren der Konditorei Demel (Abb. 294), aber auch Geschäftskarten und Verschlussmarken (vgl. Abb. 255, 256).

Durch den Binder-Nachlass kamen 1978 bzw. 1995/1996 etliche Warenetiketten in die MAK-Sammlung, die der Grafiker im Zuge einer umfassenden Corporate-Design-Kampagne[4] ab 1931 für die Firma Arabia entwickelt hatte (Abb. 296–298). In ihrer Verwendung waren sie bereits 1935/1936 im ÖMKI zu sehen, als der Neue Österreichische Werkbund hier seine Weihnachtsausstellung veranstaltete. „As part of that exhibit, Professor Oswald Haerdtl designed an own room to show my work", schildert Binder in seinen Erinnerungen und führt aus: „There was a modern window display with the newly-designed packages for Arabia Coffee and Tea Imports."[5] (Abb S. 233.) So verknüpfen und ergänzen sich Ausstellungs- und Sammlungstätigkeit eines Museums über einen langen Zeitraum hinweg.

4   Dombrowski, André, „Joseph Binder: Grafiker, Lehrer, Werbetheoretiker", in: Peter Noever (Hg.), *Joseph Binder. Wien – New York*, MAK Studies 1, Wien 2001, 56–60.

5   „Als Teil der Ausstellung gestaltete Professor Oswald Haerdtl einen eigenen Raum für meine Arbeiten. Es gab ein modernes Schaufenster mit den neu entworfenen Verpackungen für Arabia Kaffee und Tee Import." Übersetzt von Anne-Katrin Rossberg. Englisch in: Binder, Carla, *Joseph Binder. An artist and a lifestyle from the Joseph Binder Collection of posters, graphic and fine art, notes and records*, Wien/München 1976, 60.

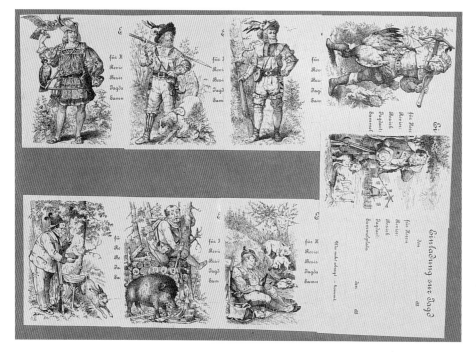

269
Hugo Gerard Ströhl
Acht Einladungen zur Jagd
Wien, 1880–1885
Strichätzung
Eight Invitations to Go Hunting
Vienna, 1880–1885
Line etching
Je 88 x 138 mm each
KI 7752-375, Schenkung donation from
Hugo Gerard Ströhl 1910

Wiener Werkstätte (WW), which organized the 1906 exhibition *Der gedeckte Tisch* [The laid table] (ill. 290, 291). Among the printed matter produced for this purpose was also the escorting card—though at that time already out of fashion, it was revived by the WW (ill. 293).

Wine labels by Josef Divéky also attest to the WW's interest in the artistic design of occasion graphics (ill. 295). The time before the WW is documented by carefully arranged sample tables by the Johann Klein printing house in Vienna from the period between 1870 and 1887, when the company was located at Ungargasse 11 in the city's third district. They predominantly comprise labels, e.g. for candy boxes from the confectioner Demel (ill. 294), but also business cards and sealing stamps (cf. ill. 255, 256).

Via the Binder estate, quite a number of goods labels entered the MAK Collection in 1978 and 1995/1996, which the graphic artist had developed over the course of a wide-ranging corporate design campaign[4] for the Arabia company in 1931 (ill. 296–298). They could be seen in use at the ÖMKI as early as 1935/1936, when the New Austrian Werkbund organized its Christmas exhibition there. "As part of that exhibit, Professor Oswald Haerdtl designed an own room to show [sic!] my work," Binder describes in his memoirs, and explains: "There was a modern window display with the newly-designed packages for Arabia Coffee and Tea Imports."[5] (ill. p. 233) In this way, the museum's exhibitions and collections are connected and complement one another over a long period of time.

4 Dombrowski, André, "Joseph Binder: Graphic Designer, Teacher, Advertising Theorist," in: Peter Noever (ed.), *Joseph Binder. Vienna—New York*, MAK Studies 1, Vienna 2001, 57–61.

5 Carla Binder, *Joseph Binder, An artist and a lifestyle from the Joseph Binder Collection of posters, graphic and fine art, notes and records*, Vienna/Munich 1976, 60.

270
Rolf Schott
Einladung zum Tee bei Artur Wolf
München, um 1928
Radierung
Invitation for Tea at Artur Wolf's
Munich, ca. 1928
Etching
130 x 95 mm
KI 9136-103, Legat bequest from Artur Wolf 1933

271
Koloman Moser
**Entwurf einer Einladung
zum Kostümkränzchen**
Wien, 1894
Bleistift, Deckweiß, Aquarell
Design for an Invitation to a Costume Party
Vienna, 1894
Pencil, opaque white, watercolor
425 x 303 mm
KI 8674-19, Ankauf purchased from
Leopoldine Steindl 1929

272
Ferdinand Laufberger
**Eintrittskarte zum Gschnasball
im Künstlerhaus**
Wien, 1870
Ausführung: Druckerei Reiffenstein & Rösch
Lithografie
**Admission Ticket for the Gschnas Ball
at the Künstlerhaus**
Vienna, 1870
Execution: Printer Reiffenstein & Rösch
Lithograph
222 x 462 mm
KI 4625-1, inv. inventoried 1886

273
Franz Karl Delavilla
Einladung zum Alpenglühn-Kränzchen
Wien, 1908
Ausführung: Chwala's Druck
Klischee
Invitation to the Alpenglühn Party
Vienna, 1908
Execution: Chwala's Druck
Cliché
230 x 102 (328) mm
KI 15848-16-2-1, Ankauf Teilnachlass
purchased from part of the estate of
Chwala's Druck 2008

274
Franz Karl Delavilla
Eintrittskarte zum Alpenglühn-Kränzchen
Wien, 1908
Ausführung: Chwala's Druck
Klischee
Admission Ticket for the Alpenglühn Party
Vienna, 1908
Execution: Chwala's Druck
Cliché
222 x 100 mm
KI 15854-39-3, Ankauf Teilnachlass
purchased from part of the estate of
Chwala's Druck 2008

275
Hansi Lehner-Rosner
Einladung zum Souper Dansant im Hotel Imperial
Wien, um 1935
Klischee
Invitation to the Souper Dansant at the Hotel Imperial
Vienna, ca. 1935
Cliché
205 x 120 mm
KI 9305-6, Schenkung donation from Hansi Lehner-Rosner 1936

276
Charles Wilda
Probedruck für die Einladung zu einem Gschnasball
Wien, 1895
Ausführung: Druckerei C. Angerer & Göschl
Autotypie, Siebdruck
Test Print of an Invitation to a Gschnas Ball
Vienna, 1895
Execution: Printer C. Angerer & Göschl
Halftone, screen printing
285 x 210 mm
KI 14393-5, Ankauf purchased from
Wolfgang Prohaska 1985

277
Hubert von Zwickle
**Einladung zum Kostümfest der
Wiener Kunstgewerbeschule**
Wien, 1901
Lithografie
**Invitation to a Costume Party
at the Viennese School of
Arts and Crafts**
Vienna, 1901
Lithograph
169 x 70 (210) mm
KI 14393-11, Ankauf purchased
from Wolfgang Prohaska 1985

278
Leopold Forstner
**Einladung zum Kostümfest
der Wiener Kunstgewerbeschüler
in den Sofiensälen**
Wien, 1902
Klischee, Buchdruck
**Invitation to a Costume Party of the
Students of the School of Arts and Crafts
at the Sofiensäle**
Vienna, 1902
Cliché, letterpress print
147 x 108 mm
KI 14393-14, Ankauf purchased from
Wolfgang Prohaska 1985

279
Franz Wacik
**Einladung zum Unterhaltungsabend der
Kunstakademiker im Künstlerhaus**
Wien, 1907
Lithografie
**Invitation to an Evening of Entertainment
of the Members of the Art Academy at
the Künstlerhaus**
Vienna, 1907
Lithograph
365 x 168 mm
KI 14393-27, Ankauf purchased from
Wolfgang Prohaska 1985

280
Leopold Schmid
Einladung zur Gschnas-Redoute
im Künstlerhaus
Wien, 1931
Klischee, Buchdruck
Invitation to a Gschnas
Masquerade Ball at the Künstlerhaus
Vienna, 1931
Cliché, letterpress print
153 x 120 mm
KI 14393-65, Ankauf purchased from
Wolfgang Prohaska 1985

281
Bertold Löffler
Einladung zur Gschnas-Revue im
Künstlerhaus
Wien, 1929
Lithografie
Invitiation to a Gschnas Revue
at the Künstlerhaus
Vienna, 1929
Lithograph
154 x 116 mm
KI 14393-58, Ankauf purchased from
Wolfgang Prohaska 1985

282
Eduard Stella
Einladung zum Kinderfest im
Künstlerhaus
Wien, 1932
Offsetdruck
Invitation to a Children's Festival
at the Künstlerhaus
Vienna, 1932
Offset print
152 x 112 mm
KI 14393-71, Ankauf purchased from
Wolfgang Prohaska 1985

283
Joseph Binder
Programmheft der Wiener Opernredoute
Wien, 1928
Autotypie
**Program Booklet for the Viennese
Opera Masquerade Ball**
Vienna, 1928
Halftone
197 x 142 (284) mm
BI 101879, Ankauf purchased from
René Schober 2012

284
Anonym Anonymous
**Tanzordnung zum Mummenschanz des
Männer-Turnvereins Klosterneuburg**
Wien, 1909
Ausführung: Chwala's Druck
Buchdruck
**Dance Sequence for the Mummers'
Plays of the Men's Gymnastics Club
Klosterneuburg**
Vienna, 1909
Execution: Chwala's Druck
Letterpress print
115 x 70 (140) mm
KI 15854-38-2, Ankauf Teilnachlass Chwala's
Druck purchased from part of the estate of
Chwala's Druck 2008

285
Sign. Signed Schmidt
**Illustration zur 5. Quadrille in der
Tanzordnung zum Kränzchen der
Kunstgewerbe-Schüler mit Eintrag
„Jos. Hoffmann"**
Wien, 1895
Lichtdruck
**Illustration for the 5th Quadrille in the
Dance Sequence of a Party of the Stu-
dents of the School of Arts and Crafts
with the Inscription "Jos. Hoffmann"**
Vienna, 1895
Collotype
153 x 90 mm
KI 8687-2, Ankauf purchased from
Leopoldine Steindl 1929

286
Josef Hoffmann
**Einband für *Das neue Narrenschiff*,
Ballspende zum Concordia-Ball**
Wien, 1911
Leder, geprägt
**Book Cover for [The new ship of fools],
ladies' gift at the Concordia-Ball**
Vienna, 1911
Leather, embossed
150 x 108 mm
BI 61025, Ankauf purchased from
Antiquariat Wögenstein 1997

287
Jan van Beers
**Menükarte, gezeigt auf der Pariser
Weltausstellung 1900**
Paris, 1900
Ausführung: Druckerei Nathan Weill
Lithografie, Prägedruck
**Menu Card, shown at the 1900 Paris
World's Fair**
Paris, 1900
Execution: Printer Nathan Weill
Lithograph, embossing
165 x 108 mm
KI 7476-83, Schenkung donation from
k. k. Handelsministerium 1901

288
Anonym Anonymous
**Menükarte, gezeigt auf der
Pariser Weltausstellung 1900**
Paris, 1900
Ausführung: Druckerei Nathan Weill
Lithografie
**Menu Card, shown at the
1900 Paris World's Fair**
Paris, 1900
Execution: Printer Nathan Weill
Lithograph
175 x 118 mm
KI 7476-98, Schenkung donation from
k. k. Handelsministerium 1901

289
Alfons Mucha
**Menükarte, gezeigt auf der Pariser
Weltausstellung 1900**
Paris, 1900
Ausführung: Druckerei Nathan Weill
Lithografie
**Menu Card, shown at the 1900 Paris
World's Fair**
Paris, 1900
Execution: Printer Nathan Weill
Lithograph
210 x 143 mm
KI 7476-123, Schenkung donation from
k. k. Handelsministerium 1901

292
Arnold Nechansky
Tischkarte der Wiener Werkstätte
Wien, 1912
Lithografie
Place Card from the Wiener Werkstätte
Vienna, 1912
Lithograph
78 x 88 mm
KI 13771-23, Ankauf purchased from
Alexandra Ankwicz-Kleehoven 1964

291
Anonym Anonymous
Menükarte der Wiener Werkstätte
Wien, um 1906
Klischee
Menu Card from the Wiener Werkstätte
Vienna, ca. 1906
Cliché
105 x 40 mm
KI 13771-18, Ankauf purchased from
Alexandra Ankwicz-Kleehoven 1964

290
Anonym Anonymous
Menükarte der Wiener Werkstätte
Wien, um 1906
Klischee
Menu Card from the Wiener Werkstätte
Vienna, ca. 1906
Cliché
127 x 51 mm
KI 13771-15, Ankauf purchased from
Alexandra Ankwicz-Kleehoven 1964

293
Anonym Anonymous
**Tischführungskarte der
Wiener Werkstätte**
Wien, 1906
Lithografie
**Escorting Card of the
Wiener Werkstätte**
Vienna, 1906
Lithograph
54 x 82 mm
KI 13771-25, Ankauf purchased from
Alexandra Ankwicz-Kleehoven 1964

294
Anonym Anonymous
Etikett der Konditorei Demel
Wien, um 1880
Ausführung: Druckerei Johann Klein
Lithografie
Label of the Pastry Shop Demel
Vienna, ca. 1880
Execution: Printer Johann Klein
Lithograph
Durchmesser Diameter 171 mm
KI 22214-39, alter Bestand, inv.
old holdings, inventoried 2015

295
Josef Divéky
Weinetikett der Wiener Werkstätte
Wien, 1904–1905
Lithografie
Wine Label of the Wiener Werkstätte
Vienna, 1904–1905
Lithograph
106 x 106 mm
KI 13771-6, Ankauf purchased from
Alexandra Ankwicz-Kleehoven 1964

296
Joseph Binder
Etikett für *ARABIA Frühstückstee*
Wien, 1931–1935
Offsetdruck
Label for [ARABIA Breakfast Tea]
Vienna, 1931–1935
Offset print
34 x 210 mm
KI 14145-201, Legat bequest from
Carla und and Joseph Binder 1978

297
Joseph Binder
Etikett für *ARABIA India-Ceylon-Tee*
Wien, 1931–1935
Offsetdruck
Label for [ARABIA India Ceylon Tea]
Vienna, 1931–1935
Offset print
43 x 345 mm
KI 14145-940-2, Legat bequest from
Carla und and Joseph Binder 1995/96

298
Joseph Binder
Etikett für *ARABIA Finest Old Jamaika Rum*
Wien, 1931–1935
Offsetdruck
Label for *ARABIA Finest Old Jamaika Rum*
Vienna, 1931–1935
Offset print
98 x 137 mm
KI 14145-940-8, Legat bequest from
Carla und and Joseph Binder 1995/96

EINLADUNGEN ZU AUSSTELLUNGEN UND BESICHTIGUNGEN

Nach dem Tod des langjährigen Bibliotheksleiters Hans Ankwicz-Kleehoven 1962 sowie seiner Frau 1969 kam ein Teil seines Nachlasses an das Österreichische Museum für angewandte Kunst (ÖMAK). Darunter befanden sich auch Einladungen zu Wiener Künstlerfesten, Atelierschauen und Vorträgen. Ankwicz-Kleehoven selbst lud jahrelang zwischen Jänner und Mai einmal im Monat zum Tee ein, um Kunstschaffende und -interessierte zusammenzuführen, ebenso wie der gleichgesinnte Walter von Zur Westen in Berlin zu „Sammlungstee" und Ausstellung bat (Abb. 308, 309). Die Einladungen sind aufwendig gestaltet und ausgeführt – als Holzschnitt, Radierung, Lithografie oder Fotomontage. Zwei Originalentwürfe für die Wiener Werkstätte (WW) stammen aus deren Archiv, das 1955 von Alfred Hofmann, dem letzten Geschäftsführer der WW, in die Sammlung übernommen wurde (Abb. 303, 304). Sie zeigen die Stilentwicklung unter dem Einfluss Dagobert Peches im Vergleich zu den frühen Drucksachen, entworfen von Koloman Moser (Abb. 301). Zwei Einladungen zur Besichtigung von Schülerarbeiten wiederum machen die Veränderungen deutlich, die die Verbindung von Schrift und Ornament zwischen Historismus und Moderne erfahren hat: von der nobilitierenden Geste hin zur inhaltlichen Aussage (Abb. 299, 311).

Darüber hinaus sind die Einladungen oft ein Fundus für die Alltagsgeschichte. Man erfährt etwa, dass die kunstaffine Frauenrechtlerin Marie Lang eine persönliche Einladung zur Eröffnung der 13. Secessionsausstellung erhielt, bei der die Herren im Gehrock zu erscheinen hatten (Abb. 302), dass das Österreichische Museum für Kunst und Industrie einst täglich geöffnet und bis auf zwei Tage in der Woche gratis zu besuchen war (Abb. 300), dass die Grafiker Gaertner, Kloss und Weyr um die Vermittlung der modernen Kunst bemüht waren und dafür im Inflationsjahr 1923 monatlich 100.000 Kronen (Wert von ca. 2 kg Kaffee) verlangten (Abb. 305), dass einmal eine Straßenbahnlinie B durch den 2. Wiener Bezirk fuhr (Abb. 307) und dass sich der seit 1930 international reüssierende Maler Sergius Pauser 1935 ein neues Atelier am Schwarzenbergplatz leisten konnte (Abb. 310). Zeitgleich mit der Einladung zur Ausstellung *Joseph Binder New York. Nonobjective Art* im ÖMAK 1972 ereignete sich der plötzliche Tod des prominenten Grafikers (Abb. 313). Sein letzter Brief an den damaligen Direktor Wilhelm Mrazek datiert vom 14. Juni und kündigt die Ankunft in Wien für den 22. Juni an; hier wollte er gemeinsam mit seiner Frau den Ausstellungsaufbau und die Katalogproduktion betreuen.[1] Vier Tage später erlag Binder einem Herzinfarkt. So wurde es eine Gedächtnisausstellung, die von vornherein nicht der Gebrauchsgrafik, sondern Binders Malerei der letzten Jahre gewidmet war.[2] Ihr folgte 1976 eine Präsentation von frühen Aquarellen aus den USA als weiteres Beispiel dafür, dass sich das Museum auch immer wieder der bildenden Kunst annahm.[3]

Eine zeitgenössische Einladung wiederum zeigt, dass diese Art Gelegenheitsgrafik für die MAK-Sammlung bis heute relevant ist (Abb. 314). Im Jahr 2014 gehörte die damalige Grafik-Studentin Dasha Zaichanka mit ihrem Sujet für die Jahresausstellung der Universität für angewandte Kunst *The Essence 14* zu den PreisträgerInnen des Wettbewerbs *100 BESTE PLAKATE*, dessen Ergebnisse jährlich im MAK-Kunstblättersaal präsentiert werden. In der Einladung ist das Plakatmotiv – aus einer Banane wächst und schält sie eine Banane und eine zweite und eine dritte ... – durch Aufklappen erweiterbar: Das Bild für einen permanenten Lernprozess[4] wird damit noch einmal schlüssiger.

[1] MAK-Archiv, Aktenzahl 1972/50.

[2] „Joseph Binder. Nonobjective Art", in: *Alte und moderne Kunst* (XVII) 124/125 1972, 86.

[3] „Joseph Binder. Amerikanische Impressionen 1933–1935", in: *Alte und moderne Kunst* (XXII) 150 1977, 50.

[4] Vgl. Posting auf dashazaichanka.tumblr.com (4.2.2016).

INVITATIONS TO EXHIBITIONS AND VIEWINGS

After the death of the long-standing head of the library, Hans Ankwicz-Kleehoven, in 1962 as well as his wife in 1969, part of his estate arrived at the Austrian Museum of Applied Arts (ÖMAK). It included invitations to Viennese artists' parties, studio shows, and lectures. For many years Ankwicz-Kleehoven himself extended invitations to tea once a month between January and May in order to bring together those who created and/or were interested in art, just as the like-minded Walter von Zur Westen in Berlin invited people to "collection teas" and exhibitions (ill. 308, 309). The invitations are elaborately designed and executed—as woodcuts, etchings, lithographs, or photomontages. Two original designs for the Wiener Werkstätte come from its own archive, which was transferred to the collection by Alfred Hofmann, the last manager of the WW, in 1955 (ill. 303, 304). They illustrate the stylistic development under the influence of Dagobert Peche in comparison with the early printed matter, which had been designed by Koloman Moser (ill. 301). In turn, two invitations to view students' works make clear the changes pertaining to the relationship between text and ornament in the period from historicism to modernity: from a dignifying gesture to a declaration of content (ill. 299, 311).

Furthermore, the invitations are often stock for everyday history. For example, one discovers that the campaigner for women's rights and art enthusiast Marie Lang received a personal invitation to the opening of the 13th Secession exhibition, at which the dress code for gentlemen was a frock coat (ill. 302); that the Austrian Museum of Art and Industry was once open daily and admission was free on all but two days a week (ill. 300); that the graphic designers Gaertner, Kloss, and Weyr endeavored to support modern art and for this they charged a monthly rate of 100,000 Kronen (the value of ca. 2 kg of coffee) in 1923, the year of inflation (ill. 305); that the B tram once went through Vienna's second district (ill. 307); and that painter Sergius Pauser—who had enjoyed international success since 1930—could afford a new studio on Schwarzenbergplatz in the city center in 1935 (ill. 310).The invitation to the exhibition *Joseph Binder New York – Nonobjective Art* at the ÖMAK in 1972 arrived at the same time as news of the sudden death of this prominent graphic designer (ill. 313). His last letter to the then director, Wilhelm Mrazek, was dated 14 June and announced that he would arrive in Vienna on 22 June, where he wanted to supervise the setting up of the exhibition and the production of the catalog together with his wife.[1] Four days later Binder would suffer a heart attack. The show therefore became a memorial exhibition, which from the outset had been dedicated not to ephemera but to Binder's recent paintings.[2] It was followed in 1976 by a display of early watercolors from the U.S.A.—a further example of the museum also attending to fine art.[3] On the other hand, a contemporary invitation shows that this type of occasion graphic is still relevant for the MAK Collection today (ill. 314). In 2014 the then graphic design student Dasha Zaichanka and her subject for the end-of-year exhibition at the University of Applied Arts Vienna, *The Essence 14*, was one of the award-winners of the competition *100 BEST POSTERS*, the results of which are announced in the MAK Works on Paper Room every year. In the invitation the poster's motif—a banana is peeled and grows out of another banana and another and another—is extended when it is unfolded: the symbol of a permanent learning curve[4] is thus made even more conclusive.

[1] MAK Archive, reference number 1972/50.

[2] "Joseph Binder. Nonobjective Art," in: *Alte und moderne Kunst* (XVII) 124/125 1972, 86.

[3] "Joseph Binder. Amerikanische Impressionen 1933–1935," in: *Alte und moderne Kunst* (XXII) 150 1977, 50.

[4] Cf. post on dashazaichanka.tumblr.com (4 Feb 2016).

299
Hugo Gerard Ströhl
**Einladung zur Besichtigung von Schülerarbeiten
der gewerblichen Fortbildungsschule in Hernals**
Wien, 1883
Ausführung: Druckerei C. Angerer & Göschl
Strichätzung
**Invitation to View Student Works from the
[Industrial continuation school] in Hernals**
Vienna, 1883
Execution: Printer C. Angerer & Göschl
Line etching
123 x 190 mm
KI 7752-234, Schenkung donation from Hugo Gerard Ströhl 1910

300
Anonym Anonymous
**Einladung zur Eröffnung der *Ausstellung
der österr. Tapeten-Industrie* im ÖMKI 1913**
Wien, 1913
Ausführung: Chwala's Druck
Buchdruck
**Invitation to the Opening of the [Exhibition of the
Austrian wallpaper industry] at the ÖMKI 1913**
Vienna, 1913
Execution: Chwala's Druck
Letterpress print
112 x 175 mm
KI 15854-13-5, Ankauf Teilnachlass
purchased from part of the estate of Chwala's Druck 2008

301
Koloman Moser
**Einladung der Wiener Werkstätte zur Besichtigung
neuer Arbeiten**
Wien, 1907
Ausführung: Chwala's Druck
Klischee
Invitation by the Wiener Werkstätte to View New Works
Vienna, 1907
Execution: Chwala's Druck
Cliché
140 x 90 mm
KI 15848-10-1-5, Ankauf Teilnachlass
purchased from part of the estate of Chwala's Druck 2008

302
Koloman Moser
**Einladung zur XIII. Ausstellung
der Secession**
Wien, 1902
Klischee
**Invitation to the 13th Exhibition
of the Secession**
Vienna, 1902
Cliché
150 x 80 (160) mm
WWGG 404-1, Nachlass bequest from
Hans Ankwicz-Kleehoven 1963/64

303
Maria Likarz
**Entwurf für eine Einladung der
Wiener Werkstätte**
Wien, 1917
Bleistift, Tusche, Deckfarbe
**Design for an Invitation of the
Wiener Werkstätte**
Vienna, 1917
Pencil, ink, coating paint
340 x 207 mm
KI 12281-17, Schenkung donation from
Alfred Hofmann 1955

304
Mathilde Flögl
**Entwurf für eine Einladung der
Wiener Werkstätte**
Wien, um 1927
Bleistift, Tusche, Deckfarben auf Transparentpapier
**Design for an Invitation of the
Wiener Werkstätte**
Vienna, ca. 1927
Pencil, ink, coating paint on transparent paper
160 x 200 mm
KI 11812-2, Schenkung donation from
Alfred Hofmann 1955

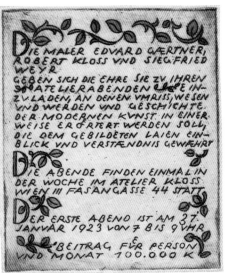

305
Eduard Gaertner
**Einladung zu Atelierabenden der
Maler Eduard Gaertner,
Robert Kloss und Siegfried Weyr**
Wien, 1923
Radierung, koloriert
**Invitation to Studio Evenings
by the Painters Eduard Gaertner,
Robert Kloss, and Siegfried Weyr**
Vienna, 1923
Etching, colored
143 x 122 mm
KI 9136-81, Legat bequest from
Artur Wolf 1933

306
Ernst Ludwig Franke
**Einladung zur Atelierschau
von Ernst Ludwig Franke**
Wien, 1924
Klischee, Holzschnitt
**Invitation to a Studio Show
by Ernst Ludwig Franke**
Vienna, 1924
Cliché, woodcut
118 x 127 mm
KI 13369-17-3, Ankauf purchased from
Ilka Franke 1959

307
Vermutl. Prob. Franz von Zülow
**Einladung zur Verkaufsausstellung
von Ernst Huber, Josef Dobrowsky,
Sergius Pauser und Franz von Zülow**
Wien, 1929
Lithografie
**Invitation to a Sales Show by
Ernst Huber, Josef Dobrowsky,
Sergius Pauser, and Franz von Zülow**
Vienna, 1929
Lithograph
272 x 220 mm
WWGG 456, Nachlass bequest from
Hans Ankwicz-Kleehoven 1963/64

308
Karl Michel
Einladung zum Tee bei Walter von Zur Westen
Berlin, 1927
Holzschnitt
Invitation to Tea at Walter von Zur Westen's
Berlin, 1927
Woodcut
139 x 165 mm
KI 9136-95, Legat bequest from Artur Wolf 1933

309
Vermutl. Prob. Rudolf Köhl
Entwurf für eine Einladung zum Tee
Wien, um 1931
Tusche
Design for an Invitation to Tea
Vienna, ca. 1931
Ink
162 x 100 mm
WWGG 503-1, Nachlass bequest from
Hans Ankwicz-Kleehoven 1963/64

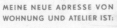

310
Anonym Anonymous
**Einladung zur Atelierschau
von Sergius Pauser**
Wien, 1935
Rasterdruck
**Invitation to a Studio Show
by Sergius Pauser**
Vienna, 1935
Halftone
190 x 175 mm
WWGG 440, Nachlass bequest from
Hans Ankwicz-Kleehoven 1963/64

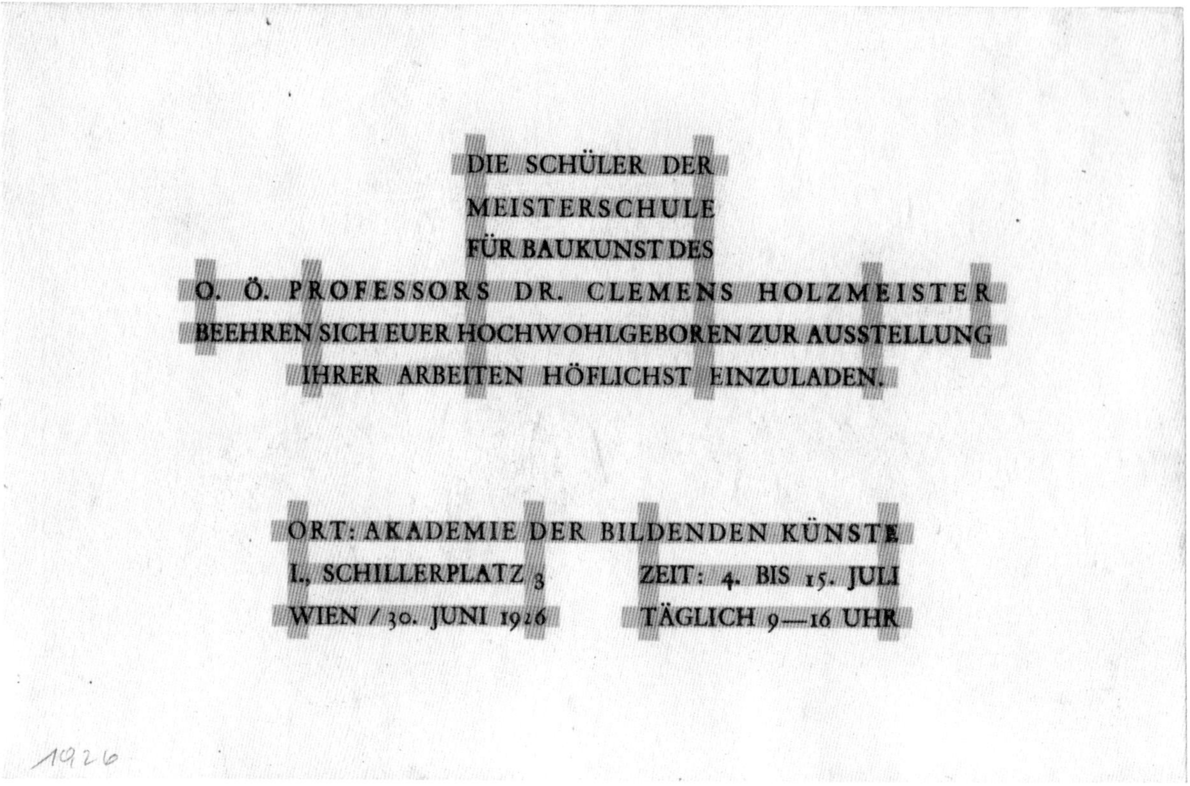

DIE SCHÜLER DER
MEISTERSCHULE
FÜR BAUKUNST DES
O. Ö. PROFESSORS DR. CLEMENS HOLZMEISTER
BEEHREN SICH EUER HOCHWOHLGEBOREN ZUR AUSSTELLUNG
IHRER ARBEITEN HÖFLICHST EINZULADEN.

ORT: AKADEMIE DER BILDENDEN KÜNSTE
I., SCHILLERPLATZ 3   ZEIT: 4. BIS 15. JULI
WIEN / 30. JUNI 1926   TÄGLICH 9—16 UHR

1926

311
Robert Haas
**Einladung zur Ausstellung der Meisterschule
für Baukunst von Prof. Clemens Holzmeister**
Wien, 1926
Klischee
**Invitation to an Exhibition of the [Master school
of architecture] of Prof. Clemens Holzmeister**
Vienna, 1926
Cliché
110 x 174 mm
KI 8895-6, Schenkung donation from
Robert Haas 1930

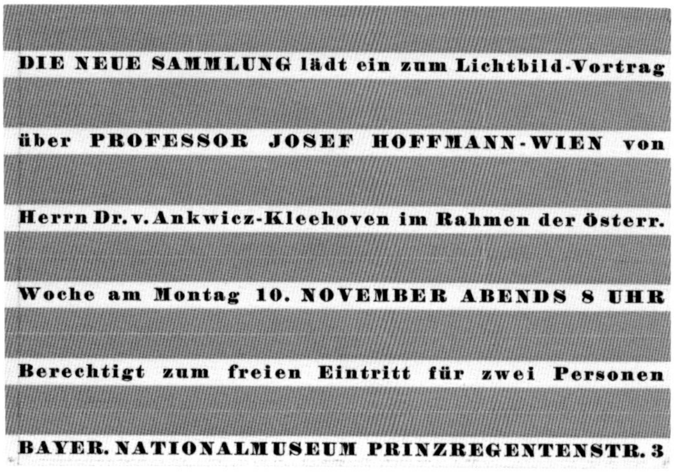

DIE NEUE SAMMLUNG lädt ein zum Lichtbild-Vortrag

über PROFESSOR JOSEF HOFFMANN-WIEN von

Herrn Dr. v. Ankwicz-Kleehoven im Rahmen der Österr.

Woche am Montag 10. NOVEMBER ABENDS 8 UHR

Berechtigt zum freien Eintritt für zwei Personen

BAYER. NATIONALMUSEUM PRINZREGENTENSTR. 3

312
Anonym Anonymous
**Einladung zu einem Vortrag von
Hans Ankwicz-Kleehoven über Josef Hoffmann**
München, 1930
Klischee
**Invitation to a Talk by Hans
Ankwicz-Kleehoven on Josef Hoffmann**
Munich, 1930
Cliché
82 x 124 mm
WWGG 479, Nachlass bequest from
Hans Ankwicz-Kleehoven 1963/64

das österreichische museum für angewandte
kunst und die gesellschaft der kunstfreunde
erlauben sich, zur eröffnung der ausstellung
joseph binder, new york, nonobjective art —
bilder und pastelle, höflichst einzuladen.

die gedenkausstellung wird donnerstag,
den 14. september 1972, um 18 uhr von
frau dr. hertha firnberg, bundesminister für
wissenschaft und forschung, in der
ausstellungshalle des museums, 1010 wien,
weiskirchnerstraße 3, eröffnet werden.

JOSEPH BINDER NEW YORK
NONOBJECTIVE ART

die ausstellung steht unter dem ehrenschutz von
dr. hertha firnberg, bundesminister für
wissenschaft und forschung,
gertrude fröhlich-sandner, vizebürgermeister
der stadt wien, stadtrat für kultur, volksbildung
und sport,
john p. humes, außerordentlicher und
bevollmächtigter botschafter der vereinigten
staaten von amerika.

313
Anonym Anonymous
**Einladung zur Ausstellung *Joseph Binder
New York. Nonobjective Art* im ÖMAK 1972**
Wien, 1972
Offsetdruck
**Invitation to the Exhibition *Joseph Binder New
York. Nonobjective Art* at the ÖMAK 1972**
Vienna, 1972
Offset print
200 x 97 (195) mm
KI 14145-881-31-1, Legat bequest from
Carla und Joseph Binder 1995/96

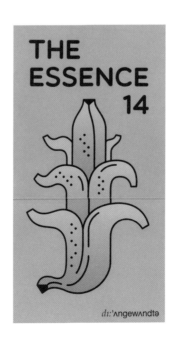

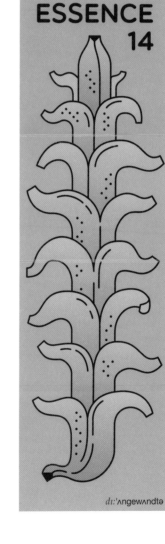

314
Dasha Zaichanka
**Einladungskarte zur Eröffnung der Jahresausstellung
The Essence 14 der Universität für angewandte Kunst Wien**
Wien, 2014
Offsetdruck
**Invitation Card to the Opening of the Annual Exhibition
The Essence 14 at the University of Applied Arts Vienna**
Vienna, 2014
Offset print
190 (350) x 100 mm
KI 19540, Schenkung Universität für angewandte Kunst Wien
donation from the University of Applied Arts Vienna 2014

EIN SAMMLER IST EIN SAMMLER IST EIN SAMMLER. Seine Leidenschaft richtet sich auf Objekte, die ihm etwas bedeuten. Was veranlasst einen, ausgerechnet Exlibris zu sammeln? Für den passionierten Büchersammler Walter Benjamin ist nicht der Gebrauchswert des gesammelten Dinges wichtig, sondern „das Theater seines Schicksals", das er „studiert und liebt". „Zeitalter, Landschaft, Handwerk, Besitzer, von denen es stammt – sie alle rücken für den wahren Sammler in jedem einzelnen seiner Besitztümer zu einer magischen Enzyklopädie zusammen, deren Inbegriff das Schicksal seines Gegenstandes ist." Für Benjamin sind die gesammelten Dinge Erinnerungen an eine frühere Welt, ihr Besitz ist für ihn „das allertiefste Verhältnis".[1] Wie weit gilt das auch für einen Exlibrissammler wie mich?

Der Reiz eines Exlibris liegt für mich darin, dass es mit Büchern zu tun hat und dass neben der optischen Faszination des Bildgehalts und der Technik auch ein Eigner angegeben wird, der als Person durch seine Kooperation mit dem Kunstschaffenden in das Blatt mit eingeht. Jedes Blatt bietet also neben der Bildwirkung auch das Rätsel der Person, für die das Exlibris gestaltet wurde: Diesem Rätsel nachzugehen, ist mir ein wichtiges Bedürfnis geworden. Für mich als Literaturwissenschaftler sind es Exlibris von DichterInnen wie Rilke, Morgenstern oder Ebner-Eschenbach, die ich meiner Sammlung gern einverleibe. Ein kleines Blatt mit einem Wappen und der Bezeichnung *Bibliotheque de Coppet*, das mir in die Hände fiel, stellte sich als Exlibris der berühmten Madame de Staël heraus, die auf ihrem Schloss in der Schweiz mit bedeutenden Persönlichkeiten ihrer Zeit verkehrte. Da spiegelt die Fantasie dem Sammler das Theatrum Mundi einer früheren Zeit, er imaginiert die Bibliothek, in der das Buch mit jenem Exlibris stand, und fragt sich, in welchem Buch das Blatt wohl klebte.

Hinter solchen Funden jagt jeder Sammler her. Lange Zeit wusste ich beispielsweise bei einer nicht signierten Lithografie, die ich in einem Buch auf dem Flohmarkt beim Wiener Naschmarkt fand, nicht, wer sie gemacht hatte, bis ich sie in einem Aufsatz als erstes Exlibris von Ernst Barlach identifizierte und so die Beziehung zwischen KünstlerInnen und EignerInnen erforschen konnte.

Zu den Kategorien Benjamins kommt bei der Exlibrisgrafik für den forschenden Sammler auch noch der Stil hinzu. Das Sammeln von Exlibris öffnet ein Schlupfloch in die Kunst- und Kulturgeschichte. Freunde des Jugendstils finden auf Exlibris quer durch Europa die ganze Vielfalt dieser europäischen Stilbewegung vertreten. Spannend ist ebenso, wie sich die Exlibris-Grafik in der Postmoderne entwickelt.

Exlibris-Sammeln hat auch mit Beziehungen zu tun. Man kann auf jedem Blatt der Beziehung zwischen den KünstlerInnen und den EignerInnen nachgehen. Und auch zu den Tauschpartnern in den Sammelvereinigungen, die seit 1891 in Europa existieren, ergeben sich für den Sammler Beziehungen, die zu Freundschaften werden können. Sicher haben sich auch für den Sammler und Verleger Artur Wolf viele solche Beziehungen und Freundschaften ergeben.

Für mich ist meine Sammlung in der Tat zu einer „magischen Enzyklopädie" geworden, aus der sich immer wieder neue Erkenntnisse schöpfen lassen.

Heinz Decker, Träger der Walter-von-Zur-Westen-Medaille der Deutschen Exlibris-Gesellschaft, Frankfurt/Main

[1] Benjamin, Walter, *Ich packe meine Bibliothek aus. Rede vom Sammeln*, http://gutenberg. spiegel.de/buch/kurze-prosa-6570/2 (8.9.2015).

Ankwicz Alexandra

1. Exlibris (Radierungen und Klischees) von Prof.
   Richard Teschner.
   Exlibris v. Alexandra Ankwicz, (Klischee)

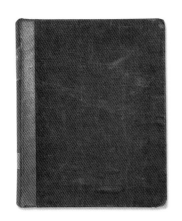
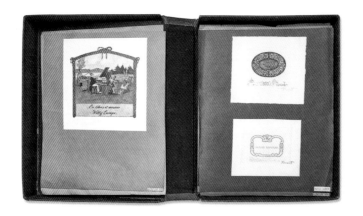

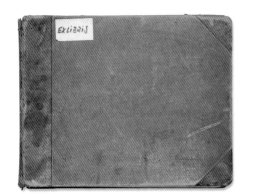
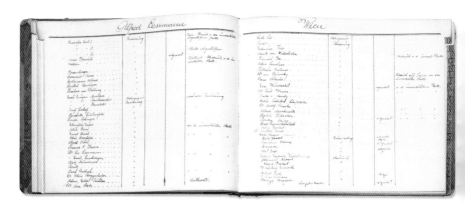

[1] "Unpacking My Library: A Talk about Book Collecting," in: Benjamin, Walter, *Illuminations*, transl. by Harry Zohn, New York 1969, 60, 67.

A COLLECTOR IS A COLLECTOR IS A COLLECTOR. Their passion is directed at those objects, which mean something to them. What induces someone to collect ex libris, of all things? For the avid book collector Walter Benjamin, the practical value of the collected object was not important, but rather "the stage of their fate," which he "studies and loves." "The period, the region, the craftsmanship, the former ownership—for a true collector the whole background of an item adds up to a magic encyclopedia whose quintessence is the fate of his object." For Benjamin, collected objects are reminders of an earlier world; owning them is for him "the most intimate relationship."[1] To what extent can that also be said of an ex libris collector like myself?

For me, the allure of ex libris lies in the fact that they are associated with books and that—in addition to the optical fascination of the image's content and technique—they also name an owner who—due to their cooperation with the artist—becomes part of the plate. Thus alongside the impact of the image, every plate also presents the mystery of the person for whom the ex libris was designed: attempting to solve this mystery has become a compulsion for me. As a literary scholar, it is the ex libris of poets such as Rilke, Morgenstern, and Ebner-Eschenbach, which I personally like to assimilate into my collection. A small plate with a coat of arms and the designation *Bibliotheque de Coppet,* which fell into my hands, turned out to be an ex libris of the famous Madame de Staël, who socialized with the important personalities of her age at her palace in Switzerland. Looking at it the collector's imagination reflects the Theatrum Mundi of an earlier age; they imagine the library in which the book bearing this ex libris was kept, and ask themselves in which book this plate might once have been stuck.

Every collector chases such finds. For example, for a long time I did not know who had signed the lithograph I had found in a book on the flea market at Vienna's Naschmarkt—until I identified it in an article as the first ex libris by Ernst Barlach and hence was able to research the relationship between Barlach and its owner.

In addition to Benjamin's categories, the researching collector of ex libris graphics must add the category of style. Collecting ex libris opens a bolt-hole into the history of art and culture. Fans of art nouveau will find the entire spectrum of this European stylistic movement on ex libris from across Europe. It is equally fascinating to see how ex libris graphics develop in the age of postmodernism.

Collecting ex libris is also a question of relationships. On every plate one can trace the relationship between artist and owner. Collectors who exchange objects in collecting societies—which have existed in Europe since 1891—also enter into a relationship, which could become a friendship. The collector and publisher Artur Wolf undoubtedly made many relationships and friendships in this way.

My own collection has indeed become a "magic encyclopedia" filled with an unending wealth of new insights.

Heinz Decker, Holder of the Walter-von-Zur-Westen medal of the Deutsche Exlibris-Gesellschaft, Frankfurt/Main

„… NUR GEGEN ERSTE KÜNSTLER"
DER VERLEGER ARTUR WOLF ÜBER DAS EXLIBRISSAMMELN MIT ANMERKUNGEN SEINER GESPRÄCHSPARTNERIN
CLAUDIA KAROLYI

WIE ES GEWESEN SEIN KÖNNTE

Richtig losgegangen mit dem Sammeln ist es 1913. In diesem Jahr erlebte Wien quasi einen Exlibris-Frühling. Denn die Österreichische Exlibris-Gesellschaft veranstaltete anlässlich ihres zehnjährigen Bestehens im k. k. Österreichischen Museum für Kunst und Industrie „die vermutlich spektakulärste Exlibrisschau der Zeit … 56 öffentliche und private Leihgeber"[1] stellten damals ihre Blätter für eine „Historisch-retrospektive Ausstellung" in der Säulenhalle und „Das moderne Exlibris" auf der Galerie des Museums zur Verfügung, und ich gehörte zu den Ausstellern (Abb. 315). Insgesamt – im Laufe der Schau wurden die Exlibris ausgewechselt – waren ca. 3 000 Bucheignerzeichen zu sehen. Und weil man „manchen Tag etwa 600 Besucher"[2] zählte, wurde sie sogar um drei Wochen verlängert. Über 20 000 Menschen besuchten die Ausstellung! Warum schauen Sie so skeptisch? Das Exlibris war damals modern, genauer gesagt: Es war wieder modern, nachdem es in der ersten Hälfte des 19. Jahrhunderts in die Bedeutungslosigkeit versunken war. Kein Wunder, hätten Sie ein grafisch gestaltetes Blatt mit Ihrem Namen in ein liebos gestaltetes Billigprodukt kleben wollen? Wenn sich die von England ausgehende Buchkunstbewegung in den 1880er Jahren nicht für das Exlibris interessiert hätte … Wie bitte? Das Wappenexlibris sei von den Heraldikern bereits ein bisschen früher wiederentdeckt worden? Richtig, aber glauben Sie wirklich, es wäre ab 1900 so leidenschaftlich gesammelt worden, wenn auf ihm lediglich der Name des Buchbesitzers und sein Wappen zu sehen gewesen wären? Mein Freund Richard Braungart[3] erklärte das heraldische Wappen für den modernen Menschen bereits in den 1910er Jahren für gegenstandslos. Lesen Sie nach, was er im Geleitwort zu meiner 1922 verlegten Exlibris-Mappe *100 deutsche Meisterexlibris* schreibt: „An seine Stelle ist eine Art von geistig-künstlerischem Wappen getreten, in dem der Künstler versucht, das Wesentliche eines Menschen in der Gestalt eines graphischen Symbols oder einer graphischen Formel festzuhalten."[4] Die Künstler und ein sammelfreudiges Bildungsbürgertum befreiten das Exlibris aus seinen heraldischen Fesseln und ermöglichten die heutige Vielfalt an Bildmotiven! Aber Braungart hat 1913 auch darauf hingewiesen, dass mit dieser neuen Freiheit eine Art Anarchie einherging, weil so gut wie alles „von irgendeinem Künstler einmal für ein Exlibris verwertet worden wäre". Tja, da hat er nicht Unrecht. Sehen Sie, ein Exlibris entsteht in Zusammenarbeit von Auftraggeber und Künstler. Der Besteller überlässt es dem Künstler, ein geeignetes grafisches Symbol für seine Person zu finden, oder gibt ein konkretes Thema vor, möchte zum Beispiel über seinen Beruf, sein Hobby oder als Naturfreund charakterisiert werden. Nun gibt es Auftraggeber, die sich auf ein völlig banales Motiv kaprizieren, und irgendwann wirft der Künstler das Handtuch … Ehrlicherweise muss man zugeben: Es war nicht immer die erste Garnitur von Künstlern, die sich auf dem weiten Feld des Exlibris tummelte. Trotz alledem haben wir es beim modernen Exlibris mit kleinformatiger Künstlergrafik zu tun und nicht mehr mit einem Eignerzeichen im engeren Sinne. Braungart war diese Entwicklung suspekt, weil „sehr viele von ihnen im Grunde genommen gar keine wirklichen Bibliothekzeichen sind". Lesen Sie weiter vor! „Sie sind schon infolge ihres oft sehr großen Formates und auch aus Gründen ihrer äußeren ‚Aufmachung' nur wenig geeignet, in ein Buch

[1] Tauber, Henry, *Der deutsche Exlibris-Verein 1891 bis 1943. Seine Geschichte im Kontext von Exlibrisbewegung und Exlibriskunst vornehmlich in Deutschland* (= Jahrbuch 1995 der Deutschen Exlibris-Gesellschaft), Frankfurt/Main 1995, 235.

[2] Hoschek, Rudolf Freiherr von, „Exlibris-Ausstellung Wien Frühjahr 1913", in: Österreichische Exlibris-Gesellschaft (Hg.), *XI. Jahrbuch 1913*, Wien 1913, 5–14, hier 13. (Die Jahrbücher der Österreichischen Exlibris-Gesellschaft, die seit 1903 unter wechselndem Namen erscheinen, werden im Folgenden mit dem Kurztitel „ÖEG-Jahrbuch" zitiert.) – Artur Wolf wird in Hoscheks Bericht (S. 8) und in der Begleitbroschüre zur Schau als Leihgeber aufgelistet, vgl. Österreichische Exlibris-Gesellschaft (Hg.), *Exlibris Ausstellung. Unter dem Protektorate Sr. kaiserl. und königl. Hoheit, des durchlauchtigsten Herrn Erzherzogs Karl Franz Josef. Veranstaltet von der österreichischen Exlibris-Gesellschaft anläßlich ihres zehnjährigen Bestandes. 4. März bis 11. April 1913*, Ausst.kat. k. k. Österr. Museum für Kunst und Industrie, Wien 1913, o.S. Die Ausstellung wurde aufgrund des Publikumsinteresses bis 4. Mai verlängert.

[3] Braungart, Richard (1872–1963), Schriftsteller und Journalist, publizierte mehr als 220 Aufsätze über Exlibris und Gebrauchsgrafik und zahlreiche Bücher zum Thema, vgl. Tauber 1995 (s. Anm.1), 448.

[4] Braungart, Richard, „Geleitwort", in: *100 deutsche Meisterexlibris*, Grafikmappe, Artur Wolf Verlag, Wien 1922, o. S.

"… ONLY FOR FIRST-RATE ARTISTS"
THE PUBLISHER ARTUR WOLF ON COLLECTING EX LIBRIS, WITH COMMENTS BY HIS INTERVIEWER
CLAUDIA KAROLYI

HOW IT MIGHT HAVE BEEN

The craze for collecting really began in 1913. That was the year when Vienna experienced an ex libris spring, as it were. It was when the Austrian Bookplate Society organized "probably the most spectacular ex libris show of the age" to celebrate the tenth year since its founding; that show was hosted by the Imperial Royal Austrian Museum of Art and Industry. "56 public and private lenders"[1] made their plates available for a "Historic and retrospective exhibition" in the Columned Main Hall and "The modern ex libris" in the museum's gallery—and I was one of the exhibitors (ill. 315). The ex libris were exchanged over the course of the show, meaning that, in total, ca. 3 000 bookplates were on display. And because "on some days [there were] approximately 600 visitors,"[2] it was even extended for three weeks. Over 20 000 people visited the exhibition! Why do you look so skeptical? Ex libris were fashionable then, or more precisely: they were back in fashion, after having faded into insignificance during the first half of the 19th century. Which was hardly surprising—after all, would you have wanted to stick a graphically designed plate bearing your name in a carelessly designed, low-quality product? If the book art movement ensuing from England in the 1880s hadn't shown any interest in ex libris … I beg your pardon, what did you say? The heraldic ex libris was discovered somewhat earlier by the heraldists? True, but do you really believe bookplates would have been collected with such passion from 1900 if all that they showed were the name of the book's owner and their coat of arms? My friend Richard Braungart[3] declared heraldic coats of arms to be irrelevant to the modern population back in the 1910s. Read what he wrote in the preface to the ex libris portfolio I published in 1922, *100 deutsche Meisterexlibris*: "It has been replaced with a kind of spiritually artistic coat of arms, in which the artist attempts to capture a person's essence in the form of a graphic symbol or a graphic formula."[4] The artists and the educated middle class—who were avid collectors—liberated the ex libris from its heraldic fetters and facilitated today's wide variety of image motifs! But Braungart also pointed out in 1913 that this new freedom went hand in hand with a kind of anarchy, because almost everything "would have been exploited by some artist or another for an ex libris." Well, he wasn't wrong. You see, an ex libris is created in cooperation between the artist and their customer. The customer leaves it up to the artist to find a suitable graphic symbol of themselves, or names a specific theme—they might want, for example, something about their profession, their hobby, or to be characterized as a nature lover. Now, there are customers who insist on a completely banal motif, and at some point the artist will throw in the towel … To be honest, I have to admit: it was not always first-rate artists who explored the wide field of ex libris. Nevertheless, modern ex libris revolve around small-format works on paper by artists and are no longer an ownership label in the narrower sense. Braungart was suspicious of this development, because "a large number of them are—strictly speaking—not actually bookplates at all." Read on! "As a result of their often very large format and due to their external 'layout,' they are but little suited to being stuck in a normal-sized book. And it is not seldom that their material value considerably exceeds that of the book itself."[5] He's right, though admittedly my friend Richard

1   Tauber, Henry, *Der deutsche Exlibris-Verein 1891 bis 1943. Seine Geschichte im Kontext von Exlibrisbewegung und Exlibriskunst vornehmlich in Deutschland* (=1995 yearbook of the Deutsche Exlibris-Gesellschaft), Frankfurt/Main 1995, 235. Translated by Maria Slater.

2   Hoschek, Rudolf Freiherr von, "Exlibris-Ausstellung Wien Frühjahr 1913," in: Österreichische Exlibris-Gesellschaft (ed.), XI. Jahrbuch 1913, Vienna 1913, 5–14, here 13. Translated by Maria Slater. (The yearbooks by the Austrian Bookplate Society, which were published under various names from 1903, are quoted in the following using the abbreviation "ÖEG Yearbook.") Artur Wolf is listed as a lender in Hoschek's report (p. 8) and in the brochure accompanying the show, cf. Österreichische Exlibris-Gesellschaft (ed.), *Exlibris Ausstellung. Unter dem Protektorate Sr. kaiserl. und königl. Hoheit, des durchlauchtigsten Herrn Erzherzogs Karl Franz Josef. Veranstaltet von der österreichischen Exlibris-Gesellschaft anläßlich ihres zehnjährigen Bestandes. 4. März bis 11. April 1913*, exh.cat. Imperial Royal Austrian Museum of Art and Industry, Vienna 1913, n.p. The exhibition was extended until 4 May due to public interest.

3   Braungart, Richard (1872–1963), writer and journalist, published more than 220 articles on ex libris and ephemera, as well as numerous books on the topic, cf. Tauber 1995 (see note 1), 448.

4   Braungart, Richard, "Geleitwort," in: *100 deutsche Meisterexlibris*, portfolio of graphic art, Artur Wolf Verlag, Vienna 1922, n.p. Translated by Maria Slater.

5   Braungart, Richard, *Neue deutsche Exlibris*, Munich 1913, 9 f. Translated by Maria Slater.

von normaler Größe geklebt zu werden. Und meistens übersteigt auch ihr materieller Wert den des Buches nicht selten sogar um ein Vielfaches."[5] Stimmt, allerdings besaß Freund Richard selbst Exlibris, die sich nicht als Besitzvermerke eigneten, schau'n Sie mal in meiner Sammlung nach! Übrigens warnte der deutsche Grafiker Erich Büttner vor diesen Pseudoexlibris: „Offenes Geheimnis: Große Exlibris mit breitem Papierrand sind Attrappen"[6] (Abb. 316). Ob es einem gefällt oder nicht, um 1900 gab das Exlibris seine existenzielle Verbindung zum Buch auf. Grafiken, die sich vom Format her als Bücherzeichen eigneten, nannte man Gebrauchsexlibris und die, die gesammelt und getauscht wurden, Luxusexlibris. Natürlich getauscht. Es handelte sich um private Grafiken, die nicht in Kunsthandlungen herumlagen. Zwar konnten Sie auf Auktionen einzelne Blätter oder gar ganze Sammlungen kaufen. Aber bedenken Sie, wie viele Dubletten oder uninteressantes Zeug man sich da einhandelte. Deshalb tauschte man seine eigenen gegen Exlibris von anderen Sammlern. Abhängig von der Auflagehöhe der eigenen Blätter, den Künstlern und Motiven, besaß man binnen kurzer Zeit eine Kleingrafiksammlung. Gratuliere, Sie haben das System begriffen! Natürlich mussten die Sammler in regelmäßigen Abständen neue Exlibris in Auftrag geben, die waren schließlich ihr Tauschmaterial, manche besaßen über 100 Exlibris auf ihren Namen. Und wie man an diese Sammler herankam? Tja, einem unbedarften Neuling konnte es da ganz schön übel ergehen. Zum Beispiel schickte Hansi Ehrenfeld, die langjährige Sekretärin der österreichischen Gesellschaft, ihr erstes Exlibris einfach ins Blaue. Und was passierte? „… einige antworteten gar nicht, andere sandten mir für meine schöne Radierung einen schlechten Holzschnitt oder ein Klischee, und nur ein oder zwei schöne Blätter kamen ein. Das sah ich jetzt ein, auf diese Art würde es nicht gehen, und ich wurde Mitglied der Österreichischen Exlibris-Gesellschaft, die es mir nun möglich machte, in einen geordneten Tauschverkehr einzutreten."[7] Ja, Sie haben richtig gehört: geordneter Tauschverkehr. Warum, glauben Sie, wurden um die Jahrhundertwende in der ganzen Welt Exlibris-Gesellschaften gegründet? Die betrieben nicht nur Exlibrisforschung, sondern organisierten auch den Tausch. Wenn man sich verpflichtete, „Zusendungen durch Tausch oder Rücksendung"[8] zu beantworten, konnten die Mitglieder in den regelmäßig erscheinenden Tauschlisten ihre Exlibris offerieren, am besten mit dem Zusatz „nur gegen erste Künstler" oder „nur gegen Bestes".[9] Sie haben ja keine Ahnung, welche Unsäglichkeiten einem da ins Haus flatterten. Nein, die Profis schickten keine Exlibris durch die Gegend. Die bahnten ihre Tauschgeschäfte mit Übersendung einer gedruckten Liste ihrer Exlibris an. Da stand das Wesentliche drauf: Künstler, Motiv, Drucktechnik, Entstehungsdatum … 1927, als ich bereits ziemlich viel Tauschmaterial besaß, bot ich ebenfalls ein „Verzeichnis auf Wunsch" an. Nein, bei den Österreichern war ich nie Mitglied. Nachdem ich mich an ihrer Exlibris-Ausstellung beteiligt hatte, wäre dies naheliegend gewesen. Doch die Zusammenarbeit mit dem Arbeitskomitee zur Auswahl der Exponate war mühsam. Rudolf Hoschek von Mühlhaimb hat es in seinem Bericht angedeutet: „… rein künstlerische Prinzipien kamen in Widerstreit mit sammlerischen und historischen Anschauungen, und mit solchen älterer und extrem-moderner Kunstrichtung."[10] Extrem-moderne Kunstrichtung! Was soll das denn heißen? Wenn Sie einen Blick ins erste Jahrbuch der Österreichischen Exlibris-Gesellschaft werfen, werden Sie begreifen, warum ich dort nicht hinpasste. Die Publikation listet österreichische Sammlungen mit über 1 000 Blättern auf. Und was sammeln die Herren und Damen vornehmlich: alte Blätter bis 1890![11] Nein, nein, mit denen wollte ich nicht über moderne Kunst diskutieren. Der Exlibris-Verein zu Berlin war aufgeschlossener, sein Präsident, Walter von Zur Westen, verstand etwas von zeitgenössischer Buchkunst und Grafik …

5 Braungart, Richard, *Neue deutsche Exlibris*, München 1913, 9 f.

6 Büttner, Erich, *Exlibris. Erlebnisse und Erfahrungen*, Berlin 1921, 13.

7 Ehrenfeld, Hansi, „Das Sammeln", in: *ÖEG-Jahrbuch* 1911, 100.

8 „Tauschrubrik", in: *Mitteilungen des Exlibris-Vereins zu Berlin* (9) 3/4 1915, o. S. Die Mitteilungen des Vereins wurden dem jeweiligen Jahrbuch beigebunden, vgl. Exlibris-Verein zu Berlin (Hg.), *Exlibris, Buchkunst und angewandte Graphik* 25, 1915. – Die Jahrbücher des Exlibris-Vereins zu Berlin, die ab 1891 unter wechselndem Namen erschienen, werden im Folgenden mit dem Kurztitel „EVB-Jahrbuch" zitiert, die beigebundenen Mitteilungen mit „EVB-Mitteilungen".

9 Formulierungen, die Artur Wolf mehrmals in seinen Tauschanzeigen verwendete, vgl. die jeweilige „Tauschrubrik" bzw. „Tauschliste" in den EVB-Mitteilungen 1915–1929.

10 Hoschek 1913 (s. Anm. 2), 6.

11 Vgl. Dillmann, Eduard, „Österreichische Ex libris-Sammlungen", in: *ÖEG-Jahrbuch* 1903, 7–12.

6 Büttner, Erich, *Exlibris. Erlebnisse und Erfahrungen*, Berlin 1921, 13. Translated by Maria Slater.

7 Ehrenfeld, Hansi, "Das Sammeln," in: *ÖEG Yearbook* 1911, 100. Translated by Maria Slater.

8 "Tauschrubrik," in: *Mitteilungen des Exlibris-Vereins zu Berlin* (9) 3/4 1915, n. p. The society's announcements were included in the respective yearbook, cf. Exlibris-Verein zu Berlin (ed.), *Exlibris, Buchkunst und angewandte Graphik* 25, 1915. The yearbooks of the Exlibris-Verein zu Berlin, which were published under various names from 1891, are quoted in the following using the abbreviation "EVB Yearbook," the included announcements "EVB announcements."

9 Expressions frequently used by Artur Wolf in his exchange advertisements, cf. the respective exchange column ("Tauschrubrik") or exchange list ("Tauschliste") in the EVB announcements 1915–1929.

10 Hoschek 1913 (see note 2), 6. Translated by Maria Slater.

11 Cf. Dillmann, Eduard, "Österreichische Ex libris-Sammlungen," in: *ÖEG Yearbook* 1903, 7–12.

himself owned ex libris, which were not suited to being used as ownership labels—just have a look in my collection! Incidentally, the German graphic artist Erich Büttner cautioned against these pseudo ex libris: "It is an open secret: large ex libris with a broad paper margin are a sham"[6] (ill. 316). Whether or not we like them, around 1900 ex libris abandoned their existential connection to books. Works on paper whose format made them suitable bookplates were called practical ex libris, and those which were collected and swapped, luxury ex libris. Obviously swapped. They were private works on paper, which didn't lie around in art dealers' shops. Though you could buy individual plates or even entire collections at auction. But consider how many duplicates or uninteresting things you were bartering for. Which is why we exchanged our own ex libris for those of other collectors. Depending on the number of copies published of one's own plates, the artists, and the motifs, you could soon own a collection of minor works on paper. Congratulations! You've understood the system! Of course, collectors had to commission new ex libris at regular intervals— after all, they were their exchange currency—meaning that some people owned over 100 different ex libris in their own name. And how did we gain access to these collectors? Well, an inexperienced newcomer could make some serious blunders. For example, Hansi Ehrenfeld, the longstanding secretary of the Austrian society, simply sent her first ex libris off into the void. And what happened? "… some didn't answer at all, others sent me a bad woodcut or a stereotype for my beautiful etching, and only one or two beautiful plates arrived. So then I realized it wouldn't work that way, and I became a member of the Austrian Bookplate Society, which then made it possible for me to enter into an organized system of exchange."[7] Yes, you heard right: organized system of exchange. Why do you believe ex libris societies were founded all around the world at the turn of the century? They didn't only research ex libris, but also organized swaps. If you pledged to respond to "deliveries with exchanges or returns,"[8] the members could offer their ex libris in the regularly published exchange lists, preferably with the additional information "only for first-rate artists" or "only for best."[9] You honestly have no idea what unmentionables would flutter into your house otherwise. No, the pros didn't send ex libris all over the place. They initiated swaps by sending out a printed list of their ex libris. It contained all the essentials: artist, motif, printing technique, date it was made … In 1927, when I already owned quite a large quantity of exchange currency, I also offered a "catalog upon request." No, I was never a member of the Austrian society. Seeing as I had participated in their ex libris exhibition, it would have been the obvious next step. Yet dealing with their working committee to select the exhibits was tedious. Rudolf Hoschek von Mühlhaimb implied as much in his report: "… purely artistic principles came into conflict with collectors' and historians' opinions, and with those of older and extremely modern art movements."[10] Extremely modern art movements! What's that supposed to mean? If you cast a glance at the first yearbook of the Austrian Bookplate Society, you'll understand why I didn't belong there. The publication lists Austrian collections with over 1 000 plates. And what do those ladies and gentlemen principally collect? Old plates from pre-1890![11] No, no, I did not want to discuss modern art with them. The Exlibris-Verein zu Berlin was more open-minded; its president, Walter von Zur Westen, had a certain understanding of contemporary book art and graphic art … Whether economic considerations might not have played a part? Obviously. I published so-called "beautiful books" and certainly not cheap portfolios of works on paper. Who buys such luxury editions? Correct, bibliophiles! They were rare, though, so I had to establish myself on the considerably larger German market for books and works on paper, including

Ob dabei nicht auch ökonomische Überlegungen eine Rolle gespielt hätten? Selbstverständlich. Ich verlegte sogenannte „schöne Bücher" und nicht eben preisgünstige Grafikmappen. Wer kauft solche Luxusausgaben? Richtig, Bibliophile! Die waren rar, ich musste im wesentlich größeren deutschen Buch- und Kunstblättermarkt Fuß fassen, auch über den Umweg des Exlibris. Wissen Sie eigentlich, wie viele Mitglieder der Verein damals hatte? Ich wurde 1913 als Nr. 659 geführt. Zwei Jahre später inserierte ich erstmals in der Tauschrubrik, bot aber natürlich nicht alle neun Exlibris auf meinen Namen an. Warum nicht? Nun, 1915 besaß ich vier erotische Blätter von Franz von Bayros (Abb. 318), ein Monogramm-Exlibris von Rudolf Geyer (Abb. 317), ein Klischee nach einem Motiv von Félicien Rops, ein Akt-Exlibris von Alfred Soder, ein redendes Exlibris von Moritz von Gruenewaldt und ein Vanitas-Motiv von Alfonso Bosco. Was ein redendes Exlibris ist? Sein Bildinhalt visualisiert den Eignernamen, also in meinem Fall einen Wolf. Ich habe übrigens selbst ein redendes Exlibris auf meinen Namen gezeichnet, einen Wolfskopf. Ja, den können Sie sich auch in meiner Sammlung ansehen, ich ließ ihn allerdings nie drucken, obwohl er gar nicht so schlecht gezeichnet war (Abb. 319). Aber zurück zu meinem Tauschangebot. Mit den Blättern von Bayros konnte ich bei den Erotik-Sammlern punkten, weibliche Akte waren in der Sammlergemeinde heiß begehrt, das Exlibris von Gruenewaldt war 1913 im deutschen Jahrbuch gelobt und im selben Aufsatz auch das Blatt von Bosco abgebildet worden, die waren also bekannt.[12] Aber das Wichtigste, das allen Grafiken eignete: Sie waren Tiefdrucke. Die Radierung war zu dieser Zeit „die unbestrittene Königin unter den Techniken des modernen Exlibris", schrieb mein Freund Braungart treffend. „Leider hat diese doch wohl etwas übertriebene Wertschätzung häufig dazu geführt, daß eine Exlibrisidee nur dann etwas gilt, wenn sie mit der Radiernadel ausgeführt ist. Radierung – das ist für viele eine Wertbezeichnung, die durch nichts überboten werden kann."[13] Sie begreifen: Auf den Geyer- und Rops-Exlibris, beides Hochdrucke, wäre ich sitzengeblieben. Lediglich in der Tauschliste von 1917 bot ich ein als Klischee ausgeführtes „Ex musicis" von Mathilde Ade an. Warum? Die Illustratorin der *Meggendorfer Blätter* war seinerzeit sehr beliebt, außerdem konnte ich damit Sammler bedienen, die sich auf Musik-Exlibris spezialisiert hatten. Danach inserierte ich bis 1925 neben meinen eigenen Exlibris vor allem Grafiken von Erhard Amadeus-Dier (Abb. 321) und anderen Verlagsmitarbeitern. Ich verlegte nämlich vor allem Klassikerausgaben, für deren Gestaltung ich zahlreiche Künstler engagierte.[14] Der britische Maler und Grafiker William Russell Flint, der Münchner Radierer und Lithograf Rolf Schott, aber auch junge österreichische Grafiker wie Stefan Eggeler, Eduard Gaertner, Alfred Hagel oder Franz Wacik entwarfen Einbandvignetten, Illustrationen und eingebundene Originalgrafiken. Was Sie nicht sagen! Der Verlag „bemühte sich offenbar auch bewusst um die Förderung junger, aufstrebender Künstler"[15], hätte ein Herr Heller vor nicht allzu langer Zeit geschrieben? Endlich jemand, der die Verleger nicht als Ausbeuter verteufelt. Der kennt sicher meinen Verlagsalmanach von 1921. Darin bewarb ich meine Bücher und Exlibris-Mappen und ermahnte meine Kunden: „Jeder, der Bücher besitzt, sollte auch ein Eignerzeichen dazu haben."[16] Um ihnen zu einem ordentlichen Exlibris zu verhelfen, erklärte ich mich sogar bereit, für meine künstlerischen Mitarbeiter „Aufträge zur Herstellung von Exlibris"[17] zu übernehmen. Exlibris „bester deutscher Graphiker, insbesondere Bayros und E.A. Dier", konnten von Sammlern ab 1924 auch „einzeln bezogen werden".[18] Die Vermittlung von Exlibrisaufträgen an meine Mitarbeiter wäre wohl nicht gänzlich uneigennützig gewesen, meinen Sie? Kindchen, die Zeiten waren schlecht, insbesondere für Künstler. Die waren über jedes kleine Zubrot dankbar! Na, sicher sind für die Vermittlungen

12 Vgl. Corwegh, Robert, „Exlibrisschau", in: *EVB-Jahrbuch* 1913, 206–208.

13 Braungart, Richard, *Deutsche Ex Libris und andere Kleingraphik der Gegenwart*, München 1922, 41.

14 Die Firmengeschichte und Verlagsproduktion des Artur Wolf Verlages ist ausführlich beschrieben in: Hall, Murray G., *Österreichische Verlagsgeschichte 1918–1938. Bd. II: Belletristische Verlage der Ersten Republik*, Wien u.a. 1985, 476–480.

15 Heller, Friedrich C., *Die bunte Welt. Handbuch zum künstlerisch illustrierten Kinderbuch in Wien 1890–1938*, Wien 2008, 414.

16 Artur Wolf Verlag (Hg.), *Das illustrierte Buch. Ein Almanach*, Wien 1921, 28.

17 Ebd.

18 Artur Wolf Verlag (Hg.), *Der Almanach vom schönen Buch*, Wien 1924, 72.

315
Anonym Anonymous
Einladung zur Ausstellung der Österreichischen Exlibris-Gesellschaft
im ÖMKI 1913
Wien, 1913
Ausführung: Chwala's Druck
Buchdruck
Invitation to the Exhibition to the Austrian Bookplate Society
at the ÖMKI 1913
Vienna, 1913
Letterpress print
Execution: Chwala's Druck
125 x 193 mm
KI 15854-11-2, Ankauf Teilnachlass purchased from part of the estate
of Chwala's Druck 2008

316
Hanns Bastanier
Exlibris Richard und Jeannette Braungart
Berlin, 1907
Radierung
Ex Libris Richard und Jeannette Braungart
Berlin, 1907
Etching
157 x 118 mm
KI 9136-363, Legat bequest from Artur Wolf 1933

317
Rudolf Geyer
Entwurf eines Exlibris für Artur Wolf
Wien, vor 1910
Tusche, Deckfarbe
86 x 84 mm
Design for an Ex Libris for Artur Wolf
Vienna, before 1910
Ink, coating paint
86 x 84 mm
KI 9136-2236, Legat bequest from Artur Wolf 1933

318
Franz von Bayros
Exlibris Artur Wolf
München, 1911
Heliogravüre
Ex Libris Artur Wolf
Munich, 1911
Photogravure
139 x 123 mm
KI 9136-660, Legat bequest from
Artur Wolf 1933

319
Artur Wolf
Entwurf für ein Eigenexlibris
Wien, o. J.
Bleistift
Design for a Personal Bookplate
Vienna, n.d.
Pencil
143 x 117 mm
KI 9136-7053, Legat bequest from Artur Wolf 1933

320
Ephraim Moshe Lilien
Neujahrswunsch für 1913
Dresden, 1912
Radierung
New Year Greetings for 1913
Dresden, 1912
Etching
200 x 130 mm
KI 9136-289, Legat bequest from Artur Wolf 1933

321
Erhard Amadeus-Dier
Exlibris Dr. Karl Johannes Schwarz
Wien, um 1920
Radierung
Ex Libris Dr. Karl Johannes Schwarz
Vienna, ca. 1920
Etching
125 x 78 mm
KI 9136-1329, Legat bequest from Artur Wolf 1933

via the indirect route of ex libris. Do you know how many members the society had back then? I was listed as no. 659 in 1913. Two years later I advertised in the exchange column for the first time, but naturally didn't offer all nine ex libris under my own name. Why not? Well, in 1915 I owned four erotic plates by Franz von Bayros (ill. 318), a monogramed ex libris by Rudolf Geyer (ill. 317), a stereotype after a motif by Félicien Rops, an ex libris with a nude by Alfred Soder, a canting bookplate by Moritz von Gruenewaldt, and a vanitas motif by Alfonso Bosco. What is a canting bookplate? The image's content visualizes the owner's name, so in my case it was a wolf. Incidentally, I myself have drawn a canting bookplate for my name, a wolf's head. Yes, you can see that in my collection, too, though I never had it printed, despite the fact that the drawing isn't bad at all (ill. 319). But back to the exchange I offered. With the plates by Bayros I was in luck with collectors of eroticism; female nudes were highly coveted in the collecting community; the ex libris by Gruenewaldt had been praised in the German yearbook in 1913 and the plate by Bosco was also illustrated in the same article, so they were well known.[12] But the most important thing that made all of the works suitable for swapping was that they were intaglio prints. Etching was "the undisputed queen of modern ex libris techniques" at that time, as my friend Braungart aptly put it. "Unfortunately this probably somewhat exaggerated appreciation frequently led to an idea for an ex libris only being deemed valid when created using an etching needle. Etching—lots of people see that as a term of value, which nothing can surpass."[13] You realize: I wouldn't have been able to swap the Geyer and Rops ex libris as they are both relief prints. It was only in the exchange list of 1917 that I offered an "ex musicis" by Mathilde Ade, executed as a stereotype. Why? The illustrator of the *Meggendorfer Blätter* was very popular in her day, and besides, it meant that I could also serve collectors who specialized in music ex libris. Between then and 1925 I advertised, in addition to my own ex libris, mostly works on paper by Erhard Amadeus-Dier (ill. 321) and other colleagues from the publishing company. You see, I mostly published editions of classics, and I engaged numerous artists to design them.[14] The British painter and graphic artist William Russell Flint, the Munich-based etcher and lithographer Rolf Schott, but also young Austrian graphic artists like Stefan Eggeler, Eduard Gaertner, Alfred Hagel, and Franz Wacik designed cover vignettes, illustrations, and integrated original works on paper. You don't say! The publishing house "obviously consciously tried to support young, up-and-coming artists,"[15] didn't a Mr. Heller write not that long ago? Finally, someone who wasn't demonizing publishers as exploiters! He must know my publisher's yearbook from 1921. In it I advertised my books and ex libris portfolios and urged my customers: "Everyone who owns books should also have ownership labels for them."[16] In order to help them find decent ex libris, I even declared that I was prepared to accept "commissions to produce ex libris"[17] on behalf of my artistic staff. Ex libris "by the best German graphic artists, especially Bayros and E. A. Dier" could even "be purchased individually" by collectors from 1924.[18] Mediating commissions for ex libris by my staff wouldn't have been entirely altruistic, you think? Child, times were hard, especially for artists. They were grateful for any small source of extra income! Well of course there were some under-the-counter deductions for the mediations. Like the overprints from my eleven portfolios of ex libris, they formed the exchange currency with which I made collectors' mouths water in those years. Incidentally, my artistic staff gave me lots of plates anyway. If you flick through my collection, you'll be amazed how many designs, states, but also graphic art you'll find by them there. Artists who were hoping for a commission by the publishing house sent their latest

[12] Cf. Corwegh, Robert, "Exlibrisschau," in: *EVB Yearbook* 1913, 206–208.

[13] Braungart, Richard, *Deutsche Ex Libris und andere Kleingraphik der Gegenwart*, Munich 1922, 41. Translated by Maria Slater.

[14] The company history and the publications of the Artur Wolf Verlag are described in detail in: Hall, Murray G., *Österreichische Verlagsgeschichte 1918–1938. Bd. II: Belletristische Verlage der Ersten Republik*, Vienna et al. 1985, 476–480.

[15] Heller, Friedrich C., *Die bunte Welt. Handbuch zum künstlerisch illustrierten Kinderbuch in Wien 1890–1938*, Vienna 2008, 414. Translated by Maria Slater.

[16] Artur Wolf Verlag (ed.), *Das illustrierte Buch. Ein Almanach*, Vienna 1921, 28. Translated by Maria Slater.

[17] Ibid.

[18] Artur Wolf Verlag (ed.), *Der Almanach vom schönen Buch*, Vienna 1924, 72.

Abzüge über den Tisch gewandert. Sie bildeten wie auch Überdrucke aus meinen elf Exlibrismappen das Tauschmaterial, mit dem ich in diesen Jahren den Sammlern den Mund wässrig machte. Übrigens schenkten mir meine künstlerischen Mitarbeiter viele Blätter ohnehin. Wenn Sie meine Sammlung durchblättern, werden Sie staunen, wie viele Entwürfe, Zustandsdrucke, aber auch freie Grafiken Sie von ihnen dort finden. Sogar Künstler, die auf einen Verlagsauftrag hofften, ließen mir ihre neuesten Arbeiten zukommen, schließlich war bekannt, dass ich Exlibris sammelte. In kreativen Berufen lässt sich das Private eben nicht fein säuberlich vom Geschäftlichen trennen. Warum, denken Sie, befinden sich von einigen der angesehensten Künstler der Zeit nicht nur Exlibris, sondern auch Neujahrswünsche (Abb. 320) oder Einladungen zu Vernissagen und Atelierfesten in meiner Sammlung? Ich kannte sie persönlich. Als Verleger hielt ich mich regelmäßig in München, Berlin und Leipzig, wo ich ein zweites Verlagsbüro unterhielt, auf. Und wann immer sich die Gelegenheit bot, ging ich dort in die Ateliers der Künstler. Als das *Neue Wiener Tagblatt* 1932 meinen plötzlichen Tod meldete, schrieb es nicht zufällig: „Er verkehrte viel in Künstlerkreisen."[19] Jammerschade, dass Sie nicht in meinem Gästebuch mit „vielen Handzeichnungen, Aquarellen, Pastellzeichnungen etc. bekannter Künstler u. einer großen Anzahl Widmungen"[20] blättern können. Sie entdeckten viele Namen, die sich auch in meiner Sammlung finden. Keine Frage, die freundschaftliche Verbundenheit mit Braungart war meiner Sammlung ebenfalls zuträglich. Der kannte doch Gott und die Welt und reichte mich weiter ... Wie ich zu meinem Brangwyn-Exlibris gekommen bin, wollen Sie wissen? Ah, das ist eine schöne Geschichte. Im Grunde genommen ist es ein Abfallprodukt meiner verlegerischen Tätigkeit. 1921 wandte sich die in Wien lebende englische Kunsthistorikerin und Journalistin Amelia Sarah Levetus[21] im Auftrag von Frank Brangwyn an mich. Die Genossenschaft der bildenden Künstler Wiens plane, im Dezember 1922 Arbeiten des international gefeierten Peintre-graveur auszustellen. Ob ich bereit wäre, im Vorfeld Arbeiten des Künstlers aus der Albertina und aus englischem Privatbesitz zu verlegen. Was für eine Frage! Mit Blick auf die Ausstellung im Künstlerhaus würde sich das kostspielige Unternehmen schon lohnen. Die Großfoliomappe enthielt 20 grafische Arbeiten Brangwyns, die von Miss Levetus eingeleitet wurden, und „Titel und Kopfleisten dieser Einleitung" wurden von „eigens geschnittenen Originalholzstöcken" des Meisters gedruckt.[22] Das Titelblatt hat mich begeistert (Abb. 322). Es zeigt zwei Männer vor dem Sternrad einer Tiefdruckpresse, die eine soeben gedruckte Grafik kontrollieren, und vom rechten Rand beobachten Kunstinteressierte diese Szene. Einige Monate später entdeckte ich in der Brangwyn-Schau im Künstlerhaus ein nahezu identes Motiv als Kreidezeichnung – nur die Herren am Rand fehlten.[23] Wie oft stand ich selbst in einer Druckerei neben der Presse und begutachtete Drucke! Diese Grafik beschrieb wie keine andere meine berufliche Tätigkeit. Dass Brangwyn das Motiv nochmals aufgriff und mir zu einem standesgemäßen Berufsexlibris verhalf – unglaublich! (Abb. 323) Naturgemäß war das Blatt bei Sammlern, die etwas von Grafik verstanden, ein großer Erfolg. Wolfgang Born, der nach meinem Tod die von Hans Ankwicz-Kleehoven kuratierte Ausstellung meiner Exlibris im *Neuen Wiener Journal* besprach, schrieb gar, dass es „zu den besten der ganzen Sammlung"[24] gehöre. Warum ich meine Exlibrissammlung 1930 dem Österreichischen Museum für Kunst und Industrie vermachte? Ach, 1929 verlor ich das Interesse am Exlibris, seine große Zeit war ohnehin vorbei ... außerdem heiratete ich und wollte meine freie Zeit mit Käthe verbringen. Aber selbst wenn man des Sammelns müde geworden ist, möchte man seine Anhäufungen an einem Ort unterbringen, wo sie geschätzt werden und vielleicht auch nützlich sind. Als Spielart der angewandten

[19] „Plötzlicher Tod eines Wiener Verlegers", in: *Neues Wiener Tagblatt*, 17.10.1932.

[20] Wiener Auktionshaus J. Fischer (Hg.), *Kunstsammlung und Wohnungseinrichtung aus dem Nachlasse Artur und Katharina Wolf (Gräfin Attems), Wien, I., Seilerstätte 1 (Palais Coburg): Auktion 14., 15., und 16. März 1933*, [Wien 1933], Nr. 806 und: http://digi.ub.uni-heidelberg.de/diglit/fischer_wien1933_03_14 (11.1.2016). Artur Wolf erlitt am 16.10.1932 während des Reitens einen tödlichen Herzinfarkt. Wolfs Testament bestimmte seine Ehefrau, Katharina (Käthe) Wolf (geb. Winkler, geschiedene Gräfin Attems) zur Universalerbin. Katharina Wolf, geb. 1898, schied am 11.12.1932 freiwillig aus dem Leben, vgl. *Gothaisches Genealogisches Taschenbuch der Gräflichen Häuser. Zugleich Adelsmatrikel der Deutschen Adelsgenossenschaft* 115, Teil A, Gotha 1942, 36. Alleinerbe des Nachlasses des Ehepaares und des Artur Wolf Verlages war Katharina Wolfs minderjähriger Sohn aus erster Ehe, Christoph Ferdinand, Graf Attems, vgl. dazu Hall 1985 (s. Anm. 14), 477 f.

[21] Amelia Sarah Levetus (1853–1938) war Brangwyns „agent in Austria", vgl. Brangwyn, Rodney, *Brangwyn*, London 1978, 190; zu Amelia Sarah Levetus vgl. www.mackintosh-architecture.gla.ac.uk/catalogue/name/?nid=LevAS&xml=peo und https://de.wikipedia.org/wiki/Amelia_Sarah_Levetus (5.1.2016), dort unter „Weblinks" Informationen zu ihren Aktivitäten als Volksbildnerin.

[22] Kolophon von *Frank Brangwyn. 20 graphische Arbeiten in Mappe, eingeleitet und herausgegeben von A. S. Levetus*, Wien [1921/1922].

[23] Vgl. Genossenschaft der bildenden Künstler Wiens (Hg.), *Brangwyn Ausstellung, Dezember 1922 bis Jänner 1923*, Wien [1922], 7, Nr. 58 A: „Studie zu einer Adresse für eine Kunstausstellung. Zwei Männer vor einem großen Rade einer Druckerpresse betrachten ein Druckblatt. Kreide"; das Blatt stammt aus einer früheren Schenkung Brangwyns an die Albertina, die Levetus im Auftrag von Brangwyn durchführte, vgl. dazu 2 und 5.

[24] Born, Wolfgang, „Exlibris-Ausstellung in Wien", in: *Neues Wiener Journal*, 16.8.1933, 4.

322
Frank Brangwyn
Titelblatt zu *Frank Brangwyn.*
Zwanzig graphische Arbeiten
Wien, 1921–1922
Holzschnitt
Titel Page of [Frank Brangwyn.
Twenty graphic works]
Vienna, 1921–1922
Woodcut
470 x 392 mm
BI 23175, Schenkung donation
from Maria Helbig 1944

323
Frank Brangwyn
Exlibris Artur Wolf
London, 1922–1925
Weichgrundätzung
Ex Libris Artur Wolf
London, 1922–1925
Soft-ground etching
154 x 114 mm
KI 9136-966, Legat
bequest from Artur Wolf 1933

324
Felix Hollenberg
Exlibris Dr. Rud. [Rudolf] Erhard
Stuttgart, 1910
Radierung
Ex Libris Dr. Rud. [Rudolf] Erhard
Stuttgart, 1910
Etching
107 x 101 mm
KI 9136-2903, Legat bequest from Artur Wolf 1933

325
Karl Ritter
Exlibris Jorge Monsalvatje
Berlin, 1921
Radierung
Ex Libris Jorge Monsalvatje
Berlin, 1921
Etching
178 x 116 mm
KI 9136-5416, Legat bequest from Artur Wolf 1933

326
Robert Budzinski
Exlibris Géza Herzog
Konitz, 1916
Radierung
Ex Libris Géza Herzog
Konitz, 1916
Etching
137 x 96 mm
KI 9136-1118, Legat
bequest from Artur Wolf 1933

327
Michel Fingesten
Exlibris Hopkins Jazzband
Berlin, o. J.
Lithografie
Ex Libris Hopkins Jazzband
Berlin, n. d.
Lithograph
250 x 230 mm
KI 9136-1704, Legat bequest from Artur Wolf 1933

19 "Plötzlicher Tod eines Wiener Verlegers,"
in: *Neues Wiener Tagblatt*, 17 Oct 1932.

20 Wiener Auktionshaus J. Fischer (ed.),
*Kunstsammlung und Wohnungseinrichtung
aus dem Nachlasse Artur und Katharina Wolf
(Gräfin Attems), Wien, I., Seilerstätte 1
(Palais Coburg): Auktion 14., 15., und
16. März 1933*, [Vienna 1933], No. 806 and:
http://digi. ub.uni-heidelberg.de/diglit/fis-
cher_wien1933_03_14 (11 Jan 2016).
Translated by Maria Slater.
Artur Wolf suffered a fatal heart attack while
riding on 16 Oct 1932. Wolf's will named his
wife, Katharina (Käthe) Wolf (née Winkler,
divorcée of Count Attems) as sole heir.
Katharina Wolf, b. 1898, chose to depart this
life on 11 Dec 1932, cf. *Gothaisches Genealogisches Taschenbuch der Gräflichen Häuser. Zugleich Adelsmatrikel der Deutschen
Adelsgenossenschaft* 115, part A, Gotha
1942, 36. The sole heir of the couple's estate and the Artur Wolf Verlag was Katharina
Wolf's son from her first marriage, Christoph
Ferdinand, Count Attems, who was still a
minor; cf. Hall 1985 (see note 14), 477 f.

21 Amelia Sarah Levetus (1853–1938) was
Brangwyn's "agent in Austria," cf. Brangwyn,
Rodney, *Brangwyn*, London 1978, 190; on
Amelia Sarah Levetus cf. www.mackintosh-
architecture.gla.ac.uk/catalogue/
name/?nid=LevAS&xml=peo und
https://de.wikipedia.org/wiki/
Amelia_Sarah_Levetus (5 Jan 2016).

22 Kolophon von *Frank Brangwyn. 20 graphische Arbeiten in Mappe, eingeleitet und
herausgegeben von A. S. Levetus*, Vienna
[1921/1922].

23 Cf. Genossenschaft der bildenden Künstler
Wiens (ed.): *Brangwyn Ausstellung, Dezember 1922 bis Jänner 1923*, Vienna [1922], 7,
No. 58 A: "*Studie zu einer Adresse für eine
Kunstausstellung. Zwei Männer vor einem
großen Rade einer Druckerpresse betrachten
ein Druckblatt. Kreide";* the plate comes
from an earlier donation by Brangwyn to
the Albertina, which Levetus carried out
on behalf of Brangwyn, cf. 2 and 5.

24 Born, Wolfgang, "Exlibris-Ausstellung
in Wien," in: *Neues Wiener Journal*,
16 Aug 1933, 4. Translated by Maria Slater.

25 Cf. Karolyi, Claudia/Smetana, Alexandra,
"Die Geschichte der Exlibrissammlung der
k. k. Hof- und Nationalbibliothek in Wien von
den Anfängen bis 1938," in: *Österreichisches
Jahrbuch für Exlibris und Gebrauchsgraphik*
(66) 2009/2010, 36–59.

works my way, too—after all, it was common knowledge that I collected ex libris. In creative professions, there's no clear cut between work and private life. Why do you think there are not just ex libris, but also New Year's greetings (ill. 320) and invitations to vernissages and studio parties in my collection by some of the most esteemed artists of the age? It's because I knew them person- ally. As a publisher, I regularly stayed in Munich, Berlin, and Leipzig, where I operated a second publishing office. And whenever the opportunity arose, I went to the artists' studios there, too. When the *Neues Wiener Tagblatt* reported my sudden death in 1932, it was no accident that they wrote: "He moved in many artists' circles."[19] It's a terrible pity that you can't leaf through my guest book with its "many drawings by hand, watercolors, pastel drawings, etc. by famous artists & a large number of dedications."[20] You would have discovered lots of names, which you can also find in my collection. Needless to say, my friendship with Braungart was also beneficial to my collection. He knew all and sundry and introduced them all to me ... You want to know how I came to own my Brangwyn ex libris? Ah, that's a nice story. In principle, it's a by-product of my work as a publisher. In 1921 the Vienna-based English art historian and journalist Amelia Sarah Levetus[21] came to me on behalf of Frank Brangwyn. She told me the association of Viennese fine artists was planning to exhibit works by the internationally acclaimed *peintre-graveur* in December 1922. Asked me whether I would be prepared to publish works by the artist from the Albertina and English private collections in advance of the show. What a question! In view of the exhibition at the Künstlerhaus, the expensive undertaking would certainly be worthwhile. The large portfolio contained 20 works on paper by Brangwyn, which were introduced by Miss Levetus, and the "title and headpieces of this introduction" were printed from "specially carved original wood blocks" by the master.[22] The title page captured my imagination (ill. 322). It shows two men in front of the star wheel of an intaglio press who are examining a work, which has just been printed, with people interested in art watching the scene from the right-hand edge. A few months later at the Brangwyn show at the Künstlerhaus, I discovered an almost identical motif as a chalk drawing—only the gentlemen at the edge were missing.[23] How often had I myself stood and examined prints next to the press in a printing house! This work described like none other my professional tasks. That Brangwyn took up the motif once again and helped provide me with a professional ex libris, which befitted me personally—incredible! (ill. 323) Naturally the plate was a great success among collectors who had an understanding of works on paper. Wolfgang Born, who reviewed the exhibition of my ex libris— curated by Hans Ankwicz-Kleehoven after my death—in the *Neues Wiener Journal*, even wrote that it was "one of the best in the entire collection."[24] Why I bequeathed my ex libris collection to the Museum of Art and Industry in 1930? Oh, in 1929 I lost interest in ex libris; anyway, its golden age was already over ... Besides, I got married and wanted to spend my free time with Käthe. But even when you've grown tired of collecting, you still want to house everything you've amassed somewhere they'll be appreciated and where they might be useful. As a variant form of applied arts, ex libris could serve as visual aids for the students of the School of Arts and Crafts, I thought. What other institution should I have given them to? The gentlemen at the National Library were only interested in old plates[25] ... What, another question? OK, but that really must be the last one. Whether these small private plates also reflect the course of time? Find out for yourself. These works on paper tell lots of little stories. And they are all part of the bigger story, aren't they? Browse, my love, browse ...

Künste könnten Exlibris den Studenten der Kunstgewerbeschule vielleicht als Anschauungsmaterial dienen, dachte ich. Wohin hätte ich sie sonst geben sollen? Die Herren in der Nationalbibliothek interessierten sich ja bloß für alte Blätter[25] … Was, noch eine Frage? Gut, aber das ist jetzt wirklich die letzte. Ob diese privaten Blättchen auch die Zeitläufte widerspiegeln? Finden Sie es selbst heraus. Die Grafiken werden Ihnen viele kleine Geschichten erzählen. Und diese sind doch alle Teil der großen Geschichte, oder? Blättern Sie, meine Liebe, blättern Sie …

[25] Vgl. Karolyi, Claudia/Smetana, Alexandra, „Die Geschichte der Exlibrissammlung der k. k. Hof- und Nationalbibliothek in Wien von den Anfängen bis 1938", in: *Österreichisches Jahrbuch für Exlibris und Gebrauchsgraphik* (66) 2009/2010, 36–59.

ANMERKUNGEN DER GESPRÄCHSPARTNERIN VON ARTUR WOLF

Artur Wolf, geb. 1887 in Mährisch-Weißkirchen, stammte aus einer Fabrikantenfamilie und begann, wie ein Vermerk auf dem Vorsatz seines handschriftlichen Exlibrisverzeichnisses belegt, 1908 Exlibris zu sammeln. Seit einem Jahr Buchhändlerlehrling beim Wiener Verlag Dr. Rudolf Ludwig, dürfte er im selben Jahr bei Rudolf Geyer, einem Schüler von Rudolf von Larisch, sein erstes Exlibris bestellt haben, insgesamt sind 14 ausgeführte Exlibris auf seinen Namen nachweisbar. Die Tauschlisten des Exlibris-Vereins zu Berlin zwischen 1915 und 1929 ermöglichen, den Entstehungszeitraum bisher undatierter Blätter einzugrenzen und geben zudem Einblick in das Tauschmaterial, mit dem er seine Kleingrafiksammlung aufbaute. Denn Wolf bot in diesem Zeitraum nicht nur seine eigenen Exlibris, sondern auch Arbeiten der künstlerischen MitarbeiterInnen seines 1911 gegründeten Artur Wolf Verlages zum Tausch an. Bis zu seinem überraschenden Tod 1932 häufte der Verleger knapp 7700 Exlibris, Gebrauchsgrafiken und freie Grafiken an[26], die 1933 per Legat an das Österreichische Museum für Kunst und Industrie (ÖMKI) gingen. Mehr als die Hälfte der Grafiken fiel einem Bombenangriff im Zweiten Weltkrieg zum Opfer, rund 3800 „überlebten". Die künstlerischen bzw. motivischen Schwerpunkte der ehemaligen Sammlung festzumachen, ist daher nur eingeschränkt möglich. Ein Abgleich der vorhandenen Blätter mit jenen, die Wolf in seinem handschriftlichen Verzeichnis auflistete, kann der Rekonstruktion des ursprünglichen Bestandes dienlich sein, allerdings muss in Betracht gezogen werden, dass das Verzeichnis vermutlich nicht vollständig ist und der Sammler dort vermerkte Blätter bereits während seiner Sammlertätigkeit wieder abgestoßen haben könnte. Die erhalten gebliebenen Grafiken erlauben den BetrachterInnen einen Blick in die Welt des Exlibris der 1910er und 1920er Jahre. Sie sind überwiegend deutscher, österreichischer und Schweizer Provenienz, auch Exlibris von britischen, französischen, belgischen und spanischen KünstlerInnen sind vertreten, während die tschechische Exlibriskunst unterrepräsentiert ist. Selbst wenn die Sammlung gute Beispiele für das Gebrauchsexlibris bietet und alle druckgrafischen Techniken vom Holzschnitt bis zu aktuellen fotomechanischen Verfahren widerspiegelt, dominiert das radierte Luxusexlibris. Motivisch gesehen, beherrschen die beiden großen Themen des deutschen Exlibris – die Landschaft und der Akt – die Sammlung. Zahlreiche Exlibris von Georg Broel, Felix Hollenberg (Abb. 324) oder Adolf Kunst visualisieren die Sehnsuchtsorte der SammlerInnen, Akt-Exlibris von Hanns Bastanier, Bruno Héroux, Alois Kolb oder Karl Ritter (Abb. 325) feiern das Weibliche als Verkörperung des Schönen und Sinnlichen und bestätigen die Rolle des Mannes als Weltgestalter. Gestört wird dieses Idyll von Grafiken, die die Verheerungen des Ersten Weltkriegs festmachen (Abb. 326), im Wandel begriffene Geschlechterverhältnisse thematisieren oder den lebenshungrigen „Tanz auf dem Vulkan" der Roaring Twenties visualisieren (Abb. 327).

Das insbesondere in Österreich gepflegte Schriftexlibris ist lediglich mit einigen wenigen Beispielen vertreten, ebenso die puristische Buchmarke. Hingegen belegen mit Anmerkungen versehene

[26] Zu den Zahlen vgl. MAK-Bibliothek und Kunstblättersammlung, Inventarbuch KI 9136 und 9136a (1934).

COMMENTS BY ARTUR WOLF'S INTERVIEWER

Artur Wolf, born in Mährisch-Weißkirchen (now Hranice, Czech Republic) in 1887, came from a manufacturing family and started to collect ex libris in 1908, as evidenced by a remark on the endpaper of his handwritten ex libris catalog. Having been an apprentice bookseller for a year at the Dr. Rudolf Ludwig publishing house in Vienna, he appears to have ordered his first ex libris during the same year from Rudolf Geyer, a student of Rudolf von Larisch; in total 14 completed ex libris can be traced in his name. The exchange lists of the Exlibris-Verein zu Berlin between 1915 and 1929 make it possible to narrow down the period when as yet undated plates were created, while also providing an insight into the exchange currency with which he grew his collection of minor works on paper. During this period, Wolf not only offered his own ex libris for exchange, but also works by the artistic staff of his Artur Wolf Verlag, which he had founded in 1911. Until his surprising death in 1932, the publisher amassed almost 7 700 ex libris, ephemera, and graphic art,[26] which arrived at the Austrian Museum of Art and Industry in 1933 via his bequest. Over half of these works on paper fell victim to a bombing raid during the Second World War; around 3 800 "survived." It is therefore not entirely possible to determine the artistic or motif foci of the former collection. A comparison of the remaining plates with those Wolf listed in his handwritten catalog can be beneficial when trying to reconstruct the original holdings; however, it must be taken into consideration that the catalog is probably incomplete and the collector might have dispensed with some of the plates noted there before he ceased collecting.

The surviving works permit their observer an insight into the world of ex libris during the 1910s and 1920s. They are predominantly of German, Austrian, and Swiss provenance, though ex libris by British, French, Belgian, and Spanish artists also feature, whereas Czech ex libris art is underrepresented. Even if the collection offers good examples of practical ex libris and reflects all printing techniques from woodcuts to contemporary photomechanical processes, the majority are etched luxury ex libris. From the perspective of their motifs, the collection is dominated by the two main themes of German ex libris: landscape and nudes. Numerous ex libris by Georg Broel, Felix Hollenberg (ill. 324), and Adolf Kunst visualize the places collectors yearned to visit, while the nude ex libris by Hanns Bastanier, Bruno Héroux, Alois Kolb, and Karl Ritter (ill. 325) celebrate femininity as the embodiment of beauty and sensuality and confirm the role of men as organizers of their world. This idyll is destroyed by those works which capture the ravages of the First World War (ill. 326), record the changes in gender relations, or visualize the zest for life of the roaring twenties' "Tanz auf dem Vulkan" [Dance on the volcano] (ill. 327).

Particularly cultivated in Austria, the text-based ex libris is represented by only a few examples, as is the purist book label. In contrast, the collector's attachment to his favorite artists is documented in his annotations on ex libris, proofs, plates before they have been given any text, occasion graphics and graphic art by Alfred Soder, Hubert Wilm, and Erhard Amadeus-Dier, who was artistic staff members of the publishing house. The works by Franz von Bayros enjoy a special status. It was presumably when he was an apprentice that Wolf met the artist via his master, who published twelve ex libris by Franz von Bayros in 1911.[27] The portfolio *Ex-Libris. Neue Folge* was published by Wolf's company as early as 1912; five other portfolios and 172 works on paper by Bayros in the publisher's collection are testament to their longstanding friendship. Personal relationships can also be assumed from 118 plates by Willi Geiger (ill. 328), 74 by Michel Fingesten, 49 by

26 On this number cf. MAK Library and Works on Paper Collection, inventory KI 9136 and 9136a (1934).

27 Cf. Bayros, Franz von, *Ex-libris*, Vienna: Verlag Dr. Rudolf Ludwig 1911.

Exlibris, Probedrucke, Blätter vor der Schrift, Gelegenheits- und freie Grafiken von Alfred Soder, Hubert Wilm oder Erhard Amadeus-Dier, einem künstlerischen Mitarbeiter des Verlages, die Verbundenheit des Sammlers mit von ihm favorisierten Künstlern. Eine Sonderstellung nehmen die Arbeiten von Franz von Bayros ein. Wolf lernte den Künstler vermutlich bei seinem Lehrherrn kennen, der 1911 zwölf Exlibris von Franz von Bayros veröffentlichte.[27] Die Mappe *Ex-Libris. Neue Folge* erschien 1912 bereits in Wolfs Verlag – fünf weitere Mappen und 172 Grafiken von Bayros in der Sammlung des Verlegers bezeugen eine langjährige Freundschaft. Auf persönliche Beziehungen lassen auch 118 Blätter von Willi Geiger (Abb. 328), 74 von Michel Fingesten, 49 von Georg Jilovský und 48 von Emil Orlik (Abb. 330), dessen Arbeiten bereits zur Zeit ihrer Entstehung als Rara gehandelt wurden, schließen.

Obgleich Artur Wolfs Sammlung vor allem die Welt des deutschen Exlibris widerspiegelt, bietet sie einiges an Material zum Exlibrisschaffen österreichischer KünstlerInnen. Als Sensation kann gewertet werden, dass in der Sammlung Wolf erstmals ein Druck des 1903 entworfenen und im *Ver Sacrum* abgebildeten Exlibris von Josef Hoffmann für Fritz Waerndorfer nachgewiesen werden kann[28] (Abb. 329). Eine weitere Überraschung sind unbekannte Arbeiten der Grafikerin, Illustratorin und Kunstgewerblerin Marianne Steinberger-Hitschmann, deren verwunschene Radierserie *Melodien* zu Werken österreichischer und deutscher Komponisten Artur Wolf 1913 verlegte (Abb. 331). Der deutsche Sammler Heinz Decker, aufgrund dessen akribischer Recherche wir von 32 Exlibris der Künstlerin wussten, kann nun das Werkverzeichnis ihrer Bücherzeichen[29] weiterschreiben.

Dass Artur Wolf der *Magie des Kupferstichs* von Alfred Cossmann und seinen SchülerInnen nicht erlegen ist, dürfte der konservativen Formensprache der Cossmannschule geschuldet sein. Fasziniert haben ihn allerdings die fantastischen Landschaften und Szenerien des Cossmannschülers Franz Taussig, dessen poetische Reise-Impressionen er 1929 in der Grafikmappe *Spanische Reise* (zehn Radierungen) herausgab. Hans Ankwicz-Kleehoven, ab 1925 Vorstand der Bibliothek und Kunstblättersammlung des ÖMKI und einer der führenden Vertreter der österreichischen Exlibrisbewegung der 1920er und 1930er Jahre, wies die Community bereits 1934 darauf hin, dass sich in der Sammlung Wolf eine „der vollständigsten Taussig-Kollektionen"[30] befindet, die neben ausgeführten Exlibris, Entwürfen und Probedrucken auch viele freie Grafiken enthält (Abb. 332, 333). Dennoch gehört die Aufarbeitung seines Werks bis heute zu den Desideraten der Exlibrisforschung wie auch eine Analyse der grafischen Arbeiten des Malers und Komponisten Erhard Amadeus-Dier, die in der deutschen und österreichischen Exlibrisliteratur bislang nur beiläufig erwähnt wurden. Wer zu den Tauschpartnern des Verlegers zählte, ist nach einmaliger Durchsicht der Sammlung kaum zu beantworten. Licht ins Dunkel könnten die Analyse seiner Mappe *100 deutsche Meisterexlibris* (1922), für die KünstlerInnen und SammlerInnen ihre Druckplatten zur Verfügung stellten, und eine EDV-unterstützte Abfrage mehrfach aufscheinender Exlibris-EignerInnen bringen. Wolf dürfte vornehmlich mit deutschen und Schweizer Exlibristen getauscht haben, auch mehrere Blätter des katalonischen Sammlers Jorge Monsalvatje weisen auf Tauschkontakte hin (Abb. 334). Zu den Mitgliedern der Österreichischen Exlibris-Gesellschaft bzw. Funktionären des Vereins der 1920er Jahre scheint Artur Wolf konsequent Distanz gehalten zu haben. Exlibris von Hans Anwicz-Kleehoven fehlen überhaupt, und zwei von Fingesten bzw. Arthur Paunzen ausgeführte Eignerzeichen für Marco Birnholz – der mit Exlibrisaufträgen zahlreiche junge österreichische KünstlerInnen förderte[31], die

27 Vgl. Bayros, Franz von, *Ex-libris*, Wien: Verlag Dr. Rudolf Ludwig 1911.

28 Smetana, Alexandra/Karolyi, Claudia, „Der Künstler und seine Mäzene. Unbekannte Exlibris und Exlibrisentwürfe von Josef Hoffmann für Otto und Mäda Primavesi", in: *biblos* (49) 2 2000, 356–358 und Fußnote 31.

29 Decker, Heinz, „Werkliste der Exlibris von Marianne Steinberger-Hitschmann", in: www.exlibris-austria.com/index.php/men-home-de/men-artists-de/men-artistindex-de/men-artist-wor-de/46-art-steinberger-marianne-wer-de?limitstart=0 (12.1.2016).

30 Ankwicz-Kleehoven, Hans, „Der Graphiker Franz Taussig", in: *Österreichisches Jahrbuch für Exlibris und Gebrauchsgraphik* (29) 1934, 18. Zur Biografie Hans Ankwicz-Kleehovens vgl. Karolyi, Claudia/Mayerhofer, Alexandra, „Das Glück des Sammelns. Die Exlibris-Sammlung Ankwicz-Kleehoven in der ÖNB", in: *biblos* (46) 1 1997, 91–114.

31 Zu Marco Birnholz vgl. Jobst-Rieder, Marianne/Karolyi, Claudia, „,Birnholziana'. Geschichte, Raub und Restitution der Exlibris-Sammlung Marco Birnholz", in: *Österreichisches Jahrbuch für Exlibris und Gebrauchsgraphik* (64) 2005–2006, 45–77.

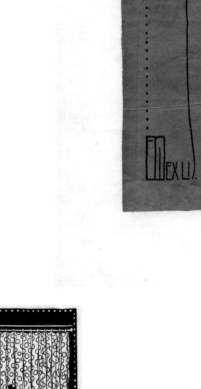

328
Willi Geiger
Exlibris Martha Lehmann
Rom, 1905
Klischee
Ex Libris Martha Lehmann
Rome, 1905
Cliché
142 x 110 mm
KI 9136-2119, Legat bequest from Artur Wolf 1933

329
Josef Hoffmann
Exlibris F[ritz] W[aerndorfer]
Wien, 1903
Klischee
Ex Libris F[ritz] W[aerndorfer]
Vienna, 1903
Cliché
174 x 80 mm
KI 9136-3860, Legat bequest from
Artur Wolf 1933

330
Emil Orlik
Exlibris Emil Orlik
Prag, 1902
Lithografie
Ex Libris Emil Orlik
Prague, 1902
Lithograph
98 x 78 mm
KI 9136-3953, Legat bequest from Artur Wolf 1933

331
Marianne Steinberger-Hitschmann
Exlibris Wilhelm von Klastersky
Wien, vor 1911
Holzschnitt
Ex Libris Wilhelm von Klastersky
Vienna, before 1911
Woodcut
143 x 82 mm
KI 9136-2801, Legat bequest from Artur Wolf 1933

vermutlich das Interesse des Verlegers geweckt hätten –, könnten über die Entwerfenden oder Exlibristausch in die Sammlung gekommen sein. Abschließend sei darauf hingewiesen, dass diese nur im Kontext von Artur Wolfs verlegerischer Tätigkeit und mit Blick auf seine 1933 versteigerten Kunstschätze[32] beurteilt werden kann. Denn der Auktionskatalog belegt Wolfs große Wertschätzung für österreichische KünstlerInnen, deren Grafiken man bei Durchsicht seiner Exlibrissammlung vermisst.

[32] Wiener Auktionshaus J. Fischer 1933 (s. Anm. 20).

332
Franz Taussig
**Entwurf eines Exlibris
für Maria Kreitner**
Wien, o.J.
Bleistift
**Design for an Ex Libris
for Maria Kreitner**
Vienna, n.d.
Pencil
104 x 81 mm
KI 9136-6319, Legat bequest
from Artur Wolf 1933

333
Franz Taussig
Exlibris Maria Kreitner
Wien, o.J.
Kupferstich, Radierung
Ex Libris Maria Kreitner
Vienna, n.d.
Copper engraving, etching
82 x 56 mm
KI 9136-6276, Legat bequest
from Artur Wolf 1933

334
Josep Triadó i Mayol
Exlibris Josep [Jorge] Monsalvatje
Barcelona, 1916
Radierung
Ex Libris Josep [Jorge] Monsalvatje
Barcelona, 1916
Etching
253 x 171 mm
KI 9136-6454, Legat bequest from Artur Wolf 1933

Georg Jilovský, and 48 by Emil Orlik (ill. 330), whose works were treated as rarities the moment they were produced.

Although Artur Wolf's collection predominantly reflects the world of German ex libris, it also offers some material on the creation of ex libris by Austrian artists. It can be considered a sensation that a print of the ex libris by Josef Hoffmann for Fritz Waerndorfer—designed in 1903 and illustrated in *Ver Sacrum*—can be documented for the first time in the Wolf Collection[28] (ill. 329). Another surprise is the unknown works by the graphic artist, illustrator, and craftswoman Marianne Steinberger-Hitschmann, whose enchanting series of etchings *Melodien* [Melodies] Artur Wolf published alongside works by Austrian and German composers in 1913 (ill. 331). The German collector Heinz Decker, thanks to whose meticulous research we knew of there being 32 ex libris by the artist, can now continue writing the catalogue raisonné of her bookplates.[29]

That Artur Wolf did not succumb to the *Magie des Kupferstichs* [Magic of copperplate engraving] by Alfred Cossmann and his students, must be due to the Cossmann school's conservative language of forms. Despite this fact, he was fascinated by the fantastical landscapes and scenery of Cossmann's student Franz Taussig, whose poetic travel impressions he published in the graphic portfolio *Spanische Reise* [Spanish Journey] (ten etchings) in 1929. As early as 1934 Hans Ankwicz-Kleehoven, head of the Library and Works on Paper Collectionat the Austrian Museum of Art and Industry from 1925 and one of the leading advocates of the Austrian ex libris movement in the 1920s and 1930s, made the community aware that the Wolf Collection contained one "of the most complete Taussig collections,"[30] which in addition to executed ex libris, designs, and proofs also included several works of graphic art (ill. 332, 333). Nevertheless, a reappraisal of his work is still a desideratum of ex libris research, as is an analysis of the works on paper by the painter and composer Erhard Amadeus-Dier, which have as yet only been mentioned in passing in German and Austrian ex libris literature.

The question as to who the publisher's exchange partners actually were can hardly be answered upon a cursory perusal of the collection. An analysis of his portfolio *100 deutsche Meisterexlibris* (1922)—for which artists and collectors alike made available their printing plates—could shed some light on the matter, as could an IT-supported survey of frequently appearing ex libris owners. Wolf must have predominantly exchanged ex libris with German and Swiss collectors; several plates from the Catalonian collector Jorge Monsalvatje also suggest a connection for purposes of exchange (ill. 334). Artur Wolf appears to have consistently kept his distance from the members of the Austrian Bookplate Society or rather functionaries of the society in the 1920s. Ex libris from Hans Anwicz-Kleehoven are entirely lacking, and two ownership labels executed by Fingesten and Arthur Paunzen for Marco Birnholz—who supported numerous young Austrian artists with commissions for ex libris[31] and who had presumably attracted the attention of the publisher—could have entered the collection via the designers themselves or an exchange of ex libris. In conclusion it can be noted that this can only be judged in the context of Artur Wolf's profession as a publisher and in view of his art treasures, which were auctioned in 1933[32]: the auction catalog attests to Wolf's great appreciation of Austrian artists, the absence of whose works can be felt when perusing his ex libris collection.

[28] Smetana, Alexandra/Karolyi, Claudia, "Der Künstler und seine Mäzene. Unbekannte Exlibris und Exlibrisentwürfe von Josef Hoffmann für Otto und Mäda Primavesi," in: *biblos* (49) 2 2000, 356–358 and note 31.

[29] Decker, Heinz, "Werkliste der Exlibris von Marianne Steinberger-Hitschmann," in: www.exlibris-austria.com/index.php/men-home-de/men-artists-de/men-artistindex-de/men-artist-wor-de/46-art-steinberger-marianne-wer-de?limitstart=0 (12 Jan 2016).

[30] Ankwicz-Kleehoven, Hans, "Der Graphiker Franz Taussig," in: *Österreichisches Jahrbuch für Exlibris und Gebrauchsgraphik* (29) 1934, 18. On the biography of Hans Ankwicz-Kleehoven cf. Karoly, Claudia/Mayerhofer, Alexandra, "Das Glück des Sammelns. Die Exlibris-Sammlung Ankwicz-Kleehoven in der ÖNB," in: *biblos* (46) 1 1997, 91–114.

[31] On Marco Birnholz cf. Jobst-Rieder, Marianne/Karolyi, Claudia, "'Birnholziana.' Geschichte, Raub und Restitution der Exlibris-Sammlung Marco Birnholz," in: *Österreichisches Jahrbuch für Exlibris und Gebrauchsgraphik* (64) 2005–2006, 45–77.

[32] Wiener Auktionshaus J. Fischer 1933 (see note 20).

DER AUFBAU DER SAMMLUNG DURCH HANS ANKWICZ-KLEEHOVEN

Obwohl das Museum seit 1912 Mitglied der Österreichischen Exlibris-Gesellschaft war und 1913 in der Säulenhalle deren große Exlibrisschau stattfinden ließ, wurde bis 1925 – als Hans Ankwicz-Kleehoven die Leitung der Bibliothek und Kunstblättersammlung übernahm – kein einziges Bucheignerzeichen in die Sammlung aufgenommen. Dabei erschien in der Museumsschrift *Kunst und Kunsthandwerk* ein zwölfseitiger Artikel von Rudolf Freiherr von Hoschek, einem der Kuratoren der Ausstellung, der darin das allgemeine Interesse an dieser Kleinkunst in Wien beteuerte. Einer abfälligen Bemerkung des Berliner Sammlers Walter von Zur Westen in dessen Exlibris-Monografie 1901 hielt er entgegen, dass in Wien schon damals „eine ganze Anzahl von Persönlichkeiten [existierte], welche das Sammeln von Exlibris mit Geschmack und Verständnis pflegten".[1] Dazu gehörte auch der Verleger Artur Wolf (1887–1932), der als Leihgeber der Ausstellung womöglich das in Hoscheks Artikel abgebildete Exlibris von Willi Geiger borgte (Abb. 337), welches 20 Jahre später durch sein Legat in die Bibliothek gelangte.

Weshalb der Verleger seine Sammlung dem Museum vermachte und welche Rolle Hans Ankwicz-Kleehoven (1883–1962) dabei spielte, ist nicht überliefert. Aus den Archivalien geht nur hervor, dass Wolf die ständige Präsentation der Grafiken in einem eigenen Raum verfügte. Aus Platzmangel und wohl auch konservatorischen Gründen wurde dem nicht nachgekommen, Ankwicz-Kleehoven richtete jedoch im Sommer 1933 eine Ausstellung ausgewählter Blätter aus. „Da ist zunächst Emil Orlik, der kurz vor dem Sammler selbst verstorbene Meister. Er hat Max Reinhardts Exlibris entworfen. Es ist eine Radierung, die noch deutlich das Gepräge des Jugendstils trägt […] – das Ganze sichtlich von den Shakespeare-Inszenierungen des großen Regisseurs inspiriert", heißt es in einer Rezension im *Neuen Wiener Journal* (Abb. 345). Darin werden etwa auch das Blatt von Käthe Kollwitz für ihren Sohn, das Herxheimer-Exlibris von Hans Thoma sowie eine frühe Arbeit von Julius Klinger erwähnt (Abb. 335, 339, 343).[2]

Durch das Legat Artur Wolfs vergrößerte sich die Exlibris-Sammlung 1933 um mehr als 7 000 Blätter.[3] Zuvor hatte Ankwicz-Kleehoven die Sammlung durch Ankäufe und Schenkungen aus seinen eigenen Beständen aufgebaut. Zu den frühesten Erwerbungen gehören Exlibris von Dagobert Peche aus dem Besitz seiner Witwe bzw. des Holzschneiders Friedrich Skurawy sowie Entwürfe von Koloman Moser aus dem Besitz seiner Schwester Leopoldine Steindl. Ankwicz-Kleehoven war den Künstlern der Wiener Werkstätte (z. T. Professoren an der dem Museum angeschlossenen Kunstgewerbeschule) besonders verbunden und setzte viel daran, den Museumsbestand an WW-Erzeugnissen zu vermehren.[4] Aus seiner eigenen Sammlung steuerte er immer wieder Exlibris aus der WW und deren Umkreis bei (Abb. 340–342). Im Zusammenhang mit Ditha Mosers *Whist*-Spiel (s. Abb. 226) ist ein Familien-Exlibris ihres Mannes interessant, das im Format einer Spielkarte ähnliche Gestaltungsprinzipien zeigt (Abb. 338). Darüber hinaus stiftete Ankwicz-Kleehoven der Bibliothek mehrere der bemerkenswerten Exlibris von Alfred Kubin (Abb. 350, 352), für ihn selbst angefertigte Buchzeichen sowie etliche Beispiele des von ihm als „Vater des modernen österreichischen Exlibris"[5] verehrten Alfred Cossmann und dessen Schule (Abb. 348, 351, 353). Den Großteil seiner Sammlung vermachte er der Graphischen Lehr- und Versuchsanstalt in Wien, die den Nachlass schließlich zur Bearbeitung der Österreichischen Nationalbibliothek übergab.

[1] Hoschek, Rudolf Freiherr von, „Exlibrisausstellung in Wien 1913", in: *Kunst und Kunsthandwerk* (XVI) 3 1913, 191.

[2] Born, Wolfgang, „Exlibris-Ausstellung in Wien", in: *Neues Wiener Journal*, 16.8.1933, 4–5.

[3] Im Zweiten Weltkrieg wurde durch Bombentreffer und Löscharbeiten im Trakt des alten Lesesaales, wo die Exlibris zur Anschauung in Laden untergebracht waren, mehr als die Hälfte der Blätter zerstört.

[4] Vgl. Karolyi, Claudia/Mayerhofer, Alexandra, „Das Glück des Sammelns. Die Exlibris-Sammlung Ankwicz-Kleehoven in der ÖNB", in: *biblos* (46) 1 1997, 99–100.

[5] Ebd., 103.

HANS ANKWICZ-KLEEHOVEN AND THE CREATION OF THE COLLECTION

Although the museum had been a member of the Austrian Bookplate Society since 1912 and their large-scale ex libris show had taken place in the museum's Columned Main Hall in 1913, not a single bookplate entered the collection until 1925, when Hans Ankwicz-Kleehoven took over as head of the Library and Works on Paper Collection. Yet a twelve-page article had appeared in the museum's publication *Kunst und Kunsthandwerk* at the time of the exhibition by Rudolf Freiherr von Hoschek, one of its curators, who asserted the general interest in this minor art form in Vienna. He reacts to a disparaging remark by the Berlin-based collector Walter von Zur Westen in the latter's monograph on ex libris from 1901 by declaring that even at that time, there were "quite a number of people [in Vienna], who used to collect ex libris—and who did so tastefully and appreciatively."[1] One such collector was the publisher Artur Wolf (1887–1932), who had loaned parts of his collection to the exhibition—perhaps including the ex libris by Willi Geiger pictured in Hoschek's article (ill. 337), which Wolf would bequeath to the library when he died 20 years later.

There is sadly no record of the reason why the publisher chose to leave his collection to the museum in his will nor what role Hans Ankwicz-Kleehoven (1883–1962) played in his decision. The only thing to emerge from the archives in this regard is that Wolf stipulated that these graphics should be on permanent display in a dedicated room. Due to a lack of space and probably also for conservational reasons, the museum did not comply with this request; however, Ankwicz-Kleehoven did organize an exhibition of select bookplates in summer 1933. "First, there is Emil Orlik, the master who passed away shortly before the collector himself. He had designed Max Reinhardt's ex libris. It is an etching, which still bears a distinctly art nouveau character [...]—the whole thing has visibly been inspired by the great director's Shakespearean productions,"[2] according to a review in the *Neues Wiener Journal* (ill. 345). It also mentions the plate by Käthe Kollwitz for her son, the Herxheimer ex libris by Hans Thoma, as well as an early work by Julius Klinger (ill.335, 339, 343).[3] Thanks to the bequest from Artur Wolf, in 1933 the ex libris collection increased by more than 7000 plates.[4] Ankwicz-Kleehoven had previously established the collection by means of purchases as well as donations from his own holdings. Among the earliest acquisitions are ex libris by Dagobert Peche belonging to his widow or the woodcutter Friedrich Skurawy, as well as designs by Koloman Moser belonging to his sister, Leopoldine Steindl. Ankwicz-Kleehoven had particularly close connections with the artists of the Wiener Werkstätte (some of whom were professors at the museum-affiliated School of Arts and Crafts) and strove to increase the museum's holdings of WW products.[5] Indeed, he repeatedly contributed ex libris by the WW and their circle from his own private collection (ill. 340–342). A family ex libris by Ditha Moser's husband is interesting in connection with her *whist* deck (see ill. 226): its format is that of a playing card and it abides by similar design principles (ill. 338). Furthermore, Ankwicz-Kleehoven endowed the library with several remarkable ex libris by Alfred Kubin (ill. 350, 352), bookplates made especially for him, as well as quite a number of examples by Alfred Cossmann—whom he venerated as the "father of modern Austrian ex libris"[6]— and his school (ill. 348, 351, 353). He left the majority of his collection to the Graphische Lehr- und Versuchsanstalt in Vienna, which ultimately transferred his bequest to the Austrian National Library for processing purposes.

[1] Hoschek, Rudolf Freiherr von, "Exlibrisausstellung in Wien 1913," in: *Kunst und Kunsthandwerk* (XVI) 3 1913, 191. Translated by Maria Slater.

[2] Translated by Maria Slater.

[3] Born, Wolfgang, "Exlibris-Ausstellung in Wien," in: *Neues Wiener Journal*, 16 Aug 1933, 4–5.

[4] During the Second World War, over half of the plates were destroyed after a bomb hit the wing of the old Reading Room where the ex libris had been displayed in drawers; that which had not been destroyed by the bomb was ruined by the firefighting operation.

[5] Cf. Karolyi, Claudia/Mayerhofer, Alexandra, "Das Glück des Sammelns. Die Exlibris-Sammlung Ankwicz-Kleehoven in der ÖNB," in: *biblos* (46) 1 1997, 99–100.

[6] Ibid., 103. Translated by Maria Slater.

336
Koloman Moser
Entwurf eines Exlibris für Ludwig Hevesi
Wien, um 1900
Bleistift, Tusche auf Karton
Design for an Ex Libris for Ludwig Hevesi
Vienna, ca. 1900
Pencil, ink on cardboard
150 x 190 mm
KI 16951-4, Ankauf purchased from
Leopoldine Steindl 1929

335
Hans Thoma
Exlibris Dr. S[alomon] Herxheimer
München, 1898
Algraphie
Ex Libris Dr. S[alomon] Herxheimer
Munich, 1898
Algraphy print
130 x 105 mm
KI 9136-6382, Legat bequest from Artur Wolf 1933

337
Willi Geiger
Exlibris Klara Weiss
München, 1904
Klischee
Ex Libris Klara Weiss
Munich, 1904
Cliché
173 x 120 mm
KI 9136-2117, Legat bequest from
Artur Wolf 1933

338
Koloman Moser
Exlibris [Koloman und Ditha] Moser
Wien, um 1905
Lithografie
Ex Libris [Koloman und Ditha] Moser
Vienna, ca. 1905
Lithograph
101 x 66 mm
KI 8910-2, Schenkung donation from
Hans Ankwicz-Kleehoven 1931

339
Julius Klinger
Exlibris S[ebastian] Malz
Berlin, 1906
Klischee
Ex Libris S[ebastian] Malz
Berlin, 1906
Cliché
112 x 92 mm
KI 9136-3134, Legat bequest from Artur Wolf 1933

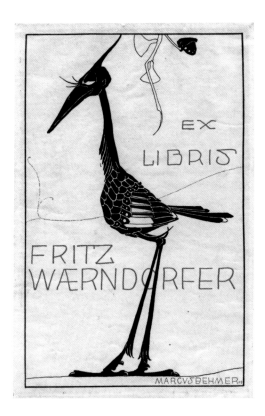

340
Marcus Behmer
Exlibris Fritz Waerndorfer
Wien, 1907
Klischee
Ex Libris Fritz Waerndorfer
Vienna, 1907
Cliché
160 x 105 mm
KI 8912, Schenkung donation from
Hans Ankwicz-Kleehoven 1931

341
Carl Otto Czeschka
Exlibris Emma Bacher
Hamburg, 1909
Klischee
Ex Libris Emma Bacher
Hamburg, 1909
Cliché
165 x 124 mm
KI 8884, Schenkung donation from
Hans Ankwicz-Kleehoven 1930

342
Koloman Moser
Exlibris Dr. Franz Zweibrück
Wien, um 1908
Klischee
Ex Libris Dr. Franz Zweibrück
Vienna, ca. 1908
Cliché
86 x 37 mm
KI 8910-1, Schenkung donation from
Hans Ankwicz-Kleehoven 1931

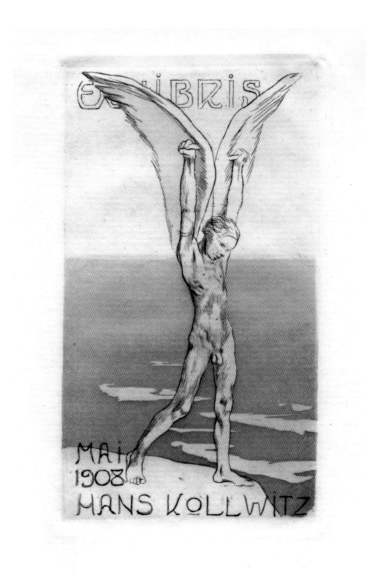

343
Käthe Kollwitz
Exlibris Hans Kollwitz
Berlin, 1908
Radierung, Aquatinta
Ex Libris Hans Kollwitz
Berlin, 1908
Etching, aquatint
124 x 73 mm
KI 9136-3224, Legat bequest from
Artur Wolf 1933

344
Dagobert Peche
Exlibris M. B. Robert
Wien, 1911
Radierung
Ex Libris M. B. Robert
Vienna, 1911
Etching
70 x 50 mm
KI 8473-2, Ankauf purchased from
Nelly Peche 1926

345
Emil Orlik
Exlibris Max Reinhardt
Berlin, 1911
Radierung
Ex Libris Max Reinhardt
Berlin, 1911
Etching
98 x 97 mm
KI 9136-3968, Legat bequest from
Artur Wolf 1933

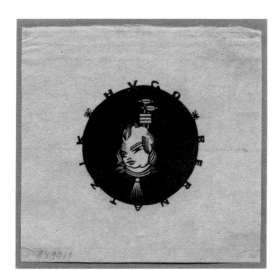

346
Dagobert Peche
Exlibris Hugo Bernatzik
Wien, um 1920
Ausführung: Druckerei Friedrich Skurawy
Holzstich
Ex Libris Hugo Bernatzik
Vienna, ca. 1920
Execution: Printer Friedrich Skurawy
Wood engraving
88 x 90 mm
KI 8490-1, Ankauf purchased from
Friedrich Skurawy 1926

347
Rudolf Junk
Exlibris
Hans Ankwicz-Kleehoven
Wien, um 1924
Klischee
Ex Libris
Hans Ankwicz-Kleehoven
Vienna, ca. 1924
Cliché
71 x 71 mm
KI 8911-6, Schenkung
donation from Hans
Ankwicz-Kleehoven 1931

348
Alfred Cossmann
Exlibris Leopold,
Therese, Walter Pasching
Wien, 1925
Kupferstich
Ex Libris Leopold,
Therese, Walter Pasching
Vienna, 1925
Copper engraving
108 x 72 mm
KI 8891, Schenkung
donation from Hans
Ankwicz-Kleehoven 1930

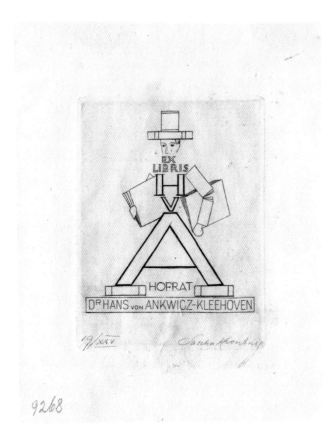

349
Sascha Kronburg
Exlibris
Hans Ankwicz-Kleehoven
Wien, 1925
Kupferstich
Ex Libris
Hans Ankwicz-Kleehoven
Vienna, 1925
Copper engraving
70 x 55 mm
KI 9268, Schenkung
donation from Hans
Ankwicz-Kleehoven 1935

350
Alfred Kubin
Exlibris
Dr. Carl Lamersdorf
Zwickledt, 1926
Lithografie
Ex Libris
Dr. Carl Lamersdorf
Zwickledt, 1926
Lithograph
132 x 103 mm
KI 8916-1, Schenkung
donation from Hans
Ankwicz-Kleehoven 1931

351
Hubert Woyty-Wimmer
Eigenexlibris
Wien, 1927
Radierung
Personal Ex Libris
Vienna, 1927
Etching
47 x 45 mm
KI 8915-2, Schenkung
donation from Hans
Ankwicz-Kleehoven 1931

352
Alfred Kubin
Exlibris Dr. Franz Heller
Zwickledt, 1936
Lithografie
Ex Libris Dr. Franz Heller
Zwickledt, 1936
Lithograph
185 x 144 mm
KI 8916-3, Schenkung
donation from Hans
Ankwicz-Kleehoven 1931

353
Hans Ranzoni
Exlibris Lisl Kemeny
Wien, 1929
Kupferstich
Ex Libris Lisl Kemeny
Vienna, 1929
Copper engraving
53 x 58 mm
KI 9001-6, Schenkung
donation from Hans
Ankwicz-Kleehoven 1932

SCHENKUNGEN VON KÜNSTLERINNEN UND KÜNSTLERN IN DER ÄRA ANKWICZ-KLEEHOVEN

Streng genommen fällt das moderne Exlibris aus den ersten drei Jahrzehnten des 20. Jahrhunderts nicht unter die Ephemera, die eine praktische Funktion und ein Ablaufdatum haben. Von Anbeginn wurde es als künstlerische Grafik behandelt, die man nicht in ein Buch klebte, sondern tauschte und sammelte. Das tat auch Hans Ankwicz-Kleehoven, der 1920 der Österreichischen Exlibris-Gesellschaft beitrat und deren Jahrbuch über lange Zeit redaktionell betreute. Bereits 1919 erschien darin sein Aufsatz über das *Wiener Humanisten-Exlibris* des 16. Jahrhunderts, das Ankwicz-Kleehovens anhaltendes Interesse an alter Exlibriskunst bezeugt.[1] Die Moderne öffnete sich ihm wohl im Zuge seiner Beschäftigung am Museum (ab 1915 als sogenannter Kustosadjunkt), welche den regen Austausch mit der angeschlossenen Kunstgewerbeschule implizierte. Sie war außerdem Thema zahlreicher Artikel, die er als Kunstreferent der *Wiener Zeitung* verfasste, ebenso wie die Biografien ihrer ProtagonistInnen, die er in über 250 Artikeln für das Künstlerlexikon Thieme-Becker festhielt.[2] Dazu gehörten auch jene von Richard Teschner, Oskar Laske (Abb. 354), Hubert Woyty-Wimmer, Rose Reinhold (Abb. 356), Franz Taussig (Abb. 358) und Rudolf Köhl – allesamt österreichische KünstlerInnen, die der Bibliothek in den 1930er Jahren etliche Exlibris spendeten und sich damit ihrem Biografen, Rezensenten und Förderer Ankwicz-Kleehoven erkenntlich zeigten. Beispiele von Teschner, dem er auch ein jahrelanger Freund war, publizierte Ankwicz-Kleehoven in seinem Aufsatz *Von jüngster österreichischer Exlibris-Kunst*, darunter auch die märchenhaften Bücherzeichen für den Exlibris-Auftraggeber Theodor Alexander (Abb. 357).[3]

Figurale und landschaftliche Motive seien immer weniger zeitgemäß, stellte Ankwicz-Kleehoven fest. „Der von der Larisch-Schule propagierte Puritanismus, der eine schöne ornamentale Schrift als ausreichenden Dekor eines modernen Exlibris erklärt […], führt mehr und mehr zu einer Vereinfachung dieses bisher allzusehr nach ‚bildmäßigen' Effekten strebenden Kunstgenres."[4] In diesem Zusammenhang fallen die Namen der Larisch-Schüler Rudolf Geyer und Rudolf Köhl (Abb. 360). Auch Otto Feil, der bei Köhl den Holzschnitt erlernte, und Otto Hurm, Nachfolger Rudolf von Larischs an der Akademie der bildenden Künste, verfolgten diese Gestaltungsweise und überließen der Sammlung zahlreiche Beispiele. Rein kalligrafischer Art sind auch die Exlibris des Larisch-Schülers Robert Haas. Der Mitbegründer des grafischen Ateliers Officina Vindobonensis, das sich dem edlen Buchdruck mit der Handpresse verschrieben hatte, bereicherte die Sammlung 1930 mit über 40 mehrheitlich als Holzstich ausgeführten Beispielen (Abb. 364).[5] Weitere Schenkungen erfolgten durch Ludwig Heinrich Jungnickel (1926), der auch im Exlibris seiner Vorliebe für das Tiermotiv nachging, durch den tschechischen Künstler Robert Herrmann (1935), dessen präzise durchkomponierte Schrift-Exlibris eine Besonderheit darstellen, durch Max Oppenheimer (1936), dessen „Nahaufnahmen" auch im Kleinformat funktionieren, oder den gänzlich unbekannten Hans Felix Kraus (1937), der vieldeutige Auftragsarbeiten für den Apotheker und Sammler Marco Birnholz fertigte. Erst viel später erhielt die Bibliothek ein ganzes Konvolut an Exlibris-Entwürfen des erwähnten Rudolf Geyer durch dessen Sohn (Abb. 365), wodurch eine Sammeltätigkeit weitergeführt wurde, die mit der Zwangspensionierung von Hans Ankwicz-Kleehoven 1939 ein abruptes Ende gefunden hatte.

[1] Ankwicz-Kleehoven, Hans, „Wiener Humanisten-Exlibris", in: Österreichische Exlibris-Gesellschaft (Hg.), *XVII. Jahrbuch 1919*, Wien 1919, 11–56; Ders., „Von alter Exlibriskunst", Sonderdruck, ca. 1938, 110–117.

[2] Vgl. Karolyi, Claudia/Mayerhofer, Alexandra, „Das Glück des Sammelns. Die Exlibris-Sammlung Ankwicz-Kleehoven in der ÖNB", in: *biblos* (46) 1 1997, 93.

[3] Ankwicz-Kleehoven, Hans, „Von jüngster österreichischer Exlibriskunst", in: *Österreichisches Jahrbuch für Exlibris und Gebrauchsgraphik* (21) 1924/25 (erschienen 1926), 19.

[4] Ebd., 20.

[5] Dem später vor allem als Fotograf erfolgreichen Haas, der 1938 in die USA emigrierte, widmete die Bibliothek 1983 eine Personale zum 85. Geburtstag. Vgl. Egger, Hanna (Red.), *Robert Haas. Schrift, Druck, Photographie*, Schriften der Bibliothek des Österreichischen Museums für angewandte Kunst 25, Ausst.kat., Wien 1983.

ARTISTS' DONATIONS DURING THE ERA OF ANKWICZ-KLEEHOVEN

Strictly speaking, the modern ex libris dating from the first three decades of the 20th century do not fall within the scope of ephemera, which have a practical function and an expiry date. From the outset, ex libris were treated as an artistic form of graphic design, which was not affixed inside a book, but rather swapped and collected. This is also what Hans Ankwicz-Kleehoven did; he joined the Austrian Bookplate Society in 1920 and for a long time edited their yearbook. As early as 1919 the publication featured his article about the 16th-century *Wiener Humanisten-Exlibris*, which attests to Ankwicz-Kleehoven's prolonged interest in the old art of ex libris.[1] His fondness for modernism probably grew over the course of his employment at the museum (where he began as a so-called assistant custodian in 1915), which entailed a lively exchange with the affiliated School of Arts and Crafts. Moreover, it was the subject of numerous articles, which he wrote as the arts correspondent of the *Wiener Zeitung*; he also recorded the biographies of the movement's protagonists in over 250 articles for the Thieme-Becker dictionary of artists.[2]

The latter included those of Richard Teschner, Oskar Laske (ill. 354), Hubert Woyty-Wimmer, Rose Reinhold (ill. 356), Franz Taussig (ill. 358), and Rudolf Köhl—all of whom were Austrian artists who donated a great number of ex libris to the library in the 1930s, arguably as a sign of gratitude to their biographer, critic, and patron Ankwicz-Kleehoven. He published examples by Teschner, who was also a long-term friend, in his article *Von jüngster österreichischer Exlibris-Kunst*; amongst others the fairy-tale bookplates for Theodor Alexander, who commissioned many ex libris (ill. 357).[3] However, figurative and landscape motifs were less and less in keeping with the period, as Ankwicz-Kleehoven observed. "The puritanism propagated by the Larisch school, which declares attractive, ornamental text to be sufficient decoration for a modern ex libris [...], is increasingly leading to a simplification of this artistic genre, which had hitherto striven all too much for 'image-like' effects."[4] In this context the names of the Larisch students Rudolf Geyer and Rudolf Köhl (ill. 360) spring to mind. Otto Feil, who learned woodcutting under Köhl, and Otto Hurm, Rudolf von Larisch's successor at the Academy of Fine Arts, also pursued this design style and left numerous examples of it to the library.

Equally of a purely calligraphic nature are the ex libris by Robert Haas, also a student of Larisch. The co-founder of the graphic studio Officina Vindobonensis, which was dedicated to high-end letter-press printing using a hand-operated press, enriched the collection in 1930 with over 40 examples predominantly created by wood engraving (ill. 364).[5] Further donations came from Ludwig Heinrich Jungnickel (1926), who also pursued his penchant for animal motifs in his ex libris; from the Czech artist Robert Herrmann (1935), whose precise and well-composed text-based ex libris are exceptional; from Max Oppenheimer (1936), whose "close-ups" also function on a small scale; and the entirely unknown Hans Felix Kraus (1937), who produced ambiguous commissions for the druggist and collector Marco Birnholz. It was only much later that an entire bundle of ex libris designs by the aforementioned Rudolf Geyer were presented to the library by his son (ill. 365), thanks to whom the collection could be resumed after having met an abrupt end with the forced retirement of Hans Ankwicz-Kleehoven in 1939.

[1] Ankwicz-Kleehoven, Hans, "Wiener Humanisten-Exlibris," in: Österreichische Exlibris-Gesellschaft (ed.), *XVII. Jahrbuch 1919*, Vienna 1919, 11–56; Id. "Von alter Exlibriskunst," offprint, ca. 1938, 110–117.

[2] Cf. Karolyi, Claudia/Mayerhofer, Alexandra, "Das Glück des Sammelns. Die Exlibris-Sammlung Ankwicz-Kleehoven in der ÖNB," in: *biblos* (46) 1 1997, 93.

[3] Ankwicz-Kleehoven, Hans, "Von jüngster österreichischer Exlibriskunst," in: *Österreichisches Jahrbuch für Exlibris und Gebrauchsgraphik* (21) 1924/25 (published 1926), 19. Translated by Maria Slater.

[4] Ibid., 20.

[5] In 1983 the library dedicated a solo show to Haas for his 85th birthday; he emigrated to the U.S.A. in 1938 and would later gain success mostly for his work as a photographer. Cf. Egger, Hanna (ed.), *Robert Haas. Schrift, Druck, Photographie*, Schriften der Bibliothek des Österreichischen Museums für angewandte Kunst 25, exh.cat., Vienna 1983.

354
Oskar Laske
Entwurf eines Exlibris
für Herbert Zucker
Wien, 1928
Federzeichnung, aquarelliert
Design for an Ex Libris
for Herbert Zucker
Vienna, 1928
Pen and ink drawing, watercolored
145 x 107 mm
KI 9045-3, Schenkung donation
from Oskar Laske 1932

355
Ludwig Heinrich Jungnickel
Exlibris Theodor Alexander
Wien, 1925
Holzstich
Ex Libris Theodor Alexander
Vienna, 1925
Wood engraving
155 x 78 mm
KI 8453-7, Schenkung donation
from L. H. Jungnickel 1926

356
Rose Reinhold
Exlibris Marco Birnholz
Wien, um 1930
Holzschnitt, koloriert
Ex Libris Marco Birnholz
Vienna, ca. 1930
Woodcut, colored
130 x 93 mm
KI 9060-5, Schenkung donation
from Rose Reinhold 1933

357
Richard Teschner
Exlibris Dr. Theodor Alexander
Wien, 1925
Handtonätzung
Ex Libris Dr. Theodor Alexander
Vienna, 1925
Tonal etching
111 x 93 mm
KI 8954-14, Schenkung donation
from Richard Teschner 1931

358
Franz Taussig
Exlibris Gustinus Ambrosi
Wien, um 1933
Radierung
Ex Libris Gustinus Ambrosi
Vienna, ca. 1933
Etching
83 x 54 mm
KI 9135-5, Schenkung donation
from Franz Taussig 1934

359
Hans Felix Kraus
Exlibris Marco Birnholz
Wien, um 1936
Holzstich
Ex Libris Marco Birnholz
Vienna, ca. 1936
Wood engraving
83 x 65 mm
KI 9452-6, Schenkung donation
from Hans Felix Kraus 1937

360
Rudolf Köhl
Exlibris Leopold Grünfeld
Wien, 1926
Weißlinienholzschnitt
Ex Libris Leopold Grünfeld
Vienna, 1926
White-line woodcut
92 x 73 mm
KI 8991-6, Schenkung donation
from Rudolf Köhl 1932

361
Otto Hurm
Exlibris Madelon de Latour
Wien, 1932
Holzstich
Ex Libris Madelon de Latour
Vienna, 1932
Wood engraving
66 x 50 mm
KI 9017-1, Schenkung donation
from Otto Hurm 1932/33

362
Otto Feil
Exlibris *Bühne der Jungen*
Wien, 1926
Linolschnitt
Ex Libris [The youth stage]
Vienna, 1926
Linocut
79 x 57 mm
KI 8906-13, Schenkung donation
from Otto Feil 1931

363
Max Oppenheimer
Exlibris W. Escher
Zürich, 1919
Radierung
Ex Libris W. Escher
Zurich, 1919
Etching
78 x 53 mm
KI 9313-3, Schenkung donation
from Max Oppenheimer 1936

364
Robert Haas
Exlibris A H
Wien, um 1925
Holzstich
Ex Libris A H
Vienna, ca. 1925
Wood engraving
31 x 31 mm
KI 8880-16, Schenkung der
donation from the Officina
Vindobonensis 1930

366
Robert Herrmann
Exlibris Josef Hanuš
Prag, 1931
Klischee
Ex Libris Josef Hanuš
Prague, 1931
Cliché
111 x 61 mm
KI 9245-8, Schenkung donation
from Robert Herrmann 1935

365
Rudolf Geyer
Entwürfe für Exlibris
Wien, 1910–1920
Bleistift, Tusche, Deckweiß
Designs for Ex Libris
Vienna, 1910–1920
Pencil, ink, opaque white
295 x 215 mm
KI 16845-55, Schenkung donation
from Georg Geyer 2005

WAS BLEIBT? Ist es bloß der Zufall, der entscheidet, welche (Druck-)Sachen eine Zeit lang fortleben und welchen vergehen? Seit Beginn meiner Tätigkeit als Büchermacher ist die Vergänglichkeit eines meiner künstlerischen Themen. Momente, Augenblicke, Fundstücke, Nebensachen, Kleinigkeiten, Splitter, Zitate, Notizen sind die idealen Partner bei der Entstehung meiner Bücher und Editionen. Daher war die Anfrage für diesen Text ein willkommener Anlass, einmal über den Prozess genauer nachzudenken, der abläuft, wenn eine Nebensächlichkeit beginnt, mich zu einem neuen (Buch-)Werk anzutreiben.

Wann habe ich verstanden, dass alles vergeht? Warum erschaffe ich trotzdem Drucksachen? Es ist der Wunsch, aus Flüchtigem Bleibendes zu formen, und der Traum – wie im Märchen – aus Stroh Gold zu machen. So taste ich mich vor und sammle und suche auf Flohmärkten, in Bibliotheken, in Geschäften, auf der Straße, im Müll nach Themen, die zu Büchern werden könnten.
Bei Wikipedia findet sich folgende Definition: „Ephemera stammt aus dem Griechischen und setzt sich aus zwei Bestandteilen zusammen, die gemeinsam ausdrücken, dass etwas nicht länger als einen Tag Bestand hat. Gemeint sind Dinge, die für einen einmaligen bzw. kurzen Gebrauch bestimmt sind. Im engeren Sinne sind damit nur Papierprodukte gemeint."

Nicht länger als einen Tag? Nun sind aber oft die Alltagsdinge viel bezeichnender für unser Leben als die Kunstprodukte. Der Moment der Umwandlung interessiert mich: Wann ist etwas noch „alltäglich", ab wann ist es „Kunstwerk"? Natürlich wissen wir alle seit Marcel Duchamp, dass der Wille (die Geste) des Künstlers dafür ausreicht. Aber so einfach ist es dann eben doch nicht, es gibt Grauzonen und subtile Abstufungen zwischen Kunst und Alltag. Ich möchte den Alltag zur Kunst machen und mit dem Flüchtigen Dauerhaftes erschaffen. Manchmal gleichen die Editionen Zeitkapseln, ich hoffe, durch meine Kunst(buch)werke in Kontakt zu treten mit den Zukünftigen, und glaube, dass dies möglichst unverstellt und durch die simplen Dinge geschehen muss.

Viele dieser „Dinge" hatten ein Leben, bevor sie von mir für ein Buchkunstwerk weiterverarbeitet wurden. Es gab ein Leben vor der Kunst. Und dieses Leben, diese Aura gilt es zu verstehen und nutzbar zu machen bei der Umwidmung zum Kunstwerk. Im besten Falle bleiben diese Objekte, was sie sind, und erwerben in Verbindung mit dem Text bzw. Kontext eine neue Bedeutung.
„Ich suche, also bin ich" ist das Motto dieses Arbeitsprozesses und von diesem Fundament aus versuche ich – frei nach Descartes – meine Erkenntnisfähigkeit weiter aufzubauen und zu erweitern. Hier ein kleiner Einblick (in alphabetischer Reihenfolge) in die verwendeten Ephemera und Alltagsobjekte, die in die Bücher von Bartleby & Co. im Wortsinne „eingebunden" sind:

ANZEIGEN	GLASPERLEN	LATEXHANDSCHUHE	REAGENZGLÄSER	TAGESGEDICHTE
ARAUKARIEN-SAMEN	GLÜCKSKEKSSPRÜCHE	LAVABROCKEN	REISEFÜHRER	TOPFLAPPEN
BUCHSEITEN	GÜRTEL	LEBENSMITTELPAPIERE	ROSENBLÄTTER	T-SHIRTS
BÜCHER	HAARNETZE	MILITÄRNAHRUNG	SAFRAN	U-BAHN-PLÄNE
CELLOPHAN	HANDTÜCHER	NOTIZZETTEL	SARDINENBÜCHSEN	VAPORETTO-PLÄNE
DRUCKE	HAUSSTAUB	PACKPAPIER	SCHOKOLADENPAPIER	VERMISSTENANZEIGEN
ECHTHAAR	HENNA	PLASTIKPALMEN	SPORTHOSEN	VERPACKUNGSMÜLL
EINWEGBESTECK	HOLZLÖFFEL	PLASTIKROSEN	STAUBTÜCHER	VOGELFUTTER
ESSPAPIER	HÜHNERKNOCHEN	PLASTIKTÜTEN	STICKEREIEN	WASCHLAPPEN
FOTOGRAFIEN	KOCHREZEPTE	POLAROIDS	SUPERMARKTKATALOGE	ZUCKERTÜTEN
GESCHENKPAPIER	KUNSTHARZ	POSTKARTEN	STEREOSKOP-BRILLE	
GESCHIRRTÜCHER	KUNSTRASEN	PUTZSCHWÄMME	STEREOSKOP-FOTOGRAFIEN	

Thorsten Baensch, Künstler und Verleger, Bartleby & Co., Brüssel

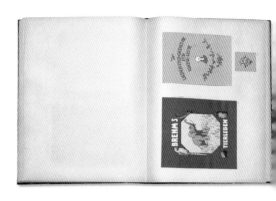

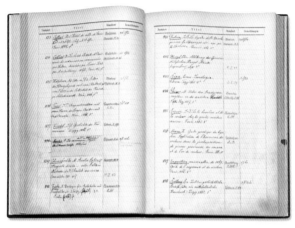

WHAT LASTS? Is it merely happenstance that decides which (printed) matter will survive for a while and which will perish? Since starting my career as a maker of books, ephemerality has been one of my artistic themes. Moments, instants, finds, irrelevancies, trivialities, fragments, quotations, and notes are all ideal assistants when making my books and editions. Which is why the request to write this text was a welcome incentive to reflect more closely on the process, which occurs when a negligible item begins to motivate me to create a new work (or book).

When did I realize that everything is ephemeral? Why do I create printed matter in spite of that fact? It is my desire to make something permanent from something fleeting, and my dream—as in the fairy tale—of transforming straw into gold. So I wander around flea markets, in libraries, in shops, on the street, rummage through the trash, collecting and searching for ideas, which could become books. Wikipedia gives the following definition: "Ephemera are any transitory written or printed matter not meant to be retained or preserved. The word derives from the Greek *ephemeros*, meaning 'lasting only one day, short-lived.'"

Only one day? Yet everyday items are often much more representative of our lives than artistic creations. That moment of metamorphosis fascinates me: When is something still considered "everyday"? At what point does it become a "work of art"? Of course, Marcel Duchamp made it clear that the will—or spirit—of the artist alone is sufficient to trigger this transformation. But in practice it is not that easy; there are gray areas and subtle nuances between art and the everyday. I want to make the everyday into art and create permanent objects from fleeting things. Sometimes my editions are akin to time capsules; I hope to reach the future through my works of (book) art, and I believe that the only way to do so is as genuinely as possible and by using simple things.

Many of these "things" had a life before I used them for a work of book art. There was a life before art. And this life, this aura, must be understood and made useful by repurposing the "thing" into a work of art. At best, these objects both remain what they are and acquire a new significance in connection with the text or context.
"I search, therefore I am," could be the motto of this work process, and it is from this foundation—loosely based on Descartes—that I try to improve and expand my cognitive faculty. Here is a short insight (in alphabetic order) into the ephemera and everyday objects used in and literally "bound" into the books of Bartleby & Co.:

3D GLASSES	DISHTOWELS	LATEX GLOVES	POSTCARDS	SUBWAY MAPS
3D PHOTOS	DISPOSABLE CUTLERY	LAVA	POST-IT NOTES	SUPERMARKET CATALOGS
ARTIFICIAL FLOWERS	DUST	MILITARY RATIONS	POT HOLDERS	SWEATPANTS
ARTIFICIAL GRASS	DUSTCLOTHS	MISSING PET POSTERS	PRINTS	TEST TUBES
BAGS	EMBROIDERIES	MONKEY PUZZLE SEEDS	RECIPES	TOWELS
BELTS	FOOD PACKAGING	NEWSPAPER ADS	RESIN	T-SHIRTS
BIRDSEED	FORTUNE COOKIE QUOTES	PACKING PAPER	RICE PAPER	VAPORETTO MAPS
BOOKS	GLASS BEADS	PAGES	ROSE PETALS	WASHCLOTHS
CANDY CONES	GUIDEBOOKS	PHOTOS	SAFFRON	WOODEN SPOONS
CHICKEN BONES	HAIRNETS	PLASTIC PALM TREES	SARDINE CANS	WRAPPING PAPER
CHOCOLATE WRAPPERS	HENNA	POEMS	SHRINK WRAP	
DISCARDED PACKAGING	HUMAN HAIR	POLAROIDS	SPONGES	

Thorsten Baensch, artist and publisher, Bartleby & Co., Brussels

DEN BÜCHERN EIN KLEID
ANITA KÜHNEL

„Der Anblick des Schaufensters einer Buchhandlung erweckt in Menschen, die als erwachsen gelten, dieselben drängenden Gefühle des Verlangens, dieselben Tantalusqualen, wie sie Kinder vor Spielzeug- oder Schokoladenläden erfaßt! Alles möchte man haben, jedenfalls fast alles! Und es ist unendlich schwer, sich überhaupt wieder von einem Schaufenster loszureißen, hinter dem solche Herrlichkeiten locken. Schuld daran sind die Verleger und ihre Grafiker, die vermittels eines teuflischen Köders, nämlich des Buchumschlages, den ‚Buchanfälligen' magisch in ihren Bann ziehen und ihn zu Käufen verlocken, die seinem Etat gefährlich werden."[1]

Besser kann man die beabsichtigte Wirkung von Buchumschlägen kaum beschreiben. Die zum Schutze des Buches erfundene Umhüllung war zunächst schmuckloses Papier, das Staub und andere äußere Schäden vom Buch abhalten sollte. Das früheste bekannte Beispiel eines Schutzumschlages, der Autor, Titel und Verlag nennt, wurde 1833 in England verwendet.[2] „Das übliche Kleid französischer Literatur"[3] war zunächst ein grellgelber Papierumschlag mit fettschwarzen Lettern, die Autor und Titel preisgaben. Bedruckt und bebildert hat der Umschlag bis in die Gegenwart den Zweck, wie jede Verpackung das praktisch Nützliche mit der Werbung zu verbinden. Wenngleich bis in die 1980er Jahre auch Plakatwerbung für Verlage und ihre neu publizierten Bücher oder Buchreihen durchaus üblich war, fand und findet die Konkurrenz gewissermaßen im Saale statt, nämlich in den Buchhandlungen selbst. Im Überangebot an Publikationen muss sich das einzelne Buch auf dem Ladentisch selbst behaupten und potenzielle Käufer ganz direkt zum Zugreifen und Blättern verleiten. Die Konzepte hierzu sind höchst unterschiedlich. Wie im Plakat reichen die Gestaltungen von schlichter, erlesener Typografie (insbesondere dann, wenn Autorennamen schon Werbung genug sind) über pointierte Bilder bis zu geschwätzigen Illustrationen. Frisch vergebene Buchpreise werden auf dem Cover kenntlich gemacht, verfilmte Literatur wird oft in Neuauflage postwendend mit dem Konterfei von Hauptdarstellern oder Szenen des Films umhüllt oder gleich als „Buch zum Film" angepriesen. Verlagsgesichter, die besonders von Schriftenreihen geprägt waren und sind, ändern sich. In den besten Fällen ließen und lassen Einband und Umschlag den Rückschluss auf eine ästhetische wie geistige Ausrichtung des verlegerischen Programms zu.

Nicht nur in privaten Haushalten verschwinden die papiernen Kleider der Bücher, wenn sie lästig, kaputt oder unansehnlich geworden sind, auch Bibliotheken werfen die losen, verführerischen Hüllen weg. Das Signaturschild – so will es die Ordnung – muss mit dem Buch direkt verbunden sein, nicht mit seiner losen Hülle. Künstlerisch wertvolle Einbände erhalten oftmals neue Schutzhüllen oder zusätzliche Bibliothekseinbände. Sie gehen so zwar nicht verloren, wie es oft das Schicksal der Buchumschläge ist, aber sie wurden oft in die Unsichtbarkeit verdammt, fristen wie abgelegte Kleider ihr Dasein im Verborgenen. Ganz ähnlich verfahren Bibliotheken selbst mit relativ stabilen Broschureinbänden. Abgesehen von privaten Sammlern richteten Kunstgewerbemuseen und gebrauchsgrafische Sammlungen ihre Aufmerksamkeit in dem Moment auf Einbände und Umschläge, als Künstler Ende des 19. Jahrhunderts begannen, das Buch wieder als Gestaltungsaufgabe zu betrachten. Für die meist systematisch angelegten Vorbildersammlungen wurden die Einbände und Umschläge vom Originalbuch abgenommen. Häufiger aber kamen sie direkt von

1 Kuh, Hans, „Die Magie des Schutzumschlages. Zu den Arbeiten von Hannes Jähn", in: *Gebrauchsgraphik* (33) 12 1962, 2–9.

2 Vgl. Weidemann, Kurt, *Buchumschläge & Schallplattenhüllen*, Stuttgart 1969, V.

3 Ehmcke, Fritz Helmuth, *Broschur und Schutzumschlag am deutschen Buch der neueren Zeit*, Kleiner Druck der Gutenberg-Gesellschaft Bd. 47, Mainz 1951, 2.

DRESSING UP BOOKS
ANITA KÜHNEL

"The sight of a bookshop window kindles the same urgent feelings of longing, the same torments of Tantalus, in people who are considered adults as those which seize children in front of toy and chocolate shops! We want everything, or at least almost everything! And it is incredibly difficult to tear ourselves away from that shop window, behind which such marvelous things beckon. The publishers and their graphic designers are to blame, who use a diabolical bait—namely the dust jacket—to cast a magic spell over the 'book-prone' and tempt them to make purchases, which are most dangerous when they find themselves in that state."[1]

It is hardly possible to better describe the intended effect of dust jackets. Originally undecorated paper, this covering was invented to protect books from dust and other external damage. The earliest known example of a protective cover naming the author, title, and publishing house was used in England in 1833.[2] "The customary clothing for French literature"[3] was initially a bright yellow paper jacket with bold black letters, which disclosed the author and title. When printed and illustrated, however, the purpose of the dust jacket has always been to connect the practical and useful with advertising—as is the case with any packaging. Even though poster advertising was entirely common for both publishing houses themselves and their latest releases—whether individual volumes or entire series of books—into the 1980s, the competition takes and took place to a certain extent indoors, i.e. in the bookstores themselves. Amid the overabundance of publications, the individual book on the shop table must assert itself and directly induce potential buyers to pick it up and flick through its pages. The approaches are highly varied. As with posters, the designs range from simple, exquisite typography (especially when an author's name is advertising enough) to pointed images and loquacious illustrations. Recently awarded book prizes are announced on the cover; filmed literature is often immediately rereleased in a new design, now encased in portraits of the main actors or scenes from the movie—or instantly touted as "Now a major motion picture." The way in which publishing houses, which can and could particularly be characterized as publishers of series, present themselves is subject to change. In the best cases the book covers and dust jackets infer and inferred that the publisher's agenda has an aesthetic and intellectual focus.

It is not only in private households that books' paper clothes disappear when they have become inconvenient, broken, or unattractive; libraries, too, throw away these loose, alluring covers. Orderliness declares that the library label be attached to the book directly, not to its loose cover. Artistically valuable book covers are often supplied with new protective jackets or additional library bindings. In that way they are not lost—as is often the fate of dust jackets—but they are often condemned to invisibility, carving out an existence in hiding, like discarded garments. Libraries behave very similarly with even relatively stable paperback covers. Aside from private collectors, museums of arts and crafts and collections of ephemera concentrated their attention on book covers and dust jackets at the time at the end of the 19th century when artists once again began to regard the book as a design challenge. For the mostly systematically arranged exemplary collections, the book covers and dust jackets were removed from the original books. More frequently, however, they entered the collections as evidence provided directly by the bookbinding

1 Kuh, Hans, "Die Magie des Schutz-umschlages. Zu den Arbeiten von Hannes Jähn," in: *Gebrauchsgraphik* (33) 12 1962, 2–9. Translated by Maria Slater.

2 Cf. Weidemann, Kurt, *Buchumschläge & Schallplattenhüllen*, Stuttgart 1969, V.

3 Ehmcke, Fritz Helmuth, *Broschur und Schutzumschlag am deutschen Buch der neueren Zeit*, Kleiner Druck der Gutenberg-Gesellschaft vol. 47, Mainz 1951, 2. Translated by Maria Slater.

den Buchbindeanstalten, Verlagen, Künstlern oder Druckereien als Belege in die Sammlungen oder gelangten aus Privatsammlungen in die Museen.

Neben den Büchern, die beispielhafte Gesamtgestaltung aufweisen, wurden Beispiele von Typografie, Illustrationen, Buchtiteln, Vorsatz, Einband und Umschlag als Einzelblätter gesammelt. Diese Art zu sammeln, hat manche Umschläge zwar vor dem Verschwinden gerettet, sie aber auch aus ihrem ursprünglichen Zusammenhang gerissen. Heute wissen wir oft nicht, ob es sich um Musterblätter handelt, die nie Verwendung fanden, ob es Andrucke oder abgenommene „Endprodukte" etc. sind. In den meisten Fällen wurden Buchumschläge und auch Einbände beschnitten, und so ist nicht immer leicht zu erkennen, ob es sich um einen richtigen Umschlag, den Titel einer Broschur oder eines Einbandes handelt. Nur selten lässt sich feststellen, ob die Rückseite auch gestaltet wurde und wie, ob es einen Klappentext gab oder nicht. Da dieselben Titel mehrfach im selben Verlag herausgegeben wurden, ist die Zuordnung der Umschläge oder Einbände zu einer konkreten Ausgabe oftmals sehr mühsam.

Zunächst war das Sammelinteresse bei den meisten Museen auf England, Frankreich und Belgien gerichtet, bis sich allmählich auch Deutschland und Österreich mit anspruchsvollen Buchproduktionen zu Wort meldeten. Während sich in Österreich aufgrund einer restriktiven Zensur und ungünstiger Urheberrechtsvorschriften das Verlagswesen vor 1918 vergleichsweise schwer entwickelte, war es in Deutschland bereits um 1900 ein geradezu prosperierender Wirtschaftszweig, der auch vielen zeitgenössischen österreichischen Autoren willkommene Publikationsmöglichkeiten bot.[4]

ENTSTEHUNG DES DEMOKRATISCHEN BUCHES

Mit der Anhebung des allgemeinen Bildungsstandes im 19. Jahrhundert war ein enorm gewachsenes Interesse am Buch schlechthin verbunden, was den Büchermarkt erheblich veränderte. Die gängige Praxis, sich die in losen, gefalteten Bögen erhältlichen Bücher privat binden zu lassen, wurde in wachsendem Maße vom Angebot fertig gebundener Bücher verdrängt. Die Entwicklung der maschinellen Buchbindungen und serienmäßigen Herstellung von Einbanddecken eröffnete Verlagen die Möglichkeit, eine größere Anzahl einheitlich gebundener Bücher anzubieten. Der sogenannte Verlegereinband im Gegensatz zum individuell angefertigten Einband war geboren und damit eine Käuferschicht gewonnen, die sich privat in Auftrag gegebene Einbände in Leder, Marmorpapier oder Pergament nicht leisten konnte. Es kamen Bücher auf den Markt, deren Ausstattung zwar komplett, aber zunächst allzu oft eher ökonomischen Zwängen geschuldet war: eng gedruckt, oft schwer lesbar, innen schmucklos mit zunächst schlichten Einbänden. Doch je größer das Angebot wurde, desto mehr sollten sich auch die preiswerten Bücher hervorheben und voneinander unterscheiden, dies umso markanter, je mehr sich auch die Verkaufsformen änderten.

Zur gediegenen Buch- und Kunsthandlung kamen in der zweiten Hälfte des 19. Jahrhunderts, insbesondere seit den 1870er Jahren, vermehrt die Kioske an Haltestellen und Bahnhöfen hinzu, die allerorten mit dem Anstieg des Eisenbahn- und öffentlichen Nahverkehrs entstanden waren. Sie boten nicht nur Zeitungen, Tabak und Ähnliches an, sondern auch Literatur, die den Reisenden die Zeit verkürzen sollte. 1867 startete der Reclam Verlag mit seinen auflagenstarken Produktionen. Die Bücher hatten keinen Umschlag, sondern einen wiedererkennbaren Broschureinband aus dünnem Papier, der später durch einen Kartoneinband und wechselnde unverkennbare Erscheinungsbilder ersetzt wurde.

4   Arthur Schnitzler, Hugo von Hofmannsthal, Adalbert Stifter, Peter Rosegger u. a. publizierten zunächst vorwiegend in deutschen Verlagen.

companies, publishing houses, artists, or printers or came to the museums via private collections. In addition to those books which bear exemplary overall designs, examples of typography, illustrations, book titles, endpapers, covers, and dust jackets were collected as individual sheets. Although collecting in this way did save some dust jackets from being lost, it did tear them from their original context. Today we often do not know whether works are sample sheets and were never used, whether they are hard proofs, or whether they were the final design detached from the end product. In most cases dust jackets as well as book covers were trimmed, meaning that it is not always easy to establish whether an item is a true dust jacket, or instead the title of a paperback or a book cover. It is only rarely possible to determine whether and how the back panel was designed, and whether or not there was a blurb. As the same titles were often released several times by the same publisher, identifying which dust jackets or book covers belong to a specific edition is often very challenging.

Initially, the interest of most museums' collections was aimed at England, France, and Belgium—until Germany and Austria also gradually started to try their hand at sophisticated book production. While the development of publishing was comparably difficult in Austria before 1918 due to restrictive censorship and unfavorable copyright provisions, in Germany it was a positively prosperous branch of the economy by the turn of the century, and this in turn offered many contemporary Austrian authors welcome publication opportunities.[4]

4   Arthur Schnitzler, Hugo von Hofmannsthal, Adalbert Stifter, Peter Rosegger, and others were predominantly first published by German publishing houses.

THE MAKING OF A DEMOCRATIC BOOK

Raising the general level of education in the 19th century was clearly linked to a vastly growing interest in books—a development which significantly changed the book market. The established practice of having the available books—with loose, folded sheets—bound privately was increasingly superseded by the offer of pre-bound books. The development of mechanical bookbinding and serial production of hardcovers presented publishers with the opportunity of offering a larger number of uniformly bound books. The so-called publisher's binding was born to contrast with the individually produced book cover and hence targeted a class of customers who could not afford to privately commission bindings in leather, marbled paper, or parchment. Books went on sale whose design was admittedly complete, but which was at first far too often subject to economic constraints: closely printed, often barely legible, entirely unembellished inside, and with predominantly simple covers. Yet the larger the range sold, the more the inexpensive books needed to stand out and differentiate from one another—all the more markedly the more that sales methods changed.

In the second half of the 19th century, especially from the 1870s, the trustworthy art dealer's and bookstores were no longer the only places where reading material could be bought: increasingly, there were also kiosks at train stations and at bus and tram stops, which had emerged everywhere with the ascent of railroad traffic and local mass transit. They not only offered newspapers, tobacco, etc., but also literature, which was intended to help travelers pass the time. In 1867 the Reclam publishing house started its high-circulation productions. Its books had no dust jackets, but rather a recognizable softcover made of thin paper, which would later be replaced with a cardboard cover and varied yet always distinctive appearances.

In 1897 Albert Langen released his *Kleine Bibliothek Langen*, which was especially tailored to the train station book trade (ill. 367), and in 1932 the Albatross Verlag in Hamburg started to issue

1897 brachte Albert Langen seine *Kleine Bibliothek Langen* heraus, die speziell auf den Bahnhofs-
buchhandel zugeschnitten war (Abb. 367). 1932 begann der Albatross Verlag in Hamburg, Taschenbücher herauszugeben. Nach seinem Vorbild erschienen ab 1935 in London die Penguin Books,
die als erste moderne Taschenbuchreihe gelten. Besonders in der 2. Hälfte des 20. Jahrhunderts
trat das Taschenbuch seinen großen Siegeszug an. Man denke etwa an die rororo-Taschenbücher
des Rowohlt Verlages (seit 1950), die Fischer-Taschenbücher (seit 1952), an die dtv-Bücher (seit
1961), die Suhrkamp-Taschenbücher (seit 1959) und die edition suhrkamp, die seit 1963 in den
regenbogenfarbenen Umschlägen erscheint. Sie alle zeichnen sich durch ihren wiedererkennbaren
Reihencharakter aus, der durch Standardlayouts und einzelne künstlerische Handschriften geprägt
ist.[5] Die modernen Taschenbücher haben in der Regel einfache Klebebindungen und einen Kartoneinband, der bisweilen cellophaniert wurde. Eine der bekanntesten Ausnahmen bildet die *Insel-
Bücherei*, die seit 1912 in gebundener Form und mit festem Einband (nur in Kriegs- und Notzeiten
als Broschur) erscheint und deren Markenzeichen wechselnde Buntpapierbezüge und das Etikett
mit dem Titel sind. Zwischen festem und Broschureinband gibt es schließlich die sogenannte
französische und englische Broschur. Bei letzterer verschmilzt der am Rücken festgeklebte Schutzumschlag mit dem Einband, um den herum er, mit Klappe versehen, gelegt wird, während im
französischen Broschureinband der Kartoneinband eine Klappe hat, Umschlag und Einband quasi
eins geworden sind.

Auf dem Weg zum preiswerten Massenbuch hatte sich das Gesicht des Verlagseinbandes innerhalb
nur weniger Jahre grundlegend geändert. Ab den 1860er Jahren erschienen aufwendig gestaltete
Verlegereinbände. In Anlehnung an historische Stile, insbesondere die Renaissance, wurden Prachteinbände mit aufwendigen Prägedrucken gefertigt, die den Anschein des Kostbaren vermitteln
sollten und mit den individuell gefertigten sogenannten Kathedraleinbänden aus der 1. Hälfte des
19. Jahrhunderts wetteiferten. „Die sogenannten Prachtbände paradierten in trüben grauen
Mustern, in denen schmutziges Braun und Gelb den Hauptanteil hatten."[6] Je mehr das Buch als
für jedermann erschwingliche Massendrucksache von unterschiedlichen, einander konkurrierenden
Verlagen angeboten wurde, desto stärker wuchs das „Bedürfnis nach einer auch äußerlich anspre-
chenden Einkleidung des Buches"[7] von großer Werbewirksamkeit. Nach 1890 setzte sich in
Abkehr vom Historismus der neue Formwille, wie er sich im Art nouveau, Jugendstil oder Modern
Style artikulierte, gerade auch in der Buchgestaltung durch. Über die Vorbildfunktion englischer
Buchkunst wurde bereits viel publiziert. Angeregt durch William Morris, Charles Robert Ashbee
und Thomas Cobden-Sanderson erlebte in England die bibliophil ausgerichtete Buchausstattung
einen großen Aufschwung, was sich auch auf die Gestaltung des Verlegereinbandes auswirkte.
Verlage wie George Bell & Sons, Macmillan & Co. oder John Lane beauftragten u.a. Grandville Fell,
Laurence Housman, Albert Angus Turbayne und Talwin Morris mit der Gestaltung von Einbänden
und Umschlägen (Abb. 368). Künstlerischer Leiter von George Bell & Sons war Gleeson White,
selbst Entwerfer zahlreicher Bucheinbände und -umschläge und 1893 Begründer der legendären
Zeitschrift *The Studio*, die über Nacht international beachtetes Sprachrohr der neuen künstlerischen
Bewegungen wurde.

Nach den Vorbildern mustergültiger Buchproduktionen in England und hervorragender Beispiele,
die von Pariser und belgischen Verlegern auf den Markt kamen,[8] begannen zunehmend auch
deutsche Verlage über künstlerische Gesamtausstattungen von Büchern neu nachzudenken

[5] Als Beispiele seien hier Willy Fleckhaus für
Suhrkamp, Celestino Piatti für dtv, Lothar
Reher für *Spektrum von Volk und Welt* und
Christian Chruxin für *das neue buch* von
Rowohlt genannt.

[6] Lux, Josef August, „Vorwort", in:
Die Fläche (1) 1902, 1.

[7] Schölermann, Wilhelm, „Deutscher
Buchschmuck. Eine zeitgemäße
Betrachtung", in: *Archiv für Buchgewerbe*
(37) 2 1900, 333.

[8] Erinnert sei an Bücher mit Ausstattungen
von Félix Vallotton, Georges Lemmen,
Théo van Rysselberghe, George Auriol,
Eugène Grasset, Charles Doudelet oder
Henry van de Velde.

367
Eduard Thöny
Umschlag für *Der Regenschirm*
von Guy de Maupassant
München, 1898
Verlag: Albert Langen
Klichee
Dust Jacket for [*The Umbrella*]
by Guy de Maupassant
Munich, 1898
Publisher: Albert Langen
Cliché
150 x 122 mm
KI 7914-421, Schenkung donation from
Franz Malota 1914

368
Laurence Housman
Einband für *Goblin Market*
von Christina Georgina Rossetti
London, 1893
Verlag: Macmillan & Co.
Gewebe, appretiert; Goldprägung
Book Cover for *Goblin Market*
by Christina Georgina Rossetti
London, 1893
Publisher: Macmillan & Co.
Textile, dressed; gold embossing
180 x 100 mm
BI 11642, Ankauf purchased from
Ernst Arnold 1896

369
Hans Nikolaj Hansen/Anker Kyster
Einband für *Aladdin eller den*
forunderlige Lampe* [*Aladin und
***die Wunderlampe*]**
Kopenhagen, 1893
Verlag: P. G. Philipsens Forlag
Lederauflage, Goldprägung
Book Cover for *Aladdin eller den*
forunderlige Lampe* [*Aladdin or
***The Wonderful Lamp*]**
Copenhagen, 1893
Publisher: P. G. Philipsens Forlag
Leather covering, gold embossing
310 x 235 mm
BI 25429, Sammlung Dr. Martin
collection 1950/51

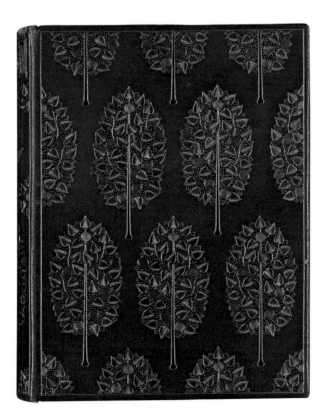

und die hervorragenden Leistungen von Schriftgestaltern, Illustratoren, Setzern, Buchbindern zusammenzuführen. So setzten der Insel-Verlag, Eugen Diederichs oder Julius Bard zunächst neue Qualitätsmaßstäbe. Sie suchten zwischen bibliophilem Anspruch und Massenbuch Mittelwege zu finden, indem sie neben den sogenannten Normalausgaben Vorzugsausgaben auf den Markt brachten. Das Buchbinderhandwerk und die damit verbundenen künstlerischen Ambitionen bei der Einbandgestaltung hatten neuen Auftrieb. Neu entstandene und bereits bestehende Großbuchbindereien begannen, handwerkliches Können, Material und Druckkunst den neuen Gestaltungsanforderungen anzupassen. Dazu gehörten u. a. in Berlin Lüderitz & Bauer, in Leipzig vor allem die Firma H. Sperling, Gustav Fritzsche und Hübel & Denck, der für Eugen Diederichs arbeitete. Kleinere Kunstanstalten und Buchbindermeister wie Paul Kersten aus Berlin oder Anker Kyster in Dänemark (Abb. 369) machten mit edlen Einbandentwürfen und farbigen Einband- wie Vorsatzpapieren von sich reden und begannen schließlich, im Auftrag von Großbetrieben zu arbeiten.

Entwürfe und die Produktion von Buntpapieren wurden auch ein Feld der Künstler, deren Impulse vom Anspruch einer künstlerischen Erneuerung aller Lebensbereiche bestimmt waren. So entfalteten beispielsweise Otto Eckmann oder Lilli Behrens, vor allem aber die Künstler der Wiener Werkstätte Josef Hoffmann, Koloman Moser oder Leopold Stolba eine reiche Buntpapierproduktion, in der das Marmorpapier zu neuen Ehren kam. Die vielerorts erscheinenden neuen Vorlagenwerke für das moderne Kunstgewerbe lieferten neben neuen Ornamententwürfen Beispiele für Vorsatz-, Titel- und Umschlaggestaltungen. Julius Klinger veröffentlichte 1901 und 1902 in seinen Büchern *Das Weib im modernen Ornament* oder *Skizzen für Lithographen und Zeichner* seine Vorschläge zu moderner Dekoration. Künstler der Wiener Secession, Koloman Moser, Alfred Roller, Josef Hoffmann, gaben ab 1902 *Die Fläche* heraus, die im Untertitel ausdrücklich auf *Entwürfe für decorative Malerei, Placate, Buch und Druck* verwies, und propagierten anhand von Beispielen die Ästhetik des neuen Stils, der sich programmatisch zu Linie und Fläche bekannte. Die als Gesamtkunstwerk gestalteten, zwölf Mal erschienenen Hefte hatten selbst Vorbildfunktion, ihr bekenntnishafter Anspruch teilt sich bereits in den Einbandgestaltungen mit (Abb. 370).

Im Gebrauchsbuch konnte sich die Idee einer Gesamtgestaltung nicht immer durchsetzen und oft genug blieb der Umschlag die einzige künstlerische „Verschwendung", die sich Verleger leisteten. In dem Maße, wie der Umschlag die werbende Funktion übernahm, trat die Einbandgestaltung zurück. Da, wo das Buch als Einheit aufgefasst ist, gibt es verbindende Gestaltungselemente. Häufig sind im Umschlag die Typografie des Einbandes, Farbformen, Ornamente oder Vignetten aufgegriffen worden. Von außen nach innen gibt es gewissermaßen einen Weg vom Lauten zum Leisen, vom Öffentlichen zum Intimen.

DER KÜNSTLERISCHE BUCHUMSCHLAG

Von Anbeginn gab es zwei Arten des Schutzumschlages: den typografisch gestalteten, oft mit Zierleisten versehenen und den illustrierten. Der illustrierte Umschlag sollte in pointierter Form auf den Inhalt des Buches aufmerksam machen. Die Verpackung sollte Rückschlüsse auf den Inhalt ermöglichen: Spannung, Mysteriöses wie Abgründiges, Dramatisches wie Leidenschaftliches sollten ebenso visualisiert werden wie Humorvolles, Sachliches oder gar Wissenschaftliches. Zur visuellen Einstimmung auf den Inhalt kam bald der Klappentext hinzu, der in knappen Worten Inhalt und manchmal Autor und Verlagsprogramm vorstellt. Häufig findet man auch die sogenannte

5   Examples include Willy Fleckhaus for
    Suhrkamp, Celestino Piatti for dtv, Lothar
    Reher for *Spektrum* by Volk und Welt,
    Christian Chruxin for *das neue buch*
    by Rowohlt.

paperbacks. It was on this model that Penguin Books were published in London from 1935, which
are regarded as the first modern paperback series. It was particularly in the 2nd half of the 20th century that the paperback started its great triumph. Consider, for example, the rororo paperbacks by
Rowohlt (since 1950), the Fischer paperbacks (since 1952), the dtv books (since 1961), the
Suhrkamp paperbacks (since 1959), and the edition suhrkamp, which has been published in
rainbow-colored jackets since 1963. All of these stand out due to their recognizable series character, which is shaped by their standard layouts and individual artistic signatures.[5] Usually, modern
paperbacks have simple perfect bindings and a cardboard cover, which was occasionally cellophane-
wrapped. One of the best-known exceptions is the Insel-Bücherei, which has been bound and had
a hardcover since 1912 (paperback only during times of war and need) and whose trademark is
alternating decorated paper covers and a label bearing the title. Finally, between hard- and
softcovers there are the so-called French flaps and English paperbacks. In the latter the protective
jacket—with flaps—is glued to the spine and merges with the book cover around which it is
wrapped, whereas in the French flaps style the cardboard cover has flaps, meaning that the dust
jacket and cover are combined as one.

On its path to becoming a low-cost mass-market book, the appearance of the publisher's binding
changed dramatically in just a few years. From the 1860s elaborately designed publisher's bindings
were released. Based on historical styles, particularly those of the Renaissance, luxury bindings
were produced with ornate embossing, which were intended to convey the semblance of expense
and emulated the individually made so-called cathedral bindings from the 1st half of the century.

6   Lux, Josef August, "Vorwort," in:
    Die Fläche (1) 1902, 1. Translated by
    Maria Slater.

7   Schölermann, Wilhelm, "Deutscher Buch-
    schmuck. Eine zeitgemäße Betrachtung," in:
    Archiv für Buchgewerbe (37) 2 1900, 333.
    Translated by Maria Slater.

"The so-called treasure bindings flaunted dull gray patterns of which the majority was dirty brown
and yellow."[6] The more books were offered as affordable printed matter for the masses by various
competing publishers, the stronger grew the "need for visually appealing clothing for the books"[7]
as effective advertising. After 1890 the rejection of historicism led to the assertion of a desire for
new forms—especially in book design—as articulated in art nouveau, Jugendstil, and modern style.
Much has already been published on the exemplary function of English book art. Prompted by
William Morris, Charles Robert Ashbee, and Thomas Cobden-Sanderson, bibliophile-oriented book
design flourished in England, and this in turn had an influence on the design of publisher's bindings.
Publishing houses such as George Bell & Sons, Macmillan & Co., and John Lane commissioned
Grandville Fell, Laurence Housman, Albert Angus Turbayne, and Talwin Morris among others to
design book covers and dust jackets (ill. 368). The artistic director of George Bell & Sons was
Gleeson White, himself the designer of numerous book covers and dust jackets, and in 1893 founder
of the legendary magazine *The Studio*, which became the internationally respected mouthpiece of
the new artistic movements overnight.

After the exemplars of model book productions in England and outstanding examples marketed

8   Consider books with designs by Félix
    Vallotton, Georges Lemmen, Théo van
    Rysselberghe, George Auriol, Eugène
    Grasset, Charles Doudelet, or Henry
    van de Velde.

by Parisian and Belgian publishers,[8] the German publishing houses, too, increasingly began to
reconsider artistic overall designs of books and combine the superb achievements of typographers,
illustrators, typesetters, and bookbinders. It was in this way that the Insel-Verlag, Eugen Diederichs,
and Julius Bard, for example, first set new standards of quality. They sought to strike a balance
between bibliophile aspirations and mass-market books by releasing deluxe editions alongside
normal editions. The craft of bookbinding and the associated artistic ambitions when designing
covers gained new momentum. Newly emerging and already existing large bookbinderies started

370
Leopold Forstner
Umschlag für *Die Fläche*, Band 1, Heft 7
Wien, 1903
Verlag: Anton Schroll & Co.
Lithografie
**Dust Jacket for [The surface], Vol. 1,
Issue 7**
Vienna, 1903
Publisher: Anton Schroll & Co.
Lithograph
309 x 205 mm
BI 12983-3, Ankauf purchased from
Anton Schroll & Co. 1903

371
Thomas Theodor Heine
**Umschlag für *Sklaven der Liebe*
von Knut Hamsun**
München, 1902
Verlag: Albert Langen
Klischee
**Dust Jacket for [Slaves of Love]
by Knut Hamsun**
Munich, 1902
Publisher: Albert Langen
Cliché
188 x 126 mm
KI 7914-346, Schenkung donation from
Franz Malota 1914

372
Bertold Löffler
**Umschlag für *Reigen*
von Arthur Schnitzler**
Wien, 1903
Verlag: Wiener Verlag
Klischee
**Dust Jacket for [La Ronde]
by Arthur Schnitzler**
Vienna, 1903
Publisher: Wiener Verlag
Cliché
193 x 139 mm
KI 7914-516, Schenkung donation from
Franz Malota 1914

373
Thomas Theodor Heine
Umschlag für *Die Haare der heiligen Fringilla* von Otto Julius Bierbaum
München, 1906
Verlag: Albert Langen
Klischee
Dust Jacket for [The hair of Saint Fringilla] by Otto Julius Bierbaum
Munich, 1906
Publisher: Albert Langen
Cliché
147 x 117 mm
KI 7914-302, Schenkung donation from Franz Malota 1914

374
Julius Klinger
Umschlag für *Die lustigen Weiber von Berlin* von Felix Meyer
Berlin, um 1900
Verlag: Eysler & Co.
Klischee
Dust Jacket for [The funny women from Berlin] by Felix Meyer
Berlin, ca. 1900
Publisher: Eysler & Co.
Cliché
202 x 145 mm
KI 7914-86, Schenkung donation from Franz Malota 1914

to adapt artisanal skills, materials, and the art of printing to the new design requirements. They included e.g. Lüderitz & Bauer in Berlin, in Leipzig above all the company H. Sperling, Gustav Fritzsche, and Hübel & Denck, who worked for Eugen Diederichs. Smaller art institutes and bookbinding masters such as Paul Kersten from Berlin and Anker Kyster in Denmark (ill. 369) became a talking point as a result of their high-quality cover designs and colorful covers and endpapers; ultimately, they began to receive commissions from large concerns.

Designs and the production of decorated paper also attracted the attention of artists who were motivated by the aspiration for artistic innovation in all spheres of life. It is for this reason that Otto Eckmann and Lilly Behrens, but above all the artists of the Wiener Werkstätte—Josef Hoffmann, Koloman Moser, and Leopold Stolba—for example developed a rich production of decorated paper in which marbled paper was held in new esteem. In many places new exemplary works for modern

Bauchbinde, eine zusätzliche Banderole mit unterschiedlichen Informationen zum Buch. Früheste Beispiele gestalteter Einbände und illustrierter Umschläge für belletristische Bücher lieferten etwa die Verlage S. Fischer (gegr. 1886), Albert Langen (1893), Eugen Diederichs (1896), der Insel-Verlag (1901) und der Wiener Verlag (1899; Abb. 372).

Parallel zum Programm der verlegten modernen Literatur sollte auch die bildkünstlerische Sprache der Ausstattung, zumindest das äußere Erscheinungsbild modern sein. Nicht selten empfahlen Autoren ihren Verlegern bestimmte Künstler für die Umschlaggestaltung, spielten persönliche Begegnungen und Vorlieben eine Rolle.[9] Das erklärt einerseits die zufällig wirkende Wahl der Zeichner und deren Vielzahl innerhalb eines Verlages. Ebenso wurden dieselben Autoren zeitgleich von verschiedenen Verlegern publiziert und von unterschiedlichen Zeichnern auf den Einbänden oder Umschlägen interpretiert.[10] Ähnlich wie im Plakat nutzten Künstler das Medium selbstbewusst als Eigenwerbung und signierten ihre Umschlagentwürfe. Wichtiges Sammelbecken für Zeichner und Illustratoren waren neu entstandene, meist satirische Zeitschriften wie der *Simplicissimus*, die *Jugend*, die *Lustigen Blätter*, *Das Narrenschiff*, die *Meggendorfer Blätter*. Mit Namen wie Thomas Theodor Heine, Julius Klinger, Emil Pirchan, Bruno Paul, Olaf Gulbransson sei hier das Spektrum an Begabungen umrissen, die sich nicht nur für Buchillustration und -ausstattung empfahlen, sondern darüber hinaus auch in der aufstrebenden Werbewirtschaft mit Plakaten und Inseraten hervortraten. Albert Langen, der seinen Verlag zunächst in Paris gründete, dann zeitweilig unter Paris und Leipzig firmierte, schließlich in München ansässig wurde, gab bereits in Paris seine ersten Bücher mit künstlerisch gestalteten Schutzumschlägen heraus. Zu den frühesten Beispielen zählen Umschläge von Théophile Alexandre Steinlen. Er vermochte es, Vorder- und Rückseite als fortlaufendes Bild zu konzipieren, rahmenlos, ausschnitthaft, ganz im Sinne der zeitgleich von ihm praktizierten freien Grafik. 1895 lernte Albert Langen Thomas Theodor Heine kennen. Er wurde Mitbegründer und Teilhaber der 1896 zum ersten Mal erschienenen satirischen Zeitschrift *Simplicissimus* und lange Zeit der wichtigste Illustrator und Gestalter des Verlages (Abb. 371). Seine illustrierten Umschläge zeichnen sich dadurch aus, dass sie einerseits den Inhalt auf eine plakative Pointe reduzieren, zugleich aber anders als ein Plakat der Intimität des Buchformates gerecht werden. Bisweilen verbindet sich die Linienführung der Zeichnung mit der ebenfalls gezeichneten Schrift zu einem spielerisch ornamentalen Klang (Abb. 373). Neben illustrierten Umschlägen lieferte er einfach gestaltete Umschläge, die stark auf Wiedererkennbarkeit setzen und den Publikationen einen Reihencharakter geben. Auf immer gleichem Format entwarf er verschieden gemusterte Papiere mit gezeichneten Titeletiketten. Sie wurden abgelöst von einfarbigen Fonds, die von einem Schachbrett-Ornament gefasst wurden, das wiederholt als Rahmen des gezeichneten Titeletiketts Verwendung fand. Auf der Rückseite war die Vorderseite gespiegelt, jedoch ohne das Titeletikett. Unten mittig findet man groß das Künstlersignet, das – selbstbewusst platziert – den Eindruck erweckt, es handle sich um das Verlagssignet.

Heine behielt sehr früh die Dreidimensionalität des Buchkörpers im Auge, während viele der Umschlaggestaltungen um 1900 noch daran krankten, dass sie lediglich auf die Vorderseite konzentriert waren. So schrieb Otto Grautoff 1903 über Otto Eckmann, dass er den dreiteiligen Buchdeckel niemals als eine Dreiteilung der ganzen Fläche behandle und infolgedessen auch den so „wichtigen, fast maßgebenden Punkt bei der Buchdeckenverzierung außer Acht" lasse, „daß im Rücken das Rückgrat des Buches liegt, das durchaus in der Anlage des Ornaments betont werden muß".[11]

[9] Vgl. hierzu Pfäfflin, Friedrich, *100 Jahre S. Fischer Verlag 1886–1986, Buchumschläge. Über Bücher und ihre äußere Gestalt*, Frankfurt/Main 1986, 10ff.

[10] Hans Loubier sprach von dieser Periode der Buchkunst als Periode des Individualismus, in: Loubier, Hans, *Die neue deutsche Buchkunst*, Stuttgart 1921, 22.

[11] Grautoff, Otto, „Der deutsche Verlegereinband", in: *Archiv für Buchgewerbe* (40) 1 1903, 54.

arts and crafts were emerging, which provided not just new decorative designs, but also examples of endpaper, title page, and dust jacket designs. In 1901 and 1902 Julius Klinger published his suggestions for modern decoration in his books *Das Weib im modernen Ornament and Skizzen für Lithographen und Zeichner*. Artists of the Vienna Secession, Koloman Moser, Alfred Roller, and Josef Hoffmann published *Die Fläche* from 1902, which made explicit reference in its subtitle to *Entwürfe für decorative Malerei, Placate, Buch und Druck* [Designs for decorative painting, posters, books, and printing], and used examples to propagate the aesthetics of the new style, which was programmatically committed to lines and blank spaces. Designed as a *Gesamtkunstwerk* (or total work of art), twelve periodicals were published in the series, which themselves functioned as exemplars; their programmatic aspirations were proclaimed on the cover designs (ill. 370). In practical books the idea of an overall design has not always been able to gain acceptance. The degree to which book cover design overtook an advertising function to the extent seen previously has subsequently diminished. Where the book is conceived of as a unit, there are connective design elements: Frequently, the typography of the cover, color scheme, decorations, or vignette are captured in the dust jacket. From the outside in, there is a path from the loud to the quiet, from the public to the intimate.

THE ARTISTIC DUST JACKET

From the outset, there were two types of protective covers: typographically designed, often furnished with decorative borders, and illustrated. The illustrated dust jacket was intended to pointedly draw attention to the content of the book. The packaging was supposed to enable potential readers to draw conclusions about the content: they aimed to visualize suspenseful, mysterious and unfathomable, dramatic and passionate stories as well as humorous, factual, and even scientific works. To visually attune the books with their content, the blurb was soon added, which introduces the content—and sometimes the author and publisher's catalog, too—in just a few words. Frequently, it is also possible to find the so-called bellyband, an additional slip of paper with different information about the book. The earliest examples of designed book covers and illustrated dust jackets for fiction books were provided by the publishing houses S. Fischer (founded in 1886), Albert Langen (1893), Eugen Diederichs (1896), the Insel-Verlag (1901), and the Wiener Verlag (1899; ill. 372), among others.

Alongside the aim of publishing modern literature, there was a desire for the pictorial language of design—at least the external appearance—to be modern. It was not rare for authors to recommend specific artists to their publishers for their dust jacket design.[9] Bearing in mind that personal encounters and preferences played a part explains on the one hand the apparently haphazard choice of draftsmen and -women and on the other their plurality within just one publishing house. Equally these authors were published by different houses at the same time and interpreted by different draftsmen and -women on the various book covers or dust jackets.[10] Similar to posters, artists used the medium self-consciously as self-promotion and signed their dust jacket designs. An important meeting place for draftsmen and -women and illustrators was the newly arising, mostly satirical magazines like *Simplicissimus*, *Jugend*, *Lustige Blätter*, *Das Narrenschiff*, and *Meggendorfer Blätter*. Names like Thomas Theodor Heine, Julius Klinger, Emil Pirchan, Bruno Paul, and Olaf Gulbransson outline the spectrum of talents, which commended itself not just for book illustration and design,

[9] Cf. Pfäfflin, Friedrich, *100 Jahre S. Fischer Verlag 1886–1986, Buchumschläge. Über Bücher und ihre äußere Gestalt*, Frankfurt/Main 1986, 10 ff.

[10] Hans Loubier spoke of this period of book art as an era of individualism in: Loubier, Hans, *Die neue deutsche Buchkunst*, Stuttgart 1921, 22.

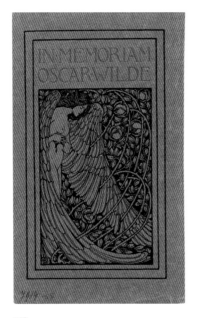

375
Walter Tiemann
Umschlag für *In memoriam Oscar Wilde*
Leipzig, 1904
Verlag: Insel Verlag
Klischee
Dust Jacket for *In memoriam Oscar Wilde*
Leipzig, 1904
Publisher: Insel Verlag
Cliché
182 x 109 mm
KI 7914-55, Schenkung donation from
Franz Malota 1914

376
László Moholy-Nagy
Einband für das *5. Bauhaus-Buch. Neue Gestaltung*
von Piet Mondrian
München, 1925
Verlag: Albert Langen
Klischee
Book Cover for the [5th Bauhaus book. New design]
by Piet Mondrian
Munich, 1925
Publisher: Albert Langen
Cliché
220 x 180 mm
BI 17911-5, Ankauf purchased 1926

So wie der Albert Langen Verlag stark von den Zeichnern des *Simplicissimus* geprägt war, beschäftigte Dr. Eysler & Co., der Herausgeber der *Lustigen Blätter,* gern Julius Klinger – nicht nur als Plakatkünstler, sondern auch für seine Buchproduktionen (Abb. 374). Klinger verzichtete auf bildmäßige
Darstellungen und fand zu markanten, flächenhaften, angeschnittenen Figuren, die er in klarer
linearer Zeichnung von fließender Eleganz asymmetrisch zur Schrift setzte.
Einer der wichtigen Erneuerer deutscher Buchkunst war Walter Tiemann. Mit seinen Arbeiten für
den Insel-Verlag, für den Verlag Eugen Diederichs und Hermann Seemann Nachfolger, den Julius
Zeitler Verlag, für Rütten & Loening u. a. etablierte er eine typografische Kultur, die Maßstäbe setzte.
Tiemann entwarf nicht nur sehr schöne Umschläge, er hatte stets das Buch als Einheit im Blick. Der
Maler, Zeichner, Schriftentwerfer, Illustrator, Exlibris-Zeichner und Entwerfer von Logos entwarf stets
aus „einem Zusammendenken heraus, aus einem Überblick über die Gesamtheit der vorliegenden
Aufgaben".[12] Die Entwicklung seiner künstlerischen Anschauungen vollzog sich von der stark den
Vorbildern der Kelmscott Press und der Präraffaeliten verpflichteten Illustration und der Lust am
Ornament um 1900 (Abb. 375) hin zu einer reduzierten, klaren Tektonik, die den Umschlägen eine
zeitlose Klassizität gab.

[12] Zeitler, Julius, „Walter Tiemann", in:
Archiv für Buchgewerbe (40) 2 1903, 466.

but moreover came to the fore in the emergent advertising industry by dint of its posters and newspaper advertisements.

Albert Langen, who initially founded his publishing house in Paris, and then temporarily traded between Paris and Leipzig before finally settling in Munich, released his first books with artistically designed protective covers during his Paris period. Among the earliest examples are dust jackets by Théophile Alexandre Steinlen. He was capable of conceiving of the front and reverse as one continuous image, without a border, and as clippings, entirely along the lines of the graphic art he simultaneously practiced. Albert Langen met Thomas Theodor Heine in 1895. The latter became co-founder and partner of the satirical magazine *Simplicissimus*, which was released for the first time in 1896, and for a long time he was the most important illustrator and designer at the publishing house (ill. 371). His illustrated dust jackets stand out on the one hand because they reduce the content to one eye-catching punchline, while on the other they do justice to the intimacy of the book format—in contrast to the poster. Occasionally, the lineation of the drawing combines with the similarly designed text to create a playfully decorative aspect (ill. 373). In addition to illustrated dust jackets, he also delivered simply designed dust jackets, which set great store by recognizability and give the publications a series character. Always in the same format, he designed various patterned papers with drawn title labels. They stood out from a monochrome background contained by a chessboard figure decoration, which was repeatedly used as the border of the drawn title label. On the reverse was a mirror of the front design, but without the title label. At the bottom center there was the artist's mark in large, which—consciously placed—gives the impression of actually being the publisher's mark.

Very early, Heine bore in mind the three-dimensionality of the physical book at a time around 1900 when many dust jacket designs still suffered from a concentration on the front alone. For example, Otto Grautoff wrote about Otto Eckmann in 1903 that he had never treated the three-part book cover as a tripartite division of the entire surface and consequently also "neglected [the so] important, almost decisive point in book cover decoration," namely "that the back is where the spine of the book lies, and the spine must be thoroughly emphasized when arranging the decoration."[11] Just as the Albert Langen publishing house was strongly influenced by the draftsmen and -women of *Simplicissimus*, Dr. Eysler & Co.—the publisher of *Lustige Blätter*—liked to commission Julius Klinger not just as a poster artist, but also for its book releases (ill. 374). Klinger eschewed pictorial depictions, instead finding striking, extensive, cut figures, which he placed asymmetrically to the text in flowingly elegant, clear linear drawings.

One of the important innovators of German book art was Walter Tiemann. With his works for the Insel-Verlag, for Eugen Diederichs und Hermann Seemann Nachfolger, the Julius Zeitler Verlag, for Rütten & Loening, and others he established a typographic culture, which laid new milestones. Tiemann designed not only extremely attractive dust jackets, but he also always had the book as a unit in mind. The painter, draftsman, typographer, illustrator, ex libris draftsman, and designer of logos always designed on the basis of "a comprehensive thinking, on the basis of an overview of entirety of existing challenges."[12] His artistic outlook developed from a style of illustration, which was strongly indebted to the exemplars of the Kelmscott Press and the Pre-Raphaelites, and the desire for ornament around 1900 (ill. 375), to reduced, clear tectonics, which gave the dust jackets a timeless classicism.

[11] Grautoff, Otto, „Der deutsche Verlegereinband", in: *Archiv für Buchgewerbe* (40) 1 1903, 54. Translated by Maria Slater.

[12] Zeitler, Julius, "Walter Tiemann," in: *Archiv für Buchgewerbe* (40) 2 1903, 466. Translated by Maria Slater.

ABSCHIED VOM JUGENDSTIL – NEUE GESTALTUNGSWEGE

Neben der Flut szenisch bebilderter Umschläge und Einbände ist seit 1910 eine wachsende Versachlichung zu beobachten. Einerseits hängt das mit einem von der Pressenbewegung beeinflussten Purismus zusammen, der sich auf noble Typografie beschränkte, andererseits mit einer endgültigen Abkehr vom Jugendstil wie der Rücknahme stark persönlich geprägter Handschriften zugunsten einer strengeren Typisierung und funktional orientierten Gestaltungsarchitektur im Buch, die klar vom Werkbundgedanken geleitet war. Erinnert sei an Umschlaggestaltungen von Peter Behrens und Fritz Helmuth Ehmcke. Gegen die axiale Ausrichtung von Titel und Ornament, die ruhige Ordnung der Typografie stellten sich die Dadaisten, Futuristen und die Künstler der russischen Avantgarde. Die bislang postulierten Gesetze der Typografie missachtend, suchten die Futuristen in der Verwendung möglichst vieler, in Gestalt und Größe verschiedener Typen und ihrer willkürlich scheinenden Anordnung der empfundenen Dynamik der Gegenwart einen zeitgemäßen Ausdruck zu verleihen. Die stärker kubistisch orientierten russischen Grafiker nutzten insbesondere seit 1919 das Gestaltpotenzial einzelner Lettern als bildnerisches Element im Spannungsfeld von Papiergrund und geometrischer Form, von Zeichnung und Buchstabe.

Seit den frühen 1920er Jahren lösten Kurt Schwitters, Walter Dexel, Jan Tschichold, Paul Renner und László Moholy-Nagy theoretische Debatten zu einer zeitgemäßen, elementaren Typografie aus. In ihren praktischen Arbeiten vereinten sie neue serifenlose Schrifttypen mit asymmetrisch angeordneten Textblöcken und -zeilen, die Text optisch nach Bedeutungen gliederten. Anstelle von Ornament setzten sie Strich, Balken und Punkt. Zur Akzentuierung und Rhythmisierung kamen unterschiedliche Strichstärken zwischen fett und mager zum Einsatz (Abb. 376). Neben Zeichnung und Typografie sollte fortan auch die Fotografie als Gestaltungselement eine wichtige Rolle spielen. Paul Renner, Hauptvertreter der Neuen Typografie und Erfinder der Futura, hob hervor: „Durch die verwendung der neuen schriften hat die neue typographie auch zum erstenmal die photographie als netzätzung in ihre flächenkomposition mit erfolg einbezogen. Das handschriftliche element der historischen schriften scheint auch das handschriftliche element der zeichnung zu fordern. Die ruhenden formen der neuen schrift fügen sich viel besser zu der photographie."[13] „Die Buchgewerbekünstler versagen ihr noch jetzt das Recht, Bestandteil eines ‚schönen Buches' zu sein", schrieb Jan Tschichold noch 1928.[14]

1922 erschien im Malik Verlag das erste Buch mit einer Fotomontage von John Heartfield auf dem Einband.[15] Heartfield hatte die Fotografie, die ihren Siegeszug durch die Journale angetreten hatte und als Dokumentarfotografie mehr und mehr in die Bücher einzog, nun auch für den künstlerischen Umschlag hoffähig gemacht (Abb. 377). Heartfield verband gezeichnete Handschrift ebenso wie gebaute Buchstabenarchitekturen oder klare Groteskschriften mit der Fotomontage. Er betrachtete den Umschlag stets als Ganzes, Vorder- und Rückseite ergänzten sich in den inhaltlich bezogenen Bildaussagen. Aufeinanderfolgende Bildmontagen wirken oft wie filmische Sequenzen. Der Einsatz von Fotografie und Fotomontage wurde ein beliebtes Stilmittel bei Grafikern, die sich dem Neuen Sehen wie der der Neuen Typografie gleichermaßen verpflichtet fühlten. Erinnert sei hier an Hans und Grete Leistikow, Alexander Rodtschenko (Abb. 378), Herbert Bayer und György Kepes (s. Abb. 411). Daneben bot sich ein ausgesprochen breites Bild in der Gestaltung gezeichneter Umschläge.[16] Einer der vielseitigsten und vielbeschäftigten Grafiker in den 1920er und frühen 1930er Jahren war Georg Salter. Er arbeitete für den S. Fischer Verlag, den Erich Reiss Verlag und den Gustav Kiepenheuer

[13] Renner, Paul, „Type und Typographie", in: *Archiv für Buchgewerbe* (65) 6 1928, 465.

[14] Tschichold, Jan, „Photographie und Typographie", in: *Tschichold, Jan, Werden und Wesen der neuen Typographie*, Berlin 1928, 89.

[15] Dos Passos, John, *Drei Soldaten*, Berlin 1922.

[16] Vgl. Holstein, Jürgen (Hg.), *Blickfang. Bucheinbände und Schutzumschläge Berliner Verlage 1919–1933*, Berlin 2005.

DEPARTURE FROM ART NOUVEAU: NEW DESIGN STYLES

In addition to the flood of scenically illustrated dust jackets and book covers, a growing reification can be observed from 1910. On the one hand, this is related to a purism influenced by the press movement, which was restricted to lavish typography; on the other hand to a definite rejection of art nouveau and the retraction of extremely personal thumbprints in favor of stricter typing and functionally oriented design architecture, which was clearly derived from the Werkbund approach. Consider, for example, the dust jacket covers by Peter Behrens and Fritz Helmuth Ehmcke. Going against the axial alignment of title and decoration, the calm organization of typography, the artists accepted the challenge posed by Dadaism, futurism, and the Russian avant-garde. Disregarding the previously postulated laws of typography, in practice the futurists attempted to provide the deep-felt dynamics of the present with a contemporary expression by using as many different types and sizes as possible and arranging them apparently at random. Particularly from 1919, the more strongly cubism-oriented Russian graphic designers used the shape potential of individual letters as a pictorial element between the poles of paper foundation and geometric form, of drawing and letters. From the early 1920s, Kurt Schwitters, Walter Dexel, Jan Tschichold, Paul Renner, and László Moholy-Nagy launched theoretical debates regarding an elemental typography that would be in keeping with the period. In their practical works, they united new sans serif typefaces with asymmetrically ordered blocks and lines of text, which optically structured text according to importance. Instead of ornament, they set dash, column, and period. For accentuation and rhythmization, various stroke widths between bold and roman were used (ill. 376). In addition to drawing and typography, photography would henceforth play an important role as a design element. Paul Renner, the main proponent of the New Typography and inventor of Futura, emphasized: "Through the use of the new fonts, the New Typography also successfully integrated photography as halftone into its surface composition for the first time. The handwritten aspect of historical typefaces also appears to call for the handwritten aspect of drawing. The latent forms of the new typeface conform much better to photography."[13] "The artists of the book trade even now deny it the right to be part of a 'beautiful book,'" Jan Tschichold wrote in 1928.[14]

In 1922 the Malik Verlag published the first book with a photomontage by John Heartfield on the cover.[15] Heartfield had now made photography—whose triumph had started via journals and had increasingly made its way into books as documentary photography—acceptable for artistic dust jackets, too (ill. 377). Heartfield combined drawn handwriting and architecture constructed from letters or clear sans serif text with photomontage. He always considered the dust jacket as a whole; the front and back panels complemented each other in their content-related pictorial statements. Serial montages often have an effect similar to film sequences. The use of photography and photomontage became a favored stylistic device among graphic designers who felt equally indebted to the Neues Sehen and the New Typography. Consider Hans and Grete Leistikow, Alexander Rodtschenko (ill. 378), Herbert Bayer, and György Kepes (see ill. 411).

Alongside there was a decidedly broad picture in the design of drawn dust jackets.[16] One of the most diverse and busiest graphic designers in the 1920s and early 1930s was Georg Salter. He worked for the S. Fischer Verlag, the Erich Reiss Verlag, and the Gustav Kiepenheuer Verlag. In what is probably his best-known dust jacket, *Berlin Alexanderplatz* from 1929 (see ill. 407), he drew the colorful blue background from the title page, which serves as a field for the title and author, around

[13] Renner, Paul, "Type und Typographie," in: *Archiv für Buchgewerbe* (65) 6 1928, 465. Translated by Maria Slater.

[14] Tschichold, Jan, "Photographie und Typographie," in: Tschichold, Jan, *Werden und Wesen der neuen Typographie*, Berlin 1928, 89. Translated by Maria Slater.

[15] Dos Passos, John, *Drei Soldaten*, Berlin 1922.

[16] Cf. Holstein, Jürgen (ed.), *Blickfang. Bucheinbände und Schutzumschläge Berliner Verlage 1919–1933*, Berlin 2005.

377
John Heartfield
Umschlag für *Das Geld schreibt*
von Upton Sinclair
Berlin, 1930
Verlag: Malik Verlag
Autotypie
Dust Jacket for [*Money Writes!*]
by Upton Sinclair
Berlin, 1930
Publisher: Malik Verlag
Halftone
223 x 128 mm
KI 8896-66, Schenkung donation from
Leihbibliothek in der Burg 1930

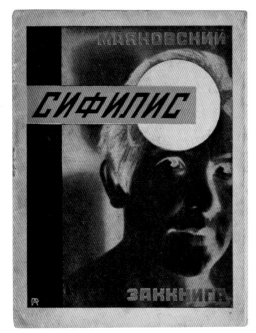

379
Joseph Binder
Umschlag für *Das Zeitalter des Films*
von Joseph Gregor
Wien, 1932
Verlag: Reinhold
Dust Jacket for [The film age]
by Joseph Gregor
Vienna, 1932
Publisher: Reinhold
153 x 143 mm
KI 9094-1, Schenkung donation from
Joseph Binder 1932

378
Alexander Rodtschenko
Umschlag für *Syphilis* von Vladimir Majakovskij
Tiflis, 1926
Verlag: Zakniga
Klischee, Autotypie
Dust Jacket for *Syphilis* by Vladimir Majakovskij
Tibilisi, 1926
Publisher: Zakniga
Cliché, halftone
170 x 130 mm
BI 47670, Schenkung donation from Angela Völker 1991

380
Richard Foster
Zeitschriftencover für
Franklin Field Illustrated
Pennsylvania, Oktober 1930
Verlag: Pennsylvania College
Klischee, Autotypie
Magazine Cover for
Franklin Field Illustrated
Pennsylvania, October 1930
Publisher: Pennsylvania College
Cliché, halftone
301 x 227 mm
KI 9000-2, Schenkung donation from
Richard Foster 1932

381
Paul Kurt Schwarz
Umschlag für *Schrei aus dem Abgrund*
von Georges Duhamel
Wien, 1953
Verlag: Herold Verlag
Autotypie
Dust Jacket for [*Cry out of the Depths*]
by Georges Duhamel
Vienna, 1953
Publisher: Herold Verlag
Halftone
203 x152 mm
KI 15610-32, Schenkung donation from
Paul Kurt Schwarz 2000

382
Paul Kurt Schwarz
Umschlag für *Steh auf und geh*
von Hervé Bazin
Wien, 1953
Verlag: Herold Verlag
Autotypie
Dust Jacket for [Get up and walk]
by Hervé Bazin
Vienna, 1953
Publisher: Herold Verlag
Halftone
196 x 150 mm
KI 15610-35, Schenkung donation from
Paul Kurt Schwarz 2000

383
gelitin
Umschlag für *Gelatin Is Getting It All Wrong Again*
Köln, 2003
Verlag: Walther König
Siebdruck
Dust Jacket for *Gelatin Is Getting It All Wrong Again*
Cologne, 2003
Publisher: Walther König
Screen printing
530 x 420 (840) mm
BI 78733, Ankauf Buchhandlung purchased
from bookstore Walther König 2004

384
Emil Rudolf Weiß
Lesezeichen für Schuster und Loeffler Berlin
Berlin, 1896
Verlag: Schuster & Loeffler
Klischee
Bookmark for Schuster und Loeffler Berlin
Berlin, 1896
Publisher: Schuster & Loeffler
Cliché
178 x 62 mm
KI 21484-7-13, Ankauf purchased from
Kunstarchiv Werner J. Schweiger 2015

Verlag. In seinem wohl bekanntesten Umschlag *Berlin Alexanderplatz* von 1929 (s. Abb. 407) zog er den farbigen blauen Grund der Titelseite, der als Feld für Titel und Autor dient, um den Rücken herum bis zur Rückseite. Der blaue Grund ist sozusagen der Fond für die Hauptinformation, während der weiße Papiergrund handgeschriebene Inhaltsangaben und kleine Vignetten trägt und den Anschein erweckt, als würde man direkten Einblick in die Werkstatt des Autors bekommen.

Inmitten der kaum zu übersehenden Vielfalt der Buchumschläge gelangte seit 1925 mit dem Art déco eine neue stilistische Bildsprache zur Blüte. Ihre Hauptvertreter A.M. Cassandre, Charles Loupot oder Jean Carlu verbanden Sachlichkeit mit sinnlicher Farbpräsenz, prägnante Form mit gestalterischer Eleganz. In Österreich folgten ihnen Joseph Binder, Hermann Kosel, Willi Willrab und Julius Klinger. Joseph Binder (Abb. 379) nutzte die Errungenschaften der modernen Typografie und integrierte sie in seine oft dynamisch aufgefassten Bildgestaltungen. Er griff auf die Fotografie ebenso zurück wie auf klare Flächenformen. Als sein amerikanisches Pendant kann man Richard Foster betrachten. Dieser fand für seine Zeitschrifteneinbände von *Franklin Field Illustrated* (Abb. 380) oder *American Printer* signifikante Formen von eindringlicher Werbekraft und moderne Zierschriften, die Sachlichkeit mit Dekorativität verbinden.

Nach dem Zweiten Weltkrieg prägte in Österreich vor allem Paul Kurt Schwarz den Buchumschlag. Schwarz steht beispielhaft für den souveränen Umgang mit allen bis dahin eingeführten gestalterischen Mitteln. Er beherrschte den Umgang mit gezeichneter und Satzschrift, mit gezeichneter Form und Fotografie und vermochte es, jedem Buch sein spezielles Kleid zu schneidern (Abb. 381, 382). Heute können Umschläge neben der traditionell werbenden Aufgabe auch Teil des Ereignisses Buch sein. Bisweilen werden die Innenseiten gestaltet. Umschläge sind aufklappbare Plakate geworden (Abb. 383), gefaltete Bilderbögen, Ergänzungen zum Buch, das Landkarten o. Ä. nicht genug Platz bietet. Christian Chruxin erfand 1963 die tragbare Galerie, indem er den abnehmbaren Kartonumschlag als Gehäuse aufbauen konnte, das als Galerieraum fungierte.

Wesentlich unabhängig von Inhalt und Gestaltung eines Buches sind Lesezeichen. In der Geschichte seit dem Mittelalter verwendet, gibt es Lesezeichen unterschiedlichster Ausführung und Materialien: als Pergament-, Leder- oder Stoffstreifen, als verzierte Klemme aus Holz, Perlmutt oder Elfenbein, Pappe, schließlich als bedrucktes Papier. Bereits im frühen 19. Jahrhundert konnten Lesezeichen als Werbeträger fungieren, als Zeichen für Kaisertreue, Königsverehrung, als Erinnerungsstück von Festen und Jubiläen etc. Mit der Zunahme von Reklame in der zweiten Hälfte des 19. Jahrhunderts wurden Lesezeichen zunehmend als Werbeträger für die unterschiedlichsten Produkte benutzt, von den Verlagen für Eigenwerbung, die, bereits in ein Buch eingelegt, auf weitere Angebote verweisen oder den Verlag als solchen bewerben (Abb. 384). Als Werbegeschenk fanden Lesezeichen über die Werbung hinaus vielseitige, ihre Attraktivität steigernde praktische Verwendungen: als Kalender, Seitenaufschneider, als Visiten- oder Postkarte.[17] Der Fantasie sind hier keine Grenzen gesetzt.

[17] Vgl. Haberland, Detlef, „Edna May oder die Sprachlosigkeit der Jahrhundertwende. Reflexionen über ein Lesezeichen", in: Zeckert, Patricia F. (Hg.), *Flachware 3. Fußnoten der Leipziger Buchwissenschaft*, Leipzig 2013, 31 ff.

the spine to the back panel. The blue background is the foundation for the main information, as it were, whereas the white paper background bears handwritten content summaries and small vignettes, and gives the impression of gaining a direct insight into an author's workshop.

Amid the hardly conceivable diversity of dust jackets, a new stylistic visual language blossomed from 1925 with the advent of art deco. Its main champions—A. M. Cassandre, Charles Loupot, and Jean Carlu, among others—combined objectivity with a sensory chromatic presence, eye-catching form with creative elegance. In Austria they were followed by Joseph Binder, Hermann Kosel, Willi Willrab, and Julius Klinger. Joseph Binder (ill. 379) used the achievements of modern typography and integrated them into his often dynamic pictorial designs. He availed himself of photography as well as of clear surface forms. Richard Foster can be considered his American counterpart. Foster found significant forms of forceful advertising appeal and modern decorative fonts for his covers for the magazines *Franklin Field Illustrated* (ill. 380) and *American Printer*, which combined objectivity with decorativeness.

In post-World War Two Austria, the dust jacket was influenced above all by Paul Kurt Schwarz. Schwarz is an exemplar of an accomplished approach to all of the creative means introduced to that point. He had mastered the art of working with designed and standard fonts, with drawn form and photography, and was able to tailor a special cover to every book (ill. 381, 382).

Today, in addition to their traditional advertising function, dust jackets can also be part of the book. Occasionally, the inside pages are designed, too. Dust jackets have become openable posters (ill. 383), folded Épinal prints, supplements to books, which do not provide enough space for maps, etc. Christian Chruxin invented the portable gallery in 1963 by making it possible to arrange the removable cardboard cover as casing, which functioned as the room of a gallery.

In contrast, bookmarks are essentially independent of the content and design of a book. Used throughout history since the Middle Ages, there are bookmarks with a wide range of designs and materials: parchment, leather, or fabric strips; adorned clips made of wood, mother-of-pearl, or ivory; pasteboard; and finally printed paper. Even in the early 19th century, the bookmark could act as an advertising medium, as a symbol of imperial loyalty, veneration of royalty, as a memento of celebrations and anniversaries, etc. With the growth in advertising in the second half of the 19th century, bookmarks were increasingly used as advertising media for highly diverse products; the publishing houses themselves utilized them for self-promotion, employing an item placed inside one book to draw the reader's attention to other works they offered or to advertise the publishing house as a whole (ill. 384). As a promotional gift, bookmarks found miscellaneous practical applications, which went beyond advertising and enhanced their attractiveness: as calendars, page openers, visiting cards, and postcards.[17] The imagination knows no bounds.

[17] Cf. Haberland, Detlef , "Edna May oder die Sprachlosigkeit der Jahrhundertwende. Reflexionen über ein Lesezeichen," in: Zeckert, Patricia F. (ed.), *Flachware 3. Fußnoten der Leipziger Buchwissenschaft*, Leipzig 2013, 31 ff.

ZUR ENTSTEHUNG DER SAMMLUNG

Dem Gründungsauftrag des k. k. Österreichischen Museums für Kunst und Industrie (ÖMKI) entsprechend, wurde das Buch in seiner künstlerischen Gesamtheit gesehen. Man war bestrebt, dafür herausragende Beispiele der Buchausstattung als Vorbild für Neuschöpfungen zu sammeln. Da zum Zeitpunkt der Gründung 1863 weder einzelne Objekte noch eine nennenswerte Sammlung vorhanden waren, betätigte sich anfangs der Kaiser selbst als Gönner und Förderer. Ein kaiserliches Handschreiben forderte Adelige und Klöster auf, Objekte zur Verfügung zu stellen. Auf diese Weise wurde der Grundstein der Sammlung von Künstlerbüchern, Supralibri, Buchdruckerzeichen, Schriftproben und Illustrationszeichnungen sowie Bucheinbänden und -umschlägen gelegt und rasch ein wertvoller Bestand von der Inkunabelzeit bis ins 18. Jahrhundert auf dem Buch-Standort „Barockbibliothek" zusammengetragen.[1] (Abb. S. 320)

Da das Museum mangels finanzieller Möglichkeiten auf Schenkungen angewiesen war, verlief die Frühzeit der Sammlungstätigkeit thematisch weniger strukturiert, vielmehr zählten als Kriterien für die Aufnahme einzelner Bücher: prachtvolle Einbände, inspirierende Schrifttypen, außergewöhnliches Material oder herausragende Illustrationen. So gelangten berühmte Standardwerke in die Bibliothek des ÖMKI, wie der rätselhafte Roman *Hypnerotomachia Poliphili* des Aldus Manutius (1499), der durch die formvollendete Antiqua und mustergültige Eleganz der Seitengestaltung als Meilenstein des frühen Buchdrucks gilt (Abb. 385). Eine außergewöhnliche Bereicherung lieferte die aus 28 Bänden bestehende Gesamtausgabe der Werke der Piranesi, die anlässlich der Silberhochzeit des Kaiserpaares 1879 von Paul Wasserburger der Bibliothek des Museums gewidmet wurde. Der Baumeister und Architekt folgte damit dem kaiserlichen Wunsch, anstelle von persönlichen Geschenken das Museum zu fördern – wohl auch in der Hoffnung, durch seine Großzügigkeit Bauaufträge an der Wiener Ringstraße zu erhalten (Abb. 386).

Für zeitgenössische Neuerwerbungen wurde im 19. Jahrhundert der Buch-Standort „Ausstattungsbücher" geschaffen. Die ersten in diese Sammlung aufgenommenen Arbeiten entstammten ausnahmslos der englischen Buchkunst. Der Vizedirektor und erste Kustos des ÖMKI, Jacob von Falke, erkannte die Stärke Englands mit seiner unvergleichlichen Tradition in der Illustrationskunst. Eines der ersten vom Museum erworbenen Bücher war Owen Jones' *The Grammar of Ornament* von 1856, für England der Inbegriff des ornamentalen Vorlagewerks (Abb. 387). Walter Crane, aus dem Kreis der Präraffaeliten kommend und ein Hauptvertreter des Arts and Crafts Movements, nahm im ÖMKI eine Sonderstellung ein. 1895 wurde dem englischen Maler und Zeichner hier die erste große Ausstellung eines englischen Gegenwartskünstlers in Wien gewidmet.[2] Auf der 500 Blätter und zahlreiche Bücher umfassenden Schau erwarb das MAK den Großteil der ausgestellten Objekte, u.a. *The Baby's Opera* von 1879 (Abb. 389). Cranes vor allem auch mit William Morris in der Kelmscott Press entstandene Bücher (Abb. 391) waren durch die Harmonie von Text, Illustration, Umschlag, Einband, Vorsatz, Titel und Verzierungen beispielgebend für die Idee des Gesamtkunstwerks und mussten schon deshalb Aufnahme in den Sammlungsbestand finden.

Man war sich aber durchaus auch Frankreichs herausragender Stellung in der Buchkunst bewusst. Jacob von Falke bereicherte durch Ankäufe auf der Pariser Weltausstellung und der Ausstellung *Imprimerie Alfred Mame* in Tours 1867 den Vorlagenbestand mit ausgewählten Ausstattungsbüchern, vor allem des französischen Buchdruckers und Verlegers Mame, der auf dem Gebiet

[1] Heute umfasst diese Sammlung fast 3 000 Bände.

[2] „Walter Crane-Ausstellung im Oesterr. Museum", in: *Mittheilungen des k. k. Oesterr. Museums für Kunst und Industrie* (X) 4 1895, 362f. Den großen Erfolg dieser Ausstellung belegt, dass das Museum bereits 1904 die nächste folgen ließ.

ON THE CREATION OF THE COLLECTION

In line with the founding mission of the Imperial Royal Austrian Museum of Art and Industry (ÖMKI), books were considered artistic wholes. The museum endeavored to collect outstanding examples of book design as exemplars for new creations. As neither individual objects nor any collection worth mentioning existed at the time of the museum's founding in 1863, at first it was the emperor himself who became involved as a patron and benefactor. A handwritten letter from the emperor invited aristocrats and cloisters to make objects available to the museum. It was in this way that the foundation was laid for the collection of artists' books, supralibros, printers' marks, handwriting specimens, and illustrations, as well as book covers and dust jackets; valuable holdings ranging from the incunabula era to the 18th century were thus rapidly compiled at the "baroque library" book repository.[1] (ill. p. 320)

Due to a lack of finances, the museum was reliant upon donations; consequently, the growth of the collection was thematically less structured during its early years, when the criteria for accepting individual books instead included magnificent book covers, inspiring fonts, unusual materials, or outstanding illustrations. Some famous standard works thus entered the library of the ÖMKI, such as the enigmatic novel *Hypnerotomachia Poliphili* by Aldus Manutius (1499), whose perfectly structured Antiqua typeface and immaculately elegant page layout mean that it is considered a milestone of early letterpress printing (ill. 385). An unusual addition was provided by the collected edition of works by Piranesi, which comprises 28 volumes and was presented to the museum's library by Paul Wasserburger in celebration of the imperial couple's silver wedding anniversary in 1879. In doing so, the master builder and architect complied with the emperor's request that well-wishers support the museum rather than giving him and his wife personal gifts—presumably his donation was also made in the hope that his generosity would be rewarded with construction contracts for Vienna's Ringstraße (ill. 386).

The repository of "design books" was created for contemporary new acquisitions in the 19th century. The first works to enter this collection were without exception examples of English book art. The vice-director and first custodian of the ÖMKI, Jacob von Falke, recognized England's forte in its incomparable tradition of the art of illustration. One of the first books acquired by the museum was Owen Jones's *The Grammar of Ornaments* from 1856—for England the epitome of an ornamental exemplar (ill. 387). Walter Crane, a Pre-Raphaelite and one of the main proponents of the arts and crafts movement, enjoyed a special status at the ÖMKI. In 1895 the first large-scale exhibition by an English contemporary artist in Vienna was dedicated to this English painter and draftsman.[2] The show comprised 500 sheets and numerous books—and the MAK acquired the majority of the exhibits, including *The Baby's Opera* from 1879 (ill. 389). Due to their harmony of text, illustration, dust jacket, endpapers, title, and embellishment, Crane's books—especially those created with William Morris at the Kelmscott Press (ill. 391)—were exemplars of the idea of the *Gesamtkunstwerk* (or total work of art) and for that reason alone simply had to be accepted into the holdings of the collection.

However, at the museum one was certainly also aware of France's outstanding position in the world of book art. Jacob von Falke enriched the exemplary holdings by purchasing select design books at the Paris world's fair and the exhibition *Imprimerie Alfred Mame* in Tours in 1867; these works were

[1] Today this collection comprises almost 3000 volumes.

[2] "Walter Crane-Ausstellung im Oesterr. Museum," in: *Mittheilungen des k. k. Oesterr. Museums für Kunst und Industrie* (X) 4 1895, 362f. The great success of this exhibition is proven by the fact that the museum held the next show on the subject as early as 1904.

der Prachteinbände Herausragendes leistete (Abb. 388). Zugleich kamen die ersten illustrierten Werke von Gustave Doré an das Museum.

Federführend für den immer größer werdenden französischen Schwerpunkt innerhalb der Sammlung des ÖMKI kurz vor 1900 war Felician Myrbach. Nach seiner Ausbildung an der Wiener Akademie der bildenden Künste jahrelang in Paris als Illustrator tätig, feierte er dort bereits 1885 mit seiner ersten Arbeit für das berühmte Jugendbuch *Tartarin sur les Alpes* von Alphonse Daudet große Erfolge (Abb. 390).

Myrbachs Berufung zum Professor für Grafik 1897 und ab 1899 zum Direktor an die dem ÖMKI angeschlossene Kunstgewerbeschule führte zu einer entscheidenden Wende in der Sammlungs-politik. Der Fokus wurde auf das institutsinterne Schaffen gerichtet und der Bestand durch Arbeiten der damaligen Schüler Bertold Löffler und Franz von Zülow sowie der Professoren Josef Hoffmann, Alfred Roller, Koloman Moser bereichert. 1902/1903 kamen Werke des Reformators der künstleri-schen Schrift Rudolf von Larisch (Abb. 392) und des um die Buchkunst hoch verdienten Carl Otto Czeschka (Abb. 393) dazu, ebenso wie Blätter von Franz Čižek, der als Initiator der „Jugendkunst-schule" schon damals Weltruhm erlangt hatte. Mit diesem Team erlebte die Druckgrafik eine nie dagewesene Hochblüte: Neben Plakaten, Postkarten, Kalendern und Geschäftskarten wurde der Buchkunst schlagartig besonderes Augenmerk zuteil.

Einer der erfolgreichsten Löffler-Schüler an der Kunstgewerbeschule war Joseph Binder, der das Grafikdesign sowohl in Europa als auch nach seiner Emigration in die Vereinigten Staaten 1938 entscheidend prägte. Die Publikation *Indianermärchen*, 1921 im Rikola-Verlag erschienen (Abb. 394), zeigt Binders reduzierte und eindrückliche Formensprache, deren Ausgangspunkt bei seinem Lehrer zu suchen ist und die stellvertretend für die neue Richtung des Grafikdesigns steht.

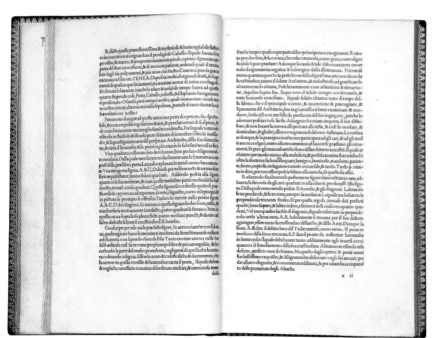

385
Franciscus Columna
Hypnerotomachia Poliphili
Venedig, 1499
Ausführung: Druckerei Aldus Manutius
Buchdruck
[Poliphilo's Strife of Love in a Dream]
Venice, 1499
Execution: Printer Aldus Manutius
Letterpress print
256 x 190 (380) mm
BI 4120, Ankauf purchased from
Buchhandlung Gerold & Co., 1873

predominantly by the French book printer and publisher Mame, whose achievements in the field of treasure binding were exceptional (ill. 388). It was at the same time that the first illustrated works by Gustave Doré arrived at the museum. Felician Myrbach was the person in charge of the ever-growing French focus within the collection of the ÖMKI shortly before 1900. After his training at the Academy of Fine Arts Vienna, he spent many years as an illustrator in Paris, enjoying great success as early as 1885 for his first work for the famous young adult novel *Tartarin sur les Alpes* by Alphonse Daudet (ill. 390).

Myrbach's appointment to professor of works on paper in 1897 and, from 1899, to director of the museum-affiliated School of Arts and Crafts led to a crucial change in collecting policy. The focus was now aimed at creativity within the institute itself and the holdings were enhanced with works by the students Bertold Löffler and Franz von Zülow, as well as by the professors Josef Hoffmann, Alfred Roller, and Koloman Moser. In 1902/1903 works by the reformer of artistic typography Rudolf von Larisch (ill. 392) and by Carl Otto Czeschka (ill. 393), who had rendered outstanding services to book art, also entered the collection, as did prints by Franz Čižek who, having initiated the "Juvenile Art Classes," was already famous the world over. With this team, printed works experienced an unprecedented golden age: in addition to posters, postcards, calendars, and business cards, particular attention was suddenly bestowed on book art.

One of the most successful students of Löffler at the School of Arts and Crafts was Joseph Binder, who had a fundamental influence on graphic design—both in Europe and after his emigration to the United States in 1938. The publication *Indianermärchen*, released by the Rikola-Verlag in 1921 (ill. 394), shows Binder's reduced and impressive language of forms, whose origins can be traced back to his teacher and which are representative of the new direction taken by graphic design.

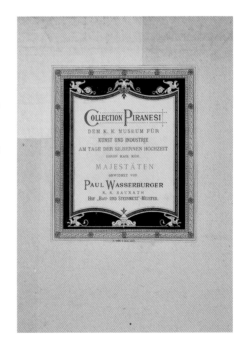

386
Giovanni Battista Piranesi, Francesco Piranesi,
Pietro Piranesi
Widmung, Collection d'ouvrages sur les antiquités et l'architecture,
gravés par eux: **Le Antichità Romane: Divisa In Quattro Tomi [Sammlung von Werken über Altertümer und Architektur], graviert von ihnen: [Römische Altertümer: unterteilt in vier Bände]**
Rom/Paris, 1800–1807
Klischee
Dedication, [Collection of works on antiquities and architecture], engraved by them: [Roman Antiquities: Divided into four volumes]
Rome/Paris, 1800–1807
Cliché
577 x 430 mm
BI 6036, Schenkung donation from
Paul Wasserburger 1879

387
Owen Jones
The Grammar of Ornament
London, 1856
Verlag: Day & Son
Chromolithografie
Publisher: Day & Son
Chromolithograph
550 x 350 mm
BI 3770, Ankauf purchased from
Buchhandlung Gerold & Co., 1873

388
Alfred Mame
Livre d'Heures [Buch der Stunden]
Tours, 1861
Ausführung: Druckerei Impr. Mame
Stahlstich
[Book of hours]
Execution: Printer Impr. Mame
Steel engraving
145 x 90 mm
BI 1689, Ankauf Ausstellung von purchased
from the exhibition of Mame in Tours 1867

389
Walter Crane
**The Baby's Opera. A book of old
rhymes with new dresses**
London, 1879
Druckerei: Edmund Evans
Verlag: George Routledge and Sons
Klischee, Holzstich
Printer: Edmund Evans
Publisher: George Routledge and Sons
Cliché, wood engraving
180 x 185 mm
BI 5975, Ankauf purchased
from Buchhandlung Gerold & Co., 1873

390
Felician Myrbach
Tartarin sur les Alpes
[Tartarin in den Alpen]
Paris, 1885
Ausführung: Druckerei A. Lahure
Holzstich
[Tartarin on the Alps]
Paris, 1885
Execution: Printer A. Lahure
Wood engraving
230 x 160 mm
BI 20540, Schenkung donation from
Karl Beitel, Wien Vienna 1903

391
William Morris
The Works of Geoffrey Chaucer
London, 1896
Ausführung: Druckerei Kelmscott Press
Holzstich
Execution: Printer Kelmscott Press
Wood engraving
432 x 305 mm
BI 13386, Ankauf purchased from
Morris & Co., London 1903

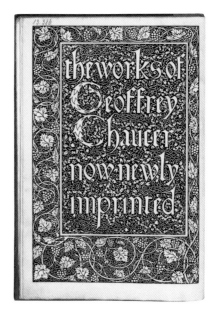

392
Heinrich Lefler, Joseph Urban
An Ehren und an Siegen reich
Wien, 1908
Verlag: Max Herzig
Leder, Metall
[Rich in honors and victories]
Vienna, 1908
Publisher: Max Herzig
Leather, metal
515 x 430 mm
KI 14336, Ankauf purchased
Wilhelm Mrazek, 1974

393
Carl Otto Czeschka
Die Nibelungen
Wien, 1908
Druckerei: Christoph Reisser's Söhne
Verlag: Gerlach & Wiedling
Strichätzung, bronziert
[The Nibelungs]
Vienna, 1908
Printer: Christoph Reisser's Söhne
Publisher: Gerlach & Wiedling
Line etching, bronzed
150 x 135 mm
BI 17990, Schenkung donation from
Christoph Reisser's Söhne 1915

394
Joseph Binder
Indianermärchen
Wien, 1921
Verlag: Rikola
Lithografie
[Native American fairy tales]
Vienna, 1921
Publisher: Rikola
Lithograph
260 x 200 mm
BI 59489, Legat bequest from
Carla und and Joseph Binder 1997

BUCHUMSCHLÄGE AUS DEM FRÜHEN 20. JAHRHUNDERT

Im Jahr 1914 erhielt die Bibliothek und Kunstblättersammlung des k. k. Österreichischen Museums für Kunst und Industrie (ÖMKI) ein großes Konvolut an Buch- und Zeitschriftenumschlägen aus den vergangenen zwei Jahrzehnten. Donator war Franz Malota, dessen Firma – Buchhandel und Antiquariat – 1904 in das Handelsregister eingetragen worden war. Das Geschäft im 4. Wiener Bezirk, Wiedner Hauptstraße 22, bestand bis 2014. Die Umschläge vorwiegend österreichischer und deutscher Publikationen haben sich, der Idee der Vorbildersammlung entsprechend, in beschnittener Form erhalten: Ohne Klappen, Rückseite und Rücken wurde ausschließlich der Titelbereich auf Untersatzkarton montiert. Anita Kühnel macht in ihrem Beitrag auf das dadurch entstandene Problem einer genaueren Analyse aufmerksam. Sind es wirkliche Schutzumschläge oder nur Titel einer Broschur? War der Umschlag durchgestaltet und gab es einen Klappentext? Um welche Ausgabe handelt es sich? Diese Fragen bleiben offen. Ablesen bzw. rekonstruieren lassen sich nur Verlage und Künstler sowie die Daten der Ersterscheinung.

Zur Zeit der Schenkung interessierte demnach primär die formale Gestaltung, und in dieser Hinsicht geben die knapp 560 erhaltenen Beispiele einen faszinierenden Überblick über die Bandbreite des Jugendstils. Der spielte klassischerweise mit Ornament und Fläche, konnte aber auch (damit) erzählerisch oder äußerst reduziert sein. In die Zukunft der Versachlichung weist etwa der Umschlag eines Romans von Alexander Roda Roda der Österreichischen Verlagsanstalt von 1904 – eines der wenigen Beispiele, dessen Gestalter unbekannt ist (Abb. 400). Im Allgemeinen beschäftigten die modernen Verlage namhafte Künstler, die sich durch Monogramm oder Signatur auf dem Cover zu erkennen gaben. Für den Wiener Verlag arbeitete neben Bertold Löffler auch Emil Orlik (Abb. 396), für den in der Malota-Schenkung stark vertretenen Verlag Albert Langen entwarfen neben Thomas Theodor Heine auch Max Slevogt oder Bruno Paul (Abb. 395, 397, 399).

Über 70 brandaktuelle Umschläge kamen 1930 als Geschenk der Leihbibliothek in der Burg (Burgpassage 14) in die Sammlung. Die Umschläge stammen mehrheitlich von Büchern aus deutschen Verlagen – Rowohlt, Malik, S. Fischer, Erich Reiss –, es sind aber auch besondere österreichische Beispiele überliefert, so ein Broschureinband von Otto Prutscher für den Katalog der Ausstellung *Buch und Raum der Gegenwart*, worin der Bibliotheksvorstand des ÖMKI Hans Ankwicz-Kleehoven einen Artikel über die „Wiener Einbandkunst" veröffentlichte (Abb. 408).[1] Bemerkenswert sind auch die Umschläge des Paul Zsolnay Verlags in der Art einer Ankündigung mit den charakteristischen Signalfarben und Streifenbändern (Abb. 410).

Eine Einmaligkeit stellt das Album mit 127 Probedrucken von Buchumschlägen aus den 1920er Jahren dar, das die Bibliothek 1966 von Michael Pabst erwarb. Der Sohn des bedeutenden Stummfilmregisseurs G. W. Pabst hatte in der Wohnung seiner Eltern am Schottenring eine Galerie eingerichtet, die später in die Habsburgergasse und 1976 nach München übersiedelte. Sein spezielles Interesse galt der Wiener Grafik um 1900, der er 1984 das gleichnamige Standardwerk widmete.[2] Das Album versammelt Umschläge von Büchern aus dem Deutschen Verlag für Jugend und Volk, der sich, 1921 in Wien gegründet, ganz dem Lehr-, Kinder-, und Jugendbuch verschrieben hatte (Abb. 403, 405). Auch dafür waren ausgezeichnete Grafiker gefragt: etwa Otto Schubert, Franz Wacik oder Richard Rothe. Josef Danilowatz gestaltete ein Cover der ab 1924 im Verlag erschienenen Familienzeitschrift *Frohes Schaffen*, für die auch Joseph Binder entworfen hat (Abb. 406, 412).

[1] Ankwicz-Kleehoven, Hans, „Wiener Einbandkunst in alter und neuer Zeit", in: *Buch und Raum der Gegenwart*, Ausst.kat. Künstlerhaus, Wien 1930, 21–36. Text und Ausstellung bezogen sich zwar nicht auf Schutzumschläge, sondern gestaltete Ledereinbände, die Schenkung der Leihbibliothek bezeugt aber Ankwicz-Kleehovens Interesse auch an diesem ephemeren Produkt.

[2] Pabst, Michael, *Wiener Grafik um 1900*, München 1984.

EARLY 20TH-CENTURY DUST JACKETS

In 1914 the Library and Works on Paper Collection of the Imperial Royal Austrian Museum of Art and Industry (ÖMKI) received a large bundle of dust jackets and magazine covers from the previous two decades. Their donator was Franz Malota, whose company—a new and used bookstore—had been entered in the commercial register in 1904. The shop at Wiedner Hauptstraße 22 in Vienna's 4th district stayed in business until 2014. The dust jackets from predominantly Austrian and German publications have been preserved only in part—they were cut to comply with the idea of an exemplary collection: without flaps, back panels, or spines, only the front covers were mounted on board. Anita Kühnel raises awareness of the resulting problems for closer analysis in her article: Are these examples really protective jackets or in fact just the front covers of paperbacks? Did the jackets have consistent designs and did they have blurbs on the back? For which edition were they made? All of these questions remain unanswered. The only information that is legible or can be reconstructed are their publishers and artists as well as the dates of the first edition.

At the time they were donated, the primary interest for the museum therefore must have been their formal design, and in this regard the almost 560 surviving examples provide a fascinating insight into the full range of art nouveau. Classically, the style played with ornamentation and blank spaces, but (these) could also be narrative or extremely reduced. The jacket of an Alexander Roda Roda novel published by the Österreichische Verlagsanstalt from 1904 points to the future of objectivity—and is one of the few examples whose designer is unknown (ill. 400). In general, the modern publishers employed well-known artists who identified themselves on the front cover by means of a monogram or signature. Not only Bertold Löffler, but also Emil Orlik (ill. 396) worked for the Wiener Verlag; a frequent feature of the Malota donation, the Albert Langen publishing house had designs by Thomas Theodor Heine as well as Max Slevogt and Bruno Paul (ill. 395, 397, 399).

Over 70 brand-new dust jackets entered the collection in 1930 as a gift from the Leihbibliothek in der Burg (a lending library at the Hofburg Palace). The majority of the dust jackets come from books by German publishers—Rowohlt, Malik, S. Fischer, Erich Reiss—though some exceptional Austrian examples have also survived. For example, there is a paperback cover by Otto Prutscher for the catalog of the exhibition *Buch und Raum der Gegenwart*, in which the head of the library at the ÖMKI, Hans Ankwicz-Kleehoven, published an article about the "Viennese art of book covers" (ill. 408).[1] Equally remarkable are the dust jackets of the Paul Zsolnay publishing house in the style of an announcement, with characteristic signal colors and striped bands (ill. 410).

A unique item in the collection is the album with 127 proofs of dust jackets from the 1920s, which the library acquired from Michael Pabst in 1966. The son of the eminent silent film director G. W. Pabst had installed a gallery in his parents' apartment on Schottenring, which later moved to Habsburgergasse and then in 1976 to Munich. He was particularly interested in Viennese works on paper from around 1900, to which he dedicated his standard reference work in 1984.[2] The album compiles dust jackets for books from the Deutscher Verlag für Jugend und Volk, which was founded in Vienna in 1921 and was entirely dedicated to textbooks, children's, and young adult books (ill. 403, 405). These publications, too, required designs by excellent graphic artists: by Otto Schubert, Franz Wacik, and Richard Rothe, among others. Josef Danilowatz designed a cover for the publishing house's family magazine *Frohes Schaffen* for which Joseph Binder had also produced designs (ill. 406, 412).

[1] Ankwicz-Kleehoven, Hans, "Wiener Einbandkunst in alter und neuer Zeit," in: *Buch und Raum der Gegenwart*, exh.cat. Künstlerhaus, Vienna 1930, 21–36. Admittedly, the text and exhibition were not concerned with protective dust jackets, but rather designed leather book covers; however, the donation from the lending library is testament to Ankwicz-Kleehoven's interest in this ephemeral product, too.

[2] Pabst, Michael, *Wiener Grafik um 1900*, Munich 1984.

395
Thomas Theodor Heine
Umschlag für *Hunger*
von Knut Hamsun
München, 1898
Verlag: Albert Langen
Klischee
Dust Jacket for [*Hunger*]
by Knut Hamsun
Munich, 1898
Publisher: Albert Langen
Cliché
190 x 128 mm
KI 7914-393, Schenkung
donation from Franz Malota 1914

396
Emil Orlik
Umschlag für *Mutter Sorge*
von Rudolf Hawel
Wien, 1902
Verlag: Wiener Verlag
Klischee
Dust Jacket for [Mother worry]
by Rudolf Hawel
Vienna, 1902
Publisher: Wiener Verlag
Cliché
178 x 117 mm
KI 7914-19, Schenkung
donation from Franz Malota 1914

397
Max Slevogt
Umschlag für *Verraten*
von Amalie Skram
München, 1897
Verlag: Albert Langen
Lithografie
Dust Jacket for [*Betrayed*]
by Amalie Skram
Munich, 1897
Publisher: Albert Langen
Lithograph
149 x 120 mm
KI 7914-422, Schenkung
donation from Franz Malota 1914

398
Emil Ranzenhofer
Umschlag für *Im dunkelsten*
Wien von Max Winter
Wien, 1904
Verlag: Wiener Verlag
Autotypie
Dust Jacket for [In darkest
Vienna] by Max Winter
Vienna, 1904
Publisher: Wiener Verlag
Halftone
169 x 130 mm
KI 7914-547, Schenkung
donation from Franz Malota 1914

399
Bruno Paul
Umschlag für *Ein Zweikampf*
von Anton Tschechoff
München, 1901
Verlag: Albert Langen
Klischee
Dust Jacket for [*The Duel*]
by Anton Chekhov
Munich, 1901
Publisher: Albert Langen
Cliché
149 x 118 mm
KI 7914-425, Schenkung
donation from Franz Malota 1914

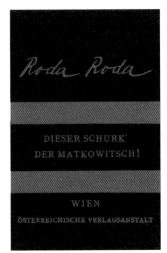

400
Anonym Anonymous
Umschlag für *Dieser Schurk'*
***der Matkowitsch!* von**
Alexander Roda Roda
Wien, 1904
Verlag: Österreichische
Verlagsanstalt
Klischee
Dust Jacket for
[Matkowitsch, the rogue!]
by Alexander Roda Roda
Vienna, 1904
Publisher: Österreichische
Verlagsanstalt
Cliché
203 x 132 mm
KI 7914-512, Schenkung
donation from Franz Malota 1914

401
Franz Wacik
Umschlag für
Wiener Kinder 1. Buch
Wien, 1923
Verlag: Deutscher Verlag
für Jugend und Volk
Lithografie
**Dust Jacket for [Viennese
children, book 1]**
Vienna, 1923
Publisher: Deutscher Verlag
für Jugend und Volk
Lithograph
253 x 181 mm
KI 13952-70, Ankauf purchased
from Michael Pabst 1966

402
Richard Rothe
Umschlag für
Die Schildbürger aus
der Reihe *Volksschatz*
Wien, 1924
Verlag: Deutscher Verlag für
Jugend und Volk
Lithografie
**Dust Jacket for
[The simpletons] from
the Series Volksschatz**
Vienna, 1924
Publisher: Deutscher Verlag
für Jugend und Volk
Lithograph
154 x 118 mm
KI 13952-42, Ankauf purchased
from Michael Pabst 1966

403
Pauline Ebner
Umschlag für *Wie Kinder
zählen und rechnen* **von
Konrad Falk**
Wien, 1923
Verlag: Deutscher Verlag für
Jugend und Volk
Lithografie
**Dust Jacket for [How chil-
dren count and calculate]
by Konrad Falk**
Vienna, 1923
Publisher: Deutscher Verlag für
Jugend und Volk
Lithograph
204 x 137 mm
KI 13952-58, Ankauf purchased
from Michael Pabst 1966

404
Otto Schubert
Umschlag für
Das Nibelungenlied
von Carl Linke
Wien, 1924
Verlag: Deutscher Verlag für
Jugend und Volk
Lithografie
**Dust Jacket for [The Song of
the Nibelungs] by Carl Linke**
Vienna, 1924
Publisher: Deutscher Verlag
für Jugend und Volk
Lithograph
178 x 127 mm
KI 13952-106, Ankauf purchased
from Michael Pabst 1966

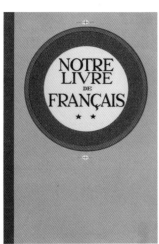

405
Anonym Anonymous
Umschlag für *Notre livre de
français* **[Unser Französisch-
buch] von Aline Furtmüller**
Wien, 1924–1925
Verlag: Deutscher Verlag für
Jugend und Volk
Lithografie
**Dust Jacket for [Our book of
French] by Aline Furtmüller**
Vienna, 1924–1925
Publisher: Deutscher Verlag
für Jugend und Volk
Lithograph
201 x 135 mm
KI 13952-64, Ankauf purchased
from Michael Pabst 1966

406
Josef Danilowatz
Umschlag für die Zeitschrift
Frohes Schaffen
Wien, 1924
Verlag: Deutscher Verlag für
Jugend und Volk
Lithografie
**Dust Jacket for the
Magazine [Happy creating]**
Vienna, 1924
Publisher: Deutscher Verlag
für Jugend und Volk
Lithograph
259 x 186 mm
KI 13952-60, Ankauf purchased
from Michael Pabst 1966

407
Georg Salter
Buchumschlag für
Berlin Alexanderplatz **von Alfred Döblin**
Berlin, 1929
Verlag: S. Fischer
Offsetdruck
Dust Jacket for
Berlin Alexanderplatz **by Alfred Döblin**
Berlin, 1929
Publisher: S. Fischer
Offset printing
214 x 133 mm
KI 8896-41, Schenkung donation from
Leihbibliothek in der Burg 1930

408
Otto Prutscher
Umschlag für den Ausstellungskatalog
Buch und Raum der Gegenwart,
Künstlerhaus Wien
Wien, 1930
Ausführung: Druckerei J. Weiner
Klischee
Dust Jacket for the Exhibition Catalog
[Contemporary books and spaces]
Vienna Künstlerhaus
Vienna, 1930
Execution: Printer J. Weiner
Cliché
193 x 165 mm
KI 8896-43, Schenkung donation from
Leihbibliothek in der Burg 1930

409
Georg Salter
Buchumschlag für *Schreib das auf, Kisch!*
von Egon Erwin Kisch
Berlin, 1930
Verlag: Erich Reiss
Offsetdruck
Dust Jacket for [Write that down Kisch!]
by Egon Erwin Kisch
Berlin, 1930
Publisher: Erich Reiss
Offset printing
210 x 134 mm
KI 8896-40, Schenkung donation from
Leihbibliothek in der Burg 1930

410
Anonym Anonymous
Umschlag für *Von Tag zu Tag*
von Ferdinand Goetel
Wien, 1931
Verlag: Paul Zsolnay
Klischee
Dust Jacket for [*From Day to Day*]
by Ferdinand Goetel
Vienna, 1931
Publisher: Paul Zsolnay
Cliché
187 x 118 mm
KI 8976-14, Schenkung donation 1932

411
György Kepes
Buchumschlag für *Bei dieser*
***Gelegenheit* von Alfred Polgar**
Berlin, 1930
Verlag: Rowohlt
Autotypie
Dust Jacket for [On this occasion]
by Alfred Polgar
Berlin, 1930
Publisher: Rowohlt
Halftone
205 x 116 mm
KI 8896-51, Schenkung donation from
Leihbibliothek in der Burg 1930

412
Joseph Binder
Umschlag für die Zeitschrift
Frohes Schaffen
Wien, um 1930
Offsetdruck
Dust Jacket for the Magazine
[Happy creating]
Vienna, ca. 1930
Offset printing
256 x 187 mm
KI 9094-2, Schenkung donation from
Joseph Binder 1932

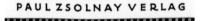

LESEZEICHEN

Schlägt man ein längst gelesenes Buch auf, stecken darin oft Lesezeichen, die als solche gar nicht gedacht waren: Kinokarten, Einkaufslisten, Kassenzettel oder Ausstellungsfolder – alles Ephemera, die erinnern helfen. Und man ist erstaunt und froh, dass Erinnerungen sich so buchstäblich wiederfinden lassen. Aus den Büchern der Historischen Bibliothek der Stadt Rastatt haben sich fast 3000 solch zweckentfremdeter Drucksachen erhalten, vom Sterbebildchen über die Gewinn-Benachrichtigung bis zum Stundenplan.[1] Doch das Lesezeichen war auch immer eine eigene Gestaltungsaufgabe. Als Perlenstickerei auf Karton aus dem 19. Jahrhundert gelangte 1917 das erste Lesezeichen in die Sammlung des Museums; die ersten gedruckten folgten 1930 mit dem Legat Artur Wolf. Bemerkenswert ist ein Konvolut von 20 Lesezeichen als Werbematerial der Wiener Städtischen Versicherungsanstalt. Sie wurden um 1930 bei Hermann Kosel sowie dem Atelier Gaertner + Kloss in Auftrag gegeben. Kosel thematisierte die drohenden Gefahren, gegen die man versichert sein sollte (Feuer, Wasser, Einbruch) und verband sie mit passenden Literaturzitaten. In den elegant-reduzierten Designs erkennt man den Plakatkünstler. Darüber hinaus suchte Kosel die Übereinstimmung von Form und Inhalt, ignorierte das übliche Rechteck und schnitt eine Welle aus (Wasserschaden, Abb. 418) oder stellte den Rathausmann in einen gotischen Spitzbogen (Wien-Serie, Abb. 419).[2] Ein sowohl senkrecht als auch waagerecht gestaltetes Lesezeichen verweist auf die zusätzliche Funktion als Lesehilfe, mit der man sich Zeile für Zeile vorarbeiten kann (Abb. 420).

Einen weiteren Zweck erfüllt das Lesezeichen als Aufschneider. Unbeschnittene gefalzte Buchseiten können damit sauber geöffnet werden.[3] Ein solches Beispiel (Abb. 414) stammt aus dem Teilnachlass des Kunstwissenschaftlers Werner J. Schweiger (1949–2011), der 2013 für die MAK-Bibliothek und Kunstblättersammlung erworben wurde. Er umfasst vor allem Material zu Schweigers 1988 publiziertem Standardwerk *Aufbruch und Erfüllung* über die Gebrauchsgrafik der Wiener Moderne, darunter zahlreiche Originale. Allein 40 Lesezeichen aus der Zeit von 1895 bis 1930 haben die MAK-Sammlung enorm bereichert. Es sind vorwiegend Werbeträger deutscher Verlage, etwa Velhagen & Klasing (Leipzig), Deutsche Verlags-Anstalt Stuttgart oder Schuster & Loeffler (Berlin), gestaltet von bekannten Grafikern wie Julius Diez, Emil Rudolf Weiß, Bertold Löffler oder Fidus (Abb. 413). Es sind aber auch Lesezeichen aus Stoff dabei oder Lesebändchen mit Werbeeinschaltung etwa in Gestalt einer Glühbirne der Firma Osram (Abb. 416, 417). Schließlich hat sich durch den Schweiger-Nachlass ein reizvoller Entwurf erhalten, der über den Lesefortschritt „Bis hie(r)her" informiert (Abb. 415).

„A bookmark need not be a fancy thing"[4], meint der britische Künstler David Shrigley (Abb. 424). Seit über 20 Jahren kreieren KünstlerInnen Lesezeichen für die Buchhandlung Walther König. Sie werden eigens entworfen oder aus vorhandenem Material gestaltet. Werner Büttners Lesezeichen bildet die beglückende Wirkung der Lektüre ab, während Martin Kippenbergers *King Size* der zweckentfremdeten alten Socke zuvorkommt (Abb. 421, 422). Christian Boltanski hingegen nutzte das Lesezeichen als Verteiler. Er reproduzierte drei Beispiele aus seiner Arbeit *Diese Kinder suchen ihre Eltern* und wandte sich an die Leserschaft mit der Bitte: „Wenn Sie sich wiedererkennen, oder wenn Sie wissen, wer die Kinder sind, schreiben Sie bitte an Christian Boltanski."[5] Auf diese Weise verlieh der französische Künstler dem „fancy thing" eine politische Dimension (Abb. 423).

1 Heid, Hans (Hg.), *100 Lesezeichen der Historischen Bibliothek der Stadt Rastatt*, Ausst.kat., Stadt Rastatt 2001.

2 Der Rathausmann bekrönt das von 1872 bis 1883 im neogotischen Stil errichtete Wiener Rathaus.

3 In früherer Zeit öfter üblich, bieten ungeöffnete Buchseiten heutzutage bei manchen Kinderbüchern einen zusätzlichen Leseanreiz.

4 „Eine Lesezeichen muss kein schickes Ding sein."

5 Die gleichnamige Ausstellung fand vom 28. November 1993 bis 28. Jänner 1994 im Kölner Museum Ludwig statt. Boltanski zeigte darin Steckbriefe von Waisenkindern aus dem Nachkriegsdeutschland.

BOOKMARKS

Whenever we open a book read long ago, it often contains items repurposed as bookmarks: movie tickets, shopping lists, receipts, or exhibition folders—all of them ephemera, which help us remember. And we are astonished and pleased that memories can be found so literally. In the books of the Historische Bibliothek in Stadt Rastatt, Germany, almost 3 000 pieces of such printed matter—used for purposes other than intended—have been preserved, from memorial card photos to prize notifications and timetables.[1] Yet bookmarks have always been a separate focus of design, too. The first bookmark to enter the museum's collection did so in 1917; it was an example of beadwork on cardboard from the 19th century. The first printed bookmarks followed in 1930 with the bequest from Artur Wolf.

A remarkable part of the collection is a bundle of 20 bookmarks produced as promotional materials by the Wiener Städtische Versicherungsanstalt. Hermann Kosel and the Atelier Gaertner + Kloss were commissioned to design them around 1930. Kosel chose as his subject the imminent dangers against which people should be insured (fire, water, burglary) and combined them with matching literary quotations. In his elegantly reduced designs one can easily recognize him as a poster artist. Furthermore, Kosel sought a correlation between form and content, ignored the customary rectangle by cutting out a wave (water damage, ill. 418), and positioned the *Rathausmann* in a Gothic ogive (Vienna series, ill. 419).[2] A vertically as well as horizontally designed bookmark points to its additional function as a reading aid, with which one can work one's way from line to line (ill. 420). Another purpose fulfilled by the bookmark is as an opener: it can be used to cleanly cut the unopened folded pages of books.[3] An example of this (ill. 414) comes from the partial bequest from the art scholar Werner J. Schweiger (1949–2011), which was acquired for the MAK Library and Works on Paper Collection in 2013. It mostly comprises material on Schweiger's standard reference work *Aufbruch und Erfüllung* from 1988 about the ephemera of Viennese Modernism, including numerous originals. Just 40 bookmarks from the period from 1895 to 1930 enormously enriched the MAK Collection. They are predominantly advertising media for German publishing houses, such as Velhagen & Klasing (Leipzig), Deutsche Verlags-Anstalt Stuttgart, and Schuster & Loeffler (Berlin), designed by well-known graphic artists including Julius Diez, Emil Rudolf Weiß, Bertold Löffler, and Fidus (ill. 413). However, there are also bookmarks made of fabric or ribbon page markers with advertising in the form of a lightbulb for the Osram company, for example (ill. 416, 417). Finally, thanks to the Schweiger bequest a delightful design has been preserved, which informs the reader about their progress „Bis hie(r)her" ["Thus far"] (ill. 415).

"A bookmark need not be a fancy thing," says the British artist David Shrigley (ill. 424). For over 20 years, artists have been creating bookmarks for the Walther König bookstore. They are either designed especially or adapted from existing material. Werner Büttner's bookmark depicts the pleasing effect of reading, while Martin Kippenberger's *King Size* ironically suggests that an old sock could be used as a page marker (ill. 421, 422). In contrast, Christian Boltanski used the bookmark as a mailing list. He reproduced three examples from his work *Diese Kinder suchen ihre Eltern* [Children in search of their parents] and appealed to his readership: "If you recognize yourself, or if you know who the children are, please write to Christian Boltanski."[4] In this way, the French artist lent this "fancy thing" a political dimension (ill. 423).

[1] Heid, Hans (ed.), *100 Lesezeichen der Historischen Bibliothek der Stadt Rastatt*, exh.cat., City of Rastatt 2001.

[2] The *Rathausmann* crowns the Rathaus (city hall) in Vienna, which was constructed in the neo-Gothic style from 1872 to 1883.

[3] Previously much more common, today unopened pages feature in some children's books to provide young readers with an additional incentive to read.

[4] The exhibition of the same name took place from 28 November 1993 to 28 January 1994 at Museum Ludwig, Cologne. In it, Boltanski showed the profiles of orphaned children in post-war Germany. Translated by Maria Slater.

413
Fidus
Lesezeichen für den Verlag
Velhagen & Klasing
Bielefeld/Leipzig, um 1900
Klischee
Bookmark for the Publisher
Velhagen & Klasing
Bielefeld/Leipzig, ca. 1900
Cliché
214 x 52 mm
KI 21484-7-22, Ankauf purchased from
Kunstarchiv Werner J. Schweiger

414
Käte Vesper-Waentig
Lesezeichen und
Aufschneider für den Verlag
Langewiesche-Brandt
Ebenhausen bei München,
1907–1908
Klischee
Bookmark and Page Cutter
for the Publisher
Langewiesche-Brandt
Ebenhausen near Munich,
1907–1908
Cliché
158 x 67 mm
KI 21484-7-19, Ankauf purchased from
Kunstarchiv Werner J. Schweiger

415
Anonym Anonymous
Entwurf für ein Lesezeichen
Deutschland/Österreich, um 1900
Deckfarben
Design for a Bookmark
Germany/Austria, ca. 1900
Coating paint
151 x 67 mm
KI 21484-7-32, Ankauf purchased from
Kunstarchiv Werner J. Schweiger

416
Anonym Anonymous
Lesezeichen
für die Marke OSRAM
Deutschland, 1912
Klischee
Bookmark for the Brand OSRAM
Germany, 1912
Cliché
93 x 34 mm
KI 21484-7-2, Ankauf purchased from
Kunstarchiv Werner J. Schweiger
2015

417
Franz Wacik
Stofflesezeichen
für das Rote Kreuz
Wien, 1914
Ausführung: Druckerei
Albert Berger
Klischee
Fabric Bookmark
for the Red Cross
Vienna, 1914
Execution: Printer Albert Berger
Cliché
239 x 50 mm
KI 21484-7-37, Ankauf
purchased from Kunstarchiv
Werner J. Schweiger

418
Hermann Kosel
Lesezeichen für die Wiener
Städtische Versicherungsanstalt
Wien, um 1930
Autotypie
Bookmark for the Wiener
Städtische Versicherungsanstalt
Vienna, ca. 1930
Halftone
170 x 55 mm
KI 18100-7, alter Bestand, inv. old
holdings, inventoried 2014

IN DIESEM ALTER
LASSET EUCH VORLESEN !

ÜBER DAS
FINDEN
EINER
SCHÖNEN
STELLE
IN EINEM
BUCH.

419
Hermann Kosel
**Lesezeichen für die Wiener
Städtische Versicherungsanstalt**
Wien, um 1930
Autotypie
**Bookmark for the Wiener
Städtische Versicherungsanstalt**
Vienna, ca. 1930
Halftone
175 x 38 mm
KI 18100-3, alter Bestand,
inv. old holdings, inventoried 2014

420
Hermann Kosel
**Lesezeichen für die Wiener
Städtische Versicherungsanstalt**
Wien, um 1930
Autotypie
**Bookmark for the Wiener
Städtische Versicherungsanstalt**
Vienna, ca. 1930
Halftone
172 x 42 mm
KI 18100-14, alter Bestand, inv.
old holdings, inventoried 2014

421
Werner Büttner
**Lesezeichen für die
Buchhandlung Walther König**
Köln, nach 1990
Digitaldruck
**Bookmark for the
Bookstore Walther König**
Cologne, after 1990
Digital print
212 x 54 mm
KI 22385-1-1, Schenkung
donation from Walther König 2015

422
Martin Kippenberger
Lesezeichen *King Size* für die
Buchhandlung Walther König
Köln, 1991
Offsetdruck
Bookmark *King Size* for
the Bookstore Walther König
Cologne, 1991
Offset printing
185 x 80 mm
KI 21181, Schenkung
donation from Walther König 2015

423
Christian Boltanski
Lesezeichen für die
Buchhandlung Walther König
Köln, 1993
Offsetdruck
Bookmark for the
Bookstore Walther König
Cologne, 1993
Offset printing
211 x 43 mm
KI 22385-7-1, Schenkung
donation from Walther König 2015

2696. Name: **Paul**, Vorname: Ilse, geb. 16. 8. 44 (geschätzt), Augen: grau - grün, Haare: braun. Das Kind befand sich zuletzt im Säuglingsheim Wilkischen, Kr. Mies (Sudetenland). Der Vater des Kindes soll gefallen und die Mutter verstorben sein.

2739. Name: **unbekannt**, Vorname: unbekannt, Augen: blau, Haare: blond, geb. etwa 4. 12. 1943. Das Kind wurde in Tilsit in der Jägerstraße aufgefunden und fand in der Kinderklinik Tilsit Aufnahme. Später kam es in eine Pflegestelle. Über Eltern oder Angehörige ist nichts bekannt.

424
David Shrigley
Lesezeichen für die
Buchhandlung Walther König
Köln, 2004
Digitaldruck
Bookmark for the
Bookstore Walther König
Cologne, 2004
Digital print
142 x 28 mm
KI 22385-3-1, Schenkung
donation from Walther König 2015

2733. Name: **Falaska**, Vorname: Edith, geb. 3. 8. 44 in Bromberg?, Augen: grau-braun, Haare: dunkelblond. Das Kind kam mit einem Transport aus einem Kinderheim in Bromberg. Näheres über die Angehörigen ist nicht bekannt.

A BOOK-
MARK

A BOOK-
MARK NEED
NOT BE
A FANCY
THING

DIE INSZENIERUNG EINES MODEBILDES kann je nach Bedarf einerseits und Stimmung oder kürzlich gemachten Erfahrungen anderseits sehr unterschiedlich sein. Wesentlich ist die Einstellung – die Freude oder Kritik –, die man an einer Modeserie festmachen will, und natürlich eine Einschätzung, wie weit man mit den genannten Dingen gehen kann oder möchte.

Ich trage die Themen immer über einige Zeit mit mir herum und spiele gedanklich verschiedene Möglichkeiten durch: Einmal wollte ich zum Beispiel ergründen, wie viel Platz die Darstellung der Mode im Verhältnis zum ganzen Foto einnehmen muss, damit man sie noch prominent wahrnimmt, oder wie geschmacklos oder gewöhnlich die Umgebung sein kann, ohne Anstoß zu erregen. In dieser Serie habe ich schöne und belanglose, billige Hotels und Wohnungen – jeweils mit TV im Zimmer – fotografiert. Dann fotografierte ich die Mode und montierte sie in die TV-Sets, die Mode war also im Verhältnis zu den gezeigten Räumlichkeiten wirklich sehr klein. Ein TV-Screen zieht aber immer die Blicke auf sich, auch auf dem Foto – eine Erfahrung, die seit damals bei meinen Überlegungen mitspielt.

Das hat auch mit der Kraft und Ausstrahlung des Models, das man auswählt, und den Kleidern, die es zu fotografieren gilt, zu tun. Dicke Wintermäntel sind oft formlos und verlangen ein anderes Konzept als fließende Kleider. Auch der Ort, die Location, zu der man sich entschließt, ist wesentlich. Es kann aber auch vorkommen, dass eine der drei letztgenannten Komponenten so stark ist, dass man den Rest ganz einfach unterordnen muss.

Eine andere wichtige Komponente ist der Auftraggeber. Er hat vielleicht genaue Vorstellungen, die sich im Idealfall mit meinen decken oder aber sehr gegensätzlich sein können. Letzteres wäre ein Unglück, denn dann muss man sich entscheiden, ob man unter diesen erschwerten Voraussetzungen überhaupt konstruktiv arbeiten kann. Ich kann mich schlecht den Vorstellungen anderer unterordnen, es lässt zu wenig Raum für eine gute Arbeit. Meist wird die Entscheidung aber schon im Vorfeld getroffen: Niemand wird einen Fotografen wählen, der nichts mit den eigenen Vorstellungen zu tun hat. Ich hatte meist Glück, konnte meine Geschichten und ihre Hintergründe gut erklären und ausführen.

Die Fotografie, ihre Form und Inhalte entwickeln sich andauernd weiter, das hat sowohl mit technischen als auch mit politischen und persönlichen Umständen zu tun. Mit jeder Fotoserie versuche ich, ein Stück weiterzukommen, etwas mir Unbekanntes auszuprobieren. Werbung kann auch schön und intelligent sein.

Früher wurde ein Cover fast ausschließlich nach Schönheit, technischer Perfektion und Klasse ausgesucht. Inzwischen wissen wir, dass ein ungewöhnliches Foto, ein nie gesehener Aufnahmewinkel, ein aufregendes, aber nicht schönes Gesicht viel wirkungsvoller sind. Nicht einmal schlechte technische Ausführung ist ein Hindernis. Beim Entwurf eines Covers versucht man natürlich, all dieses Wissen in einer Aufnahme zu vereinen, was sehr oft nicht gelingt. Außerdem ist es genauso wichtig, auf dem Cover Stil und Richtung des Magazins zu etablieren. Manchmal wird einfach das beste und packendste Foto aus einer Serie, die ursprünglich nicht dafür vorgesehen war, ausgewählt. Das ist heute selten, weil der Einfluss der Modeproduzenten, die im Magazin Werbung machen, das bestimmende Kriterium für das Cover ist. Sehr oft ist das Cover durch die Verantwortung, die man trägt, zu vorsichtig fotografiert und ausgewählt und daher langweilig.

Elfie Semotan, Fotografin, Wien/New York

10838

farbige
Modezeichnungen XXII a
von Mela Koehler
Deutsch 20. Jh.

Originalzeichnungen XXII b
aus Albanien
Deutsch 20. Jh.

FORSTNER

Original-Zeichnungen
von Lendecke XXII c
1 Deutsch 20. Jh.
Nr. 1 – 31

Original-Zeichnungen
von Lendecke XXII c
2 Deutsch 20. Jh.
Nr. 32 – 69

XXII c3
Deutsch 20. Jh.
Nr. 70 – 88

Lendecke

Kostümentwürfe XXII d
von Augusta Jansen
Deutsch 20. Jh.

XXII e
Bleistiftzeichnungen
Deutsch

V·LURJE
UM 1940

Originalzeichnungen
von Dagobert Peche
Innendekoration XXII g
Nr. 1 – 30
Tische u. Stühle
Deutsch 20. Jh.

Originalzeichnungen
von Dagobert Peche
2 XXII g
Nr. 31 – 63
Figurales u. Köpfe
Deutsch 20. Jh.

Originalzeichnungen
von Dagobert Peche
3 XXII g
Nr. 64 – 90
Ornamentales

Originalzeichnungen
von Dagobert Peche
XXII g
Nr. 91 – 125
Architekton., Öfen,
Goldschm., Elfenbein
Deutsch
20. Jh.

Originalzeichnungen
von Dagobert Peche
5 XXII g
Nr. 126 – 150
Möbel
Deutsch 20. Jh.

Originalzeichnungen
von Dagobert Peche
6 XXII g
Nr. 151 – 177
Mode
Deutsch 20. Jh.

MODELLMAPPE
AUS DER
MODE
AUSSTELLUNG
1916
IM K.K. ÖSTERR. MUSEUM FÜR
KUNST UND INDUSTRIE, WIEN
SONDERAUSGABE » ZEITSCHRIFT
WIENER MODE

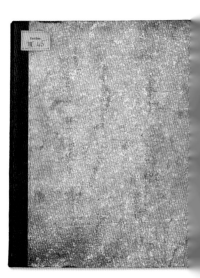

THE WAY FASHION PHOTOGRAPHY IS STAGED can differ enormously depending on the requirements of the shoot on the one hand and the photographer's mood or recent experiences on the other. What is fundamental is the mindset—the joy or the criticism—which a fashion shoot is intended to capture, and of course an estimate of how far one can or would like to go with the named items.

I always carry the subjects around with me for a while and play with various options in my mind's eye. For example, once I wanted to figure out how much space the depiction of the fashion itself needs to take up relative to the photo as a whole so that it is still perceived as the prominent feature in the image, or how tasteless or unusual the setting can be without causing offense. In that series I photographed beautiful and inconsequential cheap hotels and apartments—each with a TV in the room. Then I photographed the fashion and mounted it in the TV sets, meaning that the fashion itself was actually very small in proportion to the rooms where it was displayed. However, people's gaze is always drawn to a TV screen, even in a photo—and that experience has played a part in my approach ever since.

It is also a question of the energy and charisma of the model you decide on and the clothes you are photographing. Thick winter coats are often shapeless and require a different concept from flowing dresses. Choosing the location is crucial, too. Though it can be the case that one of those three components is so strong that the rest must come second.

Another important component is the client. They may have a clear mental image of what they want, which will ideally correspond to mine—but can contradict it entirely. The latter would be unfortunate, because you would then have to decide whether it is at all possible to work constructively under such complicated conditions. I find it difficult to abide by other people's ideas; it leaves too little space for good work to emerge. Mostly, though, the decision is made in advance: no one would choose a photographer who is entirely unrelated to the existing ideas for the shoot. Mostly, I have been lucky; I have been able to explain my stories and their backgrounds clearly enough that they could become a reality.

Photography, its form, and its subjects continue to develop; the reasons are related to technical as well as political and personal circumstances. With every series of photos, I attempt to take a step forward, to try something I have not tried before. After all, advertising can be attractive and intelligent, too.

In the past, a cover was almost exclusively selected on the basis of beauty, technical perfection, and class. Now we know that an unusual photo, a never-before-seen camera angle, an exciting but not traditionally beautiful face, can be much more effective. Even bad technical execution is not an obstacle. When designing a cover, you of course try to unite all of this knowledge in one shot, but it is rare for that to succeed. Additionally, it is equally important to establish the style and focus of the magazine on its cover. Sometimes the chosen image is simply the best and most eye-catching photo from a series, which was not originally intended for that purpose. That is rare nowadays, because the decisive criterion for the cover is the influence of the fashion labels who advertise within the magazine's pages. Very often the responsibility of choosing and shooting a cover leads to the photo and its selection being too careful—and the result being uninspiring.

Elfie Semotan, Photographer, Vienna/New York

HERR BÜCKLING AN DER ANGEL
ÜBER DEN HEILIGEN ERNST BÜRGERLICHER MASKERADE
BRIGITTE FELDERER

Im Jahr 1890 konnte die *Illustrirte Frauen-Zeitung* bereits auf ihr 25. Erscheinungsjahr zurückblicken. Man beging den würdigen Anlass mit einer Festschrift, die sich ganz der eigenen Geschichte verschrieb und ein geradezu weltumspannendes Imperium der Modepublizistik präsentierte. Das Magazin erschien in Berlin und Wien, von Beginn an in drei Sprachen. Gedruckt wurde in Leipzig. Neben Paris und London erschienen in Malmö und Stockholm, Budapest, Jungbunzlau und Prag, Den Haag, Turin und Mailand, Kopenhagen, Sankt Petersburg, Warschau, Rio de Janeiro, Porto, Madrid und Buenos Aires und nicht zuletzt in New York Ausgaben in den jeweiligen Landessprachen. Fast 400 Menschen waren für das Magazin, für Vertrieb und Herstellung, für die Texte und die Schnittmuster tätig. Allein im Wiener Büro, mit schicker Adresse im eleganten Heinrichhof in der Operngasse, waren vier Leute beschäftigt. 14 ZeichnerInnen entwarfen in der Berliner Redaktion die Bilder, Holzschneider setzten die Entwürfe um, die farbigen Abbildungen wurden zunächst noch händisch koloriert, Lithografen und Setzer gingen weiter ans Werk.

Seit der Gründung der Zeitschrift war die Zahl der Abonnements nur für die deutschsprachige Ausgabe schnell auf mehr als 300 000 gewachsen. In der Jubiläumsschrift wird das Heft als „eine grosse, universelle Zeitung für die Mode"[1] beschrieben, gewissermaßen ein modisches Zentralorgan, das nicht in der Modehauptstadt Paris, wohl aber in Berlin und Wien erschien. Die Redaktion räumte zwar ein, dass nach wie vor alle modischen Veränderungen von Paris ausgingen, zugleich wurde festgestellt, mit dieser Modeillustrierten ein bis dahin nicht dagewesenes modisches Massenmedium geschaffen zu haben, das die französischen Impulse „unter Berücksichtigung des Practischen" vereinfachte, gleichsam demokratisierte und weiter in der Welt verbreitete. Die Illustrationen zeigten vor, wie sich modische Ideen und saisonale Revolutionen auf ihre Umsetzbarkeit zurechtschneidern ließen. Nicht um die Darstellungen von Originalen ging es. Die Leserinnen bekamen Vorbilder und Anleitungen für die Schneiderin zu sehen, oder, wenn es denn sein musste, Inspirationen für die eigene Handarbeit.

In der Ausgabe vom 1. Jänner 1889 stimmte man die Leserinnenschaft auf die Ballsaison ein, und hatte auch nicht verabsäumt, all die Stoffe zu beschreiben, die für die Herstellung der „Phantasie-Costüme" benötigt wurden: Der Herr von Welt als „Bückling" trug seine Flossen aus „Tuch mit Malerei" und die „Perle" verbarg sich in einer Muschel aus „Draht mit Marzelline-Futter". Der gestandenen „Holländerin" bot ihre gestärkte Haube die beste Gelegenheit, den Familienschmuck auszuführen (Abb. 425). Doch setzten diese Maskeraden noch keine bürgerliche Konvention außer Kraft. Selbst wenn sich der Herr als Bückling karikiert, lassen feine Materialien und aufwendige Verarbeitung keinerlei Zweifel aufkommen. Hier wird nicht mit der eigenen Klassenzugehörigkeit gespielt. Der Bückling und die Holländerin sind auch bei diesem Zeitvertreib nicht aus ihrem eigentlichen Leben herausgetreten. Dieses Spiel ließe sich jederzeit unterbrechen, es bleibt auf die freie Zeit beschränkt. Dennoch ist das Spiel ein ernstgemeintes und spielt sich innerhalb bestimmter Grenzen ab, Zeit und Raum geben die Regeln vor.[2] Auf dem geweihten Tanzboden der Ballsäle formiert sich eine Gesellschaft, der auch eine solche Ausnahme von der Ordnung zusteht. Die

1   Melford, Friedrich (Vorwort und Text), *Zum fünfundzwanzigjährigen Bestehen der „Modenwelt". 1865–1890*, Berlin 1890.

2   Vgl. Huizinga, Johan, *Homo Ludens. Vom Ursprung der Kultur im Spiel*, Reinbek bei Hamburg 1987.

MR. KIPPER HAS BEEN CAUGHT
ON THE ABSOLUTE SOLEMNITY OF BOURGEOIS MASQUERADES
BRIGITTE FELDERER

1890 was the 25th year since the first edition of the *Illustrirte Frauen-Zeitung*. This honorable event was observed with a commemorative publication, which was entirely dedicated to the history of the periodical itself and presented a virtually global imperium of fashion journalism. The magazine was published in Berlin and Vienna, printed in Leipzig, and from the very outset it appeared in three languages. In addition to Paris and London, editions were released in Malmö and Stockholm, Budapest, Mladá Boleslav (then also known as Jungbunzlau) and Prague, The Hague, Turin and Milan, Copenhagen, Saint Petersburg, Warsaw, Rio de Janeiro, Porto, Madrid and Buenos Aires, and not least in New York—each in the respective national language. Almost 400 people worked on the magazine, its sales and production, its texts and sewing patterns. Four people were employed in the Vienna office alone, with its chic address in the elegant Heinrichhof on Operngasse. 14 illustrators designed the images in the Berlin editorial office, which were then realized by woodcutters. At first, the illustrations were colorized by hand; the final touch was added by lithographers and typesetters.

Since the founding of the magazine, the number of subscriptions to the German-language edition alone soon grew to over 300000. In the anniversary publication the periodical is described as "a large, universal newspaper for fashion"[1]; to a certain extent it was a pivotal fashion institution— yet it was not published in the fashion capital of Paris, but rather in Berlin and Vienna. Admittedly, the editors acknowledged that every change in fashion still emanated from Paris, yet at the same time they observed that in their illustrated fashion magazine they had created an unprecedented mass medium about fashion, which—"with due regard to what is practical"—simplified, to some degree democratized, and spread those French innovations to other parts of the world. The illustrations demonstrated how fashionable ideas and seasonal revolutions could feasibly be copied at home. The periodical was not concerned with depicting originals; instead, its readers were shown exemplars and given instructions for their dressmakers or, where necessary, inspirations for their own needlework.

The edition from 1 January 1889 set the mood for the ball season, while not neglecting to describe all of the fabrics necessary to produce the "fantasy costumes": The man of the world as a "kipper" wore fins made of "cloth with painting," and the "pearl" was hidden in a shell made of "wire with marceline lining." The seasoned "Dutchwoman" with her starched bonnet provided the best opportunity to display the family jewels. (ill. 425) Yet these masquerades did not override any bourgeois conventions. Even if a gentleman were to present himself as a cartoon kipper, the fine materials and elaborate workmanship would leave no one in any doubt about his status. This is not a case of *playing* with one's own class affiliation: The kipper and the Dutchwoman do not step out of their real-life roles during this diversion. The game could be interrupted at any time; it is restricted to the participants' free time. Nevertheless, the game is taken seriously and played out within defined limits; the time and space determine the rules.[2] On the sacred dance floor of the ballrooms a society forms, which is entitled to such an exception from the rules. The fashion plates probably

[1] Melford, Friedrich (foreword and text), *Zum fünfundzwanzigjährigen Bestehen der "Modenwelt."* 1865–1890, Berlin 1890.

[2] Cf. Huizinga, Johan, *Homo Ludens. Vom Ursprung der Kultur im Spiel*, Reinbek bei Hamburg 1987.

425
Agnes Stamer
Modebild aus *Illustrirte Frauen-Zeitung*
XVI. Jahrgang, Nr. 1, 1. Januar 1889, Tafel 768
Ausführung: Druckerei Carl Marquart, Leipzig
Stahlstich, koloriert
Fashion Plate from
[*Illustrated Women's Newspaper*]
Issue XVI, No. 1, 1 January 1889, Pl. 768
Execution: Printer Carl Marquart, Leipzig
Steel engraving, colored
405 x 292 mm
KI 8011-338, Schenkung donation from
Frieda Pollak-Sorez 1923

create a playful space, showing the correct dress code in view of the occasion—yet there is no room for maneuver. The game of fashion merely follows its (depicted) archetypes.

When the Dutchwoman takes the kipper to market, a bourgeois married couple enters the stage who are introducing their young daughter to society as a precious rarity. Mr. Kipper, possibly versed in the slippery parquet of the higher civil service, and his Dutch wife whose costume is utterly down to earth, appear en famille with the debutante, who is simultaneously concealed and presented. Later almost forgotten, these histories, these storiettes, are from a time when the social order could be suspended by inverting customary dress codes at the aristocratic masked balls of the rococo period. Women wore men's clothing, presenting themselves as soldiers or sailors, while men dressed up as women. The poor danced as bishops, lawyers, or counts; the rich masqueraded as beggars and peasants, wore Eastern costumes, or hid behind black eye masks and hoods as Venetian dominoes—perhaps unrecognized, but hopefully not unnoticed. Hidden and anonymous, it was possible to transcend the bounds of class and gender, act out erotic desires without fear of repercussions. Without the right clothes, achieving social status was only conceivable as a risky charade: When one removed one's clothes, one also removed one's power. Dressed as a beggar, a ruler might mingle with his people; the countess could arrive at a masked ball as a courtesan. Yet they were not simply disguised; they were also breaking the rules, and that could ultimately lead to social death. Once it was clothing that set the mistress apart from the lady's maid, that identified the one and the other as who they were. Those who dressed up chose a guise, which left far too much in the balance: how should one behave, if one does not know with whom one is dealing? Birth and status determined the dress codes, but in a masquerade clothes appear to have been capable of redefining the participants' social standing.

The French Revolution put a temporary end to such libertinage. In Vienna the authorities reacted disproportionately to roisterous dances and audacious masked balls as early as the beginning of the 18th century, after the successfully defeated Ottoman Wars and the subsequently blossoming celebrations. Masked balls were heavily taxed and had to be registered with the authorities. Under Maria Theresa rules were decreed for balls, which were intended to regulate the order of the dances, dress codes, manners, and much more. Only in the masked ballrooms of Vienna, Innsbruck, Linz, and Salzburg was one allowed—indeed officially permitted—to appear in disguise, and even then only in "respectable" costume. The political circumstances—whether the festive culture of the *Vormärz* or the disillusion after the defeated October revolution of 1848—found expression in the forms of representation of those who represented public life.[3] Around the mid-19th century, masked balls—once coveted aristocratic parties—also became accessible to the bourgeoisie and alleged anarchy was celebrated there. A new society had emerged, had superseded old orders, and was now defining its own, new order.

The fashionable masquerade of the honorable Mr. Kipper, caught on the fishing rod of his gracious wife the Dutchwoman, entirely complied with the standards of bourgeois unobtrusiveness. The new bourgeois self-consciousness was also expressed in the fact that there was a dictate of fashion to observe for every single social occasion. It was not at all extraordinary for ladies from Vienna's bon ton to change their outfits some six times every day.[4] Depending on the time of day, occasion, location, or society, according to duty or motto, forms were to be upheld, social attitudes

[3] Cf. Czeike, Felix, "Fasching," in: *Historisches Lexikon Wien*, vol. 2, Vienna 1993, 257 f.; Fink, Monika, "Ball," in: Flotzinger, Rudolf (ed.), *Oesterreichisches Musiklexikon*, vol. 1, Vienna 2002, 98 f.

[4] Cf. Karner, Regina/Lindinger, Michaela (eds.), *Großer Auftritt. Mode der Ringstraßenzeit*, exh.cat. Wien Museum, Vienna 2009.

Mode-Bilder entwerfen wohl einen spielerischen Raum, zeigen die richtige Toilette zum gegebenen Anlass, doch Freiheiten werden keine eröffnet. Das Spiel der Mode folgt bloß seinen Vor-Bildern. Wenn die Holländerin den Bückling zum Markt führt, tritt hier ein bürgerliches Ehepaar auf, das seine junge Tochter in die Gesellschaft einführt, als kostbare Rarität. Herr Bückling, möglicherweise auf dem glatten Parkett höherer Beamtenschaft erfahren, mit holländischer Gattin, deren Kostüm nichts an Bodenständigkeit vermissen lässt, treten en famille mit der Debütantin auf, die zugleich versteckt und vorgeführt wird. Fast vergessen die Geschichte, die dramatischen G'schichterln, als auf den aristokratischen Maskenbällen des Rokoko die soziale Ordnung durch eine Umkehrung der Kleidervorschriften außer Kraft gesetzt wurde. Frauen trugen Männerkleidung, erschienen selbst als Soldaten oder Matrosen, Männer verkleideten sich als Frauen. Die Armen tanzten als Bischöfe, Juristen oder Grafen, die Reichen maskierten sich als Bettler und Bauern, trugen orientalische Kostüme oder blieben als venezianischer Domino hinter schwarzer Augenmaske und Kapuze zwar vielleicht unerkannt, aber hoffentlich nicht unbemerkt. Verborgen und anonym ließen sich so Klassen- und Geschlechtergrenzen überschreiten, erotische Neigungen ungesühnt ausleben. Gesellschaftlicher Status ohne die rechten Kleider war nur denkbar als riskante Scharade, denn letztendlich zog man mit den Kleidern auch die Macht aus. Ein Herrscher mochte sich als Bettler verkleidet unter sein Volk mischen, die Comtesse auf einem Maskenball als Kurtisane erscheinen. Doch waren sie nicht bloß verkleidet, sie brachen mit Regeln, die letztendlich zum sozialen Tod führen konnten. Einst unterschieden Kleider die Herrin von der Zofe, ließen die eine wie die andere erst als solche erkennbar werden. Wer sich maskierte, wählte einen Deckmantel, der allzu vieles offenließ: Was, wenn man nicht mehr wusste, mit wem man es zu tun hatte? Geburt und Status gaben die Dresscodes vor, doch in der Maskerade schienen die Kleider soziale Zugehörigkeit neu festzulegen.

Mit der Französischen Revolution wurde solcher Libertinage vorübergehend ein Ende bereitet. In Wien hatten die Obrigkeiten schon zu Beginn des 18. Jahrhunderts, nach den erfolgreich geschlagenen Türkenkriegen und den in der Folge aufblühenden Festlichkeiten, empfindlich auf rauschende Tanzveranstaltungen und verwegene Maskenbälle reagiert. Maskenbälle wurden hoch besteuert und waren behördlich anzumelden. Unter Maria Theresia wurden Ballordnungen erlassen, welche die Reihenfolge der Tänze, Kleidervorschriften, Manieren und vieles mehr regeln sollten. Nur in den Redoutensälen in Wien, Innsbruck, Linz oder Salzburg durfte man – offiziell gestattet – auch maskiert erscheinen, allerdings auch das nur in „ehrbarer" Verkleidung. Die politischen Umstände – ob die Festkultur des Vormärz oder die Ernüchterung nach der niedergeschlagenen Oktoberrevolution 1848 – schlugen sich auf die Repräsentationsformen jener nieder, die das öffentliche Leben repräsentierten.[3] Um die Mitte des 19. Jahrhunderts wurden die Redouten als einst begehrte Adelsfeste auch für das Bürgertum zugänglich und auf den Maskenbällen vermeintliche Unordnungen zelebriert. Eine neue Gesellschaft war entstanden, die wohl alte Ordnungen abgelöst hatte und nun neue behauptete.

Die modische Maskerade des verehrten Herrn Bückling an der Angel seiner gnädigen Frau Holländerin folgte dabei ganz den Vorgaben bürgerlicher Unaufdringlichkeit. Das neue bürgerliche Selbstbewusstsein kam auch darin zum Ausdruck, dass es für wirklich jeden gesellschaftlichen Anlass ein modisches Diktat zu befolgen galt. Es war durchaus nicht ungewöhnlich, dass Damen

[3] Vgl. Czeike, Felix, „Fasching", in: *Historisches Lexikon Wien*, Bd. 2, Wien 1993, 257f.; Fink, Monika, „Ball", in: Flotzinger, Rudolf (Hg.), *Oesterreichisches Musiklexikon*, Bd. 1, Wien 2002, 98f.

represented and professed. During carnival time, too, the kipper wanted to be mistaken for the possibly slick citizen who he embodied on the other side of the parquet. The Dutchwoman was doubtlessly just as steadfast as her starched bonnet, and the pearl in the oyster was supposed to be elaborately sought and found, but certainly not picked up. These masquerades concealed no hidden agenda; social bounds might have been crossed or even left behind. One slipped into the roles defined by one's clothing without renouncing one's everyday role. Those who disguised themselves in this way certainly did not want to be misunderstood. This game of fashion in no way questioned social positions; it neither broke nor subverted any taboos. Those who masqueraded thus sported their conformism proudly and confidently. A fashion of this kind did not expose itself to any risks; quite the contrary, it asserted a convention, which should preferably remain unchanged. The bourgeoisie emulated the aristocracy, yet did not want to perish with them in this fashion for change. Altered social orders could be expressed by means of dress codes, yet once changed the new structures should also become firmly established.

The media snapshot of these three costumes, perhaps copied and possibly worn as depicted or differently at a Viennese carnival party, shows the two faces of fashion: Does fashion inevitably mean a "tiger's leap into the past" (Walter Benjamin) by a bourgeoisie, which has adopted the former glory of aristocratic representation? Or is a transformation happening, is future becoming present? Are clothes social mantles, which uniform a new and at once old class? Is it not the case that clothes should be representative, yes, but surely not fashionable? Is it a matter of asserting new conventions in the face of fleeting changeability? Should not a far too sophisticated lady and a refined, elegant gentleman be unmasked as social climbers? Is this really a question of fashion, or in fact mere adequacy?

The fashion plates from the MAK Collection show clothes as status symbols, as assertions of social standing. And they reveal to us what our attitude is to fashion today and how we want to behave, how we visualize this fashion, which claims eternal contemporaneity, promises individuality, and yet says so much about the groups to which we feel we belong, towards which coordinates we can and want to orient ourselves in the broad expanse of social spaces. In this sense, fashion holds up a mirror to our wishes and desires. Once again, we are reminded just how much we can learn from fashion.

der guten Wiener Gesellschaft sechs Mal täglich ihre Kleider wechselten.[4] Je nach Tageszeit, Anlass, Ort oder Gesellschaft, nach Verpflichtung oder Motto waren Formen zu wahren, gesellschaftliche Standpunkte darzustellen und zu behaupten. Der Bückling wollte auch im Fasching mit dem möglicherweise aalglatten Bürger verwechselt werden, den er diesseits des Parketts verkörperte. Die Holländerin war zweifellos genauso standhaft wie ihr gestärktes Häubchen, und die Perle in der Auster sollte aufwendig gesucht und gefunden, aber sicher nicht aufgegabelt werden. Diese Maskeraden verhehlten keine verborgenen Absichten, soziale Grenzen wurden vielleicht überschritten oder doch eher zurückgelassen. Man schlüpfte in modische Rollen, ohne die eigenen aufzugeben. Wer sich so verkleidete, wollte sicher nicht verkannt werden. Mit diesem modischen Spiel wurden gesellschaftliche Positionen keineswegs infrage gestellt, keine Tabus gebrochen oder unterlaufen. Wer sich so kostümierte, trug alle Angepasstheit stolz und selbstbewusst zur Schau. Eine solche Mode ließ sich auf keine Wagnisse ein, behauptete ganz im Gegenteil eine Konvention, die möglichst unverändert bleiben sollte. Das Bürgertum tat es dem Adel gleich, doch wollten sie im modischen Wandel nicht mit ihm untergehen. Über Dresscodes ließen sich veränderte gesellschaftliche Ordnungen zum Ausdruck bringen, doch einmal geändert, sollten sich die neuen Strukturen auch verfestigen.

Die mediale Momentaufnahme dieser drei Kostüme, vielleicht nachgeschneidert und möglicherweise so oder anders bei einem Wiener Faschingsball getragen, zeigt das Doppelgesicht der Mode: Bedeutet Modisches unweigerlich den „Tigersprung ins Vergangene" (Walter Benjamin), eines Bürgertums, das sich den einstigen Glanz aristokratischer Repräsentation aneignete? Oder wird hier ein Wandel, eine stattfindende Zukunft gegenwärtig? Sind die Kleider soziale Hüllen, die eine neue und zugleich alte Klasse uniformieren? Sollen die Kleider nicht vielmehr wohl repräsentativ, aber keinesfalls modisch daherkommen? Geht es darum, neue Konventionen gegenüber flüchtiger Veränderlichkeit zu behaupten? Sind eine allzu mondäne Dame, ein verfeinerter Elegant nicht als Aufsteiger zu entlarven? Geht es wirklich um Mode oder doch bloß um Angemessenheit?

Die Modebilder aus der MAK-Sammlung zeigen Kleider als Statussymbole, als Behauptungen gesellschaftlicher Positionen. Und sie zeigen uns, wie wir selbst uns heute zur Mode stellen und verhalten mögen, welches Bild wir uns von ihr machen, von einer Mode, die ewige Zeitgenossenschaft behauptet, Individualität verspricht und doch alles darüber erzählt, welchen Gruppen wir uns zugehörig fühlen, an welchen Koordinaten wir uns in den Weiten gesellschaftlicher Räume ausrichten können und mögen.

In diesem Sinne wirft uns die Mode die Bilder unserer Wünsche und Begehrlichkeiten zurück und es bleibt wieder einmal daran zu erinnern, wie viel sich von ihr lernen lässt.

4   Vgl. Karner, Regina/Lindinger, Michaela (Hg.), *Großer Auftritt. Mode der Ringstraßenzeit*, Ausst.kat. Wien Museum, Wien 2009.

19TH-CENTURY FASHION PLATES

"In the first half of the 19th century, fashion plates started to be distributed broadly and to gain a leading role, which removed from the creation of fashion the strict exclusivity, which it had previously maintained," as Hartwig Fischel states in his article on the fashion exhibition at the Imperial Royal Austrian Museum of Art and Industry (ÖMKI) in 1915/1916.[1] In point of fact, quite a number of magazines were established around 1800—from the well-known Weimar-based *Journal des Luxus und der Moden* (from 1786) to the *Wiener Moden-Zeitung* (from 1816)[2]. The fashion plates, Fischel continues, "initially had a strong artistic influence; they were carefully designed, engraved, printed, and colorized […], so that they became popular exemplars, but can often be appreciated and provide inspiration as achievements in graphic art, too."[3] It was in this sense—as an exemplar and inspiration—that the design for a plate for the *Wiener Moden* entered the museum's collection as early as 1868/69 via the art dealer's Miethke & Wawra; its final version was acquired in 1914 at Artaria & Co.[4] (ill. 426, 427).

These plates might have been part of the aforementioned fashion exhibition, which also included a "historical section."[5] For the latter, it was not only possible to draw on the rich collection of ornamental engravings, but also on the over 2000 recently acquired fashion plates from French and Spanish journals from the period between 1870 and 1900 (purchased from Hermine Srna in 1915). A short time later, a bundle of Biedermeier copperplate etchings on fashion from the *Wiener Theaterzeitung* were added to the collection (purchased from the antiquarian bookstore Reinhold Entzmann 1916). In 1935 Alexandra Ankwicz-Kleehoven donated almost 60 plates from the 1830s, which had originally belonged to the director of the School of Arts and Crafts, Felician Myrbach (ill. 429). The bequest from the Vienna Porcelain Manufactory containing almost 2000 patterns entered the collection as early as 1866, including pictures of costumes by the Viennese lithographer Joseph Trentsensky, editor of the *Modenbilder des Auslandes* (ill. 428).

By reference to these examples, it is possible to reconstruct not only the history of fashion, but also the changes in pictorial composition. For a long time, the *Journal des Luxus und der Moden* adhered to strict profile and frontal depictions, whose precision was supplemented by detailed descriptions. The Biedermeier models hold fans or letters in their hands and, in time, are permitted to assume a dance pose or be seated. From the 1830s, a stage is no longer built for them; instead, pieces of furniture or balustrades point to interior and exterior spaces, until genuine scenarios finally emerge. They portray Christmas and communion or a farewell on the jetty (ill. 436). Around the middle of the 19th century, group portraits become more common in order to show mens- and womenswear together; children, too, congregate in such images, as entire fashion supplements are now dedicated to this new target group within moneyed society (ill. 438). The depiction of accessories is also subject to change. While hats, collars, and neckties were still presented in the style of a product catalog in the first half of the 19th century, they were increasingly portrayed on the wearer during the era of historicism.

The collection therefore demonstrates how the fashion plate develops from an exemplar and pattern to a promise of an elegant, prestigious, and simultaneously individual lifestyle in the stories it tells—whether of the appeal of playing in a card game costume, of the delights of love in a romantic lace dress, or of social pleasures in afternoon dress.

[1] Fischel, Hartwig, "Modeausstellung im Österreichischen Museum," in: *Kunst und Kunsthandwerk* (XIX) 1/2 1916, 87. The architect Hartwig Fischel worked primarily as an expert author and, as Ludwig Hevesi's successor, wrote over 230 articles for the museum's publication *Kunst und Kunsthandwerk*. Translated by Maria Slater.

[2] Published under the title *Wiener Zeitschrift für Kunst, Literatur, Theater und Mode* from 1817 with several supplements, e.g. *Wiener Moden*.

[3] Translated by Maria Slater.

[4] The ÖMKI worked closely with the art dealer's and publishing house Artaria & Co. The museum's publication *Kunst und Kunsthandwerk* was printed by the publishing house from 1898 to 1921.

[5] *Mode-Ausstellung 1915/16 im k. k. Österreichischen Museum für Kunst und Industrie*, exh.cat. ÖMKI, Vienna 1915, 29–31.

MODEBILDER DES 19. JAHRHUNDERTS

„In der ersten Hälfte des XIX. Jahrhunderts beginnen die Modeblätter eine große Verbreitung und eine führende Rolle zu erlangen, die der Schaffung der Mode jene strenge Exklusivität nimmt, welche vorher gewahrt wurde", konstatiert Hartwig Fischel in seinem Artikel zur *Mode-Ausstellung 1915/16* im k. k. Österreichischen Museum für Kunst und Industrie (ÖMKI).[1] In der Tat etablieren sich um 1800 etliche Zeitschriften – vom bekannten Weimarer *Journal des Luxus und der Moden* (ab 1786) bis zur *Wiener Moden-Zeitung* (ab 1816)[2]. Die Blätter, so Fischel weiter, „standen vorerst noch stark unter künstlerischem Einfluß, wurden mit Sorgfalt entworfen, gestochen, gedruckt und koloriert […], so daß sie beliebte Vorbilder wurden, aber auch schon als graphische Leistung oft schätzbar und anregend sind". In diesem Sinne – als Vorbild und Inspiration – gelangte der Entwurf für ein Blatt der *Wiener Moden* bereits 1868/1869 über die Kunsthandlung Miethke & Wawra in die Sammlung des Museums; seine Ausführung wurde 1914 bei Artaria & Co.[3] erworben (Abb. 426, 427). Womöglich waren die Blätter Bestandteile der erwähnten Modeausstellung, die auch eine „historische Abteilung" beinhaltete.[4] Diesbezüglich konnte man nicht nur auf die reich bestückte Ornamentstich-Sammlung zurückgreifen, sondern auch auf über 2 000 jüngst erworbene Modebilder aus französischen und spanischen Journalen der Zeit zwischen 1870 und 1900 (Ankauf Hermine Srna 1915). Wenig später wurde die Sammlung durch ein Konvolut an Biedermeier-Mode-kupfern aus der *Wiener Theaterzeitung* ergänzt (Ankauf Antiquariat Reinhold Entzmann 1916). 1935 schenkte Alexandra Ankwicz-Kleehoven knapp 60 Blätter aus den 1830er Jahren, die ursprünglich dem Direktor der Kunstgewerbeschule Felician Myrbach gehört hatten (Abb. 429). Bereits 1866 kam der Nachlass der Wiener Porzellanmanufaktur mit fast 2 000 Vorlagen in die Sammlung, darunter auch Kostümbilder des Wiener Lithografen Joseph Trentsensky, Herausgeber der *Moden-bilder des Auslandes* (Abb. 428).

Anhand der Beispiele lässt sich nicht nur Modegeschichte nachvollziehen, sondern werden auch die Veränderungen hinsichtlich der bildlichen Inszenierung deutlich. Das *Journal des Luxus und der Moden* hält lange Zeit an strengen Profil- und Frontaldarstellungen fest, deren Präzision durch ausführliche Beschreibungen ergänzt wird. Die Biedermeier-„Models" halten Fächer oder Briefe in den Händen und dürfen im Laufe der Zeit eine Tanzpose oder einen Sitzplatz einnehmen. Ab den 1830er Jahren wird ihnen eine kleine Bühne gebaut – Möbelstücke oder Balustraden weisen auf Innen- und Außenräume –, bis schließlich richtige Szenarien entstehen. Darin sind Weihnachten und Kommunion thematisiert oder der Abschied auf den Landungsbrücken (Abb. 436). Um die Jahrhundertmitte häufen sich Gruppenbilder, um Damen- und Herrenmode gemeinsam zu zeigen; auch Kinder finden sich darin zusammen, denn dieser neuen Zielgruppe aus gut betuchten Kreisen sind nunmehr eigene Modebeilagen gewidmet (Abb. 438). Die Darstellung von Accessoires unterliegt ebenfalls einem Wandel. Wurden Hüte, Krägen oder Halsbinden in der ersten Hälfte des 19. Jahrhunderts noch in der Art eines Warenkatalogs präsentiert, werden sie im Historismus fokussiert an der Trägerin vorgeführt.

So vollzieht sich die Entwicklung des Modebilds von Vorlage und Muster hin zur Verheißung eines eleganten, repräsentativen und zugleich individuellen Lebensstils durch die Geschichten, die es erzählt – sei es vom Reiz des Spiels im Kartenspielkostüm, vom Liebesglück im romantischen Spitzenkleid oder von gesellschaftlichen Vergnügungen im Nachmittagsdress.

[1] Fischel, Hartwig, „Modeausstellung im Österreichischen Museum", in: *Kunst und Kunsthandwerk* (XIX) 1/2 1916, 87. Der Architekt Hartwig Fischel war vor allem als Fachautor tätig und verfasste in der Nachfolge von Ludwig Hevesi über 230 Artikel für die Museumsschrift *Kunst und Kunsthandwerk*.

[2] Ab 1817 unter dem Titel *Wiener Zeitschrift für Kunst, Literatur, Theater und Mode* mit etlichen Beilagen, z.B. *Wiener Moden*.

[3] Mit der Kunsthandlung bzw. dem Verlag Artaria & Co. arbeitete das ÖMKI eng zusammen. Im Verlag erschien von 1898 bis 1921 die Museumsschrift *Kunst und Kunsthandwerk*.

[4] *Mode-Ausstellung 1915/16 im k. k. Österreichischen Museum für Kunst und Industrie*, Ausst.kat. ÖMKI, Wien 1915, 29–31.

426
Philipp Stubenrauch oder or
Johann Nepomuk Ender
Entwurf für ein Modebild
Wien, 1827
Federzeichnung, laviert
Design for a Fashion Plate
Vienna, 1827
Pen and ink drawing, washed
172 x 114 mm
KI 1689-1, Ankauf purchased from
Galerie Miethke & Wawra 1868/69

427
Philipp Stubenrauch oder or
Johann Nepomuk Ender
**Modebild aus *Wiener Zeitschrift
für Kunst, Literatur, Theater und Mode*,
Beilage *Wiener Moden***
Wien, 1827
Stecher: Franz Xaver Stöber
Stahlstich, koloriert
**Fashion Plate from the [Viennese
magazine of art, literature, theater
and fashion], supplement to [Viennese
fashions]**
Vienna, 1827
Engraver: Franz Xaver Stöber
Steel engraving, colored
224 x 141 mm
KI 7931-31, Ankauf purchased from
Artaria & Co. 1914

428
Joseph Trentsensky
**Modebild aus der Beilage
zu *Modenbilder des Auslandes***
Wien, um 1834
Lithografie
**Fashion Plate from the Supplement
of [Fashion pictures from abroad]**
Vienna, ca. 1834
Lithograph
303 x 228 mm
KI 15165-103-2, Nachlass bequest from
Wiener Porzellanmanufaktur

429
Anonym Anonymous
**Modebild aus dem *Journal des Tailleurs*
[Journal der Schneider]**
Paris, 1835
Stecher: Hippolyte Damours
Kupferstich, koloriert
Fashion Plate from the [Tailors' journal]
Paris, 1835
Engraver: Hippolyte Damours
Copperplate engraving, colored
270 x 188 mm
KI 9247-19, Schenkung donation from
Alexandra Ankwicz-Kleehoven 1935

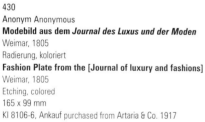

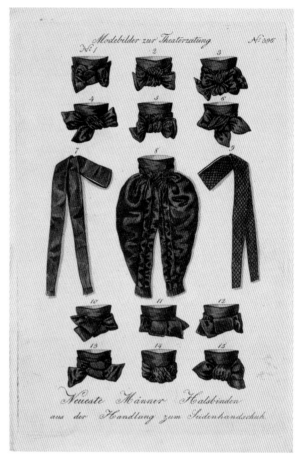

430
Anonym Anonymous
Modebild aus dem *Journal des Luxus und der Moden*
Weimar, 1805
Radierung, koloriert
Fashion Plate from the [Journal of luxury and fashions]
Weimar, 1805
Etching, colored
165 x 99 mm
KI 8106-6, Ankauf purchased from Artaria & Co. 1917

431
Anonym Anonymous
Modebild aus der *Wiener Theaterzeitung*
Wien, um 1840
Stecher: Andreas Geiger
Radierung, koloriert
Fashion Plate from the [Viennese theater newspaper]
Vienna, ca. 1840
Engraver: Andreas Geiger
Etching, colored
227 x 147 mm
KI 8025-92, Ankauf purchased from
Reinhold Entzmann 1916

432
Guido Gonin
Modebild aus *La Modiste Universelle*
[Die universelle Modistin]
Paris, 1881
Ausführung: Druckerei H. Lefévre
Kreidelithografie, koloriert
Fashion Plate from *La Modiste Universelle*
[The universal modiste]
Paris, 1881
Execution: Printer H. Lefévre
Chalk lithograph, colored
361 x 275 mm
KI 7990-46, Ankauf purchased from
Hermine Srna 1915

433
Guido Gonin
Modebild aus *La Modiste Universelle*
[Die universelle Modistin]
Paris, 1888
Ausführung: Druckerei H. Lefévre
Kreidelithografie, koloriert
Fashion Plate from *La Modiste Universelle*
[The universal modiste]
Paris, 1888
Execution: Printer H. Lefévre
Chalk lithograph, colored
380 x 274 mm
KI 7990-159, Ankauf purchased from
Hermine Srna 1915

434
Anonym Anonymous
Modebild aus *Victoria,*
Illustrirte Muster- und Modenzeitung
Berlin, 1864
Stahlstich, koloriert
Fashion Plate from [Victoria, illustrated
pattern and fashion newspaper]
Berlin, 1864
Steel engraving, colored
298 x 228 mm
KI 9231-112, Ankauf purchased from
Heimatmuseum Freistadt 1935

435
Guido Gonin
Modebild aus *L'Élégance Parisienne*
[Pariser Eleganz]
Paris, 1881
Ausführung: Druckerei H. Lefévre
Kreidelithografie, koloriert
Fashion Plate from [Parisian elegance]
Paris, 1881
Execution: Printer H. Lefévre
Chalk lithograph, colored
362 x 276 mm
KI 8011-5, Ankauf purchased from
Hermine Srna 1915

436
Anonym Anonymous
Modebild aus dem *Berliner Modenblatt*
Berlin, 1875
Stahlstich, koloriert
Fashion Plate from [Berlin journal of fashion]
Berlin, 1875
Steel engraving, colored
375 x 266 mm
KI 8011-284, Ankauf purchased from
Hermine Srna 1915

437
Jean-Baptiste Jules David
Modebild aus *L'Élégance Parisienne*
[Pariser Eleganz]
Paris, 1882
Stecher: E. Cheffen
Stahlstich, koloriert
Fashion Plate from [Parisian elegance]
Paris, 1882
Engraver: E. Cheffen
Steel engraving, colored
362 x 272 mm
KI 8011-107, Ankauf purchased from
Hermine Srna 1915

438
Anonym Anonymous
Modebild aus dem
Journal des Demoiselles
[Journal der jungen Damen]
Paris, um 1870
Ausführung: Druckerei Vapeur de Th. Dupuy
Stahlstich, koloriert
Fashion Plate from the
Journal des Demoiselles
[Young ladies' journal]
Paris, ca. 1870
Execution: Printer Vapeur de Th. Dupuy
Steel engraving, colored
182 x 268 mm
KI 9210-100, Alter Bestand, inv.
old holdings, inventoried in 1935

439
Anonym Anonymous
Modebild aus *La Moda Elegante Ilustrada*
[Illustrierte elegante Mode]
Madrid, 1893
Stahlstich, koloriert
Fashion Plate
from *La Moda Elegante Ilustrada*
[Illustrated elegant fashion]
Madrid, 1893
Steel engraving, colored
275 x 375 mm
KI 8010-309, Ankauf purchased from
Hermine Srna 1915

MODEPOSTKARTEN UND ZEITSCHRIFTENCOVER NACH 1900

Ein beliebtes – und gut verkäufliches – Motiv der um 1900 etablierten Künstlerpostkarte war der Modeentwurf. Von der Hand eines Ludwig Heinrich Jungnickel, Otto Lendecke oder Eduard Wimmer-Wisgrill, einer Maria Likarz und vor allem Mela Koehler zierte er einen Großteil der Postkarten der Wiener Werkstätte (WW), die ab 1907 in Produktion gingen.[1] Aus deren Anfangsjahren stammen kleine Serien mit Biedermeier-Moden und belegen – auch in diesem Medium – die Beschäftigung mit der Kultur der Großväter-Generation in der Zeit vor dem Ersten Weltkrieg. Generell war die historische Aufarbeitung bestimmter Themen populär geworden, was sich auch in der Gebrauchs-grafik niederschlug. Einen Abriss über die Modeentwicklung im 19. Jahrhundert liefert etwa eine zwölfteilige Postkartenserie des deutschen Grafikers Erich Gruner, entstanden um 1912, die den Einfluss der „Mode von 1800" auf die „Mode von heute" deutlich zeigt. Auch die Art der Darstellung hat hier ihre Wurzeln: Der Fokus ist – nach den Gruppen-Szenarien des Historismus – wieder auf das einzelne Modell gerichtet, die Bühne auf einen Bodenstreifen reduziert.

Vielfach als Glückwünsche fungierten die Postkarten der WW-Künstlerin Mela Koehler und erhielten entsprechende Aufdrucke durch den Verlag. Im besten Fall war hierfür ein freies Feld vorgesehen – wie bei Koehlers Postkarten-Serie für die Firma Bahlsen. Die Motive thematisierten die Lebensalter der Frau vom Baby bis zur Greisin und erschienen auch als Reklamemarken (s. S. 432). Äußerst durchdacht wird hier der lebenslange Genuss von Bahlsen-Keksen mit der aktuellen Mode verbunden und bleibt damit stets en vogue (Abb. 442).

Anlasskarte, Werbeträgerin oder Teil einer Bildergeschichte – die Modepostkarte des frühen 20. Jahrhunderts diente verschiedensten Zwecken. Das Cover eines Modemagazins hatte hinge-gen primär Sehnsüchte zu wecken, nicht nur nach dem angesagten „evening dress", sondern nach einem bestimmten Lebensstil. Während des Ersten Weltkriegs wurde auch hier noch zurück-geschaut auf bessere Zeiten (Abb. 444). Dabei bedeutete die Besinnung der Wiener Mode(rne) auf die nationalen Kulturleistungen der Vergangenheit weit mehr: Sie ermöglichte die Opposition gegen den „aufgedrängten Geschmack des Auslands"[2], besonders Frankreichs. Eigenständigkeit zu zeigen, war der dezidierte Anspruch der Initiatoren der *Mode-Ausstellung 1915/16* im ÖMKI: „Daß endlich unsere Künstler den französischen ebenbürtig sind, ja sie an Kraft und Frische übertreffen, davon müssen wir selbst überzeugt zu sein beginnen."[3] Mit Dagobert Peche als Ausstellungsgestalter holten sie sich den besten Beweis für diese Behauptung. Die Zeitschrift *Wiener Mode* gab ein Sonderheft heraus und reproduzierte für den durchgehend gestalteten Umschlag Peches Tapete *Rom*, die der WW-Künstler in den Ausstellungsräumen eingesetzt hatte (Abb. S. 364). Die Ver-wendung eines Leitmotivs (auch auf dem Katalog-Cover) für eine Museumsschau scheint neu und zugleich folgerichtig aus dem Corporate-Design-Gedanken der WW entwickelt.

Am Ende des Ersten Weltkriegs steht das gesellschaftliche Leben wieder im Mittelpunkt, vor allem aber künden die Titelblätter von der veränderten Rolle der Frau. Man sieht sie reisen, Sport treiben, Auto fahren, Zigaretten rauchen. Ihre neue Unabhängigkeit zelebriert besonders das deutsche Modemagazin *Die Dame* mit seinen Haupt-Illustratoren Paul Scheurich, Ludwig Kainer und ab 1926 Ernst Deutsch-Dryden. Der Wiener Grafiker wurde als künstlerischer Leiter der *Dame* nach Paris berufen und prägte bis 1933 nicht nur deren Erscheinungsbild, sondern äußerte sich auch in eigenen Artikeln. 2009 kamen mit dem Teilnachlass Deutsch-Drydens knapp 560 seiner Illustrationen für

[1] Vgl. Schmuttermeier, Elisabeth/Witt-Dörring, Christian, *Postcards of the Wiener Werk-stätte. A Catalogue Raisonné*, Neue Galerie New York 2010.

[2] Tilgner, Friedrich [Einleitung], in: *Mode-Ausstellung 1915/16 im k. k. Österreichischen Museum für Kunst und Industrie*, Ausst.kat. ÖMKI, Wien 1915, 3.

[3] Ebd., 6.

FASHION POSTCARDS AND MAGAZINE COVERS AFTER 1900

[1] Cf. Schmuttermeier, Elisabeth/Witt-Dörring, Christian, *Postcards of the Wiener Werkstätte. A Catalogue Raisonné*, Neue Galerie New York, New York 2010.

A popular—and readily marketable—motif on art postcards, which were established around 1900, was the fashion design. From the hand of Ludwig Heinrich Jungnickel, Otto Lendecke, or Eduard Wimmer-Wisgrill, Maria Likarz, and above all Mela Koehler, it adorned a large proportion of Wiener Werkstätte (WW) postcards, which were produced from 1907.[1] Small series bearing Biedermeier fashions originate from the early years of the WW; even in this medium, the designs bear witness to the artists' interest in the culture of their grandparents' generation during the pre-WWI period. The historical reappraisal of certain themes had become popular in general, and this was also reflected in ephemera. A survey of the evolution of 19th-century fashion is provided, for example, by a twelve-part postcard series produced around 1912 by the German graphic designer Erich Gruner, which clearly demonstrates the influence of the "Fashion of 1800" on the "Fashion of today." The type of depiction, too, has its roots in that age: the focus has returned—after the group portraits of historicism—to the individual model, the stage reduced to a strip of floor.

WW artist Mela Koehler's postcards frequently functioned as greeting cards and were given corresponding overprints by their publisher. In the best case, a blank space was designated for this purpose—as in Koehler's postcard series for the Bahlsen company. The subject of the motifs was the stages of a woman's life, from baby girl to elderly lady, and they were also released as poster stamps (see p. 433). Extremely well-conceived, the lifelong enjoyment of Bahlsen cookies is here linked to contemporary fashion and hence remains forever en vogue (ill. 442).

Occasion card, advertising medium, or part of a pictorial story, the early 20th-century fashion postcard served a wide variety of purposes. In contrast, the aim of the cover of a fashion magazine was primarily to trigger desire—not just for the popular evening dress, but also for a certain lifestyle. During the First World War, this was another place, which looked back to better times (ill. 444). Yet the fact that Viennese Modernism and fashion took stock of the nation's past cultural achievements in truth meant much more: it facilitated opposition to the "enforced taste from foreign lands,"[2] particularly from France. Demonstrating autonomy was the explicit aspiration of those who initiated the fashion exhibition at the ÖMKI in 1915/1916: "We ourselves must begin to be convinced that finally our artists are on a par with the French, indeed exceed their strength and freshness."[3] With Dagobert Peche as an exhibition designer, they had found themselves the best evidence for this claim. The magazine *Wiener Mode* published a special issue for the occasion, reproducing for the uniformly designed cover Peche's wallpaper *Rom* [Rome], which the WW artist had installed in the rooms of the exhibition (ill. p. 364). The use of a leitmotif (also on the cover of the catalog) for a museum show appears to have been a novel concept at the time and was simultaneously a development consistent with the corporate design-thinking of the WW.

[2] Tilgner, Friedrich [introduction], in: *Mode-Ausstellung 1915/16 im k. k. Österreichischen Museum für Kunst und Industrie*, exh.cat. ÖMKI, Vienna 1915, 3. Translated by Maria Slater.

[3] Ibid., 6. Translated by Maria Slater.

At the end of the First World War, social life once again took center stage; above all, however, the title pages bore witness to the new role of women. They are shown traveling, playing sport, driving cars, smoking cigarettes. Their new independence was particularly celebrated by the German fashion magazine *Die Dame* with its main illustrators Paul Scheurich, Ludwig Kainer, and—from 1926—Ernst Deutsch-Dryden. The Viennese graphic designer was called to Paris as art director of *Die Dame* and until 1933 not only influenced its visual appearance, but also expressed his opinions in his own articles. In 2009 just under 560 of his illustrations for *Die Dame* entered the

Die Dame in die MAK Bibliothek und Kunstblättersammlung. Der Großneffe seiner einstigen Geschäftspartnerin Helene Wolff hatte sie im Zuge der Räumung ihres Londoner Hauses in einem großen grünen Reisekoffer entdeckt.[4] Deutsch-Drydens experimentierfreudiger Zugang äußert sich in dominanten Schriftzügen oder ungewöhnlichen Ausschnitten. Geradezu revolutionär erscheint dabei die Werbung für eine Zigarettenmarke: das Bild wurde comicartig in zwei Teile geteilt und der Text dazwischengeschoben (Abb. 447). Wie auf Mela Koehlers Bahlsen-Postkarten ist auch hier die elegant gekleidete Frau Garantin für die Qualität des Produkts.

[4] Lipmann, Anthony, „Fragmente einer Biografie: Ernst Deutsch (1887–1938)", in: Peter Noever (Hg.), *Ernst Deutsch-Dryden. En Vogue!*, MAK Studies 2, Wien 2002, 16.

440
Erich Gruner
Postkarte *Mode von 1800*
Leipzig, um 1912
Ausführung: Druckerei
Meissner & Buch
Lithografie
Postcard [Fashion in 1800]
Leipzig, ca. 1912
Execution: Printer
Meissner & Buch
Lithograph
139 x 90 mm
KI 8876-23, Schenkung
donation 1930

441
Erich Gruner
Postkarte *Mode von heute*
Leipzig, um 1912
Ausführung: Druckerei
Meissner & Buch
Lithografie
Postcard [Fashion of today]
Leipzig, ca. 1912
Execution: Printer
Meissner & Buch
Lithograph
139 x 90 mm
KI 8876-34, Schenkung
donation 1930

442
Mela Koehler
**Postkarte aus einer
12-teiligen Serie für
die Keksfabrik Bahlsen**
Hannover, 1913
Offsetdruck
**Postcard from a
12-Part Series for the
Cookie Factory Bahlsen**
Hannover, 1913
Offset print
140 x 90 mm
KI 9121-49, Schenkung
donation from
Mela Koehler 1915

443
Mela Koehler
Neujahrskarte
Wien, 1912
Verlag: Postkartenverlag
Brüder Kohn
Offsetdruck
New Year's Card
Vienna, 1912
Publisher: Postcard
Publisher Brüder Kohn
Offset print
140 x 90 mm
KI 9121-87, Schenkung
donation from
Mela Koehler 1915

[4] Lipmann, Anthony, "Fragmente einer Biografie: Ernst Deutsch (1887–1938)," in: Peter Noever (ed.), *Ernst Deutsch-Dryden. En Vogue!*, MAK Studies 2, Vienna 2002, 16.

MAK Library and Works on Paper Collection thanks to the partial bequest from Deutsch-Dryden. The great-nephew of his erstwhile business partner Helene Wolff had discovered them in a large, green suitcase while clearing her London house.[4] Deutsch-Dryden's eagerly experimental approach is expressed in dominant lettering or unusual details. Well-nigh revolutionary in this context is the advertisement for a cigarette brand in which the image is divided in two like a comic, with the text squeezed in between (ill. 447). As on Mela Koehler's Bahlsen postcards, here too the elegantly dressed woman symbolically guarantees the quality of the product.

444
Vermutl. Prob. Josef Divéky
Titelblatt für die *Wiener Mode*
Heft 14, 1917
Verlag: Verlag der Wiener Mode
Klischee
Title Page for [Viennese fashion]
No. 14, 1917
Publisher: Publisher of Wiener Mode
Cliché
318 x 238 mm
KI 8977-88, Schenkung donation 1930

445
Anonym Anonymous
Titelblatt für *Die Kunst der Mode*
Heft 5, 1918
Verlag: Arnold Bachwitz Verlag, Wien
Klischee
Title Page for [The art of fashion]
No. 5, 1918
Publisher: Arnold Bachwitz, Vienna
Cliché
322 x 245 mm
KI 8977-94, Schenkung donation 1930

447
Ernst Deutsch-Dryden
Werbung für die Zigarettenmarke *Blaupunkt*
von Waldorf Astoria
Die Dame, Heft 6, 1928, S. 46
Verlag: Ullstein & Co., Berlin/Wien
Klischee
Advertisement for the Cigarette Brand
Blaupunkt **by Waldorf Astoria**
[The lady], no. 6, 1928, p. 46
Publisher: Ullstein & Co., Berlin/Vienna
Cliché
362 x 278 mm
BI 18146-1928-6-46, Schenkung donation from
Anthony Lipmann 2009

446
Ernst Deutsch-Dryden
Titelblatt für *Die Dame*
Heft 17, Mai 1927
Verlag: Ullstein & Co., Berlin/Wien
Klischee
Title Page for [The Lady]
No. 17, May 1927
Publisher: Ullstein & Co., Berlin/Vienna
Cliché
360 x 270 mm
KI 8977-78, Schenkung donation 1930

448
Ernst Deutsch-Dryden
Titelblatt für *Die Dame*
Heft 11, 1931
Verlag: Ullstein & Co., Berlin/Wien
Klischee
Title Page for [The lady]
No. 11, 1931
Publisher: Ullstein & Co., Berlin/Vienna
Cliché
362 x 278 mm
BI 18146-1931-11, Schenkung donation from
Anthony Lipmann 2009

449
Ernst Deutsch-Dryden
Titelblatt für *Die Dame*
Heft 12, März 1929
Verlag: Ullstein & Co., Berlin/Wien
Klischee
Title Page for [The lady]
No.12, March 1929
Publisher: Ullstein & Co., Berlin/Vienna
Cliché
362 x 278 mm
BI 18146-1929-12, Schenkung donation from
Anthony Lipmann 2009

450
Nathan Steffie
Titelblatt für *Die Dame*
Heft 20, Juli 1927
Verlag: Ullstein & Co., Berlin/Wien
Klischee
Title Page for [The lady]
No. 20, July 1927
Publisher: Ullstein & Co., Berlin/Vienna
Cliché
358 x 275 mm
KI 8977-75, Schenkung donation 1930

451
Paul Scheurich
Titelblatt für *Die Dame*
Heft 20, Juli 1918
Verlag: Ullstein & Co., Berlin/Wien
Klischee
Title Page for [The lady]
No. 20, July 1918
Publisher: Ullstein & Co., Berlin/Vienna
Cliché
360 x 282 mm
KI 8977-41, Schenkung donation 1930

MODEINSERATE AUS DEM FRÜHEN 20. JAHRHUNDERT

Der Erfolg der von Josef Hoffmann kuratierten und von Dagobert Peche gestalteten Modeausstellung im k. k. Österreichischen Museums für Kunst und Industrie – sie wurde zwischen Dezember 1915 und Februar 1916 von 71 637 Personen besucht[1] – hatte offenbar die gewünschten Auswirkungen hinsichtlich eines wirtschaftlichen Impulses auf die Wiener Modebranche, zumindest was die Wiener Werkstätte (WW) betraf: Sie eröffnete im November 1916 einen Modesalon in der Kärntner Straße 41 sowie ein Stoffgeschäft in unmittelbarer Nähe (Maysedergasse 4); letzteres wurde 1918 in die Kärntner Straße 32 verlegt. Für diese Niederlassungen wurden verschiedenste, oft ganzseitige Annoncen in der *Neuen Freien Presse* geschaltet. Abgesehen von Peche stammen sie hauptsächlich von den Künstlerinnen der WW: Vally Wieselthier und Lilly Jacobsen, Irene Schaschl oder Maria Likarz. Während des Krieges wurde das Modebild auch in die Werbung für das Zeichnen von Kriegsanleihen integriert, wie ein Entwurf von Fritzi Löw zeigt (Abb. 458).

Die WW-Inserate sind Teil eines Konvoluts, das 1933 als Schenkung von Richard Wildner in die Sammlung geriet. *Lehmanns Wohnungsanzeiger* verzeichnet zu dieser Zeit eine einzige Person dieses Namens als Textilhändler im 9. Wiener Bezirk, Hörlgasse 11; 1940 verliert sich seine Spur. Die über 200 Ausschnitte aus Zeitungen und Magazinen enthalten Reklame für Luxusartikel (Autos, Zigaretten, Spirituosen, Parfums) und neue technische Errungenschaften (Metax-Glühbirne, Wiktorin-Licht), überwiegend aber für Mode und Accessoires der WW ebenso wie der Wiener Warenhäuser Zwieback, Gerngross und Herzmansky. Insgesamt fällt die Präsenz Ernst Deutsch-Drydens als Grafiker auf, der auch für deutsche Firmen tätig war; sein Werdegang ist gleichsam anhand der Inserate ablesbar. 1887 als Ernst Deutsch in Wien geboren, ist er ab 1910 in Berlin nachweisbar und bewirbt dort etwa die renommierten Salamander-Schuhe, die so „weltberühmt" sind, dass sie gar nicht mehr gezeigt werden müssen (Abb. 459). 1918 kehrt er nach Wien zurück, nennt sich zunächst Deutsch-Dryden, ab ca. 1921 nur noch Dryden. Seine Werbegrafiken sind äußerst vielfältig, zeigen sich mal konservativ, mal abstrahierend, mal karikaturistisch – eine Bandbreite, die Dryden ab 1926 als Chef-Illustrator der Zeitschrift *Die Dame* in Paris voll ausschöpfen konnte.[2]

Für *Die Dame* sowie das Modehaus Zwieback arbeitete auch Otto Lendecke. Der bei Paul Poiret geschulte Künstler schuf etliche Modeentwürfe für die WW und verlegte kurz vor seinem Tod 1918 noch ein eigenes Magazin unter dem Titel *Die Damenwelt*. Er war künstlerischer Berater der *Wiener Mode*, die ab 1921 vom Rob-Verlag herausgegeben wurde.[3] Dessen Gründer Karl Rob[itsek], wie Lendecke eine Zeit lang in Paris ansässig, war selbst als Grafiker tätig und zeigte dabei oftmals sein Faible für die Karikatur, so etwa in den Annoncen für das Pelz-Importhaus E. Anders (Abb. 462). „Schließlich und endlich wissen wir, daß wir nicht Ewigkeitswerte, sondern nur anspruchslose Arbeiten schaffen, die naturgemäß der Mode des Tages unterworfen sind. Aber eine unbescheidene Hoffnung hegen wir: daß unsere Arbeiten vielleicht einst in 50 oder 100 Jahren starke Kulturdokumente sein werden für die Art, wie der Kaufmann Anfangs des 20. Jahrhunderts seine Ware anpries."[4] So äußerte sich der Wiener Grafiker Julius Klinger 1912 aus seiner Wahlheimat Berlin. Die wenigen hier gezeigten Beispiele verdeutlichen die mögliche Vielfalt dieser Kulturdokumente im Zusammenhang mit bedeutenden Institutionen und Persönlichkeiten.

[1] „Mitteilungen aus dem k. k. Österreichischen Museum", in: *Kunst und Kunsthandwerk* (XIX) 1/2 1916, 102.

[2] Pokorny-Nagel, Kathrin, „Kunst als Trend. Werbeillustrationen von Ernst Deutsch-Dryden", in: Noever, Peter (Hg.), *Ernst Deutsch-Dryden. En Vogue!*, MAK Studies 2, Wien 2002, 58–77.

[3] Koscher, Michael, *Der Rob-Verlag,* Seminararbeit am Institut für Germanistik der Universität Wien (Neuere deutsche Literatur, „Arisierung" im österreichischen Buchhandel), Wien 2002 [Onlinefassung], www.murrayhall.com/files/referate/rob.pdf (29.4.2016).

[4] Deutsches Museum für Kunst in Handel und Gewerbe (Hg.), *Julius Klinger. Monographien deutscher Reklamekünstler*, Bd. 3, Hagen/Dortmund 1912, o. S.

EARLY 20TH-CENTURY FASHION ADVERTISEMENTS

[1] "Mitteilungen aus dem k. k. Österreichischen Museum," in: *Kunst und Kunsthandwerk* XIX, 1916, 102.

The success of the fashion exhibition at the Imperial Royal Austrian Museum of Art and Industry—which was curated by Josef Hoffmann, designed by Dagobert Peche, and visited by 71 637 people between December 1915 and February 1916[1]—obviously had the desired effect, namely an economic stimulus for the Viennese fashion industry. This can be said for the Wiener Werkstätte (WW), at least, which opened a fashion house at Kärntner Straße 41 as well as a fabric shop close by (Maysedergasse 4) in November 1916; the latter then moved to Kärntner Straße 32 in 1918. A wide range of often full-page advertisements for these branches was published in the *Neue Freie Presse*. Aside from Peche, they mostly come from the artists of the WW: Vally Wieselthier and Lilly Jacobsen, Irene Schaschl, or Maria Likarz. During the war, the fashion plate was also integrated into advertisements for war bonds, as shown by the design by Fritzi Löw (ill. 458).

The WW advertisements are part of a bundle donated to the collection by Richard Wildner in 1933. The *Lehmanns Wohnungsanzeiger* from the time records a single person with this name: a textile dealer at Hörlgasse 11 in Vienna's 9th district; in 1940 all traces of him are lost. The more than 200 cuttings from newspapers and magazines contain promotions for luxury articles (cars, cigarettes, spirits, perfume) and new technological achievements (Metax lightbulbs, Wiktorin lamps), but they are overwhelmingly for fashion and accessories by the WW as well as by the Viennese department stores Zwieback, Gerngross, and Herzmansky. The ubiquitous presence of Ernst Deutsch-Dryden as a graphic designer of these works is striking; while he also worked for German companies, these advertisements can more or less be read as a pictorial CV. Born in Vienna in 1887 as Ernst Deutsch, he is traceable to Berlin from 1910 and there advertises for the prestigious Salamander shoes, for example, which were so "world famous" that it was not even necessary to depict them (ill. 459). In 1918 he returns to Vienna, calling himself Deutsch-Dryden at first, but from ca. 1921 he evolves into to just Dryden. His advertising art is extremely diverse, appearing at times conservative, at times abstract or caricatural—a range Dryden was able to exploit in full as head illustrator of the magazine *Die Dame* in Paris from 1926.[2]

[2] Pokorny-Nagel, Kathrin, "Kunst als Trend. Werbeillustrationen von Ernst Deutsch-Dryden," in: Noever, Peter (ed.), *Ernst Deutsch-Dryden. En Vogue!*, MAK Studies 2, Vienna 2002, 58–77.

[3] Koscher, Michael, *Der Rob-Verlag*, seminar paper at the German Studies Institute at the University of Vienna (Modern German Literature, "Aryanization" in the Austrian book trade), Vienna 2002 [online version], www.murrayhall.com/files/referate/rob.pdf (29 Apr 2016).

Otto Lendecke also worked for *Die Dame* as well as the fashion house Zwieback. Having been taught by Paul Poiret, the artist created several fashion designs for the WW and also published his own magazine entitled *Die Damenwelt* shortly before his death in 1918. He also worked as artistic adviser for *Wiener Mode*, which was published by the Rob-Verlag from 1921.[3] Like Lendecke, its founder, Karl Rob[itsek], also resided in Paris for a while, and himself worked as a graphic designer, often revealing his predilection for caricature. This is the case in his advertisements for the fur importing company E. Anders (ill. 562), for example.

[4] Deutsches Museum für Kunst in Handel und Gewerbe (ed.), *Julius Klinger. Monographien deutscher Reklamekünstler*, vol. 3, Hagen/Dortmund 1912, n. p. Translated by Maria Slater.

"Finally and ultimately, we know that we do not create eternal values, but merely unpretentious works, which are naturally subject to the fashion of the day. But we do nurture one immodest hope: that our works might at some time—in 50 or 100 years—become powerful cultural documents for the way in which retailers advertised their wares at the beginning of the 20th century."[4] These are the words of the Viennese graphic designer Julius Klinger from his adopted home city of Berlin in 1912. The few examples shown here illustrate the potential diversity of these cultural documents in connection with significant institutions and personalities.

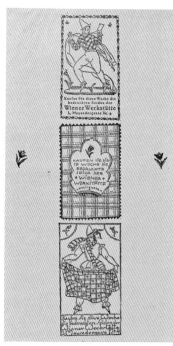

452
Dagobert Peche
Ganzseitiges Inserat
Die Stoffe der Wiener Werkstätte
Neue Freie Presse, Wien, 7. 11.1916
Klischee
Full-Page Newspaper
Advertisement [The fabrics
of the Wiener Werkstätte]
Neue Freie Presse, Vienna, 7 Nov 1916
Cliché
426 x 277 mm
KI 9079-11, Schenkung donation from
Richard Wildner 1933

453
Vally Wieselthier/Lilly Jacobsen
Inserat *Kaufen Sie diese Woche*
die bedruckte Seide der Wiener
Werkstätte
Neue Freie Presse, Wien, 1916/17
Klischee
Newspaper Advertisement
[Buy the printed silk of the
Wiener Werkstätte this week]
Neue Freie Presse, Vienna, 1916/17
Cliché
420 x 264 mm
KI 9079-12, Schenkung donation from
Richard Wildner 1933

454
Heddi Hirsch
Inserat *Wiener Werkstätte*
Frühjahrsmoden
Neue Freie Presse, Wien, um 1920
Klischee
Newspaper Advertisement
[Wiener Werkstätte spring
collection]
Neue Freie Presse, Vienna, ca. 1920
Cliché
45 x 234 mm
KI 9079-4, Schenkung donation from
Richard Wildner 1933

455
Hertha Ramsauer
Inserat *Wiener Werkstätte*
Weihnachtsverkauf
Neue Freie Presse, Wien, um 1920
Klischee
Newspaper Advertisement
[Wiener Werkstätte Christmas
sale]
Neue Freie Presse, Vienna, ca. 1920
Cliché
43 x 263 mm
KI 9079-26, Schenkung donation from
Richard Wildner 1933

456
Irene Schaschl
Inserat *Neuer Laden*
Wiener Werkstätte
Wien, 1918
Klischee
Newspaper Advertisement
[New shop Wiener Werkstätte]
Vienna, 1918
Cliché
171 x 90 mm
KI 9079-33, Schenkung donation from
Richard Wildner 1933

457
Maria Likarz
Ganzseitiges Inserat der
Wiener Werkstätte
Neue Freie Presse, Wien, 8.9.1921
Klischee
Full-Page Newspaper
Advertisement by the
Wiener Werkstätte
Neue Freie Presse, Vienna, 8 Sept 1921
Cliché
424 x 273 mm
KI 9079-15, Schenkung donation from
Richard Wildner 1933

458
Fritzi Löw
Entwurf für ein Kriegsanleihe-
Inserat der Wiener Werkstätte
Wien, 1917
Bleistift, Tusche
Design for a War Bond Newspaper
Advertisement of the Wiener
Werkstätte
Vienna, 1917
Pencil, ink
93 x 93 mm
KI 12546-6, Schenkung donation from
Alfred Hofmann 1955

459
Ernst Deutsch-Dryden
Inserat für Salamander-Schuhe
Wien, 1912
Klischee
**Newspaper Advertisement for Shoes
by Salamander**
Vienna, 1912
Cliché
138 x 225 mm
KI 9079-153, Schenkung donation from
Richard Wildner 1933

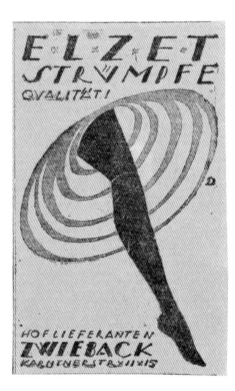

460
Ernst Deutsch-Dryden
Inserat *Elzet Strümpfe*
des Bekleidungsgeschäfts Zwieback
Neue Freie Presse, Wien, 1919
Klischee
**Newspaper Advertisement
[Elzet Stockings] by the Clothes Shop
Zwieback**
Neue Freie Presse, Vienna, 1919
Cliché
130 x 81 mm
KI 9079-76, Schenkung donation from
Richard Wildner 1933

461
Ernst Deutsch-Dryden
**Inserat für Pyjamas von Gartenberg
im Trattnerhof**
Wien, um 1921
Klischee
**Newspaper Advertisement for Pajamas
by Gartenberg in the Trattnerhof**
Vienna, ca. 1921
Cliché
122 x 91 mm
KI 9079-180, Schenkung donation from
Richard Wildner 1933

462
Karl Robitsek/Rob-Verlag
Inserat für das Wiener Pelz-Importhaus
E. Anders
Wien, 1919
Klischee
Newspaper Advertisement for the
Viennese Fur Importer E. Anders
Vienna, 1919
Cliché
81 x 166 mm
KI 9079-163, Schenkung donation from
Richard Wildner 1933

463
Anonym Anonymous
Inserat für die *Grosse Bade Schau*
im Bekleidungsgeschäft Zwieback
Wien, nach 1920
Klischee
Newspaper Advertisement for
the [Great swim show] at the
Clothes Shop Zwieback
Vienna, after 1920
Cliché
222 x 85 mm
KI 9410-9, Schenkung donation from
Richard Wildner 1936

464
Atelier Hans Neumann
Inserat für das Wiener Pelz-Importhaus
E. Anders
Wien, um 1920
Klischee
Newspaper Advertisement for the
Viennese Fur Importer E. Anders
Vienna, ca. 1920
Cliché
228 x 147 mm
KI 9079-103, Schenkung donation from
Richard Wildner 1933

465
Otto Lendecke
Inserat für Handschuhe
des Bekleidungsgeschäfts Zwieback
Neue Freie Presse, Wien, 29.8.1919
Klischee
Newspaper Advertisement for Gloves
at the Clothes Shop Zwieback
Neue Freie Presse, Vienna, 29 Aug 1919
Cliché
92 x 113 mm
KI 9410-7, Schenkung donation from
Richard Wildner 1936

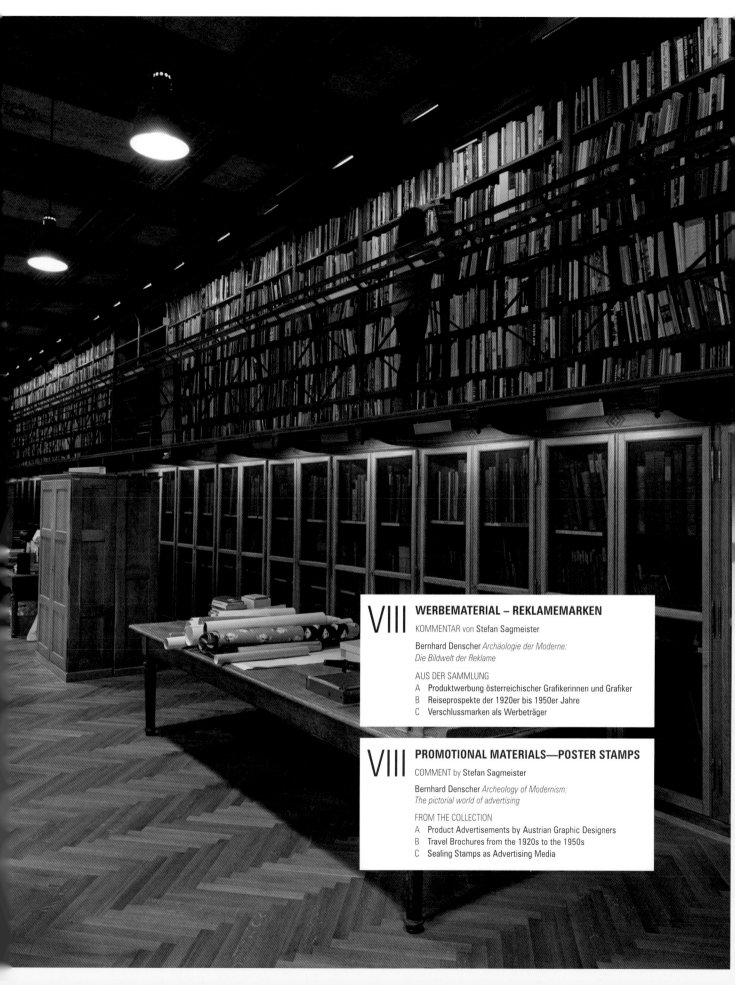

LIKE MOST PEOPLE ON THE PLANET, I LIVE IN A CITY. And like every urbanite, I am entirely surrounded by things, which were designed by someone: the socks on my feet, the flooring in my room, the room and the house, the street and the park, the neighborhood, the city and its suburbs—everything was designed. In this incredible diversity, the small things—the playing card and the travel brochure, the postage stamp and the shirt box—matter and mattered just as much as the design of the toaster and the architecture of the building.

These small things can be designed in a way that makes them a burden for people, that visually pollutes the environment, or they can be designed in a way that might provide some small delight to their beholders. The things in this book delighted someone, they were worth collecting, keeping, selecting, and publishing. They are good.

Stefan Sagmeister, Graphic designer, New York

ICH WOHNE, WIE DIE MEISTEN LEUTE AUF DIESER WELT, IN EINER STADT. Wie jeder Stadtbewohner bin ich zu 100 Prozent von Dingen umgeben, die von jemandem gestaltet wurden: Die Socken an meinen Füßen, der Fußboden in meinem Zimmer, das Zimmer und das Haus, die Straße samt dem Park, die Nachbarschaft, die Stadt und deren Vororte, alles wurde gestaltet. In dieser unglaublichen Vielfalt spielen und spielten die kleinen Dinge, die Spielkarte und die Reisebroschüre, die Briefmarke und der Hemdenkarton genauso eine Rolle wie das Design des Toasters und die Architektur des Hauses.

Diese kleinen Dinge können so gestaltet sein, dass sie für die Menschen belastend sind, dass sie die Umwelt visuell verschmutzen, oder sie können so gestaltet sein, dass sie die Möglichkeit haben, den Betrachter ein kleines bisschen zu entzücken. Die Dinge in diesem Buch haben jemanden entzückt, sie waren es wert, gesammelt, aufgehoben, aussortiert und publiziert zu werden. Sie sind gut.

Stefan Sagmeister, Grafiker, New York

ARCHÄOLOGIE DER MODERNE: DIE BILDWELT DER REKLAME
BERNHARD DENSCHER

Das „Ephemere" ist, so die ursprüngliche Bedeutung des griechischen Wortes, nur für einen Tag
bestimmt. Im heutigen Sinn, so hat der Ephemera-Sammler und -Forscher Maurice Rickards[1] in
seinem Buch *Collecting Printed Ephemera* dargelegt, tauchte der Begriff im Englischen bereits zur
Mitte des 18. Jahrhunderts auf, als der bedeutende Schriftsteller und Lexikograf Samuel Johnson[2]
in seiner Zeitschrift *The Rambler* im Zusammenhang mit „journals and gazettes" vermerkte: „These
papers of the day, the ‚Ephemerae' of learning, have uses more adequate to the purposes of common life than more pompous and durable volumes."[3] Waren mit Johnsons Feststellung in erster
Linie noch Texte gemeint, so sollten diese Beobachtungen bald auch für die Welt der Bilder gelten.
Das Ephemere ist eben nicht nur für einen Tag, sondern für *den* Tag bestimmt, das heißt im medialen
Kontext gesehen: Es sind und es finden sich darin aufschlussreiche „Ausdrucke", die besonders
intensive Extrakte des jeweiligen Zeitgeistes darstellen. So hat auch Karl Kraus rund 150 Jahre
nach Johnson in Bezug auf die ihn in Wien umgebende optische Alltagsware einen ähnlichen Ge-
dankengang verfolgt, wenn er meinte: „Als man anfing, das geistige Leben in die Welt der Plakate
zu verbannen, habe ich vor Planken und Annoncentafeln kaum eine Lernstunde versäumt."[4]
Viel früher, also wieder zur Zeit von Samuel Johnson, sind gerade für England beachtliche visuelle
Beispiele des „Graphic Design before Graphic Designers"[5] nachweisbar. Auf Dokumenten, Ankündigungen, Geschäftskarten, Inseraten und Rechnungsformularen zeigten die Drucker, dass sie nicht
nur eine entsprechende handwerkliche, sondern auch eine erstaunliche ästhetische Qualität in ihre
Arbeit einbringen konnten und wirkten damit vorbildlich für die weitere Entwicklung in Europa.
Im Laufe des 19. Jahrhunderts und zu Beginn des 20. Jahrhunderts trat aufgrund enormer sozialer,
wirtschaftlicher und technologischer Veränderungen eine nahezu explosionsartige Entwicklung der
Bildmengen ein. Die österreichische Zeitung *Die Zeit* beleuchtete 1902 in einer Artikelserie dieses
Phänomen einer sich ständig vermehrenden visuellen Medienlandschaft: „Tausende von Schnell-
pressen laufen für Reclamegegenstände, für Affichen, Innenplakate, Reclamekarten und Reclame-
kalender. Es gibt Papierfabriken und Chromopapierstreichereien, die nur von den Aufträgen dieser
Pressen leben; und große Prägeanstalten, zahlreiche Buchbindereien adjustiren die Lieferungen der
lithographischen Institute und Buchdruckereien, die von der Erzeugung der Reclameartikel ihren
Betrieb aufrecht erhalten. Eine kleine Armee von Zeichnern, Malern, Lithographen und Druckern ist
thätig, um all die vielfältigen Schauobjekte herzustellen, die uns neue oder alte Kunst- und Industrie-
erzeugnisse ankündigen."[6]
Sehr bald wurde diese Vielfalt von neuartigem Material zum Gegenstand spezieller Kollektionen.
Die Kunsthistorikerin Ruth E. Iskin weist in ihrer Studie zu den Anfängen des Plakats auf die weg-
weisende Bedeutung der Sammler für die Bereitstellung und Aufarbeitung des ephemeren,
ästhetisch interessanten und kulturwissenschaftlich überaus aufschlussreichen Materials hin.
Die Gemeinschaft jener Bildbegeisterten, der „Iconophiles", sammelte nicht bloß zum eigenen
Vergnügen, sondern angesichts der entsprechenden Zurückhaltung öffentlicher Institutionen im
überzeugten Selbstbewusstsein, wichtige kulturelle Zeugnisse für die Nachwelt zu sichern.[7] Sie
verstanden sich somit nicht als jene skurrilen Sonderlinge, als die sie oft gesehen wurden, sondern
als wichtige Dokumentare, die interessante Belege für gesellschaftliche Entwicklungen für die

1 Rickards, Maurice, *Collecting Printed Ephemera*, New York 1988, 13.

2 Vgl. McDowell, Paula, „Of Grubs and Other Insects: Constructing the Categories of ‚Ephemera' and ‚Literature' in Eighteenth-Century British Writing", in: Murphy, Kevin/O'Driscoll, Sally (Hg.), *Studies in Ephemera: Text and Image in Eighteenth-Century Print*, Lewisburg 2013, 36.

3 „Diese Tageszeitungen, die ‚Ephemera' des Lernens, bieten einen adäquateren Nutzen für die Zwecke des Gemeinlebens als aufwendigere, langlebigere Publikationen", in: *The Rambler*, Nr. 145, 6.8.1751. Übersetzt von Claudia Fuchs.

4 Kraus, Karl, „Die Welt der Plakate", in: *Die Fackel* 26.6.1909, 21.

5 Jury, David, *Graphic Design before Graphic Designers. The Printer as Designer and Craftsman 1700–1914*, London 2012.

6 „Die volkswirtschaftliche Bedeutung der Reclame", in: *Die Zeit*, 10.10.1902, 10.

7 Iskin, Ruth E., *The Poster. Art, Advertising, Design, and Collecting 1860s–1900s*, Hanover/New Hampshire 2014, 300.

ARCHEOLOGY OF MODERNISM:
THE PICTORIAL WORLD OF ADVERTISING
BERNHARD DENSCHER

[1] Rickards, Maurice, *Collecting Printed Ephemera*, New York 1988, 13.

[2] Cf. McDowell, Paula, "Of Grubs and Other Insects: Constructing the Categories of 'Ephemera' and 'Literature' in Eighteenth-Century British Writing," in: Murphy, Kevin/O'Driscoll, Sally (eds.), *Studies in Ephemera: Text and Image in Eighteenth-Century Print*, Lewisburg 2013, 36.

[3] In: *The Rambler*, No. 145, 6 Aug 1751.

[4] Kraus, Karl, "Die Welt der Plakate," in: *Die Fackel* 26 Jun 1909, 21. Translated by Maria Slater.

[5] Jury, David, *Graphic Design before Graphic Designers. The Printer as Designer and Craftsman 1700–1914*, London 2012.

[6] "Die volkswirtschaftliche Bedeutung der Reclame," in: *Die Zeit*, 10 Oct 1902, 10. Translated by Maria Slater.

[7] Iskin, Ruth E., *The Poster. Art, Advertising, Design, and Collecting 1860s–1900s*, Hanover/New Hampshire 2014, 300.

The "ephemeral" is, according to the original meaning of the Greek word, only destined for one day. The ephemera collector and researcher Maurice Rickards[1] explains in his book *Collecting Printed Ephemera* that the term emerged in the contemporary sense in English as early as the mid-18th century, when the remarkable writer and lexicographer Samuel Johnson[2] noted in his magazine *The Rambler* in the context of "journals and gazettes" that "These papers of the day, the 'Ephemerae' of learning, have uses more adequate to the purposes of common life than more pompous and durable volumes."[3] While Johnson's statement pertained in the first instance to texts, these observations would soon also apply to the world of images.

The ephemeral is in fact not just intended for one day, but rather for the day; in a media context, that is to say: there are (to be found) within that category revealing "prints," which constitute particularly condensed extracts of the respective zeitgeist. Even Karl Kraus followed a similar train of thought some 150 years after Johnson with respect to the optical everyday wares surrounding him in Vienna, when he said: "When people began to banish spiritual life to the world of posters, I missed hardly a single lesson in front of planks and advertising boards."[4]

Much earlier, i.e. in the age of Samuel Johnson, there is evidence of notable visual examples—especially in England—of "Graphic Design before Graphic Designers."[5] On documents, announcements, business cards, newspaper advertisements, and billing forms, the printers showed that they could not only contribute an appropriate artisanal but also an astounding aesthetic quality to their work, and with it they exerted an exemplary influence on further developments in Europe.

Over the course of the 19th century and at the beginning of the 20th century, an almost explosive evolution of image quantities occurred due to enormous social, economic, and technological changes. The Austrian newspaper *Die Zeit* shone a light on this phenomenon of a constantly increasing visual media landscape in a series of articles from 1902. "Thousands of high-speed presses run for promotional materials, for placards, interior posters, advertising postcards, and promotional calendars. There are paper factories and chromo paper manufactories, which live on commissions from these print media alone, and large embossing establishments and numerous bookbinderies adjust the deliveries from lithographic institutes and book printers, which manufacture promotional articles in order to support their businesses. A small army of draftsmen, painters, lithographers, and printers is employed to produce all of the diverse showpieces, which announce to us new or old products of art and industry."[6]

Very soon, this variety of novel material became the focus of special collections. The art historian Ruth E. Iskin refers in her study on the beginnings of the poster to the groundbreaking significance of collectors for the provision and reappraisal of these ephemeral, aesthetically interesting, and extremely insightful materials from a cultural historical perspective. The community of picture enthusiasts, those "iconophiles," collected not just for their own enjoyment, but rather—given the relative reticence of public institutions—with the self-assured conviction that they were securing important cultural testimony for posterity.[7] Consequently, they did not consider themselves the bizarre eccentrics for which they were often held, but rather important documenters who were

466
Ernst Deutsch-Dryden
Plakat für *Metax*-Glühlampen
Wien, 1916
Ausführung: Druckerei J. Weiner
Flachdruck
Poster for *Metax* Light Bulbs
Vienna, 1916
Execution: Printer J. Weiner
Flat print
950 x 625 mm
Pl 2090, Schenkung donation 1930

467
Ernst Deutsch-Dryden
Reklamemarke für
***Metax*-Glühlampen**
Wien, 1916
Lithografie
Poster Stamp for
***Metax* Light Bulbs**
Vienna, 1916
Lithograph
60 x 45 mm
KI 14142-2-301, Ankauf purchased
from Maria Landa 1980

468
Ernst Deutsch-Dryden
Inserat für *Metax*-Glühlampen
Neue Freie Presse, Wien, 11.6.1916
Klischee
Newspaper Advertisement
for *Metax* Light Bulbs
Neue Freie Presse,
Vienna, 11 Jun 1916
Cliché
217 x 267 mm
KI 9079-85, Schenkung donation
from Richard Wildner 1933

469
Ernst Deutsch-Dryden
Inserat für *Metax*-Glühlampen
Wien, um 1916
Klischee
Newspaper Advertisement
for *Metax* Light Bulbs
Vienna, ca. 1916
Cliché
257 x 82 mm
KI 9079-194, Schenkung donation
from Richard Wildner 1933

8 Cf. Stammers, Tom, "The Bric-a-Brac of the Old Regime. Collecting and Cultural History in Post-Revolutionary France," in: *French History* (22) 3 2008, 314.

9 Iskin (see note 7), 264.

10 *Die Sammlung angewandter Graphik*, Handbücher der Reklamekunst 1, Berlin-Charlottenburg 1919.

11 Grohnert, René, *Hans Sachs und seine Plakatsammlung, der Verein der Plakatfreunde und die Zeitschrift "Das Plakat" im Prozess der Herausbildung, Bedeutungswandlung und Konsolidierung des Plakates in Deutschland zwischen 1890 und 1933*, Berlin/Neersen 1993; id., "The Final Chapter: the collections of Dr Hans Sachs between 1898 and 2013," in: Le Coultre, Martijn F. (ed.), *Hans Sachs and the Poster Revolution*, Hoorn 2013, 27 f.

12 Denscher, Bernhard, "Ottokar Mascha, a Viennese Connoisseur," in: Le Coultre, Martijn F. (ed.), *Hans Sachs and the Poster Revolution*, Hoorn 2013, 41 f.

13 Schweiger, Werner J., *Aufbruch und Erfüllung. Gebrauchsgraphik der Wiener Moderne 1897 -1918*, Vienna 1988, 159. Translated by Maria Slater.

preserving interesting evidence of social developments for future generations.[8] This assessment would soon prove to be very accurate, since many of the large public collections are substantially founded on what were originally private collections. Even the corresponding holdings of "everyday prints"[9] at the MAK were to no small extent initially collated by private individuals and only later entered the museum's Works on Paper Collection.

Published in 1919, the *Handbuch der Reklamekunst* lists the collectors who were members of the renowned Verein der Plakatfreunde [Society of poster fans] in Berlin and also states the foci of their collections.[10] It becomes apparent that prominent poster collectors such as Hans Sachs[11] in Germany and Ottokar Mascha[12] in Austria had a broader interest than is often assumed. For example, Mascha's collection—to whose initiative the poster collections of the Austrian National Library as well as the Albertina can be traced—comprised not only 4000 posters, but also 3000 items of "small advertising art and ephemera." Hans Sachs, on the other hand, could list 8000 posters ("only artistic, 2000 of which are war posters"), 1200 magazine covers, 2000 items of "small advertising art," 1000 items of "private occasion graphics," 400 calendars, literature on advertising art ("80 books, 700 individual articles"), and 400 "plagiarisms of ephemera" as his property.

The two individuals just named are also prototypical of a newly emerging scene of collectors in terms of their social position: Hans Sachs was a dentist, Ottokar Mascha a lawyer. While acquiring expensive artworks was restricted to the aristocracy in the early decades of the 1800s and later the upper classes, in the second half of the century a strengthened middle class began to copy the feudal attitude to collecting, but had to concentrate on other materials due to their limited financial means—and in this respect advertising could quite literally be found on the street. Yet even preserving these cheap materials required a certain effort, both in terms of free time and space. Neither were they particularly available to the proletariat, although even here there occasionally emerged the possibility to collect smaller materials, which also promised a certain distinction—for example picture postcards or postage stamps.

That the interest of great collectors and collections was not just limited to posters understandably arose from the professionalization of the advertising industry. Graphic designers increasingly focused on their customers' publicity campaigns as a whole and consequently also designed brochures, newspaper advertisements, and other materials, which they frequently furnished with the same subjects. This phenomenon can be observed very clearly in poster stamps, which experienced a veritable boom around 1900 and on which many posters of the age are depicted in miniature—the name "poster stamp" is no coincidence. Werner J. Schweiger, to whose collection a considerable part of the respective holdings at the MAK can be traced, located the beginnings of these "micro posters" in Austria. In his work *Aufbruch und Erfüllung. Gebrauchsgraphik der Wiener Moderne*, he wrote: "After 1900, poster stamps were among the most prevalent, known, and mainstream advertising media in the history of advertising and publicity there had ever been. Their beginnings can be found in promotional stamps for exhibitions, of which Vienna can proudly claim to be the 'inventor': the oldest exhibition stamp dates from the year 1845 and advertised the 'Third general Austrian trade products exhibition.'"[13]

In the German Empire, an equivalent scene developed in the years between 1910 and 1914—and hence substantially later, yet all the more vehement, than in Austria. Over just a few years, 100000

Nachwelt bewahrten.[8] Es war dies eine Einschätzung, die sich bald als sehr zutreffend erweisen sollte, denn viele der großen öffentlichen Sammlungen basieren im Wesentlichen auf ursprünglich privaten Kollektionen. Auch der entsprechende Bestand an „everyday prints"[9] im MAK wurde zu einem nicht unerheblichen Teil zuerst von Privaten zusammengetragen und gelangte erst später in die Kunstblättersammlung des Museums.

Das im Jahr 1919 erschienene *Handbuch der Reklamekunst* listet jene SammlerInnen auf, die Mitglieder des renommierten Berliner Vereins der Plakatfreunde waren, und gibt auch deren Sammelgebiete an.[10] Es zeigt sich, dass prominente Plakatsammler, wie Hans Sachs[11] in Deutschland oder Ottokar Mascha[12] in Österreich, ein weiter gestreutes Interesse hatten, als oft angenommen wird. So beinhaltete etwa die Kollektion von Mascha, auf dessen Initiative die Plakatsammlungen der Österreichischen Nationalbibliothek sowie der Albertina zurückgehen, nicht nur 4000 Plakate, sondern auch 3000 Stück „kleine Werbe- und Gebrauchsgraphik".

Hans Sachs wiederum konnte 8000 Plakate („nur künstlerische, davon 2000 Kriegsplakate"), 1200 Zeitschriftenumschläge, 2000 Stück „kleine Werbegraphik", 1000 Stück „private Gelegenheitsgraphik", 400 Kalender, Literatur zur Reklamekunst („80 Bücher, 700 Einzelaufsätze") und 400 „Plagiate der Gebrauchsgr[aphik]" als sein Eigentum auflisten.

Die beiden genannten Persönlichkeiten sind auch von ihrer sozialen Stellung her prototypisch für eine neu entstandene Sammlerszene: Hans Sachs war Zahnarzt, Ottokar Mascha Anwalt. War es in früheren Jahrhunderten nur dem Adel und später dem Großbürgertum vorbehalten, teure Kunstwerke zu erwerben, so begann in der zweiten Hälfte des 19. Jahrhunderts ein erstarkter Mittelstand die feudale Attitüde des Sammelns zu kopieren, musste sich aber aufgrund der begrenzten finanziellen Möglichkeiten auf andere Materialien konzentrieren – die Reklame war diesbezüglich im wahrsten Sinne des Wortes auf der Straße zu finden. Aber auch das Bewahren dieser billigen Materialien bedurfte eines gewissen Aufwandes, und zwar sowohl an Freizeit als auch an Raum. Dem Proletariat stand beides kaum zur Verfügung, obwohl sich auch hier fallweise das Sammeln von kleinerem Material, das doch auch eine gewisse Distinktion versprach, zum Beispiel von Bildpostkarten oder Briefmarken, herauskristallisierte.

Dass sich das Interesse der großen Sammlungen nicht bloß auf Plakate beschränkte, ergibt sich nachvollziehbar aus der Professionalisierung der Werbebranche. Die Grafiker beschäftigten sich immer mehr mit dem gesamten Werbeauftritt ihrer Auftraggeber und entwarfen daher auch Prospekte, Inserate und weiteres Material, das sie häufig mit denselben Sujets versahen. Sehr deutlich ist dieses Phänomen bei den Reklamemarken zu beobachten, die um 1900 einen wahren Boom erlebten und auf denen viele Plakate der Zeit im Miniformat zu sehen sind – nicht zufällig heißen sie im Englischen „poster stamps". Werner J. Schweiger, auf dessen Kollektion ein attraktiver Teil des diesbezüglichen Bestandes im MAK zurückgeht, ortete die Anfänge dieser „Mikro-Plakate" in Österreich. In seinem Werk *Aufbruch und Erfüllung. Gebrauchsgraphik der Wiener Moderne* schrieb er dazu: „Reklamemarken gehörten nach 1900 zu den am meisten verbreiteten, bekanntesten und populärsten Werbemitteln in der Geschichte der Werbung und Reklame überhaupt. Der Beginn lag bei Propagandamarken für Ausstellungen, wobei Wien sich die ‚Erfindung' zugute halten kann: Die älteste Ausstellungsmarke stammt aus dem Jahre 1845 und warb für die ‚Dritte allgemeine österreichische Gewerbe-Producten-Ausstellung'."[13]

8   Vgl. dazu: Stammers, Tom, „The Bric-a-Brac of the Old Regime. Collecting and Cultural History in Post-Revolutionary France", in: *French History* (22) 3 2008, 314.

9   Iskin (s. Anm. 7), 264.

10 *Die Sammlung angewandter Graphik*, Handbücher der Reklamekunst 1, Berlin-Charlottenburg 1919.

11 Grohnert, René, *Hans Sachs und seine Plakatsammlung, der Verein der Plakatfreunde und die Zeitschrift „Das Plakat" im Prozess der Herausbildung, Bedeutungswandlung und Konsolidierung des Plakates in Deutschland zwischen 1890 und 1933*, Berlin/Neersen 1993; Ders., „The Final Chapter: the collections of Dr Hans Sachs between 1898 and 2013", in: Le Coultre, Martijn F. (Hg.), *Hans Sachs and the Poster Revolution*, Hoorn 2013, 27 f.

12 Denscher, Bernhard, „Ottokar Mascha, a Viennese Connoisseur", in: Le Coultre, Martijn F. (Hg.), *Hans Sachs and the Poster Revolution*, Hoorn 2013, 41 f.

13 Schweiger, Werner J., *Aufbruch und Erfüllung. Gebrauchsgraphik der Wiener Moderne 1897–1918*, Wien 1988, 159.

470
Julius Klinger
Reklamemarke der
Wiener Internationalen Messe
Wien, 1921–1922
Klischee
Poster Stamp for the [International
Trade Fair of Vienna]
Vienna, 1921–1922
Cliché
55 x 34 mm
KI 21484-3-100, Ankauf purchased
from Kunstarchiv Werner J. Schweiger
2015

471
Julius Klinger
Plakat der II. Wiener
Internationalen Messe
Frühjahr 1922
Wien, 1922
Ausführung: Druckerei J. Weiner
Flachdruck
Poster for the [2nd International
Trade Fair of Vienna Spring 1922]
Vienna, 1922
Execution: Printer J. Weiner
Flat print
1160 x 940 mm
PI 1146, Schenkung donation 1929

Im Deutschen Reich entfaltete sich eine entsprechende Szene in den Jahren zwischen 1910 und 1914 – und somit erheblich später, doch umso heftiger. In nur wenigen Jahren wurden 100 000 verschiedene Sujets in Millionenauflage gedruckt.[14] In Österreich begann der Einsatz der Reklamemarke nicht nur sehr früh, sondern er war hier auch von einer erstaunlichen Beständigkeit. Endete der Boom in anderen Ländern bereits mit dem Ersten Weltkrieg, so waren die Reklamemarken in Österreich noch Ende der 1920er Jahre ein populäres Werbemedium.

Im Bereich der Prospekte und Inserate gab es keine derart organisierte Sammlerszene wie bei den Marken. Auch wenn einige Sammler im *Handbuch der Reklamekunst* angaben, „kleine Werbegraphiken" aufzubewahren, so konnte dieses Material bei weitem nicht einen derartigen Boom auslösen, wie das etwa bei den Reklamemarken oder den Plakaten der Fall war. Hatten die Plakate in ihrer Nähe zu den kostbaren Originalgrafiken und die Reklamemarken zu den oft teuren Briefmarken eine gewisse Aura, so schien die „Wertlosigkeit" der Inserate und mehr noch der Prospekte offenbar vielen doch zu deutlich erkennbar. Auch viele öffentliche Sammlungen versagten darin, die Qualitäten dieser Objekte zu erkennen. Doch gerade historische Werbung kann ein – im buchstäblichen Sinn – anschauliches Quellenmaterial zu den vielfältigsten Aspekten der politischen, ökonomischen und kulturellen Entwicklung einer Gesellschaft sein. Über den ästhetischen Reiz und kunsthistorischen Wert hinaus vermag die gedruckte Reklame Aufschluss über Beeinflussungsstrategien, Mentalitäten und allgemein über das Alltagsleben mit seinen Produktentwicklungen und dem Konsumverhalten der Menschen zu geben.

Aber trotz widriger Umstände konnten sich bedeutende Kollektionen an Ephemera in öffentlichen Institutionen – wenn auch oft wenig beachtet – erhalten. Nicht von ungefähr spricht die Kunsthistorikerin Ruth E. Iskin in diesem Zusammenhang von einschlägigen Sammlungen als von „Collecting as Salvaging an Archeology of Modernity".[15] Sie beruft sich dabei auf den französischen Ephemera-Sammler Alfred Frigoult de Liesville, dessen Nachlass größtenteils im Pariser Musée Carnavalet aufbewahrt wird und der im Sammeln von Zeitungen, Liedern, Bildern, Karikaturen oder Münzen eine neue Art von „Archäologie" sah.[16] Aus diesem Statement ergibt sich, dass man – so wie man anhand von Artefakten die Antike erforscht – genauso die Ephemera der neueren Zeit auswerten kann. Insbesondere können Alltagsdrucke wie Prospekte oder Inserate als oft optisch reizvolle Objekte bei richtiger „Befragung" sehr viel über die industrielle Massengesellschaft des 19. und 20. Jahrhunderts „aussagen". Es dauerte jedoch relativ lange, bis eine professionelle Historiografie jene Leistungen der frühen sammelnden Amateure zunehmend zu schätzen wusste. Lange hatte etwa die etablierte Kunstgeschichte Probleme damit, „Gegenstände serieller Ästhetik den Werken der ‚hohen' Kunst gleichgestellt und mit ähnlich hohem Interpretationsaufwand gewürdigt zu sehen".[17] Gerade die Ansätze der Cultural Studies und einer modernen Bildwissenschaft haben in dieser Frage zu einem entscheidenden Umdenken beigetragen, das es ermöglicht, anhand der frühen Artefakte der Wirtschaftswerbung eine „Archäologie der Moderne"[18] zu entwickeln.

14 Jüdisches Museum Berlin (Hg.), *Sammelwut und Bilderflut. Werbegeschichte im Kleinformat*, Berlin 2014, 2.

15 Iskin (s. Anm. 7), 295f.

16 Liesville, Alfred Frigoult de, *Histoire numismatique de la Révolution de 1848, ou description raisonné des médailles, monnaies, jetons, repoussées etc. relatifs aux affaires de la France*, Paris 1877, 7. Vgl. dazu auch: Stammers 2008 (s. Anm. 8), 315.

17 Gries, Rainer/Ilgen, Volker/Schindelbeck, Dirk, *„Ins Gehirn der Masse kriechen!" Werbung und Mentalitätsgeschichte*, Darmstadt 1995, 7.

18 „Archäologie der Moderne" ist ein Begriff, der sich seitdem vor allem im Rahmen der Kulturwissenschaften in verschiedenen Bedeutungen manifestiert. Vgl. dazu etwa: Emden, Christian, *Walter Benjamins Archäologie der Moderne. Kulturwissenschaft um 1930*, München 2006; Markgraf, Monika (Hg.), *Archäologie der Moderne. Sanierung Bauhaus Dessau*, Edition Bauhaus 23, Berlin 2006.

[14] Jewish Museum Berlin (ed.), *Sammelwut und Bilderflut. Werbegeschichte im Kleinformat*, Berlin 2014, 2.

different subjects were printed there by the million.[14] In Austria the use of the poster stamp not only began very early, but was also astonishingly persistent there. While the boom ended in other countries with the First World War, in Austria poster stamps were still a popular advertising medium at the end of the 1920s.

In the field of brochures and newspaper advertisements, there was no organized collectors' scene comparable to that for stamps. Even though some collectors claimed to keep "small advertising art," this material was nowhere near able to trigger the kind of boom enjoyed by poster stamps or posters. While posters had a certain aura due to their similarity to the precious original graphics and poster stamps were akin to often expensive postage stamps, the "worthlessness" of newspaper advertisements—and brochures even more so—apparently seems indeed to have been too clearly discernible. Even many public collections failed to recognize the qualities of these objects. Yet it is precisely historical advertising, which can serve as a—literally—graphic source material for the most diverse aspects of the political, economic, and cultural development of a society. Beyond the aesthetic appeal and cultural historical value, printed advertising is capable of shedding light on manipulation strategies, mentalities, and on everyday life in general with its product developments and people's consumer behavior.

[15] Iskin (see note 7), 295f.

[16] Liesville, Alfred Frigoult de, *Histoire numismatique de la Révolution de 1848, ou description raisonné des médailles, monnaies, jetons, repoussées etc. relatifs aux affaires de la France*, Paris 1877, 7. Cf. also: Stammers 2008 (see note 8), 315.

[17] Gries, Rainer/Ilgen, Volker/Schindelbeck, Dirk, *"Ins Gehirn der Masse kriechen!" Werbung und Mentalitätsgeschichte*, Darmstadt 1995, 7. Translated by Maria Slater.

[18] "Archeology of modernity" (or "archeology of modernism") is a term, which has predominantly appeared in the context of the cultural sciences and has a range of different meanings. Cf. e.g.: Emden, Christian, *Walter Benjamins Archäologie der Moderne. Kulturwissenschaft um 1930*, Munich 2006; Markgraf, Monika (ed.), *Archäologie der Moderne. Sanierung Bauhaus Dessau*, Edition Bauhaus 23, Berlin 2006.

Yet despite adverse circumstances, significant collections of ephemera have been able to survive in public institutions—though they have often been paid little heed. It is not by chance that the art historian Ruth E. Iskin speaks in this context of pertinent collections being a case of "Collecting as salvaging an archeology of modernity"[15]. In saying so, she invokes the French ephemera collector Alfred Frigoult de Liesville, the majority of whose bequest is preserved at the Musée Carnavalet in Paris and who saw a new kind of "archeology" in collecting newspapers, songs, pictures, caricatures, and coins.[16] It follows from this statement that one can analyze the ephemera of modern times in much the same way as one researches antiquity on the basis of artefacts. As optically often appealing objects, everyday prints in particular—such as brochures and newspaper advertisements—can reveal a great deal about the industrial mass society of the 19th and 20th centuries when correctly "consulted." However, it took a relatively long time for a professional historiography to progressively come to appreciate the services of early amateur collectors. Conventional art history, for example, long had problems with "seeing objects of serial aesthetics being treated as equal to the works of 'high' art and being paid tribute with a similarly high degree of interpretative effort."[17] In this regard, the approaches of cultural studies and modern pictorial science in particular have contributed to a crucial change in thinking, which in turn has enabled the development of an "archeology of modernism"[18] based on the early artefacts of commercial advertising.

PRODUKTWERBUNG ÖSTERREICHISCHER GRAFIKERINNEN UND GRAFIKER

Eine Auswahl aus fast 1000 Objekten zum Thema Waren- und Firmenwerbung in Form von Broschüren, Foldern, Annoncen oder Schildern zu treffen, kann nur unter dem Aspekt erfolgen, die Besonderheiten der Sammlung vorstellen zu wollen. Der Schwerpunkt in diesem Zusammenhang liegt auf österreichischen Arbeiten, bedingt durch die umfangreichen (Teil-)Nachlässe etwa eines Joseph Binder, Ernst Ludwig Franke oder der Buch- und Steindruckerei August Chwala. Da sie zum Teil große Zeiträume abdecken, dokumentieren diese Nachlässe persönliche wie allgemeine Stilentwicklungen, Biografien und Zeitgeschichte, lassen sich also vielfach befragen – wozu Bernhard Denscher in seinem Artikel anregt. Im Sinne der von ihm beschriebenen „Archäologie der Moderne" mithilfe der Reklamekunst können jedoch an dieser Stelle nur die obersten Schichten freigelegt werden. Der wohl radikalste österreichische Gebrauchsgrafiker des 20. Jahrhunderts war der 1876 in Dornbach bei Wien geborene Julius Klinger, der 21-jährig nach Berlin auszog, um dort zu einem der gefragtesten Plakatkünstler zu werden. Nach dem Ersten Weltkrieg wieder in Wien ansässig, zeichnete er für den Werbeauftritt der Marke *Tabu* verantwortlich und prägte damit das Wiener Straßenbild. Nicht nur eine Serie von Plakaten warb für das Zigarettenpapier, der Name füllte ganze Feuerwände aus.[1] In den Zeitungen wurde mit zahlreichen Inseraten nachgesetzt, in denen Klinger entweder die Plakatmotive variierte (Abb. 474) oder eigene Formate schuf (Abb. 472, 473). Darin zeigt sich seine Vorliebe für das Spiel mit Schrift: Die Buchstaben werden als Gesicht angeordnet oder von Max und Moritz gestohlen und bilden – AU! – eine eigenes Wort. Beliebtes Motiv ist auch die Großstadt: Klinger erfindet eine urbane Szenerie mit *Tabu*-Feuermauer und -Reklametafel und thematisiert damit die Wirkung großer öffentlicher Werbeflächen in einer von Tempo und Kurzlebigkeit geprägten Zeit. Dabei vergisst er nicht, auch den Gestalter werbewirksam einzubauen. „Man könnte Julius Klinger den Peter Behrens der Plakatkunst nennen. Denn wie dieser […] besitzt er eine stark ‚technisch' empfindende Phantasie, gemischt mit einer tüchtigen Portion Amerikanismus, die […] stets auf Einfachheit und Größe ausgeht", urteilte der spätere Leiter der Bibliothek Hans Ankwicz-Kleehoven 1923.[2] Joseph Binder, 22 Jahre jünger als Klinger, orientierte sich an diesem Vorbild und war in seiner Wiener Zeit amerikanischer als später in den USA. Der Erfinder des „Meinl-Mohren" (Abb. 475 zeigt eine Version noch ohne Fes) arbeitet wie Klinger gerne mit Schwarz-Weiß-Rot-(Blau-)Kontrasten und setzt Buchstaben bildhaft ein. So ist das „A" seiner Arabia-Kampagne (s. S. 256) in den Körper bzw. Turban jener Figur eingeschrieben, die Indien als Importland der Kaffee-Firma repräsentieren soll (Abb. 478), seine Initialen JB wiederum gestalten das Staffeleibild in einer Eigenwerbung (Abb. 479).

Kurzzeitige Mitarbeiterin Binders war Margit Doppler (damals Kováts), bekannt durch das Blockmalz-Männchen der Firma Kirstein. „Im Atelier Binder habe ich schöne Frauengesichter für die Tabakregie gemacht", schilderte sie in einem Interview mit Bernhard Denscher.[3] Das geben ein Entwurf (Abb. 476) und zwei Inserate wieder, die 2011 durch Dopplers Tochter Xenia Katzenstein[4] in die MAK-Kunstblättersammlung gelangten und in ihrer Ästhetik das Klischee von den verruchten 1930er Jahren bestätigen. Ein Mitarbeiter von Julius Klinger wiederum war Hermann Kosel, bekannt durch seine Tourismus-Plakate und jene für das Schuhhaus Humanic. In einem Reklameblatt für die Wiener Städtische Versicherungsanstalt 1930 (Abb. 480) verwendete Kosel Piktogramme – eine

[1] Ein berühmtes Beispiel ist die Feuermauer des Loos-Hauses am Michaelerplatz, die nach Abriss des benachbarten Palais Liechtenstein entstand. Ihre Bemalung zeigt ein Baugerüst, in das die Buchstaben TABU eingehängt sind. Erst über zehn Jahre später sollte an dieser Stelle das erste Hochhaus Wiens entstehen (Theiss & Jaksch, 1931–1933). Abb. in: Kühnel, Anita, *Julius Klinger. Plakatkünstler und Zeichner*, Bilderheft der Staatlichen Museen zu Berlin – Preußischer Kulturbesitz 89, Berlin 1997, 13.

[2] Ankwicz-Kleehoven, Hans [Rezension zweier Klinger-Publikationen], in: *Mitteilungen der Gesellschaft für vervielfältigende Kunst* (55) 4 1923, Beilage zu: *Die Graphischen Künste* (46) 1923.

[3] Denscher, Bernhard, „Margit Doppler: ‚Man muss sich zur richtigen Zeit etwas einfallen lassen!'", Interview aus Anlass ihres 90. Geburtstags 1999. www.austrianposters.at/2011/04/10/2515/ (7.4.2016).

[4] Als „Karin Sommer" reüssierte auch Xenia Katzenstein in der Werbebranche: Zwischen 1971 und 1985 pries sie in Fernsehspots und Printmedien „das große Aroma" von Jacobs Kaffee an.

PRODUCT ADVERTISEMENTS BY AUSTRIAN GRAPHIC DESIGNERS

A selection of almost 1000 objects promoting wares and companies in the form of brochures, folders, advertisements, and signs can only be introduced when presenting the distinctive features of a collection. The focus in this context is on Austrian works, by virtue of wide-ranging (partial) bequests from Joseph Binder, Ernst Ludwig Franke, and the Buch- und Steindruckerei August Chwala, among others. As some of them cover large intervals, these bequests document personal as well as general stylistic developments, biographies, and contemporary history; they can therefore be consulted on a number of matters—as Bernhard Denscher encourages in his article. However, when it comes to the "archeology of modernism" with the aid of advertising art, which he describes, only the top layers can be unearthed at this point.

Probably the most radical Austrian designer of ephemera in the 20th century was Julius Klinger, who was born in Dornbach near Vienna in 1876 and moved to Berlin aged 21, where he became one of the most sought-after poster artists in the area. Living in Vienna again after the First World War, he was responsible for the advertising campaign of the *Tabu* brand, with which he left his mark on the Vienna streetscape. Not only did a series of posters promote the cigarette paper, but the name filled entire firewalls.[1] The campaign also continued in newspapers, where the numerous advertisements by Klinger were either variations on the poster motifs (ill. 474) or specially created formats (ill. 472, 473). They reveal his fondness for playing with text: the letters are arranged into a face or stolen by Max and Moritz to create a single word—AU! (in English: OW!). Another favorite motif is the metropolis: Klinger invents urban scenery with *Tabu* firewalls and billboards, thereby using as a central theme the effect of large, public advertising surfaces in an era characterized by tempo and transience. Yet he never fails to remember to incorporate the designer himself, too, without compromising any advertising appeal.

"One could call Julius Klinger the Peter Behrens of poster art since, like the latter, [...] he possesses a strong, 'technically' sentient imagination, combined with a sound portion of Americanism, which [...] always aims at size and simplicity": this was the judgment of the later head of the library, Hans Ankwicz-Kleehoven, in 1923.[2] Joseph Binder, 22 years younger than Klinger, followed in this exemplar's footsteps and was more American during his time in Vienna than he was later during his time in the U.S.A. Like Klinger, the inventor of the "Meinl Moor" (ill. 475 shows an early version without a fez) enjoyed working with black, white, and red (and blue) contrasts and introduced letters pictorially. For example, the "A" of his Arabia campaign (see p. 257) is inscribed in the body or in the turban of the figure who is intended to represent India as the coffee company's country of importation (ill. 478); his initials JB, on the other hand, transform the easel painting into a self-promotion (ill. 479).

A short-term colleague of Binder was Margit Doppler (at that time Kováts), known for the malt sugar cough drop man she drew for the Kirstein company. "At Binder's studio I made beautiful female faces for the management of the tobacco company," she described in an interview with Bernhard Denscher.[3] That is illustrated in a design (ill. 476) and two newspaper advertise- ments, which entered the MAK Works on Paper Collection in 2011 via Doppler's daughter Xenia Katzenstein[4]; their aesthetics confirm the cliché of the infamous 1930s. A colleague

[1] A famous example is the firewall of the Loos House on Michaelerplatz, which was created after the neighboring Palais Liechtenstein was torn down. Its painting shows scaffolding in which the letters TABU are suspended. It was only over a decade later that Vienna's first high-rise building would come into existence on this site (Theiss & Jaksch, 1931–1933). Ill. in: Kühnel, Anita, *Julius Klinger. Plakatkünstler und Zeichner*, Bilderheft der Staatlichen Museen zu Berlin – Preußischer Kulturbesitz 89, Berlin 1997, 13.

[2] Ankwicz-Kleehoven, Hans [review of two Klinger publications], in: *Mitteilungen der Gesellschaft für vervielfältigende Kunst* (55) 4 1923, supplement to: *Die Graphischen Künste* (46) 1923. Translated by Maria Slater.

[3] Denscher, Bernhard, Margit Doppler: "Man muss sich zur richtigen Zeit etwas einfallen lassen!," interview on the occasion of her 90th birthday in 1999. www.austrian-posters.at/2011/04/10/2515 (7 Apr 2016). Translated by Maria Slater.

[4] Xenia Katzenstein also gained success in advertising as "Karin Sommer": Between 1971 and 1985 she promoted "the great aroma" of Jacobs Kaffee in TV spots and print media.

Gestaltungsart, die kurz zuvor von dem Philosophen und Ökonomen Otto Neurath als „Wiener Methode der Bildstatistik" entwickelt worden war und seitdem die Gebrauchsgrafiker immer wieder beschäftigt hat (Abb. 481).

Klinger ließ 1923 seine für den amerikanischen Markt bestimmte Publikation *Poster Art in Vienna* von Chwala's Druck in Wien herstellen. Der 2008 erworbene Teilnachlass der Firma erlaubt einen Überblick über 70 Jahre Eigenwerbung in Form von Inseraten, Broschüren und Werbezetteln. Deren meist anonyme GestalterInnen lieferten dabei jeweils die modernsten Entwürfe: Die Beilage zu einer Mustermappe – sie diente zugleich als Löschblatt (Abb. 482) – rezipiert den Stil der Wiener Werkstätte, mit der Chwala's Druck von Anbeginn zusammenarbeitete; in den 1930er Jahren trat man in silbrig glänzendem Art déco auf und 20 Jahre später im organisch-bunten Fifties-Design. Einblick in ein Gesamtwerk gewährt auch der Teilnachlass von Ernst Ludwig Franke (1886–1948), Mitbegründer des 1926 konstituierten Bundes österreichischer Gebrauchsgraphiker (BÖG). Über 250 Arbeiten, darunter auch Linolschnitte samt Druckstöcken, sowie persönliche Dokumente erwarb das Museum 1959 von Frankes Frau Ilka. Der „Problematiker" unter seinesgleichen, dessen Arbeiten „von starker psychologischer Wirkung" seien, so ein Zeitgenosse,[5] arbeitete etwa für die Wiener Gaswerke, die Firma Olso (Schnellkocher) oder den Spielkarten- und Papierwarenerzeuger Piatnik, dessen Schutzmarke er auch entwarf (Abb. 490). 1929 leitete Franke die Vorbereitungen zur Ausstellung *Das österreichische Plakat*, die der BÖG im Museum am Stubenring ausrichtete. Darin wurde Julius Klinger gewürdigt, Hermann Kosel war beteiligt, Joseph Binder schuf das Plakat und Chwala's Druck fertigte den Katalog.

5 Lörl, Hans, „Ernst Ludwig Franke", Artikel aus einer Zeitschrift, um 1930, KI 13486, Geschenk Ilka Franke 1959.

472
Julius Klinger
Inserat für Tabu Antinicotin
Wien, 1919
Klischee
**Newspaper Advertisement
for Tabu Antinicotin**
Vienna, 1919
Cliché
98 x 223 mm
KI 9079-95, Schenkung donation from
Richard Wildner 1933

of Julius Klinger, on the other hand, was Hermann Kosel, who was known for his tourism posters as well as those for the shoe store Humanic. In an advertising brochure for the Wiener Städtische Versicherungsanstalt from 1930 (ill. 480), Kosel used pictographs—a design style, which had been developed shortly beforehand by the philosopher and economist Otto Neurath as the "Viennese Method of Pictorial Statistics" and has continued to occupy designers of ephemera ever since (ill. 481).

Klinger had his publication *Poster Art in Vienna*, which was aimed at the American market, printed by Chwala's Druck in Vienna in 1923. Acquired in 2008, the partial bequest from the company provides an overview of more than 70 years of self-promotion in the form of newspaper advertisements, brochures, and promotional leaflets. Their mostly anonymous designers each delivered extremely modern designs: the supplement to a sample portfolio—which simultaneously served as a blotter (ill. 482)—adopted the style of the Wiener Werkstätte, with whom Chwala's Druck had collaborated from the outset; in the 1930s, the company was portrayed in silvery, shiny art deco, then 20 years later in an organically colorful fifties design.

An insight into an oeuvre is also granted by the partial bequest from Ernst Ludwig Franke (1886–1948), co-founder of the Bund österreichischer Gebrauchsgraphiker (BÖG), established in 1926. Over 250 works, including linocuts complete with printing blocks, as well as personal documents, were acquired by the museum in 1959 from Franke's wife Ilka. This "problematic man" among his peers whose works had a "strong psychological effect"—according to a contemporary[5]—worked among others for the Wiener Gaswerke, the Olso company (pressure cookers), and the playing card and stationery manufacturer Piatnik, whose trademark he also designed (ill. 490). In 1929 Franke oversaw the preparations for the exhibition on Austrian posters organized by the BÖG at the museum on Stubenring. In it, tribute was paid to Julius Klinger, Hermann Kosel participated, Joseph Binder created the poster, and Chwala's Druck printed the catalog.

5   Lörl, Hans, "Ernst Ludwig Franke," article from a magazine, ca. 1930, KI 13486, gift from Ilka Franke 1959.

473
Julius Klinger
Inserat für Tabu Antinicotin
Neue Freie Presse, Wien, um 1920
Klischee
Newspaper Advertisement for Tabu Antinicotin
Neue Freie Presse, Vienna, ca. 1920
Cliché
69 x 264 mm
KI 9079-81, Schenkung donation from Richard Wildner 1933

474
Julius Klinger
Inserat für Tabu Antinicotin
Wien, um 1920
Klischee
**Newspaper Advertisement
for Tabu Antinicotin**
Vienna, ca. 1920
Cliché
118 x 89 mm
KI 9410-22, Schenkung donation
from Richard Wildner 1936

475
Joseph Binder
Inserat für *Meinl-Kaffee*
Wien, 1923–1924
Klischee
**Newspaper Advertisement
for [Meinl Coffee]**
Vienna, 1923–1924
Cliché
91 x 69 mm
KI 9079-100, Schenkung donation
from Richard Wildner 1933

476
Margit Doppler-Kováts
**Entwurf für eine Zigaretten-
werbung der Österreichischen
Tabakregie**
Wien, 1930
Bleistift, Kohle, Deckweiß, Tusche
**Design for a Cigarette
Advertisement by the
Österreichische Tabakregie**
Vienna, 1930
Pencil, charcoal, opaque white, ink
170 x 257 mm
KI 18817-1, Schenkung donation
from Xenia Katzenstein 2011

477
Joseph Binder
Das Auge kauft
Wien, um 1930
Ausführung: Gröbnerdruck
Lithografie
[The eye buys]
Vienna, ca. 1930
Execution: Gröbnerdruck
Lithograph
117 x 132 mm
KI 14145-1344-1, Legat bequest from
Carla und and Joseph Binder 1995/96

478
Joseph Binder
Werbung für *Arabia Kaffee*
Wien, nach 1931
Offsetdruck
Advertisement for [Arabia Coffee]
Vienna, after 1931
Offset print
209 x 151 mm
KI 14145-940-16-1, Legat bequest
from Carla und and Joseph Binder
1995/96

480
Hermann Kosel
Werbeblatt der Städtischen
Versicherungsanstalt
Wien, 1930
Klischee, Buchdruck
Advertising Leaflet by the Städtische
Versicherungsanstalt
Vienna, 1930
Cliché, letterpress print
234 x 189 mm
KI 17026-4, alter Bestand, inv.
old holdings, inventoried in 2013

479
Joseph Binder
Eigenwerbung Joseph Binder
Wien, um 1926
Offsetdruck, Lithografie
Self-Advertisement Joseph Binder
Vienna, ca. 1926
Offset print, lithograph
302 x 227 mm
KI 14145-937-1-1, Legat bequest from
Carla und and Joseph Binder 1995/96

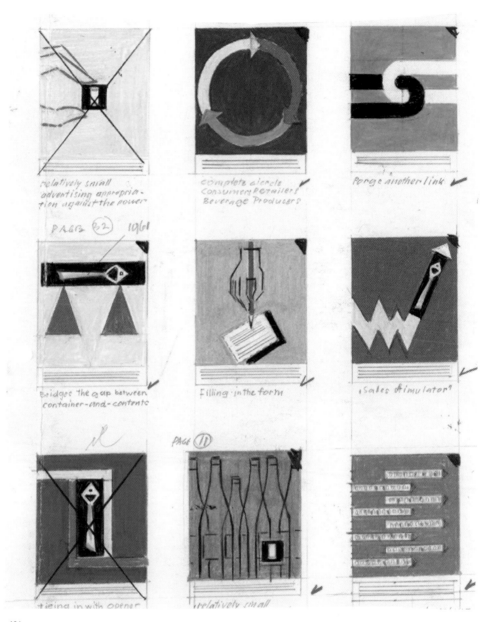

481
Joseph Binder
Entwurf für einen Prospekt
der American Can Company MiraCan
USA, 1960
Bleistift, Pastellfarbe
Design for a Brochure
by the American Can Company MiraCan
USA, 1960
Pencil, pastel color
238 x 194 mm
KI 14145-567-1, Legat bequest from
Carla und and Joseph Binder 1995/96

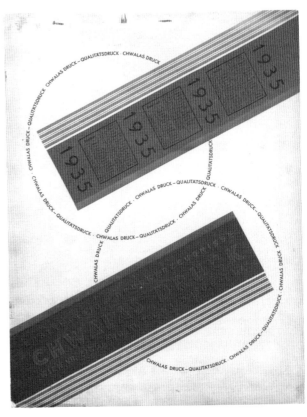

482
Anonym Anonymous
Werbeblatt der Druckerei Chwala
Wien, 1911
Klischee
**Advertising Leaflet by the
Printer Chwala**
Vienna, 1911
Cliché
268 x 200 mm
KI 15853-16, Ankauf Teilnachlass
purchased from part of the estate
of Chwala's Druck 2008

483
Anonym Anonymous
Werbeblatt der Druckerei Chwala
Wien, 1935
Klischee
**Advertising Leaflet by the
Printer Chwala**
Vienna, 1935
Cliché
325 x 249 mm
KI 15853-20, Ankauf Teilnachlass
purchased from part of the estate
of Chwala's Druck 2008

484
Anonym Anonymous
Werbeblatt der Druckerei Chwala
Wien, 1953
Offsetdruck
**Advertising Leaflet by the
Printer Chwala**
Vienna, 1953
Offset print
200 x 240 mm
KI 15853-1, Ankauf Teilnachlass
purchased from part of the estate
of Chwala's Druck 2008

485
Ernst Ludwig Franke
Eigenwerbung Ernst Ludwig Franke
Wien, um 1920
Klischee
Self-Advertisement Ernst Ludwig Franke
Vienna, ca. 1920
Cliché
90 x 140 mm
KI 13369-5-2, Ankauf purchased from
Ilka Franke 1959

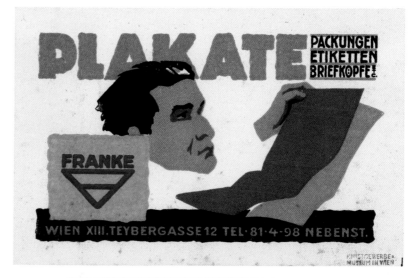

486
Ernst Ludwig Franke
Werbeanzeige für die Tageszeitung
Der Tag
Wien, um 1923
Lithografie
Advertisement for the Daily Newspaper
[The day]
Vienna, ca. 1923
Lithograph
285 x 207 mm
KI 13377-7, Schenkung donation from
Ilka Franke 1959

487
Ernst Ludwig Franke
Werbebroschüre für die Stadt-Gaswerke
der Gemeinde Wien
Wien, um 1928
Autotypie
Advertising Brochure for the Municipal
Gasworks Vienna
Vienna, ca. 1928
Halftone
287 x 171 mm
KI 13370-41, Ankauf purchased from
Ilka Franke 1959

488
Ernst Ludwig Franke
Werbeanzeige für Olso Kohlen-Schnellkocher
Wien, um 1925
Klischee
Advertisement for a Coal-Fired Pressure
Cooker by Olso
Vienna, ca. 1925
Cliché
234 x 179 mm
KI 13377-4, Schenkung donation from
Ilka Franke 1959

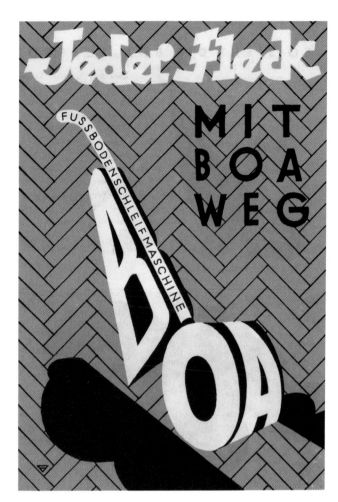

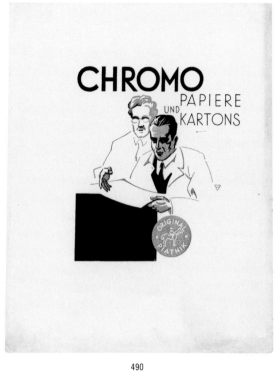

490
Ernst Ludwig Franke
**Werbeanzeige für Papier und
Kartons der Firma Piatnik**
Wien, um 1925
Klischee
**Advertisement for Paper and
Cardboard by the Company Piatnik**
Vienna, ca. 1925
Cliché
208 x 227 mm
KI 13377-16, Schenkung donation frum
Ilka Franke 1959

489
Ernst Ludwig Franke
**Werbebroschüre für die
Fußbodenschleifmaschine *Boa***
Wien, um 1930
Klischee
**Advertising Brochure for the
Floor Sanding Machine *Boa***
Vienna, ca. 1930
Cliché
215 x 150 mm
KI 13370-32, Ankauf purchased from
Ilka Franke 1959

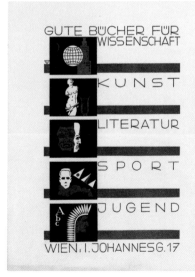

491
Ernst Ludwig Franke
Werbeanzeige für eine Buchhandlung
Wien, um 1930
Klischee
Advertisement for a Bookstore
Vienna, ca. 1930
Cliché
250 x 204 mm
KI 13377-19, Schenkung donation from
Ilka Franke 1959

REISEPROSPEKTE DER 1920ER BIS 1950ER JAHRE

Der Grafiker Paul Kurt Schwarz vermachte der MAK-Bibliothek und Kunstblättersammlung 2008
an die 300 Werbeprospekte, überwiegend zum Thema Reisen: mit Zug, Schiff oder Flugzeug, an
die See, in die Berge oder in verschiedenste Städte, europa- und weltweit. Sie umfassen nahezu
das ganze 20. Jahrhundert, wobei der Schwerpunkt auf der im Titel genannten Zeitspanne liegt.
Namhafte Künstler, unbekannte Künstlerinnen und viele anonyme Gestaltungen prägen eine ungemein qualitätsvolle Phase der Werbegrafik. Oft wurde das Motiv zunächst für ein Plakat entwickelt
und dann für Broschüren und Folder abgewandelt.

Das betrifft etwa Eric de Coulons Reklame für die Gornergrat Bahn, Joseph Binders Raxbahn-Motiv
oder die Werbekampagnen des Norddeutschen Lloyd Bremen. Binders 1927 entstandenes Plakat
erfuhr zehn Jahre später allerdings gröbere Veränderungen: Wiederholte Blau-Rot-Kontraste und
ein Strahlenglanz über der Bergwelt untergraben die Wirkung des bedeutungstragenden Pfeils
(Abb. 494). Zeitgleich mit Binders Plakat entwarf Oswald Hengst ein Motiv für die Innsbrucker Nord-
kettenbahn und markierte deren Verlauf ebenfalls, wenngleich viel zaghafter, mit einer roten Linie
(Abb. 495). Sich verjüngende Zugstrecken oder Landebahnen sind bevorzugte Gestaltungselemente
in der Zwischenkriegszeit, um Dynamik und Fortschritt zu signalisieren (Abb. 496) – später legte
sich die Euphorie und wich einem verstärkt technischen Zugang (Abb. 500).

Der Norddeutsche Lloyd schrieb 1929 eine Plakat-Konkurrenz aus, um seine drei schnellsten Turbi-
nenschiffe Europa, Columbus und Bremen zu bewerben. Sie fand unter reger Anteilnahme österreichischer Grafiker statt, u. a. Hanns Wagula, Hermann Kosel, Joseph Binder und Ernst Ludwig Franke.
Eine Ausstellung präsentierte am Ende „12 Preisträger, 9 Ankäufe und 38 Entwürfe engerer Wahl".[1]
Der 4. Preis ging an den Wiener Lois Gaigg, der 7. an den Wahlbremer Bernd Steiner – beide stilisie-
ren die Monumentalität der Lloyd-Dampfer in den bildfüllenden roten Rümpfen (Abb. 497, 498).
1930 organisierte die berühmte Passagier-Reederei eine Amerika-Fahrt für deutsche Reklamefach-
leute und signalisierte damit erneut ihr besonderes Interesse an der Förderung der Werbeindustrie
(Abb. 499).

Der Großteil der Reiseprospekte gilt Destinationen am Meer oder in den Bergen. In der Zwischen-
kriegszeit überwiegen die Art-déco-Darstellungen sportlich-eleganter Damen am Strand, auf der
Promenade oder im Ski-Dress – insofern könnten sie auch als „Modebilder" firmieren. Dem Stil
entsprechend, aber doch überraschend in ihrer extravaganten Einfachheit ist eine Broschüre von
Ilse Lagerfeld (Abb. 501), von der ähnlich abstrahierende Zigaretten-Werbungen überliefert sind.
Ein Hotspot des Wintersports ist St. Moritz, das sich 1930 die Sonne als Markenzeichen wählte.
Bis heute treten Signet und Namenszug in den Wappenfarben des Ortes Blau und Gelb auf. Der
deutsche Grafiker Christoph Niemann, dem das MAK 2015 eine Personale im Kunstblättersaal
widmete,[2] arbeitet seit einigen Jahren für die Tourismusorganisation Engadin St. Moritz und erweist
dabei der Dreißigerjahre-Ästhetik seine Referenz (Abb. 503). Hanns Wagulas Österreich-Werbung
sei hierfür beispielhaft: Mit seinen kristallinen Landschaften schuf der Grazer Plakatkünstler jene
glatte, stumme Schönheit, die dem heutigen Gebot der Coolness so entgegenkommt (Abb. 502).
Das von Paul Kurt Schwarz gesammelte Material bietet außerdem zahlreiche Städte-Prospekte,
wobei vor allem jene aus Deutschland künstlerisch hervorstechen. Sie dokumentieren das
kontrastreiche Art déco eines Ludwig Hohlwein, den Bauhausstil eines Herbert Bayer oder das

[1] Kain, Robert, „Die Entwürfe zum Plakat-
Wettbewerb des Norddeutschen Lloyd", in:
Bremer Nachrichten 1929, KI 14145-907-23,
Legat Carla und Joseph Binder 1995/96.

[2] *Christoph Niemann. Unterm Strich*,
MAK-Kunstblättersaal, 1.7.–27.10.2015.

TRAVEL BROCHURES FROM THE 1920S TO THE 1950S

The graphic designer Paul Kurt Schwarz bequeathed almost 300 advertising brochures to the MAK Library and Works on Paper Collection in 2008, most of which are related to travel: by train, ship, or plane, to the sea, the mountains, or various cities all over Europe and the world. They span almost the entire 20th century, though the focus is on the time period named in the title above. Famous male artists, unknown female artists, and many anonymous designers left their mark on this tremendously high-quality phase of advertising art. Often the motifs were originally designed for posters before being modified for brochures and leaflets.

That is the case with Eric de Coulon's promotion of the Gornergrat Bahn, Joseph Binder's Raxbahn motif, and the advertising campaigns for the Norddeutscher Lloyd Bremen, for example. Admittedly, Binder's poster from 1927 was subjected to crude alterations ten years later: repeated red and blue contrasts and beams of light over the mountainous landscape undermine the effect of the symbolic arrow (ill. 494). At the same time as Binder's poster, Oswald Hengst designed a motif for Innsbruck's Nordkette Cable Railways and likewise marked their course—albeit much more faintly—with a red line (ill. 495). Juvenescent railroad lines or runways are the preferred design elements of the inter-war period, chosen to signalize dynamism and progress (ill. 496); later the euphoria subsided and made way for a more technical approach (ill. 500).

In 1929 the Norddeutscher Lloyd announced a poster competition to advertise its three fastest turbine-powered ships: Europa, Columbus, and Bremen. It was greeted with a lively response from Austrian graphic designers, including Hanns Wagula, Hermann Kosel, Joseph Binder, and Ernst Ludwig Franke. An exhibition at the end presented "12 award winners, 9 purchases, and 38 designs from a narrower selection."[1] The 4th prize was awarded to the Viennese artist Lois Gaigg, the 7th to Bremen-based Bernd Steiner; both stylized the monumentality of the Lloyd steamships by filling their posters with red hulls (ill. 497, 498). In 1930 the famous passenger ship company organized a trip to America for German advertising professionals, hence once again signalizing its particular interest in supporting the advertising industry (ill. 499).

The majority of travel brochures is given over to destinations at the seaside or in the mountains. The interwar period is dominated by art deco depictions of sporty and elegant ladies on the beach, on the promenade, or dressed to ski—and to this extent they could serve a dual purpose as "fashion plates," too. Stylistically appropriate yet surprising in its extravagant simplicity is a brochure by Ilse Lagerfeld (ill. 501), whose similarly abstract cigarette advertisements have also survived.

A hotspot for winter sport is St. Moritz, Switzerland, which chose the sun as its symbol in 1930. Even now, the signet and town name appear in the resort's colors, blue and gold. The German graphic designer Christoph Niemann, to whom the MAK dedicated a solo exhibition in the Works on Paper Room in 2015,[2] has worked for the tourism organization of Engadine St. Moritz for several years, and in his work he makes reference to the aesthetics of the 1930s (ill. 503). Hanns Wagula's advertisement for Austria is exemplary in this regard: with his crystalline landscapes, the Graz-based poster artist created that smooth, silent beauty, which so well conforms to the contemporary demand for coolness (ill. 502).

Furthermore, the material collected by Paul Kurt Schwarz comprises numerous city brochures, among which it is predominantly those from Germany, which stand out on an artistic level. They

[1] Kain, Robert, "Die Entwürfe zum Plakat-Wettbewerb des Norddeutschen Lloyd," in: *Bremer Nachrichten* 1929, KI 14145-907-23, Bequest Carla and Joseph Binder 1995/1996. Translated by Maria Slater.

[2] *Christoph Niemann: Drawing the Line*, MAK Works on Paper Room, 1 Jul – 27 Oct 2015.

geometrische Design eines Theodor Paul Etbauer. Alfred Mahlau, von 1920 bis in die 1950er Jahre für die Hansestadt Lübeck und deren Unternehmen tätig, ist ebenso vertreten wie Max Burchartz, dessen Werbung für das Ruhrgebiet mit den Mitteln der Fotocollage den bauhausnahen Künstler erkennen lässt. Im Unterschied zu Bayer montiert er die Bilder jeweils zu einem Gesamtmotiv und erzeugt damit äußerst suggestive Wirkungen (Abb. 508, 509).

Was für St. Moritz die Sonne, ist für Dresden das Auge, das Franz von Stuck 1911 anlässlich der ersten *Internationalen Hygiene-Ausstellung* entwarf. Es wurde 1929 von Fritz Petzold adaptiert und ist in dieser Form bis heute Signet des Deutschen Hygiene-Museums (Abb. 505). Ausstellungen und Messen waren und sind eng mit dem Städte-Tourismus verknüpft. Ihre Bewerbung erfolgt meist auf höchstem Niveau – das zeigen auch die Reklamemarken der Wiener Messe über einen Zeitraum von 40 Jahren (s. folgendes Kapitel).

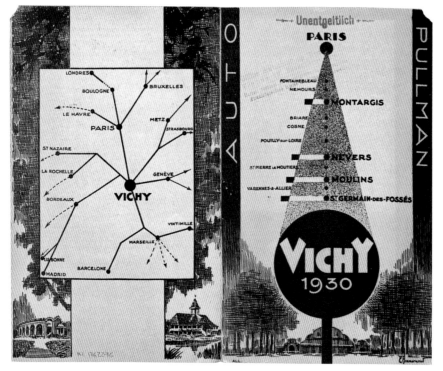

492
Pierre Commarmond
Reisebroschüre *Paris–Vichy 1930*
Vanves (FR), 1930
Ausführung: Druckerei Imprimerie Kapp
Klischee
Travel Brochure *Paris–Vichy 1930*
Vanves (FR), 1930
Execution: Printer Imprimerie Kapp
Cliché
216 x 132 (264) mm
KI 17622-96, alter Bestand, inv. old holdings,
inventoried in 2013

document the rich contrasts in the art deco of Ludwig Hohlwein, the Bauhaus style of Herbert Bayer, and the geometric design of Theodor Paul Etbauer, among others. Alfred Mahlau is represented, who worked for the Hanseatic City of Lübeck and its companies from 1920 to the 1950s, as is Max Burchartz, whose use of photo collage in his advertisement for the Ruhr Valley is indicative of his Bauhaus links. In contrast to Bayer, he always assembles the images to create an overall motif and in doing so produces extremely evocative effects (ill. 508, 509).

Just as the sun symbolizes St. Moritz, the eye represents Dresden; it was designed by Franz von Stuck in 1911 on the occasion of the first international hygiene exhibition. It was adapted by Fritz Petzold in 1929 and has been used in this form as the signet of the Deutsches Hygiene-Museum ever since (ill. 505). Exhibitions and fairs are and were closely connected to city tourism. Consequently, their advertisements are usually of the highest quality—as is demonstrated also by the poster stamps for the Vienna Trade Fair over a period of forty years (see next section).

493
Eric de Coulon
Reisebroschüre *Zermatt Gornergrat*
Zürich, 1929
Ausführung: Druckerei Gebr. Fretz
Lithografie, Kupfertiefdruck
Travel Brochure *Zermatt Gornergrat*
Zurich, 1929
Execution: Printer Gebr. Fretz
Lithograph, copper intaglio print
150 x 110 (219) mm
KI 17556-75, alter Bestand, inv. old holdings,
inventoried in 2013

494
Anonym Anonymous
(nach Joseph Binders Plakat von 1927)
(based on Joseph Binder's Poster from 1927)
Winterfahrplan der Raxbahn 1936/37
Wien, 1936
Ausführung: Druckerei Steyrermühl AG
Lithografie
Winter Timetable for the Raxbahn 1936/37
Vienna, 1936
Execution: Printer Steyrermühl AG
Lithograph
227 x 123 mm
KI 17881-57, alter Bestand, inv. old holdings,
inventoried in 2013

495
Oswald Hengst
Werbebroschüre _Innsbrucker_
Nordketten-Bahn
Innsbruck, 1927
Ausführung: Druckerei Tyrolia
Autotypie
Advertising Brochure _Innsbrucker_
Nordketten-Bahn
Innsbruck, 1927
Execution: Printer Tyrolia
Halftone
186 x 121 mm
KI 17881-35, alter Bestand, inv. old holdings,
inventoried in 2013

496
Anonym Anonymous
Reisebroschüre _Im Flugzeug von ... Wien_
Mailand, um 1940
Offsetdruck
Travel Brochure
[On an airplane from ...Vienna]
Milan, ca. 1940
Offset print
223 x 119 (238) mm
KI 15876-19, Schenkung donation from
Paul Kurt Schwarz 2008

497
Lois Gaigg
Reisebroschüre des Norddeutschen
Lloyd Bremen
Berlin, 1929
Ausführung: Druckerei Otto Elsner AG
Kupfertiefdruck
Travel Brochure of the Norddeutscher
Lloyd Bremen
Berlin, 1929
Execution: Printer Otto Elsner AG
Copper intaglio print
243 x 202 mm
KI 17216-22, alter Bestand, inv.
old holdings, inventoried in 2013

498
Bernd Steiner
Fahrplanheft des Norddeutschen
Lloyd Bremen
Bremen, 1929
Ausführung: Druckerei Carl Schünemann
Kupfertiefdruck
Timetable Booklet of the
Norddeutscher Lloyd Bremen
Bremen, 1929
Execution: Printer Carl Schünemann
Copper intaglio print
210 x 135 mm
KI 17216-14, alter Bestand, inv.
old holdings, inventoried in 2013

499
Franz Gustav Arnold
Reisebroschüre des Norddeutschen
Lloyd Bremen *Amerika Fahrt*
Deutscher Reklame Fachleute 1930
Bremen, 1930
Ausführung: Druckerei Carl Schünemann
Autotypie
Travel Brochure of the Norddeutscher
Lloyd Bremen [Journey to America for
German advertising specialists 1930]
Berlin, 1930
Execution: Printer Carl Schünemann
Halftone
288 x 225 mm
KI 17216-35, alter Bestand, inv.
old holdings, inventoried in 2013

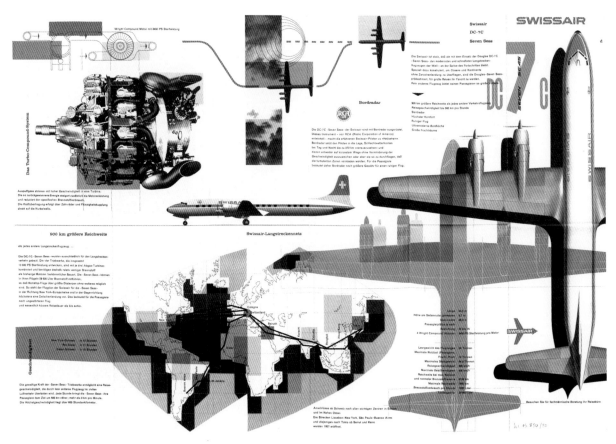

500
Kurt Wirth
Prospekt der Swissair
Laupen, 1956
Ausführung: Druckerei Polygraphische
Gesellschaft Laupen
Offsetdruck
Brochure for Swissair
Laupen, 1956
Execution: Printer Polygraphische
Gesellschaft Laupen
Offset print
210 x 102 (420 x 610) mm
KI 15880-80, Schenkung donation from
Paul Kurt Schwarz 2008

501
Ilse Lagerfeld
Werbebroschüre *Kurhaus-Abbazia*
Leipzig, um 1930
Ausführung: Spamersche Buchdruckerei
Klischee, Autotypie
Advertising Brochure [Opatija spa resort]
Leipzig, ca. 1930
Execution: Spamersche Buchdruckerei
Cliché, halftone
247 x 129 mm
KI 17769-10, alter Bestand, inv. old holdings,
inventoried in 2013

503
Christoph Niemann
Werbeanzeige für St. Moritz
Urlaubsmagazin Sylt, 2015
Offsetdruck
Advertisement for St. Moritz
Holiday magazine Sylt, 2015
Offset print
297 x 207 mm
KI 23030, Schenkung donation from
Anne-Katrin Rossberg 2015

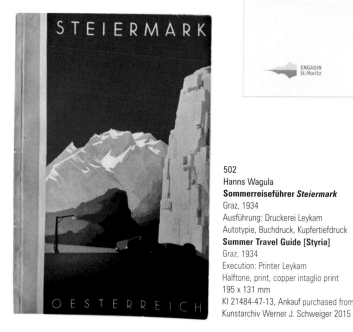

502
Hanns Wagula
Sommerreiseführer *Steiermark*
Graz, 1934
Ausführung: Druckerei Leykam
Autotypie, Buchdruck, Kupfertiefdruck
Summer Travel Guide [Styria]
Graz, 1934
Execution: Printer Leykam
Halftone, print, copper intaglio print
195 x 131 mm
KI 21484-47-13, Ankauf purchased from
Kunstarchiv Werner J. Schweiger 2015

504
Louis Christiaan Kalff
Reisebroschüre *Scheveningen.*
The Hague-on-Sea. Holland
Amsterdam, 1930
Ausführung: Druckerei C. A. Spin & Zoon
Autotypie
Travel Brochure *Scheveningen.*
The Haag-on-Sea. Holland
Amsterdam, 1930
Execution: Printer C. A. Spin & Zoon
Halftone
208 x 105 (210) mm
KI 17768-3, alter Bestand, inv. old holdings,
inventoried in 2013

505
Wilhelm Limpert
Prospekt für die *Internationale*
***Hygiene-Ausstellung* in Dresden, 1930**
Dresden 1929–1930
Autotypie
Brochure for the [International
hygiene exhibition] in Dresden, 1930
Dresden 1929–1930
Halftone
220 x 100 mm
KI 17030-14, alter Bestand, inv.
old holdings, inventoried in 2013

506
Franz Heinrich Neundlinger
Prospekt für die Wiener Herbstmesse 1934
Wien, 1934
Klischee, Buchdruck
Brochure for the [Autumn Trade Fair of Vienna 1934]
Vienna, 1934
Cliché, letterpress print
200 x 116 mm
KI 15878-6, Schenkung donation from Paul Kurt Schwarz 2008

507
Ludwig Hohlwein
Reisebroschüre *Germany*
München, um 1930
Ausführung: Druckerei Carl Gerber Verlag
Autotypie
Travel Brochure *Germany*
Munich, ca. 1930
Execution: Printer Carl Gerber Verlag
Halftone
225 x 103 mm
KI 17406-16, alter Bestand, inv. old holdings,
inventoried in 2013

508
Max Burchartz
Reisebroschüre *Bochum*
Deutschland, 1930
Offsetdruck
Travel Brochure *Bochum*
Germany, 1930
Offset print
195 x 119 (238) mm
KI 17882-41, alter Bestand, inv.
old holdings, inventoried in 2013

509
Herbert Bayer
Reisebroschüre *Dessau*
Dessau, 1926
Autotypie, Buchdruck
Travel Brochure *Dessau*
Dessau, 1926
Halftone, letterpress print
210 x 105 mm
KI 17882-55, alter Bestand, inv.
old holdings, inventoried in 2013

510
Alfred Mahlau
Reiseprospekt *Lübeck*
Lübeck, um 1955
Ausführung: Druckerei Lübecker Nachrichten
Autotypie, Buchdruck
Travel Brochure *Lübeck*
Lübeck, ca. 1955
Execution: Printer Lübecker Nachrichten
Halftone, letterpress print
208 x 98 (395) mm
KI 15877-20, Schenkung donation from
Paul Kurt Schwarz 2008

511
Theodor Paul Etbauer
Reisebroschüre *Hamburg*
Hamburg, um 1931
Ausführung: Druckerei H. O. Persiehl
Offsetdruck
Travel Brochure *Hamburg*
Hamburg, ca. 1931
Execution: Printer H. O. Persiehl
Offset print
220 x 100 (200) mm
KI 17882-78, alter Bestand, inv.
old holdings, inventoried in 2013

VERSCHLUSSMARKEN ALS WERBETRÄGER

Kleine bemalte oder geprägte Aufkleber zum Verschließen der Briefkuverts gab es bereits im frühen 19. Jahrhundert, sie ersetzten Wachs und Siegellack und versprachen schöne Inhalte: „Il a beau dire" oder „L'interieur est douce" (Abb. S. 397). Im Laufe der Zeit verwandelten sich diese persönlichen Botschaften in Ankündigungen zunächst von Ausstellungen, bis die Verschlussmarke im frühen 20. Jahrhundert zu einem bedeutenden Werbeträger für alle Branchen avancierte. Etwas überspitzt beschreibt Hans Sachs diesen Boom in einem 1913 erschienenen Artikel: „Und wenn man dann […] einer Druckerei einen Besuch abstattet und ihren Inhaber ein bisschen über das flaue Geschäftsjahr stöhnen hört, während gerade durchs Telefon drei neue Kinoplakate und von einer grossen Zigarettenfirma ‚5 Millionen Reklamemarken in 30 verschiedenen Sujets nur erster Künstler' bestellt werden, dann ist man über das Schicksal unserer Reklamekunst ganz beruhigt […]."[1] Hand in Hand mit dem Aufschwung ging eine regelrechte Sammelwut, gefördert durch die Konzeption ganzer Serien, die auf Tauschbörsen ergänzt und in Sammelhefte eingeklebt wurden. Bis heute ist diese Werbestrategie äußerst erfolgreich.

1980 erwarb die Bibliothek 1 590 Reklamemarken aus dem ehemaligen Besitz des Malers Hubert Landa (1870–1938); mit dem Teilnachlass von Werner J. Schweiger kamen 2013 noch einmal 1 330 Marken hinzu. Um ihren Entstehungszeitraum zu illustrieren, seien zwei Beispiele einander gegenübergestellt, die ein halbes Jahrhundert trennt: Hatte sich die Reklamemarke mit der Ausstellungswerbung etabliert, so findet sie darin auch ihre längste Verwendung (Abb. 512, 513). Dazwischen sind ihre Aufgaben vielfältig. Sie huldigt berühmten Persönlichkeiten – etwa Marie von Ebner-Eschenbach, zu deren 80. Geburtstag Koloman Moser eine Gedenkmarke entwarf. Sie betreibt politische Propaganda, etwa für die Reichstagswahl 1938. Sie demonstriert soziales Engagement als Wohltätigkeits- oder Bausteinmarke (Abb. 516, 517). Und sie kommuniziert Verhaltensregeln (Abb. 526) oder feiert einfach nur ein einmaliges Datum (Abb. 530). Ungewöhnlich ist eine Glückwunsch-Enthebungsmarke (Abb. 535), die auf das 19. Jahrhundert zurückgeht, wo die Annahme von Wunschkarten mit einer Spende an die Überbringer verbunden war (s. S. 134).

Die Gestaltung der Reklamemarke hängt naturgemäß von den AuftraggeberInnen und KünstlerInnen ab und reicht von (bewusst) antiquiert bis avantgardistisch. So steht die Marke zum Regierungsjubiläum von Kaiser Franz Joseph 1898, als der Jugendstil bereits alles überformte, noch in der Tradition des Historismus, während Bertold Löffler zehn Jahre später für eine zeitgemäße Erscheinung sorgte (Abb. 514, 515). Die Marke zur Exlibris-Ausstellung im k. k. Österreichischen Museum für Kunst und Industrie 1913 greift ein barockes Motiv auf und verweist damit auf die Geschichte ihres Gegenstandes, während sich Österreich auf der *Internationalen Ausstellung für Buchgewerbe und Graphik* in Leipzig 1914 ausdrücklich modern präsentierte (Abb. 532, 534). Die sogenannte Bugra hatte dem „unscheinbare[n] kleine[n] Ding" einen eigenen Pavillon gewidmet, wenngleich man „das grosse Rennen nach der Reklamemarke" als beendigt ansah.[2] Tatsächlich ist der Großteil der künstlerisch wertvollen Marken der MAK-Sammlung vor dem Ersten Weltkrieg entstanden, verbunden mit bedeutenden – auch weiblichen – Namen: Änne Koken etwa, aus Hannover stammend mit Beziehungen zu Wien,[3] entwarf für die Hannoveraner Unternehmen Bahlsen und Appels ebenso wie für Julius Meinl – womöglich lieferte sie die Inspiration zum „Meinl-Mohr" von Joseph Binder (Abb. 524). Fritz und Clara Ehmcke sind zu nennen, die der Klebstoff-Marke *Syndetikon* ihren

1   Sachs, Hans, „Reklamemarkenausstellung in Berlin", in: *Das Plakat* (4) 1913, 253.

2   Kirsten, Arthur, „Reklamemarken", in: *Das Plakat* (5) 1914, 111.

3   Vgl. Bleistein, Rudolf, „Aenne Koken", in: *Das Plakat* (4) 1913, 177–179.

SEALING STAMPS AS ADVERTISING MEDIA

Small painted or embossed stickers to seal envelopes have existed since the early 19th century; they replaced (sealing) wax and promised that kind words would be found within: "Il a beau dire" or "L'interieur est douce" (ill. p. 397). Over the course of time, these personal messages evolved into sealing stamps bearing advertisements—initially announcing exhibitions and later, in the early 20th century, developing into an important advertising medium for all branches. In a somewhat exaggerated tone, Hans Sachs describes this boom in an article published in 1913: "And if one then [...] pays a visit to a printer's and briefly listens to the owner moaning about the sluggish financial year, while at the same time orders are made via the telephone for three new movie posters and '5 million poster stamps bearing 30 different subjects by only the best artists' for a large cigarette company, then one will be thoroughly reassured about the fate of our advertising art [...]."[1]

Hand in hand with this boom, there was a veritable rage for collecting stamps—encouraged by the conception of entire series, which could be completed at swap meets and affixed in collector's books. Even today, this advertising strategy remains extremely successful.

In 1980 the museum's library acquired 1 590 poster stamps formerly owned by the painter Hubert Landa (1870–1938); with the partial bequest from Werner J. Schweiger, a further 1 330 stamps were added in 2013. To illustrate the period when they were created, compare two examples, which are separated by half a century: just as the poster stamp had become established as a medium to advertise exhibitions, it is for that purpose that it is used longest (ill. 512, 513). In between, its tasks are varied. It pays homage to famous individuals such as Marie von Ebner-Eschenbach, for whose 80th birthday Koloman Moser designed a commemorative stamp. It engages in political propaganda, such as for the Reichstag election in 1938. It demonstrates social engagement as a charity or construction stamp (ill. 516, 517). And it communicates rules of etiquette (ill. 526) or simply celebrates a unique date (ill. 530). What is unusual is a greeting apology stamp (ill. 535), which dates back to the 19th century when the acceptance of greeting cards was coupled with a donation to the deliverers (see p. 133).

The design of the poster stamp naturally depends on the customer and the artist, and thus ranges from the (intentionally) antiquated to the avant-garde. For example, the stamp for the jubilee of Emperor Franz Joseph in 1898—at a time when art nouveau was reshaping everything—still followed the tradition of historicism, whereas ten years later Bertold Löffler guaranteed a design, which was in keeping with the times (ill. 514, 515). The stamp for the ex libris exhibition at the Imperial Royal Austrian Museum of Art and Industry in 1913 took up a baroque motif and thereby made reference to the history of its subject, while Austria presented itself as emphatically modern at the *Internationale Ausstellung für Buchgewerbe und Graphik* [International exhibition of the book trade and graphic art] in Leipzig in 1914 (ill. 532, 534). The so-called Bugra had dedicated an entire pavilion to this "unimposing little thing," even though "the great race for poster stamps" was considered finished.[2] In point of fact, the majority of the artistically valuable stamps in the MAK Collection were indeed created prior to the First World War, and are associated with significant—sometimes female—names: Änne Koken, for example, from Hannover but with connections to Vienna,[3] designed for the Hannover company Bahlsen and Appels as well as for Julius Meinl—it is possible that she provided the inspiration for the "Meinl Moor" by Joseph Binder (ill. 524).

1   Sachs, Hans, "Reklamemarkenausstellung in Berlin," in: *Das Plakat* (4) 1913, 253. Translated by Maria Slater.

2   Kirsten, Arthur, "Reklamemarken," in: *Das Plakat* (5) 1914, 111. Translated by Maria Slater.

3   Cf. Bleistein, Rudolf, "Aenne Koken," in: *Das Plakat* (4) 1913, 177–179.

Stempel aufdrückten, und jene Grafiker, die für die Berliner Druckerei Hollerbaum & Schmidt mit sich selbst warben: Lucian Bernhard, Julius Klinger oder Hans Rudi Erdt (Abb. 527–529).

Ab 1910 erschienen die Reklamemarken vermehrt als Serien. Ihrer oft bemängelten Qualität versuchte die Keksfirma Bahlsen durch die Herausgabe exklusiver Künstlermarken entgegenzuwirken. Neben Änne Koken, Heinrich Vogeler oder Lucian Bernhard wurde auch die Wiener-Werkstätte-Künstlerin Mela Koehler beauftragt und verfolgte in der „Serie E" das Leben einer Konsumentin über zwölf Altersstufen (Abb. 533); ausgewählte Motive wurden 1914 als Postkarten herausgegeben (s. S. 380).[4] Von dem wenig bekannten Carl Willy Vogt stammt eine Zwölferserie für die Stettiner Buch-, Steindruckerei und Kartonagen-Fabrik F. M. Lenzner, in der der Maler und Grafiker werbewirksam Sachlichkeit und Karikatur kombinierte (Abb. 525).

Neben vollständigen Serien verwahrt die MAK-Sammlung Reklamemarken, die es ermöglichen, den Werbeauftritt eines Produkts oder einer Institution über Jahrzehnte zu verfolgen. Die früheste Marke etwa für die Wiener Messe datiert aus dem Jahr 1914 (1. Messe), die späteste aus dem Jahr 1962 (75. Messe). Bekannte Gestalter zeichneten für die Kampagnen verantwortlich, darunter Julius Klinger, Hermann Kosel oder Hans Neumann (Abb. 538). Aber auch weniger bekannte wie August Fischinger oder Hans Thomas lieferten überzeugende Arbeiten (Abb. 537, 539). Eine Besonderheit sind darüber hinaus intakte Streifen oder gar ganze Bogen aus dem Nachlass Werner J. Schweigers. Solche Bogen weisen eine eigene Gestaltung auf und transportieren oft zusätzliche Informationen. So wurde ein Set von neun Marken für die Wochenschrift *Zeit im Bild* buchstäblich in den Rahmen einer Werbeanzeige eingebunden und dadurch selbst zum Bildinhalt (Abb. 541).

Der Titel der Wochenschrift mag abschließend an die Bedeutung der Gelegenheitsgrafik erinnern: Ephemera sind nicht nur Wegwerfprodukte, sondern durch SammlerInnen und Sammlungen erhalten gebliebene Zeitzeugen.

[4] S. dazu: Meyer, Reiner, *Die Reklamekunst der Keksfabrik Bahlsen in Hannover von 1889–1945*, Phil. Diss., Münster 1999, 194–199, http://d-nb.info/961524944/34 (22.4.2016).

512
Anonym Anonymous
Reklamemarke der *II. Int. Kochkunst-Ausstellung* in Wien 1898
Wien, 1898
Stahlstich
Poster Stamp for the [2nd International exhibition of culinary art] in Vienna 1898
Vienna, 1898
Steel engraving
41 x 87 mm
KI 21484-2-79, Ankauf purchased from
Kunstarchiv Werner J. Schweiger 2015

Fritz and Clara Ehmcke are also noteworthy, who left their mark on the glue brand *Syndetikon*, as are those graphic designers who advertised for the Berlin-based printer's Hollerbaum & Schmidt with themselves: Lucian Bernhard, Julius Klinger, and Hans Rudi Erdt (ill. 527–529), among others. From 1910 poster stamps were increasingly published in series. The cookie company Bahlsen attempted to counteract their often criticized quality by publishing exclusive artists' stamps. Alongside Änne Koken, Heinrich Vogeler, and Lucian Bernhard, the company also commissioned the Wiener Werkstätte artist Mela Koehler and followed a consumer through twelve stages of life in the "E series" (ill. 533); select motifs were also released as postcards in 1914 (see p. 381).[4] A twelve-part series for the F. M. Lenzner book printer's, lithographer's, and cardboard cover factory in Szczecin, Poland, was created by the little-known painter and graphic designer Carl Willy Vogt, in which he combined objectivity and caricature to create advertising appeal (ill. 525).

In addition to complete series, the MAK Collection also holds poster stamps, which make it possible to trace the advertising campaigns for a product or institution across decades. The earliest stamp for the Vienna Trade Fair, for example, dates from the year 1914 (1st fair), the latest from 1962 (75th fair). Famous designers were responsible for the campaigns, including Julius Klinger, Hermann Kosel, and Hans Neumann (ill. 538). However, less well-known names such as August Fischinger and Hans Thomas also delivered convincing works (ill. 537, 539). Furthermore, one special feature of the collection is intact strips or even entire sheets from the bequest of Werner J. Schweiger. Such sheets exhibit a separate composition and often convey additional information. One such set of nine stamps for the weekly *Zeit im Bild* was quite literally incorporated into the border of an advertisement and hence itself became part of the image content (ill. 541). In conclusion, the title of the weekly *Zeit im Bild* [Time in images] may serve as a reminder of the significance of graphic design as a whole: Ephemera are not just disposable products, but when preserved by collectors they are witnesses of the age.

4   See: Meyer, Reiner, *Die Reklamekunst der Keksfabrik Bahlsen in Hannover von 1889–1945*, PhD dissertation, Münster 1999, 194–199, http://d-nb.info/961524944/34 (22 Apr 2016). ˙

513
Wolfgang Edel
Reklamemarke der *Deutschen Gastwirts- und Konditoren-Messe Berlin 1951*
Deutschland, 1951
Klischee
Poster Stamp for the [German Trade Show for Restaurateurs and Confectioners Berlin 1951]
Germany, 1951
Cliché
50 x 35 mm
KI 21484-3-404, Ankauf purchased from
Kunstarchiv Werner J. Schweiger 2015

514
Anonym Anonymous
Reklamemarke zur Ausstellung anlässlich des 50. Regierungs-jubiläums Kaiser Franz Joseph I.
Wien, 1898
Ausführung: Druckerei Philipp & Kramer
Lithografie
Poster Stamp for the Exhibition on the Occasion of the Golden Jubilee of Emperor Franz Joseph I
Vienna, 1898
Execution: Printer Philipp & Kramer
Lithograph
53 x 38 mm
KI 21484-2-98, Ankauf purchased from Kunstarchiv Werner J. Schweiger 2015

515
Bertold Löffler
Reklamemarke zu den Festlichkeiten anlässlich des 60. Regierungs-jubiläums Kaiser Franz Joseph I.
Wien, 1908
Ausführung: Druckerei Christoph Reissers Söhne
Klischee
Poster Stamp for the Celebration on the Occasion of the Diamond Jubilee of Emperor Franz Joseph I
Vienna, 1908
Execution: Printer Christoph Reissers Söhne
Cliché
37 x 23 mm
KI 21484-2-2, Ankauf purchased from Kunstarchiv Werner J. Schweiger 2015

516
Anonym Anonymous
Wohltätigkeitsmarke des Ottakringer Lehrer-hilfskomitees
Wien, 1905
Stahlstich
Charity Stamp for the Ottakringer Teacher Aid Committee
Vienna, 1905
Steel engraving
43 x 26 mm
KI 21484-3-703, Ankauf purchased from Kunstarchiv Werner J. Schweiger 2015

517
Anonym Anonymous
Bausteinmarke des I. Oesterr. Blinden-Vereins
Österreich, um 1910
Klischee
Building block stamp for the [1st Austrian Society for the Blind]
Austria, ca. 1910
Cliché
40 x 32 mm
KI 21484-3-680, Ankauf purchased from Kunstarchiv Werner J. Schweiger 2015

519
Koloman Moser
Gedenkmarke zum 80. Geburtstag von Marie von Ebner-Eschenbach
Wien, 1910
Ausführung: Druckerei Albert Berger
Lithografie
Commemorative Stamp for the 80th Birthday of Marie von Ebner-Eschenbach
Vienna, 1910
Execution: Printer Albert Berger
Lithograph
35 x 38 mm
KI 21484-2-365, Ankauf purchased from Kunstarchiv Werner J. Schweiger 2015

518
Koloman Moser
Entwurf für eine Gedenkmarke zum 80. Geburtstag von Marie von Ebner-Eschenbach
Wien, 1910
Tusche, Deckweiß
Design for a Commemorative Stamp for the 80th Birthday of Marie von Ebner-Eschenbach
Vienna, 1910
Ink, opaque white
127 x 132 mm
KI 8981-3, Schenkung donation 1932

520
Änne Koken
Reklamemarke für Appels Delikatessen
Hannover, um 1910
Lithografie
Poster Stamp for Delicacies by Appel
Hannover, ca. 1910
Lithograph
40 x 53 mm
KI 14142-1-539, Ankauf
purchased from Maria Landa 1980

521
Fritz Helmuth Ehmcke
Reklamemarke für
***Syndetikon*-Klebstoff**
Deutschland, um 1910
Lithografie
Poster Stamp for Glue by
Syndetikon
Germany, ca. 1910
Lithograph
50 x 35 mm
KI 14142-2-87, Ankauf
purchased from Maria Landa 1980

522
Clara Ehmcke
Reklamemarke für
***Syndetikon*-Klebstoff**
Deutschland, um 1910
Lithografie
Poster Stamp for Glue by
Syndetikon
Germany, ca. 1910
Lithograph
50 x 35 mm
KI 14142-1-257, Ankauf
purchased from
Maria Landa 1980

523
Georg Räder
Fünf zusammenhängende Reklamemarken
von Produkten der Firma Georg Schicht
Deutschland, um 1910
Klischee
Five Related Poster Stamps for Products
by the Company Georg Schicht
Germany, ca. 1910
Cliché
55 x 187 mm
KI 21484-3-676, Ankauf purchased from
Kunstarchiv Werner J. Schweiger 2015

524
Änne Koken
Reklamemarke für Julius Meinl
Wien, um 1910
Lithografie
Poster Stamp for Julius Meinl
Vienna, ca. 1910
Lithograph
30 x 45 mm
KI 14142-1-168, Ankauf
purchased from Maria Landa 1980

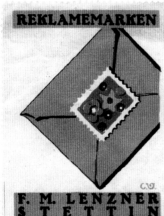

525
Carl Willy Vogt
Reklamemarken aus einer 10-teiligen
Serie der Druckerei und
Kartonagen-Fabrik F. M. Lenzner
Stettin, um 1912
Lithografie
Poster Stamps from a 10-Part Series
for the Printer and Carton Factory
F. M. Lenzner
Stettin, ca. 1912
Lithograph
Je 63 x 48 mm each
KI 14142-2-40, KI 14142-2-25,
Ankauf purchased from Maria Landa 1980

526
Fritz Schönpflug
Reklamemarke aus der Aufklärungs-
kampagne „Sicherheit in der Tramway"
Wien, 1911
Farblithografie
Poster Stamp from the Awareness-Raising
Campaign ["Safety on the tramway"]
Vienna, 1911
Chromolithograph
43 x 57 mm
KI 21484-2-457, Ankauf purchased from
Kunstarchiv Werner J. Schweiger 2015

527
Julius Klinger
Reklamemarke für Werbung
nach Entwurf von Julius Klinger
Berlin, um 1912
Ausführung: Druckerei Hollerbaum & Schmidt
Lithografie
Poster Stamp for Advertisements
Designed by Julius Klinger
Berlin, ca. 1912
Execution: Printer Hollerbaum & Schmidt
Lithograph
46 x 66 mm
KI 14142-2-238, Ankauf purchased from
Maria Landa 1980

528
Lucian Bernard
Reklamemarke für Plakate
nach Entwurf von L. Bernhard
Berlin, um 1912
Ausführung: Druckerei Hollerbaum & Schmidt
Lithografie
Poster Stamp for Posters Designed
by L. Bernhard
Berlin, ca. 1912
Execution: Printer Hollerbaum & Schmidt
Lithograph
46 x 66 mm
KI 14142-1-339, Ankauf purchased from
Maria Landa 1980

529
Hans Rudi Erdt
Reklamemarke für Werbung
nach Entwurf von H.R. Erdt
Berlin, um 1912
Ausführung: Druckerei Hollerbaum & Schmidt
Lithografie
Poster Stamp for Advertisements
Designed by H.R. Erdt
Berlin, ca. 1912
Execution: Printer Hollerbaum & Schmidt
Lithograph
45 x 65 mm
KI 14142-1-325, Ankauf purchased from
Maria Landa 1980

530
Anonym Anonymous
Marke zum 11. Dezember 1913
Vermutl. Deutschland, 1913
Klischee
Stamp for 11 December 1913
Prob. Germany, 1913
Cliché
56 x 34 mm
KI 21484-3-223, Ankauf purchased
from Kunstarchiv Werner J. Schweiger
2015

531
Emil Pirchan
**Gedenkmarke aus einer
mehrteiligen Serie zum
100. Geburtstag von
Richard Wagner**
München, 1913
Ausführung: Druckerei Oscar Consée
Klischee
**Commemorative Stamp from
a Multi-Stamp Series for the
100th Birthday of Richard Wagner**
Munich, 1913
Execution: Printer Oscar Consée
Cliché
55 x 41 mm
KI 21484-3-174, Ankauf purchased
from Kunstarchiv Werner J. Schweiger
2015

532
Anonym Anonymous
**Reklamemarke zur Ausstellung
der Österreichischen Exlibris-
Gesellschaft im ÖMKI, 1913**
Wien, 1913
Lithografie
**Poster Stamp for the Exhibition
of the Austrian Bookplate Society
at the ÖMKI, 1913**
Vienna, 1913
Lithograph
65 x 71 mm
KI 21484-2-26, Ankauf
purchased from Kunstarchiv
Werner J. Schweiger 2015

534
Vermutl. Prob. Heinrich Kathrein
**Reklamemarke des Österreich-
hauses auf der *Internationalen
Buchgewerbeausstellung
Leipzig 1914***
Wien, 1914
Farblithografie
**Poster Stamp of the Austrian
pavilion at the [International book
trade exhibition in Leipzig 1914]**
Vienna, 1914
Chromolithograph
39 x 39 mm
KI 21484-2-11, Ankauf purchased
from Kunstarchiv Werner J. Schweiger
2015

533
Mela Koehler
**Reklamemarken aus einer
zwölfteiligen Serie der
Keksfabrik Bahlsen**
Hannover, 1913
Klischee
**Poster Stamps from
a 12-Part Series for the
Cookie Factory Bahlsen**
Hannover, 1913
Cliché
55 x 39 mm
KI 21484-2-220, KI 21484-2-225,
Ankauf purchased from Kunstarchiv
Werner J. Schweiger 2015

535
Anonym Anonymous
Glückwunsch-Enthebungsmarke
vom Reichsverein für Kinderschutz
Österreich, 1916
Lithografie
New Year's Apology Stamp
from the Reich Society for
Child Protection
Austria, 1916
Lithograph
54 x 38 mm
KI 14142-1-634, Ankauf purchased
from Maria Landa 1980

536
Anonym Anonymous
Propagandamarke zur
Reichstagswahl am
10. April 1938
Deutschland, 1938
Lithografie
Propaganda Stamp for
the Reichstag Election
on 10 April 1938
Germany, 1938
Lithograph
70 x 64 mm
KI 14142-1-781, Ankauf purchased
from Maria Landa 1980

537
Vermutl. Prob. August Fischinger
Reklamemarke der Wiener
Frühjahrsmesse 1924
Wien, 1924
Druckerei: Papier- u. Blechdruck
Industrie
Lithografie
Poster Stamp for the Spring
Trade Fair of Vienna 1924
Vienna, 1924
Printer: Papier- u. Blechdruck Industrie
Lithograph
60 x 45 mm
KI 14142-1-270, Ankauf purchased
from Maria Landa 1980

538
Atelier Hans Neumann
Reklamemarke der Wiener
Herbstmesse 1928
Wien, 1928
Lithografie
Poster Stamp for the Autumn
Trade Fair of Vienna 1928
Vienna, 1928
Lithograph
59 x 40 mm
KI 21484-3-102, Ankauf purchased
from Kunstarchiv Werner J. Schweiger
2015

539
Hans Thomas
Reklamemarke der Wiener
Herbstmesse 1958
Wien, 1958
Klischee
Poster Stamp for the Autumn
Trade Fair of Vienna 1958
Vienna, 1958
Cliché
42 x 32 mm
KI 21484-3-115, Ankauf purchased
from Kunstarchiv Werner J. Schweiger
2015

540
Wilhelm Jaruska
Reklamemarke der Wiener
Herbstmesse 1960
Wien, 1960
Offsetdruck
Poster Stamp for the Autumn
Trade Fair of Vienna 1960
Vienna, 1960
Offset print
40 x 32 mm
KI 21484-3-116, Ankauf purchased
from Kunstarchiv Werner J. Schweiger
2015

541
Thomas Theodor Heine
**Bogen mit neun Reklamemarken
der Wochenschrift** *Zeit im Bild*
München, 1913
Druckerei: G. Schuh & Cie.
Klischee
**Sheet of Nine Poster Stamps
for the Weekly [Time in images]**
Munich, 1913
Printer: G. Schuh & Cie.
Cliché
226 x 160 mm
KI 21484-3-167, Ankauf purchased
from Kunstarchiv Werner J. Schweiger
2015

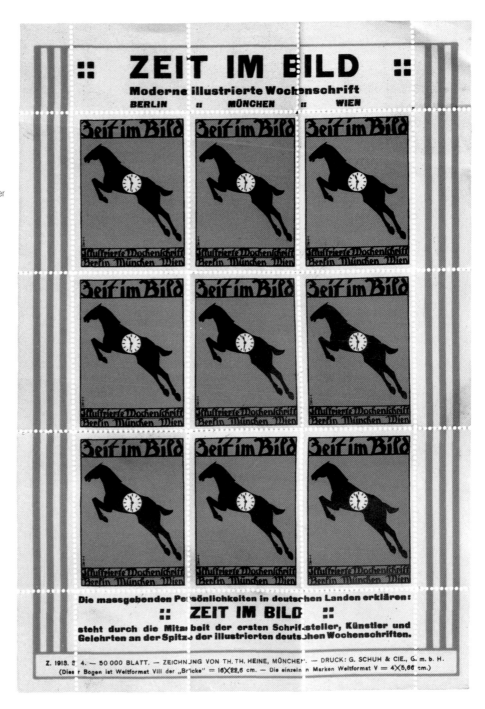

AUSGEWÄHLTE LITERATUR
ABKÜRZUNGEN, REGISTER

SELECT BIBLIOGRAPHY,
ABBREVIATIONS, INDEX

AUSGEWÄHLTE LITERATUR SELECT BIBLIOGRAPHY

ALLGEMEIN GENERAL

Binder, Carla, *Joseph Binder. An artist and a lifestyle from the Joseph Binder Collection of posters, graphic and fine art, notes and records*, Wien/München Vienna/Munich 1976.

Durstmüller, Anton, *500 Jahre Druck in Österreich*, 3 Bde. vols., Wien Vienna 1982–1989.

Evers, Bernd (Hg. ed.), *Kunst in der Bibliothek. Zur Geschichte der Kunstbibliothek und ihrer Sammlungen*, Ausst.kat. exh.cat., Berlin 1994.

Gebrauchsgraphik. Monatsschrift zur Förderung künstlerischer Werbung (1) 1 1924 – (42) 12 1971, München Munich.

Hall, Murray G., *Österreichische Verlagsgeschichte 1918–1938*, 2 Bde. vols., Wien Vienna/Graz 1985.

Heller, Friedrich C., *Die bunte Welt. Handbuch zum künstlerisch illustrierten Kinderbuch in Wien 1890–1938*, Wien Vienna 2008.

Hudson, Graham S., *The Design & Printing of Ephemera in Britain & America*, London 2008.

Jury, David, *Graphic Design before Graphic Designers. The Printer as Designer and Craftsman 1700–1914*, London 2012.

Kern, Anita, *Joseph Binder. 1. Protagonist der Moderne*, Wien Vienna 2012.

Kern, Anita, *Joseph Binder. 2. Art director in the USA*, Wien Vienna 2016.

Kern, Anita/**Reinhold,** Bernadette, *Grafikdesign von der Wiener Moderne bis heute. Von Kolo Moser bis Stefan Sagmeister. Aus der Sammlung der Universität für angewandte Kunst Wien*, Wien Vienna/New York 2010.

Klinger, Julius, *Skizzen für Lithographen und Zeichner. 100 Entwürfe im Charakter der Neuzeit: Plakatmotive, Einladungskarten, Menüs, Schlusszeichen, Flächenfüllungen, Buchschmuck, Leisten, Umrahmungen, Etiquetten und sonstige Ideen für lithographische Zwecke*, Berlin, um ca. 1900.

Lewis, John, *Printed Ephemera. The changing uses of type and letterforms in English and American Printing*, Ipswich 1962.

Maillard, Léon, *Les menus & programmes illustrés. Invitations – billets de faire part – cartes d'adresse – petites estampes du XVIIe siècle à nos jours*, Paris 1898.

Murphy, Kevin/**O'Driscoll,** Sally (Hg. eds.), *Studies in Ephemera. Text and Image in Eighteenth-Century Print*, Lewisburg 2013.

Noever, Peter (Hg. ed.), *Joseph Binder. Wien – New York Vienna—New York*, MAK Studies 1, Wien Vienna 2001.

Pabst, Michael, *Wiener Grafik um 1900*, München Munich 1984.

Pérez, Rosario Ramos, *Ephemera. La vida sobre papel, colección de la Biblioteca Nacional*, Ausst.kat. exh.cat. Biblioteca Nacional, Madrid 2003.

Pieske, Christa, *Das ABC des Luxuspapiers. Herstellung, Verarbeitung und Gebrauch 1860 bis 1930*, Ausst.kat. exh.cat. Museum für Deutsche Volkskunde Museum of German Folklore, Staatliche Museen zu Berlin/Preußischer Kulturbesitz, Berlin 1984.

Rickards, Maurice, *Collecting Printed Ephemera*, New York 1988.

Rickards, Maurice (Hg. ed.), *The Encyclopedia of Ephemera. A guide to the fragmentary documents of everyday life for the collector, curator, and historian*, fertiggestellt von compl. by Michael **Twyman,** London 2000.

Schmidt-Bachem, Heinz, *Aus Papier. Eine Kultur- und Wirtschaftsgeschichte der Papier verarbeitenden Industrie in Deutschland*, Berlin/Boston 2011.

Schweiger, Werner J., *Aufbruch und Erfüllung. Gebrauchsgraphik der Wiener Moderne 1897–1918*, Wien Vienna 1988.

Stiftung Nordfriesland, Schloss vor Husum (Hg. eds.), *Papier im Reiche des Luxus und der Phantasie*, mit Beiträgen von with contributions by Christa **Pieske** und and Rolf **Kuschert,** Husum 1987.

Zur Westen, Walter von, *Berlins graphische Gelegenheitskunst. Berliner Exlibris, Besuchskarten, Privatanzeigen, Glückwunschkarten, Notentitel, Reklamekunst in Vergangenheit und Gegenwart*, 2 Bde. vols., Berlin 1912.

BUNTPAPIER DECORATED PAPER

„Ausstellung von Buntpapieren in der Kunstgewerbeschule des Österreichischen Museums", in: *Kunst und Kunsthandwerk* (XIII) 5 1910, 319, 320–324 (Abb. ill.).

Bánszky-Kiss, Eva, „Die Konfiserie Altmann & Kühne, 1935", in: *Alte und moderne Kunst* (XXX) 203 1985, 30–33.

Benson, Jake, „The Art of Abri: Marbled Album Leaves, Drawings, and Paintings of the Deccan", in: Haidar, Navina Najat/ Sardar, Marika (Hg. eds.), *Sultans of Deccan India 1500–1700*, New York 2015.

Bierbaum, Otto Julius, „Künstlerische Vorsatzpapiere", in: *Dekorative Kunst* (I) 3 1898, 111–129.

Egger, Hanna/Lechner, Gregor M., *Europäische Buntpapiere. Barock bis Jugendstil*, Schriften des Museums für angewandte Kunst 26, Wien Vienna 1984.

Exner, Wilhelm F., *Die Tapeten- und Buntpapier-Industrie für Fabrikanten und Gewerbetreibende, sowie für technische Institute*, Weimar 1869.

Haemmerle, Albert, *Buntpapier. Herkommen, Geschichte, Techniken, Beziehungen zur Kunst*, München Munich 1977.

Hevesi, Ludwig, „Die Ausstellung von Bucheinbänden und Vorsatzpapieren", in: *Kunst und Kunsthandwerk* (VI) 4 1903, 121–148.

K. k. Österreichisches Museum für Kunst und Industrie Imperial Royal Austrian Museum of Art and Industry (Hg. ed.), Ausstellung von Bucheinbänden und Vorsatzpapieren, Ausst.kat. exh.cat. ÖMKI, Wien Vienna 1903.

Krause, Susanne/Rinck, Julia, *Buntpapier – ein Bestimmungsbuch Decorated Paper – A Guide Book, Sierpapier – Een Gids*, Stuttgart 2016.

Krist, Gabriela, *Leopold Stolba (1863–1929) und seine Tunk- und Kleisterpapiere*, Phil. Diss. PhD thesis, Salzburg 1989.

Kunstgewerbe-Museum Berlin (Hg. ed.), *Führer durch die Sonderausstellung Buntpapiere*, Ausst.kat. exh.cat. Königliche Museen Berlin, Kunstgewerbemuseum, Berlin 1907.

Neiser, Wolfgang, *Luxuspapier, Buntpapier und Ephemera. Die Sammlung Helmut und Dr. Juliane Färber im Historischen Museum der Stadt Regensburg*, Regensburg 2015.

Oettingen, Dirik von, *Verhüllt um zu verführen. Die Welt der Orange*, Potsdam 2007.

Radunsky, Clara, *Marmorpapier. Vom Gebrauchsgegenstand zum Kunstobjekt, am Beispiel der Sammlung Charles Ernest Clerget im Museum für angewandte Kunst in Wien*, Diplom-Arbeit degree thesis, Wien Vienna 2012.

Schmidt, Frieder, „Buntpapier – Forschungsansätze und Arbeitsergebnisse", in: *Leipziger Jahrbuch zur Buchgeschichte* (21) 2013, 153–171.

Schmidt, Frieder/Feiler, Sigrid (Red. eds.), *Franz Bartsch: Papiersammler aus Wien. Rekonstruktion seiner Ausstellung Stuttgart 1909*, Deutsches Buch- und Schriftmuseum German Museum of Books and Writing, Begleitmaterialien zur gleichnamigen Ausstellung materials accompanying the exhibition of the same name, Frankfurt/Main 1998.

Segieth, Clelia, *Pop Art mit Orangenduft. Orangenpapiere aus der Sammlung Buchheim*, Feldafing 2008.

Wolfe, Richard J., *Marbled paper. Its history, techniques, and patterns. With special reference to the relationship of marbling to bookbinding in Europe and the Western World*, Philadelphia 1990. „Zu unseren Bildern. Leopold Stolba", in: *Dekorative Kunst* (VII) 12 1904, 72f. (Abb. ill.), 77.

GLÜCKWUNSCHKARTEN – BRIEFPAPIER GREETING CARDS—LETTER PAPER

Anderegg, Johannes, *Schreibe mir oft! Das Medium Brief von 1750 bis 1830*, Göttingen 2001.

Böhmer, Günter, *Sei glücklich und vergiß mein nicht. Stammbuchblätter und Glückwunschkarten*, München Munich 1973.

Doosry, Yasmin, *Käufliche Gefühle. Freundschafts- und Glückwunschbillets des Biedermeier*, Ausst.kat. exh.cat. Germanisches Nationalmuseum, Nürnberg Nuremberg 2004.

Egger, Hanna, *Herrn Biedermeiers Wunschbillet*, Ausst.kat. exh.cat. Österreichisches Museum für angewandte Kunst Austrian Museum of Applied Arts, Wien Vienna 1978.

Egger, Hanna, *Glückwunschkarten im Biedermeier. Höflichkeit und gesellschaftlicher Zwang*, München Munich 1980.

Ehret, Gloria, *Freundschafts- und Glückwunschkarten im Biedermeier*, München Munich 1982.

Ertel, Susanne, *Anleitung zur schriftlichen Kommunikation. Briefsteller von 1880 bis 1980*, Tübingen 1984.

Giuriato, Davide, „Briefpapier", in: Bohnkamp, Anne/Wiethölter, Waltraud (Hg. eds.), *Der Brief – Ereignis & Objekt*, Ausst.kat. exh.cat. Freies Deutsches Hochstift Frankfurt – Frankfurter Goethe-Museum, Frankfurt am Main/Basel 2008, 1–18.

Gugitz, Gustav, „Alt-Wiener Neujahrswunschkarten", in: *Jahrbuch für Exlibris und Gebrauchsgraphik* (34) 1939, 10–20.

Korzus, Bernard (Hg. ed.), *Fabrik im Ornament. Ansichten auf Firmenbriefköpfen des 19. Jahrhunderts*, Ausst.kat. exh.cat. Westfälisches Landesmuseum und and Stiftung Westfälisches Wirtschaftsarchiv Dortmund, Münster 1980.

Pazaurek, Gustav E., „Künstlerische Besuchskarten", in: *Mitteilungen des Württembergischen Kunstgewerbevereins* (6) 2 1907/1908, 53–74.

Pazaurek, Gustav E., *Biedermeier-Wünsche*, Stuttgart 1908.

Rammler, Otto Friedrich/Traut, Heinrich Theodor (Bearb. rev.), *Otto Friedrich Rammlers Universal-Briefsteller oder Musterbuch zur Abfassung aller in den allgemeinen und freundschaftlichen Lebensverhältnissen sowie im Geschäftsleben Briefe, Documente und Aufsätze*, 46. Aufl. edition, Leipzig 1876.

Schmuttermeier, Elisabeth/Witt-Dörring, Christian, *Postcards of the Wiener Werkstätte. A Catalogue Raisonné*, Neue Galerie New York 2010.

Schoppe, Amalie, *Briefsteller für Damen. Ein Fest- und Toilettengeschenk für Deutsche Frauen*, 2. Aufl. edition, Berlin 1837.

Stiftung Nordfriesland, Schloss vor Husum (Hg. eds.) *Papier im Reiche des Luxus und der Phantasie*, mit Beiträgen von with contributions by Christa Pieske und and Rolf Kuschert, Husum 1987.

Witzmann, Reingard, *Freundschafts- und Glückwunschkarten aus dem Wiener Biedermeier*, hg. vom Historischen Museum der Stadt Wien ed. by Historical Museum of the City of Vienna, Dortmund 1979.

Zur Westen, Walter von, „Zur Kunstgeschichte der Besuchs- und Glückwunschkarte", in: *Exlibris, Buchkunst und angewandte Graphik* (18) 3/4 1908, 90–126.

Zur Westen, Walter von, *Vom Kunstgewand der Höflichkeit. Glückwünsche, Besuchskarten und Familienanzeigen aus sechs Jahrhunderten*, Berlin 1921.

SPIELKARTEN PLAYING CARDS

Altfahrt, Wolfgang, *Wiener Kartenmacher des 19. Jahrhunderts*, Studien zur Spielkarte 3, Berlin 1990.

Breitkopf, Johann Gottlob Immanuel, *Versuch, den Ursprung der Spielkarten, die Einführung des Leinenpapieres, und den Anfang der Holzschneidekunst in Europa zu erforschen*, Leipzig 1784.

Chmelarz, Eduard, „Die Spielkarten in der Bibliothek des Oesterr. Museums", in: *Mittheilungen des k. k. Oesterr. Museums für Kunst und Industrie* (XVII) 207 1882.

Deutsches Spielkartenmuseum Bielefeld (Hg. ed.), *Die Cotta'schen Spielkarten-Almanache 1805–1811*, Bielefeld 1968.

Dornik-Eger, Hanna [spätere later Egger], *Spielkarten und Kartenspiele*, Schriften der Bibliothek des Österreichischen Museums für angewandte Kunst 10, Wien Vienna 1973.

Dornik-Eger, Hanna [spätere later Egger], „Spielkarten und Kartenspiele im Österreichischen Museum für angewandte Kunst", in: *Alte und moderne Kunst* (XIX) 135 1974, 15–21.

Eitelberger, Rudolf von, *Über Spielkarten. Mit besonderer Rücksicht auf einige in Wien befindliche alte Kartenspiele*, Wien Vienna 1860.

Fenz, Werner, *Ditha Moser Whist*, Begleitheft zum Kartenspiel booklet accompanying the deck of cards, Piatnik Edition, Wien Vienna 1985.

Hevesi, Ludwig, „Das Spielkartenwerk von H.-R. D'Allemagne", in: *Kunst und Kunsthandwerk* (IX) 12 1906, 730–734.

Hoffmann, Detlef, „Vier Spielkarten aus Lyon und ein Kabinettschränkchen aus Spanien", in: *Alte und moderne Kunst* (XVI) 116 1971, 18–21.

Hoffmann, Detlef, *Kultur- und Kunstgeschichte der Spielkarte. Mit einer Dokumentation von Margot Dietrich zu den Spielen des Deutschen Spielkarten-Museums Leinfelden-Echterdingen*, Marburg 1995.

Hoffmann, Detlef/**Noggler-Gürtler,** Lisa, *Spielkarten aus dem Biedermeier*, Ausst.kat. exh.cat. Technisches Museum Wien, Wien Vienna 2000.

Husband, Timothy B., *The World in Play. Luxury Cards 1430–1540*, The Metropolitan Museum of Art, New York 2015.

Köger, Annette, *Spielend lernen – Lehrkarten aus vier Jahrhunderten*, Ausst.kat. exh.cat. Schlossmuseum Aulendorf, Leinfelden-Echterdingen 1998.

Köger, Annette, „Musikalische Spielkarten", in: **Bauer,** G. G. (Hg. ed.), *Musik und Spiel. Homo Ludens – Der spielende Mensch*, Intern. Beiträge des Institutes für Spielforschung u. Spielpädagogik an der Hochschule Mozarteum Salzburg (10) 2000, 287–304.

Köger, Annette, „Spielkarten", in: *Lexikon des gesamten Buchwesens*, Bd. vol. 7, Stuttgart 2007, 170f.

Koreny, Fritz, *Spielkarten, ihre Kunst und Geschichte in Mitteleuropa*, Ausst.kat. Grafische Sammlung der Albertina exh.cat. Graphic Arts Collection of the Albertina, Wien Vienna 1974.

Philidor, François Danican, *Die Kunst die Welt mitzunehmen in den verschiedenen Arten der Spiele, so in Gesellschaften höhern Standes, besonders in der Kayserl. Königl. Residenz-Stadt Wien üblich sind*, 2 Bde. vols., Wien/Nürnberg Vienna/Nuremberg 1756.

Radau, Sigmar, „Makulatur im Grenzbereich zwischen Spielkarten- und Einbandforschung", in: *Einbandforschung, Informationsblatt des Arbeitskreises für die Erfassung, Erschließung und Erhaltung historischer Bucheinbände (AEB)* (19) 37 2015, 20–27.

Ragg, Ernst Rudolf, *Jugendstiltarock Ditha Moser*, Begleitheft zum Kartenspiel booklet accompanying the deck of cards, Piatnik Edition, Wien Vienna 1972[1], 1982[2].

Reisinger, Klaus, *Tarocke. Kulturgeschichte auf Kartenbildern*, Bde. vols. 1–5, Wien Vienna 1996; Bd. vol. 6, Wien Vienna 1999.

Ulm, Dagmar (Hg. ed.), *Diese Karden seind zu finden bey – Spielkarten aus Oberösterreich*, Kataloge der catalogs of the Oberösterreichischen Landesmuseen, N. S. 105, Linz 2010.

VISITENKARTEN VISITING CARDS

Ankwicz-Kleehoven, Hans, „Künstlerische Visitkarten", Sonderdruck offprint, Wien Vienna 1926.

Guglia, Eugen, „Die Besuchs- und Gelegenheitskarten der Sammlung Figdor in Wien", in: *Kunst und Kunsthandwerk* (XIV) 2 1911, 73–121.

Pazaurek, Gustav E., „Künstlerische Besuchskarten", in: *Archiv für Buchgewerbe* (44) 11/12 1907, 445–452.

Poppenberg, Felix, „Berlin. Chronik der angewandten Künste" [Kleine Nachrichten], in: *Kunst und Kunsthandwerk* (XI) 11 1908, 608f.

Weittenhiller, Moritz von, „Einiges über illustrierte Besuchskarten" [I und II], Sonderdrucke aus dem VI. und VII. Jahrbuch der Österreichischen Exlibris-Gesellschaft offprints from the 6th and 7th yearbooks of the Austrian Bookplate Society, Wien Vienna 1908; Wien Vienna 1909.

Willrich, Erich, „Künstlerische Besuchskarten", in: *Die Woche* (10) 30 1908, 1315–1317.

Zur Westen, Walter von, „Zur Geschichte der Besuchskarte", in: *Exlibris, Buchkunst und angewandte Graphik* (29) 1919, 1–14.

EXLIBRIS EX LIBRIS

Ankwicz-Kleehoven, Hans, „Wiener Humanisten-Exlibris", in: Österreichische Exlibris-Gesellschaft Austrian Bookplate Society (Hg. ed.), *XVII. Jahrbuch 1919*, Wien Vienna 1919, 11–56.

Ankwicz-Kleehoven, Hans, „Von jüngster österreichischer Exlibriskunst", in: *Österreichisches Jahrbuch für Exlibris und Gebrauchsgraphik* (21) 1924/1925 (erschienen published in 1926), 18-22.

Ankwicz-Kleehoven, Hans, „Der Graphiker Franz Taussig", in: *Österreichisches Jahrbuch für Exlibris und Gebrauchsgraphik* (29) 1934, 17–22.

Ankwicz-Kleehoven, Hans, „Von alter Exlibriskunst", Sonderdruck offprint, um ca. 1938, 110–117.

Born, Wolfgang, „Exlibris-Ausstellung in Wien", in *Neues Wiener Journal*, 16.8.1933, 4f.

Braungart, Richard, *Neue deutsche Exlibris*, München Munich 1913.

Braungart, Richard, „Geleitwort", in: *100 deutsche Meisterexlibris* (Grafikmappe portfolio of graphic art, Artur Wolf Verlag), Wien Vienna 1922.

Hoschek, Rudolf Freiherr von, „Exlibris-Ausstellung Wien Frühjahr 1913", in: Österreichische Exlibris-Gesellschaft Austrian Bookplate Society (Hg. ed.), *XI. Jahrbuch 1913*, Wien Vienna 1913, 5–14.

Hoschek, Rudolf Freiherr von, „Exlibris-ausstellung in Wien 1913", in: *Kunst und Kunsthandwerk* (XVI) 3 1913, 191–203.

Jobst-Rieder, Marianne/**Karolyi**, Claudia, „‚Birnholziana'. Geschichte, Raub und Restitution der Exlibris-Sammlung Marco Birnholz", in: *Österreichisches Jahrbuch für Exlibris und Gebrauchsgraphik* (64) 2005–2006 45–77.

Karolyi, Claudia/Mayerhofer, Alexandra, „Das Glück des Sammelns. Die Exlibris-Sammlung Ankwicz-Kleehoven in der ÖNB", in: *biblos* (46) 1 1997.

Karolyi, Claudia/Mayerhofer, Alexandra, *Aufbruch und Idylle. Exlibris Österreichischer Künstlerinnen 1900–1945*, Wien Vienna 2004.

Karolyi, Claudia/Smetana, Alexandra, „Die Geschichte der Exlibrissammlung der k. k. Hof- und Nationalbibliothek in Wien von den Anfängen bis 1938", in: *Österreichisches Jahrbuch für Exlibris und Gebrauchsgraphik* (66), 2009–2010, 36–59.

Österreichische Exlibris-Gesellschaft Austrian Bookplate Society (Hg. ed.), *Exlibris Ausstellung. Unter dem Protektorate Sr. kaiserl. und königl. Hoheit, des durchlauchtigsten Herrn Erzherzogs Karl Franz Josef. Veranstaltet von der österreichischen Exlibris-Gesellschaft anläßlich ihres zehnjährigen Bestandes. 4. März bis 11. April 1913*, Ausst.kat. ÖMKI, Wien Vienna 1913.

Smetana, Alexandra/Karolyi, Claudia, „Der Künstler und seine Mäzene. Unbekannte Exlibris und Exlibrisentwürfe von Josef Hoffmann für Otto und Mäda Primavesi", in: *biblos* (49) 2 2000, 356–358.

Tauber, Henry, *Der deutsche Exlibris-Verein 1891 bis 1943. Seine Geschichte im Kontext von Exlibrisbewegung und Exlibriskunst vornehmlich in Deutschland*, Jahrbuch 1995 der Deutschen Exlibris-Gesellschaft, Frankfurt/Main 1995.

Zur Westen, Walter von, *Exlibris. Bucheignerzeichen*, Bielefeld 1925.

BUCHKUNST – LESEZEICHEN BOOK ART—BOOKMARKS

Grautoff, Otto, „Der deutsche Verlegereinband", in: *Archiv für Buchgewerbe* (40) 1 1903, 46–56.

Haberland, Detlef, „Edna May oder die Sprachlosigkeit der Jahrhundertwende. Reflexionen über ein Lesezeichen", in: Patricia F. Zeckert (Hg. ed.), *Flachware 3. Fußnoten der Leipziger Buchwissenschaft*, Leipzig 2013.

Hansen, Thomas S., *Classic Book Jackets. The Design Legacy of George Salter*, New York 2005.

Heid, Hans (Hg. ed.), *100 Lesezeichen der Historischen Bibliothek der Stadt Rastatt*, Ausst.kat. exh.cat. Stadt City of Rastatt 2001.

Holstein, Jürgen (Hg. ed.), *Blickfang. Bucheinbände und Schutzumschläge Berliner Verlage 1919–1933*, Berlin 2005.

Kuh, Hans, „Die Magie des Schutzumschlages. Zu den Arbeiten von Hannes Jähn", in: *Gebrauchsgraphik* (33) 12 1962, 2–9.

Loubier, Hans, *Die neue deutsche Buchkunst*, Stuttgart 1921.

Pfäfflin, Friedrich, *100 Jahre S. Fischer Verlag 1886–1986, Buchumschläge. Über Bücher und ihre äußere Gestalt*, Frankfurt/Main 1986.

Schölermann, Wilhelm, „Deutscher Buchschmuck. Eine zeitgemäße Betrachtung", in: *Archiv für Buchgewerbe* (37) 2 1900, 333–339.

Tschichold, Jan, *Werden und Wesen der neuen Typographie*, Berlin 1928.

Zeitler, Julius, „Walter Tiemann", in: *Archiv für Buchgewerbe* (40) 2 1903, 465–471.

MODEBILDER FASHION PICTURES

Ferber, Christian, *Die Dame. Ein deutsches Journal für den verwöhnten Geschmack 1912–1943*, Berlin 1980.

Fischel, Hartwig, „Modeausstellung im Österreichischen Museum", in: *Kunst und Kunsthandwerk* (XIX) 1/2 1916, 69–93.

Mode-Ausstellung 1915/16 im k. k. Österreichischen Museum für Kunst und Industrie, Ausst.kat. exh.cat. ÖMKI, Wien Vienna 1915.

Noever, Peter (Hg. ed.), *Ernst Deutsch-Dryden. En Vogue!*, MAK Studies 2, Wien Vienna 2002.

Rücker, Elisabeth, *Wiener Charme. Mode 1914/15, Grafiken und Accessoires*, Ausst.kat. exh.cat. Germanisches Nationalmuseum, Nürnberg Nuremberg 1984.

Semotan, Elfie/Woltron, Ute, *Eine andere Art von Schönheit*, Wien Vienna 2016.

WERBEMATERIAL – REKLAMEMARKEN PROMOTIONAL MATERIALS—POSTER STAMPS

Bäumler, Susanne (Hg. ed.), *Die Kunst zu werben. Das Jahrhundert der Reklame*, Ausst.kat. exh.cat. Münchner Stadtmuseum, Köln Cologne 1996.

Bleistein, Rudolf, „Aenne Koken", in: *Das Plakat* (IV) 4 1913, 177–179.

Bund Österreichischer Gebrauchsgraphiker (Hg. ed.), *Das österreichische Plakat. Werbekunst-Ausstellung des Bundes österreichischer Gebrauchsgraphiker im Österr. Museum für Kunst und Industrie*, Ausst.kat. exh.cat. ÖMKI, Wien Vienna 1929.

Denscher, Bernhard, „Ottokar Mascha, a Viennese Connoisseur", in: Le Coultre, Martijn F. (Hg. ed.), *Hans Sachs and the Poster Revolution*, Hoorn 2013, 41–44.

Deutsches Museum für Kunst in Handel und Gewerbe (Hg. ed.), *Julius Klinger, Monographien deutscher Reklamekünstler*, Bd. vol. 3, Hagen/Dortmund 1912.

Gries, Rainer/Ilgen, Volker/Schindelbeck, Dirk, „Ins Gehirn der Masse kriechen!" *Werbung und Mentalitätsgeschichte*, Darmstadt 1995.

Grohnert, René, *Hans Sachs und seine Plakatsammlung, der Verein der Plakatfreunde und die Zeitschrift „Das Plakat" im Prozess der Herausbildung, Bedeutungswandlung und Konsolidierung des Plakates in Deutschland zwischen 1890 und 1933*, Berlin/Neersen 1993.

Grohnert, René, „The Final Chapter: the collections of Dr Hans Sachs between 1898 and 2013", in: Le Coultre, Martijn F. (Hg. ed.), *Hans Sachs and the Poster Revolution*, Hoorn 2013, 27–38.

Iskin, Ruth E., *The Poster Art. Advertising, Design, and Collecting 1860s–1900s*, Hanover/New Hampshire 2014.

Jüdisches Museum Berlin Jewish Museum Berlin (Hg. ed.), *Sammelwut und Bilderflut. Werbegeschichte im Kleinformat*, Berlin 2014.

Kirsten, Arthur, „Reklamemarken", in: *Das Plakat* (V) 3 1914, 111–113.

Kraus, Karl, „Die Welt der Plakate", in: *Die Fackel* (11) 283/284 1909.

Kühnel, Anita, *Julius Klinger. Plakatkünstler und Zeichner*, Ausst.kat. exh.cat. Staatliche Museen zu Berlin – Preußischer Kulturbesitz 89, Berlin 1997.

Maryška, Christian, *Kunst der Reklame. Der Bund Österreichischer Gebrauchsgraphiker von den Anfängen bis zur Wiedergründung 1926–1946*, Salzburg 2005.

Meißner, Jörg (Hg. ed.), *Strategien der Werbekunst 1850–1933*, Ausst.kat. exh.cat. Deutsches Historisches Museum, Berlin/Bönen 2004.

Meyer, Reiner, *Die Reklamekunst der Keks-fabrik Bahlsen in Hannover von 1889–1945,* Phil. Diss. PhD thesis, Münster 1999.

Noever, Peter (Hg. ed.), *Hans Neumann. Pionier der Werbeagenturen Pioneer of Advertising Agencies,* MAK Studies 14, Wien Vienna 2009.

Sachs, Hans, „Reklamemarkenausstellung in Berlin", in: *Das Plakat* (IV) 6 1913, 253f.

Schweiger, Günter/**Spicko,** Gerlinde, *Die Reklamemarke. Das Werbemittel der Gründerzeit,* Wien Vienna 2008.
„Die volkswirtschaftliche Bedeutung der Reclame", in: *Die Zeit,* 10.10.1902, 10.

Uebe, Fritz Rudolf, *Die Sammlung ange-wandter Graphik,* Handbücher der Reklame-kunst 1, Berlin-Charlottenburg 1919.

Wündrich, Hans, *Der Prospekt als geschäftliches Werbemittel,* Wien Vienna/Leipzig 1927.

Zur Westen, Walter von, *Reklamekunst aus zwei Jahrtausenden,* Berlin 1925.

ABKÜRZUNGSVERZEICHNIS LIST OF ABBREVIATIONS

ÖMKI	k: k. Österreichisches Museum für Kunst und Industrie
	Imperial Royal Austrian Museum of Art and Industry (1863–1918)
	Österreichisches Museum für Kunst und Industrie
	Austrian Museum of Art and Industry (1918–1938)
KGM	Staatliches Kunstgewerbemuseum in Wien
	State Arts and Crafts Museum in Vienna (1938–1947)
ÖMAK	Österreichisches Museum für angewandte Kunst
	Austrian Museum of Applied Arts (1947–1987)
MAK	MAK – Österreichisches Museum für angewandte Kunst
	MAK – Austrian Museum of Applied Arts (1987–2001)
MAK	MAK – Österreichisches Museum für angewandte Kunst / Gegenwartskunst
	MAK – Austrian Museum of Applied Arts / Contemporary Art (seit since 2001)
ÖEG	Österreichische Exlibris-Gesellschaft Austrian Bookplate Society
WW	Wiener Werkstätte

REGISTER

INDEX

EPHEMERA
Die Gebrauchsgrafik der MAK-Bibliothek und
Kunstblättersammlung
The Graphic Design of the MAK Library and Works
on Paper Collection

MAK Studies 24

HerausgeberInnen Editors
Christoph Thun-Hohenstein, Kathrin Pokorny-Nagel

MAK
Stubenring 5, 1010 Wien Vienna, Austria
T +43 1 711 36-0, F +43 1 713 10 26
office@MAK.at, MAK.at

MAK Center for Art and Architecture,
Los Angeles at the Schindler House
835 North Kings Road, West Hollywood,
CA 90069, USA

Mackey Apartments
MAK Artists and Architects-in-Residence Program
1137 South Cochran Avenue, Los Angeles,
CA 90019, USA

Fitzpatrick-Leland House
Laurel Canyon Boulevard/Mulholland Drive
Los Angeles, CA 90046, USA
T +1 323 651 1510, F +1 323 651 2340

office@MAKcenter.org, MAKcenter.org

Josef Hoffmann Museum, Brtnice
Eine Expositur der Mährischen Galerie in Brno
und des MAK, Wien
A joint branch of the Moravian Gallery in Brno
and the MAK, Vienna
náměstí Svobody 263, 588 32 Brtnice,
Tschechische Republik Czech Republic
T +43 1 711 36-220
josefhoffmannmuseum@MAK.at, MAK.at

Redaktion Editing
Kathrin Pokorny-Nagel, Anne-Katrin Rossberg

Mitarbeit, MAK-Bibliothek und Kunstblättersammlung
Assistance, MAK Library and Works on Paper Collection
Monika Angelberger, Gabriele Iwanicki, Peter Klinger,
Barbara Kochschitz, Ingrid Krassnitzer, Aline Müller,
Fernanda Romero-Velasquez

Klärung Bildrechte Clarification of Image Rights
Thomas Matyk

Englische Übersetzung English Translation
Maria Slater, Christina Anderson

Lektorat Copy Editing
Bettina R. Algieri (Leitung Head), Cornelia Malli, Esther Pirchner

Grafische Gestaltung Graphic Design
Eva Dranaz, Jochen Fill; 3007, Wien Vienna www. 3007wien.at

Reproduktionen Reproductions
Pixelstorm, Wien Vienna

Papier Paper
Buchcover Book cover: Crush Corn, 120 g/m²
Kern Interior: Design Papier Crush Corn, 120 g/m²,
produziert von produced by Favini, Italien Italy;
Kunstdruckpapier Art paper: GardaPat Kiara, 135 g/m²,
produziert von produced by Cartiere del Garda, Italien Italy.

Alle Papiere in diesem Buch sind exklusiv erhältlich bei
All papers in this book are available exclusively at
Europapier Austria GmbH. www.europapier.at

Wir bedanken uns bei Sandra Schmidt von Europapier
für die kompetente Papierberatung. We would like to thank
Sandra Schmidt at Europapier for her expert advice on paper.

Vorsatzpapier Book endpaper
Redesign/Bearbeitung Redesign/alteration: 3007, Wien Vienna,
nach Vorlagen von after models by
Maria von Zeiller-Uchatius, Josef Manfreda, Koloman Moser,
Karl Massanetz, Hugo Falkenstein

Druck und Bindung Printing and Binding
Produktionsberatung Production advice: Ulrike Arnold
REMA Print Litteradruck, Wien Vienna
Buchbinderei Papyrus, Wien Vienna
Farbschnitt Edge coloring: J. Steinbrener KG, Schärding

Bildnachweis Photo Credits
© 3007wien: S. pp. 013, 025, 027, 105, 106, 169, 171,
229, 230, 277, 279, 317, 319, 361, 363

© Akademie der bildenden Künste Wien, Kupferstichkabinett
Academy of Fine Arts, Graphic Collection: Abb. ill. 017

© Bildrecht, Wien Vienna, 2017: Abb. ill. 070, 079, 139, 280, 317,
322, 323, 328, 337, 350, 352, 362, 365, 377, 378, 395, 399, 404,
413, 421, 423, 424, 504, 507, 508, 509, 528, 541

© Estate of Martin Kippenberger, Galerie Gisela Capitain, Cologne:
Abb. ill. 422

© Gedruckt mit Genehmigung von Printed by permission of Janet
Salter Rosenberg: Abb. ill. 407, 409

© GNM, Germanisches Nationalmuseum Nürnberg Nuremberg:
Abb. ill. 001, 089

© MAK/Georg Mayer: S. pp. 028, 109, 172, 233, 280, 320, 364,
397; Abb. ill. 021–025, 066, 077, 95, 100, 102, 111, 112, 114,
121, 261, 263, 285, 286, 383, 386, 387, 390, 392, 501

© MAK/Mona Heiß: Abb. ill. 002, 018–020, 026, 027, 094,
109, 110, 113, 115, 117–119, 122, 290, 291, 314

© mumok, museum moderner kunst stiftung ludwig wien:
Abb. ill. 008

Alle anderen Abbildungen All other illustrations © MAK

Trotz intensiver Recherche war es nicht in allen Fällen möglich,
die RechteinhaberInnen der Abbildungen ausfindig zu machen.
Berechtigte Ansprüche werden selbstverständlich im Rahmen der
üblichen Vereinbarungen abgegolten. Despite intensive research,
it was not possible to identify the right holders of every illustration.
Justified claims will of course be compensated in line with
customary arrangements.

Mit Dank an With thanks to
Designstudio 3007, Wien Vienna
Europapier Austria GmbH, Wien Vienna
Buchbinderei Papyrus, Wien Vienna
Pixelstorm, Wien Vienna
REMA Print Litteradruck, Wien Vienna

Erschienen im Published by
Vfmk Verlag für moderne Kunst GmbH
Salmgasse 4a, 1030 Wien Vienna
hello@vfmk.org, www.vfmk.org

ISBN 978-3-903131-94-1

Vertrieb Distribution
D, A und Europa and Europe: LKG, www.lkg-va.de
CH: AVA, www.ava.ch
UK: Cornerhouse Publications, www.cornerhousepublications.org
USA: D.A.P., www.artbook.com

Das MAK bemüht sich in seinen Publikationen um eine
gendergerechte Schreibweise. The MAK strives for
gender-sensitive language in its publications.

Bibliografische Information der Deutschen Nationalbibliothek
Bibliographic information published by the Deutsche
Nationalbibliothek
Die Deutsche Nationalbibliothek verzeichnet diese Publikation
in der Deutschen Nationalbibliografie; detaillierte bibliografische
Daten sind im Internet über http://dnb.d-nb.de abrufbar.
Die Deutsche Nationalbibliothek lists this publication in the
Deutsche Nationalbibliografie; detailed bibliographic data is
available online at http://dnb.ddb.de.

Für die großzügige Unterstützung danken wir
For their generous support we would like to thank

Gustav Belousek und and Andrew Demmer /
Legat Bequest of Joseph und and Carla Binder

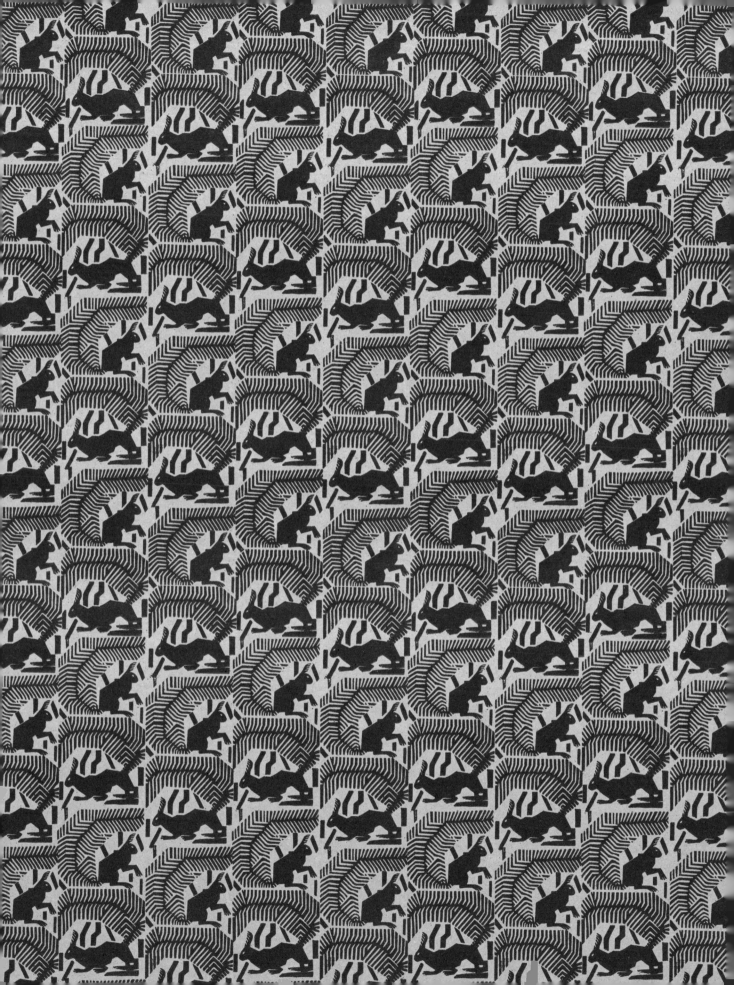

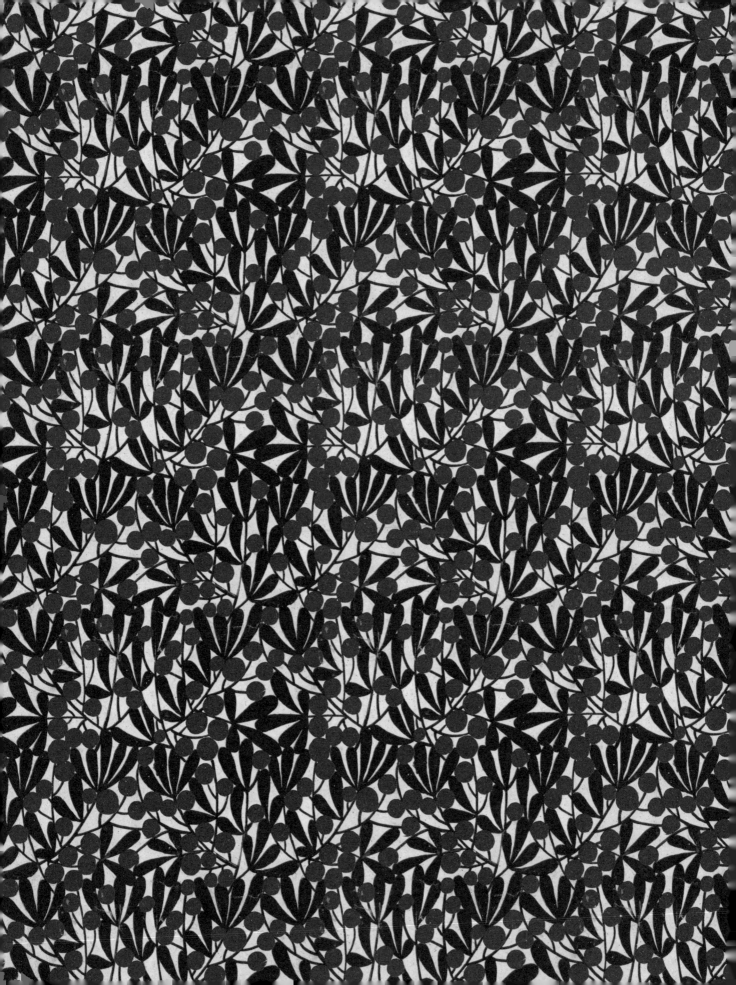

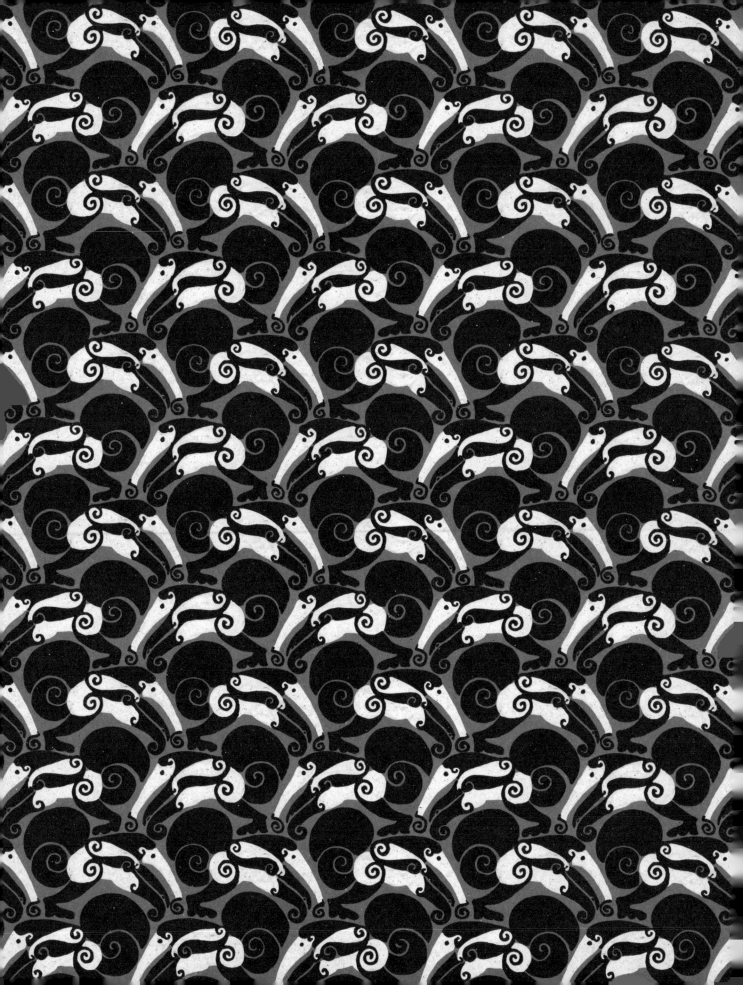